H.V. Jones

A Newspaperman's Imprint on Minneapolis History

H.V. Jones

A Newspaperman's Imprint on Minneapolis History

John Koblas

North Star Press of St. Cloud, Inc.

ISBN: 0-87839-191-6 Paper
ISBN: 0-87839-200-9 Hardcover

First Edition: December 2003

Printed in the United States of America by Versa Press, Inc.,
East Peoria, Illinois.

Published by
North Star Press of St. Cloud, Inc.
P.O. Box 451
St. Cloud, Minnesota 56302

DEDICATION

This book has come to fruition through the efforts of many people. There are two, however, who stand out for their labors, getting the project started and making it happen.

Waring Jones was instrumental in initiating the idea to produce a book about Herschel V. Jones. The idea took hold shortly after the passing of Herschel's eldest daughter, Tessie, and it has been through Waring's perseverance that the book took on its initial form.

The book remained idle for a few years until Waring's brother Winton continued its push towards publication. Winton drew cousins together to help identify people in the newly added pictures, uncovered and corrected historical inaccuracies and provided a new look for the book.

Both Winton and Waring shared a mutual interest and desire—to produce a book about their grandfather. This common desire was based on an appreciation for the role Herschel played in the formative years of Minneapolis history, its politics, commerce, and cultural foundations, as well as providing a testimony of heritage for the successive Jones generations to reflect upon.

The efforts presented herein are dedicated to these two gentlemen.

Winton and Waring Jones as boys c. 1929.

ACKNOWLEDGMENTS

The author wishes to thank the following persons and their organizations for their generous assistance in producing this book on Herschel V. Jones: Vickie Edman, Marianne Meyer, and Rick Bliss, Anchor Bancorp, Inc., Wayzata, Minnesota; Nina Archibald, Craig Wright, and Pat Coleman, Minnesota Historical Society, St. Paul, Minnesota; Christine M. Palmatier, Schoharie County Historical Society, Schoharie, New York; Dr. Lisa Dickinson Michaux, Associate Curator, Department of Prints and Drawings, The Minneapolis Institute of Arts, Minneapolis, Minnesota; Edina Historical Society, Edina, Minnesota; Hennepin County Historical Society, Minneapolis, Minnesota; Hennepin County Registrar of Deeds, Minneapolis, Minnesota; Ramsey County Registrar of Deeds, St. Paul, Minnesota; Longville Area Chamber of Commerce, Longville, Minnesota; Jacci Krebsbach, Shoreview Historical Society, Shoreview, Minnesota; and Mary Jean Levine, White Bear Lake Historical Society, White Bear Lake, Minnesota.

I also wish to extend my gratitude to the following persons for sharing memories, letters, photographs, and helping to shape this volume: Steve Anderson, Joyce Bahr, Kenneth Bailey, Midred Bailey, Roger Brezina, Thirza Cleveland, Susan Jacobson, Christopher Jones, Janet Jones, Jefferson Jones, Jr., Waring Jones, Winton Jones, Deborah Morse-Kahn, J. Harold Kittleson, Sally Koerther, Art Larson, Ann Dwight Lewis, Judy Luchsinger, John McCauley, Donna Gág, Raymond, Julie Russell, Mary Lou Schmitt, Frances and Alfred Siftar, Mrs. Raymond Sina, Bob Ulstrom, and Dave Wood.

TABLE OF CONTENTS

H.V. Jones

A Newspaperman's Imprint
on Minneapolis History

CHAPTER ONE

A CATSKILL BOYHOOD

"My object in living is to unite
My avocation and my vocation"
—Robert Frost

URING 1919-1920, JUAN CARLOS ORENDAIN, a Philippine journalist and lawyer, was attending classes at the University of Minnesota while visiting the United States. Orendain would spend eight years in the country, and, during his stay, he made many friends. The Filipino later recalled a friendship he made via a very curious situation.

"The *Minneapolis Journal* was published by Herschel V. Jones, and the *Minneapolis Journal* was dyed-in-the-wool Republican," remembered Orendain. "The Republicans, according to the feelings of the Filipinos, were not very much interested in our independence as the Democrats were. You see, when McKinley and Bryan campaigned against each other—Bryan campaigned against McKinley, I think in 1900—American imperialism in the Philippines was the subject. So the Filipinos had fallen in love with Bryan. I remember my father would come and say, if "Breean"—that's the way they pronounced it—if Breean could become president of the United States, why the Philippines would get their independence."[1]

With the assassination of President William McKinley, Theodore Roosevelt took office. According to Orendain, Roosevelt, working with William Howard Taft, then chairman of the second Philippine Commission, did a marvelous job. Together they

Opposite: Four generations of Jones men. Seated is Chauncey Jones; bearded man is William Jones, H.V. on right with mustache, Carl is the baby.

1

strove for economic development and they were very popular with the Philippine people. Taft became a hero when he told the Filipinos that the Philippines was for the Filipinos to develop and rule because it was their own country. Accordingly, the Filipinos worked hard for self-government.

Orendain discovered that most Minnesotans were Republicans, and it was next to impossible for a Democrat to get elected in the state. The Farmer-Laborite party was in its infancy, but, nonetheless, their senatorial candidate, Magnus Johnson, was elected over Frank B. Kellogg, a Republican.

"Now, Herschel Jones, who was a Republican, was more or less misinformed about the Philippines," insisted Orendain. "Off and on, we would read an editorial in the *Minneapolis Journal* against the Philippines. There were about, at that time—this was about 1919-1920—we had about twenty (Filipino) students in the University of Minnesota, and one day in our meeting it was decided that we would challenge Herschel Jones. We were kids, and we were hot heads, so I was chosen with Mr. Celedonia Maglaya to challenge Mr. Jones to a debate. I wrote Mr. Jones asking him for a debate on the Philippine question to show him that the *Journal* was wrong, but Mr. Jones never answered our letter. So, in our next meeting, the boys sort of despised Maglaya and myself because we could not do anything to get the Philippines heard, and it was decided that I should go and see Mr. Jones."[2]

The young Filipino stopped at the *Journal* office and was ushered in to see Mr. Jones by a young employee. The publisher, however, was out. "Those were the days when a swivel chair was quite new, and I was admiring Mr. Jones' swivel chair, and after looking at it carefully I tried and sat on it, and I was sitting on Mr. Jones' chair when he came in," recalled Orendain. "He was in a cutaway coat and he said, 'What's the big idea?' I stood up, and I said, 'Mr. Jones, my name is Orendain and I'm a student at the University of Minnesota. I'm a Filipino and I came here to talk to you because I don't think you are informed about the Philippines.'"[3]

Herschel V. Jones seemed quite hurt by his young visitor's accusations but admitted he did not like Francis Burton Harrison, U.S. Governor General of the Philippines (1913 to 1921). Harrison had declared the Democratic Party's intention to seek independence for the Philippines and locally introduced a number of reforms that brought more Filipinos into responsible administrative positions and added other elements of self-government. Jones said he felt the Filipinos were very far behind, and he, like most Americans, thought it would be best if the Philippines stayed under the American government for some time.

"I was quite hurt by the way he talked about the Filipinos," said Orendain, "so I asked him to give me the floor . . . he said, 'All right, come on, tell me.' Jones was quite a tough person, but he was reasonable. I said, 'Look, Mr. Jones, we have been under the American government for over twenty years from 1898 to now. We have people that are well prepared now. We have good leaders, we have Filipinos that graduated in the American schools, and they are now back home teaching our people but for twenty years you Americans have been teaching us from grade one through college through the university, and if you Americans couldn't teach the Filipinos in twenty years, why I am sorry for you. The way you write your editorials . . . you are writing against the American teachers that served in the Philippines. In the Philippines are graves of American teachers who, they must have loved the Filipinos because they died there, stayed there teaching us. Now you sit here behind your desk writing editorials like this, making the world believe the Filipinos are barbarians."[4]

Orendain knew at this point he had reached the man behind the desk as he stared at the publisher waiting for him to answer. Recalled Orendain: "He said, 'Son, tell me more,' so I stayed there, and we talked about it and Herschel Jones could let his temper go . . . and he pounded on his table and he said, 'Blankety blank.' He said, 'we have a lot of demagogues in this country, but I'm glad that we have pedagogues that trained you people in the Philippines,' Before I left he said, 'All right, tell me what I can do to help you.'"[5]

The Filipino was moved. He told Jones that all his people wanted was for the *Journal* to understand the Philippines. He added that he and some of his fellow Filipinos were holding a Rizal Day celebration at the Radisson Hotel, and they wanted him to be their speaker. The annual celebration was held to honor the life of Jose y Alonso Rizal, the physician, poet, novelist, and national hero martyred by the Spanish in 1896. His martyrdom had convinced Filipinos that there was no alternative to independence from Spain.

Jones could not attend the Rizal Day honors because he planned to be in Chicago where he wanted to see General Leonard Wood nominated as the 1920 Republican presidential candidate. Regarded by many as the political heir of Theodore Roosevelt, he had made quite an impression on H.V. Jones. Opposing Wood for the nomination was Frank Orren Lowden, born in Sunrise City, Minnesota. Wood and Lowden would become hopelessly deadlocked, and on the ninth ballot, they would both give way to Warren G. Harding. Jones' favorite, however, would be appointed to the Wood-Forbes Mission to the Philippines the following year. The mission reported that a grant of immediate independence to the islands would be premature and urged the United States government not to be left in a position of responsibility without authority. Wood would serve as Governor General of the Philippines from 1921 to 1927.

Jones said he would be glad to help, however. He urged Orendain to contact a Universalist pastor he knew. The pastor was known as a very eloquent orator and considered one of the two best speakers in the city of Minneapolis at the time. Orendain did not change any views held by H.V. Jones, but he did get him to listen and, with the speaker sent by the newspaperman, did, in effect, get his help in a small degree. Said Orendain, "The pastor of the Universalist church was the one that spoke in place of Mr. Jones, but that interview was very fruitful in that Mr. Jones understood the Philippines, and we made good friends with a leading Minnesotan."[6]

This "leading Minnesotan" who entertained opposite views from Juan Carlos Orendain but who still made a lasting impression is the same H.V. Jones columnist/author Barbara Flanagan called one of Minnesota's "memorable three Jones boys."[7]

Home of William S. and Helen Merchant Jones, Jefferson, Schoharie County, New York. This is the house where Herschel V. Jones was born on August 30, 1861.

4

Herschel V. Jones was born August 30, 1861, in the village of Jefferson, Schoharie County, New York. He was the son of William S. Jones and Helen Merchant Jones of good Welsh, English, and Scotch stock dating back to the American Revolution.[8]

Alice Webber Child wrote Tessie Jones in 1916 that "I do not doubt that the Jones[es] came from Wales. All your father's [Herschel's] characteristics agree with those I saw given in a Jones Genealogy. Too long to write. I saw where the author went to London and met a Miss Jones and asked her how far back her family had been traced. She said, 'Well, we only consider it authentic [to] about six centuries before Christ.' Another told of a pedigree being given for the Jones in Ireland. I think, probably Welsh, and they were given Thomas, the son of John, down the whole page and someone had written on the margin about half way down, 'About this time the world was created.'"[9, 10]

The Jones family has been traced to the mid-seventeenth century. Alice Webber Child, researching the recorded origins of the Jones family in 1922, could find no Welsh record of the family. As she began to doubt the family had come from Wales, she discovered the records in New England. She wrote of her discovery in a jubilant letter to Tessie Jones, Herschel's oldest daughter. "I did some work on the Jones family, along the line of any guise that Nathaniel Jones did not come from Swansea, Wales. And Tessie— I could shout for I have found the head of the Jones family you come from. I looked first at Swanzey [sic], Nebraska, and found nothing. Then I tried Swansea, Massachusetts, and there they were. It is a very interesting history."[11]

Swansea, Wales, was the district seat and county seat of West Glamorgan. It is located on the Bristol Channel at the mouth of the River Tawe. In the early twelfth century, the Norman Henry De Newburgh built a castle in Swansea, which was later destroyed by Owen Glendower. Up to the early eighteenth century, Swansea was a small market town but already a significant coal port. It grew slowly as an industrial center. Locally outcropping coal was used in the smelting of imported copper after 1717, and the industry prospered so much, that by the mid-nineteenth century, its Metal Exchange had become the center of world trade in copper.

Following the Civil War and execution of Charles I, Oliver Cromwell (1599 to 1658) became the first chairman of the Council of State of the new republic. Cromwell waged war on Ireland and Scotland, and after dissolving Parliament, he became lord protector. While serving in that office, he concluded the Anglo-Dutch War (1654), sent an expeditionary force to the Spanish West Indies (1655), and opposed the monopolies established under the Tudors.

During the first two years of Cromwell's Protectorate—1648 to 1649—a Baptist church was organized in Swansea, Wales, under Reverend John Myles. He became the leading minister in Wales. When the monarchy was restored, Reverend Myles and some members of his church came to America in 1663. Settling twice in New England, they were ordered to "desist and remove," so they moved across the colonial line into Massachusetts and built a new house of worship. The new settlement was given the name of their Welsh birthplace—Swansea—meaning "Sea of Swans." Here they at last found religious freedom, while back in Wales 8,000 others had been imprisoned.[12]

Nathaniel Jones purchased a tract of land and established a new town called Bristol, a kind of religious redoubt for Rehoboth and Swansea. Jones was a zealous Puritan but a generous, free-spirited citizen. He endowed a school in Bristol, which still bears his name, and built another in Essex County. The parish of the latter covered Newbury, Georgetown, and Rowley.

The Swansea records listed a John Jones, buried June 24, 1675. Also listed were John Padock and Anna Jones, who had married October 21, 1673; Joseph Lewis and Mary Jones, wed June 13, 1671; Benjamin Jones (wife Elizabeth), born January 10, 1699; Rebecca Jones, born April 9, 1705; Robert Jones "was a signer" in 1699; and Simeon and Encom [sic], both of whom fought in the Revolution. Nathaniel, Amos, Theophilus, Nehemiah, Ephraim, Gershom, Robert, and William Jones were listed as living in Frederickstown, Duchess County, while another Nathaniel, plus a Squire Jones, lived in Ballstown, Albany County. Ephraim, John, Jonathan, and Thaddeus Waring resided in the same town.

Genealogist Eugene Bouton, while searching the New Jersey Historical Society for Jones family information, found members of the family living in Swansea, Wales, before 1705—namely Benjamin Jones and his wife, Elizabeth. He also found an Aaron or Amos Jones living in Jefferson, New York, about the time the town was founded. Bouton discovered a Nathaniel Jones of New York who had fought in the American Revolution with the Third Regiment. According to Bouton's research, a Henry Jones married Hannah Hill in Stonington, Connecticut, in 1705. His grandson Henry married Eunice Minor in Stonington, January 19, 1749. Among their eleven children were Amos, born May 2, 1762, and Hannah, born July 4, 1764. This family, Bouton believed, moved to Jefferson, New York, where their children Hannah, Jacob, and Eli joined the Presbyterian Church in 1822.[13]

After studying *Military Minutes of the New York State Council of Appointments* by Hugh Hastings, Bouton found a list of soldiers from the 104th Regiment, composed mostly of men from Blenheim and Jefferson. Among them were Caleb Jones, Ensign (1805); a Captain Caleb Jones, and Lieutenant Russell Jones (1807); Russell Jones, first major, vice "Efner" promoted; and in 1819, a Colonel Russell Jones, who resigned in 1821.

Herschel's grandfather, Chauncey Jones, a shoemaker, had come to America from Wales in 1812 and ridden into Jefferson on horseback from one of the river counties.[14] His Welsh paternal line descends directly from those colonists who founded the town of Swansea in the Massachusetts Bay Colony in 1663. His ancestry, the Warings, from his father's mother's family (Phebe Waring married Nathaniel Jones in 1791), and the Merchants, the Smiths, and the Brainerds from his mother's side, stemmed from the first New England settlers.[15]

His grandparents on both sides left New England in the early part of the nineteenth century and were among those who founded the village of Jefferson, situated on the western face of the Catskill Mountains. His grandfather, Chauncey, moved in with his brother Eli Jones in Jefferson some time prior to 1820. Eli had built the first tannery in the town in 1810, which later became the Galt Blacksmith Shop. In 1820, the brothers tore down the log cabin in which they lived and erected a farmhouse. Recalled Eli's daughter: "Eli Jones bought the second stove with oven in Jefferson and tried to start the fire in the oven. It would not burn. He paid forty dollars for it."[16]

This same Eli, Herschel's great-uncle, and his daughter, Emeline, gained recognition circa 1819 for sailing the Hudson River as passengers on Robert Fulton's first steamboat, the *Clermont,* on route for New York and the Independence Day celebration. Clumsy little side-wheeler *Clermont* took thirty-two hours to paddle the 150 miles between Albany and New York.[17]

But Chauncey and Eli were not the only Joneses living in the Jefferson area during that time. Gazetteers state an Aaron (or Amos) Jones was among Jefferson's first settlers but there is no additional data to confirm this. But a Jacob Jones lived in the town and entered into real estate deals with Eli. Jacob, and his wife, Sally, sold the northwest corner of the Potter Hill and Harpersfield roads to Eli. Both men joined the same Presbyterian Church in 1822. Another family, headed by S.S. Jones, lived on the Westkill Road in Jefferson. These Joneses had come from the town of Westerlo in Albany County and S.S. became one of the most honored supervisors in Jefferson. Another Jeffersonian was Abraham Jones whose second wife was Betsey Foote, whose ancestors fought in the Revolutionary War. Elisha Jones was the name of a father and a son who lived toward South Jefferson. This family held less prestige than the other Joneses, although it came from the notable Jones family of Weston, Massachusetts. The elder Elisha had been an early settler in Pittsfield, Massachusetts, in 1752. Elisha, Sr., however, chose to be on the "wrong" side during the Revolution and took refuge in Canada, leaving his wife and son to face disaster. Wife and son quickly moved to New York and the Jefferson area. Elisha lived to be ninety-six and his wife, Hannah Odell, succumbed at eighty-eight. They are both buried in what is called the Welch Cemetery.[18]

Herschel's father, William Stephen Jones, was born in Jefferson in 1836. He commenced a successful business career in 1857, assuming a half interest in the mercantile firm of Twitchell & Jones with partner, Charles Twitchell. In 1860, William married Helen E. Merchant, daughter of highly respected town pioneer and semi-retired New England farmer, Reuben Merchant, born November 18, 1794, in Waterbury, Connecticut, and Ellis Smith Merchant, born in 1796.[19]

The Merchants have been traced to 1755 to the birth of Thomas Merchant in Connecticut. Thomas and his wife joined a church in Watertown in 1795. Thomas Merchant, however, became difficult to trace beyond this, although it was known that he sired thirteen or fourteen children. Two Thomas Merchants were listed as being "taxpayers" in *A History of Plymouth, Connecticut.*[20]

Although highly respected, Reuben Merchant had been highly controversial as town postmaster. Monthly audits within the postal department during 1831 seldom matched those figures kept by Mr. Merchant. The audit of November 22 is typical of the month's inaccuracies: "Herewith you have memorandum of such errors as have been discovered and corrected in your quarterly returns for the quarter ending July 1, 1831. If you need any explanation of these errors you will give immediate notice, directed 'Post Office Department, Examiner's Office.' The balance of the return, when corrected, is found to be $13.11, which is charged to your account."[21]

A report on September 25 found a discrepancy of $3.20, and another on December 8, moved the chief examiner to write Merchant that, "you should of course *charge* yourself with the same in your next return. Otherwise this department is deprived of the difference."

When these and similar "mistakes" continued on into 1832, correspondence between Merchant and the Examiner's Office became almost a monthly ritual. Merchant wrote to the chief registrar in August: "Their [sic] appears to be a mistak [sic] respecting my account commencing February 15 and ending April 1, 1831, stating letters remaining lost are omitted—$4.65 deducting $1.39 leaves

$3.26. If by the $4.65 you had reference to letters which remained in the office last autumn, I should think you would have to call on the late postmaster, Aaron Tyler, for a settlement for that for there was [sic] no accounts handed over from him to me when I took the office. But those was [sic] letters. But when I took the office to the amount of $4.37 and which you will perceive I charged myself with in the account of Mails Received which left balance due the general post office agreeable to my return of $9.73. I am now called upon from the Solicitor's office for $12.99. You will perceive that this return for a half quarter amounts to nearly as much as they do for a full quarter. But if the mistake is in my return I am willing to allow it."[22]

Following several additional exchanges of letters, Merchant was able to convince the post office he was only doing his duty to the best of his ability. In February, 1833, he received both a pat on the back and a light warning from the Assistant Postmaster General: "The Postmaster General is pleased with your diligence and attention to the faithful and prompt delivery of the mails, as mentioned in your letter of the 13th instant. When the contractor fails to deliver the mail in proper season, by reason of snowstorms or impassable roads, although he is excusable, it is nevertheless the duty of postmasters to report the fact of the detention of the mail, with the cause thereof.

"You were correct in charging double postage upon the letter which was rated only as single postage, but which, on being opened in your presence, you discover to contain a one dollar bill (see *Instructions to Postmasters*, Section 134)."[23]

Two months later, Reuben Merchant's position as postmaster was on the line following a threatened removal from office. He did, however, receive a reprieve from the Assistant Postmaster General: "The various statements for and against you have been examined. The Postmaster General has come to the conclusion that sufficient cause for your removal does not appear in this case. The act of selling temperance papers was by the regulations of the department. In most cases it is distinctly condemned by the Postmaster General. But under the explanation given by many of your fellow citizens, some of whom are known by the department and known to be highly respectable, it does not appear to have been done with any improper motive in references with the department or the cause of temperance—but on the contrary is understood to be so far as it had any effect beneficial to both. But as it is contrary to standing regulations the Postmaster General confidently expects that it will not be repeated. The Postmaster General looks to you for the [illegible] of good feeling and good policy with the view of allaying the excitement that has been raised in Jefferson in regard to your continuous in office. Personal attention to your duties and affability of demeanor towards those having official transactions with you will exert a happy influence in preventing further discontent, or rendering it harmless to you, if it arises."[24]

Another discrepancy appeared for the quarter ending July 1, 1834. Merchant was notified in November that the "Balance due to the Post Office Department" was $18.82.[25]

During 1835, Reuben Merchant was removed from duty as postmaster of Jefferson. Several Jefferson citizens had circulated a petition for his removal and for relocation of the post office in another town. While this action was taken because it was "the general wish of the inhabitants in the immediate vicinity of the post office," many of the petitioners had second thoughts. One citizen who signed his letter simply "S.C," wrote the Postmaster General that Merchant's removal had caused "a general dissatisfaction in town." He added, "it is my earnest desire that you will reinstate the office in the hands of Reuben Merchant, late postmaster in said town, knowing that he always has and I believe is still a warm supporter of the present administration."[26]

Merchant began sticking up for himself as evidenced by a letter he wrote postal authorities that same year: "I have read a communication from Mr. Hobbie, your assistant postmaster general, stating accusations that are alleged against me in the discharge of my duties as postmaster in the office at Jefferson as follows: 1. 'That the business of said office is loosely and irregularly conducted,' in reply to which I shall refer you to the [illegible] affidavits accompanying this letter and to my quarterly returns. 2. That the mail communications sent to my delivery are kept in an open box so placed within the bar of a common bar room, that they are within reach of everyone disposed to handle them; to this I say is incorrect. My bar is [seven] feet by [eighteen], it was made large for the accommodation of the post office and bar, for the front of the bar is a counter and from the floor up to the counter . . . is a swing grate which is always bolted down except on holidays when some one of us are required in the bar continually. The desk that had been furnished by the department previous to my appointment as postmaster I found to be insufficient to contain the papers and letters. I got a case made with small apartments (at my own expense) for papers sent to my delivery. It was first calculated for a door in front of the case with a lock, but finding that the door would be inconvenient, as the outer door of the bar is always kept locked except [when] myself or someone is in the bar capable of attending to the business, it was thought not necessary. My change drawer is in the bar without any lock. As to the papers being allowed to be handled, I would refer you to the certificate of M.G. The case spoken of is fastened up on the backside of the bar so that any person disposed to reach and handle them, as is stated in the complaint, must require an arm seven feet long. 3. That the business of said office is entrusted to boys not able to class charge them. To this I shall refer you to affidavits accompanying this and other opinions. 4. That the place in which said office is kept is objectionable as being a place of common resort where females cannot with propriety visit. In reply to this I will say that my house is sixty-eight feet long and fronting the road there is [sic] two front doors, one of which opens into the bar room and the other into a hall which leads to the Letting room where Mrs. Merchant is generally to be found. Mrs. Merchant is one of my room assistants and this fact is generally known in the vicinity and it is often allmost [sic] daily that females call on her to dispatch or receive letters, and she is always ready to wait on them or commiserate to me."[27]

Reuben Merchant dispatched his letter along with signed affidavits from supporters. He asked that the Postmaster General review his case and conduct another investigation into his removal. The case was reopened and a hearing was later held to determine whether any or all charges against merchant were valid. While little is known about the outcome, several Merchant supporters testified and supplied signed affidavits. One of these, Orrin Thomas of Jefferson, stated that Merchant had never over-charged him for a letter as alleged by "witnesses." Thomas also pooh-poohed the accusation that Merchant had not "refunded extra postage in money" and compelled him "to take the same or a part in whiskey."[28]

A petition was passed about town and signed by several hundred supporters that "Reuben Merchant as Postmaster may be reinstated in said office." The petition was signed on July 22, 1836, and sent to Postamster General Amos Kendall. Presumably, the petition got results, for an audit revealed that in September 1836, the "Balance due to the United States" by Reuben Merchant was $22.17.[29]

By the time William Jones married Reuben Merchant's daughter, Helen, in 1860, William was becoming a very successful businessman. About this same time, he took full charge of the mercantile firm of Twitchell & Jones and prospered through the Civil War.[30]

During the initial year of his mercantile career, he was appointed postmaster by United States Postmaster General Aaron V. Brown, November 25, 1857.[31] He held this term for seven years. All surviving documents indicate that Jones was an astute postmaster and was highly regarded. According to a local newspaper, "In Dec[ember] 1864, the auditor of the department discovered an error of $9.64 excess in remittance to the department in settlement of the quarterly account, and this amount was returned to Mr. Jones by Auditor Sells."[32]

Jones never used a clerk for any departmental correspondence. He addressed all his correspondence himself.

About 1865, William Jones sold his mercantile business to a Mr. Olmstead and, for health reasons, went to work on his twenty-six-acre farm near the village. Regaining his health, he again entered local mercantile circles by forming a partnership with Beriah H. Avery. In 1870, Jones built a new store, and his business flourished over the next twenty-three years until his death in 1894. Although he entered into a brief partnership with Watson S. Taylor, he became sole proprietor of the business when Taylor moved to Crookston, Minnesota.

Although active in the Republican Party, Herschel's parents swung their allegiance to the northern Democrats during the election of 1860. Herschel, in fact, was named for Herschel Vespasian Johnson of Georgia, a pro-Union sympathizer and candidate in 1860 for the vice-presidency of the United States on a ticket with Stephen A. Douglas. However, during the 1864 presidential election, William returned to the Republican fold over the slavery issue and voted for Lincoln. He continued his allegiance to the Republicans until Harrison was nominated for the first time. In that campaign, he voted for Fisk, the prohibition candidate, acting solely on the liquor question. Throughout his entire life, he was a strong anti-liquor advocate. When it became apparent that people would not rally against the liquor issue, he then returned to the Republican Party. He served in the role of town supervisor four times—in 1865, 1877, 1878, and 1879, and acted as town clerk, in addition to several other local offices.[33]

In addition to town services, William was frequently engaged to handle family affairs of outsiders, as evidenced by an 1874 letter: "The letter from Mr. Merchant coppied [sic] by yourself is received. Of course you know that he recommended you as the best person to attend to the collection of my notes and I agree with him. Will you take them and collect them for me? Will you also take care for the present of such other old accounts as he may turn over to you which we hold together? We have written him to do so, if he desires to be entirely free from the care of them. William, if you will take care of this business for us for the present we shall esteem it a great favor to us, and will pay you whatever is right for the care of the same."[34]

William Jones was also a devout Christian and "had for [thirty-five] years been a member of the Presbyterian Church, and for [fourteen] years he was an elder. He gave liberally towards the support of the church, and it devolved upon him to quite an extent to look after the interests of the society, because in the past death has thinned the ranks."[35]

He was considered by the church to be a "sure suppor" during the period when church membership was declining and he was always proud to acknowledge his religious faith. As a representative of the town on the Board of Supervisors in 1878, he was asked to address the board on the death of Peter Lawyer of Cobleskill, one of their members. In his closing remarks, Jones said:

"We know we can offer nothing adequate to the occasion, for affection will weep on, and for a time even our best words can be of little comfort, but I hope by this dispensation of the Divine Being we shall have at least learned a lesson, that though we may be in the very prime of life, and actively engaged in its busy scenes, we may be suddenly cut off and our life-work brought to a close. May we all, each and every one, learn that only in this life can we make preparation for that which is beyond."[36]

In a letter written to Herschel's oldest daughter, Tessie, a cousin, Ella M. Ferguson, granddaughter of Eli Jones, discussed Herschel's father and the early members of the family. "It was a happy surprise to mother and myself to receive a letter from the granddaughter of William Jones who we used to know so well," wrote Ella Ferguson. "He often came to see us when in the city, and after his death, we missed his pleasant calls for a long time. We were very glad that you spoke of your grandmother, we often think of her, we enjoyed her visit so much. My mother's people and her [sic] people were very intimate friends when they lived in Jefferson long ago. Mother had her [ninety-first] birthday on the 16th of October. . . . Well now, as regards the Jones family away back, mother says there were two brothers and one sister that came to this country from Wales. One of the brothers and the sister died, leaving only Nathaniel—your great-great-grandfather—who married Phebe Waring and settled in the town of Berne, Albany County, not far from the city. They had a family of six sons and three daughters. Four of the sons—Eli, Chauncey, Ebenezer, and Caleb were given trades as was the custom of those days—and two, the oldest Thaddeus and youngest Ensign, were farmers. The daughters married very well indeed. Sally and Lydia married men by the name of Haight—Polly married a Cornell of Schoharie. Eli Jones, my grandfather, built the house in Jefferson that your great-grandfather moved and occupied at the time of his death."[37]

Another letter to Tessie from Ella Ferguson was mailed the following month. Like the other, it was mostly concerned with genealogy, especially with the Nathaniel Jones' Swansea, Wales, connection. An excerpt read, "Mother has since found her family record and finds that Eli Jones, the second of Nathaniel Jones' children was born 1794. So we think your great-great-grandfather may have been married about 1791 and probably soon after crossing to this country as he would no doubt be anxious to make a home for himself. He very likely came not long after the Revolutionary War. He was from Swansea, Wales."[38]

Family documents suggest other Jones family members came to America from Swansea, Wales. A James Jones, as well as another William Jones, both born circa 1816, went to England and set sail for America in 1832. James, presumably, married Ellen Cahill of Irish descent, and the marriage produced six children. Mrs. Jones passed away in 1861. A Margaret Jones, born in the Baptist Church of Coffin Summit, in 1810 married Nicholas Haight. Another entry lists a pioneer, David Jones, who had four sons. One of these was also a David—Colonel David Jones—who served under General John Burgoyne in the British army during the Revolution.[39]

The year Herschel Jones was born, the town of Jefferson boasted two churches and twenty-five houses. The town, situated in a hilly upland, saw its first white settlers trickle in during 1803 when they appropriated a portion of the village of Blenheim. In 1819, a part of Summit Village was added to the new community of Jefferson. While many of the principal mountain peaks in the area loom 1,000 feet above the valley and twice that above sea level, Mine Hill to the south is about 3,200 feet above sea level. A high ridge extending northeast and southwest of the village forms the Delaware and Mohawk rivers watershed. Utsyantha Lake is situated to the south.[40]

Jefferson, New York, in 1910.

Views from Jefferson, New York.

A northerly branch of the Catskills runs along the southern border of Schoharie County, with extended spurs extending northward, covering most of the county. In the north, these hills tend to be rounded and are arable to their summits; but in the center and to the south, the declivities are steep and often precipitous. The high ridge forming a wall on the eastern border is known as the Hellebark Mountains.

The word Schoharie comes from the original Indian name "Towosschoher," signifying "driftwood." Deep within the hills and valleys, the Line Kil and Little Schoharie flowed into Schoharie Creek from opposite directions; and here driftwood was said to accumulate in large quantities, forming a natural bridge. Schoharie Creek flows just east of the center of the county and, during Herschel Jones' boyhood, was fed by many tributaries including Foxes Creek, Stony Brook, Little Schoharie Creek, Keysers Kil, Platter Kil, Manor Kil, Cripplebush Kil, Cobles Kil, Line Kil, Panther Kil, West Kil, and Mine Kil. The Charlotte River, a branch of the Susquehanna, rises in the western part of the county, and Catskill Creek, has a source in a marsh called the Vlaie. Utsyanthia Lake, 1,900 feet above seal level, and Summit Lake, even higher at 2,150 feet, comprise, surprisingly enough, the only two bodies of water in Schoharie County.

The mountains provided beautiful vistas as evidenced by the following account: "The top of Utsayantha, before and after its observatory was there, was a pleasant afternoon walk. One evening trip to its summit, which Mr. Churchill led, rewarded a good-sized party with wonderful views over near and distant peaks and valley flooded with all the charm and mystery a full moon could shed upon them. One Fourth of July a little party of us went up the gentle slope to the north of the village, and from its top feasted our eyes on the beautiful scenes to the east and north until the lengthening shadows warned us to return. The clear evening clothed the view toward Hobart with almost more than earthly beauty."[41]

Another account, older but just as enthusiastic, attests to the wild beauty of the Catskill "park" in and around Jefferson:

"The roads traversing this park lead in all directions from Stamford; the most important being to Gilboa and Prattsville along the Schoharie Kil, to Jefferson over Potter's Hill or around Mine Mountain, to Harpersfield and Lake Odell over the old drover's turnpike, to Hobart and 'over the mountain.' It is extremely doubtful if anywhere within 150 miles of New York anything so grand and constantly delightful in its varied scenic effort and so delicately beautiful in its natural state as modified only by agriculture, can possibly be found that is afforded by a drive through this natural park."[42]

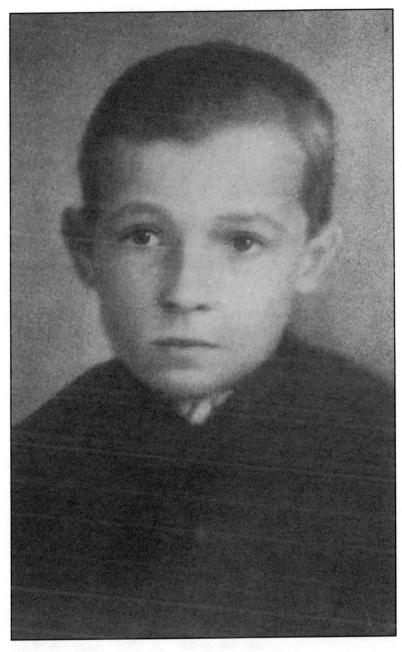

Herschel at eight years of age.

Growing up in the Catskills, a land rich in history, provided a healthy upbringing, especially for a boy like Herschel Jones, who had an intense hunger for knowledge. The county where he lived had originally been settled by the Schoharie Indians, which consisted of Mohawks, Mohicans, Delawares, Tuscaroras, and Oneidas, all living together as a single tribe. Their head chief was Karighondontee, who had once been a prisoner of the French in

17

Canada and had married a Mohawk woman. Subordinate to the Six Nations, Karighondontee's warriors, 600 strong, were allies of the British. With the aid of the colonial government, they erected several forts to protect themselves from the Canada Indians. About 200 Indians remained in the valley, but when the American Revolution broke out, the British induced them to turn on their neighbors.[43]

There was an Indian path leading into the Schoharie Valley from the Hudson River near Catskill. Over this trail, came the first white settlers in the county, a group of 600 to 700 German Palatinates, in 1711. The Indian path saved the settlers about three weeks by avoiding the circuitous route via Albany. The Dutch followed with a settlement called "Vroomansland," only a few miles above their German neighbors. When hostilities broke out between the French and British, the Germans in Schoharie aided the French. During the American Revolution that followed, many of these same Dutch and German settlers defended their land against what they considered a British invasion.[44]

While there were numerous battles in Schoharie County, the largest British raid occurred on October 17, 1780, when Chief Joseph Brant and Colonel John Johnson entered the valley and set fire to barns and crops, homes and churches. An old stone fort, which guarded the valley with its unlimited strategic overlooks, was stockaded. Besieged on all sides by the British, Tories, and Indians, the attackers failed to gain the fort and had to be content with devastating the valley.[45]

In the mid-nineteenth century "the old Catskill turnpike was a great line of travel. It seems to have been laid out from the top of one hill to the top of the next. Then was the day of the old time four-horse mail coach, which covered the route both ways daily, carrying passengers and the mail."[46]

During the early twentieth century, writers of historical romance and adventure novels drew on the Schoharie area for a setting. Among those was the distinguished novelist, Robert W. Chambers (1865 to 1933), who penned two dozen novels, most of them on the American Revolution. Two of these were made into silent movies. Chambers utilized such elements as the Six Nations of the Long House—the Iroquois—for his novels and short stories, some of which were published in *Adventure Magazine*. One of his better novels with a Schoharie locale was *The Little Red Foot* (1920).[47]

Even American fantasist and creator of Conan the Barbarian, Robert E. Howard (1906 to 1936) adopted Chamber's Schoharie milieu in several stories including *Beyond the Black River* (1935) in the last year of his life. Borrowing Chambers' real place names of Schoharie, Canajoharie, Caughnawaga, Oriskany, Sacandaga, and

Thendara, they became in Howard's tales: Schohira, Conajohara, Conawaga, Oriskonie, Scandaga, and Thandara.

In a letter to fellow author, H.P. Lovecraft, Howard penned:

"In the Conan story I've attempted a new style and setting entirely—abandoned the exotic settings of lost cities, decaying civilizations, golden domes, marble palaces, silk-clad dancing girls, etc., and thrown my story against a background of forests and rivers, log cabins, frontier outposts, buckskin-clad settlers, and painted tribesmen."[48]

But young Herschel Jones was undoubtedly a realist, not a fantasist. There were only nine books in the family library, but he found them fascinating. But one day, while on an errand to a neighbor five miles away, he saw a book like none he had ever seen before. The book was Jacob Abbott's *Life of Cyrus the Great,* and he asked the farmer what it was. The farmer informed him it was a library book, but the startled youngster did not know what a library book meant. He was told that for the small sum of five dollars a year, he could take a book and keep it for two weeks. Then he could either renew or return it for another. When the farmer let him borrow the book, Cyrus immediately became the boy's hero.

Cyrus, king of Persia and founder of Achaemenid power and the Persian Empire, conquered Media between 559 and 549 B.C., Lydia in 546, and Babylonia in 538, and laid the basis for future Persian victories in Egypt. The New Testament speaks approvingly of him because he placed Jews in power in Palestine, creating a buffer state between Persia and Egypt. Cyrus was a hero to most boys Jones' age because he respected the religion and customs of each part of his empire.

It took the twelve-year-old Herschel a year to scrape up five dollars doing odd jobs for a library membership. He soon read an entire series on the lives of great men, all authored by Jacob Abbott.[49]

Abbott, born in 1803, was well known for his many books for young readers. He was the sole author of 180 books and co-author or editor of thirty-one others, plus twenty-two volumes of biographical histories and ten volumes of *Franconia Stories.* Like most American boys growing up in the second half of the nineteenth century, young Jones read Abbott's popular "Rollo" series that included *Rollo at Work, Rollo at Play,* and several others. By following Rollo's travels about the world with his all-knowing Uncle George, the young reader could improve his knowledge of ethics, geography, science, and history.

Herschel's grandfather, at the time, subscribed to a New York newspaper, and Herschel read not only every issue, but, nearly every word.

"One feature of the news that interested me intensely," Jones recalled later, "was the obituaries! You smile at that. But I learned some very important lessons from those brief sketches. I noticed, for example, that in some men's careers there were long periods of time when they held the same position. They seemed to be standing still. And yet, in the end, these very men often reached a high place."[50]

Herschel also learned that most men do not begin to make money until after they turn forty years old. He decided that he would not worry about making money until he reached that age, and he devoted his time to preparation for the things he would need when he it was his turn. From the obituaries, he learned to have patience. He also discovered that credit was based on character and integrity and was very essential in the lives of the successful men about whom he had read. He was disturbed when he read Benjamin Franklin's precept, "Pay as you go."

"But that precept didn't seem to me to fit in with the facts in the obituary notices," recalled Herschel. "I thought a great deal about the matter, and finally decided upon a precept of my own. 'Never pay as you go—but pay!'"[51]

At the age of ten, he began publication of his own newspaper, printed with a lead pencil. Each issue contained a story he had written himself, and the story would be continued in each installment of the newspaper. He also wrote other articles for his one-man operation. Then there was the question of circulation, which was really no question at all. Herschel "printed" six to eight copies of the newspaper and distributed them to his friends. Thus, he served as editor, writer, and, of course, delivery boy.[52]

"At twelve I was haunting the printing shop which was next to my school," recollected Jones. "During recess, I would go in and set a little type from an old type case which they let me use. At fifteen I got a job in that same shop at three dollars a week; and when I was eighteen I bought the paper."[53]

For a young newspaper owner, Herschel Jones lacked a formal education. The public schools taught him only up to the age of fifteen, although he also attended the Delaware Literary Institute in the nearby village of Franklin. But he did not let his education stop him. He set two goals, which he resolved to attain one day—be the proprietor of a great newspaper and the owner of a great library.

The newspaper eighteen-year-old Herschel Jones purchased was the *Jeffersonian*. It had originated with Dr. A.W. Clark, who, in 1871, had taken a small office known as the Allen Gibbs office. Advised to rest because of his health, Clark used the office to occupy his leisure time by printing auction bills, letterheads and small job printing. In the fall of 1871, some of the businessmen of Jefferson asked him to start a local paper. Clark proposed that if enough money could be raised to purchase a printing press, he would provide the other needed supplies. Only half the money was raised by the townspeople. Nonetheless, Clark with no experience in the field and with only the aid of a small boy, furnished the needed supplies. On March 6, 1872, he issued the first paper the town of Jefferson had ever seen under the name of the *Jeffersonian.*[54]

The newspaper was an immediate success. On October 23, 1872, Clark increased the newspaper to five columns to accommodate his customers, and the columns were increased again December 13 of the same year. The goals of the newspaper during the Clark "regime" were literary culture, morality, truth and social entertainment, and to attain success.

On December 8, 1880, Clark sold the *Jeffersonian* to Herschel V. Jones and a partner. The newspaper on that day ran Editor Clark's "Farewell," which began:

"It is not with pleasure but with feelings of deep regret, that we announce to our many friends and patrons, that owing to poor health it becomes our duty to lay aside the pen and the many responsibilities attending the editing and publishing of a weekly newspaper. With this number we sever our connection as editor and proprietor of the *Jeffersonian*, having sold the same to H.V. Jones."[55]

In William E. Roscoe's *History of Schoharie County, New York, 1713-1882*, an entry under newspapers reads:

"The *Jeffersonian* is published at Jefferson, being started as the *Jeffersonian* by A.W. Clark, as editor and publisher, on March 1, 1872, and December, 1880, was purchased by Jones & Holmes, who changed the name to *Jefferson Courier*. It is a wide-awake, spicy, independent and reliable sheet, and receives a flattering patronage from the surrounding towns. The first sheet was [eighteen by twenty-four] and enlarged to [twenty-one by twenty-eight]."[56]

In addition to his editorial endeavors, the youthful newspaperman became an active member of the community. He was, by his own admittance, a self-taught musician, but, nonetheless, he played the organ in the Presbyterian Church and the coronet in the village band.[57]

Herschel had begun playing the organ at a very young age. A letter to his father from a friend, written when Herschel was only thirteen years old, reads: "Suppose Helen has banished you to the garret or to some other place out of her way while she is cleaning, dusting, and scrubbing below. Watson [Judd] can sympathize with you rather better than I can as I am more of the opinion of Helen. We are having very pleasant weather at present and very little rain.

Suppose Herschie can play almost any piece on the organ expect [sic] he has given up all idea of me answering his letter."[58]

Mr. Salisbury, the pastor of the Presbyterian Church that "Herschie" attended in Jefferson, had purchased the first stove with an oven in the town. "After one year, it became very rusty, so he painted [it] red," recalled Herschel's mother in 1904. "The old church that was burned was heated by two little box-stoves, placed on high blocks, giving no heat to feet, only to the hands. There became a division in building the old church, so it was boarded up, and remained so for about six months. One morning the people read the words on each side of the church, written in chalk: 'North America' and 'South America.'"[59]

The first year of the *Courier* was an important one for H.V. Jones. Only months after purchasing the newspaper, he bought out Holmes' interest and became sole owner of the paper. Little is known about the partner, Holmes, also spelled "Holms" in some accounts, but his money was perhaps used to help Herschel acquire the newspaper.

Herschel Jones later reflected on his purchasing of the newspaper from Dr. Clark: "The price was seven hundred dollars. Of course I had nothing like that much money; but my grandfather gave me two hundred and fifty dollars, which I paid in cash, giving my notes for the balance. In due time I paid these notes out of earnings; and when I sold the paper a few years later I had about seven hundred dollars clear, including the money my grandfather had given me."[60]

Heeding the call of Horace Greeley, "Go West, young man, and grow up with the country," Jones turned his attention to the Midwest at the age of twenty-two. He visited Chicago, Kansas City, Omaha, St. Louis, Bismarck, St. Paul, and Minneapolis in 1882, taking a survey of newspaper opportunities. He liked Minneapolis and decided he wanted to live in the city. He was greatly impressed with what he saw there and especially with the future of Minneapolis as the gateway of a great empire. He also found the newspaper he one day hoped to own—the *Minneapolis Journal*—which was then a small publication in a fairly big city. He returned to Jefferson in 1883, and before long, he sold his newspaper to P.T. Hoagland. Jones then left the Catskills for the city of his choice—Minneapolis.[61]

Minneapolis and its newspaper were not the only infatuations Herschel entertained during this period of his life. He had fallen in love with Lydia Gaylord Wilcox, a teacher in the Intermediate Department at the Schenevus Union School and Academy in Schenevus, Otsego County, New York.[62] Teaching had been in the

Wilcox blood over several generations, and two of her aunts had
served at Mt. Holyoke—one as dean and one as teacher.

According to a scrapbook kept by Lydia, she resigned her position at the school shortly after meeting Herschel. The following
notice appeared in the Jefferson newspaper: "Miss L. Augusta
Wilcox, perceptress of the Intermediate department of the Union
school, has resigned her position, resignation to take effect at the
close of the present term. She is one of the best teachers in the
school, and during her short stay in Schenevus has won many warm
friends in the village, as well as among the scholars. Miss Grace H.
Trickey has been engaged to take her place."[63]

Lydia, born in Delhi, New York, September 27, 1861, wrote of
her resignation to a friend on March 18, 1883. "Well am I not

enough to try the patience of Job himself were he on the face of the
earth," wrote Lydia. "You will see by this that I have returned again
to the parental roof. I came home from Schenevus the Thursday
before Christmas and since that time have been sitting in this
romantic place but the spoils one gets here turn—its beyond

Lydia Wilcox Jones' birthplace,
Delphi, New York. Lydia was born
September 27, 1861, and lived until
1942.

description. I do occasionally go to church and that's about all. Such an 'elegant' time I had at Schenevus. I was on the go all the time and have been sorry and sorry over again thousands of times. I did not stay but the wages I did not consider as enough so I handed in my resignation. Professor Thomas and the 'Board' seemed very unwilling I should leave. This Thomas even said he would cry if that would do any good."[64]

Lydia also mentioned that she liked the idea of moving west. She said she had been offered a position in a school somewhere, and although she "was so in love with her profession," she didn't know if she would accept. She referred to having had "a fearful, awful, dreadful" time but did not elaborate upon the problem. She was, however, suffering from a case of two boyfriends—Del Hoagland of Schenevus and Herschel Jones of Jefferson.

"[I] guess I told you of Del Hoagland of Scenevus," wrote Lydia. "Well, we did get pretty bad gone during my stay there, and after I returned home, we corresponded, and the last of February he came over and stayed three days. O hear, such a time as I have had, my hair has most all come out (but was out before he came). I didn't know who would come out with a head on. Hersch did take on so like a burnt cat. I actually thought he'd commit suicide. Just think how romantic. So I had to take him back to my arms and now Del is urgent. But Del is lovely, he has given me several beautiful presents—but gracious me, I don't want—but *one* fellow at a time again, *no* never nor hardly ever."

Lydia's letter appears to never have been sent. It was left unfinished and still remained in her possession at the time of her demise. She did, however, solve the "problem" of having two boyfriends. While poor Del rode off into the sunset, Lydia became engaged to Herschel.

A clipping pasted in Lydia's scrapbook shows Herschel's determination to finish first. This was, perhaps, a quality of Herschel's that Lydia admired. The clipping reads: "A correspondent writing from Jefferson says: 'The telephone is in operation between Jefferson and Albany, and H.V. Jones was the first one to use the line. He telephoned to Albany to send him a bird cage to put his birdie in.'"[65]

Another clipping on the same page of the scrapbook told of a visitor: "Miss Jones, of Hollyoke [sic], Mass., is visiting her former class-mate, Miss L. Augusta Wilcox." Whether this Miss Jones was a relative of Herschel's is speculative.

Lydia collected articles bearing upon everything from Charles Dickens to the various kinds of nails and tacks. She also included a curious piece called "Mount Holyoke." The piece began: "Perhaps one of the most interesting features of this place is its system of doing domestic work. Some ladies think it is too hard for a girl while engaged in hard study, but all the men think it is a most excellent plan; for is not housework the peculiar province of woman?"[66]

Lydia did some writing of her own—perhaps in conjunction with her school studies—and appeared to be especially interested in music and philosophy. At any rate, her writing skills were not wanting as evidenced from a fragment that survives from her New York days: . . . "and grandest scenes of human life, and review some of the most magnificent forms of beauty and grandeur, which the world can boast. The multiplicity and the diversity of subjects which it presents to the expanding mind afford matter for endless contemplation. It gives the scholar noble and exalted views of the reality of virtue, and will arouse from a state of inactivity the dormant mind to a sensibility of all that is most amiable and heroic in life, and will kindle in every breast a desire to imitate that word excellence which they so much admire in others.

"We can but reflect upon the condition of the world, in its early history, with no written language, and the consequent perplexity in attempting to communicate their ideas one to another."[67]

But Lydia's early writings also reflected a dark side—a lonely, insecure young lady dreading death of dear ones with a fear of the unknown. One piece of composition revealed a fear for her mother's death that would leave her walking an uncertain path. The following excerpt from her essay "Memories" stated, "With these bright and joyous memories come ones of sadness; we see that loved form laid low by the hand of death. We stand again by that dying bedside of the one of all the earth most dear to me; we clasp her hand as she gently slides over the stream of Death. Then all is over, we are pressed on by the current through this cold and dreary world alone; no gentle voice and loving hand to guide our footsteps. We miss the daily counsel and advice, and many times our feet stumble and we fall; we rise but to press on alone."

The only dated piece in Lydia's scrapbook is a newspaper clipping dated April 28, 1880, some three years before she and Herschel began dating. The piece reads: "Mrs. M.S. Wilcox received a few days since, from her daughter, Miss Augusta [Lydia], of Mt. Holyoke, a box containing a Trailing arbutus in full blossom, a bouquet of which adorns the editor's table. Please except [sic] thanks."

About the time of her courtship by Herschel, Lydia attended a wedding of a friend. An article written by Reverend F.D. Kelsey reported: "A very pleasant wedding ceremony took place Wednesday in the parlors of Rev. E.C. and J.B. Baldwin on Grove

The house and law offices in Jefferson, New York, of Moses Swift Wilcox, Lydia Augusta Wilcox's father.

Street. Rev. Edward D. Kelsey, a recent graduate of New Haven Theological Seminary, now supplying at Weston, was married to Julia C., daughter of the officiating clergyman, Rev. E.C. Baldwin, who was assisted by Rev. F.D. Kelsey of New Gloucester, Maine, brother of the bridegroom and Rev. Dr. Todd of this city. After an interesting social entertainment and repast, the bridal party started west to visit in Columbus and Cincinnati, O., carrying with them the best wishes of their many friends."[68]

The wedding of the friends must have rubbed off on Lydia and Herschel. The two were married in Jefferson on September 30, 1885. About forty guests assembled at 7:30 P.M. at the house of M.S. Wilcox. "At [eight] o'clock, the notes of the 'Wedding March' were struck, and the bridal party entered the parlor, the bride leaning upon the arm of her father and the groom walking with her mother. The groom received the bride at the hand of her father, and the couple took position beneath a beautiful floral bell, suspended from the ceiling. The ring ceremony was employed; Rev. D. Herron officiated, after which the happy couple received the hearty congratulations of the friends present."[69]

Lydia was attired in a light blue corduroy gown trimmed with Spanish lace. She wore diamonds that were a gift from Herschel. The presents were numerous and amounted to about $1,200. The following day amid a fanfare of farewells from friends and relatives, the couple left for a brief honeymoon in Albany, then were off to their new home in Minneapolis.[70]

Lydia's family was of good English stock traced back to William Willcoxon (1601 to 1652), who emigrated to the colonies from Hertfordshire, England. The earliest recorded traces of the Wilcox name, however, are found in Cornwall and Wales with a William Wilkoks recorded deceased before 1305. Another William turns up as executor of the will of Sir William Golafree in 1393. At a later date, the name spelled Willcocks is found in numerous English records and is sometimes prominent as in the name of Puritan author, Thomas Wilcocks whose books reached many editions. Another prominent name is that of Joseph Wilcocks, Bishop of Rochester, who, while dean of Westminster, restored the west front of that historical edifice. In the earliest continuous catalogue of Oxford University—from 1508 to 1528—the name is found eight times in various spellings.[71]

The name Wilcox is believed to be of Saxon or Celtic origin. A "Wilcox" or "Wilcott" was engaged in the Battle of Agincourt and is recorded as furnishing three men at arms. Another of the name was a court physician to one of the Kings Charles. Two centuries ago, another was a bishop of the Church of England and dean of Westminster Abbey, where he lies buried. A monument erected by his son commemorates his memory.[72]

The great-grandfather of Herschel's wife, Lydia, was Samuel Wilcox, born January 27, 1761. His wife, Sally Hunt, was born September 16, 1764. The Wilcoxes moved to Harpersfield, Delaware County, New York, shortly after the Revolutionary War. Samuel was active in the affairs of the town and he and his wife are buried in the cemetery of the Baptist church there.[73] Lydia's great-grandfather, A.B. Wilcox, and her grandfather, M.S. Wilcox, were both born in the house in Harpersfield. The Wilcox house was built in 1790.[74]

"For several years the settlers went to mill, first to Schoharie and then to N. Blenheim carrying their grains on horseback," states a journal belonging to Lydia Wilcox. "Mrs. Wilcox once was frightened by the howling of wolves when returning from the mill with a bag of flour. Mr. Wilcox shot a wolf one Sunday morning that was prowling about the sheep pen, the noise of the gun making quite a stir in town. It was thought at first that Indians must be around but when it was found to be only a wolf, it was seriously questioned whether the Holy Sabbath had not be desecrated by the good

Baptist deacon but it was finally considered proper to shoot wolves on Sunday providing the wolves were hunting your property and you were not really hunting the wolf."[75]

Lydia's father, Moses Swift Wilcox, was the son of Alonzo Wilcox and Hannah Swift.[76] Moses had attended school at Harpersfield Union Academy and soon became a teacher there and elsewhere.[77] In a 1851 letter to a friend, Moses described the academy as being "situated at the north west extremity of Harpersville centre. It was built by its proprietor in the year 1851. It consists of a main building and a wing on each side. It is divided into six rooms, three above and three below. Those above are to be used for music apparatus. Of those below the room in the centre is appropriated to the gentlemen. The room in the right wing to the ladies."[78]

According to Moses' grade reports, he was an exceptional student, and his compositions reveal a bit of the romantic poet. For instance, a written piece he turned in at the academy was called "Astronomy: A Delightful Study." An excerpt from the essay stated "how beautiful to trace the planets as they move, how glorious to see the stars in their loveliness, that give light to the weary traveler by night."[79]

Moses Swift Wilcox, father of Lydia Augusta Wilcox.

Moses did pen some fairly nice verse including this:

Perhaps it might afford a pleasing recollection
The name of your teacher to behold
When she shall have left this lower habitation
Or the hand that now writes this is cold.

Wilcox was also interested in politics and wrote letters to political candidates to air his feelings. One of these, an April 1852 epistle began, "Feeling somewhat interested in the coming presidential election and confidently believing that you will be the democratic candidate, I anxiously hope that you will not be wrongfully defeated as you were four years ago by the pretended honesty of the free soilers."

The Swift (Swyft) branch of the family can be traced back to Rotherham, England, and boasts some highly prominent members. An English newspaper account stated:

"One of the most interesting monuments in Rotherham Parish Church is undoubtedly that of the first of the Swyfts, who was a mercer in the town. This altar tomb, which is in the north chancel in an arched recess, is ornamented with quatrefoils, within which is a square plate of brass, and engraven thereon are the effigies of Robert Swyft, Ann, his wife, and his four children, Robert, William, Ann, and Margaret. The father is represented in a furred gown, his hair formally cut, and his hands joined as if in prayer. The lady has a square head-dress, her hands uplifted, but not joined.

"From the mouth of Swyft proceeds a scroll, with these words inscribed on it: 'Christ is ouer lyfe, And death is o'r advantage.'"[80]

Three shields have been removed from the front of the tomb, but two remain within the recess, bearing the arms of Swyft. Large numbers of rubbings from the beautiful brass have been made and have been carried off by visitors. The inscription on the tomb-face is well worth reproducing in its entirety, of course, if only to illustrate some curious differences in spelling between today and that of three hundred years ago.

The inscription on the tomb reads, "Here under this tombe are placyd and buried the bodies of Robarte Swifte, esquire, and Anne his fyrste wife, who lyvyde manye yeares in this towne of Rotherh'm in vertuous fame, grett wellthe and good woorship. They were pytyfull to the poore and relevyd them lyberally, and to their friends no less faythfulle than bountyfulle. Trulye they fearyd God, who plentiuslye powyred His blessings uppon them. The Sayd Ann dyed in the moneth of June, in the yere of o'r Lorde 1539 in the 67th year of her age; and sayd Robarte dep'tyd ye viii. Day August in the yere of our Lorde 1561 in the 8rth yeare of his age. On whose sowlles, will all Chrystan sowlls, the' omnipotent Lorde have mercey. Amen."[81]

William Swyft and his family of Sandwich, Massachusetts, undoubtedly came from England to America during the great Boston Immigration of 1630-1631, most likely from Bocking County, Essex. Swyft was living in Watertown, Massachusetts, in 1634, sold his property there in 1637, and moved to Sandwich where he died in January 1644. His will, as well as that of his wife, Joan, who survived him by twenty years, are recorded in the Plymouth County records. Swyft's farm in Sandwich was the largest farm in the town as late as 1887. The farm, that year, was occupied by his lineal descendant Shadrack Freeman Swift, Esquire.[82]

Lydia's mother, Lydia Gaylord Beard (Baird), was the daughter of Ezra Gibbs Beard and Lois Gaylord. The Gaylords or Gaillards were especially prominent. Two main streams of emigration of the Gaillards came from France. The first, during an early period of religious troubles there, took its course into the western counties of England, principally Somerset and Devon, before heading to New England in America. They first appear in Connecticut in 1630 and spread through Massachusetts and New York.[83]

Moses Swift Wilcox and his wife, Lydia Gaylord Beard, parents of Lydia Augusta Wilcox.

While of Gallic origin, the name comes from the old commune of Gaillard-bois in Normandy, France, and literally translated into English, the name is Gaylord. Chateau Gaillard was in this commune and the king passed some time in Normandy at a house called Gaillardbois—in A.D. 1475. The stronghold was built by Richard Coeur de Leon for the defense of the Normandy frontier.

At the beginning of the seventeenth century, the Chateau Gaillard was still in its entirety, and was considered the most complete and magnificent specimen of military architecture in Europe. Edward VI commenced his reign in 1547. In 1550, or 1551, the first Gaillards arrived in England. Following the accession of Edward, several religious congregations were organized by the refugees. French and Walloon churches were founded in London, Glastonbury, Somerset and other counties.

The Gaillards enjoyed religious freedom until the accession of Mary, a Papist and persecutor of the reformers. King James I extended his protection to these foreign Protestants, as did Queen Elizabeth, but in the reign of Charles I, they were again persecuted. Many emigrated to the British Colonies in North America, long known for their valuable fur trade and fisheries and regarded as a place of sanctuary.

Foremost, perhaps, of all the colonies after Plymouth was that of Dorchester, The colony later removed to Windsor, Connecticut. This honorable settlement, consisting of many Gaillards, was derived from the English colonies of Devon, Dorset, and Somerset.

William Gaillard, born in 1585 in Exeter in the county of Devon, England, emigrated to New England with his brother John in the spring of 1630. He was of good family and good estate. Gailliard had been chosen deacon of the gathering at Plymouth, Devon County, England, in March 1630, when the church was organized under Reverend John Maverick and Reverend John Warham. He sailed to America on the ship *Mary & John*, arriving in Nantucket, Boston Bay, May 30, 1630, and was made freeman October 19.

Deacon William Galliard and Deacon William Rockwell signed the first land grants in Dorchester, and Galliard's own grant was recorded there in 1633. He was selectman and representative of the General Court from 1635 to 1638, when he removed to Windsor with Warham's Company. He represented Windsor in nearly forty sessions to 1664 in the General Assembly, and died there July 20, 1673. Lydia Augusta Wilcox was a direct descendant of William Galliard.

Many of her family members settled in Delaware County, New York, in 1771 after Colonel Harper removed his family from Cherry Valley to Harpersfield, or the "Bush" as it was generally called. A survey was completed in 1772. In the list of earliest known settlers were the names Joel Gaylord, Jedidiah Gaylord, William Beard, Abijah Baird, Samuel Wilcox, Aaron Wilcox, Eliah Wilcox, and David Wilcox. The settlement was thriving when the Revolutionary War broke out, and in Harpersfield, nearly all the settlers sided with the Colonies. But in 1777, Indians and Tories commanded by Brant and Butler attacked, and nearly all the settlers fled. At the close of the war, Colonal Harper and many of the settlers returned.

Genealogist Donald Lines Jacobus of New Haven, Connecticut, located a line of direct Gaylord ancestors in 1935 and signed a sworn deposition that Benjamin Gaylord and Jerusha Frisbie were married by a Mr. Russell, January 8, 1729. The couple had three children—Levi, born January 10, 1730; Jerusha, July 1, 1731; and

Enos, January 27, 1733. Following the death of Benjamin's wife Jerusha in 1734, Benjamin married Mary Ashley, and the nuptials were performed by a Mr. Stanley, February 14, 1738. The union produced only one child—Molly, born August 29, 1739.[84]

Tessie Jones established a direct seven-generation link to Benjamin and Jerusha Gaylord. She established Benjamin's year of birth as 1692 and Jerusha's date of birth as March 10, 1712. But Tessie was also able to go beyond Benjamin three additional generations to the tenth generation ancestor, Deacon William Gaylord, who she wrote was born in England in 1585. A son, Walter Gaylord, born about 1622, became the father of Joseph Gaylord, born May 13, 1649. Joseph became the father of Benjamin.[85]

The surname of Baird, from Lydia's maternal side, originated in the south of France during the reign of Louis IV. Many of these Bairds sailed to England and Scotland from Normandy with William the Conqueror. When King William was released from his captivity in England in 1174, he returned to Lyon with some of the Bairds accompanying him. The other Bairds remained in England and Scotland. The archaic spelling of "Baird" was Bard, Barde, Beard, Byrd, and Bayard. The "Baird" spelling was not used until the latter sixteenth century. Thomas the Rhymer once prophesized that "there would be an eagle in the crags while there was a Baird in Auchmedden."

According to material gathered by genealogist Eugene Bouton, most members of the Beard family of Jefferson, New York, came from Blandford, Hampton County, Massachusetts. In 1735, when Blandford was settled, James Beard, an original settler, "took home lots 33 and 24." Soon after, there was a John Beard also living in the settlement, as well as another James Beard, probably the son of his namesake.[86]

In "Ye Story of Ye Memorial," Nathan G. Pond wrote of one Martha Beard, mother-in-law of James Stream, whose name is engraved on one of the coping-stones of the bridge erected as a memorial to the founders of the town of Milford, Connecticut:

"Lambert says she brought with her three sons and three daughters; that James died in 1642, and his estate was settled by Captain Atwood, and it was the first estate administered upon in Milford. Jeremy probably died without issue, as his estate was divided between his brother, Captain John Beard, John Stream, and Nicholas Camp, 'husbands of his sisters,' says the record. They may have let their wives have a little of it. All of the names in Milford descend from her son John, who had the military title of Captain. Her husband probably died on the ship (*Martin*?) on passage over, and on consideration of her affliction the town gave her an extra amount of land in the division."[87]

Herschel and Lydia could both take pride in their family heritage. When they left the village of Jefferson to begin anew in the city of Minneapolis, they left behind scores of family members and friends. Many of these persons would visit the Joneses in the city, and, occasionally, Herschel and Lydia would visit Jefferson.

Even to the present day, Herschel V. Jones is highly regarded by some Jefferson citizens. When his name did not appear in a 1976 history of the town of Jefferson, one disappointed reader wrote the author of the book:

"The biography of one person born in Jefferson might not fit in the concept of village history, but it could be interesting to keep in the town records. The reason I say this is that if one equates outstanding success with great wealth and international fame, the most successful person to have been born and spent his formative years in Jefferson was Hershel [sic] V. Jones."[88]

Notes

[1]Juan Carlos Orendain interview with Helen McCann White, March 20-21, 1959. Transcript pp. 35-37, Minnesota Historical Society.

[2]Ibid.

[3]Ibid.

[4]Ibid.

[5]Ibid.

[6]Ibid.

[7]Barbara Flanagan, *Minneapolis City of Lakes and Skyways,* Minneapolis, The Nodin Press, 1973, no page numbers given.

[8]Mildred Bailey, *A History of the Town of Jefferson 1771-1976.*

[9]Alice Webber Child letter to Tessie Jones dated February 19, 1916.

[10]Mrs. Child also found a problem when she discovered the name "Squire Jones" in the genealogical accounts. She wrote, "When I found Squire Jones I said to myself, Squire? Does that mean a name or is he an old man and that a title? A long time afterward I found in Connecticut a Jones named "Justice," and I said here is Squire. Of course if he was your man I should have to prove it. I suppose your head is whirling so I will stop."

[11]Alice Webber Child letter to Tessie Jones dated February 25, 1922.

[12]Ibid.

[13]Eugene Bouton letter to Tessie Jones dated March 16, 1945.

[14]Winton Jones letter to Mrs. Mildred L. Bailey dated February 2,

1985; *Jefferson Courier,* Thursday, January 11, 1894, "A Respected Citizen Gone."

[15]Edward C. Gale, "Herschel V. Jones," A memorial read on January 21 at the eightieth meeting of the Minnesota Historical Society; Herschel V. Jones, Lee Brothers Historical Collection of Portraits registration form, February 28, 1923; Mildred Bailey, *A History of the Town of Jefferson 1771-1976*; Alice W. Child letter to Tessie Jones dated Saturday Evening, February 19, 1916.

[16]1904 Recollections of Mrs. Helen Merchant Jones; *Jefferson Courier,* date unknown, "Rode on the *Clermont.*"

[17]*Jefferson Courier,* date unknown.

[18]Eugene Bouton letter to Tessie Jones dated February 1, 1945; Eugene Bouton letter to Tessie Jones dated March 16, 1945.

[19]Papers of Vista Beard Wilcox.

[20]Ida J. Turner letter to Tessie Jones dated February 27, year not given. Ida Turner stated that Thomas Merchant became an old man whom "the children of Samuel called Uncle."

[21]W.G. Eliot, Chief Examiner United States Post Office Department, letter and statement to Reuben Merchant dated November 22, 1831.

[22]Reuben Merchant letter to D. Saunders, Chief Registrar, United States Post Office Department dated August 9, 1832. Letters indicating "discrepancies" were sent to Merchant on March 20 and September 3 of that year.

[23]J.R. Hobbie, Assistant Postmaster General, letter to Reuben Merchant dated February 26, 1833.

[24]J.R. Hobbie, Assistant Postmaster General, letter to Reuben Merchant dated April 29, 1833.

[25]W.G. Eliot letter to Reuben Merchant dated November 20, 1834.

[26]"S.C." letter to Postmaster General Amos Kendall dated July 26, 1836.

[27]Reuben Merchant letter to Postmaster General Amos Kendall dated May 13, 1836.

[28]Signed affidavit of Orrin Thomas of Jefferson, New York.

[29]Petition signed by citizens of Jefferson, July 22, 1836; Auditor's Report for 3 September 1836.

[30]*Jefferson Courier,* Thursday, January 11, 1894, "A Respected Citizen Gone."

[31]Copies of Appointment Document and Requirements Form in Waring Jones Collection.

[32]*Schoharie County Chronicle,* Tuesday, January 9, 1894, "In Memoriam."

[33]*Jefferson Courier,* Thursday, January 11, 1894.

[34]Sarah A. Judd letter to W. S. Jones dated May 21, 1874.

[35]*Jefferson Courier,* Thursday, January 11, 1894.

[36]*Schoharie County Chronicle,* Tuesday, January 9, 1894.

[37]Ella M. Ferguson, letter to Tessie Jones, dated February 12, 1908. Ella apologized in her letter for being so tardy in answering a letter from Tessie. She said she had been suffering from an attack of grippe.

[38]Ella M. Ferguson, letter to Tessie Jones, dated March 15, 1908. Ella Ferguson vowed to make a trip to Wales in the near future since "people now go over the country like birds."

[39]Family records indicate that several of these Jones boys took Irish wives.

[40]J.H. French, *Historical and Statistical Gazetteer of New York State,* 1860, reprinted in 1993.

[41]Eldora Baird, Fannie McCracken and Eugene Bouton, *History of Stamford Seminary and Union Free School 1796 to 1931,* The Stamford Press, Inc., Stamford, New York, 1931, p. 18.

[42]*Stamford in the Catskills,* no author given, Stamford Printing and Publishing Company, no date given.

[43]J.H. French, *Historical and Statistical Gazetteer of New York State.*

[44]William E. Roscoe, *History of Schoharie County, New York, 1713-1882 with Illustrations and Biographical Sketches of Some of Its Prominent Men and Pioneers,* two volumes, D. Mason & Company, Syracuse, 1882, reprinted by Heritage Books, Bowie, Maryland, 1994, pp. 9-36.

[45]Old Stone Fort brochure published by Schoharie County Historical Society, Schoharie, New York.

[46]*Jefferson Courier,* Thursday, September 17, 1891, "And the Desert Shall Rejoice and Blossom like the Rose."

[47]L. Sprague de Camp, Catherine Crook de Camp, and Jane Whittington Griffin, *Dark Valley Destiny,* Bluejay Books, New York, 1983, pp. 279-280.

[48]Robert E. Howard letter to H.P. Lovecraft c. October 1934.

[49]Edward C. Gale, "Herschel V. Jones; James H. McCullough, "What a Youngster Learned from his Grandfather's Newspaper," *The American Magazine,* January, 1924, pp. 16, 74.

[50]James H. McCullough, "What a Youngster Learned from his Grandfather's Newspaper," p. 16.

[51]Ibid.

[52]Ibid, p. 74.

[53]Ibid.

[54]Mildred Bailey, *A History of the Town of Jefferson 1771-1976,* p. 84.

[55]Ibid, p. 85.

[56] William E. Roscoe, *A History of Schoharie County, New York, 1713-1882, Volume 1, p. 82.*

[57] Family History compiled by Mrs. Kenneth H. Bailey.

[58] Sarah A. Judd letter to W.S. Jones dated May 21, 1874.

[59] 1904 Recollections of Mrs. Helen Merchant Jones.

[60] James H. McCullough, "What a Youngster Learned from his Grandfather's Newspaper," p. 74.

[61] Ibid.; *Minneapolis Journal,* Thursday Evening, May 24, 1928, "H.V. Jones, Owner and Publisher of the *Journal*, Dies."

[62] Schenevus Union School and Academy booklet for 1882-1883.

[63] Scrapbook of Lydia Augusta Wilcox. Note: None of the entries in the book are dated. The book appears to have been her father's business ledger. Lydia pasted her favorite poems and clippings from the newspaper over the existing business figures of her father.

[64] Lydia Augusta Wilcox, letter to "Joe," dated Sunday afternoon, March 18, 1883.

[65] Scrapbook of Lydia Augusta Wilcox.

[66] Ibid., under "Mount Holyoke."

[67] Fragment of an essay written by Lydia Augusta Wilcox.

[68] Scrapbook of Lydia Augusta Wilcox.

[69] *Jefferson Courier,* October 6, 1885, "Wedding Party." The article ended with the following curious statement: "One of the incidents of the wedding was the presence of four gentlemen, all over 80 years of age"; Major R.I. Holcombe and William H. Bingham, *History of Minneapolis and Hennepin County, Minnesota,* Chicago, Henry Taylor & Company, 1914, p. 382.

[70] Herschel V. Jones, Lee Brothers Historical Collection of Portraits registration form, February 28, 1923; Family History complied by Mrs. Kenneth H. Bailey; Winton Jones letter to Mildred L. Bailey dated February 2, 1985.

[71] Wilcox Family History compiled by Tessie Jones.

[72] Rev. S.P. Merrill, *The Wilcox Family From Narragansett Historical Register, July 1889*, Rochester, New York, 1889.

[73] Wilcox Family History compiled by Tessie Jones.

[74] Edward J. Wheeler, Ph. D., letter to Tessie Jones dated February 9, 1908; M.S. Wilcox letter to Tessie Jones dated January 1918.

[75] *Journal* owned by Lydia Wilcox.

[76] Bowman's Ancestral Chart of Wilcox Family found in the H.V. Jones Collection.

[77] Letters of certification registering Moses Wilcox as a teacher by G.B. Selig, November 4, 1832; Principal Robert Rogers of Harpersfield Union School, September 22, 1853; and Charles Chapman, November 15, 1854.

[78] Moses Wilcox letter to Lewis Culp dated December 1, 1851.

[79]Astronomy composition of Moses Wilcox dated February 12, 1852; "Ingenuity of Man" composition dated January 27, 1852; Grade reports for April 2, 1852, July 12, 1853, and September 17, 1853.

[80]*Rotherham Advertiser,* Rotherham England, Date Unknown. H.V. Jones Collection.

[81]Ibid.

[82]Harriet Wilcox Wheeler letters to Tessie Jones, dated November 25, 1915. The other is undated.

[83]William Gaillard, *The History and Pedigree of the House of Gaillard or Gaylord* in Waring Jones Collection; Eugene Bouton letter to Tessie Jones dated April 23, 1945.

[84]Donald Lines Jacobus letter to Mrs. M.D. Field dated March 7, 1935.

[85]Tessie Jones, Proof of Eligibility to the Board of Managers of the Colonial Dames of the State of Connecticut, October 15, 1934.

[86]Eugene Bouton letter to Tessie Jones dated April 23, 1945. This same Eugene Bouton, writing in 1945, states to Tessie that he worked for Ezra G. Beard on a summer vacation in 1816 or 1817. Obviously he had his centuries confused.

[87]According to the Beard-Baird records of the Blandford town clerk, John Beard married Agnes Brown June 27, 1754. Elsewhere in the document, Jacob Jones and Ezra Beard contributed money and joined the Board of Directors to establish the Jefferson Academy in 1812.

[88]Mrs. Kenneth H. Bailey undated letter to Mildred Bailey; Christine M. Palmatier, Librarian/Archivist/Registrar Schoharie County Historical Society letter to author dated May 15, 1998.

CHAPTER TWO

BIRTH OF THE *JOURNAL*

"News, news, news, my gossiping friends,
I have wonderful news to tell."
　　　　　—Owen Meredith

newsboys rushed into the streets with still damp papers shouting, "Paper! Your *Evening Journal*." They scattered to deliver their newspapers in a town of "straggling homes, unpaved streets; a town with a few board sidewalks and a miniature horsecar system; a town growing up around the city hall at the junction of Nicollet and Hennepin avenues."[1]

Very little construction had been done north of Fourth Avenue North, or south of Cedar Avenue. When C.H. Pettit erected his home at Tenth Street and Second Avenue South in that year, many considered him a visionary. Fourth, Fifth, Sixth and Seventh Streets were the leading residential thoroughfares, but many of the town's prominent families still lived north of Hennepin Avenue along Washington, Third and Fourth Avenues North. The business district of the city spanned lower Nicollet and Hennepin avenues and extended down along Washington Avenue toward the flour milling area.

"Of sidewalks there were none, except some wooden, wobbly, plank affairs in the center of town." There were no sewers to carry off the surface water deposited by the slush, mud, and snow, and the water took its time about going. Reverend Dr. Sample, who lived on Fourth Street between Hennepin and Nicollet, entered a strong protest at city hall when Beals' Photographic Gallery proposed to move across the street from his church. The state's university boasted a faculty of nineteen and a student body of 371.

November 26, 1878, was a banner day for Charles H. Stevens, J. H. (Sidney) Rowell, and Frank E. Curtis as they watched the newsboys rushing out to the graded dirt streets of Minneapolis from the press in the Johnson, Smith, and Harrison printing office at 21 South Second Street. A fourth young owner, Clarence A. French was not present. The four had pooled their meager resources, "borrowed $200 at [twelve percent] on a short-time note from V.G. Hush," and realized their dream of an evening newspaper, *The Minneapolis Journal.*[2]

"The material end of our enterprise was meager—some lead pencils and scratch paper," recalled Frank E. Curtis fifty years later. "We owned no equipment. We had a few fonts of borrowed type and forms in a composing room in the Brackett block, and when the forms were made up, we lugged them downstairs and then upstairs to the pressroom of the neighboring building."[3]

The *Journal* venture appeared to be an "unpromising infant." A six-column folio, with both inner pages of plate matter, it was painfully apparent that the paper was started without capital and without a news franchise.[4]

That same year, Ulysses S. Grant had just completed his first term as president, and Rutherford B. Hayes was the newly elected occupant of the White House. Minneapolis fostered a population of about 35,000; comparable to present-day LaCrosse, Wisconsin. Only thirteen years earlier, Horace Greeley had visited Minneapolis, found the city made up of about 8,000 inhabitants, and predicted a rosy future for it. "The *Journal* was founded at a propitious time, for the phenomenal development of Minneapolis which took place in the eighties lay just ahead."[5]

Like most American newspapers of the era, Minnesota papers were much different from those of today. There was little attempt at objective reporting; news was bogged down with a strong dose of editorial comment. All the early newspapers were fiercely partisan, and each day they attacked political opponents. News was frequently based on nothing but conjecture or hearsay. There was little news, and the big stories were often tucked away on the second page amidst a hodge-podge of advertising, legal notices, "purple" fiction, and recipes. The papers were two to four pages long; twenty-by-twenty-five inches for weeklies, and fifteen-by-twenty-one for the dailies—both larger than today's standard newspapers. Each page held six or seven columns and rarely enough material on any single subject to fill a column. The first pages were devoted to clipped national and international news as well as fiction and poetry. The second page was composed of national and local news, as well as the aforementioned editorials, advertisements, legal notices, recipes, sensationalism, and more fiction and poetry. Advertisements filled the third and fourth pages exclusively.[6]

Early Minneapolis newspaperman Charles E. Russell later recalled, "Those were great days in Minneapolis. The character of the city in its restless activity and enterprise, its indomitable resolution, and also its high ideals, was being formed then. You youngsters see only the fruits of these things. It was something of a privilege to observe Minneapolis in its formative period. There has been no more interesting and peculiar process of evolution on the continent. I suppose a wilderness has never been conquered by men of more sterling worth than settled your region. Someone should have left a permanent record of the curious struggle that went on between the universal tendency of mankind to return to barbaric traits in primitive conditions, and the essential nobility of the men that laid the foundations of Minnesota's greatness. But men were too busy then grappling with the insistent problems of daily bread."[7]

The evening field at the time was dominated by the *Minneapolis Tribune*, founded in 1867 as a morning newspaper and adding an evening edition through an unsuccessful merger with the *St. Paul Pioneer Press*. The *Tribune*'s success had been quite an accomplishment, since, during the territorial years between 1849 and 1858, some ninety newspapers had emerged on the Minnesota frontier and nearly all of them had bitten the bullet.[8]

The first newspaper published in the future site of Minneapolis, was founded on May 31, 1851, by Isaac Atwater, a judge of the Minnesota Supreme Court. This newspaper, the *St. Anthony Express*, lived eight years and, according to Judge Atwater's account, cost him $3,000. The *Express*, like many other pre-statehood Minnesota newspapers, was circulated back East to extol the virtues of territorial life. An article, published in March 1852 warned, "Eastern cities are swarming with a useless, idle population—the prey of vice, disease, and misery. Come away from the city come to the West—come to Minnesota!"[9] A year earlier the *Express* had printed articles about the Sons of Temperance, and the early temperance reform movement, via the newspapers, had slowly begun.[10]

The *Express* was printed in the old log mess house used by the men who built the first sawmill on the east side of town. Judge Atwater, years later, reflected: "The subscribers agreed to pay two dollars a year, and really intended to do so. But, alas, the human necessity of daily bread was often greater than the necessity of a weekly newspaper. Hence they were forced to compromise on the amount of their subscriptions in farm produce, boots, clothing, and groceries, and, not seldom, promises only."[11]

Only one year after the founding of the *Express*, the paper was taken over by George D. Bowman, a Pennsylvania newspaperman. But, three years later, in 1855, Judge Atwater, who had been making cash advancements to the newspaper for the editorials he had written, took back possession of the paper to protect his investments.

During the summer of 1853, the Minneapolis area's second newspaper, the *Northwestern Democrat*, was established. When the paper moved across the river the following year, its name was changed to the *Minneapolis Democrat*. The *Democrat* was thus the first newspaper published west of the Mississippi River and north of Iowa.

In 1858, C.H. Pettit and John G. Williams purchased the recently suspended *Gazette*. Williams, serving as editor, changed the name to the *Minneapolis Journal*, but his venture was short-lived. Within a year, the newspaper was taken over by the *State Atlas* of Colonel William S. King.[12] King, a native New Yorker, was a friend of Thurlow Weed and William H. Seward in the organizational days of the Republican Party in New York. A few years later, he merged his paper with the *Weekly Chronicle,* and it became the *Minneapolis Tribune.*[13]

Suddenly, newspapers in the St. Anthony/Minneapolis area were blossoming like wildflowers. Among the pioneer fatalities were the *St. Anthony Republican, The Cataract and Agriculturalist, The Independent, The Minneapolis Plaindealer, The Rural Minnesotan,* and the *Minnesota Beacon*. These and a handful of others quickly passed into oblivion.[14]

But, in 1878, the new *Minneapolis Journal* was determined to stay afloat and grow, as evidenced in its salutatory:

"Notwithstanding that four evening newspapers have risen and fallen in Minneapolis during the past five years, the publishers of The *Journal* offer it to the people today for the favorable notice and support."[15]

It's rival, the *Tribune*, had actually begun on a sour note beginning with an apology to its readers, at the very top of the first column of its first page. It confessed with great embarrassment in its first installment that, "The lines being down most all day, we are without the greater part of our dispatches. No one can regret this accident more than we ourselves." Nonetheless, the paper flourished.[16]

Reporting was a tough business in those days, especially when only two reporters had to canvas all of Minneapolis. As one of these recalled, "In the morning we both hustled for local news and got in about noon to write the 'stuff' up, 'chop telegraph,' write the few editorial paragraphs and read proof. After the paper had gone to press there was copy to be gotten out for the next day, and we both went home at night laden down with exchanges to get out reprint, news condensations, and editorial for early copy the next day. That was the way papers were made in those days, and it was a very exceptional day that each of us did not furnish from four to six columns of 'stuff.'"[17]

Competition came also from *The St. Paul Evening Dispatch*, which had been established in 1868. Four other newspapers had entered and failed with an evening edition over the past five years. Two St. Paul morning newspapers also enlivened the competition: *The St. Paul Pioneer Press*, which began in 1849, and the *St. Paul Morning Globe*, which commenced publication the same year as the *Journal*.[18]

After the initial week of publication, the *Journal* boasted 900 subscribers, although the figure is undoubtedly inflated. The owners were compelled to renew their $200 short-term loan from Hush several times before it was finally paid. The newspaper did receive fair advertising support and five columns of "reading-notice advertising" were printed each issue.[19]

With the first issue, the editorial staff announced their intentions, stating, "The *Journal* will be a zealous adherent of all enterprises which will benefit Minneapolis and raise the standard of morality among the people." It also promised that while they did not intend "to dwell largely upon politics, the *Journal* in principle will be thoroughly Republican but without being restricted or hampered by party lines in upholding the right and integrity, and exposing and denouncing evil wherever found."[20]

The *Journal* also pledged, "Financially we will advocate a money which shall be worldwide, and tendered and received by every civilized nation—gold and silver."

Starting the newspaper in 1878 was a bold decision by the four young men of the *Journal*. The city and the railroads were just starting to recover from the depression of five years earlier, and the city was bursting at the seams to provide housing for the great increase in population. Between 1870 and 1880, the population had increased 269 percent and had reached 48,053. The influx of people inflicted pressures on the business community and brought about the development of the business blocks at such a rate "as to almost bankrupt the available supply of labor and material."[21]

Immigrants were flowing into the United States through its eastern ports, and newcomers began populating eastern cities and, eventually, the countryside. Older Americans, living in New England, New York, and in the South, began to push westward as a result of the influx. Civil War veterans, too, could not settle down peacefully in their old homes in the East and pushed west to take part in the excitement of the frontier. And Minneapolis was, of course, a frontier town in 1878.[22]

But in that first issue, the *Journal* owners were ready to face obstacles as stated in that edition:

"Obstacles and opposition are before us; but we shall meet them with a strong persistent will and with an energy born of the purpose: that of establishing a clean and interesting local paper for the people and the home."[23] The *Journal* owners, of course, were looking only to the local field, but Minneapolis was growing rapidly and was becoming the gateway to one of the richest sections of the country. As time went on, the newspaper would extend its field.

Their competitor of sorts, the *Pioneer Press*, wished them well: "The plucky trio of young journalists, who promised a few days ago to give the people of Minneapolis a new evening paper before the holidays, were promptly on hand last evening with the initial number of the *Minneapolis Journal*. Among the other good things promised, the editors say the *Journal* will be a zealous promoter of all enterprises which will benefit Minneapolis and raise the standard of morality among the people. Success and fortune to the *Journal*."[24]

The following year, 1879, the newspaper moved its offices to Room 3, Brackett Block, Second Street and First Avenue South, because George Brackett had offered cheap rent. The day of the move was intensely cold—twenty-eight degrees below zero—as the small staff trudged through the snow in heavy coats, lugging types and forms into their new facility. The newspaper was printed on the press of a former employee, Ed A. Stevens, who still printed the *Weekly Mirror*. The *Journal* owners paid for the use of the equipment and type "by setting up and printing the *Mirror*." The press cost them $1,500 and they paid an additional twenty dollars per week in securing a "skeletonized" telegraph service from a correspondent in Chicago. After payment of all their bills, including paper and rent, they divided the remainder amongst themselves and paid their own board bills. Somehow the newspaper improved both editorially and financially.[25]

"After a time we were able to establish credit and borrow money to buy a printing press and type, giving a mortgage on the equipment as security," remembered Frank Curtis. "From that time on the *Journal* went right along on the way toward prosperity."[26]

Editorially, the *Journal* pursued those principles of their platform, and, from the beginning, the stockholders had made the decision to forego liquor and tavern advertising, "although in those days such advertising was abundant and profitable," and they were personally acquainted with several "decent saloon keepers." However, a story had circulated that the founding of the *Journal* was discussed initially in the "Nicollet House barroom with Joe Murch furnishing some of the inspiration.[27] Clarence French addressed the rumor, replying, "it is a remarkable fact that three printers and one other man were found in Minneapolis in 1878 who did not drink."[28]

The *Journal* reiterated its stand for non-alcoholic drinks in its editorial column in 1879: "All hail the time when intoxicating liquors shall be banished from the land and the manufacturing thereof made a criminal offense."[29] On other editorial matters, they ridiculed the idea of woman suffrage and adopted a hard-nosed position on Indians. The *Journal* supported, in fact, the development of the proposed Northern Pacific Railroad into the Northwest "as a means of fighting and controlling the hostile Indians."[30]

That same year, "leg talent," a very important part of a local reporter's equipment, became an issue, when for the first time in history, the life of a newspaper depended upon a foot race. The walking match craze was raging all over the country, and the reporters and newspapermen of Minneapolis put together a go-as-you-please race at Market Hall. The entries were J.N. Nind, of the *Tribune*; Ed Bromley, representing the *Pioneer Press*; Ernest Sturtevant, from the *St. Paul Globe*; Fred Puhler, of the *Hotel Gazette*; and E.J.C. Atterbury, for the *Journal*.[31]

The *Journal*'s, Atterbury, was carefully trained by a professional and the tutoring paid off. Atterbury won the exciting race before a large, enthusiastic crowd of spectators by walking twenty-six miles in four hours. The *Journal* staff had been very confident of Atterbury's agility and ability as a pedestrian. Since the paper was in danger of going under, the publishers had staked the whole establishment on his winning the race. After their representative dashed across the finish line ahead of the field, the *Journal* was able to purchase a new press and increase its news facilities. Before the race, it was a question of only a few days when suspension of publication would probably have been necessary.

The *Journal*'s editorial policy by the following year advocated the building of the Northern Pacific Railroad as "a means of fighting and controlling hostile Indians," and offered the prescience of its editors in editorially envisioning Minneapolis a hundred years in the future. It predicted that in the year 1980, "the streets are thronged with people. The air, too, is full of them, for aerial locomotion has been an established fast [sic] for half a century."[32]

The *Journal* also took the side of public welfare by demanding boiler inspections on all vessels after the steamer *May Queen* blew up on Lake Minnetonka. It also addressed the subject of fairness and impartiality in its news columns during the legislative investigation of Ignatius Donnelly's bribery charges against William D. Washburn. While most newspapers at the time printed only the testimony they wished to print, the *Journal* printed the news objectively, even though it was squarely on the side of Captain Washburn.

Frank Curtis took advantage of citywide revival meetings at one of the local churches. The meetings were held over a period of several weeks, and people, among them Curtis, flocked to hear and criticize. The area newspapers were accused of not giving enough coverage to the meetings but not Curtis and the *Journal*. There were few shorthand reporters in those days, but Curtis attended the meetings every night and made a full and accurate shorthand report. Curtis recalled, "Some of the sermons were very long and the meetings were protracted to a late hour, so that it was generally well along toward morning before my notes, with the assistance of the faithful [E.J.C.] Atterbury, were transcribed and ready for the compositors. This episode helped the reputation and progress of the *Journal* very much."[33]

By the spring of 1880, the *Journal*'s circulation had accelerated to about 1,800 paid subscribers, and its advertising had spread to a seven-column folio in April. In addition, the price of the *Journal* had increased to forty cents a week or five cents a copy. This success, with the proposed return of the *Minneapolis Tribune* from the evening field back into the morning, interested several prospective buyers. Among these were the Nimocks brothers, Walter and Charles, who were about to start a new evening daily newspaper called the *Herald*. However, they were willing to forget their intended *Herald* should the *Journal* owners be persuaded to sell.[34]

The Nimocks brothers were turned down since the future of the *Journal* looked very bright. The paper had recently issued an almanac for 1880, including data on Minneapolis, the businesses, and industries, all for the cost of a five-cent stamp.

The first page of the *Journal* included a column of amusement notices and business cards, two columns of display advertising, market reports, and a half page of telegraph news. "Throughout, the paper had an air of thrift and prosperity, carrying about [fifteen] columns of advertising out of [twenty-eight]."[35]

Disaster struck on April 6, 1880, when a fire reduced the building to a heap of ashes. Not one piece of equipment had been rescued; the mortgaged printing press was destroyed, as were type, forms, and paper. Only the subscription lists survived. The owners, since they had no telephone, learned about the fire when they saw it in ruins. And, of course, their publishing dream had also been turned to ashes. They were unable to print an edition that afternoon, but they did the following day by using one of the job offices. It was a "melancholy fire edition . . . in which the publishers gallantly proposed to continue the struggle."[36] There was, however, no desire to continue. When the Minnesota Printing Company of Nimocks and Shaw offered $2,500 for what remained of the *Journal*, the owners accepted.[37]

"This was the situation in April 1880 when the disastrous fire wiped out the entire physical equipment of the *Journal*," recalled Frank Curtis. "We were left with nothing because the insurance went to liquidate the mortgage. Then the Nimocks brothers actively and eagerly began negotiations for the purchase of our good will and circulation."[38]

Clarence A. French later recalled that when they unknowingly came to work the next morning, they found their place of business surrounded by firemen and their precious press lying in a hot heap in the cellar of the gutted building, "smashed to eternal pieces." So with heavy hearts they sold all they had left to sell—the "goodwill" of those 1,700 subscribers—and after paying their bills, separated with flat pockets.[39]

The new owners brought not only experience to the *Journal*; they also brought financial support. George K. Shaw (usually referred to as Major Shaw because of his Civil War rank) stated that he and Nimocks, the new owners, invested $12,500 into their enterprise. The company quickly purchased the evening franchise of the (AP) Associated Press for $7,000 from the *Minneapolis Tribune*, which, through an earlier arrangement with the *St. Paul Pioneer Press*, had just purchased the morning franchise of the AP for $18,000. Now, in 1880, only two newspapers existed in Minneapolis—the *Journal* in the evening and the *Tribune* in the morning. This also ended the so-called Minneapolis edition of the *St. Paul Pioneer Press*, which had boasted on its front page the legend, "Published simultaneously in St. Paul and Minneapolis."[40]

The 1880s erupted into a major population explosion for Minneapolis. Some 116,600 persons descended upon the community, many of whom were immigrants. By the end of the decade, there were more than 60,000 foreign-born people living in Minneapolis, most of who had come from Sweden and Norway, as well as Canada and Germany. While there was a significant increase in *Journal* circulation, the paper did not reach many of the immigrants with a foreign language background.[41]

The population boom also affected the Minneapolis schools. In 1878, the state legislature united the two existing school boards to form the Board of Education of the City of Minneapolis. The first high school—Central—then located on Third Avenue South, between Eleventh, and Twelfth Streets, was opened.[42]

The *Minneapolis Times* of September 30, 1896, ran the following headline: "A Boom in Kids—Supt. Jordan Doesn't Know What to do with Them." According to the *Times*, the schools, which in 1878 had a staff of ninety-eight teachers and enrolled 5,270 pupils, were now capacity-filled with 769 teachers and 33,673 pupils.

The curious rushed into downtown Minneapolis in 1882 to see what Minneapolis claimed to be the world's tallest light fixture. This "fixture" was a tower 275 feet high made of tubular boiler-plates, which tapered at the top. City planners had projected this tower would light the entire city, but when the lights were raised to the very top, the light was so dissipated that it was almost ineffectual. The illumination worked best at a hundred feet above the street. The arc lights were lowered each day for trimming and then were hoisted again. The tower was razed after ten years when this method of illumination was abandoned. But, if for nothing else, the tower of lights lured thousands into the downtown business area.[43]

The business community enjoyed a renewed vigor. According to the *Journal*, "The railroad boom in Minneapolis has finally started. Tracks and freight houses are to be finished by August 15. Work on the Union depot will be begun as soon as possible. Now, who says that Minneapolis is not a railroad center?"[44]

Despite the boasts of the *Journal*, the conditions of the streets in Minneapolis were atrocious. The story of a tramp printer was widely told among Minneapolis citizens. As the tramp printer, a common breed in those years, left Minneapolis after a brief stay, he "shook off the mud and snow as a testimony against the inhabitants," claiming that the city was "no place for a white man, where 'you were over your bloomin' hankles in mud in summer and up to your blarsted 'ips in snow in winter.'"[45]

The streets were still muddy in autumn and spring, snow covered in winter, and dirty and dusty in the summer, as not a single street had been paved in Minneapolis as late as 1880. But during the next ten years, some fifty miles of streets would be paved, and the rickety planking that served as sidewalks downtown would be replaced with some 214 miles of durable planking. By 1890, there were eighty miles of stone sidewalks.

Following their takeover of the *Journal*, Nimocks and Shaw issued their proclamation concerning the "new" *Journal*: "It will be the aim of the proprietors to make a pure and readable daily newspaper, that can be safely taken into the family, and that at the same time will not lack enterprise in news gathering nor independence and boldness in the expression of opinions." Since the "proprietors are all Republicans in politics," the paper would support the Republican position, and those tenets "hallowed by the martyrdom of Lincoln and . . . incarnated in the life of a Republic saved from the assaults of Treason."[46]

Still, the *Journal* claimed it would be independent of partisan politics despite a platform concerned with politics and flag waving. The editors nonetheless wrote that politics "will constitute the smallest plank in the *Journal*'s platform. Its first and foremost aspiration is to well represent and to further the local interests, moral and material, of this city and state."[47]

Over the next few years, the *Journal* underwent changes in format, flag, style, news concepts, and publishing location. The paper was enlarged to eight columns with four pages, although the press

The first *Minneapolis Journal* Newsboys' Club, 1882. (Courtesy of the Minnesota Historical Society)

of advertising occasionally caused the publication of a blanket sheet. During the week of the Minnesota State Fair, the paper presented a double folio (eight pages). A large Roman *Evening Journal* had been used through July 16, 1880, following the fire but was replaced by a heavy, black Old English, the *Minneapolis Evening Journal*. The paper also adopted the make-up of the *Albany* (New York) *Evening Journal*. Beginning November 3, 1880, the *Journal* commenced printing a third edition at five o'clock, which was "for sale exclusively on the streets." Having purchased a new double-cylinder press and engine, the *Journal*, with new types and forms, boasted the finest production facility in the Twin Cities. Following the purchase of the paper, the business office had been separated from the editorial rooms and mechanical departments, which shared with the *Tribune* part of the old City Hall, at the intersection of Hennepin and Nicollet Avenues. As the paper grew, the *Journal* moved into a three-story brick building at 10 Washington Avenue North, recently vacated by the Merchants' National Bank.[48]

The new facility allowed greater publication capability as 12,000 four-pagers were printed hourly. Circulation increased from 1,000 to 3,000. The staff was increased with Shaw as editor and Charles Nimocks as business editor. Frank E. Hesler became city editor, A. J. Gage, Jr., telegraph editor, and George N. Loomis, state editor. A few reporters and correspondents were added as well.

In February 1883, the price of the newspaper dropped from five cents a copy to two cents, but the *Journal* continued to implement "special reduced rates" for home subscription at other times. In May, it announced the rates would be in effect for sixty days, allowing people to subscribe for four dollars a year, forty cents per month, one dollar for three months, in advance, of course, or ten cents a week.

The following blurb ran in the *Journal* that same year: "Just think of it! A daily paper giving the associated press telegraphic news, supplemented by copious special telegrams, full market reports, the local news of two great cities and all the general news for only [four] dollars per year. The *Journal*'s object, of course, is to get up a big circulation. We have such press facilities that we could print 25,000 copies of the *Journal* per day as well as 10,000, and we are going for the 25,000."[49]

In May 1883, a new managing editor took over duties at the *Journal*. Amos C. Jordan, formerly of the *Tribune*, was an experienced professional and had some time ago served as editor of the *St. Paul Pioneer* before it had consolidated with the *Press*. Major Shaw turned to other duties, and, according to A.J. Russell, all those who worked under him "liked him, hated him, feared him, laughed at him, and respected his prowess."[50]

During the spring of 1885, George K. Shaw left the *Journal* and purchased *The St. Paul Dispatch*. The Nimocks brothers paid Shaw about $50,000 for the half share he and his brother owned. "From a total investment of about $12,500 just five years earlier, the *Journal*'s worth had climbed to about $100,000. The Nimocks brothers were now in full control of a very successful and growing enterprise. But their personal involvement was to be short lived.

During the fall of that year, new interests invaded the Minneapolis newspaper field, and the threat of stiff evening competition in the city faced the Nimocks for the first time. Their response to this competition would have a profound impact on the history of Minneapolis journalism, and particularly that of the *Journal*."[51]

One year earlier, William E. Haskell had moved to Minneapolis from Boston. He and Colonel Alden J. Blethen had purchased the *Morning Tribune,* and they had their eyes on the *Evening Journal* as well. The new *Tribune* owners took control of the evening United Press service (a separate entity from today's United Press International) in 1885 and promised to meet the *Journal*'s Western Associated Press service. Blethen and Haskell were joined by Lucian Swift, Jr., and by H.W. Hawley. Swift had served as bookkeeper and cashier for the *Minneapolis Tribune* for several years before becoming business manager of the *Journal* and Hawley had become city editor.[52]

The Nimocks brothers realized they could not take on the competition. With regret they sold the newspaper for $130,000, the highest sum ever paid for a daily newspaper in a city of less than 150,000. In a long editorial, the Nimocks brothers credited them-

The Minneapolis Journal Building, 1884. (Courtesy of the Minnesota Historical Society)

selves with the success of the *Journal*. They also credited the enlarged population, support of businessmen, and the assistance of other newspapers in the metro area.[53]

The new owners took over on November 7 and made the following announcement with their first issue, "As to the principles which will govern the paper it is unnecessary to speak at length. Newspapers, like political platforms, are oftener made to be broken than kept. For this reason the *Journal* proposes to make a few promises."

As an independent Republican paper, the *Journal* would nonetheless be prepared to criticize or repudiate either men or party "when the former are less worthy of confidence, and the latter less promotive of the public good, than they ought to be." As for local affairs, the *Journal* would subscribe to a wise course "less likely to be less consistent than independent, because 'consistency,' as commonly interpreted, is the straightjacket of little minds, and is the most stubborn and ignorant foe of progress." Regarding labor, the *Journal* "will constantly befriend the cause of labor, while it will make for the safety of capital, upon which labor depends for its opportunities of thrift . . ."[54]

Lucian Swift, Jr., immediately took control of the *Journal*, serving as secretary of the corporation that owned the paper, and as the paper's business manager. Also in charge was John Scudder McLain, one of eleven reporters Blethen had brought with him from Kansas City, who were widely known as "Blethen's cowboys." McLain became managing editor from day one and was quick to make his imprint known.[55]

But Blethen did not stay with the *Journal*. Soon after acquiring the paper, he sold his interest to E.B. Haskell, the father of one of the stockholders and editor of *The Boston Herald*. Hawley followed by selling his interest to McLain and Charles N. Palmer, *Tribune* stockholder and publisher of the *Minneapolis Miller*. Palmer's share was small, as he had invested but $4,000 in the venture. The hierarchy following the reorganization included E.B. Haskell, president; McLain, vice-president and editor; Swift, secretary, treasurer, and manager. Will Haskell and Charles Palmer stayed in the background with no active roles in operating the *Journal*.

The new owners were not afraid to spend money. The staff was quickly enlarged from three reporters to five, plus six editors and correspondents. One of these reporters was Herschel V. Jones, who had joined the *Journal* staff just prior to the Nimocks brothers' sale to new owners. Hired as a reporter, he would quickly become one of the best known commercial editors in the Midwest and later would become sole owner of the *Journal*.

Notes

[1]*Minneapolis Journal,* November 25, 1928, Anniversary Issue.

[2]*Minneapolis Journal,* November 25 and 26, 1928, 50th Anniversary Issues.

[3]Ibid.

[4]No author given, *The Story of an Institutional Newspaper, 1878-1899, Being Twenty-One Years of the Minneapolis Journal,* Volume I of IV, Minneapolis, The Journal Printing Company, p. 5.

[5]*Minneapolis Journal,* Monday Evening, December 3, 1928, "Thank You."

[6]Jane Lamm Carroll, "Minnesota's Territorial Newspapers," *Minnesota History,* Vol. 56, No. 4, Winter 1998-1999, pp. 222-234.

[7]*Minneapolis Journal,* November 25, 1928.

[8]*Minneapolis Journal,* Monday Evening, December 3, 1928.

[9]Brian Horrigan, "Wild West Show," *Minneapolis Sunday Star Tribune,* November 15, 1998, p. F20.

[10]Theodore C. Blegen, "Minnesota Pioneer Life as Revealed in Newspaper Advertisements," *Minnesota History,* Vol. 7, No. 2, June 1926, p. 105.

[11]Lawrence M. Brings and Jay Edgerton, eds., *Minneapolis, City of Opportunity, One Hundred Years of Progress in the Aquatennial City,* Minneapolis, T.S. Denison & Co., 1956, p. 152.

[12]No author given, *The Story of an Institutional Newspaper, 1878 to 1899, Being Twenty-One Years of the* Minneapolis Journal, Volume I, pp. 1-2.

[13]Lawrence M. Brings and Jay Edgerton, eds., *Minneapolis, City of Opportunity,* p. 152; Joseph Stipanovich, *City of Lakes, An Illustrated History of Minneapolis,* Minneapolis, Windsor Publications, 1982, p. 334; Bradley L. Morison, "100 Years for the *Minneapolis Tribune,*" *Hennepin County History,* Winter 1968, p. 14.

[14]Ibid.; William D. Green, "Minnesota's Long Road to Black Suffrage 1849-1868," *Minnesota History,* Vol. 56, No. 2, Summer 1998, p. 76.

[15]*Minneapolis Journal,* November 26, 1878.

[16]*Minneapolis Tribune,* May 25, 1867; Bradley L. Morison, *Sunlight on Your Doorstep:* The Minneapolis Tribune*'s First Hundred Years, 1867-1967,* Ross & Haines, Inc., Minneapolis, 1966.

[17]Undated *Minneapolis Journal* column, entitled "More Newspaper Reminiscences—J. Newton Nind Recalls the Hustlers of the Old Days in the Twin Cities," in collection of Hennepin County Historical Society.

[18]*The Minneapolis Journal,* November 25, 27, 1928; George S.

Hage, *Newspapers on the Minnesota Frontier 1849-1860*, Minnesota Historical Society Press, St. Paul, 1967, pp. 127, 132-133.

[19]Ted Curtis Smythe, "A History of the *Minneapolis Journal*, 1878-1939," An unpublished thesis submitted to the faculty of the graduate school of the University of Minnesota, December 1967, pp. X, 3-4.

[20]*The Minneapolis Journal*, November 26, 1878.

[21]Ted Curtis Smythe, "A History of the *Minneapolis Journal*, 1878-1939," pp.7-8; the *Minneapolis Journal*, September 8, 1881; the *Minneapolis Journal,* November 25, 1928.

[22]*Minneapolis Journal*, November 25, 1928.

[23]*Minneapolis Journal*, Monday Evening, December 3,1928.

[24]No author given, *The Story of an Institutional Newspaper, 1878 to 1899, Being Twenty-One Years of the* Minneapolis Journal, Volume I, p. 5.

[25]Ted Curtis Smythe, "A History of the *Minneapolis Journal*, 1878-1939," pp. 7-8; *The Minneapolis Journal*, September 8, 1881 and November 25, 1928.

[26]*Minneapolis Journal*, May 25, 1928.

[27]This same Nicollet House served as a "watering hole" for members of the infamous James-Younger gang only three years earlier.

[28]*Minneapolis Journal*, November 25 and 27, 1928.

[29]*Minneapolis Journal*, July 3, 1879.

[30]Ibid.; *Minneapolis Journal*, December 12, 1928; Ted Curtis Smythe, "A History of the *Minneapolis Journal*, 1878-1939," pp. 11-12.

[31]Judge Isaac Atwater and John H. Stevens editors, *History of Minneapolis and Hennepin County, Minnesota,* Volume I, New York & Chicago, Munsell Publishing Company, 1895, p. 368.

[32]*Minneapolis Journal*, May 25, 1928.

[33]Ibid.

[34]Ted Curtis Smythe, "A History of the *Minneapolis Journal*, 1878-1939," pp. 13-14.

[35]No author given, *The Story of an Institutional Newspaper, 1878 to 1899,* Volume I, p. 7.

[36]Ibid.

[37]Ibid.; *Minneapolis Journal*, November 27, 1928.

[38]*Minneapolis Journal*, November 25, 1928.

[39]Vivian Thorp, "Here's State's Constant Reader No. 1; Took First Newspaper Off Press in 1878," *Minneapolis Journal*, Thursday, November 24, 1928.

[40]Ted Curtis Smythe, "A History of the *Minneapolis Journal*, 1878-1939," pp. 17-18.

[41]Charles E. Artman, Arthur M. Borak, Kenneth T. Setre, Rolan S. Vaile, *The Construction Industry in Minneapolis,* Volume 2, Bulletin of the Employment Stabilization Research Institute, University of Minnesota, Minneapolis, June 1934, p. 34; Calvin F. Schmid, *Social Saga of Two Cities*, Minneapolis: Bureau of Social Research, 1937, p. 134.

[42]Lawrence M. Brings and Jay Edgerton, eds., *Minneapolis City of Opportunity*, p. 168.

[43]Joseph W. Zalusky, "Nicollet . . . A Great Thoroughfare," *Hennepin County History,* Summer 1968, p. 13.

[44]*Minneapolis Journal,* June 28, 1880.

[45]*Minneapolis Journal,* November 25, 1928, p. 5.

[46]*Minneapolis Journal*, May 3, 1880; Ted Curtis Smythe, "A History of the *Minneapolis Journal*, 1878-1939," p. 21.

[47]Ibid.

[48]Ted Curtis Smythe, "A History of the *Minneapolis Journal*, 1878-1939," pp. 23-24.

[49]*Minneapolis Journal*, May 11, 1883, p. 4.

[50]*Minneapolis Journal*, May 17, 23, 1883; November 28, 1928.

[51]Ted Curtis Smythe, "A History of the *Minneapolis Journal*, 1878-1939," p. 41.

[52]Ibid., pp. 43-44; Anonymous, *Minneapolis Illustrated,* Minneapolis: Minneapolis Board of Trade, undated, p. 12; Charles B. Cheney, *The Story of Minnesota Politics*, Minneapolis, *Minneapolis Tribune*, March 1947, p. 5; *The Minneapolis Journal*, November 25, 1928, p. 2; Major R.I. Holcombe and William H. Bingham, editors, *Compendium of History and Biography of Minneapolis and Hennepin County*, Minnesota, Chicago, 1914, p. 494-495.

[53]*The Minneapolis Journal*, November 6, 1885, p. 2.

[54]*The Minneapolis Journal*, November 7, 1885, p. 4.

[55]Ted Curtis Smythe, "A History of the *Minneapolis Journal*, 1878-1939," pp. 46-47; *The Minneapolis Journal*, November 25, 1928, p. 2.

CHAPTER THREE

PURSUING THE DREAM

"Someday we'll all be gone and other
darned fools will be walking here."
—The *Journal's*, John the Janitor, when
asked about his Fourth Street[1]

he "Elegant Eighties" was an age when bearded men in
long black coats spoke in formal, decorous language, when
ladies enjoyed "afternoons at home," and "the mark of
worldly success was a well-polished carriage, with gleaming brass-
work, shiny leather, handsome horses, and a coachman. Women
wore three petticoats under heavy and elaborate dresses, and men
were strait-jacketed in boiled shirts, high stiff collars, and detachable 'hard' cuffs."[2]

Many of the elaborate dresses worn by women were made in
Minneapolis by high class dressmakers including Madames Boyd
and Worley. But these women were not casual seamstresses. According to one account, "Most of them made semiannual trips to
Europe and then Americanized Paris styles, translating them into
distinctly Minnesota products that reflected not only habit, taste,
and social niceties, but also the bloody bad weather. Not only were
they talented dressmakers, they were also consummate engineers.
Garments were built rather than sewn, each requiring an elaborate
substructure of padding, boning, and undergarments to delineate
the 'line' of each fashion era."[3]

As testimonials, one Ellen Beach Yaw praised the undergarments of Wade & Company, "I desire to express my appreciation
of the Wade Corset, which being constructed on principles allowing perfect freedom of the breathing muscles, should be endorsed

by every singer." A Julia Morlowe endorsed the undergarment by saying, "I am enjoying wearing my stays so much." And a Madame Modjeska agreed that "the corsets were perfectly satisfactory, as is always the case with anything you send."[4]

This was the period of formal notes and calling cards, where any "cultured" home had a table in the front hall bearing a silver tray and visitors were expected to leave their engraved cards. Yearning for culture, the upper crust of Minneapolis society read Ralph Waldo Emerson's *Good Manners*, and tried to emulate the standards of Boston and New York drawing rooms. Smoking in front of a lady was highly improper, and smoking on the street was the sign of the boor. The polka and waltz were immensely popular and Professor. Danz' orchestra was much in demand. Minneapolis, a frontier outpost only twenty years before, was shaping itself into a city in an attempt to shake its overgrown country town image.[5]

The frontier image had been shaken off in 1885, the year the Joneses moved to the city, when the state legislature passed a law that required every child between the ages of six and sixteen to attend school at least twelve weeks out of the year. School officials could fine any parent who did not send his or her child to school. The law was difficult to enforce, however, because "people do not like to have trouble with their neighbors."[6]

Minneapolis had spread out during the 1880s, but the city was still largely "downtown." Seventh Street and Sixth Avenue South, was considered one of the best residential areas. Nicollet Island boasted some of the finest Victorian homes in the city, especially along Grove Place. The Nimrocks, owners of the *Minneapolis Journal*, lived there, as did the DeLaittres, the Eastmans, the Eustises, and the Charles A. Heffelfingers.[7]

H.V. Jones at twenty-four years of age when he came to Minneapolis, 1885.

Across the river from downtown, near the University of Minnesota on Fifth Street Southeast, stood the opulent home of Governor John S. Pillsbury, with its "porte-cochere, elaborate woodwork, little window balconies, and towering chimneys—one of the show places of the city."[8]

Upon arriving in Minneapolis in 1885, Herschel and Lydia Jones rented a home at 347 East Seventeenth Street, on the extreme southern edge of downtown. The Joneses became one of the few families in the city to have a telephone, although the number—111-3—probably didn't ring too often, since the majority of Minnesotans couldn't afford the luxury of "being on-line."[9]

The new telephone system was anything but reliable, and the phones were hand-cranked instruments attached to the wall. The First National Bank, for instance, was on a three-party line and one of the service sharers was a liquor dealer. Because of the often-erratic service in connections, bank employees were sometimes on the receiving end of demands for "spirited" deliveries.[10]

On September 21, 1886, Lydia gave birth to their first child, a daughter they named Tessie Jones.[11] The following year, on August 24, 1887, their second child, a son, Carl Waring Jones was born.[12] Both of the children were born in Minneapolis.

The Jones home, located on the north corner of Seventeenth Street and Fourth Avenue served as their home for five years.[13] At that time, Franklin Avenue served as the city limits, and the Joneses were just three blocks north of Franklin. Park Avenue and Lowry Hill were swank residential areas at that time, but there were few houses beyond Twenty-third Street.[14]

Jones liked his location, as it was ideal for getting to work by taking the horse-drawn streetcar on Franklin Avenue. Upon entering the car, adults would drop their fares in a slot that ran across the car windows to the driver who also served as conductor. If change were needed, Jones would walk to the front of the car and pick up his change from a little cup in the door, deposited there by the driver.[15]

The area where Jones lived was called the Stevens Square neighborhood. It was platted in December 1856 into 325- or 350-foot (north-south) by 270-foot (east-west) blocks, subdivided for the most part into fifty-by-128-foot lots whose long dimensions ran east-west, usually separated down the center of the block by fourteen-foot north-south alleys. The plats typified Minneapolis subdivisions in the 1850s and 1860s laid out far in advance of any significant construction, awaiting the expanding perimeter of city growth to create a market.[16]

The bulk of the Stevens Square property was acquired by Richard J. Mendenhall and Dr. Nathan B. Hill in the mid 1870s. Mendenhall, a pioneer Minneapolis banker, owned all the land west of Stevens Avenue, including the block where the Joneses rented.

The banker had built himself a palatial mansion and gardens east of Jones' residence near Nicollet Avenue. Hill, an early Minneapolis aleopathic physician, related to Mendenhall by marriage, owned the majority of land east of Stevens. Both holdings, although platted, had no streets other than Stevens Avenue graded through them between Nicollet and Third Avenues, and between Seventeenth Street and Franklin Avenue.

Development of horse-car surface transit radically altered the city's settlement pattern, creating ribbons of housing along transit lines and clusters of new development where the lines ended. The first horse-car line, on Fourth Avenue, reached Stevens Square nine years before Jones moved into the neighborhood, terminating at East Seventeenth Street, right in front of Herschel's door. Two years later, it was extended to Twenty-fourth Street. The steam, narrow-gauge "Motor Line," intended as an excursion railway to the southwest lakes but soon a thriving commuter line, began service from downtown out Nicollet Avenue to Thirty-first Street in 1879. The neighborhood possessed ample transit service to develop as a rich residential neighborhood like the areas east and north of Jones' corner place, but for reasons unique to the area, it remained surprisingly undeveloped into the twentieth century.

In the Stevens Square area, as well as the land immediately south of Franklin Avenue and west of Nicollet, the presence of large land holdings by wealthy owners, some with "country estates," discouraged sale or rental of land for other than a few large homes on very large lots.[17]

One of these aristocrats, Richard J. Mendenhall, went into the florist business, and the quiet Quaker's greenhouses took up all the land between Eighteenth and Nineteenth Streets, First and Stevens Avenues, as well as substantial portions of the block immediately to the south. The area between First and Nicollet Avenues, just two blocks west of Jones's house, contained gardens, seedlings, and storage for Mendenhall's supply of flowers and shrubs.

Although Jones was "greened-in" for several blocks to the west by Mendenhall's greenhouses and gardens, not all the absence of development can be attributed to horticulture. Except for some large row houses in and around Jones, only forty-three houses stood in the district's twelve blocks by the time Herschel left the neighborhood. For three blocks south of his house up to Franklin, and, of course, to the west, the blocks remained entirely vacant. In fact, only three houses stood in his immediate area. Some of the lightly developed blocks west, north and south of him remained in the estate of Nathan B. Hill, and the neighborhood's lack of development may have reflected legal or practical restraints on the inability of his heirs to dispose of the land after Hill's death.

The Stevens Square neighborhood would later become another melting pot in both people and architecture, and be referred to pleasantly as a place where "there are tree-lined streets of brownstones and brick rowhouses, interspersed Victorian mansions and a town pump . . . a peaceful little community set in the center of a bustling modern city."[18]

The Joneses, however, had settled less than a block from Third Avenue, and this same Third Avenue, out south as far as the present-day Art Institute was considered one of the city's choicest neighborhoods. Just a few blocks south of the Joneses, stood the magnificent W.D. Washburn mansion—Fair Oaks—which covered more than a block between Third and Stevens Avenues, Twenty-first and Twenty-fourth Streets.[19] William Drew Washburn, a milling tycoon, had Fair Oaks built stylistically with a bit of everything—stepped gables vying with a Gothic tower, bay windows, and a crypt-styled portecochere for attention.[20]

The "Fair Oaks" area also included the mansion of Dorilius Morrison at Twenty-fourth Street and Third Avenue South, only six to seven blocks from where Herschel and Lydia lived. Morrison had spent between $700 and $800 to have his garden planted and his lawn decorated. Morrison's garden held his fellow citizens in awe with family monograms made out of flowers and Turkish rugs spread out on the lawn. This fad was extremely popular among the upper echelon during the late 1880s.[21]

The broad drive sweep was often flanked at the entrance by titanic bronze vases, filled with century plants and blossoms, and "it echoed with the roll of equipages whose occupants represented the fashion and wealth of the surrounding country."[22]

At one of the Morrison's garden parties, "the grounds presented a picture of weird beauty, where every conceivable color gleamed amid the darkness. Lights glowed in the tree tops; a crimson galre encircled the flower beds; every devious pathway was outlined; clusters of color, like fireflies, peeped from the hedges; the fountain splashed in the distance, surrounded by a crown of brilliants; and an avenue of pure white lights hung on invisible reeds led to the broad main entrance. Late in the evening a grand climax of color was attained, when calcium lights of every hue were flashed across the grounds, illuminating the remotest parts, and the Morrison mid-summer fete culminated in a blaze of glory."[23]

Elsewhere, some of the more common flowers were used to make floral initials of some of the city's leading citizens. Among these were H.L. Fletcher, F.H. Homes, Charles A. Pillsbury, Mrs.

E.J. Dibble, Mrs. W.S. Judd, Eder H. Noulton, Jessie Jones, General William D. Washburn, Colonel William King, and George R. Newell, all of whom, of course, had beautiful gardens.[24]

The Charles Pillsbury residence at 100 East Twenty-second Street subscribed to revivalism, and the interior, designed by Charles Duveen of London, was outfitted with materials from European castles. The home boasted pegged teakwood flooring and oak paneling from English manor houses, and low relief in the molded plaster ceilings. The exterior of the house, designed by architects Hewitt and Brown, was comprised of dressed limestone with high gables characteristic of Jacobean structures, stone mullions, and leaded glass windows with seventeenth-century medallions from churches and castles. All of its gaudy features stressed "a longing for the grace and apparent stability of an earlier day."[25]

Many people in the eighteen-eighties had an abundance of vacant property, and with the use of many unimproved lots, it was fashionable to have one's own cow or cows grazing on the property. At the time Jones lived on Seventeenth Street, more than a thousand cows grazed freely in yards within the city limits.[26]

Unlike many of his neighbors, who pretended to exist in fashionable big-city drawing rooms, Herschel was content to follow Longfellow's advice of "Still achieving; still pursuing. Learn to labor and to wait." His first story as a *Journal* reporter was an account of a "Negro" meeting in dialect. But Jones learned his trade over the next two years as a reporter for the *Journal*. In early 1888, however, he left the *Journal* and became assistant city editor for the *Minneapolis Tribune*, a position he would hold for two years. By 1889, he was back as a reporter for the *Journal*. The reasons for his brief tenure at the *Tribune* are unknown. Nonetheless, he and Lydia remained living at the Seventeenth Street residence for five years (1885 to 1890), for it was a short walk to the *Journal*'s office, and for that matter, the *Tribune*'s. It was also only a few blocks to where his brother Will was boarding at 116 West Fourteenth Street. When Will moved to 60 South Thirteenth Street in 1889, he was still only a few blocks from Herschel.[27]

Herschel and Lydia liked "their taste of Minnesota." They were not challenged by the Minnesota winters, having come from a climate almost as severe, and paid no heed to what others outside the state had to say. For instance, one popular New York newspaper dubbed the Twin Cities "another Siberia, unfit for human habitation in the winter."[28]

These "Siberian" accusations had their beginnings in the pioneering days of the state. In 1819, after spending a brief stint at Fort Snelling, Dr. J. Ponte Calhoun McMahon lamented, "Oh! For the dear, delightful swampy south once more. There is something balmy and renovating in even its slimy exhalations unknown to the vapid atmosphere of this Siberia—Is there no relief for the wicked? Or have I by my own folly closed the door against return to the lovely domains of yellow fever?"

Adding fuel to the fire, Governor Willis Gorman, in his 1855 message to the Minnesota territorial legislature, once stated:

> During the past year I have received almost innumerable letters from the middle states propounding a variety of questions about our territory, especially desiring to know if our winters are not very long, and so exceedingly cold that stock freezes to death, and man hardly dare venture out of his domicile [sic].[29]

But newlyweds Herschel and Lydia had come to stay.

By 1890, the city had sprawled well beyond Lake Street on its southern border. The Joneses, too, were afflicted with this "southern migration fever," and, in leaving their home on Seventeenth Street, removed to 3036 Fifth Avenue South, just a half block beyond Lake Street. Of course, they needed their precious telephone (#227-1 in 1890, and #227-3 thereafter). Here, they were but two blocks from fashionable Park Avenue.[30]

The city was changing rapidly. In March 1885, the city council granted Minnesota Brush Company permission to light by electricity four of the city's main avenues on an experimental basis. The firm built the circuits at its own expense, and the city agreed to pay seventy cents a lamp per night over a three to four month period. The council was overwhelmed by the improvement over "darkness by gaslight" that it quickly authorized a two-year contract at a minimum charge of two hundred dollars per lamp a year. By the end of 1885, 232 lamps were burning on Minneapolis streets, and by the next year, they had increased to 261. A year later, the city approved a five-year contract, and by 1888, the number of lights had increased to 463.

The election of 1885 signaled the end of unchallenged Republican supremacy. Although William R. Merriam won the victory, Democrats, Farmers' Alliance, and Prohibition candidates for governor together polled 152,781 votes to his 88,111. The change could be attributed to agrarian disaffection via the Scandinavian, namely Norwegian, farmers in the western part of the state. Thus emerged a third-party protest on a large scale in the traditionally conservative state.[32]

Minneapolis was still an oasis on the prairie, as recalled by one of Herschel's relatives who visited the newlyweds shortly upon their arrival:

> Streetcars then drawn by horses and we went out to a little
> church wedding-out towards the lakes a short walk from the
> end of the horse car-there we could look across the prairie and
> see the farmhouse of Bill King—your father [Herschel] tells
> me all built up-around Colfax and on top of a lovely hill there
> was open country mostly trees and scrub timber.[33]

Herschel and Lydia were impressed with the hill area around
Colfax and Franklin. In 1893, they bought their first home on this
very hill at 1816 Colfax Avenue South.[34] Sitting at the edge of fashionable Lowry Hill, Herschel could easily walk downtown to the
Journal office, cutting through thirty-six beautiful acres of nearby
Loring Park, which had just changed its name from Central Park
three years earlier. With the park's name change came landscaping,
whereas before "it was wild and hilly, with marshes and a spring-
fed brook running through it." Also, the area was said to have once
had "quagmires" and "bottomless pools."[35]

These parks, such as Central (Loring), were the work of H.W.S.
Cleveland, who in 1887 convinced the state legislature to approve
an act creating a Board of Park Commissioners. Besides laying out
large parks and an extensive parkway system throughout the Twin
Cities, Cleveland appealed for small parks. The parks would furnish "breathing spaces" where weary citizens could rest and become refreshed. He encouraged the acquisition of land considered
unsuitable for residential property because of steep or rocky terrain
or swamp land that could be developed into sites of beauty.[36]

But in spite of the open spaces, the city was growing before
Herschel's eyes. Only seven years before he took up residency in
the city, the Minneapolis, Lyndale, and Lake Calhoun Railroad was
built from the corner of First Avenue South and Washington Avenue downtown to Thirty-fourth Street on the east shore of Lake
Calhoun, then "way out in the country." Before the close of the
year, Colonel McCrory, the railroad's incorporator and builder,
extended it to Lake Harriet. Living but three blocks from the
Lyndale train, Jones could easily take advantage of this transportation on his way to and from the *Journal* office. In 1881, this same
line was extended all the way to Excelsior, and steam trains were
operated until 1887 when the railway failed and the Streetcar
Company acquired its property.[37]

Those not riding the rails circa 1890, rode along the line in Minneapolis in fine carriages pulled by horses, carefully guided along
by their own private coachmen. Fashionable at the time were the
games of croquet and tennis, and for those who did not own their
own courts, a relaxing ride in a carriage would take them to public
places where the games could be enjoyed.[38]

Proposals for an electric-rail line from downtown to Lake Minnetonka began in 1896 when both the Great Northern and the Minneapolis & St. Louis Railroads considered electrifying their existing routes with the addition of a third conducting rail. Twin City Rapid Transit Company realized this great opportunity and was quick to act. Soon Minneapolis citizens were riding inexpensively along what came to be known as, "The Great White Way Electric-Line."[39]

An unknown copywriter for the street car company described the trolley ride from Minneapolis to Lake Minnetonka:

> The most delightful trip you can enjoy in the Twin Cities—or, for that matter, anywhere—is the one to Excelsior on Lake Minnetonka, and if you have only a few hours to spare, avail yourself of this trip, for it includes a wonderful group of the Twin Cities' most beautiful resorts. Fare from any point in Minneapolis, each way, 25 cents: time, 45 minutes; distance, 18 miles.[40]

The ride down Lyndale through Minneapolis was one that Herschel probably enjoyed. According to the Trolley Company's copywriter, the train roared through Minneapolis. He wrote:

> Double tracks of 80-pound steel rails are laid on a perfectly graded and ballasted right of way, level and straight, except here and there where some long easy curve, planned with the most scientific skill, serves only to turn the scenic page and enhance the pleasure of the trip. Over this smooth, steel roadway the 300-horsepower car speeds along with ease at a mile-a-minute clip.[41]

Jones' salary at the *Journal* was fifteen dollars per week. "But," Herschel recalled years later, "I did not then, and I do not now, consider salary of much importance to a young man. All that he ought to have—and I mean this literally—is enough to house and feed himself comfortably. If he has more it is likely to turn his attention away from the question which is most important to him while he is young, that is: Does the job he holds lead in the right direction?"[42]

Jones based his philosophy on a personal experience of a couple years earlier. He had been sitting alone in a restaurant when he overheard a conversation between two young men at the table behind him. One man had asked the other where he was currently working and was told that he had made a change in jobs recently. He said he had been working for a hardware dealer for two years but "the old man" wouldn't pay him more than sixty-five dollars a month. So he had gone to a dry goods merchant where he received seventy.[43]

The *Minneapolis Journal* editorial staff of c. 1887. Left to right, seated: C.V. Barton, W.B. Chamberlain, W.E. Brownlee, J.S. McLain, Fred Sanders; standing: H.V. Jones, A.H. Russell, Will Wright, W.S. Harwood, J.S. Van Antwerp, and George Ledgerwood. (Courtesy of the Minnesota Historical Society)

According to Herschel, he turned and chirped in, "Look here, sir, doesn't it strike you as a mighty foolish thing to change jobs this way at your age for a mere five dollars a month? Maybe, a few months from now, a grocer or somebody else will come along and offer you five dollars more than Brown [the dry goods merchant] pays you. You'll take it, and you'll keep on changing for five-dollar raises until you're an old man. And where will you be? Now-here! What really matters for you is to gain experience that will enable you to do something big and worthwhile in a line that you know from A to Z." The listener said he had not thought of it in that light.[44]

The four-page *Journal* at the time Herschel joined the paper boasted a circulation of 10,000 readers. Jones had already made up his mind that one day he would own and edit this newspaper. When the paper took on new owners seven months after he had signed on as a reporter (E.B. Haskell, Lucian Swift, and Harry W. Hawley) and moved to the Tribune Building, he was not deterred. His mind was made up to one day own the paper.[45]

On November 11, 1885, the *Journal*'s circulation covering the past week stood at 12,275. During the next year, the circulation grew nearly half as much, so that in January 1887, circulation had boomed to 17,574 copies.[46]

The rise in circulation demanded improved press facilities. Subsequently, a new Potter press was installed with a capacity of 29,000 four-page *Journals* per hour, and when the circulation rose to over 20,000, a sixteen-page special *Journal* was issued. The size of the paper was a historic event that had never been paralleled.

But the celebration was short-lived. For some unknown reason, the new Potter had not been properly adjusted and the much-heralded issue was not completed until well after 10:00 P.M. Many persons did not get their paper delivered until the following morning. The *Journal* was flooded with people waiting for their newspapers, and the telephone rang continuously.

The issue, however, boasted a good write-up of Minneapolis, its industries, public buildings, a description of the State's natural resources, and a brilliant history of the *Journal*. The epoch issue also included many new names and staff changes. Former proofreader, Arthur J. Russell, had been promoted to news editor. W.B. Chamberlain, then news editor, was moved up to managing editor. Among the new reporters working with Herschel Jones were S. Van Antwerp, formerly the *Journal*'s Washington correspondent; Hartley C. Davis, a popular writer for the New York papers; and M.J. Mallon, former police clerk of Minneapolis. The *Journal*'s new advertising manager was Fred H. Sanders.[47]

The *Journal* that year was the only newspaper to issue an extra on the death of the vice president of the United States. In 1886, when the circulation had climbed much higher, a news gathering feat propelled the *Journal* to national recognition. A devastating tornado had ripped through the St. Cloud and Sauk Rapids area. The *Journal* rushed Jones and another reporter to the scene, while the other Twin Cities newspapers depended on the St. Cloud correspondents for their stories.[48]

The *Journal* editorials at that time objected to James J. Hill's railroad monopolies and asked the public why one man should want to own so many railroads. According to the paper, editorials objected entirely apart from any personal considerations. While praising Hill as a great railroad builder and manager, and for "his large grasp of the commercial situation," the *Journal* acted out of considerations for law and public policy to "oppose the culmination of his ambitions and dangerous scheme."[49]

The years 1887 and 1888 brought increased circulation, advertising patronage, and a general improvement in the news section.

Frequently, advertising compelled the *Journal* to resort to double sheeting so that the paper was regularly increased to eight pages.

During those same years, Herschel and Lydia began keeping a scrapbook of New York Theatre playbills. The scrapbook was maintained through 1911. The Joneses, perhaps, were looking forward to the day when they could afford to visit many of these glamorous New York theatres themselves.[50]

Lydia gave birth to their third child, Florence Purington Jones, on June 6, 1889.[51] With three children in the home, including the newborn, Mrs. Jones kept to the house most of the time. Herschel, meanwhile, worked every day although the salary of a cub reporter left quite a bit to be desired.

H.V. Jones in his thirties.

The work of a cub reporter, however, was anything but glamorous, and often, the "cubs" were sent out on unpleasant tasks. As one of Jones' fellow reporters recalled, "I was sent to ask a 'prominent citizen' certain questions about his lamentable financial failure. The cub reporter, like the fireman and the policeman, has to go where he is sent. Many are the times when I would gladly have exchanged places with either. Kindly, remember, to the cub reporter's credit, that it is another gentleman who is sending him where he would not, and where you wonder at him for going. But he goes, for the cub reporter is mortal."[52]

The reporter went to the man's office and found his quarry sitting at his desk, with every appearance of "having fought with beasts at Ephesus." The young newsman apologized, asked the questions he was told to ask, and backed away. A cynical smile danced around the businessman's nose, and the reporter had sympathized with him. "It taught me much that I might not otherwise have known, but it was in a hard school."[53]

Jones' work as a reporter brought him into contact with bankers and other commercial men. He then decided it was time to establish his own credit and went to see a banker whom he had come to know through his work. He told the banker he wanted to borrow fifty dollars for thirty days. He was afraid the banker, who could sense his fear and trembling, might not let him have the money. Jones recalled, "I was almost as surprised as I was pleased, when he said: 'Why, certainly! We'll be glad to lend you fifty dollars.'"[54]

Jones continued to borrow, for no other purpose than to establish his credit. He never used the borrowed sums, and when the notes came due, he paid them off with the very same money that had been lent him. Gradually he increased the amounts he asked for, finally receiving as much as two thousand dollars at one time. "I didn't want the money; but I did want the credit," Jones recollected. "I wanted the people to understand that when Jones borrowed, he would pay."[55]

The *Journal* had moved into the seven-story Tribune Building during the spring of 1885. One reporter recalled that life at the *Journal* was not always quiet and uneventful. This cub reporter was standing on the corner, leaning against the railing of the *Journal* when a lean, young lady strolled past him once or twice and glanced in his direction. Making a third round, she looked at him and said, "It's a mean world."

"Well," the reporter replied, rather taken aback, "it has its outs."

She looked at him again and offered, "If you haven't anything else to do, what's the matter with coming up to my room?"

"It was the first time," claimed the reporter later, "that I had been accosted in this manner on Fourth Street, and I hastened to reply in the spirit if not with the exact words of Dr. Samuel Johnson on a similar occasion." He answered merely, "No, no, my girl; it won't do."[56]

In the new facility, away from the haunts of the city's best and worst, the *Journal* and the *Tribune* shared the building with community businessmen who had offices there. The *Journal*'s counting department and editorial rooms occupied the first floor, and the composing room and printing presses were located in the basement. When Swift and McLain had taken over the newspaper, they obtained permission to use the *Tribune*'s composing room on the seventh floor. By 1889, however, this arrangement was no longer satisfactory and the *Journal* owners built a one-story addition to the Tribune Building to house their own composing room and mailing facilities.[57]

The new arrangement was short-lived. On November 30 the temperature plummeted to twenty-eight degrees below zero. Shortly after ten o'clock that evening, a fire began on the third floor, which had served as the Republican Party headquarters during a recent campaign. The flame's licking tongue quickly ignited the room, which was filled with a heap of loose papers. On the seventh floor, workers of the *Minneapolis Tribune* were busy producing a newspaper. Employees of the Minneapolis editorial offices of the *St. Paul Pioneer Press* were at work on the sixth floor. Lights were out on the street floor in the business and editorial offices of the *Minneapolis Journal*. Since the *Journal* was an evening newspaper, the staff had already gone home.[58]

In the basement, *Tribune* employees were readying their presses for last minute front-section news and sporting news from the University of Minnesota. Skid row derelicts were warming themselves in the printing rooms, waiting to stuff the sections together and in turn make a penny and get warm. Joseph Mannix, long-time Minneapolis reporter with the *Pioneer Press*, discovered the blaze and attempted to put it out. Mannix turned over a table in hopes of snuffing out the flames, but his attempt only spread the fire into other piles of paper.

Charles A. Williams, managing editor of the *Tribune*, was working in his office when a reporter rushed in and told him there was a fire on the third floor. Employees who overheard the cries were not frightened because the Tribune Building was believed to be fireproof. In fact, a few reporters and several composing room workers took an elevator down to the third floor, curious to see the spectacle.

Shortly after, reporter George Caven told Williams he was going down to check on the fire and see if there was any danger. Several reporters and editors followed Caven down the wooden stairs that circled the elevator shaft. They were gone several minutes. Still at their desks were W.W. Jermane, city editor; Millman, commercial editor; Pat Miles, daytime Associated Press wire man filling in on the night shift; and Williams in the news rooms. Across the hall, some twenty to thirty employees were still at work in the composing room.

Millman and Miles decided the situation was growing dangerous and started to leave. Pat Miles had been receiving copy from the telegraph operator at the other end of the line, when he had "broken" and passed on news of the fire to the operator. Miles instructed the operator, however, to continue sending, and he scribbled down the copy on tissue as quickly as the operator could send it. When the intense heat became unbearable, Miles ordered the operator to stop transmission.

As Miles began to leave the room, Millman paused and asked for his pay envelope that he had forgotten to pick up earlier that evening. Both men rang for the elevator, and when it did not come, started descending the stairway. About this same time, Jermane returned to Williams' office and told him the fire was advancing, and it was time to leave.

Meanwhile, on the third floor, Mannix, now aided by Caven, were attempting to extinguish the blaze but were forced from the room. The fire leaped through the open doorway and spread through the building as a raging inferno. Caven, remembering he had promised to let Williams know about any dangers, began climbing back up the stairs. Encountering a wall of flame, he was forced back. The flames, fed by gas and by the natural flue created by the open elevator shaft and stairwell, ravaged the stairs and walls, searing paint and varnish along its path. Although Mannix had telephoned the volunteer fire department, little could be done to save any part of the building. Instead, all efforts were made to save human life.

Pioneer Press employee Milton Pickett dashed from the sixth floor, just ahead of the flames, to the *Tribune*'s editorial rooms on the seventh. Stiles Jones, Harold Chapin, and Edward Barnes were trapped in the *Pioneer Press* editorial offices as the gas-fed flames filled the hallway. Their only salvation was to tiptoe across a narrow cornice along the front of the building. While firefighters were on the east side of the building, desperately trying to reach printers trapped on the seventh floor with ladders that extended only to the sixth, the trio carefully moved along the entire length of the building. The "gasping and moaning crowd of spectators," who had gathered in the snow-covered streets below, monitored every step.

Meanwhile, above them on the seventh floor, fourteen *Tribune* staff members had crowded into an office at the west end of the building, where the only fire escape ladder in the building was located. When the last of these men had entered Williams' office, he closed the door and tied down the transom, hoping to block any draft from reaching the flames. After debating who should go first, Jermane started down the lengthy fire escape, grasping the frigid metal rungs with both hands. Williams urged the others to follow and said he would be the last to leave.

Suddenly, through the smoke and flames, was heard, "For God's sake, open the door." Williams responded and Millman and Miles dashed in, blocked from their own escape attempt when the fire soared up the elevator shaft. Millman, however, caught his foot in the rug at the door and sprawled across the doorsill. Williams told him to get up, but Millman could not rise. Meanwhile, Miles did not stop and raced quickly through the door to the fire escape.

By now, the draft created by the open window through the door had fanned the flames in the hallway, and they roared into the room. Williams pulled Millman from the floor, slamming the door shut with his foot to keep out more flame. The impact of the closed door, however, shattered its glass and the flames poured in. Papers in the room were ignited as Williams pushed Millman out onto the fire escape. Millman was still weak from his fall, and in losing his balance, he slid down the ladder on top of Miles who was only five feet below him. Both lost their grips and plunged farther down the side of the building.

Below them, Milton Pickett and a Professor Olson of the University of South Dakota were struck by the falling bodies of Millman and Miles. All four plunged to their deaths on the pavement five stories below in full view of Williams, who was leaning out the window above them. As Williams reached for the ladder, he inhaled gas, flames, and smoke, and collapsed, with his body still in the room. Luckily, his head remained out the window just below the sill, and he was revived by the piercing wind. He rushed down the ladder to safety.

One *Journal* employee recalled, "On a late-in-November night in 1889, memorable forever, I saw the first slender, swaying column of flame rising perpendicularly like a great red streamer from the western end of the Old Tribune Building, now the Phoenix, and waving itself out into nothing high in the darkness above the great structure. Old friends and fellow workers are crowding out of the windows, picking their perilous ways cautiously around the narrow cornice still in place on the seventh floor of the present Phoenix Building. I see them falling from the fire escape ladder on the alley side of the building, Milton Pickett coming down as if swimming on his back, landing heavily on the pavement of the alley between the building and the present bank. I hear the cries of terror and of hurrying, and sounds of men swearing and crying!"[59]

At the other side of the building, printers on the seventh floor were trying various means to get down to the sixth where they could reach the ladders. One elderly printer hooked a belt to the seventh floor window and tried to descend. He slipped from the belt, however, and was dashed to death seven floors below. Firemen, who had glimpsed his attempt, rushed to catch him in their net, but he plunged "through it like a cannon ball through a snowpile and struck the earth a crushed and lifeless heap. . . . "[60]

Others helped each other down a piece of belt taken from a shafting. One of these, William Lown, dropped one floor to the sixth, and in breaking the window with his hands, gripped the casing. Still on the top floor was Will H. Williams, brother of the managing editor, Williams had remained behind to help all the others down. Eventually an extension ladder was hoisted to the seventh floor, and he and others were able to climb down safely.

Another man, however, was not so lucky. Separated from the others by a wall of smoke and flame, he grabbed a telegraph wire connected to the next building only twelve feet away. Moving hand over hand along the thin copper wire, he was able to endure the sharp pain of metal cutting into his hands. All went awry when he attempted to swing his legs over the wire. As thousands of spectators watched from below, he hanged suspended from two badly lacerated hands. Then he dropped and crashed to the pavement, the seventh fatality of that night.

In addition to the deaths, at least thirty men were badly burned that night. The *Journal* and *Pioneer Press* each lost a man and the *Tribune* lost five. The building on the corner of Fourth Street and First Avenue (now Marquette) was a gutted ruin. Damage was estimated at $300,000, of which only a third was covered by insurance.

Neither the *Journal*, nor the *Tribune* issued a newspaper the following day. The *Journal* made arrangements with former owner, C. A. Nimocks, then publisher of the *Times*, at 42 South Third Street, to print the afternoon *Journal* until their new building could be completed. At first it was necessary to be content with a four-page edition, but very soon the old size was resumed, and the paper showed little evidence of the experiences through which it was passing. The *Tribune*, meanwhile, began publishing on Monday through the *St. Paul Globe*.[62]

The *Journal*'s new home at 47-49 South Fourth Street was ready in only six weeks. According to the *Journal*, "During the preceding summer the owners of the paper had been looking for a site for a new building and finally had selected the [fifty] feet upon which the ancient Parcher's livery stable stood on the southern side of Fourth Street between Nicollet and First Avenue South. Plans had been drawn, and the building was nearly completed when the fire wiped out nearly all the tangible assets of the paper. It will be remembered that after the 1880 fire, what was left of the *Journal* sold for $2,000. After the fire of 1889, not $200,000 would have bought the name, goodwill and subscription lists of the paper. So much had been wrought in nine busy and eventful years."[63]

The Journal Building boasted a handsome four-story front of Bedford stone in Italian Renaissance architecture. A high basement admitted light and offered vast space for a large pressroom. In the basement were located the press room, city carriers' room, newsboys' room, engine and boiler room, and paper storage.[64]

It stood in the best known section of Fourth Street—Newspaper Row—on the south side of the street between Nicollet and Hennepin. Down the street were some of the city's most prominent buildings, like the Vendome Hotel, "a frothy French confection topped by a replica of the Statue of Liberty's head." The old Kasota Block stood at Hennepin, seething in its Richardsonian Romanesque. Farther down the street, was Spectator Terrace, where a short-lived newspaper, the *Saturday Spectator*, was published. According to writer Larry Millett, the building "was an architectural salmagundi whose unlikely ingredients included a rooftop pagoda." The rear of the building boasted a unique onion-shaped dome.[65]

The Journal Building had an excellent location. The center of the city—the business district—in 1890, was Nicollet and Washington Avenues, only two blocks away. Business interests deliberately prohibited car lines off Nicollet, and retailers advertised the convenience and safety to children. At night, these streets were lit by gaslights that illuminated the center of the city. In 1891 a giant parade was staged to celebrate that year's great harvest, and more than 200,000 people lined the parade route to gape at the Harvest Festival.[66]

The first edition from the new building hit the streets on January 25, 1890. Three Potter web perfecting presses, which could be adjusted to print four to eight pages of six, seven, or eight columns per page were installed in the high-ceiling basement. As the latest improvement in press construction, the presses had a capacity of 12,000 eight-page papers—a combined capacity of 36,000 copies per hour. A pair of seventy-horsepower engines was attached and a conveyor was put into operation to carry the printed copies to the first floor. The business offices were also located on the main floor while the editorial offices were located on the second. The third floor was rented out to weekly newspapers while the fourth contained the *Journal*'s composing room and stereotyping departments, as well as "ad alley." Pneumatic tubes delivered copy to the fourth floor and a small freight lift in back brought stereotyping forms to the basement to be printed. Minneapolis had had telephones for eleven years and the *Journal* kept up with "every modern convenience."[67]

About the time the new building was completed, the *Journal*'s circulation reached the 30,000 mark. Over 13,000 papers were delivered outside the Minneapolis area, extending principally over Minnesota, Wisconsin, Iowa, the Dakotas, and Montana.[68] The new Journal Building was erected at a time when much of America's construction was in a period of decline. The building boom had spent its force by 1890, and the financial surplus of the 1880s had been frozen or drained away. And, of course, America was on the brink of depression with the Panic of 1893. But the *Journal* was making money and was not affected by any of these factors.[69]

But accolades other than those spirited by new presses fell upon the *Journal* in 1890. Don Arnold of New York City composed some new music dedicated the work to the *Journal* called "The *Minneapolis Journal* Waltzes." The Reeves American Band at the Minneapolis Exposition of 1890 performed the piece, and the popular rendition was adapted to sheet music.[70]

Arnold dedicated his waltz to the *Journal* because it had become the leading paper of the northwest but also on account of the enterprise shown by the Journal Company in placing its perfecting press number 3 at great expense in the Exposition. This enabled "everybody to witness the marvelous work of the modern printing press in printing from a continuous roll of paper weighing several hundred pounds, an eight-page *Journal*, completely printed and folded, rate 13,000 an hour."[71]

While the *Journal* was being saluted via the new musical composition, Herschel and Lydia celebrated for other reasons. On August 27, 1890, their fourth child, Paul Merchant Jones, was born in Minneapolis. A year later, another son, Jefferson Jones, was born on April 5, 1891.[72] For Herschel, however, the celebrations were brief. The *Journal* comprised his livelihood, and the reporter was needed on his beat.

Herschel Jones' responsibilities included real estate and legislative work. He was considered a good reporter, but he was not progressing as rapidly as he had hoped. But, of course, since he was looking toward the future, he did not consider salary an important issue. While other reporters visited the theatre via complimentary tickets that came to the *Journal*, Jones took the lecture tickets. Following a series of five lectures on philosophical subjects by Boston's Joseph Cook, Jones gathered his nerve and went to the speaker's hotel room. When Mr. Cook answered the door, the young journalist said, "Mr. Cook, I want you to write down a list of books for me in the order in which you would read them yourself. I want to know what the great philosophers have said; I want their ideas about why we are on this earth, and what we ought to do while here."[73]

Jones told Mr. Cook that for years he had watched wheat spring out of the ground from a tiny seed, put forth leaves, and finally a head. From this small seed came the world's finest food for human beings. He went on to tell the lecturer how wonderful the process was and that there must be a divine and farseeing purpose behind it all. Mr. Cook was only too happy to make out the list of books.

Herschel later said he spent fifteen years reading those books before he "realized that all I had learned from them could be found in *one* book, the Bible! The greatest lesson I found there, the paramount lesson, is faith. What a man desires and deserves to have, that, according to his ability and faith, he *can* have."[74]

During those years the *Journal* waged a constant battle against free silver, advocated the building of more schools, protested against "scorching" (bicycle speeding on Park Avenue), and opposed the merger of the Great Northern and Northern Pacific Railroads. The paper suggested that the John H. Stevens House—first house built on the west side of the Mississippi River—be moved to Minnehaha Park by the school children of Minneapolis and asked that business men organize to form a central commercial body to further public interest. In addition, they sponsored a Christmas tree for school children and a most popular teacher contest.

Jones took over the commercial department, gathering information about the latest wheat market quotations, bank transactions, and data of concern to Minneapolis businessmen. In setting up this new department, Jones appealed to John Scudder McLain that the growing importance of Minneapolis as a primary grain market made this most timely, and this innovation gave the *Journal* not only prestige, but also a rapidly growing circulation.[75]

The wheat field had moved steadily westward. "The Genessee Valley (New York), afterwards Ohio, Michigan, and Iowa, successfully, have been the lands of marvelous wheat raising. Then the current veered northwestward and Minnesota and the Dakotas became the ideal wheat belt. For twenty years the northwestern ascendency has increased, until today it is known at home and abroad as 'the bread basket of the continent.'"[76]

There was in 1890 no other virgin wheat land east of the Rocky Mountains. But the valleys of Minnesota's rivers such as the Minnesota, Red, Jim, and Mouse, having been blessed with glacial deposits, were ideally suited for wheat raising. The soil here was deep and seemingly inexhaustible.[77]

When Jones came on the scene, the golden grain belt was producing 200 million bushels of wheat annually from fourteen million acres. Its barley crop, tributary to Minneapolis, represented half the product of the nation and was a quality item. Its flax seed production was also the best in the nation. Jones pointed out that the leading newspaper in the area would have to excel in its grain market news. He also stated that in 1878, when the newspaper was founded, wheat covered "nearly sixty-nine percent of the cultivated area of the state." In 1890, while Jones was establishing his new department, the wheat acreage had drastically decreased. Jones also saw a tremendous increase in wheat production in the neighboring state of North Dakota.[78]

During the 1880s, most of Minnesota's farmers had planted wheat. The State Agricultural Society had warned, "that the continual cropping of wheat, year after year, in the same field, without even a change of seed, is bad farming and ought to be discouraged." Farmers knew that they should diversify their farming—that they should plant other crops or raise some livestock. Diversified farming was good for two reasons: Firstly, it would allow the land to rest, as planting wheat every year drained the soil of the same nutrients. Secondly, the farmer lost all his money if the crop failed. By planting flax as well as wheat, he could still make some money if the wheat failed.[79]

Wheat was indeed a banner crop in the frontier states such as Minnesota. Diversification had not proceeded evenly in varying sections. It began in the older areas, synchronizing with declines in wheat yields, population growth, and rising land values. Wheat totaled between 34,000,000 and 35,000,000 bushels in 1880, then skyrocketed to 95,000,000 bushels in 1900.[80]

Always the opportunist, Jones suggested to McLain that he be sent out well before harvest time to observe the growing grain and determine a forecast of the probable yield. The task required close observation, extensive traveling, and the development of a dependable system that would produce reliable figures for estimating the whole on a basis of the fields actually visited. The job would be of great importance because the government estimates on which the farmer and the grain trade had to depend were for the most part inaccurate. The government system at the time was "dangerous and destructive," unless it could be transformed into an accurate one.[81]

Herschel was convinced he knew why the government's estimates were erroneous: "At that time, the only comprehensive crop estimates were those issued by the government," he recalled in a 1924 interview. "Wheat is a speculative commodity in the grain markets, and the price in any year depends largely on the quantity produced. Naturally, it is very important for farmers and traders to know as early as possible what the crop prospects are; but it was common knowledge that the government's estimates at that time were often erroneous.

"According to the system the government used, there were three agents in each county. That struck me as a bad plan. I figured that, taking the average of the wheat-growing areas, one of the three agents would be dishonest. He would have reasons of his own, perhaps, for wanting the estimates to be too low or too high. In his county this dishonest agent might estimate the crop at, say, eight bushels per acre."[82]

Jones figured that another of the three agents would be honest but incompetent. His estimate for that same country would probably be nine bushels. The third agent, he speculated, would be both honest and competent and would, justifiably, estimate sixteen bushels to the acre. Said Jones, "Now I was certain that when the figures reached headquarters, and one report showed sixteen bushels against two showing eight and nine respectively, the officials wouldn't be likely to give the sixteen-bushel man much credence, even though he was right."[83]

Herschel asked his editor why the *Journal* could not publish its own estimates of wheat. He added, "that if one man, who was both careful and competent, would study the whole wheat-growing area, he would make a much better estimate than dozens of men of all degrees of honesty and ability." The editor listened and told him to go out and try his idea. "And," continued Jones, "although I knew absolutely nothing about how to estimate crops, I started out to see elevator men in the area."[84]

Jones' initial venture as a crop forecaster was confined to the spring wheat area of Minnesota and the Dakotas. He began by asking elevator men how the wheat crop was. The first man he asked told him the wheat was pretty good and looked like fifteen bushels an acre. He then looked at some of the fields that he felt might yield fifteen bushels to the acre. He carefully examined the wheat for its thickness and height and moved on to the next town to duplicate the same procedure. He continued on covering the whole wheat belt and recording the figures given him by the elevator men. He then averaged them best he could and prepared his own initial estimate based on the system.

"That was in 1890—and I was pretty far wrong! The next year I repeated my effort, all the time studying and trying to learn. Again my estimate was wrong but not so far wrong as before. Then I said to myself: 'Either I can judge wheat by myself, or I can't. From now on, I am going to take my own judgment and stand or fall by it.'"[85] After that, he still asked the elevator men for their opinions but he studied the wheat thoroughly and made his own estimates.

In 1891, his first wheat crop estimate article was published, although unsigned . . . Jones estimated the crop for that year would run between 120 to 150 million bushels, giving himself considerable allowance for error.

Jones' estimates, however, were different from any of those the *Journal* had attempted before. Herschel signed all of his estimates as H.V. Jones, and he announced total production in bushels for the three-state area. He shortly thereafter provided estimated acreage. This was a significant step because he had attempted to determine the average yield per acre for each county and state. Thus, the more accurate the acreage, the more accurate the total estimated yield.

His estimates seldom varied greatly from those of the government during the 1890s. Both were frequently low in their estimates of production. Jones' estimates, however, were highly regarded because out-of-state newspapers gave them equal billing with government estimates.[86]

Jones then made an attempt to overcome his underestimates and those of the government. Believing that the crop estimates he made were accurate, the fault must lay in the government's figures on acreage. Jones recalled, "I noticed that from eight pieces of wheat to the mile in southern Minnesota, we dropped to three. I dropped my acreage accordingly. The government did not. And so things became twisted, and I began to get my acreage built up on a right basis. In other parts of the country, where development was in progress, the wheat acreage grew, and my acreage grew along the track, but the government acreage did not grow. So after two or three years I had increased two million acres over the government and distribution bore me out."[87]

But almost immediately, he established himself in the business community by gaining the confidence and friendship of the "big name" grain men, elevator operators, and railroad officials. Grain merchant, Frank H. Peavey, wrote the *Journal*: "Your market reports are very commendable, accurate and correct. I think they are unequaled by any paper in the Northwest. I take great pleasure in reading them because I have found Mr. Jones, commercial editor of the *Journal*, very correct and careful in all his statements, with no tendency whatsoever toward sensationalism."[88]

A commercial reporter at the *Journal* expressed the nature of his confidential relationship: "Jonesy is sleeping with Frank Peavey and Charlie Pillsbury." Another time, Jones entered the newsroom and was greeted with new words to an old hymn: "the song arising strongly on the office air something as follows: 'I will sing of Frank H. Peavey.'" Although Jones had little time for horseplay, he joined in the laughter.[89]

But Frank Peavey was not the only enthusiastic reader to write the *Journal*. Flour manufacturer, Charles A. Pillsbury wrote:

> Without reflecting upon the ability of the other market correspondents in Minneapolis, I wish to say that I consider Mr. Jones at the head of them all, and that the market page of *The Minneapolis Journal*, taken as a whole, year in and year out, is the best of any published by any paper in the twin cities. In saying this, I do not wish to be understood as reflecting upon the ability shown by the market correspondents in the market pages of some of the other journals in the two cities.[90]

The Washburn-Crosby Company wrote:

> We wish to acknowledge, by a voluntary testimonial, the
> working of the *Journal* in its daily presentation of a strong,
> clean cut market page. We consider the *Journal* market
> reports reliable and the best in the Northwest. They are pre-
> sented in good form and show careful work at all times. Your
> daily price diagrams, representing the market for the day, are
> a feature that no producer of wheat in the Northwest should be
> without."[91]

Accolades also came in from out of state. A Fargo, North
Dakota, man penned,

> I regard the market reports of the *Journal* as the best pub-
> lished in the Northwest, and equal to those published by the
> leading dailies of Chicago, and in passing I wish to say that I
> read no newspaper with more interest than the *Journal*. It is in
> the best sense of the word a "news" paper—always clean and
> with all of the news fresh and crisp. We receive your [five]
> o'clock edition bright and early the following morning, and
> but for the loyalty of our people to home newspapers, the
> *Journal* would have a circulation in Fargo greater than all
> other newspapers combined.[92]

Herschel was, in fact, close to the leaders of the grain trade. A
few years later, he walked into the *Journal* office with a pasteboard
shoebox under his arm, looked guiltily around the room, and asked
telegraph editor, Arthur J. Russell, if he wanted to see something.
Jones tipped the cover back and revealed row upon row of bank
bills in banded stacks of fifties and hundreds. Jones informed
Russell that one of the grain men had convinced him that "wheat
was on its way to a dollar and nothing could stop it." Jones had
been persuaded to "buy a little wheat and forget it."

When the price of cash wheat did reach the dollar point, the
grain broker, according to Russell, led a brass band into the building and "from down the hallway on the Chamber of Commerce
floor came the sound of martial music . . . the crowd broke into a
cheer as up the corridor came C.A. Pillsbury at the head of a band
of music pounding out a dollar wheat memorial march.[93]

Jones acted meticulously and learned as he went along. He found
he could base his estimates on the color of the growing grain, the
size and fullness of the heads, the probable acreage, and the probable size and quality of the crop. He worked out his own system
based on his numerous actual visits to as many widely scattered
fields as he could make, traveling by rail and by horse and buggy.
His judgment grew to be almost uncanny and he learned to strike

an average. Throughout 1891 to 1900, the *Journal* boasted about its commercial editor, claiming him as "the leading commercial writer of the Northwest . . ."[94]

Herschel Jones would always investigate the fields himself since he distrusted reports from others. He recalled an incident in July 1895: "I visited a farm that will yield over [twenty] bushels average. As late as July 10 the owner claimed in Sioux Falls that his average would not exceed six bushels." The reason, he thought, was that he wanted to keep land prices down "as he is a constant buyer."[95]

Jones was able to build up a correct acreage by keeping track of all the miles he had logged on the railroads and the wheat acreage he observed from the train window while chugging across the country. He carried a "field microscope . . . for intensive study of the structure—normal, healthy, or otherwise—of the growing wheat," and recorded the crop that would be harvested in his records.[96]

Although he lacked a background in wheat growing, he was quick in learning to determine a good crop of wheat. Once, he observed that most people were announcing a bumper wheat crop with an average of twenty bushels in the Northwest. Jones recognized that the wheat was of good height but had "no quickness of stem, and it requires thickness of stem to make a [twenty] bushel average, because there must usually be from [twenty-five to thirty] bushels, since once in a while you get down to ten, and even five, bushels on a good crop." He predicted a lower yield and was right. Although his estimates were better than those of the government, Jones admitted that nationally "not much attention was paid to what I said."[97]

As his experience and expertise grew, he extended his trips into the winter wheat areas of the Southwest. Only twice in twenty years as a crop reporter did Jones disagree with other reports. Each of these times, his opinion was vindicated. These dependable predictions established for him an enviable reputation as a forecaster of crops.[98]

The first time he disagreed with government figures was in 1900, when a dry year carried with an outlook of a poor crop. By July, the wheat fields looked badly burned up. Herschel had just returned to Minneapolis and turned in his estimates.

"But then it began to rain, and it rained for a week," Herschel later recalled. "I knew that this might change everything. While that rain lasted I sat around with my suitcase packed, waiting for it to stop. And the minute it did stop, I caught the first train out of town. I made my whole trip, more than ten thousand miles, a second time. Again I studied the condition of the wheat. And now, instead of being spindling and thin, it was in fine shape."[99]

Returning again to Minneapolis, Herschel was confronted with a government estimate of a yield of eighty-five million bushels, plus an estimate by a noted crop expert of eighty-six million. Scoffing at these reports, Herschel estimated the yield would be 140 million bushels. Although the grain trade was incredulous, the final accounting showed his forecast to be correct.

Initially, his estimate was not taken seriously. "I was laughed at," Herschel remembered. "People told me I couldn't be right. But I was not laughed at the following May! For the final figures then showed that even my estimate had been seven million bushels too low. The government's estimate had missed by sixty-two million bushels. That gave me a national reputation."[100]

Four years later, he was confronted with a similar situation. This time, however, the positions were reversed. Although the wheat fields seemed to be producing excellent stands, Jones discovered a peculiar red-dish appearance of the wheat in a South Dakota field. He had never seen rust before, but he had read a book telling about the disease. Jones learned that rust was a parasite growing on barberry bushes and was carried by the wind to nearby wheat fields, withering the wheat stalks and wheat kernels. He soon discovered that hundreds of acres in the northwest were rust-infected. Jones estimated that fields that looked good for twenty to twenty-five bushels to the acre would produce a mere three to five. Thus, he estimated that the total crop output was far below that of the government's projections. Again, he proved to be correct.

Jones had learned that he had to stand by the figures he deduced no matter how many experts told him he was wrong. He reflected, "When I was judging wheat, I never speculated. I knew that if I bought or sold against a possible rise or fall in the market price, that in itself would be enough to impair my judgment. I knew I would be inclined to think there was more wheat, or less, in the fields, if because of my speculating, I wanted more, or less, wheat to be there!"[101]

The *Journal*'s circulation was climbing. The market section of Herschel Jones boosted subscriptions, as did the superb editorial cartoons of Charles L. Bartholomew, and the *Journal* continued to move ahead of its competition. The *Journal*'s Washington office had been opened in 1885-1886; the *Tribune* did not send a reporter to Washington until 1893. In February 1893, Minneapolis' reading population was composed of Germans, Norwegians, Swedes, Danes, English, Scots, Welsh, Irish, Poles, Czechs, and Finns. The *Tribune*'s circulation in September 1894 was only about 31,000. The following year it climbed to 37,453. But the *Tribune* held many of its loyal readers with its Sunday edition. The *Journal* did not publish a Sunday paper until 1905.[102]

In May 1893, the Joneses traveled to New York, presumably stopping in Jefferson before continuing on to New York City. Lydia was seven months pregnant. On Tuesday evening of the 23rd, they attended an orchestral concert at Madison Square Garden Concert Hall, featuring members from the New York Philharmonic and Seidl Orchestras, under the direction of pianist, composer, and conductor Carl V. Lachmund, who was assisted by Xaver Scharwenka, an eminent composer and pianist. The Joneses enjoyed the program consisting of Scharwenka's "Fest Overture," Godard's "Introduction and Allegro," Mozart's "Aria-Don Juan," St. Saens' "Introduction Et Rondo Capriccioso," and Lachmund's "Fades the Rose."[103]

Richard Watson Gilder composed special words to the latter piece and dedicated them to the poet-editor of the *Century Magazine*:

"Fades the Rose"

Fades the rose; the year grows old;
The tale is told,
Youth doth depart—
Only stays the heart.

Ah, no! if stays the heart,
Youth can ne'er depart,
Nor the sweet tale be told—
Never the rose fade, nor the year grow old.

Tragedy struck shortly after their return to Minneapolis. On July 1, 1893, Lydia gave birth to another son, Herschel Veley Jones. The child, however, suffered serious medical problems and passed away a few weeks later. The young H.V. Jones was interred in Minneapolis' Lakewood Cemetery.[104]

But death was not slow in striking a second time. On January 4, 1894, Herschel's father, William Stephen Jones was confined to the house by illness.[105] The following day, he died at his home in Jefferson, New York, of acute inflammation of the bowels caused by stricture. The illness had come on very suddenly, and he suffered only a week. He had, however, been troubled for a number of years with heart problems. Since the death of Herschel's father was so unexpected, the announcement shocked the *Journal*'s young market reporter. The morning of his death, William had felt much better than he had all week. In better spirits, he even told his wife that he was considering going to his place of business.[106]

The funeral was held four days later at 11:00 A.M. at the Presbyterian Church in Jefferson. Herschel and his younger brother, William, who was also working at the *Journal*, left Minneapolis and were in attendance at the funeral. With the two boys was their widowed mother, and eighty-five-year-old grandfather, Chauncey, father of the deceased. According to the *Schoharie County Chronicle* of January 9, 1894, a nephew, C.G. Turner, of Poughkeepsie, New York, attended the funeral as well. The attendance was very large, people being present from all parts of the town and also from neighboring villages. The sermon was given by Reverend Alvin Cooper from the text, Revelations 22: 12—"And behold, I come quickly; and my reward is with me, to give every man according as his work shall be." The theme of the sermon was, "The importance of living right was communicated because at death, according to the scriptures, it brings its own reward."

The choir sang two pieces that were both favorites of William Jones, "My Heavenly Home," and "Some Sweet Day." It had been a custom of Herschel's father to take his hymnbook on Sunday afternoons and sing, and these two favorite songs of his had always been included.

The *Jefferson Courier* reported: "The deceased enjoyed to a high degree the respect of the people. His competitors always found him a fair business rival. If in the past there had been any political animosities, it was clear in the general testimonials of regard that were expressed when death came, and in the general response of the people at the burial service that these animosities were long ago forgotten, and that genuine sorrow prevailed in the community."[107]

The departed Mr. Jones left a legacy in connection with a New Year's tree at a nearby Methodist church. While on his sickbed, he had informed his wife that he had wanted to remember the children in his end of the village. He had her bring to him from the store several little baskets and mouth organs. Sitting up in his bed, he arranged his remembrances and sent for Mrs. Nathan Mann from the local Methodist society. William gave her the budget and instructed her to say nothing.

Herschel's father was buried in the family lot in Jefferson Rural cemetery, and Herschel returned to Minneapolis and the *Journal*. Lydia, however, again pregnant, had not attended William's funeral. On June 11, 1894, she gave birth to another son, Moses Chase Jones. This time the baby was healthy. The following year, a daughter, Frances Lois Jones, was born. Frances, too, was a healthy baby, but she was the last child born to Herschel and Lydia.[108]

During the next six years, Herschel's crop predictions became highly reliable, and from all over the Northwest, people in the business were turning to the *Journal* to read his projections. The name Herschel V. Jones had in only a decade become synonymous with grain. But Herschel always looked ahead.

So had William H. Seward, who had visited Minnesota one year before Herschel Jones was born. Seward, seeing great potential in the area, delivered a speech here in which he said, "I now believe that the last seat of power on the great continent of America will be found somewhere within a radius not very far from the spot where I stand, at the head of navigation on the Mississippi River and on the great Mediterranean lakes."[109]

Seward was right, and Jones was one of those to recognize this wealth. In the late 1880s, the developed waterpower of Minneapolis was worth $2,750,000 a year; principally from grinding wheat into flour. In 1898, that waterpower as the basis of the milling industry produced 14,278,915 barrels of flour, that required sixty million bushels of wheat. Minneapolis led the world in flour production and served also as the world's greatest primary wheat market. The elevators in the Minneapolis area stored a capacity of 27,585,000 bushels of grain; and the total storage capacity of the elevators, tributary to this market was over seventy-four million bushels. As a result, the wheat and flour trade in Minneapolis provided jobs to over 5,000 workers. Herschel knew the importance of accurate crop forecasting.[110]

That same year, however, tragedy reared its ugly head, when on February 15, the American battleship *Maine* mysteriously exploded in Havana, Cuba, killing 266 of the 350 sailors on board. The origin of the explosion was not immediately apparent, but the Hearst and Pulitzer papers were eager to capitalize on the incident. In their blazing headlines, they blamed the explosion on Spain. These newspaper accounts fanned American antagonism towards Spain, and even one elderly Civil War veteran wrote to the adjutant general begging, "Give me a chance like a good fellow. [I'm] just as young as ever, and would like a whack at them."[111]

On August 20, 1898, President William McKinley signed a joint resolution of Congress prepared by Senate foreign-relations commissioner chairman Cushman K. Davis of Minnesota. This joint resolution recognized Cuba's independence, demanded Spain's immediate withdrawal from the island, and directed the president to use military force if needed. Spain severed diplomatic relations with the United States, and on April 25, Congress ratified a declaration of war.

The war was over in less than four months. With the signing of the Treaty of Paris on December 10, 1898, Spain withdrew from

Cuba and ceded Puerto Rico and the Philippines to the United States.[112] An American newspaperman at the time summed up the Spanish flotilla's defeat somewhat enthusiastically: "If Spain was served as well by her statesmen and public officials as she was by her sailors, she might still be a great country."[113]

American forces in the Pacific defeated the Spanish navy at Manila Bay, and also captured the city of Manila, Spanish Guam, and Wake Island. United States troops in Cuba, including the Third U.S. Infantry from Fort Snelling, won battles at El Caney and San Juan Hill. Under the Treaty of Paris, signed on December 10, the United States was ceded Puerto Rico, Guam, and the Philippine Islands (the latter for twenty million dollars). Hawaii had been ceded to the United States just prior to the treaty. In 1899, the Filipino nationalists, who had been denied their independence by the United States, began fighting their American "captors." Three years later, Theodore Roosevelt declared the Philippines "pacified," but it was not until 1946 that the Filipinos would finally achieve their independence from the United States.[114]

All through the war with Spain in 1898, *Minneapolis Journal* cartoonist Bart attacked "America's imperialism." One of Bart's better cartoons, that ran in the *Journal* on March 17, 1898, depicted Senator Cushman K. Davis, an ardent expansionist instrumental in annexing Hawaii, telling Congressman James Tawney of Winona, "Say, Jim, if Uncle Sam doesn't want this thing we'll just put it in the upper lake at Minnetonka and annex it to Minnesota."[115]

As Minnesota soldiers headed for home, the *Journal* established an employment bureau as an intermediary between "the disarming veterans from the Philippines and a grateful and patriotic public."[116]

The United States had been at war with Spain, but it was still engaged in a bigger war with the typhoid fever epidemic of 1898. During the four months the Twelfth and Fourteenth Minnesota Regiments were in service, one-third of the men—433—of the Twelfth developed the disease. Eighteen died. The Fourteenth listed 286 "probable" cases, with eight deaths.[117]

In 1899, war news was becoming "old hat," and there was a return to normalcy both in the nation and in the press. The *Journal* gave press to artistic endeavors such as the initial print show of the Minneapolis Camera Club April 5-7. The show was highly praised by the *Journal* in an article with multiple headings: "Photographic Art; Fine Examples in the Minneapolis Camera Club's Print Exhibit; Notable Camera Achievements; Demonstrating that Photograph-Making Is Truly a Fine Art."[118]

In Minnesota, wheat was king, with a record 6,400,000 acres of wheat harvested. Over the past decade, Minneapolis had become the "Budapest of America." With such an abundance of dry wheat stored in the mills, however, there was always the great risk of fire. The Washburn "A" Mill had been destroyed in 1878, and five or six nearby mills had collapsed from explosion or had caught fire. Eighteen men had been killed and "nearby half the city's milling capacity had been destroyed at a stroke."[119]

During the rebuilding of the "A" Mill, Washburn had taken measures to control the menace of flour dust by installing dust-collecting machines, since it was believed the explosion had been caused by ignited dust.

Frank H. Peavey, in an attempt to stop fires and explosions, came up with the answer—build grain elevators out of cement. Called "Peavey's Folly" by many, hundreds gathered laughingly in May 1899 as Peavey's eighty-foot elevator was completed and filled with grain. The experiment worked perfectly, a new way of storing grain had been discovered, and no one laughed at Frank Peavey again.[120]

In August of that year, Herschel and Lydia attended not one, but five, band concerts at the Lake Harriet Pavilion. On the sixth, they listened to the Banda Rossa, the Great Band of Italy, perform Mancini's "March Addio Napoli," Auber's "Overture Zanetta," a "Mazurka, Souvenir of Minneapolis" of Sorrentino, Wagner's "Pilgrims' Chorus Tannhauser," Bellini's "Norma, Grand Selection Priests' Chorus," Verdi's "Prayer, Forza del Destino," the "Maypole Dance" of Tobani, "Marcia Fimbre" by Ponchielli, and Wagner's "Ride of the Valhyries."[121]

On the 13th, the couple listened to works by Sorrentino, Rossini, Verdi, Bizet, and Marengo, while on the 16th (German Night), works of Beethoven, Handel, Abt, Meyerbeer, Mozart, Schuman, Schubert, Mendelssohn, and Fahrbach. On Verdi Night, August 18th, they were treated to works of Verdi, Sorrentino, Loreglio, and Rossini, and on the 24th (Wagner Night), compositions by Wagner, Sorrentino, and Schubert.

Life at Lake Harriet was idyllic. The Linden Hills district comprised its own village separated from the rest of the city by lakes. The Lake Harriet pavilion served as the hub of activity during those dreamy summers. Warville Nelson was the conductor of the band concerts. Wearing an immaculate white uniform, the conductor stepped to the podium and would bow to the audience. When all chatting ceased, Nelson waved his baton, and the concerts began. These were the "glow-worm" years when members of the audience could stand on the rooftop garden and take in both the concert and canoes swishing by below. Tiny electric lights illuminated the bandstand while passing motorists "tooted" their appreciation.[122]

About this same time, Herschel and Lydia attended a performance of Puccini's Opera, "La Boheme," at the Grand Opera House of Minneapolis' Exposition Auditorium. The piece was performed by the Maurice Grau Opera Company, and following Puccini's masterpiece, they were treated to the "Mad Scene" from "Lucia De Lammermoor."[123]

The Grand Opera House, following its opening in 1883 under the management of J.F. Conklin, was referred to by New York managers as the ideal playhouse. It was redecorated four years later by John S. Bradstreet but closed on October 5, 1895, with Hoyt's "A Contented Woman." Its bookings were transferred to the Metropolitan Opera House, which like the Orpheum and the Shubert Stock Company, played the choicest productions following their Broadway runs. Later the Grand moved into the Exposition Auditorium that had been built in 1886.[124]

The Metroplitan, Grand, Pence Opera House, the Academy of Music, and the Bijou Opera House, to which the Joneses visited, were the "legitimate" theatres operating in Minneapolis during the late nineteenth century. The "less-respectable," risque variety theatres, unfortunately, were frequented by an even larger number of people and also subject to police raids.[125]

That same year, the *Journal* praised Jones for his crop estimating and thanked him for being a member of the "family" for fourteen years: "By unusual aptitude and industry, Mr. Jones has created a department which is a credit to himself and the *Journal*. His crop estimates—his own conception and execution—have given him a unique and important position in commercial lines.

"The *Journal* has been no small factor in the up-building of the Northwest, agriculturally. It has stimulated production in various ways and its market reports, for their completeness and reliability, have won the confidence of the grain-raisers and shippers from Winnipeg to Winona. It is a national authority concerning the grain trade of the Northwest."[126]

One of the staff writers pointed out that the commercial page, unlike some of its competition, also covered the livestock markets of the Northwest, having in addition to the regular reports, valuable articles concerning various phases of this important industry. Minneapolis was written up as an important produce and fruit market. As a distributing point for fruits, Minneapolis was second only to Chicago among western cities. And the trade was fully represented in the *Journal*'s commercial department.[127]

By late 1900, H.V. Jones was recognized as the expert on the Northwest wheat situation. Barnard Willis Snow, formerly assistant chief of the Department of Agriculture's Bureau of Agricultural

Statistics and newly appointed director of the Orange Judd Farmer bureau on crop statistics, had also enjoyed a highly respected reputation as a crop estimator. But in 1900, when Jones, perhaps, had his best year, Snow was off by at least thirty million bushels, or more than one third of the total production predicted. His reputation suddenly decreased, and Herschel Jones became the undisputed authority on Northwest wheat.[128]

The *Minneapolis Journal* composing room and staff, ca. 1900. (Courtesy of the Minnesota Historical Society)

Notes

[1] A.J. Russell, *Fourth Street*, Minneapolis, Minneapolis Journal Press, 1917, p. 110.

[2] Lawrence M. Brings and Jay Edgerton, editors, *Minneapolis, City of Opportunity: One Hundred Years of Progress in the Aquatennial City 1856-1956,* Minneapolis, Denison & Company, 1956, pp. 90-93.

[3] Dorothy Gimmestad, "Costume Collection Called Strong 'From Boardroom to Bedroom,'" *Minnesota History News*, p. 4.

[4] Advertisement in Grand Opera Program by the Maurice Grau Opera Company of Minneapolis, in the possession of H.V. Jones.

[5]Lawrence M. Brings and Jay Edgerton, editors, *Minneapolis, City of Opportunity*, pp. 90-93.

[6]No author given, "Going to School in Minnesota," *Roots*, Vol. 2, No. 1, Fall 1973, p. 8.

[7]Lawrence M. Brings and Jay Edgerton, editors, *Minneapolis, City of Opportunity*, pp. 90-93.

[8]Ibid.

[9]Polk Directories for City of Minneapolis, 1886-1890.

[10]Lyman E. Wakefield, Jr., "A Star Shines on Minneapolis' First National Bank," *Hennepin County History*, Spring 1968, p. 11.

[11]Tessie Jones, Proof of Eligibility to the Board of Managers of the Colonial Dames of the State of Connecticut, October 15, 1934.

[12]Winton Jones telephone interview with author January 30, 1999.

[13]Polk Directories for City of Minneapolis, 1886-1890.

[14]Lawrence M. Brings and Jay Edgerton, editors, *Minneapolis, City of Opportunity*, pp. 90-93.

[15]Joseph W. Zalusky, "Do You Remember When? Fares, Transfers, and Other Pertinent Facts About Streetcars—1873-1960," *Hennepin County History*, Winter 1961, p. 9.

[16]Minneapolis Heritage Preservation Committee findings for Stevens Square in collection of Hennepin County Historical Society.

[17]The special use of one such holding would keep Stevens Square an oasis of open land until 1912, when its sudden availability for construction would make it, ironically, the highest density neighborhood in Minneapolis—a distinction which it retains to the present day.

[18]Stevens Square Neighborhood File, Hennepin County Historical Society.

[19]Lawrence M. Brings and Jay Edgerton, editors, *Minneapolis, City of Opportunity*, pp. 90-93.

[20]Jean Adams Ervin, *The Twin Cities Perceived: A Study in Words and Drawings*, Minneapolis, University of Minnesota Press, 1976, p. 108.

[21]Joseph Zalusky, "Through the Years . . . Hotel Nicollet," *Hennepin County History*, Winter 1968, p. 13.

[22]No author given, "Full of Surprises . . . Was Mrs. Dorilus Morrison's Famous Rose Fete on July 1, 1892," *Hennepin County History*, Fall, 1961, pp. 7-9; *Minneapolis Tribune*, July 1, 1892.

[23]Ibid.

[24]Joseph Zalusky, "Through the Years . . . Hotel Nicollet," *Hennepin County History*, Winter 1968, p. 13.

[25]Jean Adams Ervin, *The Twin Cities Perceived: A Study in Words and Drawings*, p. 112.

[26]Joseph Zalusky, "Through the Years . . . Hotel Nicollet," *Hennepin County History*, Winter 1968, p. 13.

[27]Polk Directories for City of Minneapolis, 1886-1890; *Minneapolis Journal* Special, May 25, 1928.

[28]Rebecca Christian, "Cold Hands, Warm Hearts," *Home and Away Magazine*, November/December 1998, p. 20.

[29]William E. Lass, "Minnesota: An American Siberia?" *Minnesota History*, 49/4 Winter 1984, p. 149.

[30]Polk Directories for City of Minneapolis, 1890-1893.

[31]Lucile M. Kane, *The Falls of St. Anthony: The Waterfall that Built Minneapolis*, St. Paul, Minnesota Historical Society Press, 1987, pp. 142-143.

[32]Theodore C. Blegen, *Minnesota: A History of the State*, p. 388.

[33]M.S. Wilcox letter to Tessie Jones postmarked May 3, 1915 in H.V. Jones collection.

[34]Polk Directories for City of Minneapolis, 1893-1911.

[35]June D. Holmquist and Sue E. Holbert, *A History Tour of 50 Twin City Landmarks*, St. Paul, Minneapolis Historical Society, 1966, p. 39.

[36]William H. Tishler and Virginia S. Luckhardt, "H.W.S. Cleveland: Pioneer Landscape Architect to the Upper Midwest," *Minnesota History*, 49/7, Fall 1985, p. 289.

[37]Lawrence M. Brings and Jay Edgerton, editors, *Minneapolis, City of Opportunity*, p. 215; Edward A. Bromley and H.C. Chapin, *Minneapolis Portrait of the Past: A Photographic History of the Early Days in Minneapolis*, Voyageur Press, Inc., Minneapolis, 1973.

[38]Kathryn H. Moody, "The Reminiscences of Lowell Henderson Moody," *Hennepin County History*, Winter 1967, p. 7.

[39]Terry and James Elwell, "Big Island Park," Part I, *Hennepin County History*, Winter 1974-1975, p. 15.

[40]Lawrence M. Brings and Jay Edgerton, *Minneapolis, City of Opportunity*, p. 214.

[41]Ibid.

[42]James H. McCullough, "What a Youngster Learned from His Grandfather's Newspaper," *The American Magazine*, January 1924, page 16.

[43]Ibid., p. 76.

[44]Ibid.

[45]*Minneapolis Journal*, Thursday Evening, May 24, 1928, "H.V. Jones, Owner and Publisher of the *Journal*, Dies," p. 1.

[46]No author given, *The Story of an Institutional Newspaper, 1878 to 1899, Being Twenty-One Years of the Minneapolis Journal*, Volume I, Minneapolis, Journal Printing Company, 1899, pp. 18-

19.

[47]Ibid., pp. 19-20.

[48]*Minneapolis Journal,* undated article, Hennepin County Historical Society Collection.

[49]In concluding, the *Journal* stated, "Other points in Mr. Hill's interesting speech may be taken up at another time."

[50]Scrapbook of H.V. Jones. On the bottom of the first clipping in the book, advertising the play "A Hole in the Ground," the management had inserted a printed note. Aimed at a little humor, the note read, "It is the custom to interfere with the progress of a play of this description by the introduction of more or less successful attempts at music."

[51]Mrs. Frances Siftar interview with author February 25, 1999, Minneapolis.

[52]A.J. Russell, Fourth Street, pp. 26-27.

[53]Ibid.

[54]James H. McCullough, "What a Youngster Learned from His Grandfather's Newspaper," *The American Magazine,* January 1924, p. 16.

[55]Ibid.

[56]A.J. Russell, *Fourth Street,* pp. 27-28.

[57]*The Minneapolis Journal,* Vol. 1, pp. 17-18.

[58]Bradley L. Morison, *Sunlight on Your Doorstep,* p. 13; *Minneapolis Journal,* December 2 and 3, 1928; Ted Curtis Smythe, *A History of the* Minneapolis Journal *1878-1939,* pp. 68-77; Charles A. Williams, *Press Club of Minneapolis Souvenir 1904,* pp. 126-128.

[59]A.J. Russell, *Fourth Street,* pp. 28-29.

[60]Bradley L. Morison, *Sunlight on Your Doorstep,* p. 13; *Minneapolis Journal,* December 2 & 3, 1928; Ted Curtis Smythe, *A History of the* Minneapolis Journal, *1878-1939,* p. 68-77; Charles A. Williams, *Press Club of Minneapolis Souvenir 1904,* pp. 126-128.

[61]*Minneapolis Journal,* March 19, 1887.

[62]*Minneapolis Journal,* December 3, 1928; Bradley L. Morison, *Sunlight on Your Doorstep,* p. 13; Bradley L. Morison, "100 Years for the *Minneapolis Tribune,*" *Hennepin County History,* Winter 1968, p. 20.

[63]*Minneapolis Journal,* December 3, 1928; Judge Isaac Atwater and John H. Stevens, editors, *History of Minneapolis and Hennepin County Minnesota,* p. 369.

[64]No author given, *The Story of an Institutional Newspaper, 1878 to 1899: Being Twenty-One Years of the* Minneapolis Journal, Volume I, pp. 22-23.

[65]Larry Millett, *Twin Cities Then and Now*, St. Paul, Minnesota, Historical Society Press, 1996, pp. 28-29.

[66]Joseph W. Zalusky, "Nicollet . . . A Great Thoroughfare," *Hennepin County History*, Summer 1968, pp. 10, 14.

[67]Larry Millett, *Twin Cities Then and Now*, pp. 28-29.; Ed W. Mather and H.N. Blood, eds., *Illustrated Minneapolis: A Souvenir of the* Minneapolis Journal, *Minneapolis, 1891*, p. 107.

[68]Ibid.

[69]Muriel B. Christison, "LeRoy S. Buffington and the Minneapolis Boom of the 1880s," *Minnesota History*, Volume 23, Number 3, September 1942, p. 231.

[70]Gorham Carlson letter to Arnett W. Leslie dated January 4, 1955, in collection of Hennepin County Historical Society.

[71]Ibid.

[72]Mrs. Frances Siftar interview with author February 25, 1999.

[73]James H. McCullough, "What a Youngster Learned from His Grandfather's Newspaper," *The American Magazine*, January 1924, p. 82.

[74]Ibid.

[75]*Minneapolis Journal*, Thursday Evening, May 24, 1928.

[76]No author given, *The Story of an Institutional Newspaper, 1878 to 1899: Being Twenty-One Years of the* Minneapolis Journal, Volume III, p. 3.

[77]Ibid., p. 4.

[78]Laura M. Hamilton, "Stem Rust in the Spring Wheat Area in 1878," *Minnesota History*, Vol. 20, No. 2, June 1939, p. 156; Herb Paul, "Milling: Oldest American Industry," *Greater Minneapolis*, Vol. 9, No. 4, January 1958, p. 30.

[79]No author Given, "King Wheat Overthrown," *Roots*, Vol. 2, No. 2, Winter 1974, pp. 20-21.

[80]Theodore C. Blegen, *Minnesota: A History of the State,* University of Minnesota Press, Minneapolis, 1963, pp. 390-391.

[81]*Minneapolis Journal*, Thursday Evening, May 24, 1928; *Minneapolis Journal*, Sunday, May 27, 1928; *Minneapolis Tribune*, May 24, 1928; *Minneapolis Star*, May 24, 1928; *Jefferson* (New York) *Standard*, Wednesday, April 18, 1923; *The New York Times*, Friday, May 25, 1928; *Syracuse Herald*, Friday Evening, May 25, 1928; *The Art News*; June 2, 1928.

[82]James H. McCullough, "What a Youngster Learned from His Grandfather's Newspaper," *The American Magazine,* January 1924, p. 77.

[83]Ibid., p. 78.

[84]Ibid.

[85]Ibid.

[86]Ted Curtis Smythe, *A History of the* Minneapolis Journal, *1878-1939*, pp. 412-413.

[87]Ibid.

[88]No author given, *The Story of an Institutional Newspaper, 1878 to 1899: Being Twenty-One Years of the* Minneapolis Journal, Volume IV, p. 5.

[89]Ted Curtis Smythe, *A History of the* Minneapolis Journal *1878-1939,* pp. 173-174; *Minneapolis Journal*, August 15, 1891 and December 6, 1928; Arthur J. Russell, *Good-bye Newspaper Row*, Excelsior, 1943, p. 12.

[90]No author given, *The Story of an Institutional Newspaper, 1878 to 1899: Being Twenty-One Years of the* Minneapolis Journal, Volume IV, p. 6.

[91]Ibid., p. 10.

[92]Ibid., p. 9.

[93]Ted Curtis Smythe, *A History of the* Minneapolis Journal *1878-1939*, pp. 174-176; *Minneapolis Journal,* August 20, 1897.

[94]*Minneapolis Journal*, Thursday Evening, May 24, 1928 and Sunday, May 27, 1928; *Minneapolis Tribune*, May 24, 1928; *Minneapolis Star,* May 24, 1928, *Jefferson Standard*, Wednesday, April 18, 1923; *The New York Times*, Friday, May 25, 1928; *Syracuse Herald*, Friday Evening, May 25, 1928; *The Art News*, June 2, 1928.

[95]Ted Curtis Smythe, *A History of the* Minneapolis Journal, *1878-1939*, pp. 413-415.

[96]Ibid., p. 414.

[97]Ibid., pp. 414-415.

[98]*Minneapolis Journal*, Thursday Evening, May 24, 1928 and Sunday, May 27, 1928; *Minneapolis Tribune*, May 24, 1928; *Minneapolis Star*, May 24, 1928; *The New York Times*, Friday, May 25, 1928; *Syracuse Herald*, Friday Evening, May 25, 1928.

[99]James H. McCullough, "What a Youngster Learned from His Grandfather's Newspaper," *The American Magazine*, January 1924, p. 79-80.

[100]Ibid.; No author given, "King Wheat Overthrown," *Roots*, Vol. 2, No.2, Winter 1974, p. 24.

[101]James H. McCullough, "What a Youngster Learned from His Grandfather's Newspaper," *The American Magazine*, January 1924, p. 80.

[102]Bradley L. Morison, *Sunlight on Your Doorstep*, p. 17-18.

[103]Herschel Jones' program.

[104]Mrs. Frances Siftar interview with author February 25, 1999.

[105]*Jefferson Courier*, Thursday, January 4, 1894.

[106]*Jefferson Courier*, Thursday, January 11, 1894; *Schoharie Coun-*

ty Chronicle, Tuesday, January 9, 1894.

[107]*Jefferson Courier,* Thursday, January 11, 1894.

[108]Mrs. Frances Siftar interview with author February 25, 1999.

[109]Excerpt from William H. Seward's speech, "Political Equality with National Idea," delivered near Minneapolis, September 18, 1860.

[110]No author given, *The Story of an Institutional Newspaper, 1878 to 1899: Being Twenty-One Years of the* Minneapolis Journal, Vol. II., pp. 4-6.

[111]Adam Scher, "Remembering America's 'Splendid Little War,' Spanish-American War Collections at the Minnesota Historical Society," *Minnesota History*, Vol. 56, No. 3, Fall 1998, pp. 129-137.

[112]William P. Everts, Jr., *Stockwell of Minneapolis*, St. Cloud, Minnesota, North Star Press of St. Cloud, Inc., 1996, p. 83.

[113]A.B. Feuer, "Spanish Fleet Sacrificed at Santiago Harbor," *Military History*, June 1998, p. 60.

[114]Adam Scher, "Remembering America's 'Splendid Little War,' Spanish-American War Collections at the Minnesota Historical Society," *Minnesota History*, Vol. 56, No. 3, Fall 1998, pp. 129-137.; Richard E. Killblane, "Assault on San Juan Hill," *Military History*, June 1998, pp. 38-45; Miguel J. Hernandez, "San Juan Under Siege," *Military History*, April 1998, pp. 46-52.

[115]Adam Scher, "Remembering America's 'Splendid little War,' Spanish-American War Collections at the Minnesota Historical Society," *Minnesota History*, Vol. 56, No. 3 Fall 1998, p. 136.

[116]Kyle Roy Ward, *In the Shadow of Glory: The Thirteenth Minnesota in the Spanish-American Wars, 1989 to 1899*, St. Cloud, Minnesota, North Star Press of St. Cloud, Inc., 2000, p. 136.

[117]Herbert F.R. Plass, M.D., "Typhoid Fever Epidemic of 1898," *Ramsey County History*, Volume 3, Number 2, Fall 1966, pp. 4-5.

[118]Christian A. Peterson, "The Minneapolis Camera Club at the Turn of the Century," *Hennepin County History*, Volume 47, Number 1, Winter 1988, p. 6.

[119]Theodore C. Blegen, *Minnesota: A History of the State*, p. 352.

[120]Minnesota Agricultural Statistics, 1973, issued by the State Federal Crop and Livestock Reporting Service of the Minnesota Department of Agriculture; No author given, "What's Growing on Minnesota Farms?" *Roots*, Vol. 2, No. 2, Winter 1974, p. 7; No authors given, "The Waterfall That Built a City" and "Peavey's Folly," *Roots*, Vol. 3, No. 2, Winter 1974, pp. 9, 13.

[121]Herschel Jones' programs for August 6, 13, 16, 18, and 24. All five concerts, plus five others the Joneses did not attend, were billed as "The Musical Event of the Season."

[122]Beatrice Morosco, "Lew Ayres: Lake Harriet's Gift to the Cinema World," *Hennepin County History*, Volume 46, Numbers 3 and 4, Fall 1987, pp. 21-22.

[123]Grand Opera program belonging to H.V. Jones.

[124]Randolph Edgar, "Early Minneapolis Theatres," *Minnesota History*, Vol. 9, No. 1, March 1928, pp. 31-38.

[125]Lawrence J. Hill, "Dives and Diversions: The Variety Theatres of Early Minneapolis," *Hennepin County History*, Volume 46, Numbers 3 and 4, Fall 1987, p. 4.

[126]No author given, *The Story of an Institutional Newspaper, 1878-1899: Being Twenty-One Years of the* Minneapolis Journal, Vol. III, pp. 4-5.

[127]Ibid., pp. 5-6.

[128]Ted Curtis Smythe, *A History of the* Minneapolis Journal *1878-1939,* p. 419.

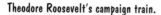

Theodore Roosevelt's campaign train.

CHAPTER FOUR

BULLY

"The use of traveling is to regulate imagination by reality, and, instead of thinking how things may be, to see them as they are."
—Dr. Samuel Johnson

n September 1883, Theodore Roosevelt first ventured "Out West" when he stepped from a train at the Little Missouri (called "Little Misery" by locals) station in Dakota Territory. He intended to hunt buffalo for a week or two but instead found himself investing in the cattle business. Roosevelt purchased two ranches—the Maltese Cross and the Elkhorn—and while he would later lose his investment and sell at a loss, he never lost his enthusiasm for the region.[1]

During 1885-1886, Theodore Roosevelt's North Dakota ranching operations were at their peak. Estimates for how many cattle he owned varied from between 3,000 to 5,000 head. The census rolls for 1885 reveal that Roosevelt was the fourth largest cattleman in Billings County. His total invested amounted to about $82,500.[2]

As early as 1899, Major John Wesley Powell, "the prophet of the arid region," warned North Dakota's constitutional convention of the dangers of plowing the central and western part of the state unless irrigation water was available. Roosevelt, learning about the vital need for irrigation and conservation measures in general, profited by his ranch life in the Little Missouri Badlands and his hunting experiences throughout the West. The passing of the frontier, considered about 1890, dramatized the need for conservation. For Roosevelt, the rich lands of the West were his country, and he would return again and again.[3]

Following the Spanish American War in 1898, Roosevelt returned home to New York. His colorful exploits, especially in the Battle of Santiago, established him as something of a national hero. Thomas C. Platt, the Republican boss of New York, was looking for a respectable candidate for governor. Platt distrusted him, but upon Roosevelt's pledge that he would not attack the machine, he was easily elected. An excellent governor, he successfully removed several corrupt politicians from office and, over Platt's opposition, secured a corporate franchise tax and a civil service system. Enraged, Platt maneuvered Roosevelt into the 1900 nomination for vice president on William McKinley's ticket and thus secured his elimination from New York politics.

Roosevelt needed to push his Republican Party, for some of the states in the "West" were not pro-Republican. A strange thing had happened in Minnesota during the election of 1898, when "Honest John" Lind, running as a fusion candidate, had won the governorship. This marked the first election since pre-Civil War times in which a Republican had failed to capture the governorship of Minnesota.[4]

Honest John, however, did not carry out large-scale reforms as governor. He monitored the state's progress, urged reforms in taxation, advocated improvement in the care of the mentally ill, pushed agriculture, forestry, and education, and voiced approval for direct Democratic control of state government by the people.

Lind, however, became a one-term governor. In 1900, he was defeated by Samuel R. Van Sant, last of the Civil War veterans to hold the office of governor. The Republicans in Minnesota were back in control, but in this state and other western areas, this hold was shaky.

On September 5, 1900, Roosevelt embarked on a six-week speaking tour of "his West." His western campaign car, the *Minnesota*, was attached to the rear end of Train 23 that left Albany that evening. With Roosevelt and others on the special train was John Proctor Clarke of New York, whose job it was to dispense oratory from the tail end of the train at unscheduled stops. According to the *New York Sun*, "while Governor Roosevelt's throat now is in fairly good condition, it is not proposed that he take any risk of overstraining it before his trip shall be ended."[5]

His first speaking stops were in Detroit and Grand Rapids, Michigan. The Michigan State Republican Committee provided special trains for him to ride between Detroit to Great Bend, Indiana. He stopped to make speeches in the Saginaw Valley and a few other points. With him was a corps of other speakers on the special trains. Many of the speakers rode along for only a portion of the trip when others of this select group came aboard and replaced them. Roosevelt had chosen his speakers from many important fields relating to politics, industry, and agriculture.

One of these elite was Herschel V. Jones of Minneapolis, who, according to the *Sun*, was already in 1900 an authority on commercial conditions in the Northwest. It was Jones' responsibility to make careful notes of the agricultural and industrial conditions in the country through which the trip was made. Jones had to pay special attention to their bearing on the political situation. Jones got aboard Roosevelt's train when it stopped in Minnesota on its way to Bismarck, North Dakota.[6]

Only two months earlier, Jones had shocked the grain men of Minnesota with a front-page estimate in the *Journal* regarding the probable yield in the Northwest. His article, "A Good Crop Result" stated, "The *Journal* feels justified in making this preliminary crop statement today because conditions are sufficiently advanced to warrant it, and also because of the unwarranted statements about the Northwest yield that have been put in circulation. They are without foundation and were never warranted."[7]

Jones had estimated a minimum crop yield of 135 million bushels, and with a good rain, perhaps 150. This completely disrupted the sanity of the grain trade and led the *Chicago Tribune* to reprint the *Journal* story the following day. According to the Chicago newspaper, part of the grain trade did not believe in Jones' wild estimate but that "reports of recognized statisticians, however, had a pronounced effect on the general trade, and prices suffered accordingly."[8]

The *St. Paul Pioneer Press* stated the estimate was a surprise to local grain and elevator men. After all, the secretary of the Minneapolis Chamber of Commerce had predicted only 100 million bushels.[9] The *Minneapolis Tribune* alleged that the *Journal*'s estimate caused a "depressing effect on prices."[10]

In Jones' August 10 estimate, he increased his 135 million-bushel to a surprising 136. In "The *Journal*'s Ninth Annual Report on the Yield in Minnesota and Dakota," he gave the reasons for backing up his estimate. From his first day on the job, he always gave his reasons behind his estimates. This time he said his July 13 report had received "such hostile criticism as has never been bestowed on a crop report before. But notwithstanding all this adverse criticism, I am unable to reduce the estimate . . . and I believe the final result will sustain the figures."[11]

Farmers in the Aberdeen, South Dakota, area vigorously denounced Jones' estimate, saying that it was too high for South Dakota. But the *Journal* editor defended its commercial editor and two days later ran a *Watertown, South Dakota*, report of scarcity of help. The *Watertown* headline ran, "No Help, Hurtful Effect of the Aberdeen Wheat Junta Calamity Talk."[12]

It was, undoubtedly, the 1900-grain crop that made Herschel Jones the best in the business in the eyes of vice presidential candidate, Theodore Roosevelt. Jones joined Roosevelt's entourage as they sped through a storm across North Dakota to Bismarck. According to the *New York Sun*, "plain rainstorms like those of South Dakota and Minnesota yesterday are bad enough, but wind cuts like a knife and carries a drizzle which is mixed with dabs of snow as has that of today and makes attempts at public speaking almost useless."[13]

A senator traveling with Roosevelt, Jones, and company, had arranged to hold meetings at small stations along the way, but the intense storm, permitted only handshakes and greetings. Jones and the passengers on Roosevelt's train were nearly as cold on the inside of the train as were those faithful waiting outside. However, the celebrities were met with red-hot enthusiasm at each station, and "the slightly contagious liveliness" of a band, which had traveled 200 miles across the state to meet Roosevelt, perked up the speakers. The band members were given a sleeper near the front of the train, and they played vigorously at each station. The musicians also played between stations, probably more to keep warm than for any other reason.

That same day, Denny Hannaford, "War Governor of Dakota," came on board. Seth Bullock, sheriff of Deadwood, left the train, although he planned to rejoin it later for the trip through Wyoming and Colorado. At his point of departure, before Roosevelt, Jones, and a cheering crowd, Bullock roared, "The coming man is the man of the West, the man of the plains. This is God's country. The Indian man will tell you that this is God's country. The down East man will tell you that the Rock Hill State of Maine is God's country. But this is the only country where God has elbowroom, and this is where He makes men. Teddy is a horse of the range."[14]

Roosevelt then addressed the crowd and started them shouting with a short speech. "We have the right to appeal to all men, who are indeed Americans, to uphold the policy that tells of national greatness," exclaimed Roosevelt. "We stand at the threshold of a new century. We began the century as one of the greatest nations of the world, standing among the forefront of the great nations. If we are true to ourselves, we shall establish for the nation during the century to come a record unequalled during the history of mankind."[15]

The train rested for two hours at Jamestown, but people had come from fifty to sixty miles away to hear Roosevelt and his party speak. The speakers went to the Opera House, which normally held a crowd of a thousand people, but arrangements had been made for another five hundred to sit in. Roosevelt and Senator Thomas Carter gave the main speeches, and the crowd was thoroughly Republican.

Roosevelt was asked to speak the next day at Medora, since his Elkhorn Ranch was located near there. Thousands of people were planning to attend in hopes of seeing their hero as a political candidate. Roosevelt refused to grant the request, however, saying that on no account would he speak on a Sunday or at a time when a church was in session.

When the train reached Bismarck at six o'clock that evening, Roosevelt left Herschel and the other members of his entourage and galloped away on a horse for a two-hour ride across the prairie before the evening speeches were to commence. When he did give his speech, he was greeted by the "Junior Volunteers of Jimtown," boys of seventeen or eighteen years old who had undertaken the military duties of the town when the real military men went away with the Rough Riders. None of them had complete uniforms, but a couple of them had fifes and drums.

Roosevelt walked out on the platform and approached them, saying that he had just come out to say, "how-do" and to express his admiration for the amount of patriotism they had managed to compress into their uniforms. He said it was a whole lot more to his mind than the uniforms that cost a whole lot more. He asked to be excused while he went to get his dinner. The boys whispered a moment and then sent their captain into the dining car to apologize to Mr. Roosevelt for disturbing his dinner. The governor got up, put his arm around the boy's shoulders, and went out and personally shook hands with each of the boys, thanking them for the parade they fashioned in his honor.

Later, the train passed a sod heap with an American flag hoisted high above it just a few feet away from the tracks. Roosevelt and his company were touched when they saw a young girl and boy standing hand in hand, waving smaller flags at the train. When the travelers reached the town of Buffalo, there were 200 eager greeters awaiting them.

In the town of Steele, Roosevelt's voice began to go. He was unable to speak the rest of the day and said little to the huge audience at Bismarck. A man named Foley had written a poem about Roosevelt, and the *Bismarck Tribune* had published it. The poem, "The Fall Round-up," was recited to Roosevelt and his fellow speakers:

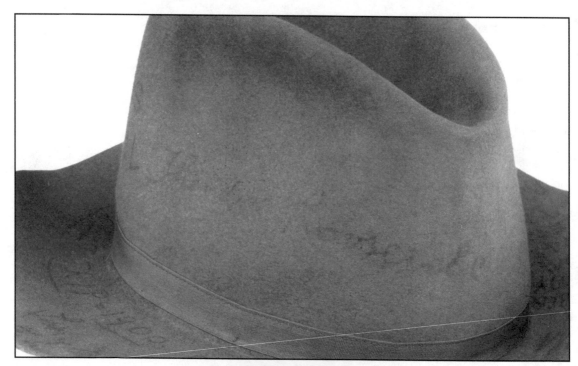

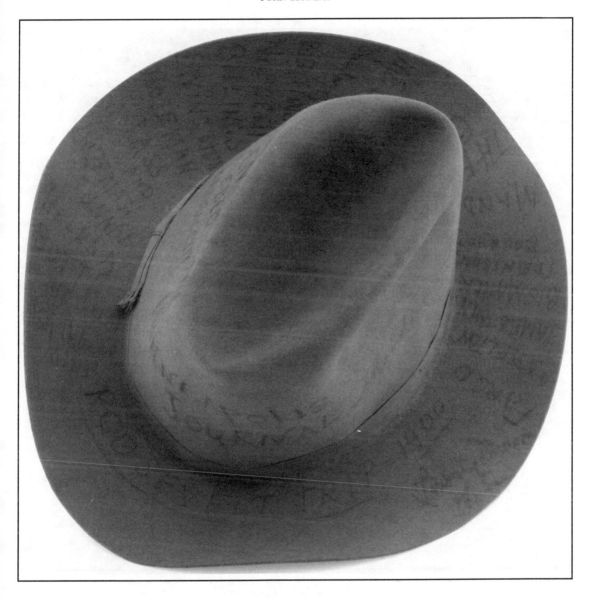

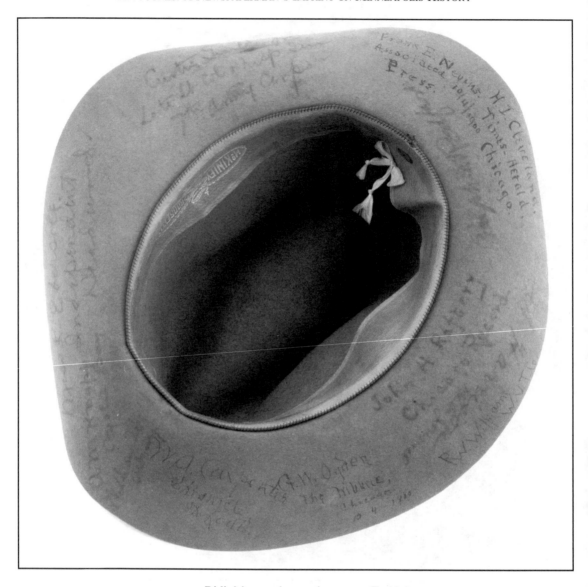

Ridin' 'cross the continent, our Teddy's on a tear;
He's got sagebrush in his haversack an' cactus in his hair.
He's out a-brandin' mavericks that's runnin' on the range,
He'll bring 'em into camp or y' may 'low it's mighty strange,
Y' can hear the boys a-shoutin',
Y' can see the cloud of dust,
Y' can hear the cry a-going up "To Washington or bust,"
So clear th' way for Teddy, he is bound to fetch up there,
For th' round-up wagon's started, and our Teddy's on a tear.

Ride the ranges careful, boys, our Teddy's on th' tramp,
Populists and Democrats, bring 'em into camp,

Ones or twos or three-year olds, every kind of breed;
Watch the leaders careful, boys, an' don't let 'em stampede.
Round 'em up and drive 'em in, every blessed steer;
Teddy's goin' to o-rate, an' they've all got t' hear,
Steady, boys, now head 'em so. That's right; now hold 'em there,
Th' round-up wagon's started, and our Teddy's on a tear.

See that little maverick that's followin'—that's Towne,
See there, now Teddy's roped him, an' he's goin' t' tie him down.
Truss his legs together-sorta shorten up his sail—
Th' ain't no livin' tenderfoot can foller Teddy's trail,
Hear that big feller bellerin', that's Bryan. See him scoot
When Teddy swings his lariat, th' ornery galoot
See 'em break and scatter for th' open ground, that pair,
Oh, they've got t' hunt th' timber when our Teddy's on a tear.[16]

Herschel Jones continued to send in his crop estimates to the *Journal* while he traveled with Roosevelt and his party. At this time, he was still under pressure to revise his August estimate. However, he had earlier taken a trip north after most of the harvesting was done and estimated the amount of damage caused by the rain. He was convinced there was no need to change his last estimate, "although it is not unlikely that yields have been reduced five million to ten million bushels; but on this basis the total could not well be placed below 130 million and this is scarcely important enough to warrant a change of the yield figures for August."[17]

As the train pulled into Medora, Roosevelt's old friend, Sheriff Folles, had a horse waiting for him. Roosevelt rode off into the plateaus of the Badlands by himself where he could rest his voice, while Herschel and the other speakers looked over the town. On the top of a rise that ended at Friburg was a sign with letters two feet high inscribed with its name and a sidetrack, nothing more. There was not a house in sight, although the site was high above the surrounding country.[18]

An article in the *New York Sun* read, "A mile beyond is where 'Badlands Charley' stands guard over his domain, as he has stood, gun in hand, since the waters washed the earth away from the petrified roots that make his form. Almost before anyone could realize it, the train was whipping in and out of the buttes and the gullies where the hills make faces at mankind and the rocks blaze out on paths of blue-gray sage brush."[19]

Joe Ferris, who had worked for Roosevelt on the Elkhorn Ranch, rode on the Minnesota train from Bismarck to Medora and sat side by side with his old friend in front of the windows. Every twisted, craggy butte reminded them of their cow-punching days. Ferris asked the governor if he remembered "the Pike," who had been Medora's bad man only twelve years earlier. They laughed as they remembered how the Pike had come into town one day threatening to lick every man in town, one at a time. He had licked two, but a third man named Snyder got him down, knelt on his chest, and pounded his face with a rock as big as a coffee cup. Snyder was familiar with the Pike's stamina, however, and began yelling, "Somebody come and hold him while I get off, he's tiring me out."

The governor wanted to know what had become of Hell Roaring Bill Jones, who had served as sheriff while Roosevelt was a deputy. The pair recalled an incident of years before when a lunatic had shot a man on a Northern Pacific train just out of Mandan. The conductor kicked the man off the train at Medora and asked if there was a peace officer on duty. Jones locked him up but a "mean man" named Bixby broke the man out. Bixby, however, was rewarded by having his nose bitten off by the escapee.

Herschel Jones, undoubtedly, took some ribbing when the subject of Hell Roaring Jones came up. H.V. had certainly raised hell with the grain trade estimators, and his cohorts on the *Minnesota* probably had a good laugh over it. Always good-natured, Herschel would have joined in as he had many times in the office of the *Journal* when the subject of Frank Peavey had come up.

After a rousing reception in Medora, the *Minnesota* pulled out of the Badlands, and within two hours, was racing across the open prairie. On the 17th, the train pulled into the foothills of the Rocky Mountains and paused in Billings, the center of Montana's sheep raising country. Near here, the "Alice Band" joined the train. The Alice Band was made up of miners who worked the Alice Mine, a competitor of the Boston and Montana Bands. The addition of the miners to the *Minnesota* placed the Livingston and Bozeman citizens in a high state of enthusiasm.

Soon the celebrities journeyed over the mountains to Bozeman and Helena. At Big Timber, a meeting was held in a warehouse where an abundance of timber had been stored. Growers claimed they were holding the timber until McKinley's victory because they believed the market would be stronger then.[20]

According to the *New York Sun*, "a little after [two] o'clock the train shot out of the Wickes tunnel and looked down on scrawny, smoky, glowing, sulphurous Butte. After a long down-hill sweeping curve by which the Great Northern enters the city, it ran past a long succession of mine entrances, smelters, and ore crushers on which were lined up hundreds of miners. In one place a group of fifty stood on the edge of an elevated ore track and waved their dinner pails at Governor Roosevelt, who saluted them by lifting his hat."[21]

As the speakers descended from the train, they were met by the Silver Bow Republican Club, who were standing ankle-deep in the sticky, unfailing mud. The greeters, despite the mud, waved their hats in the air and cheered as each speaker stepped down. Then the Alice Band climbed out, for this was their hometown, and boomed out the strains of "Hail, the Chief."

On the 19th, Roosevelt and his colleagues addressed the irrigation farmers and sheep raisers in Pocatello, Idaho. In Idaho Falls, "a quarter of a carload of fruit and flowers was loaded on the train. There were great masses of white and purple asters that were hung about the dining car and the special cars until the sides of them were covered. Branches of peach trees have been festooned over the doors and a lower berth in each car has been filled with boxes of apples, pears, peaches, and grapes. On the dining table in the *Minnesota* is a great double armful of magnificent roses."[22]

In Rexburg, Roosevelt addressed a large group of Republicans, and he was astounded to find nearly as many women in the audience as men. He spoke of the irrigation ditches and their effect:

> Why are you here? Because your fathers and some of yourselves expanded into this country. You moved here in your white-topped wagons, and came across the plains over the mountains of Utah to become miners and ranchmen, and when you got here you began to irrigate the soil. Right there is one of the problems of the nation, and the nation must help to solve it. Your forefathers came here to make the wilderness blossom like the rose. As I came up your valley this morning, I saw the rising sun throw its light not against sage brush, but against the green alfalfa fields that have been irrigated by your own efforts.[23]

Herschel Jones undoubtedly joined in the discussion in Rexburg. Much of the talk centered upon alfalfa and the irrigation process that made it such a successful crop. Jones was studying the alfalfa crop in Idaho, was better versed in the grain market than any of the other speakers, and was still sending in his reports to the *Journal*.

The first speeches delivered in Utah were held in a Mormon tabernacle in Logan, Utah. Roosevelt and his fellow speakers had been told that the Mormons were a spiritual body and never meddled in sectarian affairs. A reporter interviewed one of the church leaders and said, "Sir, I am told that the Mormon Church is at bottom a Democratic organization." The church leader flushed, and it was quite evident to the reporter, that he was angry. The man merely shook his head, undoubtedly, too angry to speak. When he recovered his composure, he snapped, "That is a lie. The Church is not in politics, and I may say, sir, that what you have said is so far from the truth that this year most of the influential churchmen are Republicans in sentiment."[24]

More than two-thousand people listened to Roosevelt and his fellow speakers in Salt Lake City where Roosevelt is said to have given one of the best speeches in his life. The only other time in history that such a sizeable crowd had gathered in that city was when it welcomed the return of the Utah Battery coming home from the Philippines with fourteen battles named on its flag.

Herschel, along with Roosevelt, addressed the folks who comprised at least thirty-one nationalities in Ogden. Before Herschel's speech, the people of various ethnic backgrounds, paraded down the street from the station to the opera house, bringing Jones and company along with them. Yells of acclaim in thirty-one languages echoed along the streets and over the Bitter Creek Hills.

In Wyoming, most of the speeches were held in towns where railroad men made up the majority of the audiences. Wyoming had 20,000 voters, and it was Roosevelt's chore to get the vote of the railroad workers. Some of these railroad towns like Rawlins, Laramie, and Cheyenne were also the headquarters of cattlemen.[25]

In Laramie, it was raining hard when Roosevelt and his men stepped into the streets. Roman candles were shot off, but their missiles landed only a few feet away, before the rain snuffed them out. However, the booming of a seventeen-gun salute and the cheering of the soaking, steaming crowd could not be stopped.

When the governor and his men walked up to the door of the Inter-Ocean Hotel, "they were confronted by a St. Bernard dog nearly as big as the governor himself. The dog urbanely put out a paw as big as a loaf of bread. Before the governor could catch his breath the dog rose and ushered him into the hotel corridor. The dog was Senator Warren's "Rex" and was said to know a heap about Wyoming politics. He was the only dog who had ever voted for a United States Senator. When the Republican caucus was considering Clark's candidacy, the dog solemnly rose to be counted every time Clark's friends rose. Notwithstanding all sorts of inducements, nothing could get him up for another candidate."[26]

As the *Minnesota* reached Colorado, a much thicker fog than they had passed through in Wyoming and a much heavier rain greeted the passengers. In Greeley, 400 persons from Denver shoved their way into the station yards. "They had come out from Denver with the famous Cook Fife and Drum Corps simply to make sure that the governor of New York should know that he [Senator Wolcott] had arrived. They whirled around the *Minnesota* in successive flying wedges until Senator Wolcott came out and made a touching appeal to them to give the Greeley folks a chance at the candidate."[27]

At Denver, on the 25th, the governor and his fellow travelers were greeted by a pelting rain. An escort of about a hundred of Roosevelt's comrades from the Spanish-American War were on hand to greet him and escort him on horseback to his hotel. The escort was truly needed to protect him from "the greedy affectation of a great mob that filled Sixteenth Street for blocks, wildly desirous to lay hands on him. With the escort he fairly had to force his way through the streets to the hotel. As far up and down as one could see through the rain, there was only a densely packed, mobbing multitude under rain-wet umbrellas and hats."[28]

In the margin of a scrapbook of clippings from the trip, the compiler, Lindsay Dreiser, who presented the book to Herschel Jones, had written, "The fare from Denver to Colorado Springs is $2.50. As to the fare from the Springs to Victor, ask Jones—he paid the freight."[29]

The trip moved along smoothly until Roosevelt's *Minnesota* pulled into Victor, Colorado, in the Cripple Creek area of the state. Tension grew as the train neared Victor because of a promised attack by a mob of Bryan supporters. In 1896, McKinley had polled only four votes in Victor, and an angry committee had stormed through the town with a bucket of tar and a feather pillow trying to find out who had cast those four votes. Roosevelt was not afraid, and he ordered the stop as planned.

When the train pulled into Victor on the 26th, the Bryan supporters were waiting as promised. Because Roosevelt did not want to waste a minute of the twenty-five minutes allotted for his speech in Victor, he did not wait for the escort to form, and he and Senator Wolcott jumped into a carriage and rode down the hill into town. They had just started down the hill when an angry woman ran out in front of them and flaunted a big piece of brown wrapping paper swinging on a piece of scantling in their faces. Written on the paper was "16 to 1."

Roosevelt and Wolcott ignored the banner. The woman, however, whose bonnet was on one side of her head exposing her hair half down her face, marched to the steps of the *Minnesota* with a swagger and rammed the paper in the faces of its passengers who were waiting for the parade to begin. Someone on the platform yelled at the woman to get away, but she refused to back down.

"She laughed shrilly," reported the *Sun*, "and asked in unprintable language who was going to make her get out, again, pushing the paper up at the men. One of them tore the paper away, crumpled it into a ball and dropped it. The woman began to scream, and a man came over from the corner and said that he was 'the lady's husband,' and wanted to fight with the man who had torn the paper from her."[30]

But the big Hungarian was moved aside and a group of Rough Riders caught up with the governor and escorted him to the meeting place. The irate lady and her husband, however, picked up the crumbled paper, remounted it and joined a crowd of toughs who were following the governor to the hall. Many men in the line cheered and applauded her loudly, yelling, "Bully for you, Mame."

With a whirl and a rush, the crowd leaped down from the street and the sewer embankments and pushed its way up the stairs screaming obscenities. Two ladies, including a niece of Senator Lodge, were in the hall with Mr. Roosevelt when the first disturbance took place. As the ladies, scenting trouble, left the hall, the angry mob marched into the meeting room. Lieutenant Sherman Bell of the First Volunteer Cavalry and General Irving Hall moved into the center of the mob and kept them away from the governor. During Roosevelt's twenty-five minute speech, the "uninvited" did everything they could to disrupt his speech. Still, Roosevelt answered them and did his best to keep order.

When Roosevelt finished his talk and was about to leave, the disturbers rushed out first. A pair of senators took hold of Roosevelt's arm, one on each side, and they marched out of the hall, down the stairs, and into the street. "As they passed out of the sidewalk door, they were greeted by a volley of eggs and decayed lemons and stones from the other side of the street," reported the *Sun*. "They were thrown by the small boys who were lined up there with boxes of missiles at their feet. Some of the escort, made a dash across the street."[31]

Twenty to thirty men suddenly rushed for the governor. One of them, a very tall man of foreign birth, carried a club in his hand and yelled, "Let me at him, damn him." The misfit swung the club at the governor twice, the second time smashing it into his chest, which knocked the candidate backwards. Postmaster Sullivan of Cripple Creek, ran to the governor, picked up the club, and bashed the assailant with it, knocking him to the ground. As another assailant rushed the governor with a similar club, E.S. Tice, part of the escort, jumped between them and knocked the man to the ground. Roosevelt shook off the escort men who were holding his arms and yelled, "Let me take care of myself." Oddly enough, his face wore an expression of radiant happiness.

The *New York Sun* summarized the incident the following day, stating that an angry mob hurled sticks, stones, and epithets, and Roosevelt was struck with a club, although not hurt seriously. "The riot, for it was nothing less than a riot, was half an hour in coming to the boiling point. In the face of its rising Gov. Roosevelt insisted on finishing what he had to say to the people of Victor, and refused to leave the hall where he was speaking until the time had been appointed for the meeting had expired."[32]

The crowd that attacked him was comprised of many former miners of the Coeur d'Alene district in Idaho, and they shouted the name of the Idaho city as an alternate battle cry with that of the Democratic party's name for president. The *Sun* stated all hell really broke loose as Roosevelt was about to board the train following his speech. "Then the clubbing and throwing of stones began and bloody heads and bruises were many and frequent in the next few seconds."

Roosevelt was struck, but the man who had committed the act, was ridden down and trampled by one of the mounted escort. The man was quickly hauled away by his friends before the police could find out who he was.

Roosevelt and his compact party continued their move to the *Minnesota*. The cursing mob was strung out on both sides of them. One of Roosevelt's companions was dragged from the group and hammered over the head with a board. Two drum corpsmen rushed into the crowd and pulled the victim back into their line.

On a hill only six hundred feet from the train, thirty men and boys pushed through the crowd waving placards bearing the name of Bryan. E.M. Solley, a former member of the Thirty-second Michigan Regiment, rode over toward the men and grabbed at their clubs, all the while shouting, "Drop those clubs." The head protester swung his eight-foot-long club at the rider and "in two seconds, everything was in a whirl. Sticks were flying through the air on both sides of the governor's group. Every moment or two a man came crawling out on his hands and knees with his face covered with blood.

"The group opened out as the fight became general, and there were hand-to-hand struggles all over the street. One man, with a ragged hat, brown beard, and no coat, zigzagged in and struck at the governor, who was walking up to the *Minnesota* with the utmost calmness between Col[onel] Guild and Mr. Clark. They were not quick enough to ward off the fellow's blow, which caught the governor on his right side near the shoulder. In another second the man was under the feet of Solley's horse and was trampled all over." As Roosevelt mounted the stairs of the train, a volley of stones was hurled at him. None, however, made their mark.[33]

"The train departed from Victor amid a shower of stones, with the governor of New York standing on the back platform despite the efforts of some of his Eastern friends to get him in the car. He courteously acknowledged the salute of every McKinley man on the outside of the circle of riotous assailants who had fought their way through to the *Minnesota*."[34]

Penciled in the margin of the scrapbook given Herschel Jones was the following statement, "And Jones! Oh where was he?"

Many of the rioters threatened to follow the train over to Cripple Creek and "make the governor sorry that he ever came into the State of Colorado." But, a force of sixty special policemen, plus a volunteer law-and-order association organized by Lieutenant Bell, was waiting in Cripple Creek. The angry mob moved away, and from a safe distance, contented itself with yelling jibes at the governor.

The rest of the week was uneventful, although there was a minor incident at Salida on the 27th, as reported by the *Sun*: "It was quite apparent that a part of the audience was bent on mischief. They were boys from [fifteen to twenty] years old. An investigation among them showed that they had been hired by a man named Thornton to break up the meeting. They caused nothing more serious than annoyance to the rest of the audience because some points of the speeches were lost by the noise."[35]

But things were different in Kansas. When the *Minnesota* roared into Kansas City, 25,000 screaming supporters met him in the convention hall. The meeting became the biggest, most successful day of the trip. Roosevelt attended church the following morning at Westminster Presbyterian Church, rode out into the country on a horse by himself, and in the evening had dinner with the editor of *The Kansas City Star.*[36]

Nebraska also cordially greeted the governor and his entourage. In Lincoln, Bryan had asked people in this, his hometown, to take down all Democratic banners in respect for Roosevelt. Roosevelt and his speaker of the day addressed a crowd of 40,000 loyal supporters, while another 50,000 marched through the streets proclaiming their support.[37]

A meeting in Deadwood, South Dakota, was said to have "broke[n] all records for political times. Following the governor's speech, a six-horse coach took a special party over to the town of Lead where Roosevelt gave another rousing speech. The Lead reception, was second only to Deadwood.[38]

In Omaha, Nebraska, a crowd of over 10,000 packed an immense tent and heard Roosevelt speak. In addition, three overflow meetings had to be held to accommodate the well wishers. But here, it was not only Roosevelt in the spotlight, as Herschel V. Jones also spoke. Here in Omaha, Jones was to leave the train and return to Minneapolis and the *Journal*.

Jones, in his farewell, said: "Business conditions always affect political sentiment. Populism in the West was a natural result of depression! When there is slow demand for farm products and prices are low, it is natural for the farmer to turn to the support of plausible theories for relief. He is told the large corporate interests are opposed to him, that he is being cut out of a fair show of profits. He believes the allegations, forgetting that all interests suffer when the farmer suffers. Policies that he fought come into play, and the farmer finds that his produce is advancing because of an increased demand for it. He makes money and pays off mortgage indebtedness. The natural result is now that he turns to the support of the political party under whose administration he has reduced his indebtedness.

"The West was never more prosperous than now. Under this improved condition, the price of land has advanced, produce has been sold for a profit, cattle and horses have brought a big profit to ranch men, and miners are at work. The voters of the West are turning to the support of the Republican candidates for reasons I have just suggested, and some of the former Bryan States west of the Missouri River will cast their electoral vote for McKinley unquestionably. In others of these states the drift toward the Republican candidates will not be sufficient to remove them from the Bryan column, but the tendency in that direction will be as marked as in the states where Republican pluralities are secured.

"Wyoming this year will dig from her mines a coal product that will be worth the price paid France for the territory of Louisiana, now the great West. Utah, Idaho, Montana, Colorado, Nebraska, and Kansas are all prosperous. Under this condition votes drift naturally toward the party in power. Workingmen employed are also a help to the party in power. There are thousands of them in the West. The political question in the West is, after all, a business question, not one of mere sentiment."[39]

Penciled in the margin of Jones' scrapbook by Dreiser, the compiler, is a hand pointing to Jones' speech in the *Sun*. On the sleeve of the arm is the word "wisdom."

Before Jones returned to Minneapolis, Roosevelt presented him with a cowboy hat that was signed by everyone on the campaign trip. While Jones departed, looking very much the part of a Rough Rider, Roosevelt and his party worked their way back to New York on the *Minnesota*. The trip would be successful, and in a few months, McKinley would be elected president of the United States with Roosevelt as his vice president.

In July 1901, Herschel wrote Roosevelt, who intended to take a trip to Minnesota, extending his hospitality:

> I shall count it a pleasure to entertain you informally for an afternoon or evening, or both, during your visit to Minnesota in September. I am embarrassed somewhat in making this suggestion lest you may choose a more sincere invitation with some that may have more sound ambitions behind them. I

assure you, Col. Roosevelt, that after my most enjoyable trip through the West as a guest on your train that I feel that I am entitled to return to you, though in the manner suggested as an acknowledgement, of the pleasure of that long ride.

If you can make it agreeable to yourself to join me in a quick way for a drive over our splendid boulevards to Minnehaha [Falls], or the lakes, or to spend an hour with me in my library—which I may say is counted as one of the two best in Minneapolis—I shall be pleased to receive your consent.[40]

In 1901, Roosevelt's life would see a major change. While President McKinley was visiting the Pan-American Exposition in Buffalo, New York, on September 6, he was assassinated by anarchist, Leon Czolgosz. Theodore Roosevelt, then, became president of the United States.

Jones wrote Roosevelt again on September 6th:

The boy tells me as I write you that the president is assassinated. Can it be possible? How strange [illegible]. I have written it with full affirmation that all is now changed. I pray the president may survive, but if it must be otherwise it is for you to carry on his great work.[41]

The same year would also see a major change in the life of Herschel V. Jones. No more would he take orders from someone else; from now on, he would be in charge of his own destiny. And Minneapolis would enjoy the fruits of his labors.

Continuing his friendship with Roosevelt, Herschel wrote the president twelve years later in reminiscence.

Do you remember that evening on the train from Kansas in 1900, when I went to you with figures in proof of the statement that you would carry Kansas, Colorado, Utah and Idaho—results you were worrying much about?

I feel I made thorough work of that canvass during progress of the trip, and I wanted you to hear me, for I never sought to trouble you unless I had something worth while. The results showed that I was less than one thousand off each in Colorado, Kansas, and Utah, and within fifteen hundred in Idaho.

And now the old "feeling'" is coming on me again, and I want to talk with you.[42]

Notes

[1] Dale L. Walker, "Teddy's Terrors: Better Known as the Rough Riders," *True West Magazine*, September 1998, p. 10.

[2] Chester L. Brooks and Ray H. Mattison, *Theodore Roosevelt and the Dakota Badlands*, National Park Service, Washington, D.C., 1958, p. 30.

[3] Ibid., p. 47.

[4] Theodore C. Blegen, *Minnesota: A History of the State*, pp. 433-434.

[5] Scrapbook containing *New York Sun* clippings presented to H.V. Jones, who journeyed with Roosevelt on the trip. In H.V. Jones Collection. While most of the clippings of that six-week period are undated, they will hereby be referred to by headings. Above material was found in "Governor Roosevelt's Campaign Trip."

[6] Scrapbook: "Omaha Greets Roosevelt" and "Roosevelt in North Dakota."

[7] *Minneapolis Journal*, July 13, 1900.

[8] *Chicago Tribune*, July 14, 1900.

[9] *St. Paul Pioneer Press*, July 15, 1900.

[10] *The Minneapolis Tribune*, July 16, 1900.

[11] *Minneapolis Journal*, August 10, 1900.

[12] *Minneapolis Journal*, August 14, 1900; Ted Curtis Smythe, *A History of the* Minneapolis Journal, *1878-1939*, p. 417.

[13] Scrapbook: "Roosevelt in North Dakota." In the margin is penciled, "Mr. Sweat's railroad assumes the burden—Jones arrives—Knappen goes."

[14] Ibid.

[15] Ibid.

[16] Ibid.

[17] *Minneapolis Journal*, September 15, 1900.

[18] Scrapbook: "Roosevelt's Day of Rest."

[19] Ibid.

[20] Scrapbook: "Roosevelt in Montana."

[21] Scrapbook: "Roosevelt Rouses Butte."

[22] Scrapbook: "Idaho Hears Roosevelt."

[23] Ibid.

[24] Scrapbook: "Roosevelt's Day in Utah."

[25] Scrapbook: "Wyoming is Stirred Up."

[26] Ibid.

[27] Scrapbook: "Speeches on the Way to Denver."

[28] Scrapbook: Roosevelt Stirs Denver."

[29] Ibid.

[30] Scrapbook: "Riot over Roosevelt."

[31] Ibid.

[32] Ibid.

[33] Ibid.

[34] Ibid.

[35] Scrapbook: "Hearing for Roosevelt."

[36] Scrapbook, "Roosevelt's Kansas Trip" and "Expect Kansas by 25,000."

[37] Scrapbook: "Good Signs in Nebraska" and "Bryan's Town turns Out."

[38] Scrapbook: "Roosevelt in Deadwood."

[39] Scrapbook: "Omaha Greets Roosevelt."

[40] H.V. Jones letter to Theodore Roosevelt dated July 1901. Courtesy of the Library of Congress.

[41] H.V. Jones letter to Theodore Roosevelt dated September 6, 1901. Courtesy of the Library of Congress.

[42] H.V. Jones letter to Theordore Roosevelt dated February 1, 1912. Courtesy of the Library of Congress.

CHAPTER FIVE

KING WHEAT

"Life is like a mountain railway,
With an engineer that's brave,
You must make your run successful,
From the cradle to the grave.
Watch the hills, the curves, the tunnels,
Never falter, never fail,
Keep your hands upon the throttle,
And your eye upon the rail."

—Old gospel hymn

Herschel Jones' success and interest in the grain field led him, in 1901, to establish the *Commercial West*, a weekly trade paper devoted to grain and finance in the Northwest. Jones was now forty years old and had gained the admiration and trust of the business leaders.[1] Contrary to many published reports, Jones did not entirely sever his connection with the *Journal*. He continued for some time to supervise the *Journal*'s commercial and financial page.[2]

Jones maintained his theory that successful men made it to the top on credit and that one should never "pay as you go." When he entertained thoughts of publishing a commercial paper of his own by starting *Commercial West*, he tested his theory to get the money for the venture. "To put such a paper on a paying basis, I needed fifteen thousand dollars—and five thousand dollars was all I had," he recalled in a 1924 interview. "I went to the cashier of a bank where I was well known through my frequent borrowings, and explained the project to him."[3]

The banker told Jones that he could probably have the ten thousand. A bank meeting was to be held in a few moments, however, and Herschel was invited to come in and tell the directors what he needed. He did so and watched the bankers, many of whom were known to him, discuss the loan. The vice president consented by saying, "I'm in favor of letting Mr. Jones have the money. If he doesn't pay, charge it to me!"

The president replied, "I am also in favor of letting Mr. Jones have the money. I don't know him very well personally, but I have noticed that for a good many years he has been a borrower from this bank and he has always paid."[4]

Jones had been following his plan for more than fifteen years, hoping that some man of consequence would respect his record when it was needed most. *Commercial West* was launched; and by the time it was on a paying basis, he had spent either "sixty-eight dollars more, or sixty-eight dollars less" than the original investment.[5]

Jones, in his trenchant and forcible style, announced his principles and policies in two editorials in the very first issue. With his original masterpiece—"The Principle of Integrity"—Jones gave an inspiration from his own splendid personality as an ideal gentleman and citizen, "like a rock," "whose word is as good as a bond," who "brings brightness to us," and who "walks up to us with a smile that has sincerity behind it."[6]

Jones, in his salutatory editorial, wrote, "These are the days when it pays to be honest. The principle of honesty is as old as the hills, but there has never been a time when it paid a better revenue to be honest than in these very days. Men who have made it a practice to be dishonest are being left in the rear, while at the front is marching the great army of young men who have learned instinctively that dishonesty can never pay at any point in the business of life.

"And, when we analyze as to what the principle of integrity is, we can understand at once why this is so. The idea of dishonest action is out of harmony with anything that is pleasant. The man who is untidy in his home is not entitled to a place in the parlor. It is under the same natural reason that we place the dishonest man outside our circle of association. No argument is necessary to suggest that he should be there; he takes his place there by his own act just as does the felon who continues to rob and murder. The instinct of those about him is to avoid him, and if dishonesty were a natural thing this would not be the case.

"We like the man who brings brightness to us; who walks up to us with a smile that has sincerity behind it; who shakes our hand with a grip that means something more than the wily hand-fondling that the hypocrite unconsciously puts forth as his effort in greeting.

"The man of integrity is like a rock. The people know him. His word is as good as a bond. What an uplift there is in the very thought of integrity. It is worth striving for from the day the young man enters upon his business life to the day when, as an aged man, he bids a farewell to earth.

"This world wants men, and it is going to have them. If there is a young man who thinks that he can forge his way to the front by trickery, he may as well come to his senses now, for it cannot be done. The Almighty made this world for honest men, and honest men are going to have the choice places in it."[7]

Jones' second article in that same issue, actually the first of the two he had composed, was undoubtedly inspired by his grain reporting on his trip West with Theodore Roosevelt less than a year earlier. Entitled,"The West," Jones wrote, "This is a great field in which to work. We need to know more about our resources, and we should not hesitate to tell the world of them. We have lands in abundance, mineral wealth beyond easy computation, great lines of railway, lumber resources, and an intelligent people. On these can be safely based predictions of growth beyond present day conceptions."[8]

Jones wrote Roosevelt on March 8, 1902:

> Your position on Cuba is fully indorsed in Minnesota. Messrs. Tawney and Morris are misrepresenting best sentiment as well as interests of the state. Our millers would export more flour were Cuba prosperous. This increased export would help make wheat higher; but outside of a narrow view, best sentiment upholds our plain duty to Cuba.[9]

Jones' principles of honesty and good will were appreciated by his employees and those that came after him as expressed in a 1928 issue of the paper: "In founding the *Commercial West*, he laid the foundations on the hard and unyielding rock of moral principle. He builded this publication in a spirit of service to the Northwest.

"He was a great publisher, but not always had printed only that which was useful, fine, delightful and good, but he also imprinted his indelible influence and brightness of soul on the mind and hearts of those who were his employees, friends and readers.

"He was a deeply religious man. It was from that Kindly Light by which he was led, that he was himself so well inspired to lead others along pathways of goodness, truth and beauty."[10]

Jones' name as owner and editor appeared on the masthead of the paper, but William A. Frisbie, city editor of the *Journal*, became assistant manager when *Commercial West* commenced. Later, Frisbie was identified as a proprietor. Frisbie may have invested some money in the enterprise and was later bought out, but within three months, he was gone from the paper and back at the *Journal* as city editor.[11]

Local newspapers were moved to pen favorable comments of the new *Commercial West* following its premier issue. The *Minneapolis Journal* was first to comment on March 16:

> The first number of the *Commercial West* made its appearance to-day. Mr. Jones and Mr. Frisbie are to be congratulated upon the typographical appearance of their new paper, its attractive make-up, its convenient form and general inviting appearance, as well upon the quality of the matter which it contains and the eminently respectable showing of business in the first number. The leading article is entitled "The West," in which it emphasized the fact that "the West has become a great investment field which has been poured already a great volume of capital from the money centers of the world," but where development "has just begun." Railroad construction, mining development and resources, agricultural and lumbering interests, the present extent and prospective greatness of the commerce of this region, and some recognition of the centers of trade and industry, are noted in the general review of the field of commercial activity to which the new paper proposes to devote its energies and facilities. Interesting correspondence appears from various western cities, financial, commercial, grain, mining, transportation, real estate and other interests. The *Commercial West* has marked out a large field for itself, but we have confidence in the ability of the publishers to occupy it profitably.
>
> It is evident from the first number that the *Commercial West* will not be a mass of dry-as-dust material, from which only an expert can derive any information. The statistics and figures necessary for exact information will all be there, but they will be presented in a manner which will make them interesting to anyone, even though he should not be directly connected with commercial enterprises. In other words, it will be a general guide book of the great west, following the movements of trade, industry and agriculture, entertainingly written with sympathetic and observant care.[12]

One day later, the *Minneapolis Times* offered the following information:

> The *Commercial West*, an investment journal conducted by H.V. Jones as editor and manager, with W.A. Frisbie, D.E. Woodbridge and Milton O. Nelson as assistants, made its initial

appearance yesterday. As its name implies and its editorial heading announces, it is a "weekly journal representing western investments, manufacturing and development." Its publication office is at Minneapolis and its southwest office at Kansas City. Each of these cities is a gateway to a great and growing region; the commercial metropolis of its section, and the *Commercial West* representing both, will have as its territory the most important and most rapidly growing part of the United States which lies west of the Mississippi River. The new journal will be a valuable aid to investors and to their customers. Its first number, though not as complete as its publishers could have wished, is replete with valuable commercial information and its advertising patronage gives gratifying promise of substantial support. As the editors and publishers are well known newspaper men of tested ability and especially trained in the classes of work demanded by their venture, its excellence is assured and its success correspondingly certain.[13]

Milton O. Nelson, the assistant referred to in the *Times* article, served as "a brilliant editorial contributor to the *Commercial West*" and also for a period as its business manager. It was later said of the well-liked Nelson that, "The *Minneapolis Journal* as well as the *Commercial West* had made much use of his great abilities as an editorial writer. He had a most lovable disposition and an earnest Christian character. His practice of high ideals made his life one of perpetual sunshine for those with whom he had contacts."[14]

The *Minneapolis Tribune* also delivered a fitting tribute to Jones' new trade journal:

> The *Commercial West*. The first issue of the above paper, whose advent was heralded some weeks ago, and the appearance of which has been looked for by the business public with an unusual degree of interest, is before us. It is a handsomely printed paper, in convenient magazine form, and bears every evidence of a promising start upon a prosperous career.
>
> The editor is H.V. Jones, for many years the commercial editor of one of Minneapolis' daily papers, a man who has acquired considerable reputation as a reliable crop expert as well as an accomplished purveyor of information valuable to the business and financial community. His assistant manager is William A. Frisbie, for some ten years connected with the local department of the daily press in this city in a responsible capacity, in which he has made a high record for careful and intelligent work. The editor of the important department of mines and mining is D.E. Woodbridge, who is one of the best posted men in that line in the Northwest.
>
> In its initial number the *Commercial West* draws a striking picture of the great progress made by the Western country and

of its potential development, and announces its aims and objects thus: "It is in this great country west of the Mississippi river that the *Commercial West* has pitched its tent. It is time that there should be located in this field of activity a paper whose work it will be to bring together into a few pages a summary of the commercial life of these states and of the growing towns and cities that give them business color."

It will thus be seen that its field is a very broad one, and we believe that the *Commercial West* will cover it in a manner that will make it a valuable, if not an indispensable weekly visitor to every store, business office, bank, and counting room. We shall watch the career of this representative business periodical with interest, and feel justified in predicting for it an abundant and far-reaching success.[15]

Immediately upon establishing his paper, Jones took off on a tour of Northwestern wheat areas. He had to be doubly careful now of forecasting a wrong estimate, for both his reputation as crop estimator and as editor of a commercial publication were at stake. In inspecting the fields, Jones was convinced that reports of a bumper crop were all wrong. Taking an unpopular stance against public and government estimators, he announced a projected production of 183 million bushels, seventeen million under the lowest estimate of his competitors. He based his decision on the heat he found to be causing withered grain in parts of the northeast and was convinced excess water would cut yields in the Red River Valley.[16]

Colonel Rogers of the Chamber of Commerce and Herschel's old friend, Frank H. Peavey, predicted a 200 million-bushel crop. The *Duluth Commercial Record* claimed that "there never has been a time since anything was known of the crop when the prospect was as low as 200,000,000 bus[hels]. We don't care to put an exact estimate on the crop, but present conditions warrant minimum figures of 225,000,000 bus[hels]."[17]

Because of Jones' low estimate, a cartoon built around a poem on a crop-killing managing editor, was directed at him in an issue of the *Northwestern Miller*. For sake of a possible lawsuit, Jones was not mentioned by name, but it was more than apparent to everyone in the business that it was he who was being laughed at. The poem ran thusly:

> It is the season of the year
> When always, without fail,
> The Crop Destroyer finds it pays
> To tell a Bullish tale.
> He takes his trusty pen in hand
> And works his daily scare.
> Hot Dry Wind, at his command,

Comes roaring from its lair,
Forth comes the Chintz Bug, fierce and
Anon, there comes the drouth,
Wheat, at once turns into straw.
Obedient to his mouth,
As up and down he walks the fields
They shrivel at his breath.
He blights them here and shrinks them there
And marks the path of death.
He sums it up, and puts it down,
 He quotes it east and west:
His words are final, terse and grim
And thrown out like his chest.
And good Dame Nature dare not raise
A bushel more or less:
She always stands around and waits
Til he has made his guess.
Then, when he's killed the wheat crop
And all the land's bereft,
His friend, the Chintz Bug, finishes
The little that was left.
The foolish farmer who don't know
The Chintz Bug has been there,
Goes on upon his silly course
Not asking bull nor bear:
And some way, no one knows just how
He gathers up a crop
That staggers all the estimates,
And makes the markets drop.
The moral of this halting rhyme
Is easy, don't you think?
Is—in short—you can't keep wheat
By drowning it in ink.[18]

Although the poem was meant to discredit Jones' estimate, many of the estimators moderately lowered their own forecasts. But it was Jones who had the last laugh, for when all was said and done, his estimate was easily the closest to the total.

Herschel Jones poured his heart and soul into the grain estimates, studying every element, including that of the importance of protein. The protein content of wheat varied from year to year; depending mostly on weather conditions, though seed wheat and soil should also be considered. In a year when the average protein content was particularly low, millers, in order to secure sufficient quantities of high protein wheat to blend with other wheat to produce the kind of flour needed by bakers, pay premiums often amounting to fifty cents per bushel. When there is a good supply of protein for blending purposes, the premiums for high protein wheat are low or not paid at all.[19]

According to "The Sharp Shooter" in his "Bull's Eye" column of *Commercial West*, "In the spring wheat states of the Northwest, where there is a better average of protein than in the winter wheat states, the question of securing fair values for extra protein for blending purposes, is particularly important.

"But though the millers in proportion as they have extra need of protein, will pay generous premiums to secure it, yet the difficulties of farmers or local elevators knowing what the protein content is at the time of sale or shipment, have prevented the producers securing the premiums to which high protein wheat was entitled." And as Jones became aware, "If the Northwestern farmer can get an extra check for his protein wheat when nature gives him the high protein yield, an added something of perhaps considerable amount can be added, at least during some years, to his farm revenues."[20]

For a short time, Jones' *Commercial West* operation boasted a southwest office in Kansas City, Missouri. But from his home base in the Minneapolis office, Herschel reached out to prominent individuals from every vocation, establishing contacts for his publish-

Minneapolis Journal Sightseeing Bus, 1902. (Courtesy of the Minnesota Historical Society)

ing venture, as evidenced by the following letter penned only a few
months after he went into business:

"Dear Sir—I am sending you copy of paper of August 17th,
which, you will notice, contains an editorial complimentary to your
Duluth address. As you are not a subscriber to the paper, I thought
you might be interested in seeing this, especially as it was written

Lydia Wilcox Jones in her late forties
or early fifties.

in Chicago by a gentleman who has no acquaintance with you; hence he was entirely sincere in his complimentary expression. I intend to call on you in a few days." (The key here is "I intend to call on you in a few days.)

During 1901 and 1902, Jones enlarged his magazine while taking time each spring and summer to visit the Northwest wheat fields and examine the crops. Over this period, he was undoubtedly the most accurate estimator of wheat crops in the business and *Commercial West* became the businessman's Bible. In 1902, his estimate was 178,500,000 bushels, which he believed distributed out as 176,347,000. The revised government estimate was proclaimed as 174 million, although its original prediction of 186,597,000, was eight to ten million bushels on the high side.[22]

Jones took time out from his crop "victories" to attend the Metropolitan Opera of Minneapolis during both the 1900-1901 and 1901-1902 seasons. On October 20, 1901, he and Lydia attended a performance of Wilson Barrett's historical drama, *The Sign of the Cross,* direct from London's Lyric Theatre and presented by William Greet's Company. The following June, the Joneses were on hand for the Metropolitan's *Mme. Sans Gene* which was performed by Daniel Frawley and Company.[23]

While on a business trip to Chicago in February 1902, Herschel took time out from work to attend "high class" continuous vaudeville at the Chicago Opera House. Among those who entertained him were *Petite Cantatrice Dancer* Baby Mildred; Trapeze artists —The Edwards; Radford & Winchester, a comedy team of jugglers and dancers; Charles W. Milton, *The Richard Mansfield of Minstrelsy*; and *The Birth of the Butterfly*, Mlle. Ameta."[24]

During May, Herschel became involved in one of President Roosevelt's political appointment controversies. Roosevelt wrote on May 6th: "I have been much bothered about Haupt. Attorney General [Philander C.] Knox made some secret inquiries through some first-rate lawyers and they recommended strongly in Haupt's favor. Mr. [William Drew] Washburn, the ex-senator, is strongly against him."[25]

He wrote again on May 13th, 1902:

> Is it possible for me to get definite statements about Mr. Haupt having been drunk or been guilty of misconduct of that kind? So far the written testimony is overwhelmingly in his favor; and men like Congressman Stevens, whom I have always found trustworthy, are equally emphatic in his behalf. The Postmaster General wishes greatly to keep Purdy, who he says has done admirably. But ist is a serious thing to turn down Senator Clapp's former partner unless I can have some

information which I can particularize. If he is an unfit man, I do not want to appoint him, but the written record as made up so far is strongly in his favor. Young Washington has protested against him orally, and says he will submit written statements, but says he knows nothing of his personal knowledge.

I wish you had to deal with appointments of some of these kinds![26]

Herschel penned a reply on May 19th, 1902:

I sympathize with you. It is surely puzzling to receive conflicting statements from those who may be classed as equally reliable. I do not want to say more than I have lest you feel that I am unduly interested. I assure you that in a personal sense I have no choice for attorney. I feel that I know the kind of a man you want, however, hence I have submitted my judgment from that standpoint and I could not change it with the facts before me as to all candidates who have been mentioned.

You are justified in following the record before you, hence you are justified in appointing Haupt. I know how well you want to do your work, but for your physical good you should not dwell to long on these matters.

Purdy is good as a lawyer, but there is a reason that I have never mentioned why he does not represent your idea of a man. I have never stated this to you because I wanted you to pass upon his case without the information. This reason need not necessarily detract from his usefulness.

Minnesota is at this time as solid as a rock for your renomination; hence it is not necessary to consider appointments that have to do with political influence joined to ability. This leaves you free to appoint Haupt, [illegible] political strength.

If you know from personal contact all the facts about attorneys eligible to this nomination, you would not appoint Haupt or Purdy. Hence I shall feel that I am indorsed in the appointment of either of them, because I feel that with your knowledge [illegible] very much alike. I do not intend this remark as a familiarity.[27]

On July 9th, the president penned another letter to Jones:

You are entirely mistaken if you think I do not consult you or do not heed your advice. You are one of the men whose words I always carefully weigh. But I am sure you will realize that in my position it is simply out of the question for me always to follow any one man's advice. I follow much advice from different men after I have carefully sifted it out, and sometimes I have to set against the advice of all, but in this last case in every way I am very sure of my ground. I never consulted a human being about the reciprocity plank in the Minnesota convention any more than I did with reference to

127

Nebraska; and the action in each State convention was a genuine surprise to me. I do not think you realize how little I do in the [illegible] to manipulte party machinery. I think it legitimate and honorable if done in legitimate ways and for honorable ends, but it is not a matter in which I have any proficiency or for which indeed I have much taste. Perhaps this sounds rather "highfalutin'"; but I do not mean it so. I am trying honestly to tell you just how I am working. If I am to be renominated it must be because the bulk of the Republican party regard me as the man whom they wish as their expodent. If I am to be reelected it must be because I, together with a great many other men, have partly succeeded by our own efforts and partly been favored by fortune in bringing about a condition of affairs which will make the people at large feel that the Republican party should be invested with power.

I hope to see you in September, or earlier if you can get here.[28]

On another trip in October—this time to New York—Herschel attended the Casino (Theatre) on Thirty-ninth and Broadway for a performance of F.C. Whitney's musical, *Piff, Paff, Pouf*. The presentation featured some of the most renowned talent of the era, including Eddie Foy, Alice Fischer, Grace Cameron, Robert Graham, and the Pony Ballet.[29]

Back to work, Jones in 1903, however, made an inaccurate forecast. He presented an estimate of 147,100,000 bushels. His prediction, however, was extremely low, although this figure did not include macaroni wheat which he estimated would be five million bushels or higher. At this time, government figures did not distinguish between macaroni wheat and bread wheat, so all spring wheats in the Northwest were estimated as one. In all fairness to Herschel Jones, his estimate should be considered as 152 million of spring wheat of all kinds, which makes him slightly closer to the realistic figure.[30]

When *Commercial West* announced its estimate in August, the *Northwestern Miller*, like everyone else, was shocked at the low figure. Having blasted Herschel with the sneering poem and cartoon two years earlier, the *Miller* now praised him stating that "much importance is attached to his yearly estimates."[31]

When weather improved in August, the majority of estimators raised their estimates. Herschel Jones, however, believing his figures to be correct, refused to revise his prediction. Jones maintained his figure of 152 million (including macaroni wheat) which fell eighteen million short of the revised government estimate.[32]

Jones' failure to come through with the 1903 spring wheat crop caused a deepening breach with the *Northwestern Miller*. In a one-sided battle over the next couple of years, the *Miller*, convinced Jones had sold out to bull interests and deliberately given inaccurate estimates, declared war on him.

But Hershel Jones bounced back the following year; his reputation became international when he became the first to discover rust in the Northwestern wheat fields. Computing the amount of actual damage caused him to delay his usually punctual forecast. On September 3rd, three weeks late, he filed his estimate of 137,700,000 bushels. When his estimate proved to be the best, Jones was once more riding high.

"That was the year of the black rust," Jones later recalled. "The wheat was tall and thick. It looked fine. It headed out wonderfully. But I discovered there wasn't *anything in the heads!*"[33]

According to Jones, everyone that year had talked about the bumper wheat crop. All these men told Jones there would be at least twenty-five bushels to the acre, but he knew there wouldn't be eight. Jones said that everyone that year gave him a tough time over his low prediction. When the results were announced in Jones' favor, every railroad president in Minneapolis was out on the line for verification. One of these men stopped Herschel on the street and exclaimed, "Jones, a week ago I told my banker you were a fool. Today I said I was a fool. You're right. The wheat crop is a failure!"[34]

Jones had won a major victory which he later gloated over: "Now for the point," he said. "I am not telling these things to puff up myself. I am doing it because I have learned what is involved in becoming an expert in any one line. It means that you have got to stand by what you deduce the facts to be, *no matter how many good men tell you that you can't be right!*"[35]

Jones' victory, however, was short-lived. Unfortunately, he had just joined the brokerage firm of Watson & Company, a Minneapolis dealer in grains and provisions. Watson was thrilled, because in Jones, he could give estimates of the Northwestern yield that would provide an edge over any and all competitors. Jones was also happy because he was making money. The *Northwestern Miller* began smearing him over his affiliation with the brokerage house. Again, the *Miller* cried that Jones' estimates were not only inaccurate but deliberate as well.[36]

Never had the *Miller* ever referred to Jones by name. But on August 10th, that policy changed. While praising Jones for being a gentleman and promising the *Miller* "would never at any time question his sincerity, his honesty or purpose of his intention to report the facts accurately," the editor added that "until Mr. Jones began to make an annual estimate of the wheat crop, the northwest raised great harvests, but since that time the returns have only been moderate."[37]

Out for blood by glossing over the facts, the *Miller* editor wrote, "The *Northwestern Miller* does not remember ever to have read a single, solitary telegram from Mr. Jones, while he was off the reservation and on the warpath, to the effect that wheat was looking well. Ever the rust, the blight, the hot, dry—extra dry—wind, the deluge, the drouth, the army worm, the Hession fly, the Chintz bug, the grasshopper . . . never oh! Never—never even once-just a plain, good, honest, big, old-fashioned comfortable crop."[38]

Continuing an attack on "Crop Killer Jones," the *Miller*'s poet penned a poem that only some readers found humorous:

> "Oh, Mother," wailed the Grain of Wheat
>   Bending its dewy head,
> "My soul is chilled with sorrows
>   And my heart is filled with dread.

> "I tremble lest the Killing Frost
>   Should nip me in the germ
> And visions of the fierce Black Rust
>   Affright and make me squirm.

> "I cannot go to sleep, Mother,
>   However hard I try.
> shudder as I think, Mother,
>   The 'Long, Cold Night' is nigh."

> "Rest, Child," the mother plant replied,
>   Hushing her offspring's moans,
> The while she murmured to herself—
>   "This comes from reading Jones."[39]

Later that same month, the *Miller* accused Herschel of collusion, and alleged that Watson & Company had made "several hundred thousand dollars by the recent advance. The statement has not yet been contradicted."[40]

On August 17, the *Miller* struck again by stating that, "Direct sufferers by this iniquitous system of estimating the crop have been the millers who have had their trade in flour killed and, owing to the exorbitant price of wheat artificially stimulated by false reports, have been unable to operate their mills."[41]

Another *Miller* report announced that "some of its readers who are in the milling business have taken this journal to task because it discredited the reports of the hired crop killers and declined to become hysterical over the situation in the spring wheat districts."[42]

Even the slightest hint of collusion on Jones' part was unjustified. True, Watson had made a profit in advance of the prices, and

Lydia Wilcox Jones in her late thirties to early fourties.

he had known before hand Herschel's crop estimate. But, the accusation that Jones intended to influence the market with inaccurate reporting fell flat on its face. In attempting to establish its erroneous claim, the *Miller* sent 500 telegrams to millers in the spring wheat areas. The reports that came back, however, tended to compare with Jones' estimate and exonerated him of any wrongdoing.[43]

The *Miller*, while in all honesty, was attempting to determine the wheat crop for its customers, still saw fit to save face by stating that it "makes no pretense at being a crop estimator or wheat prophet, *but at least it has no association or affiliation with grain gamblers nor any pecuniary interest in the course of the wheat market.*"[44]

Jones did not deny his affiliation with Watson & Company, but he was totally opposed to the position that, because of this relationship, he "must represent the situation in order to favor its trade. . . . Were these critics able to analyze they would at once see how silly such an accusation is, because outside of any question of responsibility to the general public, the ex-estimator who is connected with a brokerage house would see to it that his customers were in line with the facts, which of itself would render it unnecessary that there should be misrepresentation."[45]

Most grain authorities agreed that the 1904 crop was difficult to estimate, and even the *Northwestern Miller* made several contradictory reports. Jones that year went outside his usual pattern. In the past, he said he had always given out figures "with confidence that distribution would support them very closely" and he wanted the "trade to understand this year the great difficulty surrounding an estimate, and on account of the liability of error, resulting from an attempt to estimate damage, we do not express the same confidence in these figures that we have in years preceding, although we think the total is high enough."[46]

Arguments over the 1904 crop carried on late into fall. The *Chicago Banker* criticized the *Commercial West*, stating that it cannot repair the "damage done to the Great Northwest by crop-killing predictions of its responsible editor."[47]

Jones answered by reprinting an editorial from the *Minneapolis Journal*: "Private crop estimators who are honest and capable may do great service to the country. Mr. Jones has been severely criticized for his extremely bullish reports, but later reports from time to time tend to bear him out. If the supply situation is such as to warrant higher prices to the farmer, the first man to point this out is surely not going to be scolded by the farmers or by the northwestern business men whose mainstay is the buying power of the farmer."[48]

Despite the "crop-killing" controversy, Herschel and Lydia went on with their social life. In December, they attended the Metropolitan Opera House and watched Ezra Kendall in a new play, "Weather Beaten Benson." On Monday evening, January 16, 1905, they attended the Lyceum Theatre for a performance by Madame Melba and Concert Company under the direction of C.A. Ellis.

On March 1, the Joneses were present for the Inauguration Musical Festival, marking the opening of the Minneapolis Auditorium. The program was presented by the Minneapolis Symphony Orchestra under conductor Emil Oberhoffer; the Apollo Club, then in its tenth season; the Philharmonic Club, and prima donna soprano, Madame Charlotte Maconda. To further mark the event, a great organ, manufactured by W.W. Kimball Company, was installed in the auditorium.

Of the several pieces performed, the highlight was Handel's Hallelujah Chorus from *Messiah*. Herschel and Lydia sat on the left side of the first floor in seats Q-10 and Q-12. Their carriage was checked in at space 35 of the auditorium parking lot.

On Tuesday evening, March 14, H.V. and Lydia were back at the auditorium for the Minneapolis Symphony Orchestra's sixth concert of the season. The orchestra was joined by prima donna, Madam Johanna Gadski. Herschel and Lydia were also in the audience for Richard Wagner's *Parsifal*, presented at the Metropolitan Opera House. On Wednesday evening, May 17th, they returned to the auditorium for a performance of the Pittsburgh Orchestra, Emil Paur conducting, featuring soloist Madam Gadski again. The popular Pittsburgh orchestra had indeed been busy over the past nine seasons, having given 448 concerts, 188 of which were outside of that city.[49]

Later in 1905, Jones again found black rust in the fields. When he estimated a very poor crop, the *Northwestern Miller* took advantage of the announcement and claimed Jones was trying to destroy the crop for profit. When good weather prevailed through the pre-harvest season, Herschel should have revised his forecast, but since he never had done so once the August figures were in black in white, he under-estimated the crop by twenty-five million bushels.[50]

Always eager to discredit Jones' rust claims, the *Miller* hired a special field representative, whose identity was to be kept secret, to go out and check Jones' statements. His report differed from Herschel's in that he found very little rust. In addition, the *Miller* hired Professor Harry Snyder of the University of Minnesota to follow up on Jones' reports concerning rust. Snyder did find rust although it was not spreading.[51]

Regardless of who said what, there was rust in the fields. According to Jones, several weeks before the harvest, "rust was present in the fields," and that there was "prospect of considerable damage." The damage was actually light because good weather held through this significant period.

On October 11, 1905, Herschel paid one dollar (ten cents apiece), entering him and Lydia, plus their children Tessie, Carl, Florence,

Paul, Jefferson, Moses, and Frances in the American Flag House and Betsy Ross Memorial Association. Herschel's mother, Helen Merchant Jones, was also made a member. The objects of the association were to purchase and preserve the historic building, situated at 239 Arch Street, Philadelphia, Pennsylvania. The first flag of the United States was, at the time, believed to have been made here by Betsy Ross and was subsequently adopted by Congress, June 14, 1777, to erect a national memorial in her honor.[52]

For paying ten cents per member, the Jones family received beautiful eleven-by-fourteen-inch certificates of membership signed by the officers of the association, and bearing the seal and certificate number. Artistically portrayed in the center of these certificates was a painting of the room where Betsy Ross displayed the first Stars and Stripes to the committee appointed by Congress, consisting of George Washington, Robert Morris, and George Ross. On the left was an exterior picture of the Old Flag House, while on the right, the grave of Betsy Ross at Mt. Moriah Cemetery.

Two weeks later, Herschel and Lydia visited the Metropolitan Opera House again, this time to watch Ethel Barrymore in Thomas Raceward's four-act play, "Sunday." On February 8, 1906, they returned for "The College Widow" and on March 22nd, Charles Klein's four-act play, "The Lion and the Mouse." On March 25th, they attended a performance of "Fantasma" at the Bijou Opera House in Minneapolis.[53]

The condition of the crop in 1906 looked magnificent. Jones figured extremely high and topped the gang of estimators in his August estimate. As the weather grew inclement, Jones again refused to alter his figures. He held sacredly to his estimate of 230 million bushels, and when reports of damage from hot winds in North Dakota reached his desk, he said it was "not of sufficient importance to make necessary a revision of estimate."

When the crop results for 1906 were in, Jones was out. He finished about fifty million bushels off, after being off thirty-three million the year before. The 1906 crop became the largest statistical beating of his career. Perhaps his eye had failed him, but for whatever reason, it was the last time he ever estimated the spring wheat crop. He was probably tired of grain forecasting. The *Commercial West* was growing by leaps and bounds and demanding more of his time.

During a 1928 interview, Jones acknowledged that the crops of 1900 to 1904 had given him "an international reputation, so that I had to be very careful what I said, because I could move the market." Whatever errors Jones made with his estimating, they came only over the last two years of his crop reporting. He had been at the top for four years, and he always insisted that his "figures are never revised." Perhaps he should have changed his policy those last two years, but Herschel Jones never abandoned his principles.

While Jones undertook his other editorial duties in 1906, he had little time for personal hobbies. One of his recreational endeavors, however, was genealogy, and over the years in his spare time, he worked at establishing a family tree for other members of the family as well as himself. In this critical period of 1906 when he was in transition from grain estimating to other duties, he nonetheless stayed in correspondence with relatives regarding the family tree.

In evidence is a letter addressed to "H.V. Jones, Esq., Manager the *Commercial West*" which read as follows:

> Yours of the [ninth instance] asking if I have [a] genealogical record of the Jefferson branch of the Smith family, came at a time when I was extremely busy and I have been obliged to defer replying until now. In answer will say, that several years ago, I undertook to construct a genealogical tree of that family and prepared and sent out a list of questions with blanks for answers, to various descendants of the family, but, while in some instances I received replies, there seemed to be such an apathy on the subject among the people to whom I wrote, I was compelled to abandon the scheme. However I did secure considerable information, which is in a somewhat crude and undigested form and would require an expert genealogist to straighten out-and that I am not! I will look over the papers and see how far I can satisfy your inquiry and you will be welcome to such as I have. I fear I have not time to classify it, as it should be, but we will commence with yourself and run backwards. Of course this will only be on the Smith side.[54]

The letter from a probable relative, Edward Hubbard Smith, listed several generations of "Smiths" from the eighteenth century to the time of writing. For instance, "You [Herschel] are the son of William Jones and Helen Merchant. Helen Merchant was a daughter of Reuben Merchant and Ellis Smith, Ellis Smith was a daughter of Frederick Smith and Sarah (or Sally) Brainard, Frederick Smith was the son of James Smith and Mary Hubbard, James Smith was the son of David Smith and (?)."

Herschel also kept a busy correspondence with his son Carl who was away at Princeton. Some of H.V.'s letters dealt with money—namely Carl's financial situation.

"Let me know what the custom is as to your having a bank account," wrote Herschel on September 29, 1907. "That is, if you have [fifty dollars] on hand would you prefer to carry it in your pocket or whether you could open an account and draw out [ten dollars] at a time.

"Have the room bills and the regular school bills sent to me and keep me posted as to your personal money. Do not be stingy, nor extravagant—taking a nice medium course that will show that you are a good fellow. I think you can count on [five dollars] a week for this kind of work. You may be able to get through some weeks a little less and some will run a little more. If you can keep it to $100, so much the better. Have you bought an overcoat?"[55]

In a letter of October 3, H.V. penned, "In the first place, you forget the financial trouble. Everything is all right; I can take care of you nicely, and I want you to go ahead on that theory. I like your idea of economy, and if you think $2.50 a week is all you need, it is satisfactory to me, and so much the better. I want you to be easy, without being mean or extravagant."[56]

In February 1908 H.V. went to Princeton to visit his son. Herschel stayed at the Albany Hotel on Forty-first and Broadway and had Carl come to his room. Herschel remained in the area about two weeks and left on a New York train on February 27. Evidently, a visit to Carl was only part of the agenda for he told his son, "[I] did not close the deal but think something will yet come out of it."[57]

Herschel and son Paul returned to New York in late May and spent a little time with Carl. Father and son had to catch a quick train to Chicago for an appointment that turned out to be a "false alarm." The quick trip cost Herschel and Paul a planned visit to Jefferson, of which Paul was quite disappointed. H.V. conveyed to Carl that he would try to get back his way once more before June vacation. Herschel said he had to leave in the next couple days for his crop work.[58]

The 1907 wheat crop estimate was carried in *Commercial West*, but Herschel sent another in his place. He did, however, estimate Kansas wheat production after a trip through that state. On May 6 he left for Texas where he stayed through Decoration Day. Three weeks later, he journeyed to Zanesville, Ohio, also on business. H.V. tentatively planned to visit Carl, stating in a letter, "you never can tell what I may do, I am just as apt to run over the mountains and see you as not."[59] Herschel did not make it to Princeton, however. The closest he came was Newark, Ohio.[60]

During the first week of June, Herschel traveled to Nashville, Tennessee, and Decatur, Alabama, on business. A few days later, he went to Louisville, Kentucky, and stayed at the Seelbaugh Hotel. He had hoped to meet his son Carl in Columbus, Ohio, during his business travels, but there is no record of whether they connected.

Carl was undoubtedly on his way home to Minneapolis for summer break, and his father's rash of business meetings may have meant he was looking for a newspaper to buy. Still, he always took the time to meet with his son whenever possible.[61]

Herschel was proud of his son and the way he handled his financial encounters. One of H.V.'s letters stated, "I like your coolness and confidence. Your [sic] are not turned off your feet, easily, by argument from the opposite side. This is a good sign."[62]

The following year, H.V. Jones would take on another responsibility that would turn out to be the most exciting ride of his life. His dream come true would be another success and a giant step forward, to lay new foundations, but as always, in the light of moral principle. But, behind him, "in founding the *Commercial West* he laid the foundations on the hard and unyielding rock of moral principle. He built this publication in a spirit of service to the northwest."[63]

Notes

[1] Edward C. Gale, "Herschel V. Jones," *Herschel V. Jones*; *Minneapolis Tribune*, May 24, 1928; *Syracuse Herald*, Friday Evening, May 25, 1928; *New York Times*, May 25, 1928; *Minneapolis Journal*, May 27, 1928.

[2] *Minneapolis Journal*, May 1, 1929; *Commercial West*, September 3, 1904.

[3] James H. McCullough, "What a Youngster Learned from His Grandfather's Newspaper," *American Magazine*, January 1924, p. 16.

[4] Ibid.

[5] Ibid.

[6] *Commercial West*, "Integrity the Theme of H.V. Jones in *Commercial West* First Edition," reprinted Saturday, June 2, 1928, p. 20.

[7] Ibid.

[8] Ibid.

[9] H.V. Jones to Theodore Roosevelt dated March 8, 1902. Courtesy of the Library of Congress.

[10] *Commercial West*, Saturday, May 26, 1928.

[11] *Commercial West*, March 16, 1901.

[12] *What the Minneapolis Daily Papers Say of the* Commercial West, pamphlet published in 1901 by Hahn and Harmon, Printers, Minneapolis, under Editorial, *Minneapolis Journal*, March 16, 1901.

[13] Ibid., under Editorial, *Minneapolis Times*, March 17, 1901.

[14]*Commercial West*, Saturday, July 21, 1928, p. 5.

[15]*What the Minneapolis Daily Papers Say of* Commercial West, under Editorial, *Minneapolis Tribune*, March 18, 1901.

[16]*Northwestern Miller*, 52:224, July 31, 1901; *Commercial West*, August 10, 1901.

[17]Ibid.

[18]Aimed at Herschel V. Jones, this combination cartoon-poem first appeared in the *Northwestern Miller*, 52:221, July 31, 1901.

[19]"The Bulls Eye" by "The Sharp Shooter," *Commercial West*, Saturday, July 14, 1928.

[20]Ibid.

[21]Herschel V. Jones letter to Hon. William B. Dean dated August 26, 1901. Minnesota Historical Society.

[22]Ted Curtis Smythe, *A History of the* Minneapolis Journal, *1878-1939,* p. 421.

[23]Metropolitan programs belonging to H.V. Jones. As an "extra enticement," perhaps, was the following statement printed below the evening's program: "NOTE—This theatre is disinfected by the Ozonet Company, to the entire satisfaction of the Management."

[24]Chicago Opera House playbill belonging to H.V. Jones.

[25]President Theodore Roosevelt's letter to H.V. Jones, dated May 6, 1902. Courtesy of the Library of Congress.

[26]President Theodore Roosevelt's letter to H.V. Jones, dated May 13, 1902. Courtesy of the Library of Congress.

[27]H.V. Jones letter to President Roosevelt, dated May 19, 1902. Courtesy of the Library of Congress.

[28]President Theodore Roosevelt's letter to H.V. Jones, dated July 9, 1902. Courtesy of the Library of Congress.

[29]Casino playbill belonging to H.V. Jones.

[30]Ted Curtis Smythe, *A History of the* Minneapolis Journal, *1878-1939,* p. 421.

[31]*Northwestern Miller*, 56:349, August 12, 1903.

[32]Ted Curtis Smythe, *A History of the* Minneapolis Journal, *1878-1039,* p. 423.

[33]James H. McCullough, "What a Youngster Learned from His Grandfather's Newspaper," *American Magazine*, January 1924, p. 80.

[34]Ibid.

[35]Ibid.

[36]Ted Curtis Smythe, *A History of the* Minneapolis Journal, *1878-1939,* pp. 424-425.

[37]*Northwestern Miller*, 59:310, August 10, 1904.

[38]Ibid.

[39]Ibid.

[40]*Northwestern Miller*, 59:425, August 24, 1904.

[41]*Northwestern Miller*, 59;367, 368, August 17, 1904.

[42]*Northwestern Miller*, 59:607, September 14, 1904.

[43]Ted Curtis Smythe, *A History of the* Minneapolis Journal, *1878-1939*, p. 427.

[44]*Northwestern Miller*, 59;425 & 428, August 24, 1904.

[45]*Commercial West*, September 3, 1904.

[46]Ibid.

[47]Ted Curtis Smythe, *A History of the* Minneapolis Journal, *1878-1939*, p. 429.

[48]Ibid.; *Commercial West*, October 1, 1904.

[49]Playbills of Metropolitan Opera House, Minneapolis Auditorium, and Lyceum Theatre belonging to H.V. Jones. Included in the inaugural program are the seating and parking ticket stubs.

[50]Ted Curtis Smythe, "A History of the Minneapolis Journal, 1878-1939, pp. 182-183.

[51]Ibid., p. 431.

[52]American Flag House and Betsy Ross Memorial Association certificates and official register of Jones family.

[53]Metropolitan and Bijou programs belonging to H.V. Jones.

[54]Edward Hubbard Smith letter to Herschel V. Jones dated February 24, 1906.

[55]H.V. Jones letter to Carl Jones dated September 28, 1907. A random sampling of Herschel's letters to his son are included in this text.

[56]H.V. Jones letter to Carl Jones dated October 3, 1907.

[57]H.V. Jones letter to Carl Jones dated February 27, 1908.

[58]H.V. Jones letter to Carl Jones dated April 1, 1908.

[59]H.V. Jones letter to Carl Jones dated May 6, 1908. Herschel also told his son, "I wrote you about your money but you are the hardest fellow to get anything out of, on that question, that I ever dealt with."

[60]H.V. Jones telegram to Carl Jones dated May 22/23, 1908.

[61]H.V. Jones letter to Carl Jones dated June 3, 1908.

[62]H.V. Jones letter to Carl Jones dated April 29, 1908.

[63]*Minneapolis Journal*, May 25, 1928.

Spectators at a University of
Minnesota football game held in front
of the Journal Building, 1904.
(Courtesy of the Minnesota Historical
Society)

CHAPTER SIX

THE AMERICAN DREAM

"As boy, I thought myself a clever fellow,
    And wish'd that others held the same opinion;
They took it up when my days grew more mellow,
    And other minds acknowledged my dominion."
                                        —Lord Byron

Old ideas mingled with new ones as people in America welcomed the twentieth century. While most Americans were awed by the wonders of the developing machine age, the problems and dangers it posed also intimidated them. The new century was a time of enterprise, invention, and industrial concentration, but it was also a time of trust-busting, added public control, and a regression from old time faith in *laissez faire*.[1]

Americans in 1904 sang "Meet Me in St. Louis" and "In the Good Old Summertime," while reading such bestsellers as *Rebecca of Sunnybrook Farm*, *Beverly of Graustark*, and the latest adventures of Sherlock Holmes, and Churchill's *The Crossing*. *Raffles* was a big hit on stage, but on a more sophisticated front, Arnold Daly was performing Shaw's *Candida,* and Minnie Maddern Fiske was tantalizing in Ibsen's *Hedda Gabler*. Fads swept the country, including jujitsu and Charles Wagner's *Simple Life*, as well as Theodore Roosevelt's contribution to support simplified spelling. Popular magazines, taking advantage of wood pulp, photography, and sensationalism, multiplied. Journalism took off in a spirited cartoon phase, and "one of the most adept artists of the time was "Bart" of the *Minneapolis Journal*.[2]

These opportunities in the business world did not go unnoticed by Herschel Jones. In 1908, E.B. Haskell of Boston, one of the owners of the *Minneapolis Journal*, passed away, and his estate and partners offered the newspaper, now grown to metropolitan size and character, up for sale at a rumored price of $1,200,000. Following his brief excursion into the business world via *Commercial West*, Jones recognized his dream of a lifetime and decided to purchase the paper. He had little capital, although with the sale of *Commercial West*, he was anything but destitute.[3]

"I knew that I had enough experience, and that in other ways the time was ripe," recalled Herschel Jones years later. "But I also knew the owner of the *Journal* was keen. Naturally, if he was aware that I wanted the paper, the price of it would be high. One day my telephone rang. It was Vanders [Lucian Swift, Jr.] himself, the owner of the *Journal*, asking me to come to his office. Of course I went."[4]

According to Herschel, the conversation began, "'Jones,' he [Vanders] said, 'I want to sell the *Journal*. And I want you to buy it. You know more about the paper than anyone else.'

"'Is that all you want of me?' I asked.

"'Yes.'

"I put on my hat and walked out! It took nerve, but it was the most eloquent way I could think of for conveying to him the idea of how futile it was, apparently, for me to think of paying him the million and a half dollars he was then asking for the paper."

Jones heard nothing from the *Journal* for several weeks. Meanwhile, he decided to go out and get some money together. He had $25,000 in his own bank and another $800,000 "promised" him from other sources. One of the "affluent" whom he approached was James J. Hill, the "Empire Builder" and owner of the Great Northern Railroad. Hill, of course, was not only a magnate in the field of railroading, but also in banking, lands, iron ore, agriculture, and education as well.[5]

As early as 1896, Herschel had acquired a promise of a small loan for a new venture. When he went to meet with Hill, he said, "I don't want to borrow money because I think there is going to be a panic, and I wouldn't be able to pay you back."

Hill replied, "You are the most honest man I have ever met. If you ever need anything in the future, come back and see me."[6]

According to Herschel's granddaughter, Frances Siftar, Jones deliberately boarded a train he knew Hill was on and cornered him to make his plea for a loan.[7]

Herschel's son, Moses, later told author, Ted Curtis Smythe, that "Nobody loaned my father $1,250,000 to buy the paper. My father paid $1,000,000 for the *Journal,* and he borrowed the $1,000,000 from James Hill of St. Paul. Bonds were issued by Mr. Hill's bank in Chicago . . . and were completely sold in two days mostly to Minneapolis businessmen."[8] Undoubtedly, Hill considered Jones a very good risk.

Swift called Jones into the *Journal* again and told him he was serious about wanting him to buy the newspaper. He claimed he had given a potential buyer an option that would go into effect August 31st, but stated emphatically that he still wanted Herschel to buy the paper before that date. Herschel replied that the offer was useless to discuss because he did not have the money for such an outrageous purchase. He added that even if the paper was to sell for a million dollars, which he insisted, it was worth, he still would have trouble raising the cash.[9] Jones was told he could get the money if he really tried by calling upon some of his friends.

Meanwhile, Herschel was writing in his checkbook. Swift had no idea that what Jones was writing was a check to him for twenty-five thousand dollars. As the conversation progressed, mostly on Swift's side, Jones wrote out a memorandum of sale for one million dollars.

"Well," said Jones finally, "if you really want to sell, and want me to buy, *sign there!*"

According to Jones, "When he recovered from his surprise, he did sign. I managed to get the other two hundred thousand I needed, and thus the thing I had set out to do, twenty-three years before, was done."[10]

But, of course, it was through the good graces of James J. Hill that Jones acquired the necessary wealth to purchase the *Journal.* When he met again with the Empire Builder, Hill took out his checkbook, asked Jones how much he needed, and wrote him a check. Hill's trust in Chicago had issued bonds on the *Journal* for one million dollars, backed by deposits from four businessmen. That money was then turned over to the *Journal* owners, who, in turn, presented Herschel with ownership of the *Journal.* Jones, of course, would have to pay back the stockholders more than $50,000 a year to cover principal and interest.[11]

But from past business experience, Jones knew approximately how much capital it would take to improve the *Journal.* One of his first acts as new owner was the installation of a new elevator from the basement to the fourth floor. The expense paid off with improved staff relations, better internal communications, and greater efficiency.

A different version as to how Jones acquired the *Journal* came from Arthur J. Russell, who was employed by the *Journal* at the time:

"When the Haskells and other owners of the *Journal* were ready to sell the paper in the early years of this century, Mr. Jones, with no great amount of money of his own, paid them a million and a quarter dollars for the property. How he accomplished this Napoleonic feat was simple. The men with whom he had 'slept' in his newspaper days and who had watched his career and had confidence in him were ready to back him in borrowing the money.

"Mr. Jones is a safe man! Let him have anything he wants!'

"He needed a million and quarter dollars and got it without difficulty. The debt was financed on twenty annual payments and was repaid considerably before the twenty years passed."[12]

The James J. Hill version of the sale holds more credibility, of course, since statements of immediate family members backed it. It must also be taken into consideration that Hill, like other leading businessmen, trusted Herschel Jones.

But, was Herschel the sole owner of the *Journal*? All of his later statements insisted that he had been owner, indeed sole owner, of the *Journal*. What is confusing, however, is a September 1908 *Journal* article entitled, "Who Owns the Journal?" The article ran thusly: "The *Journal* is owned and controlled absolutely by H.V. Jones and W.S. Jones, both of whom have been engaged in the publishing business in Minneapolis for [twenty-five] years. For the first time in the last [twenty] years of its history, the *Journal* is owned wholly in the city where it is published."[13]

William S. Jones, named after his father, was Herschel's younger brother and a longtime resident of Minneapolis. He had served as business manager of the *Northwest Commercial Bulletin* from 1886 to 1903, when he became president and owner of the publication. The *Bulletin* and other publications owned by William Jones had been tough competitors of Herschel's *Commercial West*. In spite of the "friendly" competition, Herschel became a frequent editorial contributor to Will's publication, the articles printed on the editorial page of the *Bulletin* under the title "Plain Facts Told Plainly." In 1906, Will sold his publication to the Root Newspaper Association for $75,000 to $100,000.[14]

According to Moses C. Jones, Herschel's son, Will Jones was never a co-owner of the *Minneapolis Journal*. "My uncle, William S. Jones, was discharged by my father. . . . He owned no shares of the *Journal* at any time. My father was the sole owner."[15]

Moses Jones' insistence that his father was sole owner of the *Journal* was probably correct. Will Jones' 1939 obituary stated that Herschel was owner of the *Journal* with Will serving as business manager. Had Will Jones had any ownership in the paper, it would, undoubtedly, have been stated at his death.[16]

Opposite: The Journal Building decorated for the national encampment of the Grand Army, 1906. (Courtesy of the Minnesota Historical Society)

144

Although Will definitely served as business manager and may have invested some money into the enterprise, his role as a possible partner is sketchy at best. A longtime friend of the two brothers told author Ted Curtis Smythe in a 1966 interview that the pair was a good combination, because Will was "gentle, keen, ethical and slow to commit himself, a perfect complement to his brother. He had a ready smile and easy manner and was just the right man for business manager for a paper of which Herschel Jones was the editor. H.V. was a short, stocky, clean cut, emphatic, voluble and articulate publisher who had definite ideals and never compromised with his conscience in the running of the paper." Herschel would "sometimes lose his perspective and antagonize people. Will Jones always smoothed it out."[17]

Herschel V. Jones in his forties to fifties.

The day Herschel took over the *Journal*, he unfurled a flag from the *Journal* towers, bearing the inscription, "The principles that should govern the publication of a newspaper are honesty and fairness. The decision on any question should be submitted to this test—is it fair and is it honest?" From day one, Jones endeavored to give his newspaper a high moral tone. In its news, advertising, and editorials, the *Journal* adopted a serious tone, and it featured daily quotations from the Bible.[18]

Jones' first act as owner came about on September 1, 1908. On that first day, he expelled from its columns all liquor, internal medicine, unsound financial and other objectionable advertising. This took a great deal of courage for a man who had just borrowed a million dollars, for it meant the turning away of large revenues through these would-be campaigns.[19]

According to a *Journal* article, "The underlying principle was that a newspaper is just as much responsible for what appears in its advertising as in its reading columns. This principle, under his direction, has been rigidly adhered to. It has helped to make the *Journal* a clean newspaper; one that could be taken into the home, there to have its influence in the forming of an intelligent public opinion."[20]

The *Journal*'s policies in public affairs were "buttressed with the foundation of rightness," rather than with what might be popular with some readers. Above all else, Jones wanted to establish a morally right position. "Sometimes he found himself out of step with the fervor of the moment, but, in the end, he usually had the satisfaction of time's endorsement." Jones said he would never dodge an issue but would always meet it squarely. He hoped his readers would learn to expect forthrightness and enjoy it even when it went counter to their personal convictions.[21]

In one of his first days at the office, Jones was sitting at his desk looking over the advertising, when employee Arthur Russell entered the room. Jones had compiled two lists of advertisements he found unsuitable for the *Journal*—one of a sexual nature and the other of patent medicines. "This sex stuff has got to go out, and I guess the others too," he informed Russell.

"Why not start the reform on the sex stuff and see how it works," answered Russell. "Later on the others may go."

Jones jumped to his feet with a red face, took a deep breath, and bellowed, "They are all going out—NOW!"[22]

But while the *Journal* was adopting a policy of morality, its competitors were sharpening their fangs for battle. The *Minneapolis Tribune*, more than the others, began attracting readers with a regular quota of crime and sex sensationalism. Headlines such as "Night Revelry Bared by Maid," "Corset Must Go Is Preacher's

Edict," "Summer Girl Comes High," "Bar the Kissing Games," and "Woman Stops a Wedding" lured expectant thrill seekers to their front step every morning. Murder trials lingered on and on in bold print and gaudy stories such as "Deed of a Friend," "Jack the Ripper Loose," and "Was She Insane?" shocked not always unsuspecting housewives.[23]

Yet, early in 1908, the *Tribune*'s masthead still boasted, "The *Minneapolis Tribune* is a paper which any father or any mother may welcome into the home circle as they would a friend—an interesting, intensely entertaining, well-intentional family friend whose presence is cheerful as the sunlight."[24]

But, Jones, undaunted by his sensationalist competitors, published his platform in the *Journal*'s first issue on September 1: "The *Journal* will have no mission other than to present daily a clean strong newspaper, with its news columns impartial, regardless of editorial opinion. It will in no particular be a vehicle for exploiting some man's personal ambition; it will represent no clique either of corporations or individuals. It has no obligation to perform to any interest. Its essential purpose will be to present the news in clean form, to hold its advertising columns to the closest censorship consistent with decency and morals, to build up in the Northwest a great newspaper, in which the public will learn that honesty and fairness are to control. The *Journal* will seek to excel as a home paper. It will not publish, beyond existing contracts, advertisements of whisky or beer, fake investments, nor the line of medical and other objectionable advertising, as the term is generally understood."[25]

This abrupt change in advertising policy resulted in a yearly loss of $30,000 to $50,000. But Jones did not care; he was making morality an issue. Like in the days of wheat crop estimating, Jones firmly believed "that you have got to stand by what you deduce the facts to be, *no matter how many good men tell you that you can't be right!*"[27]

Jones' stand of limiting his advertisers, even though this policy cost him thousands of dollars yearly, brought widespread public and professional support. The Minnesota Editorial Association in Luverne, Minnesota, as an example, wrote, "It is well worth while in satisfaction alone to have a newspaper for the character of whose ads you need make no apology."[28]

The Better Business Bureau, in fact, originated in part from the *Journal*'s ban on fraudulent advertising. By eliminating advertisements of quack doctors, patent medicines, fake bargains, blue sky stocks, whiskey, beer, and other objectionable matter, the *Journal* gained a national reputation. This action caused the *Journal* to be called "The Northwest's Greatest Newspaper" by the Pure Food

Herschel V. Jones in his forties to fifties.

and Drug Administration. Following Jones' takeover of the *Journal*, a "safe and sane" Fourth of July was sponsored as the circulation soared to 70,000.[29]

Jones seemed to disregard the pressures of meeting the steep annual repayments. Russell witnessed Jones talking with some of the women employees—"a dozen or more hard-working little women who not only supported themselves but sometimes families as well. And they were none of them overpaid. I asked one of them about it," Russell remarked later.

"She looked around cautiously then in a sort of trembling whisper she said, 'He has raised all our salaries.'"

Russell returned to work, concluding that, "for a man with a debt of over a million dollars on his shoulders, that was doing pretty well."[30]

In one of Jones' first editorials, he thanked both his predecessors, Swift and McLain: Swift because he "always exercised an energetic business policy," and McLain for adhering to that policy with a "vigorous and independent editorial policy." According to Jones, the *Journal* "went into the homes of the people because it stood for something" and Swift and McLain had "built a newspaper. They have done great work."[31]

When Swift and McLain sold the newspaper, many of their high ranking staff members were sent packing. William Barbour left the *Journal* advertising department and found a home with the *Tribune*, and Jones' former associate, William A. Frisbie gave up his position as managing editor. As in any buyout, other employees were also afraid of losing their jobs. When A.J. Russell, who had been a reporter with Jones on the *Journal*, remarked to a fellow employee that "nobody knew what might happen to a small fry now," he must have been overheard. He was called into Jones' office.

"Sit down!" ordered Jones. "Do I have to assure my old friend and newspaper comrade that his position is secure on this paper?"

"Well, Jonesy," answered Russell, "you never can tell what cobwebs a new broom will sweep down or what barnacles will have to be scraped from the keel of an old ship."

"Jones replied, "Go back to your work and stop worrying."[32]

Russell also recalled the case of John the Swedish janitor who had "always been there." John had grown old, one of his eyes had become infected and had to be removed. John couldn't get around very well, and someone in the janitorial department fired him. John wandered about town for a couple weeks until his money gave out. Whenever he became hungry, he would drop by the *Journal* office and ask anyone he saw for a quarter. Since everyone loved him, he would always get it. On one of these visits, he saw Herschel in the corridor and asked for help. Jones stopped, gave him a serious, but warm, look and asked what was wrong.

"Maester Yones, I ain't had nothin' to eat today," replied John. Herschel told him to come into the office, and John did, saying, "I can't get nuthin' to do, Maester Yones, and not much to eat lately."

"Is that the only suit of clothes you've got?" asked Jones.

"Yes, Maester Yones."

"Jones scribbled a note with his pencil on a pad of paper, tore off the page, and handed it to the Swede. He told him to take the note to a certain clothing store and they would give him a new suit of clothes. "Then you come back here tomorrow," said Jones. "You're on the payroll."

The Swede nearly collapsed, according to Russell. He returned the next day for work in his new set of clothes. Herschel, meanwhile, had called up the janitorial head and informed him that John was back on the payroll.

The janitorial head sputtered, "He's no good, Mr. Jones' he can't do anything."[33]

"Give him a broom and let him hang around," roared Jones. "He's back on the payroll."

Following some personnel changes, Jones quickly installed Charles R. Adams as managing editor and his brother, George, as city editor. Both of these men had come over from *Commercial West* with Jones. Winthrop "Cham" Chamberlain gave up his reviewing and Sunday newspaper work to devote his full-time energy to the editorial page, a change that he welcomed. Charles Tuller, the *Journal*'s business manager under Swift, retained his employment with the paper but was demoted to assistant business manager under William S. Jones, who took over his duties.[34]

Whereas McLain had ripped the railroads for their safety practices and rate schedules in his editorials, Jones, initially, simply didn't mention them. Rumors circulated that railroads and steel interests were the real owners of the paper, but Herschel reiterated that "the paper was not controlled by any clique, either of corporations or individuals." While at *Commercial West*, he had claimed that rebate laws should be enforced, but the railroads should not be punished for past deeds. Said Jones, "Rebating was a necessity under the cut-throat policy, formerly enforced upon the railways by shippers." He probably meant to impress James J. Hill and other signers of *Journal* notes, when he stated, "There is a great need today for a fearless press to set the public mind right on this question."[35]

But Hill certainly had his critics. Charles A. Lindbergh, while he had a great respect for Hill's abilities and judgment, felt that Hill was misusing his position. If, said Lindbergh, Hill could handle his administrative functions without prejudice, equitable rates could be achieved. "But," charged Lindbergh, "Mr. Hill is not specifically interested in fixing freight rates for the people" or in securing a fair return for farmers or businessmen in small towns. "What he is specifically interested in is to see that the volume of business is enough to give the railways all they can do."[36]

On September 5th, the *Journal* reported on the wheat rate to Anoka question that involved Hill. The Pillsbury-Washburn Company filed a claim with the interstate commerce commission against the Great Northern Railroad Company for a $9,000 refund paid mostly over the past year for the transportation of wheat between Minneapolis and Anoka, where the company's Lincoln Mill was located. The complaint stated that an 1879 agreement between W.D. Washburn and the Manitoba Railroad Company, predecessor of Hill's Great Northern, was still binding. The agreement ordered the railroad to pay a proportional rate of one-cent per hundred on through shipments of wheat from northern and western points manufactured at Anoka and sent through Minneapolis to destinations outside of Minnesota under the "milling in transit" privilege.[37]

According to the Pillsbury-Washburn Company, this agreement had been renewed in 1901, and had been in operation through the winter of 1906-1907. Because of the inability and failure of the Great Northern to transport and deliver at Anoka, wheat purchased by the mill company at stations along the railroad north and west of Anoka, was in jeopardy. The mill was forced to ship wheat from Minneapolis to Anoka, then the flour made from that wheat had to be forwarded with bill of lading to eastern and foreign ports.

It was alleged that all these shipments were carried out under a transit penalty arrangement made in early December 1906. It was specifically agreed, according to the millers, that such shipments should be continued under these same conditions. The complaint stated that after these conditions had been agreed upon, Hill's Great Northern, as a means of adjusting their account with the Anoka station, asked the mill company to pay the established rate of four and one-half cents per hundred. The railroad, it was charged, had agreed to refund three and one-half cents.

Supposedly, an open account had been maintained in which shipments were charged. Since the time the agreement had been reached, large shipments of grain had been transported. The milling company asked the Interstate Commerce Commission to intervene and order the railroad to pay the refund and establish the one-cent rate as the legal rate for shipments between Minneapolis and Anoka.

Jones did not print an editorial referring to the Minneapolis-Anoka wheat battle. He seems to have remained neutral. Officially taking the side of either his milling friends or benefactor, James J. Hill, may have placed him in a very uncomfortable position. The next day, however, the *Journal* printed a story about Hill and his shipments entitled, "Steady Gain in the Business Showing Says James J. Hill."[38]

According to what Hill told the *Journal*, there had been a steady improvement in business conditions, and the outlook for the future was most optimistic, especially in the northwest. Hill admitted business had been a little slower than the following year but expressed confidence of further improvement in conditions.

"Business is slowly but certainly improving," Hill told the *Journal*. "It is lighter this year than it was during the corresponding period last year, before the stringency, but it is steadily improving. With a reasonable good crop, the purchasing power of the people of the northwest will this year be greater than in several years past. Information which I have received shows that the yield of grain in the northwest will be at least 10,000,000 in excess of last year, and the general average price of grain is higher than it was a year ago."[40]

Hill added that railroad shipments were on the increase, which pointed to greater prosperity ahead: "General business is improving and with the prospect of good crops, people will have more money to spend in the immediate future than they did last year." He did not mention the issue with the milling company.

Herschel Jones did not comment on the railroad or wheat questions in his editorial that day, but instead, turned to writing about "The Wonders of Acetylene," "New Laws for Lawyers," "Hats and Halos Matched," and other subjects. One of his better editorials that day was called "Life on the Farm." Jones reported on President Theodore Roosevelt forming a commission that would look into and report upon conditions of farm life. It would then recommend improvements. Said Jones, "There is still room for activity on the part of such a commission, but very likely the telephone, free rural delivery, modern housing, ice for the summer, and a furnace for the winter have anticipated it."[41]

According to Jones, the conditions of farm life had changed for the better. Only a generation earlier, boys and girls had left the farm for town, but in now finding the town and city overcrowded, the trend had reversed itself:

> The farmer has learned to take care of his family; to give
> his wife a decent place to work; to make her kitchen at least
> as good as his tool shop; to pay some attention to ventila-
> tion, heat and light, and most of all, to regulate his hours of

work so that every member of the family has some rest time, even in the busy harvest season. The changes that have taken place on the conditions of life on the farm were not slavish imitation. They were not sentimental. They were business. The farmer was losing his best and most reliable help.[42]

Jones believed that President Roosevelt's commission would do its best service by finding better farming methods. He reminded the reader that these methods were the basis of farm life, for the farmer's income was based on them. He also felt that "if the great weakness of poor farming can be emphasized by the president's commission, it would go a long way toward arousing the poor farmers of the country to better work."

In another H.V. Jones editorial entitled, "As to Condensed Literature," he disagreed with a statement published in the *New York World*. The *World* had written, "Terseness is the watchword. Romance, like power or perfume, must be condensed, boiled down, and offered in essence." H.V. felt that terseness in literature had been overdone. He wrote that many a publisher was still doing ruthless condensation. He felt that the book should be printed as written and that the reader would do his or her own condensing. As fuel, he stated that the only writer that had ever succeeded in condensing Shakespeare was Charles Lamb, but until another Charles Lamb was born into the world, the novel should be left alone.

Referring to the *World* newspaper, H.V. wrote, "Chairman Mack grows more confident every day. Before committing himself too deeply, Mr. Mack should read the unpublished works of James K. Jones and Thomas Taggart. His confidence is but a faint echo of their superb exhibitions." H.V. Jones was still, undoubtedly, reading the great works that influenced his own way of life.

But H.V. was writing for a much larger audience than the *Journal*. Other newspaper publishers admired his sparkling style, and he was soon writing a column that appeared in out of state papers as well as the *Journal*. The column would feature not only Jones' writing but that of boys writing in from all parts of the country. In his first column published in the *Southern Bay*, New Orleans, Louisiana, Jones wrote his first in a series of articles called, "Our New Departure." Wrote Jones, "We have at the request of the publishers of this paper, accepted the charge of this column. In doing this, we hope to meet with the hearty support of all its readers. We propose to publish good, solid composition from the boys of the United States, and hope they will take an interest in it, this making not only an interesting and useful column, but an instructive one, and perhaps be the means of doing a little good in some way. It remains for the boys of today to make the nation of the future, and now is the time to commence to improve our minds. Let us try and make this column as interesting as possible, and all work together. We hope to receive contributions from our boy friends, from any part of the country. Hoping you will overcome our faults, and try and aid us, we remain, Yours truly, H.V. Jones."[43]

On October 19, H.V. Jones wrote his son Carl in Princeton that he had sent him a check for fifty dollars, but with having taken over the *Journal*, he was just too busy to write. His letters for the next couple months amounted to but one or two sentences.[44]

Carl W. Jones, in his twenties.

Herschel did not hold anything back in his letter of November 11. "Pay these bills yourself," he demanded of Carl. "You are very weak in leaving everything until the last minute. I knew you were going out to Dartmouth and Yale and that you must be broke, although I have given you $100 since I saw you, so on Friday I wired you $100. Pay these bills at once and let me know what your balance is."[45]

On November 15, Herschel and Lydia attended "The Top O' th' World," which James M. Allison presented at the Metropolitan Opera House in Minneapolis.[46]

Two days later he wrote Carl that Florence was going to New York on the Wednesday before Thanksgiving. He instructed his son to go himself to New York, pick up Florence, and take the train from the Grand Central Station to Holyoke, Massachusetts, "without charge." At Holyoke, Carl and Florence were instructed to take a streetcar to South Hadley, some four miles away. Their mother, Lydia, would be meeting them in South Hadley that evening.[47]

By late in the year the paper was booming. The *Journal*'s circulation that first year under Jones was about 76,000 with daily issues from fourteen to thirty-two pages. The Sunday Edition, which was only a couple years old, was much larger, usually over fifty pages. Jones had about 350 employees on the paper and the editorial department boasted forty-seven editors, copy men and reporters, and five artists. The advertising department, on the other hand, employed forty men and women, and there were an additional forty-two in the business department.[48]

In December, the Joneses could afford to travel, and the bulk of Herschel's work at year's end was behind them. Again, presumably, they stopped off in Jefferson to visit relatives and friends and continued on to New York City. Getting around New York was easy and inexpensive in a Hansom Coupe or Brougham with a charge for waiting time of one cent per minute. H.V. and Lydia visited theatres and churches, attended lectures, and visited the Hippodrome on Sixth Avenue between Forty-third and Forty-fourth Streets. Shows at the Hippodrome included "Sporting Days," "Bird Ballet," and "Battle in the Skies," the performances costing between twenty-five cents and a dollar-fifty, depending on desired seating. That week there were lectures on James Russell Lowell and the novels of George Eliot.[49]

While in New York, they also attended the New Amsterdam Theatre for a production of "The Silver Star," starring Adeline Genee. The theatre provided booklets to assist the well-dressed men and women in how to prepare for an evening out in the big city. Color was coming in for men, although "not without control." Only conservative tints, like plum, dark green, blue, and a rich brown were suggested, and a waistcoat of rich brocade with the same hue as the business suit. For shoes, the "soles are even with the shoe—not extending a sixteenth of an inch, the patent leather fits as smoothly as a glove, and the dull kid tops are laced closely with inconspicuous silk strings."[50]

Women were instructed that while wide bands, stomachers, and loops of jeweled embroidery were trimming the street gowns, Persian lamb was trimming some of the tailor-mades. A wide braid about six inches long was more than acceptable on a tailor-made, the braid making a line around the skirt below the knees, the line being broken at the front and back by "panels prettily braided."

In January, the snow in Minneapolis began to thaw. Lydia had been suffering for about a week with an attack of lumbago but was getting better. On January 19, Lydia and Tess attended a local production of *Rose Stahl* and were "delighted with it." H.V., in the meanwhile, was quite busy with the newspaper.[51]

Early the next month, Herschel returned to New York on business and spent some time with Carl. H.V. also took a Pullman from Philadelphia to Washington, D.C., where he stayed at the Shoreham Hotel.[52] Upon his return to Minneapolis, it was local business as usual.

But Herschel was not the only "successful" newspaper publisher in Minneapolis. The Jones children, under the guiding genius of Carl Jones, began writing their own little newspaper and circulated it among family and friends. The first issue of *The Ant Hill Circle* was published on Sunday, January 10, 1909. Carl then left the "paper" temporarily as reflected in the initial installment: "*Ant Hill* is minus one greasy grind out of its population, Carl W. Jones of Princeton University." Other hot stories included "Jeff Jones washed his neck yesterday, Hoorah for Jeff," and another, "Florence Jones of Ant Hill, who is attending school at Miss Bang's & Whiton's school for girls in New York, saw her lover 'Irish Man' Ed smoking a cigar; she went into convulsions." Another item stated, "Tessie Jones of Ant Hill has been engaged to marry Donald Brewster of the same town in the spring.

Herschel V. Jones in his forties to fifties.

157

They have planned to take a round trip to Anoka, Minnesota, and back. Donald Brewster is now working in the West Anoka slaughter house cutting cow's tongue. A NEW REMEDY JUST OUT— If anyone wants to die, try Jeff Jones new remedy—Take one smell of Jeff Jones breath and you will die instantly." The kids charged four dollars for a one-year subscription, two dollars for a half-year, and a nickel for a single copy. The paper even contained ads for the *Minneapolis Journal* and *Commercial West.*[53]

The weekly "newspaper" changed its name to the *Bugville Bugle* with the next issue and the paper lasted for at least three more months. One big story claimed that "H.V. Jones while coming home from the Baptist Church Sunday night slipped on an icy walk and spilled some of the words he had just heard in church." Another in the same issue, while more of an editorial, stated, "The Authors Club met last night at Mrs. Hiram Goodspeeds. The meeting lasted till about 10:30. They are trying to raise money to get a statue of Chaucer for the public square and should be encouraged tho we would rather see a statue of Rex Beach than have one of a dead one like Chaucer."[54]

Two weeks later, Paul Jones made the news when he "bought himself a new suit of clothes yesterday. Who said times were not prosperous?" George Washington was the subject of the main story in the following issue: "Today is the anniversary of the birth of George Washington. He is the boy who never got licked because he never told a lie but he's making up for it now by being licked more than any other great man. That's what he gets for having his picture on a two-cent stamp." H.V.'s oldest son was again in the news in the same issue: "Carl Jones, who has been drawing covers, etc. for the *Princeton Tiger* is home for the year and is trying to see if he can draw a salary." In the March 10 issue, "Tifford Jones received a table this week from the American Tobacco Co. for 320 tags of Lone Star Plug 'Turbaker.'" Subscriptions had also decreased to a dollar a year "IN ADVANCE REMIT—In stamps, coin, bill, bank-note or by money order."[55]

Herschel Jones maintained a good relationship with his children, and he always had time to listen to what they had to say. About 1908, he bought his youngest child, a daughter, Frances, a horse, which she quickly named "Dixie." All members of the family, including the Jones' dog, were fond of Dixie. When Frances wasn't riding Dixie, she boarded the horse at Gavin's Livery Stable near Park Avenue. A groom named Harry would hitch Dixie to a buggy and bring him to the Jones house.

Frances wrote her father in June during one of his trips out-of-state: "Yesterday was my birthday. Beulah [Sutherland], Fran's

Opposite: Frances Jones (Leslie), 1907 or 1908, age twelve, with horse "Dixie."

best friend] gave me a necklace and some beautiful flowers. Helen Northrup gave me a pin, and grandma gave me a set of dolls' clothes. I ordered the dinner and this is what I had. Chicken pie, asparagus, cucumbers, ice cream, birthday cake. It all tasted very good. My dog is fine. Dixie sends you her love. Write and send me the cigars [sic] brands you have saved me. Troll [Carl Jones] got her[e] all right. We were glad to see him. Harry has left Gavins. He is never going back their [sic] again. Mama would not let me go on my Sunday School picnic because she said you would not like it. But I thought of what you said that we would take a ride through the 'old mill' so I did not care. I would not care if we did not go because I know that we can not do everything."[56]

On January 29, 1909, the *Journal* ran a story defending President-elect William Howard Taft. The incoming chief had made a statement, "I want the very nicest inauguration in history," to a half dozen colleagues in the House of Representatives. An article probably written by Jones, appearing on page one of the *Journal* should have been placed, perhaps, on the editorial page. Referring to Taft's wanting the nicest inauguration, the writer stated that "it goes to show that folks don't know what they are talking about when they say that the president-elect is trying to dodge all the frills and fuss and feathers attending his induction into office."[57]

According to the writer, "Judge Taft didn't say he wanted the most sensational inauguration, or the most magnificent, or the most ornate. He said he wanted the 'nicest,' and with that clean English word before them, every member of the inaugural committee is working to make the ceremonies of the inaugural period of 1909 as nearly ideal as possible."

One month later wheat was again the issue as indicated in a *Journal* article, "May Wheat Is at Top Notch Price." May wheat in Minneapolis was sold at $1.14 and one-half, which set a new high point. Chicago May wheat was quoted at $1.18, while wheat for May delivery in Liverpool was $1.18 and one-half. For one of the few times in history, Chicago and Liverpool were practically the same price. Ordinarily, Liverpool wheat ruled from thirteen to fifteen cents higher than that of Chicago. When such a difference existed, the United States was said to be on an export basis, the difference about what representing what it costs to ship wheat from Chicago to Liverpool and insure it in transit.[58]

According to the *Journal*, old calculations were valueless. At the time, disarrangement of prices was so great that none of the old-time calculations were of any use in determining market action. Over the previous month, a cliqué of speculators, who had been governing their actions by the export difference between the

American and English markets, had been selling wheat short. The *Journal* believed that this was done by the theory that the difference was too small to be legitimate, and the American prices would have to go down. However, the "Chicago Bull"—James A. Patten—was operating on the theory that the United States was permanently off an export basis and would act independently of Europe. Patten said this was so because he had figured out that there was only enough wheat left for home requirements until another crop was raised and nothing was left to sell to Europe.

Many speculators believed Patten was wrong and that wheat would one day go down all of a sudden without warning. In the past, these same speculators had lost money when acting on such feelings, as the "Chicago Bull" had always screwed the market up another notch. That same day, Patten had wired Charles E. Lewis, his Minneapolis correspondent, that he believed that wheat would sell at $1.50 a bushel before another crop could be raised in the United States.

Said the *Journal*: "Old speculators in Minneapolis only raised their eyebrows and shrugged their shoulders when this prediction was heard. One element contends that the present price of wheat is legitimate, another argues that it is manipulative. Meanwhile Patten keeps shoving it up a bit one day after another."[59]

Jones was back in New York City in December. While there, he attended the Liberty Theatre on Forty-second Street west of Broadway and saw Mabel Taliaferro in "Springtime." The play, written by Booth Tarkington and Harry Leon Wilson, centered on Louisiana in the year 1815. That same week, Jones journeyed to Washington, D.C., and attended the Belasco Theatre for a performance of Lew Dockstader and his Minstrels.[60]

Herschel was home for Christmas and so were all the children. Carl, who attended Princeton University, wrote in his diary an entry for Sunday, January 2, 1910, during his holiday stay with the family that he was "up at [one], disgraced. Talked all day. Home at [five] to see Jeff off for Lawrenceville. Went down in Pope with ma." His entry for the following day, Monday, January 3, read "Made another costume for Triangle show. Went to Orpheum with Florence in afternoon. Fair show. All but pa over to Mrs. Chase's for supper. Played at piano with Florence and Marjorie and also two games of pool with ma and the boys. Very cold going home in auto."[61]

After long days at the *Journal*, Herschel, joined Lydia and Tessie to attend several performances at the Shubert Theatre in Minneapolis. One of these presentations was *Miss Nobody from Starland* with Olive Vail. Later in the year, they saw *La Saison des Ballets Russes* (*Season of Russian Ballets*) presented by Gertrude

Tessie Jones, late twenties to early thirties.

Hoffman. They also enjoyed *Cleopatra* with Wanda Howard, a choreographic drama in one act.

On one occasion, Herschel, Lydia, and Tessie were on their way to the Shubert when H.V. became suddenly ill. Reaching Hennepin Avenue, he did not feel well enough to continue, so he turned around and went home. Lydia and Tessie, meanwhile, continued to the theatre, undoubtedly, much concerned about Herschel. Their hearts probably were not in *The Passing of the Third Floor Back* with Forbes-Robertson and his London Company.[62] Herschel, however, was fine in a few days.

The Joneses spent many evenings at the Metropolitan Opera House taking in such programs as *The Other Woman* with Blanche Walsh, Cohan's *The Man Who Owns Broadway* with Raymond Hitchcock, *Madame Butterfly*, which they had seen performed in the East, the farewell appearance of E.S. Willard, *Forty-Five Minutes from Broadway* with the renowned Fay Templeton, *The Free Lance* with Joseph Cawthorn and the Sousa Opera Company, and *The Girl and the Governor* with the Jefferson De Angelis Opera Company.[63]

April found H.V. back in New York for a mixture of business and pleasure. At the Bijou Theatre, he saw Cyril Scott in *The Lottery Man,* a comedy in three-acts by Rida Johnson Young. He also attended the Broadway Theatre for a Lew Fields' production of *The Jolly Bachelors* starring Nora Bayes. The musical was presented in two acts and seven scenes.[64]

During that summer, Carl and Jefferson went to Montana and Canada to work for the Great Northern Railroad in the Glacier Park Area.

In November, *Leslie's Illustrated Weekly* published 209,600 copies of a special Twin Cities issue. On one of its large pages, *Leslie's* ran an article entitled, "Some of Minnesota's Prominent Public Officials and Widely Known Editors." Not only were Herschel V. Jones and his brother Will S. Jones both mentioned, but photographs of the two brothers were published as well.[65]

While the Bible was often quoted in the *Journal*, so were the words of many men Jones admired. In a Sunday issue in April 1910, Jones quoted Dr. Samuel Johnson: "He that would pass the latter part of his life with honor must, when he is young, consider that he shall one day be old; and remember, when he is old, that he has been young. In youth he must lay up knowledge for his support when his powers of acting shall forsake him; and in age forbear to animadvert with rigor on faults which experience only can correct."[66]

In his editorial, Jones advocated "Great Novels, Not 'Society' Novels." Most society novels, Jones said, were nearly sure of becoming bestsellers, and in a few occasions, like Edith Wharton's *The House of Mirth,* they deserved to be. He added that what Thackeray "would style the unmitigated and ineradicable snobbishness of human nature, the 'society novel' is a most popular form of novel, especially if a glamor of illusion is cast over the 'exclusive circles' with which it deals."[67]

Carl W. Jones with Mrs. Willie Tailfeathers, wife of the Indian chief, Blackfeet Reservation, Montana, 1910. Carl, along with his brother, Jefferson, were surveying for the Great Northern Railroad in the Glacier Park area.

Jones questioned what part of society was Society? He quoted Balzac who had affirmed that for true poetry of human life, one must go to the poor, and Jones reminded us that Balzac was neither a Democrat nor a Socialist. H.V. insisted that the great novels of the world did not deal with the world of high fashion. Jones wrote that even an admirable "society" book like that of *The House of Mirth*" has its defect," and is "concerned with men and women of the fashionable world, who are mostly so uninteresting, petty, dull and flat, that were we not told they were faithful transcripts of the 'very rich' of Manhattan, we should be a bit bored."[68]

According to Jones, the great novels of the world do not confine themselves to society, "that one-hundredth fraction of the human comedy." He then listed what he considered great books of the world which were not "society" novels: *Don Quixote, Gil Blas, Wilhelm Meister, Tom Jones, The Heart of MidLothian, Middlemarch, The Scarlet Letter, The Woodlanders, Richard Feverill, Eugenie Grandet, Consuelo, Madame Bovary, Fathers*

and Sons, and War and Peace. He closed his piece saying that "Society affords too little scope to genius, is too essentially prosperous and little and mean to afford drama of passion and action and suffering and death."[69]

That same day's news page offered good news for farmers and businessmen. After thirteen years of research, Professor H.L. Bolley of the agricultural college of the University of North Dakota had discovered the five distinct types of fungi parasites that cause the various kinds of wheat sickness. According to Professor Bolley, who had already discovered a cure for flax sickness, the fungi preying on wheat had left lands barren throughout the world, and was gradually lessening the pro-rata crops in wheat countries then growing wheat.[70]

Professor Bolley claimed to have identified the fungi and that it resembled, in shape and in reaction on plant life, the tuberculosis germs which affect human life. The cure for wheat, however, was much easier, involving merely a correct rotation of crops, namely

Carl W. Jones and his brother, Jefferson, at the Blackfeet Reservation, 1911-1912, "hamming it up" with an Indian woman. Carl is in the center under the striped blanket. Jeff is on the right.

corn, clover, and potatoes. Water and wind carried the parasites further and further out over the world until they threatened to destroy the world's supply of wheat and bread. Wheat lands, he said, could be rescued from the fungi still lying dormant in the soil and be made to raise wheat with the same quantity as in the past. He also declared that all disappearance of plant life from the soil was a result of diseases, and not by chemical exhaustion of those soils as previously believed. All waste lands throughout Minnesota, Wisconsin, and neighboring states' former wheat acreage, he added, could be restored to their full quota of wheat yield for years to come.

The following day, Jones offered an editorial in the *Journal* entitled, "Conservation's Other Side." According to Jones, conservation had had such a run in the magazines, in current thought composed by conventions of governors, and conventions of men "who believe they are as competent as governors, that it is really refreshing to learn that there is another side to the question." George L. Knapp, a Minnesota man and then employed as an editorial writer for the Denver newspapers, wrote Jones, very tersely printed this other side, in the *North American Review*. "Mr. Knapp," concluded Jones, "is sarcastic and flings defiance at the conservationists quite as we imagine Secretary Ballinger would like to fling it if he could bring himself to face the storm. Mr. Knapp is not afraid of a ruction, and says at the outset that he proposes to speak for those 'exiles in sin who hold that a large part of the conservation movement is unadulterated humbug.'"[71]

The Joneses were back in New York City for the New Year. On January 2, 1911, they attended Lew Field's Herald Square Theatre for a production of *The Girl and the Kaiser*. The operetta, in three acts, starred Lulu Glaser.[72] Back in Minneapolis that same month, they attended a Men's Club function of the Hoevel String Quartet at the First Unitarian Society's church at the corner of Eighth Street and Mary Place.[73] Later in the year, they attended performances at the Metropolitan Opera House to see Ethel Barrymore in the new four-act play, *The Witness for the Defense*, and John Hyams and Leila McIntyre (*The Quaker Girl*) in a new musical play, *The Girl of my Dreams*.[74]

While putting together his editorial program, Jones began a series of articles on January 11, 1911, in which he called, "Opportunities in Minnesota—Get in on the Ground Floor." This editorial and news campaign stressed the importance of Minnesota and the Northwest, and presented the opportunities that existed on the area to the *Journal* readers. The series consisted of articles and editorials, and related factual statistical information about farming and land usage. According to the *Journal*, Minnesota "has seen the people of Ohio, Illinois, and the Eastern States flowing like a broad river over her prairies and surging on to the lands beyond. She has made almost no effort toward getting her share of that migration." Jones also asked the state's Immigration Bureau to spend the $100,000 that had been authorized for publicizing Minnesota.[75]

The initial articles in the series focussed upon cheapness and fertility of the soil, and were followed by pieces on climate, water supply, stock, poultry raising, fruit farming, market gardening, and grains. Jones also asked the state government to appoint a statistician who could gather information on land by counties, "with information as to the number of acres of state lands, unoccupied private lands, character of soils or the price per acre." In addition, he asked for larger appropriations for demonstrative projects to increase the land's productivity.[76]

Many persons, including United States Secretary of State Frank B. Kellogg, lamented the loss of manpower on the farms. Kellogg knew how hard life was on the prairie farm, how farmers were exposed to blizzards, price manipulation, rail rate discrimination, and falsified weights and grading. Years later he addressed his Senate colleagues and told them of the wonders of the farm, but he warmed considerably in recalling the "golden returns" in the "opulent cities."[77]

"The concentration of wealth," said Kellogg, "the marvelous accomplishments of science and invention, the increase in manufacture and world commerce, and the increase in communication and rapid transportation have afforded opportunities in the cities for large incomes, the amassing of great fortunes, and that, together with the attractiveness of city life, have taken from the farm much of the best blood of the nation."[78]

The Minnesota Populists were becoming strong at this time, and, according to what was called the Omaha Declaration, gave but one answer for land usage: The land, including all the natural resources of wealth, is the heritage of all the people and should not be monopolized for speculative purposes."[79]

During the summer of 1911, the *Journal* departed briefly from its stand to limit sensational headlines although it probably did so from a standpoint of a moral "I told you so." On July 28, the following lurid headlines greeted the faces of *Journal* readers: "Shakeup for Bars and Restaurants," "Warrants and orders Mark Sudden Activity by Mayor and Police," "Women Barred from Eleven More Cafes," and "Three Waiters Accused of Illegal Liquor Sales—Private Dining Rooms Closed."[80]

The article began, "Supplementing warrants charging the sale of liquor after hours in three of the largest downtown restaurants,

Mayor James C. Haynes today issued a series of drastic orders designed to restrict the sale of liquor to women. Eleven places which maintain 'restaurants' in connection with barrooms are forbidden to allow women to enter private dining rooms in the National hotel café and McCormick's café are ordered closed, and women are barred from Hartman's beer garden. The orders follow a conference late yesterday with License Inspector A.B. Gray and are the most stringent issued by the mayor since last November, when he issued an order barring women from saloons."[81]

The women's rights movement was addressed by Jones in an editorial, entitled "Woman's Social Ambition," only two days after the barroom "shake-up." According to Herschel, the part that the ambition of women had played in the rearrangement of the British Constitution could not be overlooked. The Lords, he said, were in crisis, with a minority fighting for the legislative functions of the Lords, and a majority fighting against an influx of new peers. One Lord, reflecting the feminine idea of the situation, expressed, "What if this bill does pass, we are still on the steps of the throne. Our children are still privileged." Any loss of legislative power was secondary to a loss of social prestige.[82]

According to Jones, "Behind the struggles for wealth and office in this country is the social ambition of our women. It is this which urges the husbands and fathers on. It is a curious and rather childish ambition to separate yourself from your neighbors just far enough as to be able to neglect them or patronize them, but is there visible anywhere in the world a more real motive? Granted that it exists, is there any need to demonstrate that it is largely a feminine motive?"[83]

Jones attacked men as being "naturally lazy, democratic and philosophical." If men cannot have what they want, they will do everything possible to take what they can get. Women, he said, were not that way because of their "eternal spirit" which always strives and never knows defeat. They have pushed men into the wilderness in quest of nature, "bound them to the soil," and "hitched them to the wheel." But," Jones concluded, "curiously enough it tends always to die out in social eddies where, the circle having been formed, the ambition of the woman exercises itself exclusively in keeping somebody else out."[84]

Any change for women was slow in coming. In 1910, a Swedish-born Republican, Adolph O. Eberhart, succeeded John A. Johnson as governor, and he remained in office over the next four years. A skilled politician, he adjusted himself adeptly to the growing progressive swing emerging in 1912. Reforms were adopted the following year that included mothers' pensions, workmen's compen-

Minneapolis Journal touring car around Lake Harriet, 1910.

sation, preference primaries for both national and state offices, and the elimination of partisan political designation for Minnesota's legislative candidates.[85]

Eberhart's successor, Winfield S. Hammond, a Democrat, was a man of many interests and champion of reform. He planned to implement a new policy of reforestation, a reorganization of the state government, a settlement of the problem involving liquor traffic, and, especially, reforms for woman suffrage. At that time, Mrs. Andreas Ueland was leading the suffrage crusade in Minneapolis and she and Hammond joined forces. However, Governor Hammond's career was cut short, the woman's movement with it, when he died suddenly only a year after his inauguration.[86]

As Jones had written, women, still, refused to be defeated and many remained optimistic. Fanny Brin, who had moved to Minneapolis from Romania in 1884, and considered herself a disciple of Mrs. Ueland, wrote, "We seem to be moving very slowly. I have faith that someday women will make a great contribution to civilization. The need for women's participation grows daily. . . . I believe they can do more than they realize . . . women working side by side with men can push forward for a better world."[87]

169

But other changes were coming about swiftly in the pre-war years and these included the "monster," that was racing about Minnesota streets and roads. The automobile was described as "a curiosity, a contrivance for the rich, a blatant educator of the nerves of horses, a noisy phenomenon that nobody quite knew how to control." The license law had been passed in 1908, and one year later, 7,000 automobiles and 4,000 motorcycles were licensed. The automobile, undoubtedly, was a spur to the "Good Roads" movement which was officially adopted in 1913 by the inauguration of a Minnesota "Good Roads Day," the third Tuesday in June.[88]

H.V. Jones would also make changes in both his personal and business life during 1912. And some of these changes would both directly and indirectly affect the people living in and about the city of Minneapolis for years to come. But as former *Journal* owner, Clarence A. French, proclaimed, that the *Journal* "is a good paper—the best—I like its makeup, its type and everything about it. I've watched it grow and improve with the keenest interest." And regarding all the *Journal*'s various publishers, the greatest econiums from him were for H.V. Jones, "a grand man whose word was as good as its bond."[89]

Notes

[1]Theodore C. Blegen, *Minnesota: A History of the State*, pp. 461-462.

[2]Ibid.

[3]Edward C. Gale, "Herschel Jones;" Family history compiled by Mrs. Kenneth H. Bailey.

[4]James H. McCullough, "What a Youngster Learned from His Grandfather's Newspaper," *American Magazine*, January 1924, pp. 80-82.

[5]Ibid.; Theodore C. Blegen, *Minnesota: A History of the State*, p. 302.

[6]Waring Jones interview with author, November 3, 1999, Minneapolis.

[7]Frances Siftar interview with author, March 3, 1999, Edina, Minnesota.

[8]Ted Curtis Smythe, *A History of the* Minneapolis Journal, *1878-1939*, p. 190.

[9]James H. McCullough, "What a Youngster Learned from His Grandfather's Newspaper," *American Magazine*, p. 82.

[10]Ibid.

[11]Ted Curtis Smythe, *A History of the* Minneapolis Journal, *1878-1939,* pp. 190-191.

[12]Arthur J. Russell, *Good-Bye Newspaper Row: Incidents of Fifty Years on the Paper*, Excelsior, Minnesota, Minnetonka Record Press, 1943, pp. 13-14.

[13]*Minneapolis Journal*, September 2, 1908. Many other sources list William S. Jones as co-owner of the *Journal* including Lawrence M. Brings and Jay Edgerton, *Minneapolis, City of Opportunity: One Hundred Years of Progress in the Aquatennial City*, p. 152.

[14]Ted Curtis Smythe, *A History of the* Minneapolis Journal, *1878-1939*, p. 188.

[15]Ibid. The statement of Moses Jones was given to author Smythe, August 12, 1966.

[16]*Minneapolis Star-Journal*, Tuesday, August 1, 1939.

[17]Ted Curtis Smythe, *A History of the* Minneapolis Journal, *1878-1939*, p. 188. This personal communication was given by Maurice Wolff to author Smythe on August 5, 1966.

[18]Edward C. Gale, "Herschel Jones."

[19]*Minneapolis Journal*, undated article in H.V. Jones Collection.

[20]Ibid.

[21]Ibid.

[22]Arthur J. Russell, *Good-Bye Newspaper Row*, p. 15.

[23]Bradley L. Morison, *Sunlight on Your Doorstep*, pp. 20-21.

[24]Ibid.

[25]*The New York Times,* Friday, May 25, 1928; *Syracuse Herald*, Friday Evening, May 25, 1928.

[26]Arthur J. Russell, *Good-Bye Newspaper Row*, p. 15.

[27]James H. McCullough, "What a Youngster Learned from His Grandfather's Newspaper," *American Magazine*, p. 80.

[28]Ted Curtis Smythe, *A History of the* Minneapolis Journal, *1878-1939,* p. 196.

[29]*Minneapolis Journal,* May 25, 1928.

[30]Arthur J. Russell, *Good-Bye Newspaper Row*, pp. 14-15.

[31]Ted Curtis Smythe, *A History of the* Minneapolis Journal, *1878-1939*, p. 196.

[32]Arthur J. Russell, *Good-Bye Newspaper Row*, p. 14.

[33]Ibid., pp. 15-16.

[34]Ted Curtis Smythe, *A History of the* Minneapolis Journal, *1878-1939*, pp. 198-199.

[35]Ibid., pp. 200-201.

[36]Bruce L. Larson, *Lindbergh of Minnesota: A Political Biography*, New York, Harcourt, Brace, Jovanovich, Inc., 1971, pp. 90-91.

[37]*The Minneapolis Journal*, Saturday Evening, September 5, 1908.

[38]*The Minneapolis Journal,* Sunday, September 6, 1908.

[39]Hill was referring to the financial panic of the year before.

[40]*The Minneapolis Journal,* Sunday, September 6, 1908.

[41]Ibid.

[42]Ibid.

[43]*The Southern Bay*, New Orleans, Louisiana, undated letter column of H.V. Jones, in H.V. Jones Collection.

[44]H.V. Jones letter to Carl Jones dated October 19, 1908. Letters of October 22 and 29 were also very brief. All of Herschel's letters to his son that year were written on new letterhead: "The Minneapolis Journal, The Great Daily of the Great Northwest, H.V. Jones, Editor."

[45]H.V. Jones letter to Carl Jones dated November 11, 1908. In spite of lecturing Carl for his going to the football games at Yale and Dartmouth, H.V. concluded his somewhat lengthy missive with, "We shall expect you to win the Yale game this year."

[46]Metropolitan Opera House program belonging to H.V. Jones.

[47]H.V. Jones letter to Carl Jones dated November 17, 1908.

[48]Ted Curtis Smythe, *A History of the* Minneapolis Journal, *1878-1939*, pp. 208-209.

[49]Daily Attractions in New York tour booklet from the Hippodrome belonging to H.V. Jones.

[50]New Amsterdam Theatre booklet belonging to H.V. Jones.

[51]H.V. Jones letter to Carl Jones dated January 20, 1909.

[52]H.V. Jones letters to Carl Jones dated January 30 and February 15, 1909; H.V. Jones' Pullman ticket stub.

[53]"The Ant Hill Circle," Vol. 1, Sunday, January 10, 1909.

[54]*Bugville Bugle*, Vol. 1, February 1, 1909.

[55]Ibid., February 15 and 22, 1909 and March 10, 1909.

[56]Frances Jones letter to Herschel Jones dated June 19, 1908.

[57]*The Minneapolis Journal*, Wednesday, January 29, 1909.

[58]*The Minneapolis Journal*, February 26, 1909.

[59]Ibid.

[60]Liberty Theatre and Belasco Theatre programs belonging to H.V. Jones.

[61]Diary of Carl Jones.

[62]Shubert Play-Bills belonging to H.V. Jones. Tessie has written in pencil on page 2: "Father started down and got as far as Hennepin Avenue but didn't feel well enough so turned back. Said to tell you he was awfully sorry." Evidently, the tickets had been given to them.

[63]Metropolitan Opera programs belonging to H.V. Jones.

[64]Bijou and Broadway Theatre programs belonging to H.V. Jones.

[65]"Some of Minnesota's Prominent Public Officials and Widely

Known Editors," *Leslie's Illustrated Weekly*, No. 2828, November 18, 1909, p. 488.

[66]*Minneapolis Sunday Journal*, April 9, 1910.

[67]Ibid., editorial page.

[68]Ibid.

[69]Ibid.

[70]Ibid., news page.

[71]*Minneapolis Journal*, April 10, 1910.

[72]Herald Square Theatre program belonging to H.V. Jones.

[73]Men's Club program belonging to H.V. Jones.

[74]Metropolitan Opera House programs belonging to H.V. Jones.

[75]*Minneapolis Journal*, January 11, 1911 and January 27, 1911; Ted Curtis Smythe, *A History of the* Minneapolis Journal, *1878-1939*, pp. 205-207.

[76]Ibid.

[77]Roger Kennedy, *Men on the Moving Frontier from Wilderness to Civilization: The Romance, Realism, and Life-Styles of One Part of the American West*, Palo Alto, California, American West Publishing Company, 1969, pp. 136-137.

[78]Ibid.

[79]John D. Hicks, "The Persistence of Populism," Rhoda R. Gilman and June Drenning Holmquist, editors, *Selections from Minnesota History: A Fiftieth Anniversary Anthology*, St. Paul, Minnesota Historical Society, 1965, p. 284.

[80]*Minneapolis Journal*, July 28, 1911.

[81]Ibid.

[82]*Minneapolis Sunday Journal*, July 30, 1911.

[83]Ibid.

[84]Ibid.

[85]Theodore C. Blegen, *Minnesota: A History of the State*, p. 466-467.

[86]Ibid.; Theodore C. Blegen, *Building Minnesota*, Boston, D.C. Heath and Company, 1938, pp. 420-421.

[87]Barbara Stuhler and Gretchen Kreuter, editors, *Women in Minnesota: Selected Biographical Essays*, St. Paul, Minnesota Historical Society Press, 1977, p. 286-287.

[88]Theodore C. Blegen, *Minnesota: A History of the State*, pp. 464-465.

[89]*Minneapolis Journal*, Thursday, November 24, 1928.

CHAPTER SEVEN

HOME AND ABROAD

"But what on earth is half so dear—so longed
for—as the hearth of home."

—Emily Bronte

he unplanned nature of Minneapolis' development during
the 1880s found Park Avenue being built up as a stylish,
high-income boulevard. As the wealthy residential areas
along Seventh, Eighth, Ninth and Tenth Streets downtown were
taken over by new business enterprises, some of the elite decided
to move to "the country"—Park Avenue's wide, inviting, and genteel landscape. Over the following twenty years, some large, often
architect-designed, houses were spaced between Franklin Avenue
and East Twenty-sixth Street for bank officers and industry executives. But the building boom did not last, and it changed character
steadily after the turn of the century. The last of the great Park
Avenue mansions was constructed in 1921, but even by 1910,
many houses in this fashionable area were being converted into
multifamily dwellings as more areas offering high-income housing
were developed elsewhere in the city.[1]

For those lucky enough to live there and those who wished they
could, Park Avenue, the Summit Avenue of Minneapolis, was comprised of sumptuous mansions owned by the city's business leaders. Most of Park Avenue's Victorian showplaces in the 1880s were
designed by leading Twin City architects with offices between
Eighteenth and Twenty-eighth Streets. By 1887, the *Saturday
Evening Spectator*, a short-lived local newspaper, called Park
Avenue "the finest residence section of Minneapolis." This state-

ment was based not only on the avenue's convenient location just south of downtown but also to "the intelligent cooperation of an unusually enterprising class of citizens.[2]

The "intelligent cooperation" referred to the Park Avenue Improvement Association, a homeowners' group founded in the mid-1880s. This association provided money to plant trees, to install sidewalks and curbs, and to ensure that Park Avenue became the first street in Minneapolis to enjoy asphalt paving. According to author Larry Millett, the association even went so far as to purchase a house thought to be too close to the street so it could be "moved back to align with the general setback along the avenue."[3]

The more elegant mansions lay south of Franklin Avenue with "big houses sporting front porches and gingerbread trim, carriages rolling down the tree-lined avenue, well-dressed children playing amid the genteel greenery of immaculately tended lawns." A few apartment buildings were beginning to infiltrate the neighborhood, but the reigning monarchs—the lavish mansions—still dominated the avenue.[4]

Herschel V. Jones home at 2505 Park Avenue, Minneapolis. This is a winter view from the northwest. The Jones family lived here from June 1912 to June 1939.

The Joneses moved into the heart of this grand neighborhood early in 1912, selling their more modest home on Colfax Avenue,

and buying a large, fashionable house with an impressive front porch at 2505 Park Avenue South. The home, built for Alonzo H. Linton in 1891, is best described as a "colonial style residence, with tall columns spanning the entire height of the house—a unique and very pleasing feature." The home's architect was George M. Goodwin, who had built a reputation for his restrained style. According to *Northwest Architect*, he possessed "that rarest gift of an architect, the knowledge of when to stop." Goodwin, unfortunately, passed away the year the Linton home was completed. After Alonzo Linton died in 1911, his widow sold the home to Herschel Jones the following year.[5]

Entering the home, one stepped into a large reception hall. On the right, the push of a button opened a wall to reveal a vast library. At the foot of the stairway leading to the second floor was a huge landing, and an elevator could be taken to the third floor where Mrs. Jones kept all her Christmas presents.[6] During the summer, recalled a granddaughter, Herschel was occupied with his roses. "He loved roses," she recalled years later, "and had a beautiful rose garden."[7]

The Jones family, about 1915. Left to right: top row: Tessie, Fran, Paul, Lydia Wilcox Jones; bottom row: Carl, Florence, Herschel.

Between 1907 and 1920, it was fashionable to find a postcard album in the living room of nearly every American home, and the Joneses were probably no exception. Visitors no longer cared to pour over family photographs, and it was "the thing" to have the postcard album available for guests to study where the hosts, or family and friends, had been on vacation. It was also a status symbol to have postcards delivered to one's home.[8]

The new Park Avenue location was more pleasing than ever for Herschel's young daughter Frances and her horse Dixie. The stable was only a couple blocks from their new home.

"When Frances wanted to go riding or take a ride in her buggy, she would call the stable," recalled Frances' daughter, Frances Siftar. "They would saddle Dixie up, and the horse would walk over to Park Avenue all alone to Frances."[9]

Jones was not the only newspaper owner on Park Avenue. Less than a block away stood the "castle" of Swan J. Turnblad, owner of a Swedish-language newspaper, *Svenska Amerikanska Posten*. Built only five years earlier at a cost of $1,500,000, it was considered one of the grandest and most luxurious homes in the Northwest. Turnblad's mansion was "a three-story, thirty-three-room architectural smorgasbord with tower, turrets, and terraces. Of gray limestone trimmed with turquoise, it is a massive, castlelike house surrounded by a high wrought-iron fence."[10]

The Park Avenue home. A winter view from the south side.

The interior of Turnblad's dream home was heralded for its fine collection of eleven *kakelugnar* (decorative porcelain stoves), its

hand-carved African mahoganies, its superb European furniture, and its Swedish Oriental rugs. The interior was highlighted by a huge fireplace, faced in onyx with a ceiling-high mantel designed and carved by famous Polish artist Albin Polesek.

Turnblad was certainly no stranger to Jones. The wealthy Swede had appeared in the *Journal* pages several times including Tuesday, April 10, 1900, when he purchased a Waverly and became the first person in Minneapolis to put a private electric car on the streets. According to the *Journal*, "The vehicle is one of the latest patterns with all the latest improvements. It will run from thirty to forty miles without being recharged, and it can be regulated to five different degrees of speed. Mr. Turnblad has placed a small electric plant in his barn with which he recharges the carriage whenever necessary."[11]

Three months later Turnblad wrote a letter to H.V. Jones, which was published in the *Journal* as to the safety and maintenance of electric automobiles. And, undoubtedly, Jones and everyone else on Park Avenue, witnessed Turnblad driving his electric car right down the middle of the street. After all, quipped Turnblad, "I pay my half of the taxes so I will use my half of the street."[12]

Jones' own luxurious home on Park Avenue was in a good geographical location. He was in walking distance of Powderhorn Lake, which had been named by the Indians because of its shape. The lake in 1912 was much larger than the current pond, although Jones most certainly would have avoided the west side of Powderhorn Park where a slaughter house was in operation. Jones was also but blocks away from a second Minneapolis lake—Shep's Lake—which was located at the site of present-day Greeley School.[13]

It was fashionable at the time to have one's house or building designed by a prominent architect. Among the most prominent at the time were two former Ohioans who had come to Minnesota in the late nineteenth century—LeRoy S. Buffington and Cass Gilbert. Buffington had designed the Pillsbury "A" Mill, the West Hotel, several University of Minnesota buildings, and some private fashionable residences. He was noted for his skyscraper patent in 1888, which was a "braced skeleton of metal with masonry veneer supported on shelves fastened to the skeleton of each story." Because his invention made buildings as high as twenty-eight stories possible, he was called the "Father of the Skyscraper."[14]

Gilbert was known for his design of the new Minnesota State Capitol that opened in 1905—a domed structure in the Renaissance tradition. He also designed many Minnesota banks, churches, public buildings, and private residences. He would later gain esteem for designing New York's Woolworth Building, at that time, the tallest building in the world.

The first home built on Park Avenue and Twenty-fifth Street was that of Judge and Mrs. Ell Torrance. The judge was a colorful figure, renowned for his having served a term as commander-in-chief of the Grand Army of the Republic. Newspaper reporters frequently converged on him for information on his Civil War experiences or about the time he had guarded the body of President Abraham Lincoln as it lay in state in Baltimore. Judge Torrance was Herschel's neighbor for two years before, in 1914, he sold his house to Alexander A. McRae, who later became vice-president of Northwestern National Bank.[15]

Another neighbor of Herschel Jones, O.C. Wyman, lived directly across the street at 2500 Park Avenue South. When the Wymans moved into their new home in 1891, Park Avenue had yet to be paved. Immediately south of the house a field of wheat grew.

The Wyman residence was an "imposing, many-chimneyed, red-brick-and-stone building designed by Adam Lansing Dorr. A dining room with gold leaf ceiling, eight fireplaces, amber stained-glass windows, elaborate carvings, and paneling throughout—all conveyed a feeling of solidity and elegance."[16]

The third floor of the Wyman home boasted a much-used ballroom with an adjoining chaperone's room decorated with brightly figured wallpaper. The library was "lined with leather-bound classics and oak-framed portraits of American poets." In this room, Mr. Wyman hosted three of his neighbors in weekly card games. One of these neighbors after 1912 was probably H.V. Jones. Since Wyman's dry-goods firm was considered one of the best in the country, he and Jones could discuss both business and book collecting on equal footing.[17]

Herschel's favorite neighbor, however, was Anson S. Brooks, who also lived on another corner of Twenty-fifth and Park at 2445 Park. He and Herschel became the closest of friends. Brooks was the son of a prominent Winona County doctor who was involved in the grain business and was a former state legislator. After working at his father's grain business, Anson Brooks and two brothers formed their own grain firm which continued for twenty-four years. In 1901, the same year Herschel established *Commercial West*, the brothers organized the Brooks-Scanlon Lumber Company, of which Anson was vice-president.

Brooks' home had been designed by Franklin and Louis Long and was completed in 1907. It was the last great home erected on Park Avenue and, certainly, one of the most unusual. The home's squarish, monumental architecture was inspired by the famous Doge's Palace in Venice. This Venetian Goth home featured pointed arches that comprised the predominant decorative motif. The ironwork on the front door, the thirteen first-story windows, and the decorative balcony around the top of the home—all carried the pointed—arch design.[18]

Circassian walnut and marble fireplaces and mahogany-beamed ceilings blessed the interior of the house with a sense of warmness. Mr. Brooks' second floor billiard room, to which H.V. Jones was no stranger, was particularly comfortable, and a large skylight provided natural lighting.

When the Brookses moved in 1921, it was only a block farther south on Park.[19] Their son, Paul A. Brooks, continued living in the old family home until 1935 and the Jones-Brooks relationship remained a lasting friendship. In Jones' lifetime, Park Avenue had been converted from a rutted wagon road with a thriving wheat field to an avenue of luxury.

Fourth Street, downtown Minneapolis where the *Journal* was located, was also somewhat glamorous in 1912. Arthur J. Russell, *Journal* columnist, had once likened it to heaven, and the *Tribune*'s William J. McNally, called Fourth a "street filled with glamour and romance." In his "More or Less Personal" column, he added, "In all Minneapolis I doubt if you could find a better locale for a novel than Fourth Street."[20]

The *Journal* and the *Tribune* stood on the south side of Fourth Street, not quite a hundred yards apart, between Nicollet and Marquette Avenues. One writer, the *Tribune*'s Bradley L. Morison, was not as sentimental regarding those days on Newspaper Row. Until the advent of the Newspaper Guild, salaries were low, raises infrequent, vacations ever so brief, and fringe benefits hardly worth mentioning (with the "exception" of a company-financed office picnic on Lake Minnetonka). Employees sweltered in both newsrooms and those in the composing rooms were slowly "roasted on a spit."

Compensation-wise, Fourth Street had its great number of newspaper professionals, but there were "floaters" and deadbeats among them—heavy drinkers and others with no college background. "Yet most responded to the challenge of a big news story like a fire horse to an alarm; and in the heat of competitive strife, many a news triumph was forged and many a sparkling piece of copy written under deadline pressure."[21]

A road-show theatre, the Metropolitan Opera House, was located only half a block away from the *Journal* and *Tribune*. On Sunday, February 11, Herschel and Lydia attended the Metropolitan for a Flo Ziegfield, Jr., production of *Mlle Innocence* starring Anna Held.[22] Just beyond the Metropolitan Opera House, on

Third Street, stood "the dark mahogany cavern" of Schiek's Café, which had been built in 1862 during the Civil War. *Journal* writers would skip through a dim and dingy alley on the way to Schiek's, and at times, "encounter greatness at the Metropolitan's stage door."[23]

On February 24, a photograph of Herschel Jones was printed on the cover of a New York magazine, *The Fourth Estate*. The caption read, "Herschel V. Jones, publisher of the *Minneapolis Journal*, who recommends radical reform in post office department methods." An article on Jones appeared on page three. The magazine, established in 1894, took its name from Edmund Burke's statement that there were three estates in Parliament, "but in the Reporters' Gallery yonder there sat a 'Fourth Estate' more important far than the[m] all."[24]

Greatness was, however, celebrated in September 1912 when 1,200 stood in the St. Paul Auditorium and applauded as James J. Hill was given a loving cup on his seventy-fourth birthday. According to the *Journal*, William B. Dean, Hill's lifelong friend and business associate, presented the beautiful silver cup first to Hill, then to his wife for safe keeping, in what was considered the biggest birthday celebration ever held in this part of the country. During the proceedings, Hill was given the title of "Master Builder."[25]

Following the award, all of the 1,200 guests, many of them prominent professional men, were seated and given dinner. Archbishop John Ireland delivered the invocation. Following dinner, a series of motion pictures detailed development of the northwest, and the Sinclair Pipers played and marched among the tables. Louis Betz, representing the St. Paul Commercial Club, introduced the toastmaster—Pierce Butler. Palms and ferns decorated the speaker's table, with the numerals "1838" and "1912" outlined in electric bulbs which illuminated a large painting of Hill. At the conclusion of the party, in which Hill spoke on conservation of the soil and other issues, he stood and shook hands with everyone from wealthy railroad men to the younger generation from every walk of life.

In this same issue, the *Journal* also reported that Minneapolis had doubled its trade in farm implements and agricultural machinery over the past two months. The *Journal* quoted Frank S. Pool, president of the Minneapolis Traffic Club and manager for the Deere & Webber Company as stating, "I never saw such prosperity; everybody in Minneapolis is busy. Because we have been doing the business of our lives in farm implements and machinery and because Minneapolis has doubled her business in those lines from July 1 to August 31, over what was ever done before, we rather got the notion that the implement trade was doing all the business in Minneapolis. But I find every wholesale line in Minneapolis is rushed to capacity."[26]

The *Journal* also reported that northern wheat had not been hurt by frost. "Bright, balmy days, with cold, frosty nights" kept threshing activity moving with the yield of a bumper crop in Prince Albert, Saskatchewan, and from Milbank, South Dakota, a reported yield of twenty-seven bushels of wheat per acre on a field of 250 acres. In Mankato, Minnesota, the colder weather still found the corn crop assured in the main.

The big event of 1912, the presidential campaign, however, presented Herschel with a problem. Jones' old friend, Theodore Roosevelt, had split the Republican Party in 1912 and was running on the Bull Moose ticket. Because of this action, and, perhaps, because of Roosevelt's hard-line anti-trust position, the *Journal* swung its allegiance to Howard Taft, although Jones, in his half-hearted editorial support, probably didn't care who won the election, as long as it wasn't the Democratic candidate, Woodrow Wilson.

Taft's lack of political astuteness during his first term (1908) was soon revealed in his indifference toward the growing rift between conservatives and progressives within Republican ranks. The rift with Roosevelt and other progressives was encouraged by his failure to appoint any of the Liberal wing to his cabinet. His unspectacular first term was, however, honest. He took steps for the formation of an annual budget, established the federal postal-savings system, gave impetus to conservation and natural resources, and vigorously enforced anti-trust legislation. The last few months of his administration witnessed the widening, unbreachable rift between him and Roosevelt.

The *Journal* did give good coverage of the attempted assassination of Roosevelt while he was speaking in Milwaukee, but the incident did little, if anything, to change the newspaper's position. The *Journal* did, however, question Roosevelt's common sense in continuing his speech in spite of his gunshot wound and pointed out that the shooting would not affect the outcome of the voting very much.[27]

But the Republicans and Democrats had other factions to fear. By 1912, the Socialist Party was at its peak. Formed in 1892, it had polled 30,000 votes during the year of the Pullman Strike, and by 1912, was leading strikes, free-speech fights, civil-rights causes, and political struggles. There were fifty-six Socialist mayors in five states; Emil Seidel had been elected mayor of Milwaukee, and Arthur LeSueur, mayor of Minot, North Dakota. There were 1,039 dues-paying members in elected offices. Eugene Debs and Emil Seidel ran on the presidential ticket (they would poll 897,000 votes).[28]

There were daily and weekly Socialist newspapers exceeding two million circulation by 1913. There were trade and union papers as well and foreign language dailies and weeklies. The *International Socialist Review* was circulated on a worldwide basis, and the *Appeal to Reason* boasted 800,000 subscribers. Over 1,200 Populists and Socialists had been elected to office in municipalities, including seventy-nine mayors in a four-year span.[29]

On the local level in 1912, Wallace G. Nye was running against Socialist candidate Thomas H. Van Lear. While the *Journal* supported Republican candidates in most offices, it did not take a dim view of the dark horse Socialist candidates. An October 1912 article in the *Journal* stated, "The *Journal* has no quarrel with the Socialist candidates. They are doubtless public-spirited men. But Minneapolis cannot afford to submit itself to experimentation."[30]

As if to back up its editorial position, the *Journal* published a six-column article by James Gray on the Milwaukee Socialist regime of Emil Seidel, whom Gray interviewed at length, and the resulting article appeared on the front page, with three columns set in two-column measures. Gray praised several programs of the Socialist experiment but also pointed out its weaknesses.[31]

On election night, three screens were fastened to the buildings opposite the Journal Building, with two of these used for stereopticon projections of the electoral returns. The third showed nonstop motion pictures and entertained the huge crowd that had gathered in the streets. Mrs. Van Lear, wife of Socialist candidate for mayor, Thomas Van Lear, and six friends were among the many guests who had front-seat positions from the Journal windows.[32]

The *Journal*'s excellent coverage would have disappointed Mrs. Van Lear because it announced Nye's victory for mayor. The *Journal* quavered a bit, too, in proclaiming Roosevelt the winner in Minnesota and Woodrow Wilson the new president. The *Journal*'s editorial, however, was highly supportive of Wilson's victory stating, "His mental, moral and spiritual gifts are large. His Americanism is ardent. His ambition is for his Country. The Democracy has done well in giving Woodrow Wilson to the Country."[33]

Once in the White House, Wilson proceeded with amazing vigor to initiate and carry out major items of legislation he had advocated in his campaign. He delivered his first message to Congress in person, thus renewing the custom that had ended with the presidency of John Adams. In this session and later, he constantly influenced individual senators and representatives on behalf of his programs. His initial major victory came with passage of the Under-

wood Tariff, which reduced customs levies despite the bitter opposition of varied industrial interests. To counterbalance the downward drift of tariff funds, the act levied a federal income tax, under
authority of the adopted Sixteenth Amendment to the Constitution.

According to an article in the *Minneapolis Journal*, the act affected 425,000 American citizens. Every single person, whether
citizen or foreign resident, whose income exceeded $3,000 annual-
ly, and every married person whose income was above $4,000, was
expected to report his or her receipts in detail to the government
agents March 1 of each year. An estimate indicated that the income
tax would produce $82,298,000 from the persons taxed. To this
would be added the $35,000,000 or more produced by the then cor-
poration tax, which was continued as part of the law.[34]

The law provided for two methods of tax collection. One was the
individual return filed by the citizen. The second made by corporations and other employers who paid their employees' taxes. The latter would apply to salaries, rents, interest, royalties, partnership
profits, and some other sources of income. Persons receiving such
incomes had to be prepared to show that the money had its tax paid
at the source.

But James J. Hill took top billing in the *Journal* the following
week by donating $50,000 to St. Olaf's College, completing an
endowment fund of $250,000. The gift was the result of a plea from
a college committee in need of the funds earlier in the year. According to the *Journal*, Hill informed the group at the time that "if
you gentlemen will raise $200,000 within the year for that college,
come to me, and I will give you the other $50,000 necessary."
When the committee later told Hill they had not raised all the
money, Hill told them to "take six or seven months more, and if you
get the money, come to me for the $50,000." The money was even-
tually raised, and Hill followed through with his promise.[35]

The suffragettes in England continued to generate news. The
police were criticized for their handling of the Bow Baths Riot in
the East End when Sylvia Pankhurst was rescued by her followers.
The rioters boasted of their rescue to friends and the *Journal* reported that "every time a policeman grasped a suffragette, one of her
comrades would rip open the officer's coat and cut his suspenders.
Torn between conflicting senses of duty and modesty, the consta-
ble had to sacrifice his capture or his dignity, and everyone who
knows the London 'bobby,' will guess the prisoner escaped."[36]

On a much more serious note, the *Journal* carried daily news of
revolutionary Mexico's confrontation with President Wilson, which
had created a dangerously chaotic situation. Wilson's foreign policy, at least in principle, was characterized by a refusal to exert mate-

rial power against weaker countries and by a studied respect for the rights and interests. Unable to depose General Victoriano Huerta from his dictatorship, Wilson resigned himself to a policy of watchful waiting. He opposed the formal intervention being pressed on him by American and European business interests.

The *Journal*, as early as November 9, 1913, saw things differently, as did the general press everywhere in the country. The story run by the *Journal*, under the heading "Army and Navy Prepared for Immediate Action if Intervention Is Decided Upon," emphasized the growing impatience of the big European powers over America's shyness in the Mexican situation. "The first mutterings in June," reported the *Journal*, "the recent 'pressure,' and the steps which must follow are simply regarded as the logical progress toward the inevitable, and that is intervention by the United States in the interest of peace in Mexico."

Venustiano Carranza, leader of the Constitutionalists, claimed he could sweep the country in ninety days if allowed to obtain unlimited arms. The *Journal* also stated that the War Department was prepared with a probable plan of attack and the Rough Riders and the regular forces of the United States army were being called to the front. The plan called for transports to follow the ships and the army on an invasion of the five northerly Mexican states.

However, the following day's *Journal* insisted that President Wilson had considered lifting the embargo on arms and had "discussed the Mexican situation that day and cleared the atmosphere of many reports as to the intentions of the United States. He made it clear that he had no plans at present of addressing Congress because the situation was not in shape for such action, and while representations had been made to the Huerta government, no reply had been received. He declared that no time limit had been set for a reply from Huerta.[37]

Two days later, the *Journal*'s headlines sounded as if the ball for war had started rolling: "Hale, on Behalf of Wilson, Meets General Carranza," "Conference First Open Move of U.S. to Show Interest in Constitutionalists," "Gunboats Fire on the Rebel Forces at Tuxpan," "Japan to Send Cruisers—Five Federal Officers and Nine Soldiers Slain," and "Carranza Gains Support of Orozco and Blanquet, Former Huerta Allies." Those readers who opposed American intervention in Mexico were perhaps more interested in the *Journal* headline below those of the possible war—"Roosevelt Campaign Button Is Found in Stomach of Possum."[38]

The headlines in a later issue of the *Journal* sounded bleaker: "Huerta Refuses to Answer Demands of U.S.—Calls Congress," "Mexican Legislators, Elected on Oct. 26, Ordered to Assemble on

Nov. 15 by Provisional President—Wilson Decides Not to Issue
Statement 'For the Present,'" "John Lind Quits Mexico City and
Goes to Vera Cruz," "Charge O'Shaughnessy May Be Recalled and

Herschel V. Jones in his forties to
fifties.

Diplomatic Negotiations Ended," "Hale and Carranza Discuss Situation," and "Constitutionalist Leader, However, Declares He will not Accept Mediation."[39]

In April 1914, following affronts to United States sailors for which no apology was forthcoming, and to prevent the landing of munitions from a German ship, a U.S. naval force seized terminal facilities of Veracruz. The overthrow of Huerta, however, brought no settlement of the revolution, which continued to threaten U.S. business interests, and Wilson's recognition of Carranza's government did not end the problem. Pancho Villa's raids into U.S. territory in March 1916 led Wilson to authorize a punitive expedition under General John J. (Black Jack) Pershing. The Mexican revolution would plague Wilson to the end of his administration.

As attention turned away from Mexico, Jones shifted his editorial eye to Panama in November 1913. With the opening of the Panama Canal, Jones wrote in the *Journal* that the canal would open the west coast of South America to the Atlantic Ocean, and that the United States and Canada would experience something new. He added that the German experts wondered if the canal would make any difference to Suez, or snatch away from them most of the whole transport between Europe and the Far East. Japan, according to Jones, already had laid plans to invade the South Atlantic commercially, and he expected British and German liners bound for Yokahoma, Shanghai, and Hong Kong, tracking for the Caribbean and deserting the Mediterranean. In such a case, Jones inferred dislocation to world routes and an "immense alteration in a number of things" would result.[40]

Jones also conjectured that Central America would become a very significant piece of real estate both strategically and commercially. With ships from the greatest ports in the world passing "her windows," Central America would be exploited, developed, enriched, settled up at such a rate as "will astonish the nerves of her mañana-disposed people. The new Panama Canal would undoubtedly tempt the ambition of the greater powers, European or Asiatic, of the world." Jones also said that, "to watch what Panama will do and will not do is going to be one of the most interesting entertainments ever offered the observer."

In another editorial, Jones discussed "The Swarming Hordes of Asia." Focusing on the trouble in Natal, South Africa, over the East Indian indentured laborers, the soothsayer predicted the event would become one of worldwide significance. He discussed the past two centuries, which witnessed an immense expansion and emigration upon part of the European Aryan race. If that immigration had ebbed somewhat, it was only because it had done so "after about all the desirable unoccupied lands have been pre-empted by the white race." That pre-emption, he said, placed pressure upon the brown and yellow races. Said Jones, "the teeming myriads of Asia have only commenced to be mobile. But their mobility increases at a geometrical ratio, now that it is stirred. The difficulty of keeping them out of lands dedicated to the civilization of the white race has just begun."

United States foreign affairs after July 1914 were dominated by President Wilson's efforts to protect the rights of America as a neutral in World War I. A formal proclamation of neutrality was emphasized by a more personal appeal, in which he urged Americans to remain neutral in thought as well as in behavior. His offer of mediation, however, evoked no favorable response, and his attempts to enact secret peace negotiations failed miserably.

The *Journal*, upon the outbreak of war in Europe, had declared itself against preparedness as a means of keeping peace. The newspaper suggested a federation or international court be set up for the settlement of disputes. "Europe," stated the *Journal*, "was so well prepared for war that it ought to be in peace . . . "[41]

Right after the war broke out, the *Journal* placed bulletin boards in the windows at the front of the building to keep Twin Citians abreast of the latest news. *Journal* copy boys continuously updated the news as crowds gathered to catch the latest. The Associated Press and the United Press were both used by the *Journal,* and a special serviceman's edition was inaugurated. Alex Caldwell, a long-time member of the *Journal*'s copy desk, was placed in charge of the War Desk. During the war, big, black, bold type was used to stir interest, although the newspaper did not lend itself to the use of enough photography.[42]

In September 1914, Herschel and Lydia, along with their daughter Florence and son Moses, took an automobile trip to the town of Newton, Iowa. There they were guests of Mayor E.J.H. Beard who was Lydia's uncle. Moses did not return to Minnesota with them, as he instead continued on to New Jersey to take up work in the Lawrenceville Preparatory School.[43]

His brother Jefferson had also attended the Lawrenceville Preparatory School and had joined the United Press in 1914 in Chicago. Jefferson was sent to the Far Eastern Bureau at Tokyo, where he did general assignments between Manila, Peking, Harbin, and Vladivostok. When the Japanese government delivered to Germany a war ultimatum on August 23, 1914, Jefferson Jones was assigned to the Eighteenth Imperial Japanese Regiment as U.P. correspondent and sailed first to the Marshall Islands and on to Kiaochow, German Colonies.[44]

Moses Jones in his twenties.

Jefferson Jones returned to Tokyo in 1915 where he covered the so-called "Twenty-one Demands" on Peking, which would be the main issue of the U.S. Congress session in 1918. When Japan clamped down censorship, Jefferson left Japan for New York and joined the French Flying Corps. He went into training at Newport News, Virginia, but was injured in a crash landing. Following freelance work for *Nations Business*, he enlisted in the U.S. Navy when this country declared war on Germany. Jefferson saw action in the Mediterranean.

Jefferson, however, was not the only son of Herschel and Lydia to enter military service as the clouds of war drifted closer to America's shores. Carl went to work for the War Department, and Moses left Dartmouth in his sophomore year to enlist in the U.S. Army Tank Corps. When America entered the war, Moses saw action in France.[45]

On February 4, 1915, the government in Berlin, declaring the waters around the British Isles a war zone, threatened to sink all belligerent ships in that area and also gave warning that neutral ships might be sunk as well. Wilson replied vigorously six days later, warning Germany that it would be held to "strict accountability" for any lawless acts of its submarine commanders. Wilson also stated that destruction of an American vessel or human lives would be regarded as an "indefensible violation of neutral rights." The Germans, nevertheless, refused to budge from their declaration.

On May 7, the German embassy inserted a curious note in several American morning newspapers. It warned:

A *Journal* employee at the switchboard, 1915. (Courtesy of the Minnesota Historical Society)

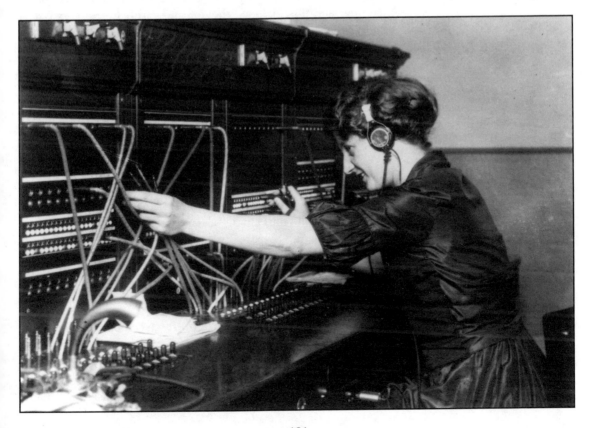

> Travelers intending to embark for an Atlantic crossing are reminded that a state of war exists between Germany and her Allies and Great Britain and her Allies; that the zone of war includes the waters adjacent to the British Isles; that in accordance with the formal notice given by the Imperial German Government vessels flying the flag of Great Britain or any of her Allies are liable to destruction in these waters; and that travelers sailing in the war zone in ships of Great Britain or her Allies do so at their own risk.[46]

That same day, however, the British liner *Lusitania* was sunk without warning by a German submarine; more than a thousand persons were drowned, among them 128 Americans. Passage on the 40,000-ton *Lusitania* had been considered safe since her top speed of twenty-five knots could outstrip any U-boat.

Still determined to avoid war at any cost, Wilson displayed long-suffering patience in the negotiations of the following weeks, but his will to compel Germany to abide by the established rules of cruiser warfare was unshakable. His protest to Germany was so strongly worded that Secretary of State William Jennings Bryan resigned rather than sign it.

The unprovoked sinking, however, had the American press screaming, and this included the *Journal*. Still, Jones' paper supported Wilson's efforts to keep the peace, and soon the angry newspaper editorials in Minnesota and the nation eased up.[47]

Following the sinking of the *Arabic* in August 1915, the German government promised that in the future liners would not be attacked without warning. The *Journal* bitterly attacked Germany's indiscriminate warfare, calling Germany an "outlaw nation" that was now "the enemy of all the world." From the time of the sinking of the *Arabic* on, the *Journal* became increasingly anti-German and declared itself a supporter of preparedness, even if America did not go to war.[48]

In the spring of 1916, when a rupture with Germany was imminent because of the torpedoing of the steamer *Sussex*, Wilson presented an ultimatum and finally evoked from Berlin a more comprehensive pledge to abandon their submarine campaign altogether. For the next seven months, relations with Germany were somewhat relaxed. This diplomatic victory not only postponed U.S. intervention in the war, but was of extreme political value during Wilson's reelection campaign of 1916. It gave support to the argument that he had vindicated America's rights successfully and had kept us out of war.

The Republicans, who had nominated Charles Evans Hughes, denounced Wilson as hesitating and cowardly because of his pampering of Germany and his handling of the Mexican revolution. But Wilson drew voting strength from the farming districts west of the Mississippi and on the Pacific Coast and support from the Progressives who refused to follow Theodore Roosevelt back to Republicanism. It was only after the late returns came in from the West that Wilson was re-elected.

The election in Minnesota saw a three-fold battle for the Republican nomination for the Senate. Moses E. Clapp, who had served in the Senate since 1901, faced the test of re-election. Clapp and his opponent, Congressman Charles A. Lindbergh, had both voted against measures that, in their judgment, carried America towards war. The third candidate, Frank B. Kellogg, had won fame in the Northern Securities case and was an advocate for preparation in the face of international danger. Kellogg won the nomination and the election while Wilson lost the state's electoral vote to Hughes.[49]

The *Minneapolis Journal* had seen little promise in Lindbergh, calling him "The Mysterious Lindbergh," saying that he had "deftly excited the public's curiosity" with his promise to solve all the political ills of the state. The *Journal* expressed an opinion that Moses Clapp would have a problem running on the Republican ticket because of his anti-Republican past. As for Lindbergh, the *Journal* penned an editorial stating that "if Mr. Lindbergh could leave his test tubes, retorts, and bottles for a few minutes, he might out of his own rich experience give Moses a little help in solving that mystery."[50]

During this same year—1916—Herschel V. Jones met Earl R. Carlson. Young Carlson had been born in Minneapolis in 1897 with a birth injury later identified as infantile cerebral paralysis, clinically known as Little's Disease (spastic cerebral diplegia), one of several ailments marked by an extreme inability to control the bodily muscles, especially under nervous tension. His father had been a stoker in a factory while his mother made a little money as a seamstress. Their home was very poor, but the parents were intelligent, and they recognized that, though their child was awkward and to many appeared mentally deficient, he actually had a good and capable mind.[51]

Earl Carlson had been so injured at birth that he never had the full use of his muscles. In taking his first step, which he did not do until long past his infancy, he was determined to learn to walk. For many years, he did not know if his ill-controlled hand would bring food to his mouth or throw it over his shoulder. He was not even master of his speech organs, nor frequently his eyes.

According to the Neurological Institute, "The movements are generally exaggerated. In reaching for an object, the arm will wander aimlessly. The hand, attempting to grasp something, may remain fixed in that position, and is relaxed with difficulty. In the early years the patient may learn to walk after a fashion, and the gait is quite characteristic. The toes scrape along the floor, the heels are not brought down, and the spasm of the thigh muscles forces the individual to move in a cross-legged fashion. Speech is difficult, and not infrequently profuse salivation with drooling tends to reflect against the normal mentality of the patient. On some occasions, these reactions may not be apparent, or may be limited to only one or two muscle groups, while on others the entire body musculature is thrown into a chaos of writhing movements with such violence that one would think the entire store of volitional impulses within the central nervous system had been set loose. Yet, as long as the mentality remains intact, the possibilities of re-education are unlimited."[52]

Young Carlson hated school as the other children often made fun of his jerking motions. He wore sweaters, boots, and other clothing that required no lacing or buttoning. A character in Shakespeare's *Richard III*, suffering from this same Little's Disease, snarled,

> "I am deformed, unfinished, sent before
> my time
> Into this breathing world, scarce half
> made up."

Yet, Carlson's mother tutored him, and he was able to get through school. Through a friend, he was able to secure a position cataloging old manuscripts at the University of Minnesota library, and then to study for a degree. While he was struggling through the first stages of his college career, both of his parents died, and, left without family, he needed a friend to help him complete his academic course. Despite his handicaps, he wanted to go on to Princeton where a possible job awaited him in a geology library, and finally, Yale, to obtain a medical degree. Still, he was not sure if he should make the move or stay in his position at the library in Minnesota.[53]

No one wanted the "disordered cripple" until help was administered from Herschel Jones. Young Carlson went to see Herschel in hopes of procuring a summer job to hold him over for a while. He informed the newspaper owner why he needed money and asked for his advice. Jones had Carlson tell him "all the factors in the situation, and then reflected for a while," Carlson reminisced. "Finally he asked me if I could get along on $10 a week. When I replied that I could very easily, he said: 'Well, I have no job for you, but I'll give you that if you will do nothing except get into the best possible shape to go to Princeton in the fall and do a good job when you get there. If the job doesn't turn out well, you needn't feel that you've burned your bridges behind you by refusing the Minnesota offer. You can fall back on me; I want you to feel that I'm taking the place of your father. But understand this: I shall expect you to pay me back when you can."[54]

Later on, Carlson learned what he termed "the remarkable story" of Mr. Jones' life. He was astonished to find that Jones had started work as a typesetter and made his own way to the proprietorship of a newspaper for which he had refused an offer of five million dollars. He discovered that, in his early years, Jones had borrowed $100, put it into the bank, and returned it six month later with the interest that had accumulated. Jones had done the same with a $500 loan, and over the years built up his credit standing and the bankers' confidence in him to such an extent that he was actually lent money to purchase his own paper.

"It was typical of him that he never acknowledged my checks as I gradually repaid his loan to me," recalled Carlson, "but when the indebtedness was completely paid off, he told me to come to him whenever I had need of 'some healthy lucre.' Thanks to Mr. Jones' help, I spent a restful summer building up my health."[55]

At Princeton, Carlson decided upon a career in medicine and selected courses in biochemistry and physiology. While on a working holiday in Maine, he wrote to Herschel about his plans and asked him if he could again help him financially, provided he could gain admission to a medical school. Carlson wanted to be sure of at least two years' freedom from financial worries while he abandoned one field and turned to another. Jones, of course, answered in the affirmative. Thanks to the kindness of Herschel V. Jones and Dr. Walter Dandy, a famous brain surgeon, Earl R. Carlson entered the Yale medical School in 1926.[56]

After becoming a doctor, Carlson worked at the Neurological Institute in New York with Dr. Frederick Tilney, who was studying the correlation of behavior with the structural development of the brain. Shortly thereafter, Dr. Carlson established a clinic for spastics at the institute, going on to founding institutions of his own in East Hampton, Long Island, and in Pompano, Florida. He also aided in the development of many schools and clinics for the birth-injured elsewhere in the United States and became a renowned author approved by authorities in fields both of medicine and psychology. And, of course, Herschel Jones was repaid, as he knew he would be.

In his book, *Born That Way*, Dr. Carlson thanked men like Herschel V. Jones and Dr. Walter Dandy, who had believed in him and made his success possible: "I have sometimes been embarrassed by being hailed as an example of what the handicapped person can do if he determines to overcome his difficulties. But what I have accomplished is really due to the help and guidance, throughout my life, of a host of teachers and friends. They kept me struggling against my difficulties and encouraged my belief that, by making the most of my opportunities, I could help other spastics to free themselves from the shackles of their handicap and to become useful citizens."[57]

Herschel Jones, sometimes anonymously, helped others in whom he saw a spark of genius. Young poet Edna St. Vincent Millay had published a few poems in *St. Nicholas*, a children's magazine, while living with her mother and sisters in Camden, Maine. Her early efforts were filled with imagery of coast and countryside. Her first acclaim came when "Renascence" was included in *The Lyric Year* in 1912; the poem brought Millay to the attention of H.V. Jones, who made it possible for her to attend Vassar. Through Herschel's financial contributions, she was able to attain a degree, and she graduated in 1917. Her poem "Renascence," full of the romantic and independent temper of youth, gave its title in 1917 to her first book, *Renascence and Other Poems*, a fitting tribute to Jones who had discovered her genius through this very poem.

On the international scene, President Wilson's determination for peace negotiations was hampered by the German decision to renew their unrestricted submarine campaign on January 9, 1917. Wilson said he was willing to negotiate practically everything but the sinking without warning of passenger and merchant ships, but Germany turned a cold cheek. Opinion in the United States was shocked by Germany's formal declaration of the submarine warfare renewal and even more so by the virtual blockade of cargoes in U.S. ports held there by fear of attack. America was infuriated by the publication of the Zimmermann Telegram that suggested a German-Mexican-Japanese alliance and a Mexican re-conquest of Texas, New Mexico, and Arizona. The sinking of the *Laconia* with the loss of American lives was the last straw as far as most Americans were concerned.

When Wilson broke relations with Germany, he received strong editorial support from newspapers across America. One of these was the *Journal*, which stated, "The American people do not want war if it can honorably be avoided; but they do not disguise to themselves the extremely critical nature of the situation, nor what may happen if Germany . . . shall wantonly tread on American rights. The American people must present a firm and united front, preferring peace with honor, but loyally supporting the Administration in whatever it may find necessary to do."[58]

Wilson could no longer resist the pressure of events and public opinion, and on April 2, he asked Congress for a declaration of war. An overwhelming majority passed his request, and on April 6, the *Journal* announced, "President Proclaims War." The United States was ill prepared for war, partly because of Wilson's reluctance to preparation, but, once in the war, he displayed outstanding leadership qualities.

Four of Minnesota's congressmen voted against the war resolution but nevertheless joined the nation with an outburst of patriotism. It was "everybody's war" as the Minnesota Commission of Public Safety declared. The commission, established by the legislature in April 1917, consisted of the governor, attorney general, and five appointed members. In so far as protection, defense, and war support, the near-dictatorial authority was empowered to do anything not in conflict with the state and federal constitutions.[59]

Colonel J.E. Nelson of the adjutant general's office later said that Minnesotans were "represented in every important engagement" and more than 126,000 Minnesota men and women saw service during the war. Among them, the army had 104,000, the navy 12,000; 2,900 served in the Marine Corps, and more than 700 nurses and others joined special services. Of these Minnesota troops, 3,480 were killed and nearly 5,000 were wounded.

As World War I neared its climax, a bitter state election was held in Minnesota. The Nonpartisan League supported the demands of the farmers. It challenged the administration of Governor J.A.A. Burnquist and threw its support to Charles A. Lindbergh. The League was accused of being Socialistic but also pro-German and hostile to the national war effort. Meetings were broken up, and the homes of League advocates smeared with yellow paint. Lindbergh faced hostile audiences, and in the end, Burnquist was re-elected.[60]

Lindbergh's campaign was heavily damaged by the publication of his book *Why Is Your Country at War*. Lindbergh had written the book to clarify his view of economics, politics, and the war, which, he felt, had been started by an inner circle of big business interests. The *Journal*, in March, quipped an article called "Nonparty Governor Candidate Author of Antiwar Book," which Lindbergh felt made him look disloyal. The Twin City newspapers called the book "a disgraceful performance," "disloyal bolshevism," "an ignominious book," and "a political mistake." On June 4, the *Journal* quipped, "O, that mine enemy would write a book."[61]

During the last year of the war, Herschel V. Jones of the *Minneapolis Journal*; Edgar Bramwell Piper of the *Oregonian* of Portland, Oregon; and Edward H. O'Hara, publisher of the *Syracuse Herald*, were among a group of several distinguished

American editors invited to visit the war fronts, both on land and sea, as guests of the Allied governments. When word circulated around Minneapolis, H.V. Jones received a letter from his old neighbor William Garland Crocker. Crocker, who lived at 1821 Colfax Avenue South, had resided across the street from Jones before the newspaperman moved to Park Avenue. "My dear old playmate," wrote Crocker, "Will you kindly put this small package in your old kit bag and take it with you to Europe? As the smoke wafts upward, please think of your old friend. Know that you still occupy a large place in my heart. Bon voyage with all good wishes and a safe return."[62]

Whatever the object sent by Crocker was is unknown, and it is also a mystery whether Jones did, in fact, carry it with him to the shores of war. It is probable that Crocker had sent Jones some kind of good-luck charm or perhaps he, himself, wanted the object returned as a souvenir from a European battlefield.

Jones, Piper, and O'Hara left for the battlefields of Europe under the protection of the British government. They spent two and one-half months in 1918 inspecting war fronts in France and Belgium. Near Arras, France, Piper and O'Hara were badly smashed up in an automobile crash. Jones, following in another automobile, rescued them, and the trio made a perilous journey alone through a war zone. The other four automobiles in the party were far ahead when the accident occurred and did not learn of it until twelve hours later.[63]

The feisty trio was in London on their way home to America on Armistice Day. "We three were regarded as inseparable, and that intimate companionship has continued in all the years between and shall now remain the richest memory in this writer's career," wrote Edward H. O'Hara years later.[64]

With its chief in London, the *Journal* beat all opposing Minneapolis newspapers to the street with an extra, only three minutes after the initial flash came through from the Associated Press. The headlines of that issue of the *Journal* bleated out, "The War Is Over," "German Empire Torn Asunder By Revolt; Hohenzollerns Fly," "Armistic Signed; Terms Announced; Fighting Stopped," "Minneapolis Gets Up in Dark to March, Sing, Cheer End of War," "U.S. Heavy Guns Join in Parting Shot at War End," "Teutonic Dispatches May Be Colored to Deceive World," "Wilson Cancels All Draft Calls; Minnesotans Go," and, of course, the big one- "Journal First with Big News."

The Journal telephoned Fire Chief Ringer, who began ringing bells throughout the city. The chimes at city hall began playing patriotic melodies and a siren above Donaldson's Department Store shrieked its way across downtown Minneapolis. Joyous crowds filled the streets to read and hear the news in the middle of the night when the armistice was announced.[65]

During the Armistice Day celebration in Minneapolis, nearly all businesses closed. The streets were scenes of parades, clanging bells, blowing horns, and screaming people. Churches held special services of thanksgiving. Not all Minnesotans, however, were part of the celebration, as many had lost sons, brothers, husbands, and fathers. And some welcomed home men injured in combat, many of whom would be handicapped for the remainder of their lives.[66]

Wilson went to the Peace Conference in Paris to fight for his peace program. This program, announced in his Fourteen Points Address of January 8, 1918, included an end to secret alliances, a settlement of colonial claims with an aim to satisfy the people involved, restitution of Belgium, the return of Alsace-Lorraine to France, autonomy for the peoples of the Austro-Hungarian and Ottoman empires, nonintervention in the Russian Civil War, and establishment of a League of Nations. The president gained only part of his objectives at the Treaty of Versailles and, after losing

Journal employee working at his desk, 1918. (Courtesy of the Minnesota Historical Society)

199

control of Congress, challenged Republicans over the treaty's ratification.[67]

For Jones, his investigation of battlefields in Europe became the first step in his national recognition. Three years later, he was elected a director of the Associated Press, replacing A.C. Weiss, former publisher of the *Duluth Herald*. Jones began the first of two terms in office during 1923.[68]

Notes

Minneapolis Journal Building, 1920. (Courtesy of the Minnesota Historical Society)

[1]John R. Bochert, David Gebhard, David Lanegran, and Judith A. Martin, *Legacy of Minneapolis Preservation Amid Change*, Bloomington, Voyageur Press, 1983, p. 66.
[2]Larry Millett, *Twin Cities Then and Now*, pp. 82-83.

[3]Ibid.

[4]Ibid.

[5]David A. Wood, "Park Avenue-Showcase of a City," *Lake Area*, Vol. 4, No. 8, September 1982, pp. 1, 24.

[6]Mrs. Sally Koether telephone interview with author, November 1, 1998; Waring Jones interview with author in Minneapolis December 4, 1998; Polk Directories City of Minneapolis.

[7]Mrs. Sally Koether interview with author, November 1, 1998.

[8]Fred Korotkin, "Postcards Show Minneapolis in the Early 1900s," *Hennepin County History*, Spring 1964, p. 28.

[9]Frances Siftar interview with author, March 3, 1999.

[10]June D. Holmquist and Sue E. Holbert, *A History Tour of 50 Twin City Landmarks*, pp. 42-43.

[11]*Minneapolis Journal*, April 10, 1900; Gertrude Gump, *The Story of Swan Johan Turnblad*, Minneapolis, The American Swedish Institute, 1969, pp. 2-3.

[12]*Minneapolis Journal*, July 25, 1900; Gertrude Gump, *The Story of Swan Johan Turnblad*, pp. 3-4.

[13]Recollections of Peter A. Cummings, Phillips Neighborhood File, Hennepin County Historical Society.

[14]Theodore C. Blegen, *Minnesota: A History of the State*, pp. 496-497.

[15]David A. Wood, "Park Avenue—Showcase of a City," *Lake Area*, Vol. 4, No. 8, September 1982, pp. 1, 24.

[16]Ibid.

[17]Ibid.

[18]Ibid.

[19]Thompson Brothers Funeral Parlor now occupies their new house, and it is the last of the great houses on Twenty-fifth Street and Park Avenue.

[20]Bradley L. Morison, *Sunlight on Your Doorstep*, p. 47.

[21]Ibid., p. 48.

[22]Metropolitan Opera House program belonging to H.V. Jones.

[23]Bradley L. Morison, *Sunlight on Your Doorstep*, pp. 48-49.

[24]"Herschel V. Jones," *The Fourth Estate*, No. 939, Saturday, February 24, 1912.

[25]*Minneapolis Journal*, Tuesday Evening, September 17, 1912.

[26]Ibid., "Farm Implement Trade Doubles in Two Months."

[27]*Minneapolis Journal*, October 15, 1912 and October 18, 1912.

[28]Meridel Le Sueur, *Crusaders, the Radical Legacy of Marian and Arthur LeSueur*, St. Paul, Minnesota Historical Society Press, 1984, pp. 22-26.

[29]Ibid, pp. xvii, 22-26.

[30]*Minneapolis Journal*, October 30, 1912.

[31]Ted Curtis Smythe, *A History of the* Minneapolis Journal, *1878-1939*, pp. 217-218.

[32]Ibid., p. 218; *Minneapolis Journal*, November 5 and 6, 1912.

[33]*Minneapolis Journal,* November 6, 1912.

[34]*Minneapolis Journal*, October 5, 1913.

[35]*Minneapolis Journal*, October 12, 1913.

[36]*Minneapolis Journal*, Sunday, November 9, 1913.

[37]*Minneapolis Journal*, Monday, November 10, 1913.

[38]*Minneapolis Journal*, Wednesday, November 12, 1913.

[39]*Minneapolis Journal*, Thursday, November 13, 1913.

[40]*Minneapolis Journal*, Sunday, November 30, 1913.

[41]*Minneapolis Journal*, August 12, 1914.

[42]Ted Curtis Smythe, *A History of the* Minneapolis Journal, *1878-1939*, pp. 232-233.

[43]*Des Moines* (Iowa) *Leader*, September 3, 1914.

[44]*Santa Barbara Press*, December 7, 1965; *Minneapolis Star*, December 7, 1965.

[45]Arnett Leslie, "Memorial to Carl Waring Jones, Minneapolis Rotary Club," January 11, 1957; *Santa Barbara Press*, date unknown.

[46]No author given, "Sinking of the *Lusitania*," *Headlines*, No. 4, December 1971, pp. 8-10.

[47]*Minneapolis Journal*, May 8, 1915 and May 15, 1915.

[48]*Minneapolis Journal*, August 20, 1915; Franklin F. Holbrook and Livia Appel, *Minnesota in the War with Germany*, St. Paul, Minnesota Historical Society, 1928, Vol. 1, pp. 25-26.

[49]Theodore C. Blegen, *Minnesota: A History of the State*, pp. 467-468.

[50]Bruce L. Larson, *Lindbergh of Minnesota*, p. 191.

[51]Earl R. Carlson, M.D., *Born That Way*, New York, The John Day Company, 1941, pp. 1-19.

[52]"Birth-Spoiled Babies," *Time Magazine*, May 30, 1932, pp. 43-44.

[53]Earl R. Carlson, M.D., *Born That Way*, pp. 1-19.

[54]Ibid., pp. 48-50.

[55]Ibid.

[56]Ibid., pp. 62-65.

[57]Ibid., p. 174.

[58]*Minneapolis Journal*, February 3, 1917.

[59]Theodore C. Blegen, *Minnesota: A History of the State*, pp. 470-474. According to Blegen, some 40,000 Minnesotans enlisted in several branches of the armed services during the war.

[60]Ibid, pp. 476-477.

[61]Bruce L. Larson, *Lindbergh of Minnesota*, p. 229.

[62]William Garland Crocker letter to H.V. Jones dated September 12, 1918.

[63]*Syracuse Herald*, Friday Evening, May 25, 1928.

[64]Ibid.

[65]*Minneapolis Journal,* November 11, 1918; Ted Curtis Smythe, *A History of the* Minneapolis Journal, *1878-1939,* pp. 234-235.

[66]Theodore C. Blegen, *Minnesota: A History of the State,* p. 475.

[67]Arthur S. Link, editor, *Woodrow Wilson: A Profile,* New York, Hill and Wang, 1968, pp. xx-xxi; Gene Smith, *When the Cheering Stopped: The Last Years of Woodrow Wilson,* New York, Time-Life Books, 1964, pp. 49-51; Robert H. Wiebe, *The Search for Order 1877-1920,* New York, Hill and Wang, 1967, pp. 280-281.

[68]Ted Curtis Smythe, *A History of the* Minneapolis Journal, *1878-1939,* p. 229; Edward C. Gale, *Herschel V. Jones.*

CHAPTER EIGHT

AMERICAN BOOKMAN

"What is a Home without a library? What
is a Library unless one lives in it?"

—A. Edward Newton

Two book dealers dominated the Minneapolis book scene during the first quarter of the twentieth century. Leonard H. Wells ran one of these dealerships, located on the main floor of Powers Department Store. Born in Oklahoma, he was called "Doc" Wells by friends and customers because he had made a living selling patent medicines out West in the late 1880s and 1890s. When Powers bought out S.E. Olson Company, Doc Wells initially became the head of the pharmacy in the store.[1]

Wells, who was not formally educated, took over the store's book department about 1895 and began selling new books. He quickly added used books and specialized in fine bindings and rare tomes. He purchased several hardbound rarities from George Bayntun, one of the fine binders of England at the time. Wells, in fact, made several buying trips to England, visiting Bayntun and other rare book dealers. He also bought artifacts including silver candle sticks, works of art, and treasured items that had belonged to George Eliot and Charles Dickens.

Wells always dressed the part and, more often than not, was formally attired in a tail coat, vest, and pince nez glasses, a real product of the Horatio Alger story. The books he sold were neatly arranged within glass door casings and the shelves were covered with velvet. Wells was a member of the Minneapolis Club, and he and his wife lived south of downtown on Blaisdell Avenue.

The other dealer in Minneapolis was Edmund D. Brooks. While Doc Wells sold both new and used books, Brooks specialized only in rare books. In 1925, six years after Brooks' death, Joseph Warren Beach, speaking at the dedication of a reading room in memory of the poet Arthur Upson at the University of Minnesota Library, referred to Brooks as "that pioneer in old and choice books, who did so much to form the taste of all of us in Minneapolis."[2]

Arthur J. Russell of the *Minneapolis Journal* once wrote of Brooks: "I watched with interest and some awe a muscular and well-dressed young bank clerk cautiously prowling . . . from old bookstore to old bookstore. I scraped an acquaintance by rubbing along the neighboring bookshelves and Mr. E.D. Brooks explained to me the why and wherefore of 'first editions,' of 'rare and valuable' books, and of 'association books,' and of 'autographed books.' For the first time I listened to the soul-warming palaver of the book-hunter and collector. During these lectures . . . Mr. Brooks sold me four first editions of Thoreau that he had concealed under his sofa. They were not the rarer ones but rare enough to start one on the downward path . . ."[3]

In 1900, Brooks opened his shop at 605 First Avenue South (now Marquette). The store was "unassuming in appearance, a dingy, dim place, dusty in summer, draughty in winter, primitive and unprepossessing. It was "sort of big and a little barnlike because his stuff didn't quite fill the shelves alongside and some glass cases."[4]

Only seven years later, Brooks moved his shop from the plain old quarters to the new Handicraft Guild Building at 89 South Tenth Street. His new shop was luxurious, one of the better book havens in the country. The center room boasted a large fireplace, over which hung a pastel portrait of Tennyson. Beautiful bookcases, some with open leaded glass doors, lined the walls. The ceiling was composed of beamed plaster. An Oriental rug covered the floor, a refectory table stood in the middle of the room, and there were other book-laden tables with straight-backed as well as rocking chairs. Brooks also had a rare book room, adjoined by a shipping room.[5]

Many wealthy and ardent book collectors bought from Brooks in the years when the titans of collecting were at work and the libraries of Europe were being ransacked for the seemingly endless American purchasing power. Some of these avid titans, steady customers of Brooks, included Henry C. Folger of the Folger Shakespeare Library of Washington, D.C., for whom Brooks obtained early Elizabethan volumes; Harry Elkins Widener, whose collection went to the Harvard College Library; John Quinn, author, art connoisseur, and defender of the freedom of the press; A. Edward Newton, author of *The Amenities of Book—Collecting and Kindred Affections* and other essay collections; Beverly Chew, who influenced numerous collectors; Frederick W. Lehmann and William K. Bixby, noted St. Louis collectors; Luther Brewer, the world's greatest collector of Leigh Hunt and his circle; George Edgar Vincent, former president of the University of Minnesota and later of the Rockefeller Foundation; and George Peavey, James Wilson Falconer, and Herschel V. Jones, renowned Minneapolis collectors.

Jones had the unique distinction of having acquired during his lifetime four notable book collections, and at least two of these were preeminently great. He was referred to as "The Miracle Man" —a title which would have delighted him—by his generation of book collectors.[6]

In his pre-collecting days, while still a young boy in New York, Jones made his first literary purchase—a copy of Tennyson's poems. Although the book had no real value, young Jones slowly added to his juvenile collection. As an adult and serious collector, he became a customer of the leading booksellers of the United States and Europe. He attended many of the important exhibitions and sales and "added rapidly and judiciously to his literary treasures."[7]

Arthur J. Rusell recalled once, just prior to Jones' book collecting "fever," that the "Chief" had walked into the office and noticed a book on a desk of one of the staff members. The book was Herman Lotze's *Microcosmos*. After Jones looked at the title page, then leafed through the book, he said, "I looked into this matter of philosophy once. Nothing in it!"[8]

But, according to Russell, Herschel soon developed an interest in books and art, especially in the former. He studied the subjects of rare books, association books, and of "odd and curious" books and visited with rare book dealers, collectors, and bibliophiles in this country and in Europe. Jones became an expert in prices and auction sales and, in a short time, an authority. His first endeavor began in the field of collecting first editions of modern authors after he had picked up a first edition of Browning's *Inn Album*. He collected about 600 volumes in this collection, which was later sold at auction.[9]

Arthur J. Russell recollected another time when Herschel came into the office for "a matter of consultation." Jones had just purchased for five hundred dollars a rare book he needed in his collection. Both Jones and Russell studied the book adoringly, but the latter was concerned more, perhaps, with the money spent for its acquisition. "A man will do almost anything for $500," thought Russell, "but he will do almost more for the book that he simply must have to fill out a gap in his collection. Without this particular book, the collection, though rare and valuable indeed, is, for the moment as nothing."[10]

Russell asked Jones if his wife was aware of the transaction. Jones said she wasn't, but as long as he thought it was right, she would offer no objection. "I burned a little incense at her shrine," Russell told himself. Jones retied the book in its brown wrapping and left the office. Russell knew Herschel was doomed. From that day on, he would be the bookseller's meat and drink.

According to the *Minneapolis Journal*, "As newspapers swung into a period of greater earnings and became more than ever before business enterprises, the *Journal* prospered to a point where Mr. Jones' hobby of book collecting could be given a freer reign and occupied more of his attention. His activities in this field in turn became an enterprise that attracted world-wide attention, though little known in Minneapolis."[11]

"There was nothing too precious that we couldn't see or touch or hold," Herschel's daughter Frances later recalled. "Father believed in living with fine things and enjoying them. You could be in his library and he would say, 'Now, I'm going to show you a nugget.'

"He would select one thing and tell you a story about it. Not a lecture, but a story so fascinating that you would never want to leave. And, yet, he was a very simple, modest man. He loved to share his collections with people."[12]

Jones particularly enjoyed humor in his art and was a staunch believer that humor existed in even the highest form of literature. In a 1913 editorial from the *Minneapolis Journal*, Jones wrote, "Humor, in the view of Tennyson, was not in consonance with the highest art. He, therefore, excluded it from his poetry almost as completely as did the humorless Wordsworth. But he was saved by his own sense of humor from some of the banalities of which his predecessor was guilty."[13]

Jones admitted that Homer, Eschylus, Vergil, Lucretius, Dante, Milton, Corneille, and Goethe were humorous, although not humorless. But, he felt, there were several great names among the real humorists, including Aristophanes, Moliere, Shakespeare, Cervantes, and Swift. "Therefore," Jones concluded, "it can't be true that humor does not enter into the highest art." He believed that Americans tended to overestimate the value of humor. Said Jones, "Great humorous master that Mark Twain was, the brother to Cervantes, he tends at times to degenerate into the mere 'comic devil,' a sort of unintellectual Mephistopheles." But he believed

Herschel V. Jones, late fifties.

that humor was not a necessary ingredient, as our two American masters, Poe and Hawthorne, had little of it.

Jones' style as a book collector has been called "eclectic, energetic, or even meandering." Doubtless, he sold more books than any of his contemporaries. The numerous books that constituted his first purchases were sold at Merwin's in 1906. Over the next decade he collected a broad spectrum of American and English literature, fifteenth-century printing, fine bindings, and manuscripts.[14]

According to Waring Jones, grandson of H.V. Jones, his grandfather loved to talk about books. "When he was lonely and wanted to talk about books, he would telephone one of the Mayo brothers in Rochester, and they would send him a letter stating it was time for his annual physical," recalled Waring. "Once he spent several days in the clinic just talking about books with the Mayos."[15]

Jones turned to incunabula and the early English poets and dramatists with vigor. In this collection, H.V. accumulated over two thousand volumes, which was easily one of the outstanding private collections in the world. Among the famed gems of the collection were a first edition of Shakespeare's *Sonnets* and a copy of Milton's *Comus* which was printed in 1637 and originally owned by John Egerton, second Earl of Bridgewater, for whom the poet wrote the masque. Also in his collection was one of the three existing copies of the 1594 edition of *The Tradgedie of Dido, Queene of Carthage,* by Marlowe and Nash; and Cicero's *Tullye of Old Age,* that Caxton printed in 1841. During the renowned third Jones sales of 1918 and 1919, this collection sold at auction for about $400,000.[16]

An article in the *Publishers' Weekly* years later referred to the successful 1918 sale: "Not since the Herschel V. Jones sale immediately following Armistice Day in 1918 has the success of a sale meant so much to those interested in rare books. In 1918 the war had just come to a close, and collectors were expecting an avalanche of rare books from war-stricken Europe from which they could buy rarities at bargain prices. It was felt quite generally that it was a bad time to sell such rare books as the Jones collection contained. But before the end of the first session the temper of the American collector was apparent. From that day until the climax was reached in the Jerome Kern sale in 1929 there never was any doubt that American buyers would pay good prices for genuine rarities."[17]

At one point, Herschel Jones was the focus of a controversial rarity argument. J.P. Collins in "In Memoriam Charles J. Sawyer," (Supplement to the *Clique Magazine,* July 11, 1931), stated that one of the late Sawyer's most important discoveries was the original manuscript that Caxton used when printing his *Chronicles of*

England, and that it went to the Herschel Jones collection. But it was also possible that the manuscript passed from Brooks to Hellman to Huntington and Collins. Some historians claimed that Collins was in error in believing the piece came from the Jones collection since the coincidence of there being two such manuscripts with such parallel histories was unlikely. Brooks had met Sawyer in one of his early trips to London.[18]

But during his book buying and selling career, Jones was frequently at the center of controversy, judging from a 1918 article in the *New York Sun*: "There was much guessing at the time of the sale of the Bridgewater Comus as to whom George D. Smith bought it for. H.V. Jones, editor of the *Minneapolis Journal*, was the fortunate person. Mr. Jones is said to be the owner of one of the finest collections of English literature in America, accumulated in a comparatively short time and so quietly that not many have known he was so engaged. It is further said that his collection exceeds in value and interest the Hagen books, which were probably the finest ever offered for sale in this country."[19]

The *Boston Evening Transcript* concurred: "That the finest copy of this work should pass into the hands of a private collector who did not care to make his identity known puzzled many of the dealers and collectors. Speculation may be at rest, however, by H.V. Jones of Minneapolis, editor of the *Minneapolis Journal*, who is the fortunate possessor of this copy. It forms one of the gems of Mr. Jones's private library of English literature, which is one of the very finest private libraries in this country, and which has been built up so quietly that few collectors are aware of its richness. As a hint of its value, it may only be stated that this library contains no less than forty of the Shakespeare quartos, a large number of early English plays of which only one or two copies are known, and practically all the great masterpieces of Elizabethan literature. The library of Winston H. Hagan, dispersed at the Anderson Galleries last season, was considered the finest of its size ever sold in this country, being chosen with unusual judgment, but the Jones library far surpasses it in interest and richness. Mr. Jones is not merely a book-collector, but a lover of books, and actually reads them."[20]

The *New York Herald Tribune* stated in 1928 that "the best known of the fine ex-Jones books are probably: the now famous copy of the first edition of Milton's *Comus*, 1637, owned originally by John Egerton, second Earl of Bridgewater, Viscount Brackley, for whom Milton wrote this 'Maske, presented at Ludlow Castle,' 1634, and to whom he probably presented this very copy. Very strange to say, it was nevertheless sold as a mere 'duplicate' in the Huntington sale of April 1918, where Mr. Jones bought it for $9,200—and sold it again in January 1919, for $14, 250."[21]

The *Herald Tribune* also praised another Jones gem, the Jolley-Utterson-Halliwell-Tite-Locker copy of Shakespeare's *Sonnets*, 1609 with its title and dedication leaves in facsimile, which sold for $10,500.

As his enthusiasm for the Elizabethans soared, his interests in the former fields of interests began to pale. He again began to collect in earnest. Jones later wrote, "It is thirty years since I purchased Browning's *The Inn Album* in first edition, and entered the line as a book buyer. I bought six hundred American first editions and sold them many years ago to make way for volumes that covered the Dickens-Thackeray period. These went in turn, because I had caught the spirit of the Elizabethan collector, and it became my desire to own a representative number of the world's great volumes."[22]

Jones said his initial plan had been to collect about two thousand books, which he would sell when he became sixty years old. "I have not quite the full number of volumes called for in my forecast and a few months are lacking in the age limit, but both volumes and years will serve."

He never intended to buy all the books of any given writer, but only the rarer tomes. He wanted his books to have a historical background, and while they were examples of fine literature, he wanted them also as examples in the development of fine binding, of printing, of illustration, and of leathers. Jones said his collection boasted a very rare Spanish manuscript from the tenth century among other precious items.

Said Jones, "My book of earliest date is Fust and Schoffer of 1460, only ten years after printing. I was able to secure several rare and notable books to cover the first fifty years' printing period, two of them presentations, one by Pannertz, the first printer of Italy, the other by Zainer, the first printer of Augsburg. There are included several volumes from Italy, the rare Serbian liturgy, examples of Spanish, Montenegrin, Russian, and Turkish, a considerable number of French and Dutch, some German and many very rare English volumes."[23]

Jones addressed many of his rarities as "monuments" and said he had acquired them from direct sources in Europe. But in his sale book, he also wanted to acknowledge the obligation to several dealers in the United States—Edmund D. Brooks, James F. Drake, Walter M. Hill, Lathrop C. Harper, A.S.W. Rosenbach, George D. Smith, W.M. Voynich, and Gabriel Wells. In selling his collection, Jones lamented, "For me the time of parting has come. I bid these volumes an affectionate farewell."[24]

Herschel wrote Theodore Roosevelt in 1902 regarding book collecting:

> You know of my love for books. I now have 350 first editions. I bought the copy of Walt Whitman's *Leaves of Grass*, 1855 edition, in New York three weeks ago at the record price of $62. I think it will sell at $180 within three years. There are only twelve copies known. I bought today a beautiful copy of Lee Casas on Spanish cruelties, published 1699, and bound by Bedford, paying $30.
>
> What I set out to discuss has to do with your books. An agent of Putnam called on me last week and offered me what was claimed to be a first edition. For the general public the edition is all right but from the standpoint of the bookman, there is little in it to attract. For myself I prefer the first editions in the original cloth.
>
> I believe that your books would sell in a limited edition of say 250 copies at $10 to $15 a volume, or even $20 maybe. I shall be pleased if you will give this a little consideration, not that you would find the profit large in such an edition, but rather that you are almost bound to give book lovers a fine edition of your works.
>
> And this leads me to say one more thing to you on this point, confidentially of course. Putnam cannot print an edition such as I refer to. To my mind, only two firms can—Houghton, Mifflin & Co. and Little, Brown & Co., both Boston. Scribner and Harper would dispute this, of course, but for some reason I have never found high-class bookmaking coming under their imprints.
>
> And now for a personal request somewhat out of the ordinary. I want you to present me with a copy of the first edition of your new book on "The Deer," [illegible]. I want it as one of many interesting autograph books that I have not to exhibit to the public.[25]

Roosevelt wrote back on March 12, 1902:

> I thank you cordially for your letter and am very glad to hear from you.
>
> Indeed you shall have a copy of my volume on deer just as soon as it comes out.[26]

Many treasures from his English collection had been sold earlier through the Anderson Galleries of New York at the huge Jones second sale, November 20, 1916, which included rare books, manuscripts, autographed letters, original drawings, and fine bindings. Among the manuscripts sold by Jones were two *Book of Hours* with beautiful miniatures; a curious manuscript of the Koran; an unpublished manuscript by William Combe, with watercolors by

Lane; and six manuscripts by William Harrison Ainsworth, including *The Tower of London, Jack Shepard,* and *Crichton.* Other pieces included the original manuscripts of *The Shadowy Waters* by William Butler Yeats and *The Waif Woman* by Robert Louis Stevenson; manuscripts by Lord Byron and Thomas Moore, and the lengthy and complete manuscript of Mark Twain's *A Curious Expreience.*[27]

Autographed letters by Charles Dickens and U.S. Grant were sold as well as a signed document by Henry of Navarre and other Protestant leaders. The *Poems of Burns,* printed in Edinburgh in 1787, containing manuscript additions by the author expressly for his friend Robert Ainslie, and a letter to him from the poet, were also sold.

Early English literature sold by Jones included first editions of Betterton, Chapman, Crowne, Dennis, Doggett, Dryden, Garrick, Otway, Prior, and Van Brugh. Other items Herschel let go were books of later writers—Lamb, Shelley, Byron, and others. Many of these rare books boasted color plates. Jones even sold a lock of Thackeray's hair. Original drawings were offered as well, among them those of Cruilshank, Leech, and Rowlandson.

Jones also sold Beverley's *Virginia,* London, 1722; Bishop's *New England Judged*; Browning's copy of White's *Middle State of Souls*; Southey's copy of the *Life of Wesley,* presented by Coleridge with many notations by the latter; and Boswell's copy of *Rutty's Diary,* to which he refers in his *Life of Johnson.*

Throughout his life, Jones embarked upon many book-buying trips to New York City. He always made it a point to visit fellow bookman Abraham Simon Wolf Rosenbach when in the city. According to authors Edwin Wolf, II, and John F. Fleming, Rosenbach had "plump pink cheeks, a twinkle in his eye, walked-as a friend once said—as a penguin would walk if a penguin could walk like Rosy, puffed everlastingly on a pipe or a cigar, drank a bottle of whisky a day, and was the greatest antiquarian bookseller the world has seen. Without much pressing he would admit as much."[28]

During Jones' first buying trips to Rosenbach's store, the newspaper owner purchased a copy of Blake's *For Children, The Gates of Paradise* for well over $5,000, as well as some rarities in English literature. Throughout 1917, Jones spent most of his New York hours in Rosenbach's rooms on Fortieth Street discussing books. When he returned to Minneapolis, he would be loaded down with books. He did not mind paying Rosenbach a profit on what the New Yorker had picked up at Huth and Huntington sales.[29]

Jones held a great deal of faith in Rosenbach and was always pleased with his purchases. Late in 1917 and the following year, he bought a copy of *The Historie of the Two Valiant Knights Sir Clyomon and Clamydes*, 1599, for $975. Jones sold the book for $1,420 eleven months later. Jones also purchased *A Pleasant Conceyted Comedie of George a Greene the Pinner of Wakefield*, 1599, for $710. He later sold the volume for $2,150.

At a 1918 sale, Rosenbach paid a record price of $10,000 on behalf of H.V. Jones for a first edition of *Much Ado About Nothing*. He paid double that amount for the same copy only seven years later.

In May 1919, Herschel stayed with the Rosenbachs at their Philadelphia home. He later wrote the Doctor, as Rosenbach was called by his friends, and asked him to put away the slippers he had forgotten in a closet for future use, for he would be a steady visitor. Regarding book transactions, he added, "You have an intelligence about your work that is appealing to one who is as sympathetic with the subject as I am."[30]

On another visit, Rosenbach invited Herschel to his home to attend a party for book collector and sometimes author Amy Lowell. Jones later recalled the dinner appreciatively, "Some dinner—some terrapin—some Amy—some cigar Amy smoked."[31]

During a visit in the spring of 1921, Herschel dropped in on his friend Rosenbach's showroom. Important men from all over the world made a habit of dropping in, and, during 1920, Rosenbach's showroom averaged about $100,000 a month. Herschel spent a happy week with Rosenbach, and when they began tearing down Jones' old stamping ground, the Manhattan Hotel, Dr. Rosenbach reminded him that he always had "a smaller and more comfortable home" at Madison Avenue.[32]

Early in the fall, Dr. Rosenbach found his relationship with H.V. Jones somewhat reversed. Rosenbach told Jones that he was in need of urgent money and asked for a note for $10,000, which he could discount. But Herschel had seen Rosenbach cry poor before, and he was certain that things were quite prosperous since the Doctor had asked for only $10,000. So he offered Rosenbach his print collection of old masters and moderns. His Zorns alone would double their value in a year and his Rembrandt "Hundred Guilder Print" was worth between $13,000 and $15,000. Rosenbach, however, would not bite.

Jones then shifted his tactics and hinted at his early English books, since he had lost interest in them. Rosenbach, however, said the deal was too big. Jones informed the Doctor that he was finishing his catalogue of them, and found it impossible to hold the amount to $100,000 without excluding some of the books he knew Rosenbach dearly wanted.

"It would be suicide for you not to make the deal because it would give you the greatest collection in the world," wrote H.V. Jones to

Rosenbach. "You can fix up F. and H. and still have a nice little bunch for the boys, including Clawson."[33] Since two large book buyers had not paid their accounts, Rosenbach balked, reluctant to go further into debt even for his friend Jones and his wonderful books.

During the first week of January 1921, Rosenbach agreed to buy some of Jones' collection if the books sold could be converted quickly into cash. Rosenbach reiterated to Jones that his business was down and conveyed for Jones' "private ear that Mr. Huntington has been quite ill during the last week, and it has worried me considerably. There are very few collectors today, and Mr. Huntington has been a great prop to the market." What he failed to whisper to Jones was that total sales for the firm that year exceeded $900,000, his best year in history.

Jones sent the Doctor eleven titles. He carefully calculated that by selling these volumes to Rosenbach for $18,700, they could be sold in turn for $29,000. But Jones grossly underestimated Rosenbach's profit. A month later, Rosenbach visited Huntington in California and sold him one of Jones' books with three rare English versions of Seneca's tragedies; one of the rarest of all early Scottish poems, Alexander Montgomerie's *The Cherry and the Slaye*, 1597; Markham's *The Famous Whore, or Noble Curtizan*, 1609; and one of the most celebrated pre-Shakespearean tragedies, Thomas Kyd's translation of *Pompey the Great*, 1595, for $20,000. All the rest was Rosenbach's gravy.

During the summer of 1921, Rosenbach wrote to Herschel and informed him that, "prices in London are steadily falling and there are bargains to be picked up if one has the courage and the money. The latter article is as rare as Folger's unique Titus. Nearly all our dear friends, the assassins," Drake, Harper, Wells, and Kenall, "are on their way to Europe." But Jones relished the reference to the assassins and wrote back, "They all have my money, and I have their books at 200 percent of present value. However, I am an optimist. After two or three years go by they will be around wanting some of Jones' books."[34]

Early in July 1923, Jones and Rosenbach had what was perhaps, their only serious disagreement. Jones sent the bookseller $20,000 towards his somewhat complicated balance with Rosenbach. Jones had been purchasing books, and against these buys, had applied through Anderson's auction, part of Rosenbach's bill for what the Doctor had bought at the Jones sale. Rosenbach thanked Jones for his check but, in a state of agitation, reminded Herschel that he still owed him $55,000. An exchange of rather cool business letters followed. In a bitter letter, Jones sarcastically stated, "I can see that I am wholly at fault. I regret that I did not realize more quickly that the days pass. I am going to tell you something. You made one mistake in dealing with Jones. Jones has his peculiarities. He has no bookkeeper on his book purchases. He has carried all this $800,000 in his mind. He has paid for these books without the dispute of a dollar with anybody. Had you got the point, as I think you should have, you would not have put in that sentence about my being unfriendly. I think I have shown my faith in you by paying you a very large part of the $800,000. And so we come to a cash basis. That will relieve you of all trouble and annoyance."[35]

Obviously hurt, the Doctor wrote Herschel that he had never expected such a letter from a friend, "a startling revelation to me written by someone whom I did not know, by a Mr. Jones whose acquaintance I have yet to make. You now propose to stab me with a rapier stained with money. This I will not permit from anyone whom I consider a friend. You say you will pay cash in the future. I do not know if you realize there will be no future if you persist in this attitude. I do not care a jot for your money or your business in comparison with your friendship. Of all the collectors I have known, this relationship has been the most intimate, the warmest, certainly the brightest."[36]

Jones explained to the Doctor that he should have just asked for a larger payment instead of sending a "sharp dun." Jones continued by saying, "Which brings me to your statement wherein you do not care for my money or my business in comparison with my friendship. That strikes the chord. Therefore, I will not try to injure the 'pleasant relations of all these years.' I have felt the intimacy that existed between us, because that intimacy brought from you the closest and most sacred confidences, which is the test. Not for the world would I say anything to wound you. All through the years I have had from you unfailing courtesy and the most kindly consideration. Your loyalty has been expressed many times in the book room. I know it, and you know it, and it is that very quality in you, which is not commercial, but natural to you, that has given you the great success you now enjoy. And so we will leave matters until my next visit, when we will both decide not to discuss this further. There is no reason to discuss it further. You and I are friends."[37]

The matter ended on July 31st with a note from Rosenbach that read, "Enough said!"

At the end of the year, Jones, his old self again, visited Rosenbach, hoping to sell him three items left out of a recent sale. "I assume you want them, and I shall charge you a good price, but one that I think you can scalp ten thousand off from, more or less," Jones told Rosenbach. "As you have scalped me so long and so frequently it will do no harm if you don't have much scalping room left for this."

Herschel jokingly asked the Doctor if he was the Rosenbach he had seen a picture of in the *New York Times*, referred to as "the largest buyer of books in England and other countries." If so, he wanted the title of the book Rosenbach was holding as he considered buying it from him. Said Jones, "I have always wanted to own a book that this Rosenbach I have mentioned has owned."

Rosenbach laughed and told Herschel his was the 8,416th request he had had, but if Jones would send a certified check on a rep-

Herschel V. Jones in his mid-sixties.

utable bank in the amount of $2.35, he would sell him the book. Rosenbach offered him a copy of the Declaration of Independence for $165,000, but instead Jones purchased $30,000 worth of Americana.

A third collection put together by H.V. Jones was in the field of general literature. Jones collected a library of some three thousand books, many of which were rare first editions. But Jones was still buying Elizabethan volumes, although this time with a very select list.

When Herschel reached the conclusion that he wanted to sell his Elizabethan collection, he wrote Rosenbach and offered him a list of titles to present to Huntington. The Doctor took some of the tomes to sell to Folger, and although Jones questioned the decision, he left it to the expert. Jones began removing the Elizabethans from his shelves and filling them with Americana.

"Kindly look through that secret drawer in Philly and send me a little approval package," wrote H.V. Jones to Dr. Rosenbach. "You were kind to me in New York when you gave me the Joel Palmer. That consideration covers a multitude of sins on your part."[39]

Jones also wrote Mitchell Kennerley, president of the Anderson Galleries on October 1, 1922: "After the disposal, four years ago, of my library of English literature, I proceeded to collect one hundred rare Elizabethan books, with accompanying minor but important volumes, for the sole purpose of giving me comfort in the time of bereavement over the loss of my friends.

"Instead of their proving a comfort, I find myself miserable in being compelled to face the impossibility of collecting another English library."

"I shall be happier with none than with the few. Therefore, I am sending them to you for disposal." Jones received $137,865 for the sale of his collection.[40]

One of the three known copies of *The Tragdie of Dido, Queene of Carthage*, by Christopher Marlowe and Thomas Nash, printed in 1594, was purchased by Dr. A.S.W. Rosenbach for $12,900. This play was considered to be the most important with the exception of Shakespeare's own ever offered for sale. Other purchases by Dr. Rosenbach from the Jones Collection were a first edition of *Amoretti and Epithalamion*, by Edmund Spencer for $8,600; a Caxton Press edition of *Tullye of Old Age*; *Tullis de Amicicia*, by Marcus Tullius Cicero, for $5, 850; a superlative copy of the rare first edition of the only print of Shakespeare's poems made during the seventeenth century, for $4,800; a first edition of *The Tritameron of Loue* by Robert Greene, for $3,200; a probable first issue of the first edition of *A Most Excellent Comedie of Alexander, Campaspe and Diogenese* by John Lyly, for $4,300; a rare issue of

Sapho and Phao, by John Lyly, for $3,450; and *Midas* by the same author for $2,100. In all, Rosenbach bought scores of works in the "above $1,000" range from the Jones collection.[41]

Following the sale, an article in *The Bibliographer* stated, "Knowing Mr. Jones, we are inclined to think that even after this sale he will not try to get along without books and as he still has the prospect of many years of life before him, he will again be seen in the bookshops where rare things are sold, and be represented at the great auctions."

And, indeed, they were correct for Jones then devoted his attention and dollars to a fourth collection, this one consisting of Americana. In less than six years, while much of the time in ill health, H.V. purchased some seventeen hundred volumes, largely original first editions, covering a four-hundred-year period from Columbus to the Klondike.[42]

Jones, undoubtedly, focused on very rare, quality items. Doctor Rosenbach described an original manuscript signed by the Emperor Charles V, wherein Hernando Cortes, Adelantado of the Indies, was appointed Knight of the Order of Santiago. "Today this magnificent document is in the collection of my dear friend, Mr. H.V. Jones, in Minneapolis," wrote Dr. Rosenbach. "Mr. Jones in a surprisingly short time has formed one of the finest libraries of books relating to this country."[43]

An article in *The Bookman* stated, "In the conversations between New York dealers, regarding this latest collection formed by Mr. Jones, the uppermost question was, 'How did he do it?' Nearly all the leading dealers had sold one or more rare books to Mr. Jones, but many are still wondering where all these rarities came from and how Mr. Jones managed to get them before other collectors had a chance. For, while there are weak spots—books of no great importance which reflected Mr. Jones's personal likings—the number of great rarities is such that when it is sold, as it probably will be, there will be another dispersal which will long be known as 'the Jones Americana sale.'"[44]

The article cautioned those dealers and collectors who pointed to Jones as a commercial type of collector. Jones, it said, was a "shrewd and courageous" buyer who bought books for the character of his collection and not for probable profit. He had bought and sold Conrads before the Conrad cult had even started. He purchased many cheap Eugene Fields editions, because he knew and liked Fields. He collected Bret Harte and Joaquin Miller because they reflected the West he knew, and he bought George Bernard Shaw because he found him stimulating and amusing.

"These were not the kind of books that the purely commercial collector would buy to sell again, ten years ago," the article continued. "But in the exercise of his collecting faculty this 'miracle man' had the same vision which made him successful in his newspaper business, and which built the Northwest. He had vision."[45]

During an evening visit to Rosenbach's showroom, Jones and the Doctor sat contentedly talking books. One of Rosenbach's book salesmen, Harry Hymes, however, continuously showed the *Journal* owner filler books he needed for his Western collection. Handing Jones a book, he asked, "What do you think it is worth?" Jones replied, "About five dollars." Crossing the room, Hymes told the Doctor that Jones said the book wasn't worth more than five dollars. The Doctor answered, "Hell, then let him have it for that." Jones remarked to one of the staff that the book was marked sixty-five dollars. He was told to let the five dollars figure stand; the firm could take a joke, too.[46]

Rosenbach's good friends spent a great deal of time at his home, especially in his personal library. The room was almost filled by a long refectory table, and there was room for only three or four persons to sit. In this room with the perennial bottle of whisky on the table, the Doctor spent long evenings with Lawrence Wroth, Clarence Brigham, Bill Elkins, Randolph Adams, and Herschel Jones.

In 1925, Dr. Rosenbach purchased the original manuscript of Norman Douglas' *South Wind*, which he almost immediately sold to Jones. On Christmas Day, Herschel returned the book with a note: "A Christmas remembrance for my friend of thirty years, A. S.W. Rosenbach—In business he adds fifty, but he repays in kindness manyfold. This little gift expresses my appreciation. May the 'South Wind' blow gently many years for both of us."[47]

Shortly thereafter, Herschel purchased the little quarto volume of Holford's American tracts that were broken out and enshrined in Morocco. Jones paid $48,670 for eight of them and a few other less spectacular items.[48]

When Rosenbach stopped in Minneapolis to visit Jones, the Doctor was asked for his advice. Herschel wondered if it was time for him to sell his Americana collection. Rosenbach was horrified and told him he would not advise it. When the Doctor returned home, he wrote Jones that one more purchase would give him "a halo of commercialism." When Jones went East to spend Thanksgiving with the Rosenbachs, the Doctor convinced him that the only thing to do with a great collection was to add to it. Jones went home with manuscript rarities for which he paid $14,850.[49]

But Jones could give advice as well as take it. During the spring of 1924, Rosenbach wrote his friend that he was ill. Herschel responded with a lecture: "I cannot help reaching the conclusion that there has been too frequent hooch in the latter months. You are not built for it; your system does not need alcohol. I trust your doctor agrees with this view."[50]

Just prior to Herschel's death he supervised the preparation of a deluxe catalogue in two volumes of about three hundred of the most valuable of these books. The venture was entitled *Adventures in Americana, 1492-1897: The Romance of Voyage and Discovery from Spain to the Indies, the Spanish Main and North America; inland to the Ohio Country; on towards the Mississippi; through to California; over Chilkoot Pass to the Gold Fields of Alaska.* The cataloguing was performed by Miss Helen Fagg under the advice of Dr. Eames of the New York Public Library who contributed a brief introduction. The two-quarto-volumed edition, printed by William Edwin Rudge of New York, had its title page designed by Bruce Rogers. Limited to two hundred copies, it was "a beautiful piece of book-making." This collection comprises, perhaps, the most notable private collection of Americana in the United States.[51]

In his preface to the catalogue, Dr. Eames touches upon the scope of Herschel Jones' collection: "The three hundred pictures of title pages which illustrate this catalogue give a good idea of what a remarkable collection of seventeen hundred volumes the owner has succeeded in bringing together in less than half a dozen years. The full period of American exploration is covered by original or contemporary publications, in chronological order, for about three hundred and seventy-five years, from the beginning by Columbus and Vespucci to the gold diggers of California, the Great West and Alaska."[52]

According to the *New York Times Book Review*, there were only four more lines to Dr. Eames' preface. "As a matter of fact," said the *Times*, "the entire text of the catalogue is a somewhat reticent or laconic affair. This will come as a distinct relief to those who have suffered from the all too expansive bibliographers whose passion for fine points or enthusiasm for their own notes, has encumbered their pages and added to the difficulties of the embattled collector. And, after all, what really could one say that has not already been said about this array of well-known and well-documented books?"[53]

The article referred to Jones' "dim days of book collecting" some fifteen years earlier when he owned one of the great "small" libraries of English literature which he had sold to the Anderson Galleries in 1917. The *Times* then stated that, "no sooner was it dispersed than he began, heart-brokenly, we think, to gather up the pieces. For Mr. Jones was an ardent collector, and books he had to have. The stepchild did not, however, thrive so well; it suffered chiefly from malnutrition. For the books Mr. Jones had sold yester-year were no longer to be had—certainly not at the old prices—and after he had collected 200 or so, he renounced his ambition to form another library of English rarities and in 1923 sold what he had so slowly and painfully acquired. But Mr. Jones, ever a zealous collec-tor, renewed his allegiance to the flag and set out after Americana."[54]

There were several other collectors looking for the same items as Jones, but despite the competition, he succeeded in gathering a library of rare Americana never before equaled. The *Times* described his Americana treasures: "Take the Church and Brown catalogues, the B.A.V., Sabin (to Smith, since one can go no further), mix with some 'uniques,' add a dash of Cowan, Medina, and Wagner, stir these ingredients thoroughly, skim off the cream and there you have a taste of the Jones library. Any thoughtful examination of the cata-logue will show that this is hardly an exaggeration. For of the 10,000 possibilities of books that treat of America, Mr. Jones has shown a nice understanding of what ones are really meritorious."[55]

The *New York Herald Tribune* praised the Jones collection and catalogue as well: "If there ever was an *embarras de richesses* in an American catalogue it is here presented, beyond doubt. Nearly every item seems to require mention even in the present general notice, and our original list of very special items would alone fill far more than our entire space today. So after all we can only select a few typical books merely as characteristic specimens. And must then let it go at that, for the present at least."[56]

The *Herald Tribune* disagreed with the *Times* over the length of Wilberforce Eames' preface. While the *Times* had praised the brevity of the preface as a "relief" to collectors, the *Herald Tribune* felt the opposite would have been more effective. Referring to Dr. Eames' piece, the *Herald Tribune* wrote, "This is certainly the real truth, but we should have greatly appreciated much more of it from the same most authoritative source."[57]

The Americana collection can be divided roughly into three groups, according to Lathrop C. Harper who had examined the Jones Americana Library: The Discovery Period and Early Voyages, 1492-1608; the Early Settlement, including wars and relations with the Indians, 1608-1784; and the Exploration and Settlement of the West, 1784-1898.[58]

In the Discovery Period, Jones owned three of the printed letters of Christopher Columbus"—the Rome Latin edition, the Strassburg German edition, and the illustrated version printed at Basle in 1494. The epistle written by Columbus aboard the *Nina*, which he ad-dressed to Gabriel Sanchez, the Royal Treasurer of Spain, is the second issue of a first edition known as the Fernandi and Helisabet, a translation from the Spanish into Latin. Another of the books bearing upon Columbus and his expeditions was written by his illegitimate son, Fernando, who accompanied him on his fourth voyage and, upon returning to Spain, gathered together books and manuscripts called the *Biblioteca Coulmbina*.

The three printed letters of Columbus had been purchased from Rosenbach, who had written Jones about them. Herschel wrote Rosenbach the following day, "On receipt of your letter yesterday, I note the suggestion 'if I decide to purchase.' Good Godfrey! I thought I had purchased them. The price (it was $63,000) sounds big, but what can I say? . . . I cannot spare these books. Of course, I do not ever expect to pay for them, but that would not be of any interest to you."[59]

Rosenbach recalled the Strassburg German edition he sold to Herschel: "The Germans enhanced their edition with one of the most amusing woodcuts I have ever seen. It is a picture of the King of Spain and Columbus, who seems to be explaining their great achievement (doubtless as an offering) to Jesus Christ." Rosenbach went on to point out that, until recently, only six copies of it were known to exist. During a visit to an old friend's library in the west of England, he discovered two more copies. "One is now in the collection of that great lover and connoisseur of books, Mr. Grenville Kane, of Tuxedo Park, New York, who is now the doyen of American collectors; the other is cherished by my old friend Mr. H.V. Jones.[60]

Herschel also had collected three of the printed letters of Americus Vespuccius printed in 1503 and 1504. The second of these pieces is a Latin translation of the *Mondus Novus*, upon which is based the information about his voyage. This is addressed to to his Florentine patron, Lorenzo di Piero Francesco de' Medici, and was printed in Paris.[61]

Other Jones gems included a commentary by Johannes Gloveniensis on a work by a noted English mathematician and geographer, John Holywood, printed in Cracow in 1506—the first piece of Americana to be printed in Poland. Another important work was the collection of initial voyages by Francanzio da Montalboddo, including Columbus' first three voyages and the third of Vespucci's. Another rarity was Martin Fernandez de Enciso's account of the West Indies and part of the American coast. This piece was printed for the instruction of Charles V and in the Jones copy showed a deletion ordered by the Spanish Inquisition, in a conversation among the Cenu chieftains, who declared, "the pope must have been drunk and the King was an idiot."

He also owned *Cosmoggraphia Introductio*, a little book printed at St. Die in 1507, which was the first tome to suggest the new continent be called America, as well as *Globus Mundi*, Strassburg 1509, the first book in which the name America was really used. Other rarities in Jones' collection included the *Peter Maryr*, 1511, the first book on the history of America; the *Enciso Oviedo*, 1535, the first history of America written by one who had been there; the *Hernando Cortez*, 1524, the first Latin edition of his earliest letter; the *Gomara*, 1522; the *Pre-Columbians—the Solinus*, 1473 and the *Ptolemy* of 1482, and several Mexican and South American rarities.

Jones also owned the first book in English relating mostly to America—Eden's *Treatyse of the New India*—which was published in London in 1553. Only two other copies of this book were known to exist, one of these in America at the Brown Library. Jones' pre-settlement English volumes included an English translation by Thomas Hacket of Andre Thevet, printed by the translator in London in 1568, the first book to contain reference to Canada. The lavishly bordered title page described the subject matter as "The new found worlde, or Antarctike, wherein is contained wonderful and strange things, as well of human creatures, as Beastes, Fishes, Foules, and Serpents, Trees, Plants, Mines of Golde and Silver: garnished with many learned authorites."[62]

Others were *Frobisher's Voyage*, 1577; the English *Cartier's New France*, 1580, and the English edition of *Hariot's Virginia*, 1590, printed at Frankfort by De Bry. There were also 111 volumes of the De Bry Voyages in various versions and different languages. H.V. also owned a fine copy of the 1589 first edition and 1599 second edition by Hakluyt of *Virginia Richly Valued*—a treatise by a Portuguese on the country south of Virginia. Other early English voyages included Drake's *West Indian Voyage*, 1589, by Captain Walter Briggs and his alleged lieutenant, Master Crofts; and *The Verie Two Eyes of New England Historie*—Brereton (1602) and the *Rosier* (1603). John Brereton had accompanied the original party of Englishmen who landed with settler intentions on the New England coast and hailed as the "north part of Virginia." James Rosier's account of Captain George Waymouth's voyage to Maine first aroused English interest in that part of the New England coast. Jones also owned John Nicholl's *Houre Glass of Indian Newes*—"Or a true and tragicall discourse, shewing the most lamentable miseries and distressed Calamities indured by 67 Englishmen, which were sent for a supply to the planting in Guina in the yeare, 1605. Who not finding the saide place, were for want of victuall, left a-shore in St. Lucia, an Island of Caniballs, or Men-eaters in the West Indyes, under the Conduct of Captain Sen-Johns, of all which said number, only 11 are supposed to be still living, whereof 4 are lately returned into England." Besides Jones' copy, only four existed.[63]

Among other early works of American exploration were the *Descriptio ac Delineatio Geographica Detectionis Freti*, edited by eminent Dutch cartographer Hessel Gerritsz and printed in Amsterdam in 1612, which describes Henry Hudson's voyage to discover the Northwest Passage; the observations of Sir Richard Hawkins, who made the first known voyage to the Guinea coast for blacks and bestows curious information regarding the Florida Indians; and *The Strange and Dangerous Voyage of Captaine Thomas James in his intended Discovery of the Borthwest Passage into the South Sea*.

The Settlement Period consisted of Captain John Smith's *True Relations*, 1608, only one of two copies in private hands of the first book on America's first permanent settlement. Several volumes of *Virginia Tracts*, 1609-1650, were part of the rare collection as were two books by Thomas Hughes, 1615 and 1621, Captain John Smith's *History of Virginia*, 1625, and Brooke's *Massacre in Virginia*, 1622 (the only known copy). Among other rare New England antiquities were Wood's *New England Prospect*, and works by Levett, Peckham, and Mason.

William Penn's copy of a map of the New Netherlands, New England, and part of Virginia, was also in Herschel Jones' valuable collection. Engraved by Nicholas Visscher about 1651, and having on its back, in Penn's handwriting, the following message: "The map by which the privy Council 1685-[168]8 settled the Bounds between the Lord Baltimore and I, & Maryland & Pennsylvania & Territorys or annexed counties.—W.P." In Penn's own handwriting also were ink drawings where those boundaries were.

An interesting book, the first in English relating to New York, was published in London in 1653. This piece of "propaganda" was entitled, *The Second Part of the Tragedy of Amboyna; or, a True Relation of a Most Bloody, Treacherous, and Cruel Design of the Dutch in the New Netherlands in America. For the total Ruining and Murdering of the English Colonies in New England*. This work focused upon an alleged Dutch plot to massacre English colonists in the manner of the East Indies massacre of 1624.

Jones also counted as precious two letters by Dr. John Mitchell of the proceedings in regard to Captain Kidd. The Earl of Bellemont financed most of Kidd's expeditions against pirates, and the author, a kinsman of the earl, attempted to prove the unfairness of Kidd's trial.

Herschel V. Jones owned several works on English colonization in America by Robert Johnson, Thomas West (Baron De La Warr), Alexander Whitaker, Ralphe Hamor, and Lewis Hughes, the first gentleman appointed to Bermuda, where he was sent by the

Virginia Company in 1612. Hughes' Letter was regarded as one of the rarest early books on Virginia."

Jones was not lacking in his New England Indian Wars with rarities by Underhill (1638), Hubbard, Mather, Mason, and Penhallow, and a complete set of the folio King Philip War Tracts, printed in London in 1675. His series of Indian Captivities was highlighted by the first London edition of Mary Rowlandson, 1682—the first account of a captivity to see print. Other masterpieces included the first issue of the *Nehemiah How Captivity*, 1748, and the *Norton's Redeemed Captive, John Williams*.

Herschel had at one time purchased the entire book collection of Henry R. Wagner with Spanish titles relating to the Southwest. He also had accumulated rarities relating to all the colonies, including the Southern states.

As to the eighteenth century, Jones owned an original Williamsburg edition of Washington's *Journal to the French Forces on the Ohio*, 1754, written when he was but nineteen years old. This journal included the governor's letter and a translation of the French officer's reply. This treasured piece is considered by many experts to be the most desirable piece of Americana, and Jones' copy was one of only six in existence. Herschel also had collected numerous Indian treaties and other rare Indian narratives of that historical period.

Of Benjamin Franklin press rarities, Herschel possessed *Cicero's Cato Major, or his Discourse of Old-Age: with Explanatory Notes*, published in Philadelphia in 1744. This book was considered "the finest production of Franklin's press and perhaps the finest eighteenth century printing in America." Franklin's own written piece, *A Narrative of the Late Massacres, in Lancaster County, of a Number of Indians, Friends of this Province by Persons Unknown. With Some Observations on the Same*, also reposed in the Jones collection. The book was printed in 1764 by Armbruster of Philadelphia. The "unknown persons" were the Paxton Boys, and this massacre assumed a political importance.

Another historical gem was an account in Portuguese of the English expedition against Louisburg, which opened the door to Canada and the Great West. Printed in Lisbon in 1758, the volume's title page presented a curious picture of the siege. The book was not recorded in any bibliography of Americana. Another work, totally unknown to bibliographers until 1902 when a copy was found in a volume of miscellaneous pamphlets in the Library of Congress, was a poem entitled "The American Village" by Philip Freneau. The poem was a parody of Goldsmith's "Deserted Village" and written by Freneau at the age of twenty. Jones also owned a 1776 Isaac Pinto translation, which was the earliest Jewish prayer book published in New York and probably, the first in America.

A rare aeronautics book by J. Pollard Blanchard was not mentioned in any of the Americana bibliographies. Published by Charles Cist in Philadelphia, the engraved frontispiece depicted the author in a balloon waving an American flag. Below in both French and English read: "45th Ascention and the first made in America, January 9, 1793, at Philadelphia 39 degrees 56' N. Latitude by J. P. Blanchard."

Other Americana items included a Mexican publication, *Estracto de Noticias del Puerto de Monterrey, etc.*, 1770, the earliest printed account of Spain's occupation of Northern California; Walter Marshall McGill's *The Western World: A Poem, Founded on the Facts Recorded of the Revolutionary War*, which was dedicated to General Jackson; *Life and Adventures of Timothy Murphy, the Benefactor of Schoharie*, 1839, about the life of a famous Indian scout; *The Emigrant's Guide to California and Oregon*, by James Johns, one of the earliest writings on the Overland route; John R. St. Johns' *A True Description of Lake Superior County*; *The Oregon Almanac for 1848*, believed to be the first almanac printed on the Pacific coast north of Mexico; the extremely rare *The Latter-Day Saints' Emigrants Guide*; *The Thrilling, Startling and Wonderful Narrative* of Lieutenant E.J. Harrison who had been taken prisoner by Mexicans in Texas in 1836; a very rare imprint of the Constitution of the State of California; D.F. Read's *Journey to the Gold Diggins By Jeremiah Saddlebags*; the only known copy of Joaquin Miller's *Specimens*; and the frist edition of Ernest Ingersoll's *Golden Alaska*, with its pictorial colored cover.

He owned, too, a wealth of material on the Middle West and the Mississippi River, such as Thevenot's *Voyages*, 1682, with the first map of the river. Early and rare editions of Father Hennepin's works and a unique copy of Wild's *Mississippi Scenery*, St. Louis, 1841, adorned his shelves. But Jones was also fascinated by the Far West, the Gold Rush, and the settlement and development of the new states there, which prompted him to buy the first three weeks on the settlement of California by the Spaniards in 1770. His overland narratives and early guides included most of the rarities, among them *Pattie*, 1831; Zenas Leonard: John James' *Journal* in manuscript; Edwards' *Oregon*, Joel Palmer; Johnson and Winter; and Clayton's *Mormon Guide*. He owned as well several volumes on the Gold Rush from 1848 on, such as Hastings, Duganne, Harrison, Wierzbicki (the first book printed at San Francisco), McNeil, Aldrich, Miles, John Wood (only three known), and others.

An outstanding rarity from Jones' collection was John Filson's Wilmington edition of the life of George Washington and the Philadelphia edition of a map. Filson had given copies to Daniel Boone that had become a part of the Robert Hoe Library until purchased by Jones.[64]

Harper declared the collection the finest of Americana in private hands. He based his decision on the fact that Jones owned many rarities not found in older collections, such as John Carter Brown Library, Lenox, Huntington, Ayer, and Clements. Harper wrote on July 1, 1929, "It is a great monument to the unerring judgment, courage, persistence and 'collector's luck' of Herschel V. Jones, the most beloved, and also the most astute collector of our time."[65]

The New York Times Book Review stated, "There can be no question that a great collection has been gathered here. If there be any doubts on the subject, one could go on to select even at random, from the balance of the chronology, a sufficiently impressive number of prize books to make most Americanists gnash their teeth with envy." In summing up the Americana collection, the *Times* concluded, "In short, the Jones collection may be regarded as one in which one would hardly miss a Bay Psalm Book or a Columbus autograph."[66]

While the family was faced with settling the estate upon H.V. Jones' demise, Carl, the collector's son, in a special arrangement, sold the entire Americana library for the bargain price of $225,000 to A.S.W. Rosenbach. The Jones Library was well known to many avid collectors like Everitt DeGolyer, Everett D. Graff, Thomas W. Streeter, and Herbert S. Auerbach, and, almost overnight, they became Rosenbach customers. Jones' books, realistically, sold themselves.[67]

Another source indicates the entire Americana library was not sold to Rosenbach. A few items, according to Sotheby & Company, were sold to H.E. Widener, John Carter Brown, Henry E. Huntington, and other specialist libraries.[68]

James Ford Bell of Minneapolis, whose collection of literature in commerce and trade grace a special library named in his honor at the University of Minnesota, looked to Herschel V. Jones as a role model. It was Jones, with help from Rosenbach, who once talked Bell into specializing in Americana. Impressed with the books of his book mentor, Bell could think of no one but Herschel as "the" collector, and whenever he talked of an example to follow, it was always Jones of whom he spoke. Bell also became a good friend of Herschel's son, Carl Jones, after they became neighbors on "the lake."[69]

While Bell looked to Herschel as someone to emulate, he always wondered why Jones had not kept his books and given them to an institution like the University of Minnesota instead of letting them be dispersed after his death. Bell could just not fathom why, and while he held Herschel in esteem as a great collector and the bookman to emulate, he felt his mentor had deviated through dispersal of his library. According to Jack Parker, the Bell Library's first curator, a position he held for thirty-seven years, [Bell] "thought Herschel was a great collector but someone who didn't do the right thing."

During the period 1920 to 1929, H.V. Jones was the biggest collector in town, and James Ford Bell would soon become heir to that title. Herschel, however, set an example as a collector that is still bearing fruit, because, through Bell's emulation, the James Ford Bell Library is now a world-class library.

The New York Times, upon Herschel's death, published a fitting memorial in regard to Herschel's life as a bookman: "A friendship with President Roosevelt that began when Mr. Jones was a reporter 'covering' the 1900 national campaign, first aroused Mr. Jones's keen interest in the literature of the 'Wild West' and led to his gathering a collection of books and diaries of pioneer days. Eventually he branched out into the broader field of general Americana and formed one of the famous libraries of this type. He collected in all four libraries and sold three of them. The second brought $391,854 at an average of $226.11 per lot; which George H. Sargent, the book expert, pronounced the highest average ever reached in the history of book auctions. The sale of his third library, which consisted of Elizabethan items, took place at the Anderson Galleries in 1923. It realized $137,865."[70]

The *Minneapolis Star* also took a Wild West approach to Herschel's early collecting: "His close friendship with the late Theodore Roosevelt was directly responsible for the creation of a library of 'Wild West' stories. Mr. Jones 'covered' Mr. Roosevelt's northwest campaign for election as vice president on the ticket with William McKinley. While on the tour the late president and Mr. Jones found their tastes for the 'Deadwood Dick' style of literature to be parallel. Then began Mr. Jones' quest for diaries and other accounts which dealt with the pioneer West. He gradually built up a great collection of the covered wagon literature."[71]

The *Minneapolis Tribune* paid their respect in citing Jones' magnificent manuscript collection with special attention devoted to those of Mark Twain and Bret Harte. The article went on to state that "his interest in books grew, however, to include volumes of all phases of American life, and with this growing interest, his library expanded in size. During the latter years of his life he brought together a collection of Americana that has become famous among book collectors, this library being the crowning achievement of his book-collecting hobby." The article also described his earlier libraries of English books and Elizabethan literature.[72]

Jones' own newspaper stated, "As a bibliophile he exhibited the same qualities of judgment, integrity and daring that he showed as a publisher—the same, indeed, as had brought him world-wide fame in an earlier period of his newspaper life as a crop forecaster. He sought and bought his book treasures with an insight that was registered in high figures, when his collections in later years were put up at auction."[73]

In a lengthy article about Jones and his collections in the *International Studio*, Uffington Valentine said in conclusion: "In a library of this kind almost every volume has its own personal biography, which is something like the story of the 'private life' of some great artist as compared to his public career."[74]

Jones, undoubtedly, had realized his second youthful dream—becoming the owner of a great library. But he not always made purchases for the mere spirit of gain. He was fond of his books, regarding them almost as living things, and he often collected in a field where there was little general interest, and, therefore, no expectation of monetary gain. Herschel had become a life member of the Minnesota Historical Society in 1904 and, in 1921, a member of the executive council. Upon his death, he left twenty-five thousand dollars to the society "for the purchase of books, pamphlets, and manuscripts relating to subjects, individuals and events having a bearing upon the history and development of Minnesota." His gift became the largest the Minnesota Historical Society had ever received.

Jones once remarked in a magazine interview during 1924: "There have been only two serious objects in life for me: One was to own a newspaper in a large city; the other was to build up a library. I have accomplished both these objects."[75]

Notes

[1] J. Harold Kittleson interview with author January 13, 1999, Minneapolis, Minnesota.

[2] Ruth Shepard Phelps, editor and compiler, *The Arthur Upson Room, The Four Addresses on the Occasion of its Opening, 21 February, 1925, and a List of the Books in the Room*, Minneapolis, 1928, p. 10.

[3] A.J. Russell, *Fourth Street*, p. 95.

[4] John Alden Bradford, *Books: the Shop and the Man*, Minneapolis, not dated; Lee Edmonds Grove, *Of Brooks & Books*, Minneapolis, the University of Minnesota Press, 1945, p. 7.

[5]Lee Edmonds Grove, *Of Brooks & Books*, pp. 12-14.

[6]*The Bookman*, "The Book Mart," August 1928, p. 27.

[7]Sale Catalogue, "Rare Books from the Library of H.V. Jones of Minneapolis, Minn., to be sold Monday Afternoon and Evening November 20, 1916."

[8]A.J. Russell, *Goodbye Newspaper Row*, p. 18.

[9]Edward C. Gale, *Herschel V. Jones*.

[10]A.J. Russell, *Goodbye Newspaper Row*, pp. 51-52.

[11]*Minneapolis Journal*, Sunday, May 27, 1928.

[12]Barbara Flanagan, *The Minneapolis Star*, Tuesday, December 10, 1968; Frances and Alfred Siftar interview with author March 3, 1999, Edina, Minnesota.

[13]*Minneapolis Journal*, Sunday, November 30, 1913.

[14]Donald C. Dickinson, *Dictionary of American Book Collectors*, New York, Greenwood Press, 1986, pp. 183-184.

[15]Waring Jones interview with author, February 17, 1999.

[16]Uffington Valentine, "A Notable Adventure in Americana," *International Studio*, October 1928, p. 45.

[17]Frederick M. Hopkins, "Old and Rare Books," *The Publishers' Weekly: The American Book Trade Journal*, No. 7, February 13, 1932, p. 781.

[18]Lee Edmonds Grove, *Of Brooks & Books*, p. 20.

[19]*New York Sun*, Books and the Book World, "The Bridgewater Comus," Sunday, September 1, 1918.

[20]*Boston Evening Transcript*, "The Bibliographer," August 14, 1918.

[21]Leonard L. Mackall, "Jones Americana Nuggets," *New York Herald Tribune Books*, Notes for Bibliophiles, Sunday, May 27, 1928.

[22]Sale Catalogue, "The Library of Herschel V. Jones to be sold Monday and Tuesday Afternoons and Evenings, December Second and Third [1918] at 2:30 and 8:15."

[23]Ibid.

[24]Ibid.

[25]H.V. Jones letter to Theodore Roosevelt, dated February 3, 1902. Courtesy of the Library of Congress.

[26]President Theodore Roosevelt letter to H.V. Jones, dated May 12, 1902. Courtesy of the Library of Congress.

[27]Sale Catalogue, "Rare Books from the Library of H.V. Jones of Minneapolis, Minn., to be sold Monday Afternoon and Evening, November 20, 1916"; *The American*, November 12, 1916. The latter source announced that the sale was of "especial interest and allure for the collectors of manuscripts."

[28]Edwin Wolf II with John F. Fleming, *Rosenbach: A Biography*,

Cleveland and New York, The World Publishing Company, 1960, frontispiece.

[29]Ibid., pp. 104-108.

[30]Ibid., p. 115.

[31]Ibid., p. 123.

[32]Ibid., pp. 139-144.

[33]The "F" and "H" stood for Henry Folger and Henry Huntington.

[34]Edwin Wolf II with John F. Fleming, *Rosenbach: A Biography*, p. 146.

[35]Ibid., pp. 182-183.

[36]Ibid.

[37]Ibid., pp. 183-184.

[38]Ibid., p. 193.

[39]Ibid., p. 150.

[40]Sale Catalogue, "The Later Library of Herschel V. Jones to be Sold Tuesday Evening January Twenty-Third, 1923, at eight-fifteen"; Donald C. Dickinson, *Dictionary of American Book Collectors*, p. 184.

[41]*New York Herald*, Wednesday, January 24, 1923; *New York Times*, January 24, 1923; *Minneapolis Tribune*, January 24, 1923.

[42]Lathrop C. Harper, "The Americana Library of Herschel V. Jones," *Herschel V. Jones*, no page numbers given.

[43]A.S.W. Rosenbach, *Books and Bidders: The Adventures of a Bibliophile*, Boston, Little, Brown & Company, 1927, pp. 268-269.

[44]*The Bookman*, The Book Mart, August 1928, pp. 28-29.

[45]Ibid.

[46]Edwin Wolf II with John F. Fleming, *Rosenbach: A Biography*, pp. 239-246.

[47]Ibid., p. 191.

[48]Ibid., pp. 233-234.

[49]Ibid., p. 257.

[50]Ibid., p. 205.

[51]Lathrop C. Harper, "The Americana Library of Herschel V. Jones," *Herschel V. Jones*; Uffinton Valentine, "A Notable Adventure in Americana," *International Studio*, October 1928, pp. 45-47.

[52]Ibid.

[53]"Notes on Rare Books," *The New York Times Book Review*, May 20, 1928.

[54]Ibid.

[55]Ibid.

[56]Leonard L. Mackall, "Jones Americana Nuggets," *New York Herald Tribune Books: Notes for Bibliophiles*, Sunday, May 27, 1928.

[57]Ibid.

[58]Jones also owned many fundamental items that fell in none of the above categories but were co-relative to them.

[59]Edwin Wolf II with John F. Fleming, *Rosenbach: A Biography*, pp. 254-255.

[60]A.S.W. Rosenbach, *Books and Bidders: The Adventures of a Bibliophile*, p. 272.

[61]Leonard L. Mackall, "Jones Americana Nuggets," *New York Herald Tribune Books: Notes for Bibliophiles,* Sunday, May 27, 1928.

[62]Uffinton Valentine, "The American Library of Herschel V. Jones, " *International Studio*, October 1928, p. 47-51.

[63]Ibid; Lathrop C. Harper, "The American Library of Herschel V. Jones," *Herschel V. Jones*.

[64]R.C. Ballard Thruston, "Filson's History and Map of Kentucky," *The Filson Club History Quarterly*, Vol. 8, No. 1, January 1934, pp. 12, 24.

[65]Lathrop C. Harper, "The American Library of Herschel V. Jones," *Herschel V. Jones*.

[66]"Notes on Rare Books," *The New York Times Book Review*, May 20, 1928.

[67]Donald C. Dickinson, *Dictionary of American Book Collectors*, p. 184; *Important Incunabula and Early Printed Books from the Library of the Late Herschel V. Jones, Minneapolis*, 1947.

[68]*Americana Catalogue of Valuable Printed Books, Autograph Letters, Historical Documents and Relics*, Sotheby & Company, 1957.

[69]Jack Parker, interview with author, February 1, 1999, Minneapolis.

[70]*The New York Times*, May 25, 1928.

[71]*Minneapolis Star*, May 24, 1928.

[72]*Minneapolis Tribune*, May 24, 1928.

[73]*Minneapolis Journal*, May 24, 1928.

[74]Uffington Valentine, "A Notable Adventure in Americana," *International Studio*, October 1928, p. 51.

[75]Edward C. Gale, *Herschel V. Jones*.

[76]James H. McCullough, "What a Youngster Learned from His Grandfather's Newspaper," *The American*, January, 1924, p. 74.

CHAPTER NINE

LUCRETIA AND THE ARTS

"A great etching by a great etcher is a great work of art displayed on a small piece of paper, expressed with the fewest vital, indispensable lines, of the most personable character; an impression, a true impression of something seen, something felt by the etcher, something that means a great deal to him, which can be expressed only by etching, something he hopes someone may understand and care for, as he, the artist does-for it is all his own work-and if not, well, it does not matter; he pulls a few proofs, knowing them to be good, he smashes the plate, feeling like a murderer . . ."

—Joseph Pennell

Art presented in black and white on paper was once believed to hold little interest for avid museum patrons. That myth was soon shattered when the public began attending great exhibitions of drawings here in America and in Europe. In no way competing with painting or sculpture, drawings have been a means of understanding these arts by exposing the creative impulses thoroughly hidden in a highly completed colored work. Many artists have selected the print medium to give birth to inner visions, which could not be expressed in any other form of medium. Rembrandt committed a form of artistic heresy when he executed his two most monumental plates, *The Three Crosses*, 1653, and *Christ Presented to the People*, 1655, in dry point, undoubtedly, the most expressive and colorful, but also the "most fugitive of all media on copper." In other plates, Rembrandt used dry point in addition to the more durable form of etching. The proper balance between the two was upset after only a few etchings were printed. Rembrandt, Durer, and others printed their own plates beyond the point where they would create perfect impressions, and later generations have continued to print from the worn plates. Thus, prints can be enjoyed in only early impressions of high quality.[1]

Condition of the paper is an important element in the quality of prints. The natural tone of the paper "is an integral part of the tonal scale, even the finest impression is ruined once the paper has lost its freshness." Old papers were well made but were frequently ruined by exposure to moisture, sunlight, or chemically active modern mat boards. But in certain instances, where quality of impression and condition go hand in hand, numerous works of art appear as fresh as the day they were printed despite the passing of several centuries. One needs only compare Rembrandt's famous etching *Arnold Tholinx* with his rather faded painting of the same sitter.

Art became popular in Minnesota. Theodore J. Richardson, an art teacher in Minneapolis, had established the Society of Fine Arts in 1883, with President William Watts Folwell of the University of Minnesota as a promoter. Three years later, artist Douglas Volk was appointed president of its art school. Many famous Minnesota artists received their basic training here, including Alexis J. Fournier, Adolf Dehn, Wanda Gág, Gilbert Fletcher, and John Flanagan. In 1893, German-born Robert Koehler came to Minneapolis, and a year later, he was made director of the school of fine arts. In 1911, Koehler led the way to the establishment of the Minneapolis Institute of Arts as an outgrowth of the Society of Fine Arts.[2]

The Minneapolis Institute of Arts was built between 1913 and 1915, facing Fair Oaks, the home of William D. Washburn. In those years, imperial Roman buildings were considered proper for structures of culture. The New York firm of McKim, Mead and White designed the institute with a "forbidding flight of steps" leading up to the entrance and the "expectable classical portico announced that the visitor was now entering the Church of Art, and the rotunda within either frightened him off entirely or reassured him that all was well, that the vulgar outside world was walled out. More monumental staircases and galleries with exceedingly high ceilings and poor lighting in the interior have been the despair of curators.[3]

Young Minnesota artist Wanda Gág, her brother, and sisters submitted drawings, stories, poems, and cartoons to various magazines and the *Minneapolis Journal*. The *Journal* had a Saturday supplement called *Journal Junior* slanted towards younger readers. That publication, Wanda Gág later recalled, "encouraged the creative efforts of grammar and high school students by actually paying for accepted material, and I immediately deluged them with my work." Gág earned more than $100, most of which came from the pink-paged supplement.[4]

When Wanda Gág was between the ages of fifteen to eighteen, her work appeared often in the *Journal*. Mae Harris Anson, editor of the *Journal Junior*, invited her to submit a series with text and illustrations for ten issues and offered the youngster fifty dollars for the project. From May 2 to July 4, 1909, Gág's "Robby Bobby in Mother Gooseland" graced the pages of the *Journal*.

When Arthur J. Russell became *Journal Junior* editor, he wrote Wanda Gág, wanting to lend her his copy of *Phantastes: A Fairy Story for Men and Women*, which he claimed to have read 500 times. The novel, written by George MacDonald when he was thirty-four, was published in 1858 and is considered to be by some the first imaginary-world novel. *Phantastes* was regarded as a serious attempt to describe the world of dreams and was followed by an even more important novel—*Lilith*. Russell wrote Gág, saying that if she "got it," she "got it;" if she didn't, she didn't, and it would mean that she did not have fairy blood in her as her drawings indicated. Russell also told Wanda that if she ever came to Minneapolis, he wanted to meet her personally.[5]

Wanda found the MacDonald fantasy a "queer book." It was full of mental pictures, music, and thoughts that appealed to her very much, and she was fascinated by the element of "delectable surprise." Russell told her to come by the *Journal* and bring some of her work with her. During their meeting, she was impressed by him because he did not go through "useless preliminaries" in getting acquainted. She later said they took each other from "where we were not where we seemed." Russell told her, "I can see through you, just as you can see through me."[6]

Russell paced back and forth, and he reiterated that a telephone was such an "impersonal thing." He asked her if she enjoyed poetry, and when she answered in the affirmative, he gave her a poem to read. She was, however, more interested in watching Russell, whom she described as a slight man of medium build with "queer ways." She admired his frankness.

Russell looked over the drawings she had brought with her, and he seemed to like them very much. He was especially interested in a pencil-sketched self-portrait that she called "Calm and Myself." He also picked out a drawing of a little girl standing in front of flowers and trees. Russell said he wanted to show these two pieces to Herschel V. Jones. He walked into H.V.'s office several times but Jones was busy.

Herschel V. Jones, late fifties.

Russell asked Wanda about her position at Buckbee Mears as a commercial artist. She replied that her employer liked her art but only as long as it was profitable to the firm. She said she hated keeping her originality in check. Russell advised her to never marry a man who "does not move in your world" and that there were people who would respond to her and her art.

Russell left for a minute and returned with H.V. Jones. Wanda was shocked when Herschel became very enthusiastic over her

238

drawings. She had always thought that editors were immovable and fancy, but here was Herschel Jones "jumping up and down with enthusiasm" as he looked at her art. Jones asked her what kind of work she was doing and she told him about Buckbee Mears.

Jones asked, "How much are they giving you a week?" She told him she was being paid five dollars a week. Jones turned around and looked at Russell and "they both gave a sort of snort." According to Wanda Gág, it was a "Listen to that!" sort of snort. Then Jones asked her if she would like to attend art school in Minneapolis with all expenses paid. Wanda replied, "Well of course I want badly to go to school again, but it's this way. You see we all draw, and there are six younger than I who will soon need educations in order to get that out of them what is in them, and I want as soon as possible to be in a position to earn the money which will be necessary for that." Jones told her he would look into the matter.[7]

A few days later, Wanda received a special delivery letter from Herschel Jones. The letter said that he was giving her instruction at the Minneapolis School of Art, all expenses paid, room and board included. The lessons and room and board, according to Herschel's letter, were "already engaged."

Again, Mr. Jones shocked Wanda Gág. He had talked to her for only about five minutes and looked at only eight or ten of her sketches, and it seemed "impossible that he should take me up on such scanty proof of my abilities."

Wanda stopped by the *Journal* to see Mr. Russell. He told her the room engaged for her was in the Woman's Boarding Home, which was in charge of the Y.W.C.A. This house on Tenth Street had been bequeathed as a home for girls by millionaire William H. Dunwoody. When Wanda attempted to thank Mr. Russell, he told her that she was to express her thanks personally to Mr. Jones because he was the one that had done everything for her.

He took her into Jones' office and left. Wanda recalled that she could not control her quaking knees. She thanked Herschel profusely and added, "I know I can do something worthwhile if I want to. That isn't arrogance; it's a feeling inside of me." He replied that this was the way it should be and asked her when she had thought of "all those things." She told him she had always thought that way. Herschel said abruptly, "Well, are you coming?"

She answered shyly that since she had come to the city from New Ulm, some people in St. Paul had been the first to help her on her way and, in a sense, they had first claim upon her. Jones popped out with, "We accepted your first work, didn't we?" She reminded herself that Jones was right. She reminded herself that she had made over $200 from the *Journal* and could not have gotten through high school without the newspaper's help. And, of course, that was before St. Paul had ever heard of her.

Jones smiled and said, "You'd better come. I'm the best friend you've got. When I start a thing I put it through. If your work merits it, we will see that you go East where you will have a good chance to get in the magazine field and so be able to help your sisters."

When she left his office, she rushed to Arthur Russell and told him what Herschel had said. Russell told her that Herschel had good pull with the magazine people in the East and simply being in the good graces of such a man meant much. She accepted Jones' offer and registered at the Minneapolis School of Art on December 11, 1914.[8]

A few days later, she returned to the *Journal* to see H.V. Jones. She was again, "a trifle shaky in the knees." Wanda began her conversation by telling Jones how she was getting along, when he suddenly asked her if she were ready to accept his help. Jones said he wanted to put things "on a basis" and told her to come back on Saturday.

When she returned on Saturday, Wanda was greeted with a friendly "hello" from Herschel. She liked his approach because he did not attempt to act business-like. He told her he was giving her an allowance of two dollars per week. She had been living on five dollars a week and the additional two dollars could be spent as she pleased. Jones also informed her he had opened a charge account for her at an art store for her art school materials. From that day forth, she always referred to Herschel as "her *Journal* man." Without his financial help over the years, she perhaps would not have had the opportunity to attend art school.[9]

In January the school moved from its quarters in the Minneapolis Public Library to the new building of the Minneapolis Institute of Arts. Wanda was so impressed with the great works of art around her that she spent hours studying the paintings on exhibit.

Herschel Jones needed to push her along at times because Wanda Gág could work only when she was in a drawing mood. "Life without a drawing mood is miserable, miserable, miserable," she wrote. "But when one comes and takes hold of me (it will make me miss meals and sit up all night because I have to draw, and make me forget to be polite to people because I am so enraptured by the things I see), I become done to a frazzle. My drawing mood puts me completely under its power."[10]

It took someone like H.V. Jones—"my *Journal* man"—to take hold of her and make certain her drawing mood stayed with her most of the time.

Wanda's final entry in her diary (undated) read, "My *Journal* man wrote and said that he had a room reserved at the Studio Club in New York for me. Happy, gee—"[11]

Millions of Cats, Gág's most popular book, sold over 10,000 copies in its first three months during January 1929. There was even a hassle over money when the farmer woman who contributed the cats to be drawn discovered they were Gág's models. She felt she deserved a profit from the book. *Millions of Cats* sold more than two copies per hour for every business hour the publisher had been in business. Unfortunately, Herschel V. Jones, Wanda's "*Journal* man," died shortly before it was published.[12]

It is not surprising that Jones turned his attention to the field of art, and although his interest was no less marked than his rare book collecting, it was less known. He acquired his first print in October of 1915 while visiting New York with his daughter Tessie. This was a wise purchase for the print was a superb impression of Hans Sebald Beham's, *Virgin and Child with a Parrot*. Herschel had already been collecting books, and this print purchase started him collecting art.[13]

In entering the field, Jones sought professional advice from Miss Marie Lehrs, the Minneapolis Institute of Art's first curator of the Department of Prints and Drawings, and with many dealers and museum personnel throughout the country. He purchased the majority of his prints from the Keppel Gallery and Knoedler & Company in New York, working with both Frederick Keppel and FitzRoy Carrington, the head of the print department at Knoedler's and a renowned scholar. FitzRoy Carrington first worked at Keppel Galleries in New York where he helped to place many of the prints in the Ladd Collection. Carrington was also the editor of *The Print-Collector's Quarterly* from its inception in 1911 until he passed over the reigns to Campbell Dodgson in 1921 (the journal did cease production during the war). Even after Dodgson took over as the main editor, Carrington remained as the American editor for two years. In 1912 Carrington left Keppel and went to the Museum of Fine Arts in Boston where he became the curator of Prints and Drawings on March 1, 1913. He resigned from his post in Boston in 1921 and became the head of the old master print department at Knoedler Gallery through the 1930s. In 1916 when the Ladd Collection was on the market, Carrington was in Boston. He hounded Herschel and was instrumental in placing it in Minneapolis and in keeping the collection together rather than seeing it sold off in parts. Carrington knew how important a print collection could be to a museum from his experience in Boston and wanted these works to stay together.[14] Herschel also bought from Arthur Hahlo & Company in New York, The Bresler Company in Milwaukee, and the Albert Roullier Gallery in Chicago.

Jones began by putting together a collection of modern etchings from the 1917 auction of Ladd prints held at the American Art Association in New York. He had become a trustee of the Minneapolis Institute of Arts and was influential in shaping its policies, especially in the acquisition of paintings. It was his belief that the institute should obtain great and outstanding pieces of art, whenever possible, and it was under his "dictatorship" that the institute acquired Titian's famous "The Temptation of Christ." The cost of this piece was $300,000, very high for that period. While many of Jones' associates balked at the purchase, the piece soon became one of the institute's most valuable possessions. According to one of his reporters at the *Journal*, Jones was a "benevolently bullying dictator . . . who made its trustees and benefactors buy what he thought should be bought, whether they liked it or not." But he also gave the institute financial support, a much-needed publicity, and gifts of prints.[15]

Through the *Minneapolis Journal*, Herschel gave the institute a great deal of free publicity. The *Journal*'s Sunday magazine, written in Minneapolis and printed by rotogravure in Chicago, contained many reproductions of the institute's famous paintings and prints in nearly every issue. The campaign for erecting a new building on grounds donated to the society was also given much publicity in the pages of the *Journal*.[16]

Jones also promised the Art Institute there would be a reporter from the *Journal* "whose entire time would be given to art news." When Eugene J. Carpenter, vice-president in charge of the institute's finance committee, selected a blue-ribbon advisory panel of sixty-eight members, Jones printed the names in the *Journal*. These members represented every line of activity in Minneapolis, and their common objective was to procure a new building for the institute. He deliberately printed William Hood Dunwoody, president of Washburn Crosby Company, first on the list. Dunwoody's support was crucial, of course, since he was one of the wealthiest and most respected businessmen in the state. Dunwoody was also the spokesman for the powerful milling fraternity.[17]

Jones made certain that headline after headline trumpeted the virtue of sister cities that patronized the arts: "St. Louis Museum Built by Public," "Denver's Museum Broad in Scope," "Detroit Invests Millions for Art," "Boston's Temple of Art Represents Outlay of Million and a Half," and "Worcester Boasts Fine Art Museum." The publicity campaign cleared the way for a gala banquet at the Minneapolis Club, January 10, 1911.

When the Art Institute was formally dedicated on January 7, 1915, in the city's main assembly hall of the Minneapolis Auditorium, Jones was there. The Minneapolis Symphony Orchestra performed Richard Strauss' *Festival Prelude*, and the society's newly elected president, John R. Van Derlip spoke from the podium. George E. Vincent, president of the University of Minnesota, delivered the keynote address and informed the capacity audience that the Art Institute "is our protection against provincialism, and an influence for metropolitanism."

James J. Hill followed Mr. Vincent to the podium, and at the conclusion of his speech, warned the audience to "make your standard high and try to live to it. This institute is to pitch the key. Do not pitch the key too low."[18]

Following Hill's remarks, congratulatory speeches were given by Metropolitan Museum of Art Director Edward Robinson, Minnesota Governor Winfield Scott Hammond, and Minneapolis Mayor Wallace G. Nye. The Minneapolis Symphony concluded the program with the "Star Spangled Banner."

That same evening, three thousand people attended a formal reception at the Minneapolis Institute of Arts and viewed a private showing of the Inaugural Exhibition. One lady wrote later in her diary that "silks and satins and throats glide[d] by us" at the "glittering" affair.

Jones wrote in the *Journal* the following day that the opening was "one of the most brilliant social events of the winter." He also issued a warning to the Society's board of trustees, of which he was a member: "Art is not just something attractive in a stone building where it can be visited and tea served now and then by 'the better classes.' . . . The Art Institute is for the people to make the fullest use of and to protect from false friends, if they ever arise, who would monopolize it or make it 'exclusive.'"[19]

On the first Saturday of the Inaugural Exhibition, over 12,000 visitors packed the galleries, setting a single-day attendance record for any museum outside of New York City. Herschel wrote in the *Journal* that "comparatively few automobiles were drawn up before the institute, most of the visitors being of the unpretentious sort who walk or ride streetcars. The widespread appeal of the project was manifest in the number of just plain folks who came to see and study."[20]

Soon after, the Art Institute's director, Joseph H. Breck, told Paul J. Sachs, assistant director of the Fogg Art Museum in Cambridge that he had no money in his budget for additional purchases. He also explained to Sachs, however, that he was encouraged by the fact that "one of our trustees is showing an interest in prints and has just acquired three superb examples, [including] a remarkably fine example of Durer's *St. Jerome in His Study*." That trustee was H.V. Jones.

As chairman of the Committee of Museum Development, Herschel wrote one of his early reports to the trustees of the Minneapolis Society of Fine Arts. In his three-page report, he began:

> With January first next, we shall have completed our first five years in our new Minneapolis Institute of Arts. The building, the inauguration of work there, the management, plan, and operation of the institute have been most gratifying. We can feel that a beginning has been made unusually auspicious and successful. For the past two years, it has been felt that a somewhat conservative policy has been desirable, and a practice of careful economy followed. The war is over, and we turn from the practices of war to the practices of peace. Upon those who have the guidance of its destinies, who have assumed the voluntary burden of projecting and carrying through to fruition its policies, falls the responsibility of now proceeding with the plans so wisely laid by its founders. No one thing is more clearly indicated than that the education, both industrial and liberal, must be developed. In such work the Society has a legitimate and important part to play. A sound and proud policy must govern our thought and action, that in its attainment those of a generation hence can truthfully say, "They have builded wisely and well." This is, preeminently, the time for energetic and incisive action that the Institute may be in the forefront in support of all that is wholesome and best in Art in its largest sense.

The well-written piece sounded very much like many of Jones' editorials in the *Journal*.[21]

H.V. Jones was less concerned with administrative detail than with long-range planning. It was his responsibility to prepare a twenty-five-year plan for the Art Institute's growth. Jones realized that the postwar mood of Minneapolis was not congenial to large-scale civic improvement, and his hopes for an extensive orchestra hall addition in the near future would not reach fruition. Jones and his committee, therefore, recommended that the society build, on a smaller scale than originally planned, its own auditorium space to fulfill "its educational, cultural, and social" obligations.[22]

In allocating funds for paintings, Herschel advised the trustees to concentrate on the acquisitions of a few Old Masters. Jones felt that there were several important examples available at moderate prices. Jones' interest in Old Masters was mirrored by his own print collection, which focussed upon the works of Durer, van Leyden, and Rembrandt. Following his own advice to the trustees, Jones continued buying several works of arts of the Old Masters,

George M. Adams, the *Journal*'s managing editor, wrote years after Herschel's death, "[Jones] used to make periodic trips to New York for the sole purpose of adding books and art to his great collections. He would take a suite in a hotel and every day would find him at some book or art store, relaxed and enthused over the search for new items, entirely detached from business."[23]

Late in Jones' life, he was intensely interested in art, especially etchings. Over an eleven-year period, he had been the anonymous donor of a collection of prints worth between $600,000 and $700,000 to the Minneapolis Institute of Arts. This collection consisted of 5,852 separate pieces of art and represented the entire spectrum of the graphic arts history. The gift, reputed to be the finest private collection of etchings by the old masters, in the United States, constituted the largest single donation of works of art ever made to the Art Institute, according to Russell A. Plimpton, director. It was also considered one of the greatest donations ever made in this field to any American art museum past or present.[24]

"Any endeavor to list the great number of important items in the Jones Gift," stated the Art Institute's bulletin, "would be futile in the limited space afforded in this bulletin. Nothing but a catalogue of considerate proportions would do it adequate justice. We must, therefore, confine ourselves to a brief account of its history, and a mere suggestion of the recent additions to the original anonymous donation which have made it a collection of which the Institute and the city of Minneapolis may well be proud. For it now ranks as one of the outstanding collections in America."[25]

According to the *Minneapolis Journal*, which carried news of the gift on its front page, "Many of the items are exceedingly rare, existing in only a few scattered copies. Many have never been exhibited in Minneapolis, but an extensive exhibition of prints from the gift soon will be displayed at the institute."[26] The *Journal* article said Jones had donated two additions to his Ladd Collection, in June 1926 and January 1928, which were valued at more than $120,000. He did so to "fill in the gaps" of the earlier masters. Only twelve years after Jones had purchased the Ladd for $225,000, its worth had more than tripled.

At the Art Institute, the collection became known as the "Herschel V. Jones Gift of Prints." Included in the collection, was the work of 674 artists, almost the entire known work of some of them. The bulk of these prints were acquired by Jones in 1916 when he purchased the famous collection of William M. Ladd of Portland, Oregon, a collection known for its richness in modern masters. About a dozen of the group were duplicates from the Albertina Museum in Vienna, and a few others were duplicates of collections in the British Museum. Among the outstanding pieces in the collection were Rembrandt's "Christ Healing the Sick," often known as the "Hundred Guilder Print." It was so nicknamed because the amount was so high. Others included an anonymous print of the fifteenth century; "Christ Crowned," "The Standard Bearer," by Urs Graf; four rare Martin Schongauer "Wise and Foolish Virgins," and a fine impression of Lucas Van Leyden's "Head of Maxmilian," the earliest known example of etching and engraving combined.[27]

There were 199 engravings and a complete set of woodcuts by Durer—"The Life of the Holy Virgin," in a complete first edition with the Latin text. Most of the series were made in 1503 and 1504, the final plates dating about 1510. This set was especially rare because, although the number of copies Durer published were considerable, it is seldom that complete books are found, since collectors in the past adopted the practice of tearing out and mounting single leaves.

It is believed that the piracy of this series was the occasion for Durer's visit to Venice in 1505, when, seventeen of the twenty blocks had been prepared for publication and already issued in separate copies. Durer soon discovered that Marcantonio Raimondi had engraved them on copper line for line and published them without the slightest compunction. Durer then instigated suit against Raimondi before the Signoria, although no record of it exists in the Venetian archives.

The collection boasted two of the so-called "dotted prints," which form a group far apart from the product of their contemporaries. It is believed that these were first produced about the middle of the fifteenth century. But they went out of fashion near its close, and nothing quite like them ever appeared again. Thus, they were of the greatest rarity.

There were also 108 etchings by Whistler, thirty-eight by Charles Meryon, and 245 by Seymour Haden. The group also included 122 prints by Turner, 157 by Millet, and 242 by Jacque, as well as 136 engravings by Nanteuil, 145 by Lepere, and 129 by Legros. Among the earlier masters, who made comparatively few plates, were forty-eight Van Leydens, nineteen Aldegraevers, eighteen Van Meckenems—including "St. Agatha" and "Two Wild Men Jousting," fourteen Schongauers, thirteen Burgkmairs, including four plates from the "Seven Virtues," eleven Behams, three Glockentons—one of which being the much heralded "Christ on the Cross," and two Mantagnas.

Virtually all important print makers were represented, including Bocholt's "St. Matthew" and "St. John." Of the former, only eight impressions were then listed by Lehrs in his catalogue, and of the latter only five. Zasinger was represented with seven examples, including the "St. Barabara" and the "Beheading of St. Catherine." Several others highlighted the collection, from Holbein and Duvet, of the fifteenth and sixteenth century masters through the middle centuries with Rembrandt, Claude Lorrain, and Tiepolo, to the moderns with Turner, Whistler, Cameron, and various others.

The outstanding items of the fifteenth century Italian group were highlighted by a leaf from a block book with references to "De Civitate Dei" by St. Augustine, a Zoan Andrea, "Christ before Pilare," partially colored by hand, three Jacopo de' Barbari, a Brescia, and three Campagnola.

In the collection of sixteenth century Dutch masters were forty-eight Lucas van Leyden, Durer's contemporary, including his masterpiece, the "Portrait of Maximilian" and Vellert's "St. Bernard."

Marcantonio Raimondi, the noted engraver of Raphael's works, was represented by "St. Cecilia," "Dance of the Cupids," and "David and Goliath."

According to the bulletin, "There are many others, too numerous to mention, among the older masters and some exceedingly rare moderns. In the latter class, suffice it to single out four lithographed portraits by Ingres printed on one sheet, of the utmost rarity. They are doubly noteworthy as wholly characteristic of this great artist, and as being among the earliest examples of artistic lithography produced in any country."

Jones' acquisition of the Ladd Collection is an interesting story. When he learned from private dealers that the collection was up for sale, he arranged to have it shipped to the Art Institute for Breck's inspection. When the Ladd prints arrived at the museum in January 1916, Breck immediately brought in FitzRoy Carrington, curator of prints at the Boston Museum of Fine Arts and one of the leading authorities in the field.

"My old firm, Messrs. Frederick Keppel & Company sold to Mr. Ladd the greater part of his collection," Carrington wrote Breck. "I have, therefore, not only a personal knowledge of it, but a keen personal interest in its welfare, and its being made a source of inspiration to the public. . . . [The Ladd Collection is] a 'plum' of unusual importance, [and], if you were to secure it what a proud Director you should be!"[28]

Carrington arrived in Minneapolis in March 1916 to talk over the collection with Breck. The main obstacle was the purchase price of nearly a quarter of a million dollars, which would affect the society's acquisition funds for years to come. Herschel Jones, however, was adamant that the collection should remain in Minneapolis, and he agreed to finance the entire purchase as an anonymous donation. When Jones acquired the Ladd Collection of prints, he did donate it anonymously to the institute. The remainder of his collection was added over the next nine years in eight separate gifts. Jones asked that his gifts be kept anonymous until shortly before his death.

The trustees and Society of Fine Arts were, of course, deeply grateful, and one of them declared: "Be it resolved, therefore, that this testimonial be spread upon the records of the society as renewed expression to the donor of the deep appreciation of the trustees, and, as we feel assured, on the part of the entire community—of his great gift and of the vision, the idealism and the large generosity which prompted it:'That the gift be recorded and hereafter known as The Herschel V. Jones Gift of Prints; that the name of Herschel V. Jones be recorded as a benefactor of the society, and that a copy of this resolution be forwarded to Mr. Jones.'"

The bulletin emphasized that very few of the additions had ever been exhibited at the Institute of Art. Two hundred prints, however, had just opened in the Print Gallery and three adjoining galleries on the third floor. The museum had made no attempt to showcase one man's work or arrange the prints in historical sequence, which had been the practice with its regular exhibitions. "The aim in this case," promised the bulletin, "will be to present as many as possible of the new acquisitions which have never been shown before, and to give an idea of the wide scope of the Jones Gift. Only thus can some conception of the value and beauty of this remarkable collection be given."[29]

Another bulletin called the Jones Gift of Prints, "undoubtedly the most important single gift of objects of art the museum has ever received, is well-nigh inexhaustible in its riches, and will provide new material for exhibition and study for many years to come."[30]

This Jones collection was written up in *International Studio* shortly after his death: "Although the versatile Herschel V. Jones, editor and publisher of the *Minneapolis Journal* and the first man to predict wheat yields by a personal inspection of the fields, did not live to inspect the exhibition of his notable gift of prints to the Minneapolis Institute of Art, the Minnesota gallery may now boast of one of the finest print collections treasured in America.

"As an avocation he began to collect rare books and gradually became interested in old prints. Twelve years ago he acquired the William M. Ladd collection. The Portland [Oregon] collector had amassed no fewer than five thousand etchings, engravings, woodcuts, and lithographs, the majority by masters of the nineteenth century. These Mr. Jones presented anonymously to the Minneapolis institution. But Herschel V. Jones was ambitious to complete this history of the graphic arts. In the following decade he added eight different groups, the most important of which were contributed in 1926. This gift includes works of the earliest known engravers." The article went on to list many of these famous works.[31]

The Minneapolis Institute of Arts put together an exhibition of the H.V. Jones etchings that covered five centuries of work. The exhibit began at almost the earliest point where etchings existed as an art form. It is unknown when exactly etchings were first used and who saw them as an art form. Etching was original used by goldsmiths and armorers for decorating their wares. The practice of taking impressions from these etched incisions on metal did not begin until about 1500, not long after engraved incisions were being used as a duplicative art. Between 1515 and 1518, Albrecht

Herschel V. Jones, in his fifties.

Durer experimented with the medium and produced six etchings on iron. In the Art Institute's Jones exhibition, two of these. "Christ in the Garden," 1515, and "The Cannon," 1518, were showcased.[32]

Durer made only six etchings in his lifetime and his immediate followers made only a few. But Durer's followers worked in other styles, breaking away gradually from the attempt to etch form by use of a variety of hatching and parallels. The development grew toward the sketch in which simple lines, usually outlines, suggested form. Altdorfer, Hirschvogel, and Lautensack, whose work was also exhibited in the Jones showing, left large portions of their plates unetched. This revealed the effect of careful pen drawings done for the sake of reporting visual impressions of landscape and city scene.

Etching was almost abandoned in the eighteenth century. When it was used at all, it was mostly as a facsimile medium. But etching returned with new vigor in the early nineteenth century, and with this revival, inking came to have a greater importance than ever. Mary Cassatt's "Little Girl in a Big Coat," shown in the Jones exhibit, revealed to what extent inking could be relied upon. Rebiting, too, was more extensively used for gaining contrasts of thick and thin lines.

But etching was rescued from its false attempt to secure tone in the 1830s and 1840s by the Barbizon School. Attention turned to its real forte, line. Charles E. Jacque was the most prolific of the Barbizon etchers and made etching his chief work. But Millet, in his fine and dignified study of two men digging, showed the power and mystery inherent in a highly simplified form of technique. Several artists such as Haden, Meryon, and Zorn, contributed to the renewed interest in etching. All together fifty-five etchings, representing the efforts of forty artists, were included in the Jones exhibit.

In January 1918, Jones lent some of his precious works to a New York exhibition. The *New York World* announced the event: "The coming loan exhibition of the Museum of French Art in its gallery at No. 599 Fifth Avenue for the benefit of the building fund promises to be of a unique character, especially in what is to be shown of the early Gothic period. Specimens of the time are rare, and the committee on exhibitions have been fortunate in securing early carvings and other objects that have been found by lovers of the arts of France."[33]

Herschel, this same year, was interested in the works of Peter de Hooch. He picked up a German art magazine and had a de Hooch article translated into English. Perhaps it was because of his admiration of Wilhelm Von Bode, the author of the article. Jones kept the typed translation in the book *Zeitschrift Fur Bildendekunst*. The article, important to Jones, reads:

Now Peter de Hooch appears before us in a new form and manner in a pair of recently discovered pictures. One of the last acquisitions that Karl Von Hollctacher had made before he sold his entire collection was a cleanly painted view of a Dutch courtyard between red bricks with a servant girl. This picture has been known as being by Q. Brekelenkan and had been offered to Mr. Von Hollctacher as such for the price of 20,000 marks but was refused by him. (I may give away the secret and establish the amusing anecdote of the art business.) However, as he had fallen in love with the picture, he reconsidered the purchase of it. In the meantime, however, the dealer came to the conclusion that the picture was not by Brekelenkan but by no one less than P. de Hooch, consequently he raised his price to five times the original amount and Mr. Hollctacher bought it. A few years later it was sold for double.

In his strong local color of the almost painful, faithfulness and smooth cleanliness with which all the detail is carried out in the even light, cool daylight, it was difficult to recognize P. de Hooch either in the work of his classic period or of his youth as we had studied him. Consequently it seemed at that time (before this article) that the Brekelenkan attribution had been the correct one.[34]

Not all of Herschel's etchings went to the Minneapolis Institute of Art. About this time, his interests were turning toward acquiring great paintings of the masters, and, several of Herschel's etchings were sold March 28 and 29, 1921, through the Anderson Galleries in New York. The collection featured the etchings of thirty-one different artists, among them Loren R. Barton, Eugene Delacroix, Seymour Haden, Alphonse Legros, Edouard Manet, Jean Francois Millet, Auguste Rodin, James Abbot McNeil Whistler, and Anders Zorn. On page one of the catalogue was stated the following: "The prints in this Collection are of such uniform high quality that it would be monotonous to describe the condition of each particular print. It can be accepted that Mr. Jones was never satisfied with an impression that was less than the best that could be found."[35]

In 1926, he paid $75,000 to the Reinhardt Galleries for El Greco's "Portrait of a Nobleman," done in the elongated style familiar in the works of El Greco, painted in 1608. El Greco painted the three-quarter-length nobleman in a black doublet between 1609 and 1611. Against a gray background, the patrician model was painted with a striking effect of animation. Although there are a few details in the picture, none are allowed to divert the attention from the linear design. The ruff and cuffs are merely suggested; even the face is secondary; and an ornament hanging from the neck is only for linear reasons.

According to Malcolm Vaughan of *International Studio*, "The drawing is astonishingly swift and of a fluency that is almost fluid. The dynamism of design which is today the goal of the modern school was here three centuries ago attained with a force that impresses the spectator as if he had looked on a graceful design flutteringly made by lightning. All the impatience of the aging Greek is here magnificently subjected to pictorial form rather than to poetic expression. What many others 'strive to do, and agonize to do, and fail in doing,' Greco achieves. It is not surprising that among our modern painters El Greco has come to be looked on as a god—the twentieth century god of Spanish art."[36]

Lucretia, the famous Rembrant painting Jones purchased. Now at the Minneapolis Institute of Art.

He also purchased two amazing works of art, a painting by Francisco Goya, and the most famous painting ever to grace his collection-Rembrandt's "Lucretia." In January 1927, he lent to Reinhardt his "Lucretia," which Dr. Wilhelm Bode had judged one of the master's greatest works.[37]

Bode wrote:

> The painting representing Lucretia contemplating killing herself, I consider to be a masterpiece by Rembrandt painted in his late period. It has the original large signature and the date 1666. In the color composition, in which a dullish yellow predominates, and in which delicate green and purplish-red tones are wonderfully harmonized with dull white and black, the picture is very close to the 'Jewish Bride,' painted about the same time, and is of the same high rank.
>
> The picture has been prepared and finished with the most extraordinary sureness and masterfulness-to a great extent with a palet knife-and yet in its execution it is of the greatest delicacy scarcely again achieved by Rembrandt. The glow of the colors and their luminosity, and the golden tones are emphasized by the beautiful condition of the picture, which surpasses anything that I know of Rembrandt.[38]

Wilhelm R. Valentiner, director of the Detroit Museum of Art, was so moved by "Lucretia" when he saw it on public display that he wrote Herschel Jones the following letter of tribute:

> I have been fortunate enough to . . . see your great Rembrandt . . . and I want to tell you how deeply I was impressed with it. . . . I can not remember of having in a long while been so deeply touched with a work of art as with this. The rediscovery of this work is one of the most important events for all those who are studying Rembrandt, as the painting throws an absolutely new light on the last years of this great master. To my mind, the painting is on the same level as the double portrait in Amsterdam usually called the "Jewish Bride," and the Family Group in Brunswick, and the two Yousupoff portraits in Mr. Widener's collection. For those who know the personal history of Rembrandt, this painting may be even more revealing and touching, since it is surely a work not done on any order like the portraits, but out of his own will, expressing the deep sorrow of his last years in a most glorious composition of light and color.[39]

Rembrandt's celebrated portrayal of the suicide of Lucretia was considered one of the last great expressions of Rembrandt's genius. According to the Institute's bulletin, "the expression of human emotion, the most absorbing study of the artist's life, is refined to a degree found in almost none of the other secular paintings. Lucretia, lost for a space in contemplation of the awful deed she is about to perform, stands frozen at the merging of two worlds. For a moment she pauses, her left hand closed in determination around the bell rope that will announce the deed accomplished, her right, grasping the dagger, fallen heavily, uncertainly beside her. But the agonizing period of debate is over. The magnificent eyes, wherein lies all that Rembrandt himself thought of life and death, are turned at once toward the past and future."[40]

Lucretia, a paragon of virtue, was the wife of Tarquinus Collatinus, Commander of Collatia. At a banquet given by Sextus Tarquinus, a dispute arose over the virtue of their wives. Collatinus, after glorifying the virtue of his wife, suggested the pair visit their homes by surprise. At Collatinus' home in Rome, they found his wife Lucretia spinning amid her handmaids. But Sextus became inflamed with passion and came back after Collatinus had returned to Rome. Sextus threatened Lucretia with a sword and said he would kill her if she screamed. Lucretia was then ravished by the powerful Roman nobleman. While suffering inconsolable grief, she told her husband and father of her shame, received from them an oath of vengeance, and stabbed herself to death. When her body was taken to Rome for burial, the angry people sent the Tarquin family into exile. Poets and artists have been fascinated with the terrible fourth century, B.C., deed. And, of course, it is the theme of Shakespeare's poem, "The Rape of Lucrece."[41]

Painted in 1666, Rembrandt's painting is doubly interesting because of its similarity to a painting of the same subject in the Andrew Mellon collection, done in 1664. An even earlier depiction of the suicide was shown at the Detroit Institute of Arts, a composition done in part by pupils after drawings by Rembrandt.

Dr. William R. Valentiner wrote of the two later paintings of 1664 and 1666: "In the two representations of the dying Lucretia, which are among the most magnificent creations of Rembrandt's last period, the artist has chosen a theme which is . . . concerned with the other world, and which treats still more plainly [than the 'Descent from the Cross'] of the transition from life to death. . . . Everything is concentrated upon the expression of the figure and especially of the face, and the consciousness of the present life, vanishing before the glimpse of the world to come, is delineated in an incomparable manner."[42]

Out of 175 Rembrandt paintings pictured in a book by Valentiner, only about fifteen were of superior quality, according to one reviewer. "Lucretia," of course, was among the high order. Valentiner, a worshipper of Rembrandt's "Lucretia," possessed an almost unblemished reputation in the art world, was a scholarly pupil of Von Bode and a successor to the great critic in cataloguing newly discovered Rembrandt paintings.[43]

In the conclusion of a recapitulation of Rembrandt's life and work in the bulletin, during the exhibition of Jones' painting at the Art Institute, it was written: "Not even when the tender Hendrickje died and Rembrandt had to sell Saskia's tomb to provide a burial place for her; not even with the death of his beloved Tituts; would he bow to fate. In 1664, more preoccupied than ever with the mystery of death, he painted the first 'Lucretia,' and in 1666 the version that now belongs to the Art Institute—a portrayal that in some inscrutable manner explains his own attitude toward life and death. He had finished his experiment to his own satisfaction, and in 1669 he died, forgotten and almost alone. The only notice taken of the passing of one of the greatest painters of all time was the laconic obituary, 'Tuesday, October 8, 1669, Rembrandt van Rijn, painter, on the Roozegraft, opposite the Doolhof. Leaves two children.'"[44]

Critics were highly enthusiastic during a 1927 art show at the Reinhold Galleries. Commenting on the Jones-owned painting "Lucretia," Elizabeth L. Cary, noted art critic of the *New York Times*, wrote:

> Rembrandt was sixty-three when he died, and his art was at its zenith. Into this painting he threw with his boldest gestures the elements of his mature genius. The 'old household stuff and wonderful rags,' the gleaming jewels and golden chains, to which he clung with his curious, intense love of splendor, are used in this painting with the casual ease of his ironic later years. Life was mocking his love of the material, and in his turn he mocked those who judged him dependent upon his hoarded treasures.[45]

The *Literary Digest*, announcing the exhibit, focused on Jones' "Lucretia": "Chief among all and holding a solitary place is the Rembrandt, a 'Lucretia,' painted after the inspiration of Shakespeare's pitiful heroine. Seen for the first time in America, it is almost a new revelation to the art world in general, since it has been unknown to any great authority on Rembrandt since the time Dr. Waagen cataloged it in 1854. It was recently discovered in England and has been acquired by Mr. Herschel V. Jones of Minneapolis."[46]

The Arts hailed "Lucretia" as "the great Rembrandt, the quality of which, whether as vision, painting, or noble dramatic feeling is supreme." The magazine also showcased another piece from the Jones collection—"Landscape" by Meindert Hobbema.[47]

Also highly enthusiastic, the *Art News* praised the Jones-owned painting as one of Rembrandt's finest: "In technique and dramatic power there is nothing in the exhibition and but few pictures anywhere to compare with it. No written description could give an adequate impression of the marvelous brushwork in the white gown or the superb texture of the golden brown velvet robe. Like the flesh tones which, from even a short distance, appear unbroken and simple, each part of this tragic figure achieves its simplicity by the complete subordination of infinite detail."[48]

"I think I lived at the Art Institute with him," recalled Mrs. Sally Koether, Herschel's granddaughter, who regarded the painting with a curious mixture of awe and sorrow. "He loved art so much. I was so impressed with the great big oil painting of the little girl with the knife that hung over grandpa's fireplace in his huge house on Park Avenue. He later gave the painting to the Minneapolis Institute of Art."[49]

The 1927 attendance at the Minneapolis Institute of Arts showed an increase of over 15,000 over the previous year. Many of the 125,135 visitors in 1927 were there to see the opening of a new wing, begun on September 4, 1926, and opened in July 1927. It is believed, also, that many of these were at the museum to see the Jones gifts. Nonetheless, 1927 was a banner year for the Art Institute. In general it is interesting to note that the proportion of attendance to the population of Minneapolis was considerably higher than the attendance at the British Museum in London or the Metropolitan Museum in New York. The proportion in Minneapolis was about twenty-five percent of the population while both London and New York registered only seventeen percent.[50]

Jones' newspaper stated in a 1928 article, "Gradually his interest in things artistic widened to include prints and paintings, and as a director of the Art Institute he played an active part in its policies and purchases. His lavish gift of prints made over a period of years, was kept anonymous at his request until recently.

"A forceful man and persistent one, when his interest was aroused, he put the impress of his personality and his views not only on his own immediate surroundings but on the people and the activities he touched."[51]

The *St. Paul Pioneer Press* concurred. "Although Mr. Jones was known chiefly for his share in the journalism of Minnesota, his interests were broad and varied. The development and guidance of his newspaper naturally furnished the main outlet for his unusual energy and abilities, but he was in intimate touch with all aspects of the busy commercial and intellectual life around him, and especially in the later years, he turned his attention to cultivation of his rare artistic appreciation. Side by side with his interest in the *Journal* went that in the collection of books, of prints and paintings. Few persons in the Twin Cities are aware of the worldwide fame of Mr. Jones' unique library and of his art collections, out of which he has made many priceless gifts to the public."[52]

Unique indeed were his priceless gifts to the public. In February 1939, eleven years after the death of H.V. Jones, his prints headlined a popular exhibition, "Paris in Prints" at the Institute. The two oldest prints in the exhibit were two etchings by Jacques Callot. Callot was born in 1592, when the Valois line had finally died out and Henry of Navarre was King of France. But by the time Callot made these prints, Henry had already been murdered by an assassin, and his son, Louis XIII, with Richelieu behind him, was on the throne.[53]

One of these prints shows the old Tour de Nesle, which stood where today's Institute of France "shelters its immortals." There in the tower dwelt Margaret of Burgundy, and at night she lured young students from the university, only to have them thrown into the Seine before daylight. She and her "blood-stained orgies" provided the elder Dumas with his popular drama "La Tour de Nesle."

In the background of Callot's etching is Pont Neuf—that "new bridge" which is today the oldest in Paris; and in the center, resting on a small island below, the statue of Henry IV. The bridge appeared more than once in the exhibition as it was popular by many artists, including Thomas Girtin. Girtin was represented in the Jones collection by his aquatint "The Seine with Notre-Dame in the Background." Girtin, an Englishman, sketched twenty views of Paris in 1801 and 1802. But Napoleon was in power, and although the peace between England and France had been signed, all foreigners were closely watched. For military reasons, sketching was strictly forbidden. All of Girtin's famous views had to be made on the sly. Thus, he hired closed carriages, drew the curtains tight, ordered the coachman to drive to such and such a spot, and then with one eye peering out through some convenient crack, made his sketches.

Lepere's view of the Pont Neuf, a lithograph done with freedom, portrayed the tragedy of the river in "Somebody's Drowned." The bridge is crowded with people peering down at the grim spectacle below, where men in boats search the water with long poles. Another macabre print in the Jones collection was Charles Meryon's "The Morgue," in which a careful scrutiny reveals a cadaver being carried up to the small, unimpressive building at the water's edge. Another Meryon print in the collection was "The Apse of Notre-Dame" and it was considered the finest print in the exhibition. Meryon was a gifted, but unappreciated, artist in his lifetime. Discouraged, poverty-stricken, and eventually deranged, he died in an asylum in 1868. The Aspe print, extremely valuable today, was sold by the artist for thirty-cents to Ladd, undoubtedly, a much lower price than what Jones paid for it in 1916.

The bulletin for that 1939 exhibition stated that most of the prints on display had come from the Herschel V. Jones Collection of some five thousand prints, presented to the museum in 1926. Since that time, they have "given pleasure and interest to an increasing group of visitors. One of the most important of the institute's collections, it is an endless source of enjoyment."[54]

In November 1956 and March 1957 some of Jones' prints went on loan to exhibitions at the Cleveland Museum of Arts and the Art Institute of Chicago. Among them was "Christ's Entry into Jerusalem," an engraving lent by Herschel's son, Carl W. Jones. The brilliant impression, slightly trimmed on the left side, was formerly in the collection of Friedrich August of Saxony. The mysterious artist is believed to have been Lucas Cranach (1472 to 1553).[55]

Another, "The Judgment of Solomon," by Israhel Van Meckenem (born before 1450, died 1503) was lent by Jones' daughter, Miss Tessie Jones. The piece is a copy in reverse after an engraving by a master, and the plate without monogram may be one of Meckenem's earliest works. A goldsmith-engraver, Meckenem was perhaps the most prolific engraver of the fifteenth century. Over six hundred plates of his remain today. He was well known for making copies of many other artists. Sometimes he even retouched their plates and affixed his own monogram. He also reworked his own plates whenever they were not at the printer. However, the early impressions with their fine, silvery quality reveal a hand far more than merely skillful.

Also from Herschel, came Lucas Van Leyden's "The Emperor Maximilian," 1520. This portrait was finished in the year after Maximilian's death. It is not known whether the artist ever saw the emperor or whether he merely relied on portraits by Durer. The print, however, is done mainly in etching, but the face is engraved. It is believed to be the earliest print in which the two media appear together and also probably the first instance of etching on copper.

Born in Leyden, Holland in 1494, Van Leyden studied with the painter Cornelis Engelbrechtsz. In 1521, Van Leyden met Durer in Antwerp where the master made a drawing of him. Although the artist's life was short (he died in 1553), his engraved work is extensive, comprising 174 plates. The artist was a prodigy, and already in his earliest engravings, when at the age of fourteen or fifteen, his artistic personality was formed. Although his work was heavily influenced by Durer, he never imitated the metallic brilliance and emphatic definition of German engraving. He preferred a softer and warmer over-all tone. Fine impressions of his engravings are, nonetheless, much rarer than those of Durer, and few can be found outside the great print rooms of Amsterdam, London, and Vienna. One of Rembrandt's most treasured possessions was an album of engravings by Lucas Van Leyden.

A fourth work from the Herschel V. Jones Collection was Giovanni Battista Tiepolo's etching, "The Adoration of the Magi." This lightly etched, yet colorful and luminous composition, was done after the artist's own painting for the chapel of the royal castle at Aranjuez. Tiepolo, born in Venice in 1696, died in Madrid in 1770. He studied under Lazzarini, learned from Piazetta and Sebastiano Ricci, but was influenced even more by the sixteenth-century Venetian, Paolo Veronese. Tiepolo was active in Northern Italy, in Wurzburg, and spent the last eight years of his life in Madrid.

The exhibition and the catalogue, were dedicated to Herschel's son, Carl W. Jones, "Benefactor and trustee of the Minneapolis Institute of Arts this exhibition and catalogue are dedicated in gratitude and affection." In his preface, Richard S. Davis, the Art Institute's director at the time, wrote, "Concentrated interests in prints on the part of the Minneapolis Institute of Arts dates from the year 1926 when the late Herschel V. Jones made the first of many gifts of prints to the museum's then limited collections. Primarily through his love for graphic arts, his collecting and his generous gifts the museum was soon enabled to incorporate the study and exhibition of prints into its general program. This activity, pursed and developed through the devoted interest of Carl W. Jones, attained new significance this spring with the reestablishment, through his generosity, of the Departments of Prints and Drawings. It is in grateful recognition of this event that the present exhibition has been organized."[56]

H.V. Jones was able to gather large collections in the fields of books and art because he made money from his newspaper. By 1912, the Sunday edition of the *Journal* exceeded one hundred pages each week and it averaged well over forty-five percent of this output in advertising. Even the *St. Paul Dispatch* and the *St. Paul Pioneer Press* advertised their want-ad services in the *Journal*'s want-ad section. By 1914 the *Journal* brought in almost one million dollars annually in advertising, despite the ban on liquor, patent medicine, or quack advertising, which would have added another $50,000 annually.[57]

In May 1928, Richard Davis in the bulletin of the Minneapolis Institute of Arts stated, "Mr. Jones' interest in the Institute was

Herschel V. Jones in his mid-sixties.

always keen. A trustee for fourteen years, his counsel was invariably sound in all problems involving the development of the museum. As a private collector of national reputation his advice in the matter of acquisitions was invaluable. The announcement of less than two weeks ago of his name as donor of a magnificent collection of prints, made anonymously in 1916 and since augmented by eight additional groups, placed him among the great benefactors of the society.

"Throughout his career as a journalist, Mr. Jones' proverbial modesty was only exceeded by the extent of his service to the public. In many fields his strong personal enthusiasm and broad vision did much towards the upbuilding of the Northwest."[58]

With the publication of a book on the Jones Collection in 1968, the Minneapolis Institute of Arts said of Herschel:

"Herschel Jones shares only with Alfred Pillsbury and J.J. Hill the primacy amongst Minnesota art collectors of the period in which our state's culture was founded. Of the three, Mr. Jones' activities were the most varied: he was not only one of the most gifted of painting collectors and one of the greatest print collectors America has ever produced, but also a great bibliophile. In his very active life Mr. Jones set a model of cultivated interest, patronage and devotion in an incredibly varied field, all of it serious, exciting and profoundly public-spirited. For our local culture, and not least for this museum, his model remains unsurpassed."[59]

Notes

[1] Harold Joachim, Prints 1400–1800, Minneapolis, Minneapolis Istitute of Arts, 1956-1957, Introduction.

[2] Theodore C. Blegen, *Minnesota: A History of the State*, pp. 493-494.

[3] Jean Adams Ervin, *The Twin Cities Perceived: A Study in Words and Drawings*, pp. 109-110.

[4] Karen Nelson Hoyle, *Wanda Gág*, New York, Twayne Publishers, 1994, pp. 4-5; "Wanda Gág Makes a Wish Come True," *Roots*, Vol. 8, No. 2, Winter 1980, pp. 16-19.

[5] Wanda Gág, *Growing Pains*, St. Paul, Minnesota Historical Society Press, 1984, p. 306; George MacDonald, Phantastes, New York, Ballantine Books, 1970, p. vii.

[6] Wanda Gág, *Growing Pains*, pp. 306-318.

[7] Ibid., p. 315.

[8] Ibid., pp. 323-325.

[9] Ibid., Karen Nelson Hoyle, Wanda Gág, p. 7.

[10] "Wanda Gág Makes a Wish Come True," *Roots*, Vol. 8, No.2, Winter 1980, p. 20.

[11] Wanda Gág, *Growing Pains*, p. 467; Karen Nelson Hoyle, *Wanda Gág*, p. 83.

[12] Karen Nelson Hoyle, *Wanda Gág*, p. 39.

[13] Anthony M. Clark, *The Jones Collection: The Bequests of Her-*

schel V. and Tessie Jones, Minneapolis, Minneapolis Institute of Arts, 1968, no page numbers given.

[14]Dr. Lisa Dickinson Michaux, associate curator, Department of Prints and Drawings, the Minneapolis Institute of Arts, letter to Winton Jones, dated January 15, 2003.

[15]*Minneapolis Star,* May 24, 1928; *Minneapolis Journal,* May 17, 1928; *Minneapolis Tribune,* May 24, 1928; *Bulletin of the Minneapolis Institute of Arts,* Vol. XVII, No. 22, June 2, 1928.

[16]Robert Hardy Andrews, *A Corner of Chicago,* Little, Brown & Company, 1963, p. 9.

[17]Jeffrey A. Hess, *Their Splendid Legacy: The First 100 Years of the Minnesota Society of Fine Arts,* Minneapolis, Minneapolis Institute of Arts, 1985, pp. 23-24.

[18]Ibid., pp. 33-34.

[19]Ibid.

[20]Ibid.

[21]Report, undated, by Herschel Jones to the trustees of the Minneapolis Society of Fine Arts.

[22]Jeffrey A. Hess, *Their Splendid Legacy: The First 100 Years of the Minnesota Society of Fine Arts,* p. 39.

[23]*Minneapolis Tribune-Times,* May 30, 1940.

[24]*Minneapolis Star,* May 24, 1928; *Minneapolis Journal,* May 17, 1928; *Minneapolis Tribune,* May 24, 1928; *Bulletin of the Minneapolis Institute of Arts,* Vol. XVII, No. 22, June 2, 1928.

[25]*Bulletin of the Minneapolis Institute of Arts,* Vol. XVII, No. 22, June 2, 1928.

[26]*Minneapolis Journal,* Thursday Evening, May 17, 1928.

[27]*Bulletin of the Minneapolis Institute of Arts,* Vol. XVII, No. 22, June 2, 1928; *Minneapolis Journal,* Thursday Evening, May 17, 1928.

[28]Jeffrey A. Hess, *Their Splendid Legacy: The First 100 Years of the Minneapolis Society of Fine Arts,* pp. 36-37.

[29]*Bulletin of the Minneapolis Institute of Arts,* Vol. XVII, No. 22, June 2, 1928; *Minneapolis Journal,* Thursday Evening, May 17, 1928.

[30]*Bulletin of the Minneapolis Institute of Arts,* Vol. XVII, No. 35, December 29, 1928.

[31]"Notes of the Month," *International Studio,* August 1928, p. 57.,

[32]"Art throughout America," *The Art News,* May 1, 1937, pp. 17-18 under subtitle, "Minneapolis: A History of Etching."

[33]*New York World,* January 27, 1918.

[34]Von Wilhelm Von Bode, "Ein Neu Aufgefundenes Jugendwerk Von Pieter De Hooch," *Zeitschrift Fur Bildendekunst,* 54 Jahrgang, 1918-1919.

[35]Sale Catalogue, *Modern Etchings: The Collection of H.V. Jones*, Minneapolis, Minnesota, Saturday March 19, 28, 29, 1921, p. 1.

[36]Malcolm Vaughan, "Portraits by El Greco in America," *International Studio*, March 1927, p. 102.

[37]*The New York Times*, May 25, 1928; Jones Family History compiled by Mrs. Kenneth H. Bailey; "Three Hundred Years of Painting," The *Literary Digest*, Letters and Art, Vol. 92, No. 6, Whole No. 1920, February 5, 1927, p. 28.

[38]"Three Hundred years of Painting," The *Literary Digest*, Letters and Art, Vol. 92, No. 6, Whole No. 1920, February 5, 1927, p. 28; "Old Masters from a Loan Exhibition," *International Studio*, January 1927, p. 66.

[39]Jeffrey A. Hess, *Their Splendid Legacy: The First 100 Years of the Minneapolis Society of Fine Arts*, p. 40.

[40]"Rembrandt's Prime," *The Art Digest*, February 1, 1935, p. 9.

[41]Ibid.; "Three Tapestries Representing the Story of Lucretia in the Felix Warburg Collection," *Art in America and Elsewhere*, Volume XII, Number VI, October 1924, pp. 291-292.

[42]Ibid.

[43]Frank Jewett Mather, Jr., "Rembrandt, Inc.," *Creative Art*, Volume 10, No. 2, February 1932, p. 105; Alan Burroughs, "Rembrandt Paintings," *Creative Art*, Volume 10, No. 2, February 1932, p. 109.

[44]"Rembrandt's Prime," *The Art Digest*, February 1, 1935, p. 9.

[45]"Three Hundred Years of Painting," The *Literary Digest*, Letters and Art, Vol. 92, No. 6, Whole No. 1920, February 5, 1927, p. 28.

[46]Ibid.

[47]Frank Jewett Mather, Jr., "Painting from Dan to Beersheba," *The Arts*, February 1927, pp. 71-79.

[48]"Rembrandt, El Greco, Cezanne, and Matisse," *The Art News*, January 22, 1927, pp. 1, 5.

[49]Mrs. Sally Koether telephone interview with author, November 1, 1998; Alfred and Frances Siftar interview with author March 3, 1999, Edina, Minnesota; *Minneapolis Star*, June 19, 1974; *Minneapolis Tribune*, June 13, 1974.

[50]Annual Report of the Minneapolis Society of Fine Arts for the Year 1927, May 1928.

[51]*Minneapolis Sunday Journal*, May 27, 1928.

[52]*The Pioneer Press* editorial was reprinted in the *Journal*.

[53]*Bulletin of the Minneapolis Institute of Arts*, Vol. XXVIII, No. 5, February 4, 1939.

[54]Ibid.

[55]Harold Joachim, *Prints 1400-1800*, Minneapolis, The Minneapolis Institute of Arts, 1956, pp. 11, 22-23, 28.

[56]Ibid., Preface.

[57]Ted Curtis Smythe, *A History of the* Minneapolis Journal, *1878-1939*, p. 231.

[58]*Bulletin of the Minneapolis Institute of Arts*, Vol. XVII, No. 21, May 26, 1928.

[59]Anthony M. Clark, *The Jones Collection: The Bequests of Herschel V. and Tessie Jones*, Introduction.

CHAPTER TEN

ON THE AIR

"Now I am in the public house
And lean upon the wall,
So come in rags or come in silk
In cloak or country shawl,
And come with learned lovers
Or with what men you may,
For I can put the whole lot down
And all I have to say
Is, 'Fol de rol de rolly O.'"

—William Butler Yeats

n November 1915, when the Great War was still a European war, Herschel V. Jones ran the following editorial in the *Minneapolis Journal*: "Man is a social animal. Reformers with their various reforms do not always remember that man lives here below before he ever gets to paradise—quite a number of years, many of us.

"Working, doing his duty by home and family, saving his soul in the manner of his particular creed—these things still leave some unoccupied hours and still leave unfilled some natural cravings. And the fact is that in the saloon, for want of a better place, many men do find that social intercourse which is a need of human nature. The saloon has flourished not only because it dispenses alcohol, but also because it dispenses cheer, or a sorry imitation of cheer.

"This fact, especially conspicuous in the life of cities, ought to be considered by those who would abolish the saloon. It accounts for the refusal of great cities to go dry, even when the surrounding country has done so. The men of the cities want their club, and the majority of them find it in the more or less vicious saloon. The countryman is not so insistent on a place of social assembly, but he has suffered for the lack.

"A substitute for the saloon must be found. Such substitutes have been put forward by ethical and religious bodies. But all have been prompted by some sort of uplift. Whereas a man doesn't go to a social gathering to be uplifted, saved, or bettered, but to be amused, to be relaxed, to exercise with others his human qualities. What he wants is fun, perhaps even horseplay. What he asks to hear is talk and to talk himself—vapid, nonsensical, or even vulgar talk. He wants to trot out his human conceit and human vanity and human credulity out of the cage of convention and self-interest awhile, and see them roll over as horses do when released from harness.

"The saloon is a most harmful institution, particularly when run unregulated to make as much money as quickly as it can. . . . The pity is that some better place and occasion has not been found, whereby these human, foolish, but beneficent discharges of repressed egoisms are furthered. Can it not be found?"[1]

The prohibitionists, however, did not care about replacing the saloon. Their only objective was to eliminate it. The underlying forces at work to support national prohibition included antipathy to the growth of cities (the scene of heaviest drinking), evangelical Protestant middle-class, anti-alien and anti-Roman Catholic sentiment, and rural domination of the state legislatures. Other forces included the growing corruption in the saloons and the industrial employers' concern for preventing accidents and increasing the efficiency of workers.

In 1917 the resolution for submission of the Prohibition Amendment to the states received the necessary two-thirds vote in Congress; the amendment was ratified on January 29, 1919, and went into effect on January 29, 1920. On October 28, 1919, the National Prohibition Act, popularly called the Volstead Act after its promoter, Congressman Andrew J. Volstead, was enacted, providing enforcement guidelines.

But millions of Americans continued to drink. The unpopular amendment was inconsistent, outlawing manufacture, sale and transportation of liquor but not buying, drinking, or making it at home. Since alcohol could not be dispensed legally, then it would have to be distributed illegally. The enterprising crime syndicates quickly moved in and set the country up for years of sensational lawlessness.[2] Al Capone, for example, brought in an annual bootlegging income of over $60,000,000.

Arrests for drunkenness more than doubled in the city of Minneapolis between 1920 and 1925, going from 2,500 to 7,000. Illegal stills were active in the city, but more serious was the flood of imports of Canadian whiskies being trucked in from Canada on a daily basis. Before Prohibition, Minneapolis had been a wholesaling center as well as a hub for the trucking industry. It was simple for bootleggers to hire independent drivers to make the border crossings with loads of illegal liquor. A great deal of liquor was directed to other cities such as Chicago and Kansas City, but most of the hooch was driven through Minneapolis.[3]

Having become wealthy from the liquor trade, local racketeers simply bought police and city government protection from greedy officials. Gambling, prostitution, and other rackets were upgraded, while many crooks turned to providing "protection" to small businesses via blackmail and extortion schemes. Gangland murders in Minneapolis were not unusual.

A friend told H.V. Jones, that, despite the reports of prostitution, there were no working prostitutes in the city of Minneapolis. To find out for himself, Herschel borrowed a "poor man's" clothing and ventured into the Gateway District in his disguise. The girls working the avenue thought he was just another customer from the Iron Range. H.V. took photographs with an early flash camera he had concealed in his clothing and proved that there was an abundance of "working" girls on the streets. An article bearing his findings appeared in the *Journal*.[4]

The war with Germany had ended but the war on liquor evolved into a nightmare of its own. On February 3, 1919, the Minneapolis City Council closed all the saloons in the city, even though an order of the Public Safety Commission had temporarily reopened them when the war had ended. Two months later, Minneapolis police raided four lower loop cafes and arrested eighteen people. They were charged with violating Public Safety Ordinance #7, which forbade the selling of liquor to women. The *Minneapolis Journal* covered the event thoroughly in its April 19 issue and also reported that a woman at the Miller Hotel café at Second and Washington Avenues South, threw a beer glass at a policeman.[5]

The following day, the *Journal* reported more unrest, this time over a raid on an I.W.W. meeting place. According to the *Journal* article, "Eleven men in army uniforms raided a building at 14 First Street South after I.W.W. were said to have conducted a meeting in the place, the police said today. All the windows were smashed. The attack took place late yesterday. Bricks and stones also were hurled inside, members of the I.W.W. informed detectives. The I.W.W. immediately posted a sign over the building reading 'Since our windows have been Americanized, the light shines brighter.'[6]

The *Journal* article also stated that the raiders quickly disappeared when Lieutenant J.F. Little and detectives arrived from police headquarters. The I.W.W. charged that a man dressed in the uniform of a Marine Corps. Sergeant had led the attack. The newspaper carried a quote from J.W. Bryant, secretary of the executive committee of the Northwest Warriors Association, stating, "Property owners need not expect service men to be complacent towards group who seek to tear down all they fought for."[7]

Four days later, the *Journal* reported that fifty raiders came back and wrecked the I.W.W. headquarters and beat up the Wobblies then present with clubs. Some gunfire was also reported. The leader of the mob is said to have announced before the raid that, "Minneapolis is not a healthy place for a red. . . . You failed to heed our warning to get out of town so we're back again."[8]

According to the *Journal* report, the attackers were all wearing military uniforms, and as before, they all strangely managed to escape before the arrival of the police. But the *Journal* emphasized the word "Strangely,"—the police had been out of sight during all the anti-radical incidents. The I.W.W. in Minneapolis never really recovered from the 1919 repression typified by the violence in the Gateway district.

The I.W.W. began to dissolve, not only in Minnesota, but, throughout the country. On Lincoln's birthday in 1919, fifty-four members were ordered deported. On January 2, 1920, ten thousand suspected members were arrested. One judge described them as "a mob made up of government officials acting under instructions from the Department of Justice." Transports waited in the ports for any deportation.[9]

A source of this agitation was the Ku Klux Klan. Fed by theories of white racial supremacy and a giddiness of power generated by the victory in the war, many citizens of Minneapolis joined the resurgent Ku Klux Klan in droves during the early 1920s. There were no less than ten Klan chapters in the city of Minneapolis by 1923 as well as a statewide Klan publication. The Klan boasted an anti-radical attitude of the war years in their attacks on Socialists, Wobblies, and other leftist organizations. They combined this with an anti-Semitic and anti-Catholic policy, blaming these religions somehow for the war in Europe.[10]

But Minneapolis civic leaders still struggled with the alcohol question. A border patrol was set up to prevent people from smuggling liquor into the state. In Minnesota, as in the entire nation, the prohibition law was difficult to enforce with any degree of success.

In 1929, in a successful bust, Federal agents in Minnesota seized more than 235,000 gallons of liquor and 271 stills. But the underworld rings fought to control the illegal trade.[11]

After the Salvation Army started a soft drink bar, the courts and the police hit upon the idea of licensing new establishments. On September 9, 1920, a five-dollar license ordinance for dancehall and soft drink bars was put into effect.[12] While the city had no trouble establishing regulations, it did encounter opposition from some of the regulators. According to the *Journal*, a letter from T.E. Hughes, president of the Union City Mission to A.C. Jensen, Minneapolis police superintendent, read:

> For the good of the service and for your information, I wish to report that at about nine o'clock last evening, one of your officers, in uniform, decidedly in an intoxicated condition came from the alley from the direction of Washington Avenue, crossed Second Street North in front of the St. James Hotel, and on through the alley alongside of the hotel towards First Street.
>
> While there were a number of hotel guests sitting on the sidewalk in front of the hotel who observed the officer, none of them as far as I know are able to sufficiently describe him to be of any value in his identification.

The police superintendent replied: "I wish to thank you for your letter of the [four]th inst. advising of the condition of one of our officers on the evening of Aug[ust thi]rd.

"This matter was called to my attention prior to the receipt of your letter and as soon as I can ascertain all the facts in this, I assure you that he will be disciplined.[13]

Adding to the woes of prohibition and local unrest, depression struck Minnesota and the Midwest in the early 1920s. A forerunner of what was soon to spread worldwide, Minnesota's banks were shattered. Of Minnesota's 1,160 state banks in 1921, only 675 remained a decade later. Some 320 had closed their doors between 1921 and 1929, all of these before the Great Depression.[14]

Rural Minnesota did not escape the local economic crisis, and farmers were hit extremely hard. Farm crops were valued at $506 million in 1919; ten years later they had declined to $310 million. The depression subsided a few years later and business boomed, but farming conditions improved little. Farmers turned to politics, supported a "farm bloc" in Congress, secured a federal farm board, put faith in "farm plans," and prayed that freighting on the Mississippi River would return.

Herschel Jones was very concerned with the bleak economic situation that affected the Midwest and his *Journal* as well. The price of newsprint had skyrocketed since war's end. During the war, the price had been frozen by government regulations, although it had nonetheless climbed from forty-two dollars a ton in 1916 to eighty dollars in 1918. But when price controls were abandoned, the paper manufacturers immediately hiked their prices to make up for money that was lost. When the increase stopped in 1921, the price had hit a peak of $137 a ton. This steep increase affected every newspaper in the country, many of which went broke.[15]

Still, the *Journal* made money and Herschel's book and art expeditions were not affected. In 1919, Herschel urged his son Carl to leave a promising advertising career in Chicago with Lord & Thomas, and later, Erwin Wasey, and come to work for the *Journal*. His urgings were successful. Two of Carl's brothers followed him to the *Journal*—Moses in circulation and Jefferson in editorial. Seven years later, when Herschel became ill, Carl took over operation of the paper. George B. Bickelhaupt was business manager during both regimes.[16]

With three sons on board, Herschel had more time to spend with his grandchildren. One of the granddaughters recalled: "He'd take

Crowds in front of the Minneapolis Journal Building on election night 1920, awaiting returns. (Courtesy of the Minnesota Historical Society)

me to art shows. He once bought me a lovely Mickey Mouse doll with a long rubber band tail. He loved art so much. I think he bought me the doll because he wanted to keep me quiet."[17]

One of Herschel's favorite haunts when his grandchildren visited was the local drugstore. A grand daughter, Mrs. Sally Koether, recalled the shop being partitioned by many panels. They always had sodas, and on one occasion, Herschel bought her a Brownie camera. "I always enjoyed being with him," she said. "He was so much fun."[18]

Herschel perhaps had a little more time to devote to his memberships in various clubs and organizations also. Since his early days in Minneapolis, he had become a member of the Westminster Presbyterian Church, where he helped found and was the first secretary of the Westminster Club. He had remained an active member throughout the years. In addition to his directorships of the Associated Press and the Minneapolis Institute of Arts, he held memberships in the Minneapolis Club, Athletic Club, Lafayette Club, Automobile Club, Minikahda Club, Skylight Club, and others in Minneapolis; the Minnesota Club in St. Paul; the Chicago Club, and the National Press Club in Washington. He was also a member of the Grolier Club of New York, a famous organization of book collectors and authors.[19]

It was quite an honor to be a member of most of these clubs. The Automobile Club of Minneapolis certainly had its privileges. On the backside of Jones' 1918 membership card was printed the following: "To the Arresting Officer: The officer arresting the owner of this card for violation of the law regulating automobiles, will hold this card as bail and release party at once, and deliver this card to the Chief or Superintendent of Police, and receive further orders." The card was signed by the Superintendent of Police of Minneapolis and the Chief of Police of St. Paul.[20]

The prestigious Skylight Club, of which Herschel was a member, was founded in 1890. It took its name from a skylight in the ceiling of the building on Hennepin Avenue where the members met.[21] Here in this social club for men, Herschel rubbed elbows with the Crosbys, Pillsburys, and other affluent families of the city.[22]

Flour industry giant James Ford Bell wrote seventy years after the club's establishment: "I came to Minneapolis in 1888 as a boy of nine. I lived at the old West Hotel, attended Jefferson School at Seventh Street and First Avenue North. I remembered that I was particularly intrigued by a building which stood back on Hennepin Avenue between Seventh and Eighth—a studio of a local artist. It was approached by two wooden planks laid side by side and forming a walk over which the privileged members entered the sanctity of the Skylight Club when it was in session. Once I was permitted to enter its halls. To me, it was like a house of magic, with all the trappings that the artist had managed to incorporate into his studios.

"In those days there were not many channels through which we could express both social and cultural characteristics. The Skylight Club, therefore, held an honorable place and a recognition of cultural values which meant much to a small but growing community."[23]

John Crosby, who had come from Maine in 1877 and formed a partnership with Cadwallader Washburn to form the flour milling leader, Washburn, Crosby & Company, was superbly efficient as home manager.[24] As one of the first members of the Skylight Club, he was "an urbane and original master of ceremonies," and in a very festive manner, played Santa Claus at numerous Skylight Club Christmas parties. He was heralded as a master ad-lib when it came to finding the right remarks to go along with each gift he handed out from the tree. During the meetings, the treasurer would always be called upon for a financial report, but the treasurer, Crosby's brother Franklin, would always refuse since the meetings were so informal.[25]

Another member of the group was Dr. Frank Westbrook who was responsible for the building of the University of Minnesota's new medical school. Dr. Marion B. Shutter was the storyteller of the group. George Perigo Conger, another member, was the esteemed author of an enormous volume, *Synthetic Naturalism,* that attempted to outline all the progress humankind had made. Yale professor of philosophy, William Henry Sheldon, called Dr. Conger "one of the greatest philosophers of his time."

Club member Ward Burton recalled: "My first impression of Skylight I think is the most lasting. The Skylight Club then was very small and occupied a little brick house that you've heard mentioned so often. And in the brick house with the skylight, the fire, much as it is now, was kept going all the evening; occasionally a Skylighter would get up for fuel."[26]

The Skylight was, and still is, a unique, men's club, not only because it has no formalized framework of articles or by-laws and no elected officers, but also no stated purpose. But with no rules or regulations, the Skylight boasts a rich heritage of custom and tradition and "the congeniality of its membership, which gives the Club its peculiar and distinctive character. The tie that binds is a community of interests and tastes. Town and gown are brought together in easy fireside camaraderie."[27]

272

Other clubs to which Herschel belonged were organized for a purpose, most with by-laws and elected officials. The Minneapolis Club, organized in 1883 as an outgrowth of the Silver Grays, with Charles F. Hatch as its president, met for the enjoyment of the social and literary culture of its members. The imposing structure of the Minneapolis Club's meetings was once hailed in *Leslie's Weekly* as "one of the most exclusive and progressive institutions of its kind in the West." The Minikahda Club (Uncle Billy Edgar's Sioux for "By the Waterside"), organized in 1898 with Judge Martin B. Koon serving as its president. It was organized for the "social enjoyment, mental and physical culture of its members. The emphasis in most clubs at the time was on culture—mental, literary, social, and physical.[28]

But Minnesota's "other" clubs were having a rough time of it. According to an article in the *Minneapolis Journal*, Minneapolis Mayor George E. Leach, on August 17, 1921, revoked the licenses of thirty-five soft drink bars and canceled one license. All but six of these bars were located in the Gateway District. Leach ordered Police Chief Jensen to arrest proprietors of the soft drink bars involved if they persisted in operating without a license. All of these establishments employed barmaids who did double duty as prostitutes. Future governor, Floyd B. Olson, then a young county attorney, provided Mayor Leach with a list of establishments against which he had enough evidence to obtain convictions. The majority of these canceled licenses were on Second and Marquette Avenues.[29]

Accompanying the *Journal* article was a cartoon showing properly dressed visitors to Minneapolis walking up the street from the railway station on their way to the more respectable part of the city. Their attention is drawn to a row of establishments served by lady barmaids. Women stand on the second floor of the saloons, looking out windows at them with smiling faces.

Mayor Leach banned the barmaids on September 20, 1921, according to the *Journal*. In addition to the obvious prostitution, police discovered that moonshine was secretly being sold in the soft drink bars. While the police maintained a campaign of raiding, the offenders tried to stay one jump ahead of the law. While liquor and prostitution were illegal, the law permitted gambling. That year, seven gambling houses were in operation in the city and poker games flourished from 1:00 P.M. until midnight. One "club," Moriarty's, operated a craps game with no trouble from police. Another, the Metropole Club at 26 Washington Avenue South, boasted twelve poker tables. The Author's Club, a gambling den located at 251 Hennepin Avenue, was also quite popular, or in some circles—unpopular![30]

The *Journal* also paid attention to national news with a special interest in history. A resolution adopted by the American Legion at its third national convention, held in Kansas City from October 31 to November 3, 1921, suggested the federal archives at Washington should be properly housed and administered. The legion urged "proper legislation for the erection of a suitable repository for all national archives where they may be safe from any future possibility of fire, vermin, or other causes for their destruction."

The *Journal* responded to the archives situation in Washington in its article of March 19 under the heading, "Priceless Records of World War in Peril of Destruction by Fire Because Government Neglects to Safeguard Papers."[31]

An earlier *Journal* article, "Wakened by the World War, Minnesotans at Last are Studying History," was written by William Stearns Davis, professor of history at the University of Minnesota. The *Journal* piece described the increased interest manifested in the study of history since the outbreak of the Great War and discussed some of the forty-four courses in history then offered at the university.[32] From January 15 to March 26, the *Journal* also ran a series of Sunday articles dealing with local historical subjects in Minneapolis.

Herschel Jones attended the seventy-third annual meeting of the Minnesota Historical Society, as an elected board member, on January 9, 1922. The success of the conference indicated that there was an increasing realization throughout the state of the importance of local history. The opening discussion, "Organization and Functions of Local Historical Societies and Their Relation to the State Society," focused on a speech by Dr. Solon J. Buck. Dr. Orin G. Libby then commented upon the contrast between the situation in such Eastern states as Massachusetts, New Hampshire, and Connecticut and that in Minnesota and Wisconsin. Other talks and discussions centered upon the records gathered by the Hennepin County War Records Commission, Minnesota's effort to "get out of its swaddling clothes," and the local war records in Rice County. Edward A. Bromley of Minneapolis gave a stirring lecture, "Pioneer Life in the Twin City Region," illustrated by about a hundred lantern slides made from his collection of historic pictures.[33]

On October 4, the *Journal* printed an article that presented an appeal by Edwin Clark, secretary of the Hennepin County Territorial Pioneers' Association, for the "establishment of a permanent fund to finance the care and upkeep of the [Ard] Godfrey House." Included was a brief history of the house, which was the oldest house in Minneapolis, standing at the time. Photographs of its then-present and original locations also appeared with the article.

The *Journal* also ran several other articles dealing with local history, including a January 22 piece on the changes in the names of Minneapolis streets based upon an official 1855 map of Minneapolis. An October 30 article reproduced the first page of a "copy of a long defunct newspaper," the *Minneapolis Evening News,* for June 20, 1871, as well as *Journal* comment on its contents. Another early publication, the *Minneapolis City Directory for 1867,* furnished material for a *Journal* article of February 19. The book was erroneously classed as the city's second directory, but two earlier volumes had been published.

In the area of entertainment, the 1920s became a watershed as radio, the movies, literature, and music and dance, in a new form of freedom, swept Minnesota and the country. The people of Minneapolis broadened beyond their polka horizons toward classical and popular music forms. The acceptance of jazz and blues music, performed exclusively by black musicians took its cue from the subterranean social life developed in Prohibition speakeasies. Scandalous music seemed to spawn scandalous behavior by some people. Minnesota writers such as Sinclair Lewis and F. Scott Fitzgerald described life in Minnesota, to which many Twin Citians took umbrage. But works glorifying Minnesota's pioneer heritage, such as those of O.E. Rolvaag and William Watts Folwell's *History of Minnesota*, were popular reading material. Radio was a technological revolution in entertainment, but it was also revolutionary in its form and content. News and informational broadcasts, sports, theatre, musical performances, comedy, melodrama, and events from overseas flowed into the American consciousness.[34]

Radio had suddenly brought the world into the sitting rooms of Minnesota's homes. In the early 1920s, crystal sets and earphones were standard radio equipment. In January 1922, the University of Minnesota was granted a federal license to operate a broadcasting transmitter, and under the call letters WLB, it became the first non-experimental radio station in the Twin Cities. WLB's itinerary consisted of market and weather reports and occasional concerts. A station known as "The Call of the North" (WLAG), which would be taken over by the Washburn-Crosby Company two years later and become WCCO, opened in 1922. The station would be used as an advertising arm of the firm's marketing division. The first jingle broadcast over the airwaves was for General Mills' dry cereal Wheaties, later to become the "Breakfast of Champions." Within a year, there were twelve broadcasting stations in Minnesota.[35]

When Herschel was returning from a 1922 book-buying trip in California, he glanced up at the roof of the Tribune Annex and was shocked to see a radio tower being erected. The *Tribune* had said it believed in the new medium and was constructing the tower to back its faith. It claimed "within a fortnight this station will be in operation, receiving and broadcasting things that young and old within a radius of 500 miles will wish to hear." The editorial writer also stated that this "is a great age, and the *Tribune* believes in keeping up with it when there is a chance to blaze the way. Prepare ye to cut in on W.A.A.L., the designation of the station that will be atop the Tribune Annex!"[36]

Jones met with his managing editor, George Adams, and ordered him to put a station in operation before the *Tribune* could. Adams knew little about radio but he contacted W.E. Stephenson of the Sterling Electric Company. Because they did not have a powerful transmitter, Jones and Sterling Electric borrowed one from Northern States Power Company. The *Tribune*, once it became aware of Jones' determination to broadcast first, tossed away their fortnight schedule and broadcast a brief announcement on April 20, one week ahead of schedule. The broadcast was brief because the *Tribune* was not ready to transmit music or program materials. The *Tribune* had to tune the set because "it is generally realized among radio phone users that efforts to broadcast music programs with inefficient apparatus is doing much to discourage radio beginners, who form a low opinion of radio concerts."[37]

The first program presented by a northwest newspaper station was aired the night of April 20 by the *Journal* over station WBAD. Mayor George E. Leach opened the program, and baritone Oscar Seagle, violinist George Klass, and soprano Eleanor Poehler performed music on the airwaves.

Both the *Journal* and *Tribune* maintained that they were first in operation. The *Tribune* claimed, it was "first in the field of negotiation, first to sign a contract, first to procure a government license, first to erect a station of its own on a building of its own." But the *Journal* had been first to commence regular programming, and this, the *Tribune* could not dispute. Soon the *Tribune* relinquished its claim to being the first newspaper to broadcast and boasted that it was the only newspaper in the Twin Cities to own its own station.

A day after the broadcasts of the *Journal* and the *Tribune*, the *St. Paul Pioneer Press* began broadcasting from its own station, WAAH. While never claiming to be the first radio station to broadcast, it claimed to be "first among the Northwest newspapers to recognize the value and growing importance of radio news . . . by starting a radio column in its Sunday issues." After its station went on the air, it devoted two pages each Sunday of radio news.[38]

The *Journal* followed suit by carrying a special section tabloid, "How to Make a Radio-Set" by Frank I. Solar. The supplement constituted the initial part of a booklet that could be compiled from the many articles that eventually were printed in the *Journal*. All of these had been designed for clipping and addition to the booklet. The *Tribune* published a seven-part series on how to construct a radio.[39]

Running a radio station proved to be a costly enterprise, and at least on one occasion, dangerous. A fifty-member boys choir was scheduled to perform on the *Journal*'s station one evening, but only moments before airtime, they were nowhere to be found. Bob Andrews, the *Journal*'s after-hours program arranger and stand-by announcer, "found them sitting on the cornice along the [Radisson] hotel front, leaning out above ten stories of space while dropping paper-sack water-bombs on the traffic below. "They swore they'd jump off before they'd sing for nothing," Andrews later wrote. "Several of them nearly fell." Andrews finally persuaded them to come down, but by then, the station engineer had left for the day. Andrews resigned his position.[40]

There existed at the time a growing competition between the press and radio. The main battle was for the advertising dollar. This fight eventually brought pressure from newspapers on the three American press services: Associated Press, United Press, and the International News Service. Consequently, these news agencies later notified the radio stations and networks that they would no longer provide them with the news. An agreement was not worked out between the two sides until 1934.[41]

The expense of running a radio station as well as a newspaper caused many papers to go out of the radio business as quickly as they had come into operation. Jones made his decision to quit the radio business toward the end of its first year. Although he had agreed with the Sterling Electric Company to buy a new transmitter, he backed out after it was ordered because he felt it was "not advisable to go ahead." The decision by Jones was a secret initially, but he was able to draw the *Tribune* and the *Pioneer Press* out of the radio business with him.[42]

But quitting the radio business would cultivate criticism from the people. Securing the assistance of Governor J.A.O. Preus, a plan was devised. Preus publicly requested the Twin Cities newspapers to consider a "plan for centering radio broadcasting in the Twin Cities in the University of Minnesota and under its control." Governor Preus justified the plan by stating that "as all private broadcasting stations are now ordered by the government to use the same wave length, the present stations are, by mutual agreement, operating at different times, the result being that no more service is being given than if there was but one station in continuous operation each evening."[43]

The newspapers publicly announced their decision to discontinue their stations late in June. The *Tribune* proclaimed that, "It is planned, with the discontinuance of the newspapers' stations, to have a most complete program broadcast from the University daily." The *Tribune* and the *Journal* both published a story although the *Pioneer Press* did not.[44]

On September 1, WBAD, the *Journal*'s station, left the air, followed by the *Tribune*'s station the following day. Three days later the *Pioneer Press* broadcast its final program, although its station was kept alive through the Commonwealth Electric Company that had shared the building. On September 2, 1922, Minneapolis and St. Paul newspapers discontinued their radio ownership.[45]

The year 1922 saw political changes take place in Minnesota. The Farmer-Labor Party won a great victory. At their convention, the party had nominated Henrik Shipstead to run against popular United States Senator Frank B. Kellogg, who was up for reelection. Shipstead won the election by a margin of 83,000 votes.[46] This victory was less startling to the people of Minnesota than the special election of 1923 that followed the death of Senator Knute Nelson. The popular Governor Jacob Aall Ottesen Preus entered the contest for the vacated Senate seat against Magnus Johnson, a "dirt farmer" from Meeker County. Preus lost and, thus, Minnesota's two senators in 1923 were both Farmer-Laborites.[47]

During the election, the *Journal* had backed Kellogg, but it also gave space to the positions and statements of the opposition. About a month before the election, however, the *Journal* had launched a concentrated attack on Shipstead and his Farmer-Laborites. When in that month of October, Robert M. LaFollette of Wisconsin came to the Twin Cities to endorse the Farmer-Labor candidates, the *Journal* stepped up its campaign. The "one great issue becomes clearer and clearer," reported the *Journal*. "It is the issue of radicalism. In practically every contest of moment the decision of the ballot box will be between a candidate who stands for progressive conservatism and one who, whether in some disguise or openly, stands for the schemes of radicalism." The writer concluded, "The careful voter . . . will permit himself no crosses on the ballot opposite red names, no matter how faintly pink their hue may be."[48]

In his personal life, Jones' only pink and red hues came at Christmas, which was always celebrated at the Jones house at 2505 Park. "We'd go over there on Park Avenue on Christmas Eve," recalled his granddaughter. "He'd always stand at the head of the table and recite 'The Night Before Christmas.' He would do this just for the grandchildren. The adults would have to hold their own party."[49]

She also recalled a creche banked with pine trees at the head of the wide stairs every Christmas at the Jones house. Every year Herschel and Lydia would gather the children and get their attention. "We all had our picture taken before the creche of the Christ Child and other figures. He had had the creche made in Italy."[50]

On January 15, 1923, Herschel again attended the annual meeting of the Minnesota Historical Society. This conference, which was held at 10:00 A.M. in the auditorium of the society's building, opened with a discussion of "State Parks and Memorials in Relation to Local History Interest," led by State Auditor Ray P. Chase. William E. Stoopes of the Minnesota Highway Department followed Mr. Chase in the discussion and emphasized the importance of parks in relation to the vast number of tourists who visit the state during the summer. Other highlights were talks by Carlos Avery, state game and fish commissioner; William E. Culkin, president of the recently organized St. Louis County Historical Society; Theodore C. Blegen on the society's traveling exhibition; Grace Lee Nute reading a paper on "James Dickson: A Filibuster in Minnesota in 1836; and Arthur T. Adams presenting a paper, "The Location of Radisson's Fort, 1660." The *Minneapolis Journal* published an article on January 14 based on Mr. Adams paper. The *Journal* included some of the maps prepared by the author on connection with his investigation and a picture of the supposed site.[51]

Herschel and the *Journal* stayed busy that year with more articles on the history of Minnesota. Like most everyone else in the state, the *Journal* celebrated the ninetieth birthday of Dr. William Watts Folwell. While many newspapers ran articles about the educator/historian, the keynote of these articles appeared in the *Journal*'s editorial of February 14 entitled "Dr. Folwell, Young at Ninety." Only a month before, following the Historical Society's annual meeting, the *Journal* featured another article, this one occasioned by Dr. Folwell's address at the meeting. "Myth-making and romancing have served to make many of the pioneer figures shadowy and unreal," read the *Journal*'s editorial of January 17, 1923. "Much better are they when pictured, with their warts and wrinkles. They may lose some glamour, but they gain in reality."[52]

A *Minneapolis Journal* on February 18 identified certain similarities between the legislature of 1859-1860 and that of 1923. The study was based upon a comparison conducted by Lieutenant Governor Louis L. Collins. Legislative procedure had changed but little during the intervening period, according to the study, and the proportion of farmers, attorneys, and foreign-born members was about the same over the two periods.

True to its history theme, the *Journal* ran another article on March 18 about the effect of Major Joseph Renshaw Brown's "steam wagon" upon road legislation in Minnesota. The reader's attention was called to an act of the legislature of 1870 providing for roads specially constructed to accommodate Brown's "strange" vehicle. Illustrations that accompanied the *Journal* piece included a picture of the steam wagon and a portrait of its inventor.

Other *Journal* local history articles that year included a piece on the Richfield Women's Club, which had exhibited the "treasured heirlooms of old families" in connection with a "Richfield exposition" at the Roosevelt School in Minneapolis. According to the March 18 *Journal* article, "such an exhibit of the relics of pioneer days is a genuine value, for it conveys to the onlooker a sense of reality and thus serves to arouse historical interest."[53]

Another *Journal* article ran on February 25. This piece included recollections of early employees of the old Nicollet House. The occasion for its publication was that the Minneapolis landmark was about to be razed in favor of a new and modern hotel. The *Journal* responded again on March 25 with an article containing the remi-

Minneapolis Journal newsboys, 1924. (Courtesy of the Minnesota Historical Society)

niscences of Mrs. Christine Eustis, the wife of the first owner, concerning the official opening of the Nicollet House on May 26, 1858.

The modest beginnings in Minneapolis of the use of two "modern" conveniences then looked upon as necessities formed the basis of the *Minneapolis Journal* article of February 25. The first telephones installed in the city in 1877 were mentioned, as were the difficulties experienced by those who used them. Of course, Herschel had been an early phone user upon his settling in Minneapolis, and he certainly would have been familiar with the problems encountered by their use. The *Journal* included a list of the first subscribers who installed telephones after the Northwestern Telephone Company was established in 1878.

In the second article in that issue, J.D. Robb related the account of the early automobiles. Robb, having purchased a car in 1902, owned one of the first three conveyances of its type to appear on the roads of Minneapolis. The *Journal* included a photograph of Mr. Robb seated in his automobile.

On February 28, 1923, Herschel Jones visited the studios of the Lee Brothers to have his portrait done. It was quite an honor as only a select few were chosen. H.V.'s registration form reads, "For Posterity, the Lee Brothers Historical Collection of Portraits of Prominent Citizens of Minnesota of the Twentieth Century. Galleries of the Minnesota Historical Society of St. Paul." Under creed, Jones had written, "Believer Bible cover to cover." Curiously enough, Jones also penned, "not a church member."

Despite his devotion to his newspaper, book and art collecting, and club memberships, Herschel V. Jones always had time for his family. In the unsteady times of bootleg liquor, gangsters, and the Ku Klux Klan, he remained the steady hand that guided his family, friends, and employees. As his granddaughter had said, "He was fun to be with."

Notes

[1]*Minneapolis Journal*, "The Saloon's Psychology," November 7, 1915.

[2]David L. Rosheim, *The Other Minneapolis or A History of the Minneapolis Skid Row*, Maquoketa, Iowa, The Andromeda Press, 1978, p. 97; Harrison M. Trice, *Alcoholism in America*, New York, McGraw-Hill, 1966, p. 13.

[3]Joseph Stipanovich, *City of Lakes: An Illustrated History of Minneapolis*, pp. 23-24.

[4]Waring Jones interview with author February 17, 1999.

[5]*The Minneapolis Journal*, April 19, 1919; David L. Rosheim, *The Other Minneapolis: Or a History of the Minneapolis Skid Row*, pp. 97-98.

[6]*Minneapolis Journal*, April 20, 1919.

[7]Ibid.

[8]*Minneapolis Journal*, April 24, 1919.

[9]Meridel LeSueur, *Crusaders: The Radical Legacy of Marian and Arthur LeSueur*, p. 49.

[10]Joseph Stipanovich, *City of Lakes: An Illustrated History of Minneapolis*, p. 24.

[11]Theodore C. Blegen, *Building Minnesota*, Boston, D.C. Heath and Company, 1938, p. 441.

[12]*Minneapolis Journal*, September 19, 1920.

[13]Ibid.; David L. Rosheim, *The Other Minneapolis: Or a History of the Minneapolis Sid Row*, pp. 100-102.

[14]Theodore C. Blegen; *Minnesota: A History of the State*, p. 480-481.

[15]Edwin Emery, *The Press and America*, Englewood Cliffs, New Jersey, Prentice-Hall, Inc., 1962, p. 521.

[16]James A. Alcott, *A History of Cowles Media Company*, Minneapolis, Cowles Media Company, 1998, p. 24.

[17]Sally Koether, telephone interview with author, November 1, 1998.

[18]Ibid.

[19]*Minneapolis Tribune*, May 24, 1928.

[20]H.V. Jones' membership card in the Automobile Club of Minneapolis for 1918, expiring March 31, 1919.

[21]The meeting place was later changed to the Bradstreet Building on Twelfth Street and Marquette Avenue, and, eventually, to the Edward C. Gale mansion adjacent to the "castles" of Alfred and Charles Pillsbury, Twenty-second Street and Stevens Avenue South.

[22]Harold Kittleson, interview with author, January 13, 1999.

[23]George L. Peterson, "The 70th Anniversary of a Unique Organization: The Minneapolis Skylight Club," *Hennepin County History*, Winter 1961, p. 20.

[24]Theodore C. Blegen, *Minnesota: A History of the State*, pp. 353-354.

[25]George L. Peterson, "The 70th Anniversary of a Unique Organization: The Minneapolis Skylight Club," *Hennepin County History*, Winter 1961, p. 20.

[26]Ibid., p. 22.

[27]Ibid., p. 23.

[28]Ibid; "The Famous and Flourishing City of Minneapolis,"

Leslie's Illustrated Weekly, No. 2828, November 18, 1909, p. 493.

[29]David L. Rosheim, *The Other Minneapolis: Or a History of the Minneapolis Skid Row,* p. 103; Minneapolis Journal, September 17, 1921.

[30]*Minneapolis Journal*, September 17, 1921; *Minneapolis Journal*, September 20, 1921; *Minneapolis Star*, October 17, 1921.

[31]*Minneapolis Journal*, March 19, 1921; "News and Comments," *Minnesota History Bulletin*, Vol. 4, No. 5-6, February-May 1922, pp. 278-279.

[32]William Stearns Davis, "Wakened by the World War, Minnesotans at Last are Studying History," *Minneapolis Journal*, January 15, 1922; *Minnesota History Bulletin*, Vol. 4, No. 5-6, February-May 1922, p. 279.

[33]"Notes and Documents, the Local History Conference, 1922," and "Minnesota History Notes," *Minnesota History Bulletin*, Vol. 4, No. 5-6, February-May 1922, pp. 250-252, 267.

[34]Joseph Stipanovich, *City of Lakes: An Illustrated History of Minneapolis*, pp. 24-25.

[35]Ibid; Theodore C. Blegen, *Minnesota: A History of the State*, p. 483; S.E. Frost, Jr., *Education's Own Stations,* Chicago, University of Chicago Press, 1937, p. 215.

[36]*Minneapolis Tribune*, April 15, 1922; Ted Curtis Smythe, *A History of the* Minneapolis Journal, *1878-1939*, pp. 242-245.

[37]*Minneapolis Tribune*, April 21, 1922; Ted Curtis Smythe, *A History of the* Minneapolis Journal, *1878-1939*, pp. 244-245.

[38]*St. Paul Pioneer Press*, April 23, 1922.

[39]*Minneapolis Journal*, April 20, 1922; *Minneapolis Tribune*, April 18, 1922; Ted Curtis Smythe, *A History of the* Minneapolis Journal, *1878-1939*, pp. 246-247.

[40]Ibid., Robert Hardy Andrews, *A Corner of Chicago*, Boston, Little, Brown & Company, 1963, pp. 14-15.

[41]Benedict E. Hardman, *Everybody Called Him Cedric*, Minneapolis, Twin City Federal Savings and Loan Association, 1970, p. 70.

[42]Ted Curtis Smythe, *A History of the* Minneapolis Journal, *1878-1939*, pp. 248-250.

[43]Ibid.; *Minneapolis Journal*, May 14, 1922; *Minneapolis Tribune*, May 14, 1922.

[44]*Minneapolis Tribune*, June 23, 1922.

[45]*Minneapolis Journal*, September 2, 1922; *Minneapolis Tribune*, September 2, 1922; *St. Paul Pioneer Press*, September 5, 1922.

[46]Theodore C. Blegen, *Building Minnesota*, pp. 441-442.

[47]Theodore C. Blegen, *Minnesota: A History of the State*, p. 478.

[48]*Minneapolis Journal*, August 12, 1922 and November 1, 1922.

[49]Mrs. Sally Koether, telephone interview with author, November 1, 1998.

[50]Ibid.

[51]"The 1923 Annual Meeting of the Minnesota Historical Society," *Minnesota History Bulletin*, Vol. 5, No. 2, May 1923, pp. 108-123.

[52]Ibid., pp. 153-154; *Minneapolis Journal, January* 17, 1923 and February 14, 1923.

[53]*Minneapolis Journal*, March 18, 1923; "News and Comments," *Minnesota History Bulletin*, Vol. 5, No. 2, May 1923, p. 160.

CHAPTER ELEVEN

PASSING OF AN AMERICAN ICON

"For there is no place of annihilation—but alive
They mount up each into his own order of star,
And take their appointed seat in the heavens."
—Sarah Helen Whitman

ongville, Minnesota, has been called by some a land "where the pavement ends and the North begins. Surrounded by lakes and forests, the area has been a popular vacation destination for many years. Located in north central Minnesota, the area provides some of the best fishing, boating, and hiking in the summer and fall, and cross country skiing and ice fishing in the winter and spring.[1]

Just minutes away from today's beautiful Deep Portage Conservation Reserve and Chippewa National Forest, and only three to four miles beyond Longville, lies Woman Lake. This lake, and the neighboring Girl and Child Lakes, comprise the Woman Lake Chain that begins on the shore of Longville. From any point on the lake, it is easy to travel by boat to downtown Longville. The chain offers some of the best fishing in that part of the state, especially for northern pike, walleye, and muskie. Large mouth bass, sunfish, crappie, and perch are also caught in abundance during the summer. Visitors can get pleasantly lost in miles of forest trails, and woodcocks and grouse are there for the hunting. Woman Lake has been called "One of National Geographics' top ten most beautiful lakes," "One of Minnesota's best mid-sized walleye lakes," and "One of Ron Schara's all-time top [twenty-five] walleye lakes."[2]

Woman Lake, south view.

Woman Lake has abundant structure, many rock sand points, bays, and deep holes. It is one of the few remaining natural reproducing walleye lakes in the state. On the way to the lake from Longville, visitors passed a small pasture with stately red pines and suddenly entered the woods of ghostly white birch, driving under a canopy of Norway and white pines. Perhaps the poet Robert Service said it best:

It's the great, big, broad land 'way up yonder
It's the forest where silence has lease,
It's the beauty that thrills me with wonder,
It's the stillness that fills me with peace.

Here at then-secluded Woman Lake, Herschel owned summer cabins and a great deal of property. Each summer he and the family would retreat to the lake for rest, relaxation, and summer fun. Herschel always liked to be surrounded by his family, and he par-

Woman Lake, main cabin.

ticularly enjoyed the solitude at Woman Lake, for there were few other cabins in the area.

"We'd visit them at their summer home on Woman Lake," recalled Herschel and Lydia's granddaughter. "We'd go up there and stay from May until school opened in September. There was a huge cabin for the family, plus boys' and girls' cabins. We'd frequently go over to these old Indian dwellings and also see where they were buried."[3]

Herschel's grandson, Winton Jones, recalled the Indians too. Every summer, on the Fourth of July, there would be an Indian encampment nearby with Indians setting up their teepees and sharing their culture. He also remembered going "shinny" hunting at night with a flashlight with other members of the Jones family. Today, many wealthy families live on the lake—so many, in fact, that part of the lake is called "The Gold Coast." But back in the 1920s, when Herschel and Lydia lived at the lake during the summers, the area was an uninhabited, pristine wilderness with the Jones family residing in "The Boonies."[4]

Another granddaughter of H.V. Jones recalled Woman Lake as "a neat family compound," referred to by family members and friends as "The Thicket." She especially enjoyed the many "wonderful family reunions" held on the Jones property each summer and "the fishing was always good."[5]

Herschel had purchased a drugstore for his son Paul in Brainerd, so often the Joneses would stop by on their drives to and from Woman Lake for a visit. Sally Koether recalled her northland odysseys with her grandfather, Herschel: "He'd take me up to northern Minnesota with a chauffeur when I was five or six years old. He loved headcheese steak. My uncle, Pat [Paul], owned a drugstore in Brainerd, and we'd visit him. We'd sit in the soda shop half the day."[6]

From Woman Lake, there is access to Broadwater Bay and over 5,500 acres of water. Many other secluded lakes are minutes away. Nearby Baby Lake is known for its crystal clear, green-tinted water with water clarity nearly eleven feet down. Boy Lake, or Que-wis-ans, is rich in Indian heritage. The Boy River flows through the 3,145-acre lake on its journey to Leech Lake. Long Lake, nearly

Woman Lake, Tessie Jones' cabin.

eight miles long and a quarter to a half-mile wide, is just two miles north of Longville. It is six miles long and has depths up to 110 feet. Long Lake is all spring fed, with crystal clear waters. The shoreline is irregular and beautifully wooded with white and Norway pine, birch, oak, and maple. Inguadona Lake is nearby. The lake is over four miles long and is a half mile wide on the south end. Little Boy River flows through the lake, and there is access to Rice Lake on the south through the river. Also nearby are Big Sand, Thunder, Wabedo, Cooper, Mule, and Blackwater Lakes, and directly north, lies Leech Lake, the state's second largest.

Herschel V. Jones in his late sixties.

Herschel devoted a great deal of time to his "other" summer, as well as weekend, home just southwest of Minneapolis in the Indian Hills area of Edina. This home, called "Hilltop," served as his local retreat. Perched high atop a hill, this home, according to many family members, was situated on the highest point in Hennepin County, and since no one else resided there, Herschel had the entire hill to himself. Grandson Waring Jones recalled that on special weekends his family would ride slowly up the steep, winding hill to Herschel's home. When they reached the top of the round hill, costumed family members would be standing at the end of the drive throwing flowers and waving their hands, pretending they were selling the floral pieces.[7]

The glaciation that formed Hilltop and adjacent steep hills and valleys in the central part of the state saw limited melt-water activity, according to writer-historian Deborah Morse-Kahn of the Edina Historical Society.

Hilltop (Edina, Minnesota), summer 1932.

"This rolling area begins in the southern part of Hennepin County and runs southeast," she stated. "The streams that run through Edina—Nine Mile Creek and Minnehaha Creek—have witnessed a great deal of comings and goings of Native Americans over the years. The unbroken topography remained largely undeveloped until well after World War II. From the 1880s through about 1920, there were hunting lodges on some of the hills. Many of the men from the lodges hunted wild turkeys on this heavily wooded land, and the woods were filled with migrating birds."[8]

The Roberts family, which lived near Nine Mile Creek in Indian Hills, just north of Hilltop, recalled the streams in the area: "A never-failing spring sent cold water through the spring house . . . for over 100 years there was no well on the farm. Valley View was a main trail for Indians from the Shakopee colony (on the Minnesota River), and early settlers were also refreshed at the spring and at the public watering trough beside the creek . . ."[9]

Vying for the highest point in Edina with Hilltop is nearby Krahl Hill. "It takes work to climb to the top of that hill from the hidden starting points on its north and northeast edges, but the effort rewards with the sudden opening of a perfect circle of trees at the crown of the hill," writes Deborah Morse-Kahn. "No random growth of hardwoods could have produced this ring; the planting was deliberate, and is of considerable age now." Like Hilltop, the heavily wooded summit of Krahl Hill probably provided a place of retreat for migrating Dakota tribal groups.[10]

Edina was incorporated December 18, 1888, having been previously a part of Richfield. The village derived its name from the Edina flouring mill, owned by Andrew and John Craik. The two men named the mill in memory of their boyhood home in or near Edinburgh, Scotland.[11]

The original white settlers of this area were Irish immigrants who came to America during and after Ireland's disastrous potato famine of 1846. The sale of land in what was then called Western Richfield was opened in June 1855. Patrick Carey of St. Anthony Village was the first to claim and pay for 160 acres of land in Township 116. Three weeks later, Hugh and Ellen Darcy claimed 200 acres in Sections 5 and 6, and they were followed by the McCauleys.[12] John McCauley recalled that when his father, Thomas, was in the third grade—about 1883—he and his sixteen-year-old brother, Roady, were walking through the woods near Hilltop on their way to school. A lone wolf began to follow them. As the wolf closed in on them, Roady grabbed a sturdy tree branch and killed the predator.[13]

By 1886, the area that would in two years become the Village of Edina had but 485 people living within its borders. Along the major thoroughfares, there were eighty-five residential and commercial buildings. The founding of Edina in 1888 was a reaction to the encroachments of the Minneapolis city limits. During the 1880s Minneapolis underwent unprecedented residential growth. Within less than a decade, Minneapolis expanded its borders south from Lake Street to West Fifty-fourth Street, absorbing even the old Richfield Mills community.[14]

In many families, second-generation children stayed on the farms, but most left Edina. Meanwhile, other families moved in and around Edina. By 1905 more than half the people in Edina had lived there less than five years, and 228 of the 920 residents had lived there less than a year.[15]

While the Hilltop area was still a wilderness, "downtown" Edina along Fiftieth Street and France Avenue was little more than that. Herschel and Lydia Jones were snug in their little house on the hill when produce farmers sold tomatoes, cucumbers, and other vegetables along Fiftieth Street in the 1920s. John McCauley recalled that it was not until the late 1920s that Fiftieth Street was paved:

> Our front yard had several huge oak trees and they had to cut them down to widen the street for paving. The trees were cut down with two-man crosscut saws (before the days of chain saws). It was a sad day when they cut down our favorite climbing trees.[16]

In 1921, Mayor George Leach of Minneapolis built a small house on Hilltop.[17] Mayor Leach cleared the land of trees all the way down to Arrowhead Lake. Leach, however, left a beautiful apple orchard on the property, and the trees produced beautiful fruit every year. He also drilled a well so he had water up there.[18]

"Mayor Leach stored fireworks in the stable, or as I recall, explosives that he brought home from the first world war," recollected Ann Dwight Lewis, who later lived in the Leach/Jones house on Hilltop. "There was a hunting lodge on Hilltop that Leach and others stayed at. There was a huge explosion and the stable and lodge burned down in the fire."[19]

Late in 1921, Mayor Leach sold the Hilltop home and property to Herschel and Lydia Jones.[20]

"Tom Gleason, a farmer who lived nearby, was hired to keep the dirt road open because rain could wash it away," recalled longtime Hilltop area resident, John McCauley. "Gleason did his job and kept the road open. When the road was muddy, horses were used to pull cars up the hill because they just couldn't make it up. It was unreal."[21]

John McCauley, who lived below Hilltop, on a road that is now named for the family, recalled that they were the only ones living in the area below Hilltop. Berry farms surrounded the little cottage where he and his wife lived.[22]

Mrs. Sally Koether recalled visiting Hilltop in the 1920s: "[Herschel] had a birthday party there once for our English bulldog. Uncle Will [Jones] was there. He always smoked big cigars and said, 'Don't get close to me or I'll burn you.' That's why I was always afraid of him."[23] Mrs. Koether recalled a woman present, possibly with Will. This would perhaps have been Will's wife, Amanda Jones. Their daughter Agnes would probably have been present also.[24]

According to Mrs. Koether, the winding road that led to Hilltop was gated and "you went around and around the hill" in getting to the top. The property was fenced, and the chauffeur would stop the car, get out and open the wrought-iron gate. The tedious haul up the hill was worth it to the youngsters, however, for there was always delicious ice cream awaiting them in the house. Jones' "summer" house was not a cabin. It was a "beautiful white clapboard house and it looked down at a little lake below."[25]

Two lakes are actually visible from the Jones house on Hilltop—Arrowhead Lake, as well as the more distant Indian Head Lake. "Hilltop was way out in the country, and it was a wonderful place full of big family gatherings," recalled Mrs. Siftar. "It was a big trip to go out there to our summer retreat." She said the "big white-house was like a sprawling farm house surrounded by some very tall pines."[26]

Ann Dwight Lewis recalled the Jones house: "It started out as a small cabin with a wrap-around porch and mirror-imaged rooms with French doors. There was a rose garden in a "U"-shaped patio off the living room. They had an icehouse in an adjoining shed. They used to bring ice up from Arrowhead Lake, and the ice was put in through a little door. I also remember a strange vertical building that looked like a windmill."[27]

Mrs. Lewis also recalled a much later period—the 1940s—during Sunday drives on nearby Highway 18: "You'd look up at this wonderful house on the hill, and my mother used to say, 'What kind of a fool would live in a house like that?'"[28]

Winton Jones recalled the "summer" house at Hilltop being out in the county. He also remembered it was "quite a drive" going up the hill.[29]

Ann Dwight Lewis recalled the road being little more than "a switchback trail." She added, "You'd get halfway up and you'd stop and have to go back down. There were certain curves that you just knew were there, and you'd have to press hard on the accelerator and just open it up. We had to bring up groceries on a toboggan. There were beautiful iron gates at the bottom with apple orchards on the hill, although some of the trees had been wrecked by the explosion when Mayor Leach lived there."[30]

Former Edina police patrolman Mancel Mitchell recalled that the Hilltop area was still pretty much an uninhabited wilderness as late as the 1970s. Patrolman Mitchell would park his car at the bottom of the Hilltop property and look for speeders.

"I would sit in my squad car from three o'clock in the afternoon until eleven o'clock P.M. There would only be an occasional car that would go by. I don't think the Cross View Lutheran Church had been built in the area yet, and things were pretty quiet."[31]

During the 1920s, Herschel kept his luxurious Duesenberg, "dark green and beige, great big tubes on the front fenders," in his garage at Hilltop along with some of his other automobiles. This four-door phaeton intrigued the youngsters and the adults as well.[32]

The elegant Duesenberg "was intended by its creators to be superior to the Rolls Royce Silver Ghost." It was the first American car to feature both a V-8 engine and hydraulic brakes. Brothers Fred and August Duesenberg built their first passenger car in St.

Paul in 1920. The following year, they moved their company to Indianapolis, and in September 1927, were bought out by the Auburn Automotive Company. Through 1934, thirty-five different Duesenbergs had been entered in the races at the Indianapolis Speedway. The phaeton owned by H.V. Jones was a four-door convertible with a separate back seat compartment. Thus, there was a divider between the chauffeur and passengers. These phaetons often sported two windshields, one for the chauffeur and another for the passengers.[33]

"Sometimes when I drive home at night on Highway 62 and see the lights of Southdale and all those houses, I can't help but think how things have changed," reminisced Aldora Cornelius Hallaway, who grew up in an Edina farmhouse. "Why, I can remember building sand castles in the middle of France Avenue when I was a little girl. We had about thirty-two acres of land off France Avenue. We raised vegetables for the wholesale houses in Minneapolis—parsley, carrots, cauliflower, green beans. Between France and Beard Avenues, and between Sixtieth and Sixty-second Streets, there was nothing but a large hayfield."[34]

But Herschel Jones was not content owning property "just" on Park Avenue in Minneapolis, Hilltop in Edina, and Woman Lake in Longville. On July 14, 1919, he and Lydia purchased a lot on the north shore of Turtle Lake in what is today, Shoreview, from Percy and Sadee A. Vittum. Percy Vittum lived in St. Paul and was a cattleman in one of the South St. Paul stockyards.[35]

"Vittum was a cattle commissioner," recalled one early lake resident. "I bought some feeder pigs from him down there once."[36]

The lot Herschel purchased at the lake was originally surveyed in 1847 by Isaac N. Higbee. Thomas Dolbear was issued a patent on the land on May 3, 1854, by the United States government. The land was surveyed again in 1875 by Dana King, who certified the lot size as a true copy of the original plat. On October sixteenth of that same year, S. Lee Davis, county auditor conducted a judgment sale on the land for $10.92 in favor of William F. Lindeman and his wife Rebecca. The land passed to new owners again when Augustus Barnum acquired Lindeman's land through a quick-claim deed. On May 12, 1892, William Cunningham, who lived on St. Paul's Dayton Avenue and operated a very successful woolen business, also acquired the land through a quick-claim deed. Two years later, he sold the lot to Ramsey County Deputy Sheriff Joseph Ehrmanntraut. Through 1904, other owners bought and sold the same property, and Albert Schaller, the administrator of the estate of Martin Crammer, was faced with a lien against the property for $266.63 filed by Mrs. Mary Cunningham, widow of a former owner. Mrs.

Cunningham, who owned several other lots on the lake, sold the property to Percy Vittum in 1917 for $585.[37]

During the two years Percy Vittum owned the lot, he built a handsome cottage on the property. When he sold the land to Herschel and Lydia Jones, the price had jumped from $585 to $4,200.[38]

Raymond M. Michel, Jr., whose parents later purchased the lake home from Jones, was about thirteen years old when his family moved into the house. "The house had three bedrooms, a kitchen, a living room, a bathroom, and a large porch," recalled Michel. "The screen porch had white and green trim. The Jones place also had a very large double garage and a boat ramp to bring the boat in before wintertime."[39]

But Jones owned much more than a home on Turtle Lake, according to Michel. "Herschel Jones owned more property, a great deal of it, along the lake in the name of the *Minneapolis Journal*, remembered Michel. "All these lots went to various individuals. The *Journal* used it for various promotions. You would buy a five-year subscription to the *Journal* for five dollars a year. Two dollars of this would be applied to your subscription. The other three dollars, however, would go towards property for you and your family at Turtle Lake. You could pay off the balance at your leisure. This was a common promotion in that period of time. There were so many lakes, the land was cheap—completely undeveloped and no electricity—you'd end up with a lake lot just for subscribing to the *Journal*."[40]

Michel confirmed that Herschel, Lydia, and family spent some time at the cottage during the summers. The home was among the few nice residences on the lake.

Frances Leslie and son, Wells, Turtle Lake.

Long time Turtle Lake resident, Art Larson, who was born on the lake in 1905, remembered Herschel Jones also owning a very small cottage at the edge of his property line, adjacent to land owned by Aaron Carlson. Larson recalled that the second Jones cottage was "just a cabin" of light-blue color. "It was a pretty good common square house-nothing fancy-built on piers," recalled Larson. "Twelve-by-twelve-foot timbers were set down like railroad ties. The house did not have blocks all around it and certainly no basement. It was pretty spongy land, and when they ran into peat ground, they couldn't put in a heavy foundation. The finished cabin was kind of a shell because they didn't need heat since they didn't live there in winter."[41] In the spring when the Joneses returned to the lake from the city, they had to ritualistically prime a pump for their water.[42]

Larson recalled that Herschel's smaller house was built upon thirty to forty feet of peat, especially in the back of the house. The front of the lot on County Road I, then a gravel road, was situated on solid ground, but closer to the lake there was a peat sandbar.

"I recall another lot farther down the road from Jones where the owners dug a well," Larson reminisced. "They dug through fifty feet of peat, then fifty feet of clay, before they got water."

The smaller of the Jones cottages, according to Larson, was located on a short drive, close to County Road I, the road having been filled in with dirt over the existing peat bog. Larson said there was a house about every hundred feet on Jones' side of the lake but they were all little summer homes and never permanent.

"There were no restrictions on building and no building code," remembered Larson. "You could build what you wanted by the lake. There weren't many restrictions on anything at Turtle Lake then. A guy by a name of something like 'Walkerstover' continually raced his Studebaker convertible in the neighborhood."[43]

Larson said Vittum had sold other lots to summer residents including one to a wealthy industrial contractor named Levine, who unlike the neighborhood nemesis in the Studebaker, drove a fancy Reo at proper speeds. Levine's reputation was enhanced when he built three buildings on the agricultural campus of the University of Minnesota. While Levine lived on the same road as Jones, his property was located on a small hill, safe from the peat bog below. Vittum, Larson added, had a brother, Jesse, who was a physician. "When I was sick he saved my life with a crayoline vapor lamp."

Another longtime Turtle Lake resident, Mrs. Raymond Sina, recalled that about the turn of the century, her grandparents paid fifty cents an acre for lots on the west side of the lake. A generation later, Mrs. Sina's husband's parents could have bought some of these same lots for twenty-five dollars an acre, seventy-five dollars

Herschel V. Jones, mid-
sixties.

an acre for those with shore footage. This was quality land considering that property on the south and east side was soft and very muddy. The property on the western shore, as well as that of the northern shore where Jones was located, was much more ideal since the lake there had a "real solid sand bottom."[44]

Art Larson's father sold 600-foot lots on the lake between 1910 and 1925. "He gave me one and my sister one," recalled Larson. Like everyone else, dad had a summer cabin. The fishing—ah!—it was good. We went for pretty fair-sized sunfish. All we'd use was a drop line and angle worms. You could look down ten feet, and you would see the fish. The water was so clear at that time."[45]

Herschel and Lydia owned the property where both cottages stood for one year, when on September 27, 1920, they jointly sold the lot to their son Moses Jones for the sum of five dollars. That same day, Moses sold the land back to them for the same price. The idea was, and, undoubtedly for tax purposes, to get Herschel's name off the deed of ownership. For five dollars, Lydia, and in Lydia's name only, bought back her property from her son. Perhaps the Joneses kept the property only as an investment.[46]

Jones' small Turtle Lake investment may not have been entirely coincidental. His good friend and one time benefactor, James J. Hill, spent a great deal of time at his vast North Oak country estate, where he owned between 1,000 and 1,500 acres. While Hill was blessed with a lake of his own—Pleasant Lake—on his property, his estate bordered Highway 49 and the eastern shore of Turtle lake. Jones' property was only about a half-mile away.[47]

Outside of James J. Hill's land, which bordered the highway, not the lake, the only substantial landowner on the lake was Aaron Carlson. According to another longtime lake resident, Joyce Bahr, the lake consisted almost entirely of summer homes and vacant lots. "Aaron Carlson lived in a big house and farmhouse on the northeast shore of the lake," she recalled. "He had cows and horses and a man who tended the farm. The Carlsons belonged to the Covenant Church in Minneapolis so there were mostly Covenant people living on his property. But a few Baptists got in too."[48]

Another resident, Judy Luchsinger concurred: "Aaron Carlson, who owned a big mill-working company, owned most of the eastern shore of Turtle Lake. The Carlson built two houses on the lake. It was such a long journey out there that they bought the land just to house the pastors."[49]

Art Larson also said that Carlson owned about a quarter of the lake property on the northeast corner of the lake. Carlson's property extended from the edge of Hill's land almost up to Herschel's lot. Most others in the area were farmers who owned forty- to eighty-acre lots and "everyone knew each other."[50]

Mrs. Raymond Sina remembered that Carlson frequently did work for Hill on his North Oaks estate. The work probably required the job of replacing or repairing windows since Carlson owned a sash and door company.[51]

"Turtle Lake was a long way from town," recalled resident Thomas Mowery. "Carlson went broke and had to sell some of his property."[52]

Mr. Mowery was correct about the distance from city to wilderness. Julie Russell's grandfather would take the train from St. Paul to Cardigan Junction at Turtle Lake in 1905, today's intersection of County Road E and Rice Street. From there he would walk to his cottage.[53]

Turtle Lake lore even includes its own ghost. A man dressed in orange, "but not a hunter," was seen many times over a twenty-year period by different residents. "We were never allowed to play in those woods because of the strange man dressed in orange," insisted one of these.[54]

But the Jones family and others in the area had more than ghosts to worry about. Gangsters such as Fred Barker, Alvin Karpis, and Edna "the Kissing Bandit" Murray were holed up at Harry "Dutch" Sawyer's farm on nearby Snail Lake in the early 1930s. This same Barker-Karpis gang were also at Idlewild Cottage in White Bear Lake Township where they initiated the kidnapping of wealthy William Hamm. A host of other mobsters stayed at the Plantation Nightclub in the same township.[55]

There were no gangsters or ghosts present, presumably, on February 15, 1924, when Herschel gave a dinner party for the Minnesota State Editorial Association at the Hotel Radisson in Minneapolis. Following the saying of grace by Reverend George H. Bridgman, Jones and his guests sat down to a dinner of oyster cocktail, gumbo creole, breast of guinea Radisson, Parisienne potatoes, fresh mushrooms, lettuce and grapefruit salad, fresh strawberries a la mode, cake, coffee, and good cigars.[56]

A donation was made by Walter Stone Pardee following dinner. Jones' program consisted of lectures by three prominent speakers: Melville E. Stone of New York spoke on "The Associated Press," Mrs. Thomas G. Winter delivered "A Touch on World Politics," and Reverend Thomas E. Cullen, Rector of St. Thomas College in St. Paul gave final thoughts.

But not all of Herschel's time was spent at the "retreats" of Hilltop, Turtle Lake, and Woman Lake, nor at elegant dinner parties during the 1920s. In 1924, Herschel Jones and Edward H. O'Hara, publisher of the *Syracuse Herald*, took a business trip to California where they remained for four or five weeks. Most of what they saw of the state, according to O'Hara, they saw from an automobile going from Los Angeles up the ocean road and back inland.

"In all his railroad travel to California his knowledge of the country was uncanny," recalled O'Hara of Jones. "For miles ahead he delighted to tell of the curves, the bridges, the buildings on either side of the tracks, who owned the various ranches . . .

"On our way home, Mr. Jones was asked which of his great achievements as one of the world's greatest collectors of rare books, the collector of prints (which a few weeks ago he gave to the Minneapolis Institute of Art) or the ownership of the greatest and most prosperous newspaper in the northwest he was proudest, to which with his accustomed modesty he replied, 'I've done nothing of which I should be unduly proud. However, I will say this: If I had my life to live over again I believe I'd be happiest just estimating grain.'"[57]

O'Hara always referred to Jones as a "newspaper genius" like "Otis of Los Angeles, Nelson of Kansas City, Lawson of Chicago and Ochs of New York or like Greeley Bennett of New York, Bowles of Springfield, Mass[achusetts], Watterson of Louisville of an earlier day."

That same year, St. Paul novelist, Thomas Boyd, who was at the time financially pressed, began writing book reviews for the *Minneapolis Journal*. Herschel had more than likely met Boyd earlier when the author served as manager of Cornelius Van Ness' Kilmarnock Bookshop located at 84 East Fourth Street in St. Paul. The Kilmarnock was a literary hangout for both Minnesota and out-of-town writers such as F. Scott Fitzgerald, Joseph Hergesheimer, Father Joe Barron, and Donald Ogden Stewart. Boyd, in fact, had been the literary editor of the *St. Paul Daily News* and helped keep Fitzgerald prominent on its pages. Fitzgerald, in 1923, had persuaded Scribner's to publish Boyd's war novel, *Through the Wheat*. His second novel, *The Dark Cloud*, however, sold very poorly, and Boyd, out of money, turned to editorial and book review work. His reputation must have brought a great deal of prestige to the *Journal*. His work at the *Journal* was short lived, however, as the following year, Scribner's published two more of his books, *Points of Honor* and *Samuel Drummond*, both of which brought good reviews and financial success.[58]

Jones and the *Journal* were also hailed in 1924 when *The Advertisers' Weekly* inducted the *Journal* into its Hall of Fame and ran a three-page article, "What the *Minneapolis Journal* Means to the *Advertiser*," by Jason Rogers in its September 20 issue. Rogers applauded the *Journal* as "One of the country's great outstanding evening newspapers, which has won dominance through faithful and intelligent service to its people."[59]

The article claimed that if ten advertising men were asked to name the dozen most outstanding evening newspapers in the country, the *Journal* would be selected nine times in ten. This was because, the article-writer felt convinced, Jones' first purpose was to serve his people. "H.V. Jones is a hard-headed sort of man who knowing what he wanted to do has achieved the success and influence he sought by faithful adherence to the tenets of decent journalism," continued the article. "In sharp competition with a very brilliantly progressive sort of combination newspaper, the *Tribune*, Jones has stuck rigidly to his guns, and won well merited success."[60]

The *Advertisers' Weekly* called Jones a conservative who stayed away from fireworks and gift enterprises. Jones, it further stated, had built his paper on a solid foundation, and it, therefore, wielded a great influence. Always had the *Journal* preached "sanity" and "common sense," and not reverted to illusionary schemes like many newspapers in the Northwest. Rogers said the *Journal* never feared to take an independent stand as long as it believed it was fighting for its people.

"H.V. Jones is one of the very few remaining newspaper publishers who is more a journalist than a business man, has won outstanding newspaper success and recognition," continued Rogers. "He is the sort of man who insists on hearing both sides of the story and publishing both."[61]

Rogers reported that Herschel was one of the best-informed men on Midwest business and market conditions in the country. The writer recounted Jones' twenty years of crop estimating in the Mississippi Valley and how he had traveled fifty to seventy-five thousand miles a year doing so. Rogers pointed out that these travels were carried out before the age of the automobile, and Jones had to cross the country by horse and buggy.

"This brought him into intimate contact with acreage, farm, and crop conditions from Minnesota to Texas," ran the article. "He employed no corps of assistants, but covered the acreage and made his estimates entirely himself. Because he had all factors completely under his own control, his investigations and estimates were more accurate than the government reports, which were collected by thousands of agents over the country."[62]

After praising Jones for several achievements, the article called the *Journal* "one of the soundest evening newspapers in the country." After praising the *Journal* likewise, the piece concluded by saying, "It is a pleasure to present this analysis of the *Journal* and to welcome it into our list of the real newspapers of the country for the consideration of advertisers."

Staffers at the *Journal* and the *Tribune* considered each other "unbearably smug and self-righteous" in 1924, but both papers felt the *Minneapolis Star* was a bush-league operation. Both papers felt the *Star* was a good enough newspaper, but one had to consider its strange origins, its shoe-string budgets, its workingman's clientele, and its limited news resources. Its "strange" origins referred to its being founded in 1920 by the Nonpartisan League, a five-year-old organization of agrarian revolt. The *Journal* and *Tribune* objected to the *Star*'s policy of "state socialism," while the two older newspapers protected the free enterprise system and Republican Party.[63]

The *Star* had been established at Sixth (now Portland) and Fifth Street during a time of League prosperity. Built by the Nonpartisan League, the *Star* slid gradually into receivership and, in 1924, was purchased by A.B. Frizzell, a successful farm publisher, and John Thompson, a former executive of *The New York Times*. Freed of direct League associations, the *Star*'s fortunes began to improve under its new leadership. The *Star* emphasized local news and expanded its home-carrier-delivered service. Within a few years, it broke free of the League completely, supported Herbert Hoover for president in 1928 and Franklin D. Roosevelt in 1932. But already during its initial separation from the League in 1924, both the *Journal* and the *Tribune* realized another serious competitor was knocking on their doors.

Herschel Jones probably attended the Minnesota State Historical Convention in Winona on June 16, 1925. After a luncheon in Red Wing, an automobile cavalcade of twenty-five cars descended upon historic Frontenac and Villa Maria Academy, a Catholic girls' school built on the site of the old French fort, Beauharnois. Highlights of the Winona conference included a lecture, "Minnesota: An Historical Interpretation," by Dr. Theodore C. Blegen; "Minnesota as Seen by Famous Travelers," delivered by Miss Bertha L. Heilbron; "Beginnings in Winona County," a paper read by Mary C. Goff; "A New Interpretation of the of the Voyages of Pierre d'Esprit Radisson," a lecture by Arthur T. Adams; and a paper, "Life in a Minnesota Pioneer College, Hamline University," read by Miss Helen Asher.[64]

On November 7, 1925, Arthur J. Russell returned to his desk in the *Journal* office after attending a luncheon. Scribbled on a piece of paper with a lead pencil, reposed a note on his desk, that read, "Forty years! God Bless you! H.V.J."[65]

Jones came into the office shortly and told Russell he was going to give him a banquet to commemorate his years of service to the *Journal*. Then Jones asked if he would rather go to Europe with all expenses paid. Russell replied rather feebly that he had once been to a banquet but never to Europe. In March, Russell left for Europe with two thousand dollars of the *Journal*'s money in his pocket. "Spend it freely," said Herschel, "but don't waste it!"

When Russell returned from his "holiday," he brought back nearly half the money and replaced it in the "chief's" hands. Many of Russell's cronies kidded him that he was a fool for returning the money, but he told them "If a man treats you magnificently, you should treat him at least fairly well." He had been around Jones a long time, and, undoubtedly, the philosophy of the "chief" had rubbed off on him.

Russell remembered another time when Jones was engaged in a semi-humorous controversy with one of the upper echelon of the business office. When Herschel refused to agree with the man on a certain point, Jones' "opponent" smilingly remarked, "Jonesy, you're no kind of a business man." Herschel gazed out the window, then slowly turned and replied, "Well, I bought a newspaper once!"[66]

"The chief" had convinced himself in 1926 that the *Journal* readers were tired of foreign news and urged his reporters to cover more local stories. One of these stories had to do with dancehalls in the Gateway District, which were very popular in the 1920s. Girls were available as dancing partners for the price of a dime a dance. One of these halls, located at 242 Nicollet Avenue, was specifically pointed out as being particularly seedy, but most of these operations were under fire by protesters who were considered "decent." Finally the city's license committee was forced to come out against them. The *Journal*, under Herschel's prodding, responded to the protests with a story in May.[67]

To further its investigation, the *Journal* sent an undercover reporter to the establishment on Nicollet. He climbed the two sets of rickety stairs and paid the fifty-cent admission at the door. The reporter purchased some dance tickets and danced consecutive dances with a girl he noticed had smiled at him. According to the subsequent *Journal* article, the reporter wrote, "At the far end of the large room an orchestra played. In the center of the floor thirty or forty couples were dancing. A sign said: 'System very simple— Every girl is an employee, therefore ask anyone to dance and present them with a dance ticket.' A girl could make a dollar a night, but many made more by picking up heavy-spenders as dates."[68]

During the winter of 1926, according to the *Journal*, a dynamite bomb rocked this part of the Gateway area. A person unknown

Herschel V. Jones (right) with Harvey C. Clarke, proofing the *Journal.* Jones is about sixty-five.

tossed the bomb with burning fuse into the Wonderland Theatre on Washington Avenue. Edward Oliver, the theatre manager, however, picked up the bomb and hurled it into a snow bank outside where it exploded, broke some windows but injured no one. The incident remained unexplained.[69]

Herschel attended, perhaps, his last Minnesota State Historical Convention on June 16-17, 1926, which was held in Mankato. In addition to lectures, there was a series of local historical exhibits arranged in store windows, a morning program with papers on the history of Mankato, a picnic luncheon in Sibley Park, and a conference on the progress of historical work in Minnesota. An automobile ride to nearby historic sites provided some variety, and a meeting was held with the Daughters of the American Revolution in the marking of the site of old Fort L'Huillier. A local history essay contest was held for high school students with the state and district winners announced in Sunday issues of the *Minneapolis Journal* commencing with the March 28 issue.[70]

During a 1926 trip to California, Herschel became very ill. When he announced to his *Journal* staff that he was going away to the Mayo Clinic in Rochester, Charles Tuller, who worked in the busi-

Herschel V. and Lydia Wilcox Jones (both photos), in their late sixties, vacationing in a warmer climate.

ness office, expressed his wish for an early return. Jones, who would spend the last eighteen months of his life in and out of the Mayo Clinic, answered, "It's pretty hard to die, Charlie, just when you have got things coming your way."

Arthur J. Russell later wrote, "These were the saddest words, I think, that were ever spoken in the old Journal building."[71]

When Doctor Rosenbach heard of Herschel's illness, he became very worried. He had not been able to see Jones on his way home from a recent buying trip, and although their mutual friend James F. Bell had assured him Herschel would be fine with rest, he felt he had seen the last of his old friend. Rosenbach wrote Jones letters that he hoped would keep Jones interested in books during his con-

305

valescence. In one of these, he referred to a recent sale where he had paid $4,900 for the Isham copy of Lovelace's *Poems*. The Doctor said no one but an enthusiast would pay that kind of money for the Lovelace tome, but, "I know of one who is in bed in Minneapolis, and another who is dictating this note to you. They say I am mad to have bought it at this price, but perhaps not so very mad."[72]

For the last two years of his life, H.V. Jones turned the *Journal* management over to his eldest son, Carl. Having graduated from Princeton in 1911, Carl Waring Jones was truly an intellectual. He certainly possessed the temperament, intelligence, and experience to undertake the project. Carl had inherited from his father a love of antiquarian and contemporary books, and he was a connoisseur of fine prints. Shortly after World War I, he had co-authored a book with John Day entitled *Attainable Ideals in Newspaper Advertising*. He would go on to self-publish eleven books in all, and he became one of the founders of the History Book Club.[73]

Carl W. Jones, 1920s.

In taking over the *Minneapolis Journal* for his father, he knew every facet of printing, and he knew how to produce a well-printed book on quality paper, completely illustrated and beautifully bound. He had a great love for prestidigitation and was a life-long amateur magician. Like Herschel, he had the capacity to make people do much more than they ever thought they could, and as an exacting taskmaster, he knew the end product would justify the means.

Herschel's sons Moses and Jefferson also worked at the *Journal*, Jefferson in circulation, "Moke" in editorial. Like his brother Carl, Jefferson was also an author. Houghton Mifflin Company had published his book, *The Fall of Tsingtau with a Study of Japan's Ambitions in China* in 1915.[74] By the time Herschel's illness compelled him to leave the newspaper, the three brothers were familiar with nearly every facet of the paper.

Not to be outdone by her brothers, Tessie Jones was also an author. Her collection of poems and stories, written by her over several years, were published in Paris in 1926. Her book, called *Bagatelles*, was dedicated to her parents, Herschel and Lydia Jones. The most popular piece in the book, especially to her nieces and nephews, was "Variations on a Christmas Carol," but two poems on a merry-go-round and on book collecting were also favorites.[75]

Helen Winton Jones, wife of Carl W., 1918 to early 1920s.

With assistance from business manager George B. Bickelhaupt, Carl Jones literally ran the newspaper. H.V. Jones never returned to the *Journal*; he had lost interest due to his illness and could no longer bear the pressure. He kept busy, however, building his great Americana literature collection.[76]

Carl made few changes in the *Journal*'s makeup during Herschel's illness. Less photographs seemed to be used, but in the Sunday edition, the feature stories were "displayed more dramatically with large, attractive, and eye-stopping illustrations."[77]

In the fall of 1926, Carl Jones published a series of illustrated articles on suburban districts in the vicinity of Minneapolis in these Sunday editions of the *Journal*. These articles "list educational, civic and home advantages, and give a brief review of their history." Among the communities described were Richfield, September 26; Edina, October 3; St. Louis Park, October 10; Hopkins, October 17; Robbinsdale, October 24; Columbia Heights, October 31; Osseo, November 14; Anoka, November 21; Excelsior, December 12; and Wayzata, December 19.[78]

These local historical articles, originally generated by H.V., continued as part of Carl Jones' policy. Memories of the little rural school that served Edina in pioneer days were resurrected on December 10, when the new school of Edina and Morningside was dedicated. The *Minneapolis Journal* published a sketch of the old school on December 9.[79]

On November 4, the *Journal* printed an article on the history of Acoma, a once-prosperous little dairy town in McLeod County, which had recently passed out of existence. On November 25, the *Journal* ran a story regarding the pioneer Minnesota Thanksgiving feasts of venison and cranberries, as recalled by Mr. E.J. Pond of Shakopee, a son of the missionary, Samuel W. Pond. The laying of the corner store of the new parish house of Gethsemane Episcopal Church of Minneapolis, occasioned the publication of a sketch of the history of the church and of the services of its first pastor, Reverend David B. Knickerbacker, in the October 7 edition of the *Minneapolis Journal*.

It is very doubtful that H.V. Jones attended the 1927 annual meeting of the Minnesota Historical Society. Herschel and twenty-nine other lifetime members of the society, however, were elected to serve as members of the executive council for the triennium 1927 to 1930. The new executive council, with or without Herschel, later met in the superintendent's office and elected five new officers.[80]

The *Journal*, under Carl Jones, had its share of big stories during H.V.'s illness. When Charles A. Lindbergh, Jr., flew solo over

Herschel V. and Lydia
Wilcox Jones, July 4,
1927, at 2505 Park
Avenue shortly before he
died.

the Atlantic that year, Minnesotans awaited news of their native son. On the evening of May 21, 1927, Lindbergh was reported "near France." This report came into the *Journal* office at 5:50 P.M., but the deadline for the story was six o'clock. Afraid of missing the deadline and losing the big story to the *Journal*'s competitors, Robert Hardy Andrews went to press with an "almost true" headline, "Minnesota Hero Lands in France." The sub-heading read, "Charles A. Lindbergh, Jr., of Little Falls, Minnesota, tonight successfully completed his history-making lone flight across the Atlantic from New York to Paris in his 'Spirit of St. Louis.'" Andrews' gallant gamble turned out to be right, but . . . the *Tribune* had also gambled with an extra and beaten the *Journal* to the streets.[81]

H.V. had other things to worry about. The seriousness of his illness was mentioned in a letter to his wife, Lydia, from a cousin in Albany, New York, in October 1927. The letter, which discussed the death of a mutual cousin, also referred to H.V. Jones:

> I was very glad to get your letter and a word from you, but am sorry to learn of the illness of Mr. Jones, and I suppose that you mean that Cousin Ed had passed away. I had heard nothing of it and had heard nothing of or from him since the time that he had made me a short evening call sometime in 1925, I think. It does make us feel old when classmates and friends begin to drop off.
>
> I hope the doctors may be able to get Mr. Jones in shape to live many years yet. I presume that he will have to take things easy and not exert himself in any way, and that may be very annoying for an active man. I think you ought to find a trip to Honolulu most interesting and enjoyable, if you can get along without too much worry. I can hope that it may prove beneficial for the patient. I have been alone here for the last two years. Betty is studying in Boston to become a nurse, and I have been trying to keep the house going and have taken no vacations. I find it easier to keep the machine running, than it is to stop and then try to pick up again after a vacation. Have been doing again a little genealogical work at the state library from time to time, lately have been working on descendants of Daniel Willcox and Elizabeth Cooke to see if I can't place Eliab as one of their descendants. Elizabeth Cooke was granddaughter of Francis Cooke-so if successful that would give a Mayflower line. Betty is a member of the society—through her mother, but I have never learned of any Mayflower ancestor in my lines. I am glad to know that Aunt Lydia is still well, although I suppose she must be quite a care for Lois, and then Lois' children must be grown up now and helping. Time does go fast.

I am always pleased to get a word of you and your family and hope you will think of me again sometime. Kindest regards and best wishes to his health-to Mr. Jones and yourself and remembrance to the children if they know of me.[82]

The "Aunt Lydia" referred to as being under the care of Lois was another relative with the same name as Herschel's wife. Both Herschel and his wife, Lydia, were in New York City at the time, although Herschel, perhaps, was under the care of a local clinic or hospital. The relative's letter was addressed to them in care of the Hotel Algonquin.

Knowing the end was near, Herschel had written and filed his will. While pledging most of his estate, he did not forget the Arts. Herschel wrote, "During my business life in Minneapolis, I have endeavored, to the full extent of my personal support and cooperation and those of my newspaper, to contribute to the commercial development of the city and of the promotion of its general welfare and prestige. I have realized, however, and ever increasingly, as year has followed year, that mere material growth and financial prosperity are not enough to produce the well-rounded and ideal citizen; the cultural well-being of the mind and spirit is as necessary as are pecuniary independence and physical comfort. Nothing conduces to this well-being so certainly as good literature and knowledge and apprecia-

Herschel V. Jones. "The only time he had his trousers on, on the Saturday before he died."

tion of the arts. To have a part in adding to the opportunities for the cultivation and enjoyment of the esthetic essentials and refinements of life," he bequeathed the residue of his estate in trust for the equal benefit of the Minneapolis Society of Fine Arts and the Orchestral Association of Minneapolis.[83]

On May 22, 1928, H.V. Jones slipped into a coma. Immediate members of the family were called to his bedside in his home at 2505 Park Avenue South. Unconscious for a period of forty-eight hours, Herschel passed away at age sixty-seven on May 24 of angina pectoris—a heart disease.[84]

Funeral services were conducted two days later on a Saturday, at 2:00 P.M., in Herschel's home. Dr. J.E. Bushnell, pastor of West-

Herschel V. Jones home, 2505 Park Avenue, fall view from the northwest.

minster Presbyterian Church, conducted the simple rites at the home and at Lakewood Cemetery. The bier was covered with floral blooms, while flowers in baskets, bouquets and wreaths, filled every available corner of the rooms. Nearly fifty men, friends and acquaintances of H.V. Jones, stood in two lines along the broad walk leading to Park Avenue. These were the honorary pallbearers. The active pallbearers carried the casket out across the portico, down the steps, and across the lawn, while several hundred friends stood with bowed heads.[85]

The service consisted of only Scripture reading and prayer. Gathered in tribute to their friend were many business associates, leaders in the fields of art and book collecting, and former *Journal* employees. Members of the *Journal* staff were active pallbearers: Edward I. Harlow, Edward B. McFaul, Robert P. Smith, Frank A. McInerny, A. Edward Cook, William L. Krussow, Herbert L. Foster, Harry B. Wakefield, Fred A. Thompson, Earl A. Vincent, John F. McGovern, and Neil H. Swanson.[86]

Honorary pallbearers, including Governor Theodore Christianson, were chosen from all over the state of Minnesota and scores of others from various states.

Doctor Rosenbach was in mid-ocean when he received the dis-
tressing news from Carl Jones. Carl gave a touching account of his
father's last few weeks that he had prepared for only Herschel's
closest friends. Carl informed the Doctor that the first catalogue of
the Jones Americana collection had been received but that his
father had not been in condition to read it. He had held it and knew
what it was, however, and would not let it be removed from his
bedside table. Two sets of the catalogue had been bound in full
morocco—one for Herschel, the other for Carl.[87]

Carl also told Rosenbach that "we want you to have father's
copy . . . as it is the copy he ordered for his own use, I think he
would like you to know now that you were going to keep it for him.
You gave him some of the happiest adventures he ever knew. You
know that, and you enjoyed it with him."

Jones touchingly, but almost in jest, left Rosenbach a hundred
dollars from his will "in appreciation of the pleasure and advantage
which I have derived from your friendship and as a souvenir of our
pleasant relationship." Jones had also instructed his family to consult Dr. Rosenbach regarding the disposition of his library. Tears
flowed down Rosenbach's cheek when he received the check.

Tributes to H.V. Jones poured in from not only all over the country but worldwide as well. President Calvin Coolidge sent the Jones
family a personal message expressing his sense of public loss in
Mr. Jones' death. "I am distressed at the sad news of the passing of
Mr. Jones, for whom I have always had the highest regard and
whose friendship I valued," wrote the president. "His death will be
a loss to journalism. My deepest sympathy goes to the members of
the family."[88]

Then Secretary of Commerce Herbert Hoover stated publicly,
"The death of Mr. H.V. Jones comes as a great shock. The country has
lost a great editor and a useful citizen. I have lost a very fine friend."

United States Secretary of State Frank B. Kellogg telephoned
from Washington with his expression of personal and public regret.
"I am deeply shocked to hear of the death of Mr. Jones," Mr.
Kellogg stated. "I have considered him one of the great newspapermen of America, an able, public spirited citizen. In his death
Minnesota and the northwest suffer a serious loss. I feel a sense of
personal loss also, as we have been friends for many years."

Minnesota Governor Theodore Christianson offered the following statement from his office at the state capitol: "Herschel V.
Jones was one of the outstanding figures of the northwest. He was
a man of strong convictions, and had the courage to stand up and
fight for them. He had high ideals of journalism. He insisted that a
newspaper should be clean, honest and truthful.

"He was outspoken—an expression of his honest and coura-geous nature, underneath he had a sympathetic and understanding heart.

"Minnesota has sustained a loss in his death, but she retains the gain which is hers because he lived."[89]

Accolades continued to come in from newspapermen, business leaders, and politicians—all of whom had been Herschel's friends. Frank B. Noyes of *The Washington Star*, president of the Associ-ated Press, of which H.V. had been a director, telegraphed as fol-lows: "I have greatly valued Mr. Jones' friendship for many years. Journalism suffers a great loss."

"I am deeply grieved to learn of Mr. Jones' death," said Kent Cooper, general manager of the Associated Press. "He was a great journalist and a great man besides."

Harry J. Grant, publisher of the *Milwaukee Journal*, telegraphed, "I sincerely regret the sad news of Mr. Jones' death. Journalism loses a real force and one of its sweetest and most lovable charac-ters."

Congressman Walter H. Newton sent a message by telephone from Washington. "The death of Mr. Jones grieves me deeply and comes as a shock," he said. "I knew he was seriously ill, but I hoped that the end might be deferred a long time."

"I had known him since my earliest entry into politics. I certain-ly regarded him as my friend. No one ever profited more from his advice and counsel on public questions and matters of civic inter-est than I did. I used always to advise with him on my return from Washington, and found his counsel always sane and high-minded. Personally I shall always be his debtor.

"Any man with the high ideals of Mr. Jones, who has been for so long the editor of a great newspaper, leaves an impress of those ideals and of his character on the community, which will be lasting. His leadership, as I know, extended not only to the city and state, but throughout the nation."[90]

Senator Thomas D. Schall stated, "I am very sorry to hear of the death of Mr. Jones. His death is a shock to me. His place will be very hard to fill in the estimation of the people of the state."

A tribute was even sent from London by I.W. Boehler of Munich, Germany, one of the world's foremost art authorities. The cablegram read: "The death of Mr. Jones is an irreparable loss to everybody and everything connected with him. For me he was the symbol of the American ideal of honesty and purity, of the keen appreciation of things beautiful, and of the wonderful civic spirit, which are a reve-lation to every European fortunate enough to meet a man like him. He has done great work for his country and greater work for his beloved city. His appreciation of the ethical and educational value of art, his foresight into the needs of future generations, his indefatiga-ble labor for the Art Institute, have put him in the front rank of your great men, and as a sincere admirer of your country I hope that his spirit will never die out."[91]

Hundreds of tributes from most of the nation's leading newspa-pers, the *Journal*'s competing Minneapolis papers, small state newspapers, art galleries, book dealers, and political and social agencies flooded the Jones family. It would, perhaps, fill a book to print them all. This was certainly a great testimonial to H.V. Jones as a man.

Even prominent Minnesotan Curt Carlson was moved to say, "H.V. Jones gave me the key to my life. While working for him as a newspaper carrier, he taught me the use of credit."

Herschel's newspaper, the *Journal*, like the family, felt the full impact of his loss. A very lengthy, but touching, editorial appeared in the paper on May 24. The opening paragraph read, "The *Journal*'s beloved chief is gone. His tired heart has given up its earthly task after long struggle. But his spirit lives. The work to which he gave his utmost for forty years goes on. His vision, his courage, his judgment, his policies are perpetuated in this newspa-per, of which, for the second score of those two score years, he was the owner and the guiding genius."

Herschel's last will, dated September 6, 1927, was filed for pro-bate June 1. The stock of the Journal Publishing Company was left in the hands of Mrs. Jones and her children, with the control of the company vested in Lydia Jones and three of her sons—Carl, Jefferson, and Moses. The capital stock of the company listed at 4,000 shares was divided into several shares. Herschel's widow, Mrs. Lydia A. Jones, received 2,005 shares, each of three sons, Carl, Jefferson, and Moses, 275 shares. Of the 1,170 remaining shares, held in trust by the Minneapolis Trust Company, a son, Paul, received twenty-three-and-one-half percent of the net income not to exceed $20,000 annually. Daughters Florence P. Ronald and Frances P. Leslie also received twenty-three-and-one-half per- cent, while daughter Tessie Jones, twenty-nine-and-one-half per cent.[92]

Sons Carl, Jefferson, and Moses, as well as John R. Van Derlip and the First Minneapolis Trust Company were named estate executors while the trust company was made the trustee of the var-ious trust funds created by the will.

Ruth Jones, H.V.'s daughter-in-law, was left $10,000 and the widow of Edmund D. Brooks, $5,000. Five of Herschel's valuable etchings were left to each of his children, to be selected by them, and the balance of the collection to become the property of Tessie

Jones, upon whose death it would go to the Minneapolis Society of Fine Arts. The similar disposition was made of the Jones library. The portrait of Daniel Boone, painted by American artist Thomas Sully, was bequeathed to Jefferson Jones. The bed of Herschel's great-grandfather was left to Paul Jones, while the press notices of the English library went to Carl Jones. Edward M. Taylor, of Clam Falls, Wisconsin, was left $1,000.

The major collection of etchings and prints were left to Lydia and Tessie to have during their lifetimes, and again, thereafter, bequeathed to the Minneapolis Society of Fine Arts. *The Minneapolis Star* for June 2, 1928, reported, "A collection of books known as his 'American library,' numbering 1,500 volumes relating to the discovery of America, movement of population from Europe to this country and the settlement and development of the United States, and his other books called his 'reading library,' are left to the widow for life. Upon her decease such books as relate to art subjects as are not selected by surviving children will go to the Minneapolis Society of Fine Arts. The balance of his collection is to be divided between surviving children. Miscellaneous heirlooms are left to the sons."

The *Journal* employees who had been with the newspaper for five or more years shared a fund of $110,000. The size of each share was based on years of service. Arthur J. Russell, Herschel's trusty right-hand man of many years, however, received a sum of $10,000.

According to the will, H.V. Jones: "Believing that those, who, by earnest and loyal service, have aided in developing and building up the prosperity of a business undertaking, are entitled to recognition for their contribution to the success attained in such undertaking, it has been my practice to recognize such service in connection with the Journal Printing Company, both by increasing, from time to time, commensurately with the growth of the enterprise, the salary of those contributing, and by bonus gifts. I desire to record here, however, my grateful appreciation of the faithful and valued assistance of such employees."[93]

Two personal servants, as well as Andrew Matson, chauffeur, received $500, and Anna Wittig, $1,000. Earl R. Carlson, the handicapped Yale student who went on to found his own clinic, was bequeathed $500. Malcolm H. Ornesbee and John E. O'Mara of New York were left $5,000 each, as was E.T. Trowbridge of Chicago. Numerous persons were left a sum of $100.

Jones' will also provided for the ultimate establishment of a trust fund of $40,000, the net income which was to be used for the "temporary relief of the family of any person, male or female, whose

316

sustenance and that of his family is entirely dependent upon wages earned from day to day and who, in the course of his employment, shall be killed or seriously injured by accident within the city. The will provides for the temporary care of such families or dependents if a condition of substantial destitution as a result of the accident is found, regardless of the character of the person injured or killed or whether the accident was due to his or her negligence. Income from the fund also will provide burial for persons killed in accidents."[94]

This fund, administered by the Minneapolis Foundation, was known as "The Herschel V. Jones Fund." It provided emergency relief in urgent cases and would assist in maintenance and clothing of children of deceased or injured workers who desired to continue in school but could only do so through funding. Income residue from the fund was to be used for other humanitarian projects dictated by the officers or committees of the Foundation.

In addition, a "Herschel V. Jones Journalism Fund," from a trust fund of $25,000, was paid to the University of Minnesota. The fund was given "for the purchase of newspaper files of historical or other permanent value and the purchase of books of reference relating to journalism, the history of printing and kindred subjects."

Other bequests were made to other benevolent and humanitarian trusts of public interest. Included were $20,000 to the Stony Brook School for Boys, Stony Brook, Long Island, New York; $5,000 to the Colorado Printers' Home, Colorado Springs, Colorado; $5,000 to the Little Sisters of the Poor, Minneapolis; $5,000 to Maternity Hospital in Minneapolis; $10,000 to the Animal Rescue League, Minneapolis; $5,000 to St. Mark's Church, Minneapolis, for the benefit of Wells Memorial House; and $25,000 to the Minnesota Historical Society for the purchase of book, pamphlets, and manuscripts having a bearing upon the history and development of Minnesota.

The Mayo properties Association of Rochester, Minnesota, was given $25,000 for another permanent trust fund. The trust fund became known as "The H.V. Jones Foundation for the Advancement of Medical Science." The income was to be used for the support of fellowships granted students in connection with medical research.

The *Journal*'s future, however, was on everyone's mind. Herschel had left no instructions concerning the future direction the newspaper should take. On the other hand, the *Journal* was a solid newspaper, and Herschel's three sons were trained newspapermen. But certain restrictions imposed by the will would later surface. The *Journal* would need to gather all its strengths to keep from sinking.[95]

But in June 1928, the *Journal*, still very much in mourning for its leader, was still optimistic about the future. In the concluding paragraph of its editorial eulogizing the death of H.V. Jones, the *Journal* stated, "We of the *Journal* who have gone forward under his leadership. Many of us for the full time of his ownership and more, turn to our tasks today with heavy hearts. But we shall carry on. This newspaper, molded and shaped by his vigorous hand, will continue its service to this community and to this region along the lines he laid down."[96]

Notes

[1]Longville [Minnesota] Chamber of Commerce.

[2]Ibid.; *National Geographic*, 1993; *St. Paul Pioneer Press*, May 1996; and *Minneapolis Star Tribune*, May 1996.

[3]Mrs. Sally Koether, telephone interview with author, November 1, 1998.

[4]Winton Jones, telephone interviews with author, January 30 and 31, 1999.

[5]Mrs. Frances Siftar interviews with author February 22, 1999, Minneapolis and March 3, 1999, Edina.

[6]Mrs. Sally Koether, telephone interview with author, November 1, 1998.

[7]Waring Jones, interview with author, January 26, 1999, Minneapolis.

[8]Deborah Morse-Kahn interview with author, February 27, 1999, Edina, Minnesota.

[9]Deborah Morse-Kahn, *Edina Chapters in the City History*, Edina, City of Edina, 1998, p. 17.

[10]Deborah Morse-Kahn, "Present in our Midst: Three Dakota Legacies for the City of Edina," *About Town*, Vol. 6, No.2, Summer 1995, pp. 9-11.

[11]Warren Upham, *Minnesota Geographic Names*, St. Paul, Minnesota Historical Society, 1969, pp. 221.

[12]On a current map of Edina, this land lies between West Sixty-eighth and Seventieth streets, and extends west one mile from the Soo Line Railroad tracks. The Cahill shopping center south of West Seventieth was also included.

[13]E. Dudley Parsons, "The McCauley's, the Gleesons, and Indian Hills," *About Town*, Vol. 4, No. 1, Spring 1993, pp. 8-10.

[14]William A. Scott, A.I.A., and Jeffrey A. Hess, *History and Architecture of Edina, Minnesota*, Edina, City of Edina, 1981, pp. 7-8.

[15]Paul D. Hesterman, *From Settlement to Suburb: The History of Edina, Minnesota*, Edina, Burgess Publishing, 1988, p. 36.

[16]Vern Swanson as told to Tom Clark, *From the Barber's Chair 50th & France Avenue—1936-1988*, Minneapolis, Nodin Press, 1988, pp. 16-17.

[17]Hennepin County Registrar of Deeds, Official Plat #7725.

[18]John McCauley interview with author, March 1, 1999, Edina, Minnesota.

[19]Ann Dwight Lewis interview with author, March 4, 1999, Bloomington, Minnesota.

[20]Hennepin County Registrar of Deeds.

[21]John McCauley interview with author, March 1, 1999.

[22]E. Dudley Parsons, "The McCauley's, the Gleesons, and Indian Hills," *About Town*, Vol. 4, No. 1, Spring 1993, p. 12.

[23]Mrs. Sally Koether, telephone interview with author, November 1, 1998.

[24]*Minneapolis Star Journal*, Tuesday, August 1, 1939.

[25]Mrs. Sally Koether, telephone interview with author, February 7, 1999.

[26]Mrs. Frances Siftar, interview with author, February 22, 1999.

[27]Ann Dwight Lewis, interview with author, March 4, 1999.

[28]It was after this that Mrs. Lewis, like H.V. Jones, was "fool" enough to live in the Hilltop home.

[29]Winton Jones, telephone interview with author, January 30, 1999.

[30]Ann Dwight Lewis, interview with author, March 4, 1999.

[31]Mancel Mitchell, interview with author, March 2, 1999, Edina, Minnesota.

[32]Mrs. Sally Koether, telephone interview with author, February 7, 1999.

[33]Robert C. Ackerson, "Early Days of Duesenbergs," *The Best of Old Cars Weekly*, Vol. 3, Iola, Wisconsin, Krause Publications, 1981, pp. 70-71.

[34]Deborah-Morse Kahn, *Edina Chapters in the City History*, p. 1.

[35]Registrar of Deeds Ramsey County; Mrs. Mary Lou Schmitt, interview with author, March 6, 1999, Shoreview; Art Larson, interviews with author, March 6 and 7, 1999, Shoreview. The land at the time of Herschel's ownership was in Mounds View Township.

[36]Art Larson, interview with author, March 6, 1999.

[37]Mary Lou Schmitt, interview with author, March 6, 1999. Purchase information from her property abstract. The legal description of the Jones lot reads: "All that part of Government Lot number Four (4) in said Section eleven (11) lying east of west line beginning at a point on North line of Secxtion eleven (11) Township

Thirty (30) Range Twenty-three (23), 2506.40 feet easterly from the Northwest corner of said Section, thence South at right angles to said North line to the North shore of Turtle Lake.

[38]Registrar of Deeds Ramsey County.

[39]Raymond M. Michel, Jr., telephone interview with author March 21, 1999.

[40]Ibid.

[41]Art Larson, interviews with author March 6 and 7, 1999.

[42]Mrs. Donna Michel, telephone interview with author, March 8, 1999.

[43]Art Larson interviews with author, March 6 and 7, 1999.

[44]Mrs. Raymond Sina, interview with author, March 8, 1999, Shoreview.

[45]Art Larson, interviews with author, March 6 and 7, 1999.

[46]Registrar of Deeds Ramsey County.

[47]Julie Russell, interview with author, March 8, 1999, Shoreview; Art Larson, interview with author, March 7, 1999; Mary Jean Levine, White Bear Lake Historical Society, interview with author, March 8, 1999, White Bear Lake.

[48]Joyce Bahr, interview with author, March 6, 1999, Shoreview.

[49]Judy Luchsinger, interview with author, March 6, 1999, Shoreview.

[50]Art Larson, interview with author, March 7, 1999.

[51]Mrs. Raymond Sina, interview with author, March 8, 1999.

[52]Thomas Mowery, interview with author, March 8, 1999, Shoreview.

[53]Julie Russell, interview with author, March 8, 1999.

[54]Julie Russell, interview with author, March 8, 1999; Jacci Krebsbach, Shoreview Historical Society, interview with author, March 3, 1999, Shoreview.

[55]Paul Maccabee, *John Dillinger Slept Here: A Crook's Tour of Crime and Corruption in St. Paul, 1920-1936*, St. Paul, Minnesota Historical Society Press, 1995, pp. 96-98, 141-144, 203, 299.

[56]Menu and program from Herschel V. Jones File, Hennepin County Historical Society.

[57]Edward H. O'Hara, *Syracuse Herald*, Friday Evening, May 25, 1928.

[58]Brian Bruce, "Thomas Boyd, Jazz Age Author and Editor," *Minnesota History*, 56/1, Spring 1998, pp. 14-15; John J. Koblas, *F. Scott Fitzgerald in Minnesota: His Homes and Haunts*, St. Paul, Minnesota Historical Society, 1978, pp. 37 and Appendix.

[59]Jason Rogers, "What the Minneapolis Journal Means to the *Advertiser*," The *Advertisers' Weekly*, Vol. 1, No. 38, September 20, 1924, pp. 9-11.

[60]Ibid.

[61]Ibid.

[62]Ibid.

[63]Bradley L. Morison, *Sunlight on Your Doorstep*, pp. 56-57.

[64]"The State Historical Convention at Winona," *Minnesota History*, Vol. 6, No. 3, September 1925, pp. 253-269.

[65]Arthur J. Russell, *Goodbye Newspaper Row*, pp. 17-18.

[66]Ibid.

[67]*Minneapolis Journal*, May 9, 1926; David L. Rosheim, *The Other Minneapolis: Or a History of the Minneapolis Skid Row*, pp. 109-110.

[68]*Minneapolis Journal*, March 5, 1926.

[69]*Minneapolis Journal*, April 7, 1926.

[70]"Minnesota Historical Society Notes," *Minnesota History*, Vol. 7, No. 2, June 1926, pp. 172-174.

[71]Arthur J. Russell, *Goodbye Newspaper Row*, pp. 18-19.

[72]Edwin Wolf II with John F. Fleming, *Rosenbach: A Biography*, pp. 267-268.

[73]"John Northern Hilliard, His Manuscripts and Notes," edited by Carl W. Jones and Jean Hugard, *Greater Magic*, Minneapolis, Richard Kaufman and Alan Greenberg, 1938, p. xxxvi.

[74]Jefferson Jones, *The Fall of Tsingtau with a Study of Japan's Ambitions in China*, Boston and New York, Houghton Mifflin Company, 1915.

[75]Mrs. Sally Koether, telephone interview with author, February 7, 1999.

[76]Ted Curtis Smythe, *A History of the* Minneapolis Journal, *1878-1939*, p. 275.

[77]Ibid., p. 276.

[78]"Minnesota Historical Society Notes," *Minnesota History*, Vol. 8, No. 1, March 1927, p. 111.

[79]*Minneapolis Journal*, December 9, 1926.

[80]"The 1927 Annual Meeting of the Minnesota Historical Society," *Minnesota History*, Vol. 8, No. 1, March 1927, pp. 58-59.

[81]Robert Hardy Andrews, *A Corner of Chicago*, p. 27.

[82]Edward J. Wheeler, Ph. D., letter to Mrs. H.V. Jones, dated October 24, 1927.

[83]*Minneapolis Journal*, Saturday, June 2, 1928.

[84]*Minneapolis Journal*, May 24, 1928; *Minneapolis Star*, May 24, 1928; *Minneapolis Tribune*, May 24, 1928.

[85]*Minneapolis Sunday Tribune*, May 27, 1928.

[86]*Minneapolis Journal*, May 24 and May 27, 1928.

[87]Edwin Wolf II with John F. Fleming, *Rosenbach: A Biography*, p. 296.

[88]*Minneapolis Journal*, May 24, 1928.

[89]Ibid.

[90]Ibid.

[91]*Minneapolis Journal*, May 27, 1928.

[92]*Minneapolis Journal,* Saturday, June 2, 1928; *Minneapolis Star*, Saturday, June 2, 1928.

[93]Ibid.

[94]Ibid.

[95]Ted Curtis Smythe, *A History of the* Minneapolis Journal, *1878-1939*, pp. 282-283.

[96]*The Minneapolis Journal*, May 24, 1928.

Chapter Twelve

Death of a Dream

"The man who in the view of gain thinks of righteousness . . .
And who does not forget an old agreement however far back
It extends-such a man may be reckoned a complete man."
—Confucius

ewspaper carrier Bob Ulstrom began delivering papers for
the *Minneapolis Journal* shortly after Carl Jones took over
operations. Young Bob delivered papers in the afternoon
six days a week and on Sunday morning. The carriers would pick
up their papers at a garage the *Journal* had rented on Thirty-seventh
and Girard Avenue North. The *Tribune* carrier-pickup "station"—
a galvanized steel building, was located only a few blocks away.[1]

The *Journal* carriers would gather and wait for the paper truck
to arrive. The station manager was usually "an older guy who
didn't have an active job." According to Ulstrom, "we were all
independent businessmen. We had to pay our bills on the tenth of
each month. We were charged for so many papers and the rest were
ours." The average carrier made ten to twelve dollars a month, others up to twenty-five dollars.

Delivery of the *Journal*, including the Sunday edition, cost the
subscriber seventy cents a month in 1928 and 1929. Each month a
carrier would collect money from each of his subscribers, then go
to the Circulation Department and pay for the following month's
supply of papers, based on the numbers of subscribers at the first of
each month. Most subscribers paid the correct amount, but a few
gave a dollar and said, "Keep the change."[2]

The paper truck would deliver the newspaper bundles to the carriers at each of the stations. The trucks didn't come at the same time every day, and when they did come, they merely paused long enough for a young man to throw out the bundles marked for that corner. Where the papers landed was never of interest to the drivers, so it took the cooperation of the carriers to help each other lift the bundles out of slush, mud, or wherever they landed. The camaraderie of the waiting carriers was astounding. Once the papers were assigned a carrier with the correct amounts, the boy pedaled off on his bicycle with his goods to start his route.[3]

Failure of a carrier to meet the delivery truck sometimes resulted in the bundles being stolen. If the trucks were late, when there was a malfunction of a press or an occasional holding of the presses for a last minute extra by an editor, the carriers nonetheless had to wait.

Helen Winton Jones, Carl W. Jones, with son Winton.

"On most of my days as a carrier, I lugged the papers in a proper carrier's bag with the logo of the *Minneapolis Journal* emblazoned thereon," recalled former carrier Charles B. Reif. "But on Fridays and Sundays, when the editions were larger, I used a coaster wagon or a sled. I enjoyed being a carrier through rain or snow or dark of night. . . . The only permanent thing I have to show for my effort is a left shoulder that is one inch lower than the right, the result of the newspaper bag's being slung on my left shoulder."[4]

Reif's route extended from Twenty-fifth Street down the east side of Lyndale Avenue and on either side of Garfield Avenue between Twenty-fifth and Twenty-second Streets South. Reif considered the job an "educational" experience, and in spite of its trials and tribulations, enjoyed it for the most part.

Ulstrom remembered Carl Jones as being "slender and kind of old—[forty] or more." Jones wore a bow tie and was very friendly to the carriers. The delivery boys were given incentives to procure new customers during their delivery cycle. Many of the carriers, however, considered this soliciting a chore and the worst part of their job. Carriers went from door to door asking residents if they'd like to subscribe to the *Journal*.

324

Carl W. Jones, performing a magic show. (Courtesy of the Minnesota Historical Society)

"I had the most new orders, so I won a free trip to Winnipeg to see the King and Queen circa May 1939," recalled Ulstrom. "When we arrived in Winnipeg on Banquet Night, Carl Jones was there."[5]

But Carl Jones was not only a newspaperman. In addition to his being publisher and president of the *Journal*, he was over the years one of only three Americans of non-Scandinavian descent to be decorated by the King of Norway as a Knight of St. Olaf of the First Class. This honor was in appreciation of his "distinguished and sympathetic" service to the Norwegian American people. He was a director in the Minneapolis Institute of Arts, the Minneapolis School of Art, and the Minneapolis Orchestral Association. Jones was a graduate of Princeton, and since 1913, had been associated with newspapers and advertising.[6]

Carl Jones had become interested in magic while a youngster. On a Saturday visit to the Minneapolis Public Library, he wandered into the children's room and discovered the "happiest book" of his life, *Modern Magic*. "I had the nerve to take a deck of cards—'eight kings threatened to save ninety-five queens for one sick knave,' [in the book] by Evans, the first magic book I ever owned," recalled

Carl Jones later. He responded to an ad in the *Youth's Companion*—"Catalogue of Tricks, [ten] cents."

He was thrilled when Kellar and Valadon, two internationally renowned magicians, came to town and he saw the billiard balls trick for the first time. He ordered his own billiard ball magic trip from the Bailey & Tripp catalogue for a dollar, and it took him two years to master the trick routine. From this he learned finger and hand sleights and then the use of handkerchiefs in magic. He continually fumbled with a little tube in his pocket on the way to school. Carl soon joined a half dozen other youths to form a magical club called "The Sphinx."

When he was given twenty-five dollars, "the greatest Christmas present I ever had in my life," he went to Chicago and visited his first magic shop. From the owner/professional magician Roterberg, he purchased a duck pan, coffee and milk, a few gimmicks and a half-dollar with a finger clip for the "Miser's Dream," all classical magic tricks.

"His boyhood magic had origins and development in primitive religious practices and frequently 'signs and symbols' appeared in his ever curious eyes, in paintings and prints," recalled Carl's brother-in-law Arnett Leslie. "These age-old patterns assumed deep historical significance. There was no end to his diligent search in these fields for the entertainment and edification of his fellow men. Is it any wonder that he became the world's great publisher of books on magic—Founder of the History Book-of-the-Month Club —donor of a generous gift to establish a Graphic Arts Department in Princeton's Firestone Library and longtime member of the board of the Minneapolis Institute of Arts?"[8]

When Carl Jones went to Princeton, the magic programs were "longer, more complicated, and no better." He did magical acts with the Nassau Musical Troupe of Princeton University and performed at girls' schools and state institutions. At one of these performances at the Briarcliff School for Girls, he did the Pandora's Box with a thirty to forty, large handkerchief production. As the handkerchiefs floated down, the girls screamed and grabbed them for souvenirs. According to Carl Jones, "I think I lost half of my collection."[9]

Performing in the New Jersey Insane Asylum in Trenton, he and his group were led into the auditorium from a rear door. Along the back wall were inmates in balls and chains, and the auditorium was filled to capacity with both men and women. Carl's troupe had a monologue, quartet, xylophone, comedy bit, and magical act, and the performers were sure the audience would not comprehend their college wisecracks. The audience, however, turned out to be the

Carl W. Jones, demonstrating a magic trick, 1952. (Courtesy of the Minnesota Historical Society)

most appreciative one Carl had ever had, and his "captured" audience never seemed anything but normal.

Jones' saddest and most embarrassing moment happened in Minneapolis when he was home for the holidays and did a Christmas show at an Episcopal Church. He cracked a wine bottle and accidentally killed his rabbit. The children, as well as the rector, came on stage to look things over, and Jones was shattered. His conscience hurt him for a long time, since he had known how to break the bottle without hurting his rabbit. He later found out that the rabbit may have expired from paint fumes; he had painted six mason jars the day before. Although he swore he could not have killed the rabbit, he never used one again.

Jones went to Chicago upon graduation and became a copywriter in an advertising agency. Away from magic for the next four to five years, Jones discovered the magician Thurston was going to be in town. Jones left him a note and the two met at five o'clock for dinner. Carl had always been fascinated by Thurston's feat of levitation and told him so. At one of Thurston's performances before a packed house, the master magician made Jones and six showgirls "disappear."

Later Jones, as president of the newly formed Assembly No. 12 of the S.A.M., met Houdini, who was then serving as national president. During a demonstration, Houdini passed his hand over a table and a napkin mysteriously followed his hand up off the surface. Jones and others were amazed to find Houdini's two shoes on the table where the napkin had been.

In addition to Harry Houdini, Carl Jones became acquainted with many of the greats in the field of magic. These included John Northern Hilliard, Tommy Downs, John Mulholland, Harry Blackstone, Cardini, Ted Annemann, Al Baker, Jean Hugard, Paul Rosini, Jack Gwynne, and an endless galaxy of other stars.

Carl Jones went on to self-publish eleven books of magic including his masterpiece, *Greater Magic*. Upon the death of John Northern Hilliard, his notes were delivered to Carl Jones in several suitcases, a collection of scraps of paper of all sizes and shapes, with little rhyme or reason. Jones sorted the material on the floor in his home, laying out sixty-three chapters in piles from one end of the room to the other. It was then Jones realized he could publish a mammoth tribune to Hilliard's memory.

The first edition was printed and bound by November 26, 1938, allowed to dry in the press until November 28, and then shipped to Minneapolis from a Green Bay bindery. The book featured the magic of 107 magicians, 715 tricks, 1,020 pages, and 1,120 illustrations. A thousand copies were released on December 8, and within less than three weeks, only 267 copies remained unsold. An instant success, it was hailed by many as the greatest book ever written on magic. Another magician, Genii Larsen, wrote, "Everything that has ever been done before pales into insignificance beside it. The material has been chosen by the hand of a master." Professional magician Floyd G. Thayer called it "the greatest thing I have ever seen," Al Baker revered it as "the Book of the Century," and Mihlon F. Clayton wrote, "*Greater Magic* elevates magic to a place among the Arts, which it has deserved since time began." Among Carl Jones' other published books were a sequel, *More Greater Magic* and *Memoirs of Robert Houdin: Ambassador-Author-Conjuror.*[10]

Late in life, Carl continued to do magic shows. Once during commencement exercises in Northrup Auditorium, at the University of Minnesota, he cited examples of modern magic in medicine, physics, and chemistry. Jones, then serving as president of the Minnesota Historical Society, told the students:

In the old days one dreamed of wonderful things to come and hoped for a magician to bring them. Today one dreams of wonderful things and a scientist supported by universities like this actually achieves them.

The magician of today is the product of our educational system, and we can be proud. Our positive support of education is called for now as never before.

Should we not, in our greater wisdom, look to the modern magic of science to sustain us and give us faith, not only in ourselves, but in our nation and the way of life it represents?[11]

But Carl Jones would need greater magic to keep the *Journal* afloat during the tidal wave of the next decade. The men at the helm, however, were all good captains. The editorial staff was under the direction of his brother Jefferson Jones, and Winthrop B. (Cham) Chamberlain became editor in 1929, the position Herschel maintained for twenty years. Arthur J. Russell's column "With the Long Bow" received regional attention and editorial staff members, Robert P. (Bull) Smith and Harry B. Wakefield had a combined *Journal* experience of twenty-eight years. Charles B. Cheney served as political editor with twenty-eight years as a *Journal* employee. George B. Bickelhaupt, twenty-five years with the paper, served as business manager, and his assistant, Charles B. Tuller, had been with the *Journal* since 1885.[12]

The transition from father to son was a smooth one and Carl reiterated Herschel's original principle to be as "responsible for the character of what appears in its advertising columns, as for the character of what appears in its reading columns." He wrote of public affairs how "Mr. Jones wanted, above all else, to take the morally right position. Sometimes he found himself out of step with the fervor of the moment, but, in the end, he usually had the satisfaction of time's endorsement. It was not his wont to dodge a difficult issue, but rather to meet it manfully and squarely. Readers of the *Journal* soon came to expect editorial forthrightness, to enjoy it even when it went counter to their own convictions."[13]

In less than two weeks, Carl Jones, in a signed editorial, outlined his father's basic principles in running the *Journal*. After reprinting H.V.'s original pledge, he promised to conduct the newspaper under the same guidelines: "It seems hardly necessary to add that the same policy that has built this institution to its present dimensions, will continue. The organization [Herschel] built up, its staff intact, its efficiency proved, its experience deepened, will continue along these well tested lines to make The *Journal*'s service to this community and to the whole Northwest dependable and progressive."[14]

Carl W. Jones home, 1620
Fourteenth Avenue South, 1924.
(Courtesy of the Minnesota Historical
Society)

According to writer Ted Curtis Smythe, the *Journal* ranked tenth among the nation's evening newspapers in total national advertising linage, with 1,937,520 lines, close behind the *Baltimore Sun* and the *Pittsburgh Sun-Telegraph*. It ranked sixty-ninth in the United States overall, with 6,982,617 lines of advertising. The *Minneapolis Tribune* breathed on its neck with 6,976,374. Both the *Journal* and the *Tribune* were doing very well.[15]

In 1929, Carl Jones and staff devised a means of placing the complete New York stock market quotations in the home edition. The *Journal* also undertook a campaign against the graft of aldermen. But the *Journal* focused on presenting a comprehensive market page. While H.V. Jones had concentrated on grains and flour with sparse stock marketing coverage, Carl Jones endeavored to bring complete stock market quotations to the businessman in Minneapolis.[16]

The decade of the 1920s had nearly drawn to its close. A new hotel built in the Gateway District did little to upgrade the rest of the area. The illicit booze trade still flourished in the city center. According to an October 1929 article in the *Minneapolis Journal*, federal agents moved in on soft drink bar operator George Johnson

330

and charged him with possession of liquor and "maintaining a nuisance" at his establishment at 121 Marquette Avenue South. The agents expressed surprise in discovering that liquor was the only stock the "soft drink" operator carried on his premises.[17]

The city leaders decided once again to improve the district. They came up with the idea of developing a modern transportation, communication, and civic center in the area bordered by Nicollet and Washington Avenues, South Third Avenue, and the Mississippi River. A new post office was to be the first building erected in the complex. According to the *Minneapolis Journal*, Mr. Coleman, the postmaster, said, "We are interested only in a modern utilitarian post office building which will permit the speedy handling of mails. We suggested a practical architecture with only such a decorative scheme as will harmonize with the other proposed utilitarian buildings of this group."[18]

Three other new buildings were proposed for the seedy Gateway district—a bus terminal, a Union passenger train terminal, and a municipal court building. An article in the *Journal* stated that the old post office on Third and Washington was also to be remodeled. All the land required for this project would be procured through condemnation proceedings.[19]

As the decade of the 1930s grew near, Minnesotans looked forward to even greater prosperity than they had enjoyed during the 1920s. In September 1929, the signal event in the closing of the decade was the opening of the Foshay Tower in downtown Minneapolis. The event was marked by three days of enthusiastic celebration with the John Philip Sousa Band performing a specially commissioned march to celebrate the opening. But celebrations such as this were short-lived.[20]

That same year, Minnesota and the nation were ripped apart by the Great Depression. Minnesotans were reluctant to believe that a reversal in the New York financial district could affect the Middle West. Wall Street was just too far away. On October 29, 1929, Minneapolis newspapers reported that leaders had found business still good in the Northwest and fundamentally sound. Both bankers and farmers remained optimistic.[21]

But then the roof caved in. An inflated Minnesota company went suddenly bankrupt, leaving unpaid twenty million dollars of debts. The head of the organization was sent to prison in 1934. The Depression engulfed the country, and by the spring of 1933, Wall Street had reduced the value of American stocks to below one-fifth of their October 1929 level.

As Minnesota entered the Depression, Theodore Christianson was serving his third term as governor. Christianson had been reelected in 1928—the same election that saw Herbert Hoover defeat Alfred Smith for the presidency.

On October 24, 1929, the *Journal* ran a story from the Associated Press. Special correspondents on its front page informed Minnesota investors that paper losses had reached between five and seven million dollars with some thirteen million shares changing hands. Five days later, the number of traded shares dropped more than half, but the value also declined, predicting a terrible weekend for stockholders.[22]

Carl Jones via the *Journal* blamed the crash on speculation and the growing rich that had recently entered the market. In an October 30 editorial, the *Journal* stated, "Here and there in the United States, business has receded from its record-breaking volume. The slump in the stock market means a real danger unless it is soon checked. The newspaper played down any threat to the business community. "American business has not been shaken from its sound foundation," the editorial continued. "But speculation that cannot margin its super-optimism, has been badly hurt."[23]

Already in mid-November 1929, activity at the Wall Street Exchange slowed as the "disaster" month finally ended. The wreckage of the financial machine stunned Americans and thirty billion dollars of paper values had vanished. The business leadership of Wall Street had all but collapsed. The country's credit system had begun to deteriorate, and unemployment began to rise.

According to the *Minneapolis Journal*, the city of Minneapolis was affected early. On October 24, 1929, a panic occurred at the Grain Exchange. But things were just getting started. The amount spent on Minneapolis poor relief in 1930 was $215,000. In a single year, it had risen by almost $50,000, and Minneapolis boasted the fewest unemployed and indigent of any American city in 1930.[24]

Unemployment continued to worsen, and right behind it came a massive drought in the Midwest. The ferocious winds tossed the topsoil into boiling clouds of black dust and blotted out the sun. Farmers had plowed too much land, and there had been very little rain. The Red Cross reacted to assist those starving in many states and hundreds of those newly poor roamed the streets of Minneapolis. In February 1931 these homeless numbers exploded.[25]

According to an article in the *Minneapolis Journal*, five hundred men and women led by alleged Communists rioted in the city at 6:00 P.M., Wednesday, February 24, 1931. The riot came after an "International Unemployment Day" meeting at Bridge Square where powerful speeches were made by the insurrectionists. These speakers urged the city's poor to fight for their rights. The crowd then moved down Hennepin Avenue and stormed into a grocery store and meat market, smashing plate glass windows and taking what commodities they could carry. Chester E. Doxey, owner of the grocery, confronted the rioters with a revolver, but he was beaten to the floor and later taken to the hospital.[26]

After the store break-in, homeward-bound factory and office workers encountered the disorderly crowd. Suddenly more than 3,000 people were jammed together in the city's lower loop. One hundred policemen rushed to the scene with fire hoses and tried to disperse the angry crowd with water. Nine persons were arrested and escorted off to jail.

Many of the dissidents were young people—thousands of boys and girls had become transients. These young people usually took refuge in the cities—in the case of Minneapolis, the Gateway District, but stayed only briefly before moving off to another retreat.[27]

Most of these drifters were penniless. One, however, was not, according to an October *Minneapolis Journal* article. This man, Mike Sielicki from Toledo, Ohio, was robbed in a "boxcar down by the mills." Sielicki had been eating for free at the Union City Mission and sleeping in the boxcar at night. When he reported the robbery to the police, they discovered that he possessed a bank account of $2,500. He was jailed for "future investigation."[28]

To aid the Union City Mission in providing its charity meals, the *Journal* reported that thirty-eight farmers from Lake Park had donated 1,000 bushels of potatoes.[29] In another *Journal* article, it was reported that the Minneapolis City Council had raised $570,000 through a bond issue to finance "made work" for the drifter job seeker and the homebound jobless.[30]

By 1931 the industrial depression had thrown millions of Americans out of work, and the fall in prices had begun taking its toll on the Minnesota farmers. By the winter of 1931-1932, the full impact of the Depression had shaken Minneapolis.[31]

In additional to the financial disaster, Prohibition was still in effect, and the "soft drink" bars continued to operate, barmaids and all. The *Journal* produced an article about these women in the false-fronted buildings on the south side of First Street. The block where they "worked" was destined to become Pioneer Park, a refreshing green for the new post office. The barmaids sat in sixteen shops in windows facing First Street, Marquette Avenue, Second Street, and Second Avenue South. Behind the windows, they shuffled "packs of grimy playing cards" and were joined in games by loggers, ditch diggers, camp cooks, and harvest hands that were fortunate to have jobs.[32]

The city restoration brought doom upon an old Minneapolis landmark, the Pauly Hotel, located at High Street and Nicollet

Avenue. According to the *Minneapolis Journal*, the Pauly had been a noted stopping place for tourists, and its location in the center of a growing city had been ideal. The owner, Mr. Pauly, was saddened to see his charming hotel demolished, but the post office needed the space for its parking lot.[33]

Some of the more desperate sufferers, who roamed the streets of Minneapolis with little to eat, turned to crime. The *Journal* reported that on March 2, 1931, a robber had shot his way out of the Northwestern Building at 320 Hennepin after trying to rob the City Loan Company. The fleeing man killed two detectives during the foray before he was shot to death on the streetcar tracks at Hennepin and Fourth Street, his body riddled with bullets. The gunman was identified as Leroy Martin, age twenty-six, a substitute postal clerk. Hundreds of people witnessed the killings.[34]

The *Journal* also produced a story of a stag party held on the second floor of 232 Hennepin Avenue, which was raided by Minneapolis police. Unfortunately, some police members were among the crowd of 200 spectators watching eight unclothed women dancing on a stage. Spectators fled upon the arrival of the raiding officers, but two police badges were discovered on the floor. Fifty-five men were arrested but only one of the women. The *Journal* saw some amusement in the flight of the undressed females who were much better in giving their pursuers the slip.[35]

On April 24, 1932, nearly one thousand veterans marched through the lower loop. Their march was joined by a rear guard of Communists with red banners, although they had not been asked to participate. The marchers demanded the return of beer and the payment of a special bonus to assist former service men.[36]

Some city residents lived on Prosperity Row, in a line of shacks on the banks of the Mississippi River. These crude dwellings were located half a mile from the Broadway Bridge on the south side near an emptying sewer. The average shack in "The Row" cost thirty cents to build. Olaf Larson and "Bulldog" Hans Olson, former saloon workers, lived there with a number of others who subsisted on the fish they caught in the dirty river and on stale bread they were given from restaurants and bakeries.[37]

The *Journal*, too, felt the crunch, and Carl Jones began devising methods of cutting costs. He no longer hired experienced writers and editors, hiring instead, cubs straight out of college, and in some cases, high school. Eric Sevareid was only eighteen years old when he became a *Journal* copy boy, but six weeks later, he was a reporter, "with a desk" of his own.

Sevareid later wrote, "When I broke the great news that I was to become a reporter to a rewrite man I worshipped, I received the first shock and hurt and began to learn . . . the God-like journalist looked at me coldly and said: 'For Christ's sake. The bastards." Young Severeid had discovered that experienced reporters were losing out on jobs because they were family men needing more than fifteen dollars a week. These established newsmen were losing their jobs to younger, inexperienced persons who would work for less.[38]

The *Minneapolis Journal* reported that the city had undergone another hard year. The Minneapolis City Relief Fund was running in the red by September 1932. The relief demands were costing $7,000, per day and the mayor was deeply worried. Some federal aid the previous summer had created 8,000 jobs in the city, but the radicals continued to agitate on Bridge Square, and politicians tried to no avail to inspire confidence in the minds of the voters.[39]

The Depression caused major changes in the political orientation of the citizens of Minneapolis and the entire state of Minnesota. For the first time in history, Minnesota gave its electoral votes to a Democratic nominee for the Presidency in the 1932 election. Groups such as the Non-Partisan League, Farmer-Labor Association, and unrecognized unions, found a voice in the Depression via Floyd B. Olson, a north Minneapolis native who became governor in January 1931.[40]

Although he was an avowed independent Farmer-Labor leader, Olson supported the candidacy of Franklin D. Roosevelt and became identified with the New Deal program. The *Journal* challenged Olson's campaign, however. Following Olson's sweeping victory, the *Journal* wrote, "While Governor Olson is a leader in the Farmer-Labor Party, he doubtless realizes that, as a party, it has no national future. He is too well grounded in logic and economics, moreover, to take stock in the more visionary of its projects. We believe he will carry on along safe and conservative lines for the most part, despite certain delusive and costly ideas of his party."[41]

Governor Floyd B. Olson enacted a state income tax to support state education and help limit the number of foreclosures of home mortgages. On a federal level, laws were passed that allowed the free organization of labor unions and the removal of restrictions upon them to enter into collective bargaining with their employers. This piece of legislation provided renewed life to unionization efforts in Minneapolis and the rest of the state.

During the national election of 1932, Herbert Hoover was up for reelection as president against Franklin D. Roosevelt who was seeking a first term. According to author David L. Rosheim, "The *Minneapolis Journal*, oblivious to the social conditions just outside their doorstep, endorsed Herbert Hoover for a second term, and Earle Brown for Minnesota governor.[42]

335

In its journalistic campaign to support Hoover, the *Journal* stated, "Why take a dangerous chance with a new and untried leadership, when a favorable trend in economic conditions is already under way, thanks to the measures the Hoover Administration has taken and is taking."[43] In its "Where were the Jeremiahs?" editorial, the *Journal* attacked the Democratic Party for not having foreseen the Depression themselves, and pointed to Roosevelt's spending and taxing measures in New York State.[44]

Following Roosevelt's stunning electoral victory, 472 to 59, the *Journal* published an editorial straight from the philosophy of H.V. Jones: "We have had a bitter campaign full of partisan crimination and recrimination. This was perhaps inevitable in such tense times. But that is all over. The decision has been made with unprecedented partisanism. The Nation should unitedly hold up the hands of its new President in his discharge of the momentous and critical task that has been entrusted to him."[45]

By 1934, however, Minnesota and the entire nation were devastated. Farm prices had plummeted, and workers were out of work by the thousands. Seventy percent of iron range workers were jobless, and farms were being lost through mortgage foreclosures. In Minneapolis and other cities, those fortunate to keep jobs were suffering payroll cutbacks and were working extended hours for the same pay they had received earlier. In 1933, nine million dollars in relief costs were paid; one year later, the figure reached thirty-three million.[46]

Toward the close of 1933, the trucking industry workers were putting in between fifty-three and ninety hours a week, and they were paid only twelve to eighteen dollars weekly for their service. Teamsters' Local 574 came to the conclusion that it had taken enough abuse. Minneapolis had long enjoyed the reputation of being a "pro-company" town, but now talks of striking were quite unprecedented. Transportation was a strategic key to Minneapolis' commercial life, and the union officials knew a strike would cause economic paralysis. Neither the Teamsters, nor the Citizens' Alliance, the employers' organization, were ready to back down.[47]

Local 574 organized nearly all the Teamsters in the city of Minneapolis. The organizing effort was led by Karl Skoglund, the Dunne brothers—Miles, Grant, and Victor—and William "Bill" Brown. The leadership of the group was avowedly Socialist, ideologically the adherents of Leon Trotsky's interpretation of Marxism, but throughout the strike they adhered only to the unionization effort and not ultimate political gains.[48]

The Citizens' Alliance represented more than 800 city businesses and retained a permanent staff as well as a network of paid informers. The organization boasted a long and successful record of combating unions, and it geared up immediately for a showdown with the Minneapolis truck drivers. The union leaders made preparations and called a mass meeting in April. Governor Olson attended and urged the workers to "organize and fight for their demands." Having gained the support of the governor, the workers were assured the state would not intervene and break a strike. With preparations complete, the union leaders attempted to enter into collective bargaining with the employers. The employers, however, refused to negotiate.

In May 1934, truckers, in a very good position to strike, demanded a wage increase and a closed shop town. William "Bill" Brown, president of Local 574 of the American Federation of Labor, announced the strike and claimed the closed shop issue needed attention before any discussion of rights could be worked out. Brown stated, via the *Journal*, that "Wage agreements are not much protection to a union man unless first there is a definite assurance that the union man will be protected in his job."[49]

Within days, the union literally closed the city of Minneapolis. All transportation, except for necessary foodstuffs, was non-existent, and even gas stations were picketed on the theory that truckers, wanting to ignore the strike, could obtain gas from their cars, which were free to move about the city.[50]

The strikers gained considerable support from the citizenry of Minneapolis, and within three days the union received $15,000 in contributions. Governor Olson even contributed a $500 donation. The strike proceeded under relatively peaceful conditions for several days.[51]

The *Journal* was slow to react to the strike threat. It did, however, give good coverage to the pre-strike discussions, and during the first few days of the strike, *Journal* reporters were on the scene during incidents that they decidedly reported pro-labor. One of these verbal incidents was that of picket leader Alfred Johnson who told the *Journal*, "There can't be any drinking on this job. We have to be orderly. And we aren't going to allow any agitators or troublemakers to do anything around here. We're good Americans and we don't want any of this Communist stuff."[52]

On Saturday morning, May 19, five hundred strikers attempted to halt two C. Thomas stores' trucks from making a downtown Minneapolis delivery. Twelve squad cars of club-wielding police and special deputies charged the pickets. According to the *Journal*'s report, twenty persons, sixteen of whom were strikers, were taken to the hospitals. That same evening three cars carrying men and women from strike headquarters were forced into entering Tribune Alley, next to the Journal and Tribune buildings on Fourth

Street, and were severely beaten with clubs and saps and kicked mercilessly into unconsciousness. Strikers suddenly got the message. That weekend they padded caps and gathered war clubs.[53]

Labor leaders indicated that the strikers were unarmed but the *Journal* report disagreed: "Nearly 500 strikers swooped down on the trucks moving produce with rocks and clubs. Twelve police cars were rushed to the scene. The fight was on. Strikers were clubbed and fought back with clubs. Ambulances screamed to the scene."[54]

The *Journal* pointed out in its editorial that the strike methods used by Local 574 were dividing the people of Minneapolis. According to its report, "It matters not what are the right and wrongs of this labor controversy. There are powerful and lawful methods by which to settle them. Usurpation of authority, intimidation, and violence are emphatically not in that category.

"If it be a fact that the striking truck drivers have labored under injustices that their employers refuse to correct, it does not follow that these strikers have the right to starve and abuse a whole city to bring about the redress they seek.

"The battle for civic freedom, for human rights, is on. There can be only one upshot. The reign of law and order must be, will be, restored."[55]

The employers, however, assembled an army of men, handed out billy clubs, and issued a complete set of instructions from its headquarters at 1328 Hennepin Avenue. Many of the "army" members did not consider themselves strikebreakers. Instead, they felt they were doing their duty in keeping the streets open. The men were officially made special deputies, and each wore a badge, but to the strikers, they were still strikebreakers.

The strikers, too, had become well armed. Six hundred of them moved into the market area, while special deputies were on hand to greet them. When the deputies saw the large, disciplined force, however, they retreated hastily, leaving the police to fend for themselves. Quickly, the police officers formed a square, drew their guns, and held the strikers at bay. One striker, not to be outdone, drove his car into the square and dispersed the police force. Each officer was thus exposed to the savage beatings of the strikers and the striker victory came to be called the "Battle of Deputies Run."[57]

According to one *Journal* reporter, it was "the first time since the crash that the strikers were nearly all armed. . . . They were equipped with hundreds of eighteen-inch lengths of gas pipes and with clubs and sticks." Thirty-seven persons were injured in the melee, all but seven, members of the police.[58]

One trucker, John S. Koblas, was permitted to continue driving because he gave a union official two one hundred-pound sacks of potatoes a week. Once while Koblas, his wife Susan, and two-month-old son Robert were passing through downtown Minneapolis in the truck, gunfire errupted, and Koblas pushed his family members to the floor. Although Koblas' truck was eventually allowed to pass, the family was stopped at the Mendota Bridge as strikers swarmed all over the vehicle, demanding answers.[59]

Many years later, Koblas' wife, Susan, recalled a union official coming to their home and asking Koblas if he'd like his home smashed to pieces by a "bunch of men." According to Susan, Koblas replied, "Yes, and I'll be sitting here with a shotgun across my lap waiting." Fortunately for Koblas, it was only a threat.

In the early days of the strike, the *Journal* had presented the story in an objective manner. But within days, the *Journal* became increasingly less favorable to the strikers. In a Sunday edition, Jones' paper ran a four-column photograph showing a policeman being hit in the jaw by one of the strikers.[60]

Newspapers announced there would be a movement of trucks the next day. But another clash was unavoidable when a thousand special deputies and a small number of police squared off with 2,500 strikers in the market place. The *Journal* estimated that 3,000 persons joined the crowd in case any of the trucks decided to move. A union official estimated the crowd at 60,000. Radio broadcasters were on the spot with live coverage when an unidentified person hurled a crate of tomatoes through a store window. Baseball bats, saps, and rocks smashed skulls, and as deputies and police fled, several badges were found and displayed by the strikers. Several members of the Citizens' Alliance were killed, one deputy died, and another was mortally wounded.[61]

C. Arthur Lyman, a close friend of Jefferson and Frances Jones, was an innocent bystander who happened to be in the wrong place at the wrong time. Lyman was struck by a rock thrown by one of the strikers, and he was killed. A granddaughter of Herschel Jones later recalled strikers throwing rocks from rooftops and some of the men crawling into windows of buildings. On the ground, their confederates turned over trucks. "I was not allowed to go downtown," she said. Another granddaughter remembered Mr. Lyman as a "good family friend who lived in Kenwood." She recalled his being on the strike scene as an effort to stop the violence."[62]

The *Journal*'s editorial page mourned the passing of C. Arthur Lyman, the vice-president of the American Ball Company. The piece condemned the lawlessness and overbearing actions of the strikers that had resulted in the death of an important businessman.

The *Journal* contended that Communists were in control of the strike and blamed, not the "honest American strikers, but the red revolutionaries who managed the bloody riot of Tuesday. . . . who killed Arthur Lyman."[63]

The following Sunday an agreement was reached between the Teamsters and the employers. The agreement, however, was subject only to voluntary compliance on the part of the employers. It soon became clear that the employers were not about to honor the agreement. On July 16, Local 574 leaders called for a new strike to compel the employers to honor the May agreement. On July 20 a truck carrying fifty heavily armed policeman ambushed a group of strikers, killing two of them and wounding sixty-seven others. Governor Olson declared martial law on July 26.[64]

The *Journal* published its account of the July 20th incident inaccurately, blaming the strikers rather than the police: "The strikers rushed forward. They swarmed over the truck and onto police squad cars, laying about them strenuously with fists and clubs.

"Literally fighting for their lives, the police fired once into the air in an effort to frighten off the strikers. It did no good. On they came.

"Finally one policeman aimed his gun at the crowd and fired. A striker toppled over. Then another policeman fired. Another striker fell. The mob started to move back under the more rigorous tactics of the police.

"For a moment it seemed that more gunfire would be averted, but the rioters congealed in another group again and when ordered to disperse, defied the police."[65]

The *Journal*'s fabrication of the wrong "bad guys" irked many of its subscribers. Governor Olson appointed a committee to investigate the shooting and found that police officers were at no time endangered, pickets were unarmed, pickets did not attack the officers, the truck movement was a "plant," and the police department became an agency to break the strike. "The decoy itself was dastardly; the deliberate attempt by the *Journal* to tell the public an incorrect version was reprehensible."[66]

At the end of July, Minnesota guardsmen pulled an early morning raid and peacefully arrested the leaders of Local 574, with the exception of two who had slipped away. John Belor, who had been shot by the police during "Bloody Friday," died that same day. The *Journal*'s headline read "Troops Jail Four Strike Leaders, Seize Headquarters, Arrest 25 in Truck Riots; Striker Wounded in Shooting Affray Dies." No mention was made that Belor had been shot by a policeman, and it gave the impression he had been a victim of rioters.[67]

Two days later, Governor Olson sent Lieutenant Kenneth Haycraft and a detachment of troops to raid the headquarters of the Citizens' Alliance. They found "a sheaf of dictaphone records and confidential letters." The evidence proved a close relationship had been maintained by the Citizens' Alliance and the Employers' Advisory Committee. Haycraft later found that the Alliance had been "tipped off" and four files had been removed the previous day.

The strike ended in August. Martial law was lifted by Governor Olson, troops were dispersed, and Minneapolis went back to Depression-era normalcy. The *Journal* attributed the death of the strike to secret elections. President Roosevelt, however, after meeting with Governor Olson, had issued an order "to the Reconstruction Finance Corporation to withdraw its loans to banks that were financing employer resistance. The pressure proved decisive because Twin City banks had served as the principal coercive agency of the Citizens' Alliance. Deprived of life-and-death financial power over debt-ridden employers, the Alliance could not keep the strike from collapsing."[68]

In 1936 Governor Olson was stricken with stomach cancer and died in Rochester on August 22. The Mayo brothers themselves had tried to save him with every effort of their medical knowledge expended. Minneapolis residents mourned the passing of their friend and benefactor. Hjalmar Peterson succeeded Olson as governor.[69]

The mid-1930s constituted a time of great change in the Minneapolis newspaper scene. The *Minneapolis Journal* had a daily circulation of 114,700 with a Sunday circulation of 159,200 in 1935. Of these totals, 65,700 and 76,400 represented the city circulation. The *Journal* carried 7.4 million lines of advertising daily with 1.9 million on Sunday, and was hailed as the "silk stocking" paper and the "mouthpiece of the bourbons."[70]

The *Tribune*, at the time, had a combined daily circulation of 140,500 (85,900 city circulation) and a Sunday circulation of 201,800 (108,400 city). The *Tribune* carried seven million lines of daily advertising in 1935 and 3.1 million on Sunday.

The *Minneapolis Star* had a circulation of 79,000, but 57,100 of this in the city's retail zone, constituting the highest percentage of any of the Minneapolis newspapers. Regarded as the "labor paper" or blue-collar paper, the *Star* fell a distant third in advertising with 5.5 million lines, most of which came from smaller advertisers. The *Star* had not really been a "paper of all the people," and often its editorial positions tended to influence news coverage and to dismiss opposing points of views. Its news coverage was frequently doctored to appease advertisers and the business community.[71]

When A.B. Frizzell, the *Star*'s majority stockholder died in 1934, the course of Minneapolis newspaper history was changed.[72]

The *Star* was put up for sale and initially offered to Carl Jones for a very nominal amount. Jones, however, turned down the lucrative offer stating, "We need a third newspaper in this town."

On June 18, the Cowles family of Des Moines, Iowa, purchased the *Star*, the third and weakest newspaper in the Minneapolis community. "To them that was no cause for discouragement." John Cowles was elected president, Gardner Cowles, Jr., vice president, Davis Merwin, vice president and treasurer, and John Thompson, secretary. The purchase was announced on the front page of the *Star* of June 14, with the following statement signed by the new owners:

> In purchasing control of the *Star* we are joining forces with John Thompson and George Adams and their associates to make the *Star* one of America's great liberal newspapers. All of the *Star*'s present executives and employees remain under the new ownership.
>
> The *Star* will continue to be a paper of all the people-not for just one group or class. The *Star* will continue to be politically and financially independent.
>
> It will continue to present the news fairly, accurately, concisely and honestly, to confine its own opinions to the editorial page, to respect the views with which it may not agree, to be a growing force in the development of Minneapolis as a splendid city in which to live and work.
>
> It will continue to balance enterprise with decency and to seek to be a source of information and entertainment in every home.[73]

By October, net paid circulation escalated to 88,190, rose to 94,196 in November and 100,000 by December. For the six months ending March 31, 1936, the *Minneapolis Star* had the largest daily home delivery circulation in the city with 56,286. Total circulation stood at 102,158, and 68,753 had been garnered from city circulation. Classified advertising linage during the first three months of 1936 had increased sixty-three percent, giving it the lead over both the *Journal* and the *Tribune*.[74]

These developments certainly did not go unnoticed by Lydia and members of the Jones family. But as Carl kept busy keeping the *Journal* competitive, Lydia spent time with her family. In 1937, her grandson Peter Ronald wrote her from Camp Aloha in River Falls, Wisconsin saying:

Dear Gram,

I am awful, awful sorry I have not written you much sooner, and I am very sorry. I never enjoyed anything so much as the things you brought me last Tuesday. I gave one watermelon to the camp and I gave one to our tent but I had half myself. And I just loved the candy. My clothes are just swell and so are my towels swell. Everything has gone all right. I miss you very much and hope you will come and see me soon. Please give my love to Aunt Tess and everybody.[75]

Lydia, out of a combination of love and loneliness, spent a great amount of time with her grandchildren in the 1930s. Grand-daughter Francis Siftar recalled, "She would always come visit us in her big Packard limousine. Inside the car were glass vases of flowers on either side of the back windows. My grandmother's chauffeur, named Wally, drove the car, and he always wore a gray uniform and cap. The door would open and everyone would come up to stand on the running board while she paid her respects like Queen Victoria. Grandma and Tess owned wonderful children's literature, and they always gave us a book.

"I think grandma was a great deal like Queen Victoria—morose, quiet, not outgoing or bouncy but a very sweet person. Whenever the immense car pulled up, it was a big event. The doors opened up, we rushed to her, but she wouldn't get out."[76]

Carl W. Jones with daughter Thirza H. Jones, 1930.

Every Christmas the family would gather in the big house on Park Avenue and give a toast to Herschel V. Jones. To commemorate his life, a different family member each year would recite a piece from the pen of Charles Dickens:

We had a friend who was our friend from early days, with whom we often pictured the changes that were to come upon our lives, and merrily imagined how he would speak, and walk, and think, and talk, when he came to be old. His destined habitation in the City of the Dead received him in his prime. Shall he be shut out from our Christmas remembrance?

Would his love have so excluded us? Lost friend, lost child, lost parent, sister, brother, husband, wife, we will not so

December 23, 1929, at the Park Avenue H.V. Jones House. Left to right: top row: Waring, Winton, Betty, Sally Jones, Wells Leslie; Bottom row: Chickie, Arnetta Leslie, Herschel Jones, and David Leslie.

discard you. You shall hold your cherished places in our Christmas hearts, and by our Christmas fire; and in the season of immortal hope, and on the birthday of immortal mercy, we will shut out nothing.[77]

The toast to Herschel Jones each Christmas was a moving experience, according to a granddaughter. Lydia, her children, and her grandchildren, all with tears in their eyes, would pay tribute with love and silent prayer.

In September 1938, John Cowles and his family moved to Minneapolis and bought a Georgian brick house at 2318 Park Avenue South, only one block north of the former residence of H.V. Jones. "Working quietly and with a kindly manner so characteristic of the Cowles tradition, John started a one-man campaign to win over Minneapolis," stated an article in *Editor & Publisher*. "Largely by his own effort he completely changed the picture in favor of the *Minneapolis Star*. He accomplished his mission by constant application, day in and day out. Such a personal program, combined with an excellent product, brought results in the form of advertising patronage and with it a public confidence in the management of the paper."[78]

Cowles did a great deal of entertaining in both his Park Avenue residence and his summer home, the "Pink Palace," on Lake Minnetonka. Among those with whom he fraternized were business, literary, and cultural leaders including the Pillsburys, the William McNallys, the F. Peavey Heffelfingers, the Addison Lewises, Alfred and Fefa Wilson, Harold W. Sweatt, John and Berniece Dalrymple, Hugh and Kate Wood, the Rufus Rands, John and Dorothy Rood, and author Sinclair Lewis.[79]

Between 1935 and 1939, the *Star*'s circulation reached new heights—75,770 to 150,056. The *Star* placed an emphasis on sports, using its own reporters to cover Big Ten games, furnishing air transportation to speed up its coverage and photographs.[80]

As the *Star* continued its rapid surge, replacing the *Journal* and *Tribune* as Minneapolis' premier paper, the *Journal* announced it was reversing its policy and accepting liquor ads. The following day the *Star* published its new policy of dropping all liquor advertising.

According to John Cowles, "We let every minister in the state know that the *Journal* was taking liquor ads while we were drop-

4-H Club Building, St. Louis County, August 6, 1938. Left to right: James Haley, Carl W. Jones, Elsa Johnson, Edith Johnson, and T.A. Erickson. (Courtesy of the Minnesota Historical Society)

345

ping them. I'll bet 200 preachers preached against the good old *Journal*. I'm sure it added several thousand to the *Star*'s circulation."[81]

Meanwhile, Nelson Dayton, head of the largest retail advertiser in the city, informed Carl Jones, "as a courtesy," that Dayton's [now Marshall Fields] was switching its advertising efforts to the *Minneapolis Star*. Dayton's had never advertised in the *Star* prior to this meeting, since he was a firm believer in the policy that merchants had a responsibility to support local businesses. Hitherto, Dayton's had considered the Cowles family "interlopers" who were not a part of the community.[82]

Following Herschel Jones' death in 1928, controlling interest in the *Journal* rested with his widow, Lydia, and sons Carl, Jefferson, and Moses. During the Great Depression, the *Journal* had spent little money on new promotions and innovations. No new equipment was purchased, and *Journal* staffers and employees suffered a cut in pay. Still, the *Journal* had lost money. The *Journal*'s home in the building that had been erected in 1890 was "outdated, inefficient and expensive to maintain, and inadequate for the needs of a modern metropolitan newspaper." Furthermore, the land at its location was leased rather than owned by the newspaper.[83]

Lydia Jones' concern about the *Journal* led to her installation of George Ronald as business manager, replacing George Bickelhaupt, who had been against any potential sale of the paper. The bad financial situation in 1939 prompted Mrs. Jones to act in selling the *Journal* although there was little profit to be divided between her sons, who were earning yearly salaries of $12,000 to $18,000. Carl, Jefferson, and Moses would naturally be against any purported sale of the *Journal* and were told nothing of their mother's interest in selling the paper. Lydia had, however, made up her mind and began making plans while keeping them a secret.[84]

In July 1939, Carl Jones and sons Winton and Waring flew to South Dakota with a friend, Sir Geoffrey Crowther, who served as editor of the *London Economist*. The Englishman had always wanted to see the American West, Carl was badly in need of a vacation, and so the party visited Spearfish and Deadwood in the Black Hills area. The children were shocked when, in witnessing an Indian "Sun Dance Ritual," a warrior was put to the test. As the startled children watched in awe, a small stake pierced the man's chest. A long stretch of twine fastened the stake under the warrior's muscles on one end, and the opposite end was tied to a pole in the center of the wigwam. The brave Indian leaned back and danced in a circle in a test of his endurance.[85]

In Deadwood, the Joneses attended "The Trial of Jack McCall," a play staged in the Old Towne Hall on Lee Street. Wild Bill

Hickok had been playing poker in Deadwood's Saloon Number 10 on August 2, 1876, when he was shot and killed from behind by a drifter named Jack McCall. The assassination and trial were reenacted, and Carl Jones and his English guest were chosen as two of the jurors. To the wide-eyed Jones boys, the "real" West never seemed so real.

The family and their English guest visited the Homestake Gold Mine near Lead, one of the oldest and largest underground gold mines in the Western Hemisphere. The mine had operated continuously since 1876, the year of the Custer Massacre, and today still produces 350,000 ounces of gold annually. On their way down into the mine, young Waring inquired of the tour guide as to the safety of the rope and was told, "It hasn't broken in six weeks."[86]

Near Rapid City, they visited the Stratosphere Bowl or "Strato Bowl" as it was often referred to, a deep pocket in the earth's crust. The "bowl," surrounded by a steep plateau, was a natural geological hole in the earth, which the children estimated to be about 1,000 feet deep and a half-mile wide. A road meandered down one side exposing a beautiful "Grand Canyonesque" vista. It was from this bowl that the first balloon and gondola ascended into the heavens and its occupants photographed the curvature of the earth.[87]

At the bowl, the party met renowned national rodeo champion Clyde Jones. The cowboy, no relation to the travelers, invited them to his ranch for four or five days. Waring recalled watching a "pet" rattlesnake being fed chipmunks and was shocked by the huge lump in the reptile's throat that was still there the following day.

In the midst of their stay, an urgent message reached them from Carl's secretary, Mrs. Peter Hawks. Mrs. Hawks, who had also served as secretary to H.V. Jones, urged, "Get back here right away. Your brothers and sister [Tessie] are trying to sell the *Journal*."

The Joneses rushed back to Minneapolis in an attempt to save the paper. Upon their arrival, they met with C.T. Jaffray, president of the First National Bank and founder of the Minnekahda Club, who asserted, "Carl, what is this rumor about a possible sale of the *Journal*? This must not happen. I'll get you the money this week to buy the paper."

Carl's wife, Helen Winton Jones, had two younger brothers, David and Charles, who ran a lumber company. They assured Carl, also, that they would raise the money for him to purchase the *Journal* within a matter of days.

Carl rushed to the family lawyer with his two offers but was told, "It's too late; we have already sold and signed."

The following day when Carl was called upon to sign the document of sale, giving John Cowles the newspaper, he was further shaken to find a codicil attached demanding that he could not work for another newspaper within 250 miles of the *Journal* over the next twenty years.[88]

The sale of the *Journal* had been a well-kept secret right up to the time of its announcement on the radio at 6:00 P.M. on July 31, 1939. There had been no hints, leaks, or rumors. Herschel V. Jones had sealed the fate of the *Journal* himself, perhaps, when he had willed majority control of the newspaper to his wife. As the paper began to struggle through the Depression's financial setbacks, her concerns had grown for the paper's feasibility. When her mind was made up, she was ready to sell, and some members of her family, friends, and employees of the *Journal*, were the last to know.

Arthur J. Russell, on that "fatal" morning, looked out to see nearly all of the *Journal*'s 400 employees milling on the sidewalk talking and whispering. He went out and asked, "What is it? A strike?"

"Strike, hell!" answered a compositor that had been a long-standing employee. "The paper has been sold and is closed down!"[89]

Most of the *Journal* employees learned of the sale from a notice posted on the bulletin board. Others found out the hard way. Bob Ulstrom and his fellow carriers found no newspapers that day at their station on Thirty-seventh and Girard. "We were told to go to the *Minneapolis Star* shack," Ulstrom recalled. "There they told us we were all fired."[90]

A "Statement by Carl Jones" appeared in the first issue of the *Minneapolis Star-Journal* on August 1, 1939: "The *Minneapolis Star* has purchased the *Minneapolis Journal,* and the two newspapers will be combined and published henceforth at the *Star* plant.

"The loyal support of its public for more than [sixty] years and the loyal support of the staff, many of whom have given a lifetime of service to the *Journal*, warrant a statement from the former owners of the reasons for selling the property.

"The *Minneapolis Journal* was enjoying at the present time an all time peak in daily circulation, and its advertising patronage has suffered only the natural shrinkage of the recession.

"However, there have been too many newspapers in Minneapolis to support a healthy constructive growth of any one of them. The changing times have brought revolutionary methods in mechanical equipment, news and picture gathering, handling of personnel and taxes, which required ever-increasing resources.

"Because the majority of the stockholders of the *Journal* were not engaged in operating the *Journal*, it seemed wise to the respective managements that one ownership could more effectively meet the exigencies referred to. Mr. John Cowles and his associates, desiring to further the usefulness of the Minneapolis press, made a fair offer for purchase, which was accepted by the *Journal*.

"Words fail to express our feelings in disbanding an organization that has worked side by side these many years. Many of them will soon be serving on the consolidated newspaper, others will find service elsewhere, we hope in the field of journalism where their service will be of maximum value. The *Journal* is working out generous severance pay for its regular employees.

"We extend our heartiest congratulations to the new owners for this enlarged opportunity for usefulness."[91]

Carl Jones' statement was followed by a "Statement by John Cowles," that read: "The combination of the *Minneapolis Journal* and the *Minneapolis Star*, with a fusing of all the facilities that each publication has separately enjoyed in the past, gives us, we believe, an opportunity to provide the people of Minneapolis and the Northwest with what we hope will become one of the finest papers in America."The character, the prestige and the traditions that the *Journal* has developed over the last [sixty] years will, we hope, live on stronger than ever in the new *Star-Journal*.

"To Carl W. Jones, who has served his community so well as publisher of the *Journal*, and to his able associates, we express the gratitude of Minneapolis and the Northwest for their long public service in their conduct of the *Journal*.

"The *Star-Journal* will have only one aim—to serve its readers with a clean, fair, reliable, constructive newspaper which will deserve the support of the community."[92]

Public reaction to the sale was mixed. The 135,300 subscribers of the *Journal* received copies of the new paper with a request that they continue reading the new *Star-Journal*. The *Star*'s 1938 circulation had reached 150,100, but now via the "merger," circulation stood at 241,200. One former *Journal* reporter, critical of the new paper, eulogized, "the new paper looks like the *Journal* but feels like the *Star*."[93]

Some *Journal* employees were contacted by *Star* executives and asked to work for the *Star-Journal*. Many of these employees were needed to publish the greatly enlarged daily and Sunday editions. George Ronald and Moses Jones were among the former *Journal* executives who made the move. In 1940, Ronald was elected an officer and director but resigned the following year.

Ironically, on the same day as the *Journal*'s demise, Will S. Jones, brother of Herschel, passed away in Keene, New Hampshire, at the age of seventy-five. Will had left the *Journal* in 1923 when he became business manager of the *Portland Journal* in Oregon. He later moved to Boston and retired about the time of his brother's death. Will was a member of the American Newspaper pub-

William Jones, brother of Herschel V. Jones (above), lived in Duluth. This photo was taken at the Park Avenue house. To the right: Carl W. Jones with his sisters Frances and Florence, 1915.

lishers Association and on the association's labor committee. His obituary appeared in the very first issue of the combined *Minneapolis Star-Journal*.[94]

The *Journal* was not the only family casualty. Lydia and Tessie Jones sold the Park Avenue residence to Messiah Lutheran Church in 1940 for use as a youth center and Sunday school. It was razed about 1950 to make way for a new church office and child-care center.[95]

They also sold the summer retreat at Woman Lake. In 1929, the land at Hilltop was subdivided, and on February 13, 1931, Lydia purchased additional land from George Leach. However, four years later, she sold off the entire Hilltop estate.[96]

The two cottages and the remaining lots on Turtle Lake were not spared either. About 1931 or 1932, Raymond M. Michel, Sr., his wife, Maple Georgianna Michel, and a relative, Miss Altha Wood, bought the large cottage from Lydia on a five- or ten-year payment plan.

"It sounded like a good deal to my Aunt Altha, so she pitched in with my parents and bought the place," said Raymond Michel, Jr. "We would benefit from going out there in the summer to get away from the city. I remember we purchased the place on a tax title deal from the Jones estate. We didn't have to pay very much."[97]

On June 22, 1935, Lydia sold the small lake place to Josiah Chase for "[one dollar] and other valuable considerations."[98]

After selling off all the Jones Minnesota properties, Tessie and her mother purchased a modern Italian villa on beautiful property fronting the Hudson River in Balmville, near Newburgh, New York. The large house, circled by a stone wall, was located in an area revered for its late eighteenth- through nineteenth-century buildings.[99]

According to a book published by the Minneapolis Institute of Arts in 1968, the residence was "one of the most handsome and beautifully maintained early nineteenth-century homes on the Hudson River." Through Tessie's "ideal care and love of her father's treasures, and by her exact sense of perfect taste in maintaining her mother's heritage, this house became one of the most beautiful in America."[100]

Nearby Newburgh was the site of George Washington's headquarters for more than a year, from April 1782 to August 1783, during the Revolutionary War. At this site, Washington ordered the end of the war. His military headquarters were in the 1750 Hasbrouck house, and nearby is the site of the New Windsor Cantonment, site of the last winter encampment of Washington and his Continental Army. The town later based its economy on a thriving whaling industry, and after the demise of whaling, turned its ships to other trades in the late 1800s.

Winton Jones recalled his grandmother Lydia's move to the Hudson. "I don't think she was ever happy in Minneapolis," he said. "Now this comes from a member of the family. She did not fit into the community [Minneapolis] or seem interested in it. She had always wanted to move back to her beloved Hudson River."[101]

According to Winton Jones, Lydia and Tessie lived in the "grand manner." Once a week, they went into New York City to do their shopping. Waring Jones recalled his grandmother and aunt being very happy in their Hudson villa, kept company by "the Renoir" and other paintings, Lydia's harp, and Herschel's books.

But their friends in Minneapolis kept them abreast of "family matters." In August 1939, a friend wired them that she had visited Herschel's grave. The telegram read, "Just back from cemetary [sic] grave looked nice. Love to both."[102]

Tessie, despite her move to New York, kept busy with her genealogy. Eugene Bouton, after receiving a list of ancestors, wrote to her

351

Lydia Wilcox Jones with
George Ronald.

that he had found the wife of Alonzo B. Wilcox, whose name was
Hannah Swipe, on a list of the inscriptions from the Stevens Cemetery
in Harpersfield. He then asked her how much more she knew about
Moses Swift and his wife, Hannah Hurd. He also wrote:

"I suppose you visited the Wilcox farm when you were in
Jefferson. I would like to know where in Harpersfield it was, something about its size, buildings . . . and by what roads it was reached
from Harpersfield Center and from Jefferson. I have a sort of sus-
picion it was on what was and is known as Smith Street. But that is
a guess. I assume that Alonzo B. owned and ran the farm and that
Moses S. took it from him."[103]

352

Bouton commented on Tessie's recent trip to "Les Andelys" and wanted to know about the people there related to the Beard family.

Herschel's granddaughter, Mrs. Frances Siftar, recalled her Aunt Tessie as being a very serious lady. "She had once lived in Paris and published a book there," Mrs. Siftar remembered years later. "She was brilliant and very knowledgeable, especially about art prints. She may have been so even more than Grandpa Jones. She was also a bit of a recluse. When she went out to New York, she isolated herself there. A next door neighbor, Mrs. Weed, formed a good friendship with Aunt Tess."[104]

Lydia stayed in touch with some of her friends to whom she sent Easter lilies in 1939. One family wrote back to thank her, stating:

"Again I am thanking you for a beautiful Easter lily—how the years fly by! And for how many years one of the loveliest lilies of the season has come to us from you. Please accept again our gratitude. Bert and I were glad indeed to find you so well on Saturday. The interesting pictures of your new home make it easy to imagine you and Tessie against the new background. May it bring you both continued health and joy."[105]

Although the women missed some of their Minneapolis friends, Tessie never grew lonesome for her favorite Minneapolis dentist, Dr. Charles Wiethoff, who had over the

Above: Lydia Wilcox Jones, Florence Jones, George and Peter Ronald and Wally, June 1928). Below: Lydia Wilcox Jones, 1932, Duluth.

353

Tessie Jones with Leslie's children, Arnetta, Tessie, Chickie, and Wells.

Opposite: Jefferson Jones and Admiral, mid-1930s.

years worked on her teeth. After Tessie's move to Balmville, she would send money to the dentist, and he would jump a train for New York, and with his "powerful pedal drill," perform the necessary dental work.[106]

Lydia was not to be outdone. Her favorite tree pruner in Minneapolis was sent for every summer, and he, too, made the long trip willingly to Balmville, New York. Whenever Lydia missed her favorite sweet rolls, they would be flown in from Minneapolis.[107]

Lydia Augusta Wilcox Jones passed away September 11, 1942, in her Balmville home. Services were held in her home, and she was interred in Lakewood Cemetery in Minneapolis next to her husband, Herschel. Following her mother's demise, Tessie developed a lasting friendship with Hatty Weed. The two ladies had much in common. Mrs. Weed, the widow of a major, appreciated art and literature as much as Tessie. When Tessie passed away in November 1967, Mrs. Weed was left in charge of the Balmville estate.[108]

Florence Jones and Lydia Wilcox
Jones, 1932, Duluth.

Upon Hatty's death in 1971, Moses Jones wrote, "All of us in the family felt very close to Hatty. Living so many years with my sister Tessie we all accepted Hatty as another sister. She most certainly was a major part of our family."[109]

Persons out side the family also revered Hatty Weed as evidenced by a letter from Anthony Clark, director of the Minneapolis Institute of Arts, to Hatty's niece, Mrs. Isabella Carr Leighton:

"I had the very great privilege of meeting your aunt several times and of corresponding with her extensively after Miss Tessie Jones' death. Mrs. Weed also met a number of the staff of this museum and was the most notable and thoughtful friend to all of us in the complicated arrangements about certain works of art in her beautiful home.

"I have never had the honor of greater and more sensitive aid and comfort than that your aunt gave my staff and myself, and I never experienced a more admirable lady."[110]

Tessie's brother Jefferson passed away in December 1965. When his mother had sold the *Journal* in 1939, he became associated with the Federal Cartridge Corporation. In 1946 he and his brother Moses purchased the *Bozeman Chronicle* in Montana, which they operated jointly through 1954. After selling the newspaper, he retired to Santa Barbara, California. Jefferson was a member of the American Asiatic Society, the executive council of the Minnesota Historical Society, the National Press Club in Washington, D.C., and the Minnesota Press Club.[111]

Moses Jones resigned from the *Minneapolis Star-Journal* in 1942 and enlisted in the Army Air Corps. A veteran of two world wars, he served in campaigns in North Africa, Sicily, Italy, England, France, and Holland, and rose to the rank of major. Upon his discharge from the military in 1945, he purchased the Bozeman newspaper with Jefferson and served as business manager until the paper was sold to the Scripps chain in 1954. Like his brother Jefferson, he and his wife, Pearl, moved to Santa Barbara. He was

Carl W. Jones, 1940s.

a member of the Magnolia Lodge of F & AM, a president of the Santa Barbara Shrine Club, and a member of the Al Malaikah Shrine Temple in Los Angeles. He was also a member of the Military Order of the World Wars. He passed away in 1979.[112]

Florence Purington Jones had married George W. Ronald, a vice-president of Citizens Fidelity Bank and Trust Company in Louisville, Kentucky. They lived in that city's Commodore Apartments. Florence, seventy, passed away at 11:15 A.M., November 12, 1959, at Jewish Hospital.[113]

Frances Jones married Arnett Leslie, president of John Leslie Paper Company and continued living in the Minneapolis area. She passed away in 1983.[114]

With the passing of Carl Jones, the *Journal*'s never-say-die crusader, on January 5, 1957, few of those who cherished the "pay as you go" ideals of H.V. Jones remain. Like his father, Carl Jones was cherished in life and remembered in death. As a young Wisconsin friend lamented at Carl's death, "I'm sure I never knew a great man until I met Carl Jones. That made a turning point in my life."[115]

Notes

[1]Bob Ulstrom, interview with the author, November 16, 1998, Minneapolis.

[2]Charles B. Reif, "Delivering the Minneapolis Journal," *Hennepin History*, 54/2, Spring 1995, p. 30.

[3]Ibid.; Bob Ulstrom, interview with author, November 16, 1998, Minneapolis.

[4]Charles B. Reif, "Delivering the *Minneapolis Journal*," *Hennepin History*, 54/2, Spring 1995, pp. 25-26.

[5]Bob Ulstrom, interview with author, November 16, 1998, Minneapolis.

[6]William Larsen, Sr., "Carl Jones: The Only Man for the Job," John Northern Hilliard, Carl Jones, Jean Hugard, *More Greater Magic*, pp. 1017-1018.

[7]Carl W. Jones, "My Thirty-Eight Years of Magic," John Northern Hilliard, Carl Jones, Jean Hugard, *More Greater Magic*, p. 1018.

[8]Arnett Leslie, "Memorial to Carl Waring Jones, Minneapolis Rotary Club, January 11, 1957.

[9]Carl W. Jones, "My Thirty-Eight Years of Magic," p. 1018.

[10]Flyer for *Greater Magic*.

[11]"Science Is the Magician of Today, 'U' Graduates Told," *Minneapolis Star*, July 16, year unknown.

[12]*Minneapolis Journal*, November 25, 1928.

[13]Ibid., May 24, 1928.

[14]Ibid., June 4, 1928.

[15]Ted Curtis Smythe, *A History of the* Minneapolis Journal, *1878-*

1939, p. 287.

[16]Ibid., pp. 288-289; *Minneapolis Journal*, January 14, 1929.

[17]*Minneapolis Journal*, March 9, 1929.

[18]*David L. Rosheim, The Other Minneapolis: Or a History of the Minneapolis Skid Row*, pp. 111-112; *Minneapolis Journal*, November 28, 1929.

[19]*Minneapolis Journal*, March 24, 1929.

[20]Joseph Stipanovich, *City of Lakes: An Illustrated History of Minneapolis,* p. 26.

[21]Theodore C. Blegen, *Minnesota: A History of the State*, pp. 521-522.

[22]*Minneapolis Journal,* October 24, 1929 and October 25, 1929.

[23]Ibid., October 30, 1929.

[24]Ibid., September 4, 1930.

[25]David L. Rosheim, *The Other Minneapolis: Or a History of the Minneapolis Skid Row*,p. 114.

[26]*Minneapolis Journal*, February 25, 1931.

[27]Kenneth Alsop, *Hard Travelin'*, New York, New American Library, 1967, p. 187.

[28]*Minneapolis Journal*, October 6, 1931.

[29]Ibid., October 11, 1931.

[30]Ibid., October 9, 1931.

[31]Joseph Stipanovich, *City of Lakes: An Illustrated History of Minneapolis*, pp. 26-28.

[32]*Minneapolis Journal*, April 10, 1931.

[33]Ibid., April 17, 1931.

[34]Ibid., March 3, 1931.

[35]Ibid., March 16, 1932.

[36]Ibid., April 24, 1932.

[37]Ibid., August 3, 1932.

[38]Eric Sevareid, *Not So Wild a Dream*, New York, Alfred A. Knopf, 1946, p. 29.

[39]*Minneapolis Journal*, July 24, 1932.

[40]Joseph Stipanovich, *City of Lakes: An Illustrated History of Minneapolis,* pp. 26-28.

[41]*Minneapolis Journal*, November 10, 1932.

[42]David L. Rosheim, *The Other Minneapolis: Or a History of the Minneapolis Skid Row*, p. 121; *Minneapolis Journal*, November 3, 1932.

[43]*Minneapolis Journal*, October 31, 1932.

[44]Ibid., November 4, 1932.

[45]Ibid., November 9, 1932.

[46]Theodore C. Blegen, *Minnesota: A History of the State*, pp. 524-526.

[47]Charles Rumford Walker, *American City*, New York, Farrar and Rinehart, Inc., 1937, pp. 85-88.

[48]Joseph Stipanovich, *City of Lakes: An Illustrated History of Minneapolis*, p. 179.

[49]*Minneapolis Journal*, May 17, 1934.

[50]Ibid., May 16, 1934.

[51]Joseph Stipanovich, *City of Lakes: An Illustrated History of Minneapolis*, p. 180.

[52]Ibid.

[53]Ibid., May 19, 1934.

[54]Ibid.

[55]Ibid.

[56]George H. Mayer, *The Political Career of Floyd B. Olson*, Minneapolis, University of Minnesota Press, 1951, pp. 196-198.

[57]Ibid.; Joseph Stipanovich, *City of Lakes: An Illustrated History of Minneapolis*, p. 180.

[58]George H. Mayer, *The Political Career of Floyd B. Olson*, p. 196; *Minneapolis Journal*, May 21, 1934.

[59]Mrs. Susan Jacobson, interview with author, February 14, 1999, Minneapolis.

[60]*Minneapolis Journal*, May 20, 1934.

[61]Ibid., May 22, 1934; Charles Rumford Walker, *American City*, pp. 117-122; Joseph Stipanovich, *City of Lakes: An Illustrated History of Minneapolis*, p. 180; George H. Mayer, *The Political Career of Floyd B. Olson*, pp. 198-199.

[62]Mrs. Sally Koether, telephone interview with author, February 7, 1999; Mrs. Frances Siftar, interview with author, February 22, 1999.

[63]*Minneapolis Journal*, May 24, 1934.

[64]Joseph Stipanovich, *City of Minneapolis: An Illustrated History of Minneapolis*, p. 180.

[65]*Minneapolis Journal*, July 21, 1934.

[66]Ted Curtis Smythe, *A History of the* Minneapolis Journal, *1878-1939*, p. 368.

[67]Ibid., p. 375.

[68]George H. Mayer, The Political Career of Floyd B. Olson, p. 221.

[69]David L. Rosheim, *The Other Minneapolis: Or a History of the Minneapolis Skid Row*, p. 131.

[70]James A. Alcott, *A History of Cowles Media Company*, p. 10.

[71]Ibid., pp. 11-12.

[72]Bradley L. Morison, *Sunlight on Your Doorstep*, p. 57

[73]James A. Alcott, *A History of Cowles Media Company*, pp. 9-11.

[74]Ibid., p. 13.

[75]Peter Ronald letter to Mrs. H.V. Jones postmarked July 6, 1937.

[76]Mrs. Frances Siftar, interview with author, February 22, 1999.

[77]Frances and Alfred Siftar, interview with author, March 3, 1999.

[78]"Cowles Boys Make Amazing [Six]-Year Record in Minneapolis," *Editor & Publisher*, February 13, 1943, p. 7.

[79]John J. Koblas, *Sinclair Lewis Home at Last*, Bloomington, Voyageur Press, 1981, pp. 63-64.

[80]George Hage, "Print and Broadcast Media," *Minnesota in a Century of Change,* St. Paul, Minnesota Historical Society, 1989, p. 305; James A. Alcott, *A History of Cowles Media Company*, p. 17.

[81]"Minneapolis' Family Newspaper," *The Minneapolis Star*, July 15, 1935; "Forever Curious," *The Minneapolis Star*, June 17, 1974; James A. Alcott, *A History of Cowles Media Company*, p. 19.

[82]James A. Alcott, *A History of the Cowles Media*, p. 24-25.

[83]Ibid.

[84]Ted Curtis Smythe, *A History of the* Minneapolis Journal, *1878-1939,* p. 392.

[85]Waring Jones, interview with author, February 15, 1999.

[86]Ibid.

[87]Ibid.; Winton Jones, telephone interview with author, January 30, 1999.

[88]Waring Jones, interview with author, February 15, 1999.

[89]A.J. Russell, *Goodbye Newspaper Row*, pp. 19-20.

[90]Bob Ulstrom, interview with author, November 16, 1998, Minneapolis.

[91]*Minneapolis Star-Journal*, Tuesday, August 1, 1939.

[92]Ibid.

[93]James A. Alcott, *A History of Cowles Media*, pp. 27-28.

[94]*Minneapolis Star-Journal*, Tuesday, August 1, 1939.

[95]David A. Wood, "Park Avenue—Showcase of a City," Vol. 4, No. 8, September 1982, p. 1.

[96]Hennepin County Registrar of Deeds.

[97]Raymond Michel, Jr., telephone interview with author, March 21, 1999.

[98]Ramsey County Registrar of Deeds.

[99]Waring Jones, interview with author, February 14, 1999.

[100]Anthony M. Clark, *The Jones Collection: The Bequests of Herschel V. and Tessie Jones*, Minneapolis, Minneapolis Institute of Arts, 1968, Introduction.

[101]Winton Jones, telephone interview with author, January 30, 1999.

[102]Postal Telegram sent by "Fran" to Mrs. H.V. Jones, August 30, 1939.

[103]Eugene Bouton letter to Tessie Jones dated March 22, 1945.

[104]Mrs. Frances Siftar, interview with author, February 22, 1999.

[105]"Bert and Elizabeth A." letter to Mrs. H.V. Jones postmarked April 14, 1939.

[106]Winton Jones, telephone interview with author January 30, 1999.

[107]Waring Jones, interview with author, February 14, 1999.

[108]Frances and Alfred Siftar interview with author, March 3, 1999.

[109]Moses Jones letter to Mrs. Isabella Carr Leighton dated July 20, 1971 in collection of Frances and Alfred Siftar.

[110]Anthony M. Clark letter to Mrs. Isabella Carr Leighton dated July 23, 1971 in collection of Frances and Alfred Siftar.

[111]*Santa Barbara Press*, December 7, 1965; *Minneapolis Star*, December 1965.

[112]Ibid., 1979, date unknown.

[113]*Louisville Journal*, Friday Morning, November 13, 1959.

[114]Frances and Alfred Siftar, interview with author, March 3, 1999.

[115]Arnett Leslie, "Memorial to Carl Waring Jones," Minneapolis Rotary Club, January 11, 1957.

LAMENT

"The times they are a changin'"
—Bob Dylan

Too bad that time passes so quickly on its journey into the mouth of Infinity. Herschel Jones is gone and the newspaper legacy he built on a shoestring grows fainter in memory with the passage of each generation. The laughter of loving children dressed in holiday costumes no longer echoes from atop the high ridge at Hilltop, and the Woman Lake location of their summer home is now the concrete slab of a private airstrip.

But the few that remember the man and his mission still recall Newspaper Row extending along Fourth Street from the Spectator Building between First Avenue North and Hennepin to the Globe Building between Nicollet and Hennepin; thence across Nicollet to the Minneapolis Journal building. And for some of us born too late to enjoy the heyday of Minneapolis' "Great Newspapers," there are books and periodicals and dreams. Perhaps a few "Old Newspaper Guard" survivors can still remember those good old days when a man from Schoharie County, New York, owned the premier newspaper in Minneapolis and raised his family on the city's most fashionable avenue. If there are any, they undoubtedly share the sentiment of the *Journal*'s John the Janitor when he passed the vacant parking lot once occupied by Herschel V. Jones' paper:

> "And all my mother came into my eyes
> And gave me up to tears."

PERSONAL

Oyster Bay, N.Y.,
September 15, 1903.

My dear Mr. Jones:

Come in October to Washington, and let me know in advance
and I shall have you at lunch.   I have much to talk over with
you.

I shall ask the Attorney General if he can use Somebody
for that work.   I don't know whether they have already got
somebody or not.

Sincerely yours,

Mr. H. V. Jones,

This letter to H.V. Jones from President Theodore Roosevelt and the transcriptions of letters between these two men in this chapter are courtesy of the Library of Congress.

THE HERSCHEL V. JONES/THEODORE ROOSEVELT LETTERS

(Herschel V. Jones letter to Theodore Roosevelt, dated July 1901):

Dear Sir:

I shall count it a pleasure to entertain you informally for an afternoon or evening, or both during your visit to Minnesota in September. I am embarrassed somewhat in making this suggestion lest you may choose a more sincere invitation with some that may have more sound ambitions behind them. I assure you, Col. Roosevelt, that after my most enjoyable trip through the West, as a guest on your train that I feel that I am entitled to return to you, though in the manner suggested as an acknowledgment of the pleasure of that long ride.

If you can make it agreeable to yourself to join me in a quick way for a drive over our splendid boulevards to Minnehaha [Falls], or the lakes, or to spend an hour with me in my library—which I may say is counted as one of the two best in Minneapolis—I shall be pleased to receive your consent.

After sixteen years of service at the *Minneapolis Journal*—a position secured for me by Senator Warren Miller—I left my old post after the election and am now publishing on my own account. The *Commercial West* is a paper dedicated to Western development.

I met William Davison and Thomas Cleveland this year; otherwise have seen none of the campaign party.

There I may have the opportunity of gaining a closer acquaintance with you than the luxury of the train trip permitted. If Mrs. Roosevelt accompanies you I wish her to be included in the invitation and Mrs. Jones will greet her as hostess.

Sincerely,

Herschel V. Jones

[Postscript]:

The prediction I made in my paper from Montana in Western election results was right in every instance, even to the plurality in Kansas to the Bryan plurality in Colorado. My letters share that I was very fortunate in estimates.

———————

Letter from Theodore Roosevelt to Herschel V. Jones, dated July 24, 1901:

Mr. Herschel V. Jones,
            Minneapolis, Minn.
My dear Mr. Jones—

I thank you for your letter of the 4th last. You are more than kind and I greatly wish I could accept your invitation, but I fear the entire time of my stay in Minneapolis is already engaged. I believe I am under the care of Mr. Whevlin. Would you mind coordinating with that? I should particularly like to see your library, and I should even more like to have a talk with you. It was a most genuine pleasure to have met you on the train last fall, and I shall always be glad you could come with me.
            With hearty regards, I am,
                        Faithfully yours,
                        Theodore Roosevelt
[Postscript undecipherable]

———————

August 19[01]

Hon. Theodore Roosevelt
            Oyster Bay, N.Y.

Dear Sir:

I want an early half-hour with you during your visit here, in which to suggest that you make no mistake in the men who are to look after your interests in the state, if you decide you have any. I want you to accept this suggestion in the light of its good faith and believe me that there is a good reason for it.

The situation in this state is peculiar and it is easy for one coming from outside to make missteps.

You will please treat this suggestion as confidential, as I shall anything that may pass between us.
                        Sincerely yours.
                        H.V. Jones

———————

Oyster Bay, N.Y., Aug. 28th, 1901

Mr. H.V. Jones,
      Minneapolis, Minn.

My dear Mr. Jones—
    I thank you for your favor of the 19th last. I particularly
want to see you before I do anything in Minnesota. Will you
make it a point to give me the chance as soon as I get there?
Us[e] this letter, if necessary, to get to me. See [undecipher-
able].
          With best regards,

                    Faithfully yours,
                    Theodore Roosevelt

Herschel V. Jones letter to Theodore Roosevelt, September 6, 1901:

My Dear Sir:
    Do not write Mr. Erinshaw now. I will tell you when. He
is very acrusitive [sic] over the plight. Do not write Mr.
Peterson. Write Mr. Somersby.
                    Sincerely,
                    H.V. Jones

Hon. Theodore Roosevelt
    The boy tells me as I write you that the president is assas-
sinated. Can it be possible? How strange [illegible]. I have
written it with full affirmation that all is now changed. I pray
the president may survive, but if it must be otherwise it is
for you to carry on his great work.
    You have not known me long but I assure you of my sin-
cere friendship, not as Dr. Winthrop said, because of official
position, but because of yourself. You may trust me with any
urgency.
                    Sincerely,
                    H.V. Jones

Buffalo, N.Y., September 14, 1901

My dear Mr. Jones:
    Your letter of the 16th instant was received and the
President asks me to write and say that he would be happy to
see you at any time you are in Washington.
                    Sincerely yours,
                    [secretary]

Minneapolis
Oct. 3, 1901

To Mr. President,
        Washington, D.C.

I am home from the west. I learned much that will be of interest to you and considerable that I deem of importance as bearing upon your administration. I refer especially to the temper of the people in the far northwest, to the arid land question and to the Alaskan boundary.

From the standpoint of diplomacy I think it would be well to address a letter to Judge Thomas Burke, Seattle, Wash., suggesting that you have learned of his interest in the Alaskan boundary—my name can be used or not, as you choose—and you would be pleased if he could make it convenient when east to call at the White House.

Judge Burke is a gold democrat, a man of influence, the attorney for James J. Hill, of the Great Northern, and influential with him, and a believer in you. He does not like Secretary Hay's action in this connection. A valued friend can be made, I think.

I went to the bottom of the Oregonian matter. There is nothing there that need worry you.

There are those who will seek to trip you, but I believe the work of all such can be checkmated by a careful inside organization. Believe me, I am not seeking to instruct you, but I am so entirely interested in your welfare, and sincerely so, that you must overlook any suggestion that may seem to you to be too officious. I shall go east this month.

        Sincerely,
        H.V. Jones

Oct. 14, 1901

To the President
        Washington, D.C.

Replying to your letter of October ninth.

I shall leave tomorrow for the East. It will be convenient for me to reach Washington about November first. Please write me at Jefferson, Schoharie County, New York, this week, if the date will be agreeable to you. Have considerable of importance to present, and will see you earlier if there is any reason why you may desire it.

        Sincerely
        H.V. Jones

February 22 [1902]

To the President,

Washington, D.C.

Dear Mr. President:

Permit me to say that I believe your action on the Securities company is being used in this state in a way that places you before the public here in the wrong light. You are made to appear as a partisan of Governor Van Sant. I do not understand that you are acting in any such relation.

Governor Van Sant has split the party in this state. The canvass next fall will be doubtful as to its result. The governor is posing. He is doing everything from a political motive. There are many of course who will not agree to this proposition, but I believe it most thoroughly. His secretary is a politician pure and simple and he shapes the policy. I do not believe in that kind of reform.

I want to see you the greatest president this country has had. I want to see you reelected, not from a political point of view, but because you have it within your grasp to do your country a great service; and it is clear to me what this service should be.

This week I wrote the first word of criticism on your public action that I ever thought or gave voice to. I criticized your announcement of the suit of the Northern Securities company without a public warning. It was a dangerous thing to do. It did not develop a panic, but it would under [the] right circumstances.

In this connection let me say that I believe you are acting independently of Governor Van Sant in this matter of the suit. You find the Sherman Law on the book and you believe it a duty to test its worth. The *Minneapolis Journal* and the attorney-general place you in the light of supporting Minnesota in her action, and I believe this to be an unwarranted interpretation of your position. If you feel that I can be trusted to the point of knowing the fact in this connection, the information will help me to keep my judgment right and to do you good without violating any confidence. There is no objection to your independent action in the matter, but there is objection in this state to your allying yourself with Governor Van Sant, or with any interest or faction.

I am going west in a week for a month. I have not felt like volunteering to do you a service there, because I have not understood that you care for my judgment or reports on matters like the above. I am conscious of my breach of manners, but my perfect loyalty to your interests impels me to throw rules aside and write you as one man would write another in whom he has genuine interest.

I shall take no further liberty of this sort, however, if I annoy you, and you will please make matters plain on this point. If I am not annoying you, I shall feel inclined to visit you in Washington after my return from the West, because there is much that I want to say to you that I believe is important for you to hear.

You may address me at Minneapolis,

Sincerely,

H.V. Jones

February 26, 1902

My dear Mr. Jones:

I am in receipt of your letter of the 22nd instant. It is never anything but a pleasure to hear from you, and I thank you for writing me. I do not quite understand, however, what you mean when you say that you criticised the announcement of the suit without a public warning. What we did was just exactly this; in other others, we gave a public warning that we were going to bring the suit, in order to prevent violent fluctuations and diaster in the market. How could we give public warning otherwise than in the way we did? I am sure it is unnecessary to say to you that our action was taken purely upon our own responsibility and without any reference to the State authorities of Minnesota. I am rather inclined to think it was as much of a surprise to them as to anyone.

Herschel V. Jones

Minneapolis, Minn:

BOOK TALK FOR AN IDLE MOMENT.

You know of my love for books. I now have 350 first editions. I bought the copy of Walt Whitman's *Leaves of Grass*, 1855 edition, in New York three weeks ago at the record price of $62. I think it will sell at $180 within three years. There are only twelve copies known. I bought today a beautiful copy of Lee Casas on Spanish cruelties, published 1699, and bound by Bedford, paying $30.

What I set out to discuss has to do with your books. An agent of Putnam called on me last week and offered me what was claimed to be a first edition. For the general public the edition is all right but from the standpoint of the bookman, there is little in it to attract. For myself I prefer the first editions in the original cloth.

I believe that your books would sell in a limited edition of say 250 copies at $10 to $15 a volume, or even $20 maybe. I shall be pleased if you will give this a little consideration, not that you would find the profit large in such an edition, but rather that you are almost bound to give book lovers a fine edition of your works.

And this leads me to say one more thing to you on this point, confidentially of course. Putnam cannot print an edition such as I refer to. To my mind, only two firms can—Houghton, Mifflin & Co. and Little, Brown & Co., both Boston. Scribner and Harper would dispute this, of course, but for some reason I have never found high-class bookmaking coming under their imprints.

And now for a personal request somewhat out of the ordinary. I want you to present me with a copy of the first edition of your new book on "The Deer," [illegible]. I want it as one of many interesting autograph books that I have not to exhibit to the public.

H.V. Jones

Herschel V. Jones
Minneapolis, Minn.

March 8, 1902.

Dear Mr. President:

Your position on Cuba is fully indorsed in Minnesota. Messrs. Tawney and Morris are misrepresenting best sentiment as well as interests of the state. Our millers would export more flour were Cuba prosperous. This increased export would help make wheat higher; but outside of a narrow view, best sentiment upholds our plain duty to Cuba.

I appreciate the confidence that your writing me over your name implies. It was unnecessary, as you suggest, to state to me your independence on the merger. I know you were independent, but I wanted to place it beyond all matter of thinking it.

Your statement about "public warning" suggested to me at once where the misunderstanding is—What you regarded as the warning we poor critics looked upon as the thing itself. Sometime I will suggest to you how, in my judgment, the warning could have been given publicly without the chance of causing disturbance.

I leave for the coast on Tuesday, hence this letter will not call for a reply except as you have further suggestion to make.

Sincerely yours,
H.V. Jones

March 12, 1902.

My dear Mr. Jones:

I thank you cordially for your letter and am very glad to hear from you.

Indeed you shall have a copy of my volume on deer just as soon as it comes out.

Always yours,
Theordore Roosevelt

Hotel Donnelly
Tacoma, Washington

March 24, 1902

Dear Mr. President:

Senator [Marcus A.] Hanna is making ready to run for the presidency. He is putting in the foundation work and at convention time. If things are right his name will go in.

You said to me that it was your ambition to give the people a good administration, regardless of another term. Has it occurred to you that you cannot give a successful administration without the second term? It must be yours, and you will take the course that will achieve it.

I call myself your good friend when I speak plainly. You have disturbed the confidence.

I do not own a railroad stock. I am giving you my independent judgment and you will pardon me if I say that I rate my business judgment higher than the standard among some of the purely political advisors.

I wish I might have an interview with you. I am going to New York about April 5. If you consider what I say of importance, please write me at Minneapolis that an interview would be agreeable.

Anything I have conceived as to your policy calls for no sacrifice of principle on your part. I believe in principle and should never advise a letting down of the basics on this point.

The opposition—or others hesitating support of your policy—to you is not alone among railroad managers, but among the people.

I want to talk with you and I believe I am warranted in making this suggestion.

Sincerely,
H.V. Jones

May 6, 1902

Personal.

My dear Mr. Jones:

I thank you very much. I have been much bothered about Haupt. Attorney General Knox made some secret inquiries through some first-rate lawyers and they recommended strongly in Haupt's favor. Mr. Washburn, the ex-senator, is strongly against him.

Sincerely yours,
Theodore Roosevelt

May 13, 1902
Personal
My dear Mr. Jones:

Is it possible for me to get definite statements about Mr. Haupt having been drunk or been guilty of misconduct of that kind? So far the written testimony is overwhelmingly in his favor; and men like Congressman Stevens, whom I have always found trustworthy, are equally emphatic in his behalf. The Postmaster General wishes greatly to keep Purdy, who he says has done admirably. But it is a serious thing to turn down Senator Clapp's former partner unless I can have some information which I can particularize. If he is an unfit man I do not want to appoint him, but the written record as made up so far is strongly in his favor. Young Washington has protested against him orally, and says he will submit written statements, but says he knows nothing of his personal knowledge.

I wish you had to deal with appointments of some of these kinds! [Handwritten sentence undecipherable]

Faithfully yours,
Theodore Roosevelt

May 19, [1902]
Dear Mr. President:

I sympathize with you. It is surely puzzling to receive conflicting statements from those who may be classed as equally reliable. I do not want to say more than I have lest you feel that I am unduly interested. I assure you that in a personal sense I have no choice for attorney. I feel that I know the kind of a man you want, however, hence I have submitted my judgment from that standpoint and I could not change it with the facts before me as to all candidates who have been mentioned.

You are justified in following the record before you, hence you are justified in appointing Haupt. I know how well you want to do you work, but for your physical good you should not dwell too long on these matters.

Purdy is good as a lawyer, but there is a reason that I have never mentioned why he does not represent your idea of a man. I have never stated this to you because I wanted you to pass upon his case without the information. This reason need not necessarily detract from his usefulness.

Minnesota is at this time as solid as a rock for your renomination; hence it is not necessary to consider appointments that have to do with political influence joined to ability. This leaves you free to appoint Haupt, [illegible] political strength.

If you know from personal contact all the facts about attorneys eligible to this nomination, you would not appoint Haupt or Purdy. Hence I shall feel that I am indorsed in the appointment of either of them, because I feel that with your knowledge [illegible] very much alike. I do not intend this remark as a familiarity.

With greatest sincerity
H.V. Jones

June 24 [1902]
To the President
        Washington, D.C.
Dear Mr. President:

The Hennepin County Republican convention, to elect delegates to the state nominating convention, was held here today. The only contest was as to the insertion in the county platform of a plank favoring reciprocity with Cuba. This was voted down by a three-fourths vote out of 600 delegates, after some show of feeling. Your administration in general was indorsed cordially, however. You will understand why there was opposition to the reciprocity resolution—Nelson and the house delegation, including Fletcher especially, did not want a resolution of that kind lest it should be construed as a reflection on their official action in that connection. There is likely to be a contest on this in the state convention July 1; there will be if the convention is not well stacked from Hennepin and Ramsey counties, because I believe a very large majority of the Republicans of this state are with you on the Cuban question. The Nelson chairman of today's convention has the naming of 113 delegates from this county, quite a pull.

I was surprised today to hear William Henry Eustis—formerly candidate for governor—make a strong speech against your Cuban policy—not against you. Robert Stratton led the fight in your behalf and was defeated. He made a clean-cut appeal that would have carried the convention had it not been almost wholly composed of politicians. The Nelson influence was against you. Nelson controlled the organization, and his chairman has the naming of the 113 delegates.

Van Sant will be renominated, and unless he has Lind against him—now doubtful—he will be elected big. Lind would give him a fight.

June 28, 1902

Personal

My dear Mr. Jones:

I thank you very much. You have given me just the information I desired to get. It is very kind of you.

Faithfully yours,
Theodore Roosevelt

Oyster Bay, N.Y., July 9, 1902

Personal

My dear Mr. Jones:

You are entirely mistaken if you think I do not consult you or do not heed your advice. You are one of the men whose words I always carefully weigh. But I am sure you will realize that in my position it is simply out of the question for me always to follow any one man's advice. I follow much advice from different men after I have carefully sifted it out, and sometimes I have to act against the advice of all, but in this last case in every way I am very sure of my ground. I never consulted a human being about the reciprocity plank in the Minnesota convention, any more than I did with reference to Nebraska; and the action in such State convention was a genuine surprise to me. I do not think you realize how little I do in the way of trying to manipulate party machinery. I think it's legitimate and honorable if done in legitimate ways and for honorable ends, but it is not a matter in which I have any proficiency or for which indeed I have much taste. Perhaps this sounds rather "highfalootin'"; but I do not mean it so. If I am to be renominated it must be because the bulk of the Republican party regard me as the man whom they wish as their exponent. If I am to be reelected it must be because I, together with a great many other men, have partly succeeded by our own efforts and partly been favored by fortune in bringing about a condition of affairs which will make the people at large feel that the Republican party should be intrusted with power.

I hope to see you in September, or earlier if you can get on here.

Faithfully yours,

Theodore Roosevelt

Oyster Bay, N.Y.
July 8, 1903
My dear Mr. Jones:

I was utterly at a loss what to make of your letter of the 24th instant. Most emphatically my feeling toward you has never changed in the least degree, and I am very sorry if—probably owing to some preoccupation—my manner at any time seemed changed. I never even heard of the statements that you say were made about what you had done. Mr. L--b tells me he did, but he did not even think them worth while to bring to my attention.

Be sure to let me see you the next time you get anywhere in my neighborhood.

Sincerely yours,
Theodore Roosevelt

Sept 11, 1903

The *Commercial West*
Minneapolis
To the President:

Permit me to suggest Mr. Charles W. Sommersby, attorney general's assistant, Minnesota, as one who will get the facts in connection with the Dawes Commission in Indian Territory. Our Minnesota friend down there will be watching.

I want to see you very much for a moment because I want you to know the color of some things out this way. I hope to be in Washington during the fall.

We are a pretty fair lot of people out this way and we all appreciate that you are doing many good things and not very many bad things, but when it is bad it is of good size.

You are all right in sending war ships to [illegible]. Democrats and Republicans will stick with you on that, and on about everything in your policy except the trust companies, of which there is great variance of opinion.

John Rafferty told me last week about his writing you a check in payment for *The Voter*, then framing the check and making you give up currency to pay the subscription. Pretty good, I think.

Sincerely yours,
H.V. Jones

Oyster Bay, N.Y.
September 15, 1903

My dear Mr. Jones:

Come in October to Washington, and let me know in advance and I shall have you at lunch. I have much to talk over with you.

I shall ask the Attorney General if he can use Somerby for that week. I don't know whether they have already got somebody or not.

Sincerely yours,
Theodore Roosevelt

The *Commercial West*
Minneapolis Minn.

Dec. 28, 1903.

To the President:

Fully appreciating that any analysis I may make of the electoral situation will be of but passing interest to you, I nevertheless submit my analysis herewith.

I believe the election today hinges on Massachusetts, as I suggested to you. My reason for putting the emphasis there is that you will notice by columns two and three that neither side wins without Massachusetts, and we dispose of all the states, leaving that only in doubt. I will not trouble you with an analysis of why I think this will be the result. I merely give the figures on this basis, which show that to be the decisive state. In other words, the Democrats can carry New York, New Jersey, Delaware, Connecticut and Rhode Island, and with you carrying the West and Massachusetts, you win. This shows that the Democrats have a big piece of work on hand to defeat you, and this analysis shows that I am talking to you in good faith, because, while disagreeing with our general business policy, I show that it is very difficult to cause your defeat. I think New York will vote for the Democratic candidate; I think New Jersey will. I am more in doubt about Connecticut and Rhode Island, although I have put them in the Democratic column. If you should carry those two states and lose Massachusetts, you would be elected, and lose New York. You will notice by these various combinations that New York carried by the Democrats, by no means wins them the election. You will also notice by a reasonable forcast that it is unnecessary for you to carry New York and win the election. I think it is unnecessary to say that on this account New York will not be the decisive state carried by the Democrats. If you carry it, apparently you would settle the election, but from the standpoint of the enclosed classification, Massachusetts would be the decisive state.

I can conceive of a combination whereby you could be defeated and carry New York, but it would have to be as much of a surprise as was Cleveland's election over Harrison. By May 1st I may be able to suggest some changes in this result.

Your suggestion that Indiana is doubtful does not appeal to me as much as it would to suggest some other states, such as I have indicated. While there may be Republican disaffection in Indiana, you will gain a great many votes from Democrats that in agricultural states will go far toward off-setting Republican disaffection. I presume it is fair to count Colorado, Utah, Nevada and Montana as doubtful, but I have thrown the chance in those states your way.

You have divided the party, and I am extremely sorry that such is the case, because you are too good a man from any standpoint to endanger your chance for re-election by methods that seem to me to have been unnecessary to have accomplished what you want to, and all that is for the good of the country; but I must keep in mind that it is not for me to give you counsel. It is perhaps entirely out of place for me to say as much as I have, and I appreciate that it has not been asked for.

Yours sincerely,
H.V. Jones

Maximum Roosevelt Vote Possible		My Maximum Estimate Roosevelt Vote		My Estimate Dem. Vote		Doubtful Decisive State.	
California	10			Alabama	11	Massachusetts	16
Colorado	5	California	10	Arkansas	9		
Connecticut	7	Colorado	5	Connecticut	7		
Delaware	3	Idaho	3	Delaware	3		
Idaho	3	Illinois	27	Florida	5		
Illinois	27	Indiana	15	Georgia	13		
Indiana	15	Iowa	13	Kentucky	13		
Iowa	13	Kansas	10	Louisiana	9		
Kansas	10	Maine	6	Maryland	8		
Massachusetts	16	Michigan	14	Mississippi	10		
Maine	6	Minnesota	11	Missouri	18		
Michigan	14	Montana	3	N. Jersey	12		
Minnesota	11	Nebraska	8	New York	39		
Montana	3	Nevada	3	No. Carolina	12		
Nebraska	8	New Hampshire	4	Rhode Island	4		
New Jersey	39	No. Dakota	4	So. Carolina	9		
Nevada	3	Ohio	23	Tennessee	12		
New Hampshire	4	Oregon	4	Texas	18		
North Dakota	4	Pennsylvania	34	Virginia	12		
Ohio	23	So. Dakota	4	W. Virginia	7		
Oregon	4	Utah	3		Total, 231		
Pennsylvania	34	Vermont	4				
Rhode Island	4	Wyoming	3				
South Dakota	4	Washington	5				
Utah	3	Wisconsin	13				
Vermont	4		Total, 229				
W. Virginia	7						
Wyoming	3						
Washington	5						
Wisconsin	13						
	Total, 317						

Necessary to choice, —239
Underlined states in columns 2 & 3 may change to other party.

December 31, 1903.
Personal
My dear Mr. Jones:

I thank you for your very kind note, and I much appreciate your feelings toward me. Let me say one thing, however. You state that I have divided the party and that you are sorry I have done so. I am very sorry too, if such is the case. It seems to me that if such division exists it can only be to the extent that I have divided from the party that small fraction which deems itself to be above the law; which faction and its indignation at being required to obey the law is prepared not only to defeat me but to defeat Republican policies. However, while I trust you are wrong in your views, this does not alter my profound appreciation of your personal friendship and courtesy.

Sincerely yours,
Theodore Roosevelt

Oyster Bay, N.Y.
July 17, 1905.

Personal
My dear Mr. Jones:

In the first place, as to what you say about my having lost confidence in you, surely I have told you already that it is not so. My memories of you are particularly pleasant, so much so that I had really forgotten the points upon which we differed, such, for instance, as the Northern Securities case. I know perfectly well that in any movement of that kind there is certain to be very much that is demogogic; and this fact that on some given issue the demagogues are traveling my way does not make me alter my opinion about them.

Now, as to what you say about the Agricultural Department. Can you give me any specific information or, perhaps what is better still, will you come on and meet Secretary Wilson with me?

Sincerely yours,
Theodore Roosevelt

February 1st, 1912.

My dear Colonel:

Do you remember that evening on the train from Kansas in 1900, when I went to you with figures in proof of the statement that you would carry Kansas, Colorado, Utah and Idaho—results you were worrying much about?

I feel I made thorough work of that canvass during progress of the trip, and I wanted you to hear me, for I never sought to trouble you unless I had something worth while. The result showed that I was less than one thousand off each in Colorado, Kansas and Utah, and within fifteen hundred in Idaho.

And now the old "feelin'" is coming on me again, and I want to talk with you.

I was not intending to visit New York until April, but conditions suggest that I ought to drop in pretty soon. If you feel like meeting me, can you suggest anything as to about when and where?

I am assuming that Lindsey's fiction never took hold of you, and that you will understand that I am [rest of letter missing]

February 6th, 1912.

Dear Mr. Jones:

Do come and see me if possible week after next, Wednesday or Thursday.

Faithfully yours
Theodore Roosevelt

February 9th, 1912.

My dear Mr. Jones

I received your letter but not the enclosure of which you spoke. I appreciate the letter but of course until I get the enclosures I have not an idea what the [undecipherable] is [undecipherable] said.

With many thanks,

Sincerely yours,
Theodore Roosevelt

February 16th, 1912.

Hon. Theodore Roosevelt,
New York City,

Dear Sir:

In reply to your letter of the 9th, permit me to say that I expect to be in New York about Wednesday or Thursday of next week, and will run over some figures with you.

Yours truly,
H.V. Jones

Jr Minneapolis, Minn March 24-12
Theo. Roosevelt,
  The outlook,
                New York.
  Will your address here be ready for copy or shall we pro-
vide short hand reporter answer collect.
                        H.V. Jones Editor 2:23 p.m.

May 6 [1912?]
My Dear Colonel:
  I am reminded that the Minnesota Convention comes on
soon.
  I will reach home Thursday morning and will look matters
over promptly so that you will hear from me Tuesday or
Wednesday.
  There will then be time to issue the statement you referred
to if you do it wise. And on the point I should be pleased if
you decide to send it directly to the *Journal* rather than
through your committee. We would give it best of news treatment.
  I will count on that also and express our appreciation on the
wisdom of using this [illegible] when I write.
                        Sincerely yours,
                        H.V. Jones

                                    [May 9, 1912?]
Hon. Theo. Roosevelt:
  [Robert] Lafollette issues statement for Minnesota voters
covering same ground as in North Dakota statement making
same criticism of you as in North Dakota County Conventions. Come Saturday night Minneapolis Primary, Friday
night we can handle statement from you today if rushed as late
as one o'clock your time and tomorrow we can handle anything you wish to send tonight which would make publication
twenty-four hours advance of any conventions. If you wish us
to ask you for a statement to make to the voters of Minnesota
you may use us in relation. Best information this morning is
that Lafollette is dismissing fact. Expect to see you carry
Minnesota largely.
                        H.V. Jones

May 11, 1912

Minneapolis, Minnesota

Theo Roosevelt:

You have swept Minnesota. [William Howard] Taft carred Winnona [sic] City and Mower County, Lafollette carried Redwood County alone out of nearly all counties. In state list nearly complete at eleven tonight. Think result shows I was telling you straight last Monday.

H.V. Jones

May 13th, 1912

H.V. Jones

Editor *Minneapolis Journal*

Minneapolis, Minn.

Thanks very much for your telegram and for the splendid result in Minnesota. The returns certainly carred out your prediction of the 6th.

Theodore Roosevelt

May 29th, 1912.

My dear Colonel:

Early dispatches had it that you were favoring Senator Clapp for temporary chairman.

Please do not spoil a progressive movement by placing such honor upon a man who is afraid of his shadow, who never has an opinion on anything unless he feels it is a walkaway, who changes his mind over night on every question if the wind changes. That is why he deserted LaFollette, and went to you. A man must have something in his heart, if his "reform" is consistent.

And then there is Hugh Halbert of St. Paul, another ambitious, young, Roosevelt stomach-crawler.

Let the honors go to real men up this way in so far as they are taken care of. Men like Andy Rahn, Caswell and Washburn; men who were in when it looked dark.

You can find something on the side for Clapp. The stench from his 1901 campaign is not out of the way here yet.

Understand they had a primary in New Jersey yesterday.

May 29th, 1912

I do not ask you to reply to any of these little remarks of mine. They are just for you.

Yours truly,

H.V. Jones

June 4th, 1913.

My dear Mr. Jones:

There is no truth whatever in that rumor. It looks now as if the Taft people were trying to steal the Convention.

Faithfully yours,
Theodore Roosevelt

December 20th, 1912

My dear Mr. Jones:

That is a nice editorial of yours. I am glad that you wrote it and that you sent it to me.

With thanks,

Sincerely yours,
Theodore Roosevelt

H.V. JONES, EDITOR, MINNEAPOLIS, MINN.
THERE WILL BE ADVANCE COPIES SENT OUT TO THE ASSOCIATE PRESS OF ST. PAUL SPEECH BUT MR. ROOSEVELT WILL PROBABLY NOT HAVE TIME TO PREPARE MINNEAPOLIS SPEECH BEFORE HAND.
FRANK HARPER SECRETARY

May 27, 1914

Theodore Roosevelt,
     Oyster Bay, N.Y.

My dear Colonel:

The scriptures say that the Lord "uses the weak ones of earth to confound the wise." I am one of the weak ones and though I differ with you on many points, I am sincerely your friend. I want to see your great ability used for the benefit of the Country. I was disappointed, therefore, to read your interview immediately after your arrival, in which you unnecessarily, as I see it, set up a bar between yourself and the Republicans.

I am a Republican of the right school. I am for the forward movement, but I am for it on principle, not on my stomach. When I read the list of your advisors I find names therein that make one sick from the standpoint of sincerity. I will not mention names in this letter.

I want to see you. As your friend, [I] believe I can say something helpful to you. Believe I have some political vision. I am no weakling and I am not afraid. Neither am I for the Progressive party as it has been. Now why not get together as one party on a sound platform that we can all subscribe to? If we are not willing to do this we are admitting that party is more than principle.

January 18th, 1915.

Hon. Theodore Roosevelt,
    New York City,
My dear Colonel:

I wound up the Progressive question with this editorial. I have had several compliments this week from Progressives who feel they received good treatment.

I shall be in New York next week and may venture in. If my nerve gets strong, I may invite you to luncheon to meet one or two Minneapolis men.

Sincerely yours,
H.V. Jones

January 24, 1915.

My dear Mr. Jones:

You did not enclose the editorial. By all means let me see you in New York. I am really anxious to talk over things with you.

Sincerely yours,
Theo Roosevelt

New York, February 1, 1915.

Hon. Theodore Roosevelt,
    New York.
My dear Colonel:

I have been in New York a week, but unable to get in as yet. I want to see you middle week, and will communicate with you. I am at Hotel Gotham.

Sincerely yours,
H.V. Jones

September 1st, 1916.

Mr. Theodore Roosevelt,
    Oyster Bay, N.Y.
My dear Colonel:

I take great pleasure in printing today your address in full, eight columns. Which leads me to the subject of what I have to say.

The Hughes campaign is flat. What can be done to revive it and make it a force through the country?

I picked him as dead when he spoke here much to the astonishment of some of our leaders, but I find that my opinion is now the common one. Hughes has spoken many truths, but he does not know how to make his statements effective. In this community there is danger of a split-off by many Progressives due to the fact that A.O. Eberhart, the rejected candidate for the Senate and Governor, was placed on the Hughes advisory committee of this state. Perhaps a letter to Purdy from you might help stem that break. I do not know how far this has gone, but in one ward in this city it has reached a good heighth [sic]. There were several mistakes made in the local handling of the Hughes trip, such as would never have occurred if you had been making the trip. For instance, in this city one of the leaders of the faction rode with Mr. Hughes. In North Dakota Senator McCumber, Governor Hanna and his opponent, Mr. Fraser, were on the platform when he spoke at Fargo. In the train were Mr. Fraser and Senator McCumber, but no governor. These may or may not be vital when we count the votes, but we have the right to say that the management is poor. I want to reach some one on the national committee who will take this thing up seriously. Mr. Hughes has been regarded [undecipherable] as a mere fault-finder. He was the Supreme Court Judge, and the people were ready for a message. Had that message been given without regard for details at this time, Mr. Hughes would have come home from his trip a strong candidate. Because he did not give the people what they were looking for, he has made no headway with the independent voters.

I think you will know what I am trying to say without going further. I am sincerely your friend, notwithstanding that I did not follow you in the talk, which I am sorry you made because you would now be candidate if it had not been for that. However, you have done a wonderful and patriotic work since and I believe you will be the next candidate.

Cordially yours,

H.V. Jones

September 6th, 1916.

My dear Mr. Jones:

Your letter give me real concern. It is in accord with nine-tenths of what I hear as a result of the Western trip of Mr. Hughes. Now I am absolutely in a quandary as to what to do about it. You don't need to be told that I must not give the impression that I am "butting in" or trying to boss things, or that because I was not nominated I am trying to furnish the committee with information from men who, they will think, were friends of mind and are disgruntled because I was not nominated.

Would it do for you to write me a letter which I could show to Mr. Willcox, and, if necessary, Mr. Hughes? In Maine the old standpatters had treated the Progressives so, that we were on the verge of a very serious belt. I did my best to set matters right, and think I partly succeeded; but I need not say to you that it is not possible for me to do more than a certain amount.

Faithfully yours,
Theodore Roosevelt

September 14th, 1916.

Mr. Theordore Roosevelt,
New York City,
My dear Colonel:

I am enclosing copy of letter I have just sent to the Republican National Committee.

In a very serious way, they are working me to buy one hundred eighty thousand puny pictures of Hughes at $6.00 per thousand. That fairly represents the committee's ideas of getting votes.

I have your letter this morning.

Sincerely yours,
H.V. Jones

September 14th, 1916.
Mr. Everett Colby,
Republican National Committee,
New York City,
Dear Sir:

Your proposition to print the Hughes pictures suggests to me the whole incompetency that runs through the national committee. If you took the time devoted to this piffle to analyse the sentiment in the west and get in touch with the country poeple and find their sentiment and what you need to overcome with them, you might be making some progress. Mr. Hughes must change the character of his speeches if he wants to win the independent voter. I enclose letter received this morning, anonymous, which points the way. I could send you many like this. This letter can be answered and this man can be educated. Voters can be educated. There should be two speakers in about every county seat in the United States, educating the people. That was the way Bryan was defeated.

One of the Hughes' committee called on me last week and with considerable gusto announced that the committee was going to advertise in all the dailies. I begged him not to do it as it would assure the election of Wilson. He was going to advertise in my paper, the *Saturday Evening Post* and others. Besides, it puts all the papers under the charges of having been bought by Mr. Hughes although the amount of money received would not buy postage for a week. I am talking frankly, but I want you to get to work on practical lines.

Sincerely yours,
H.V. Jones

August 30th, 1917.

Colonel Theodore Roosevelt,
      Oyster Bay, N.Y.,
Dear Colonel:

Inasmuch as we printed this poem, you might as well read it.

You are to speak here late in September. I do not want to urge any invitation upon you, but my home is open to you as a good place for rest. Can give you a good room and a dinner where some of your friends can sit down, if you choose it, or go it alone.

Sincerely yours,
H.V. Jones

September 4, 1917.

My dear Mr. Jones:

I thank you for the poem, and appreciate it; and I thank you heartily for the invitation, but I am afraid the committee that has me in charge has arranged for about every hour—and has not arranged for <u>any</u> period of rest! May the Jones and Roosevelt boys meet abroad!

Always yours,
Theodore Roosevelt

December 3rd, 1917.
Dear Sir [H.V. Jones]:

Colonel Roosevelt thought you would probably be interested in seeing the enclosed. You may publish it if you care to.

Sincerely yours,
Secretary
[of President Roosevelt]

July 1st, 1918.

Mr. Theodore Roosevelt,
        Oyster Bay, N.Y.

My dear Colonel:

I just chanced to notice your portrait, which hangs over my desk, when the thought flashed of my introduction to you in the Harvard Club of my son Jefferson and Cyrus Chamberlain, who were going [into] aviation. At the last moment my son was rejected for lack of stabilizing judgment, but Cyrus became a member of the Lafayette Escadrille. He was killed June 17th in a fierce combat.

I just thought I would mention it in passing.

In spite of three rejections, one by the Navy—on account of a bum leg—Jefferson is now in the Navy on Admiral Sim's staff.

Sincerely yours,
H.V. Jones

P.S. Cyrus told his mother of the meeting with you. He [illegible] to write Mrs. F.A. Chamberlain, Minneapolis, a word. It would help her [undecipherable].

July 8th, 1918.

Dear Mr. Jones:

I am glad to get your letter, but very sorry to learn about gallant young Cyrus Chamberlain. At any moment I may hear the same news of my own boys. Three cheers for Jefferson! I enclose a line to Mrs. Chamberlain.

Faithfully yours,
Theodore Roosevelt

October 9th, 1918

Dear Mr. Jones:

I wish to thank you again for the copy of that letter from your gallant and distinguished brother-in-law. Won't you thank him most warmly for me?

Faithfully yours,
Theodore Roosevelt

INDEX

PROPERTY OF
SEWANHAKA CENTRAL HIGH SCHOOL DISTRICT
FRANKLIN SQUARE, N. Y.

STUDENT'S NAME	H. R.	SUBJECT TEACHER
Caroline Weiss	317	Balodimas
Crystal Speckes		Balodimas

CLOTHES, CLUES, AND CAREERS

MARGIL VANDERHOFF

GINN AND COMPANY

A XEROX EDUCATION COMPANY

ACKNOWLEDGMENTS

Design and production:
Sullivan-Keithley, Incorporated
New York

Photographs:
Photo Researchers (Morton Beebe) p. 15;
Museum of The American Indian
pp. 18, 20; Howard Sochurek from Time-Life
World Library p. 19; Peter Vadnai
pp. 70, 186; The Dow Chemical Company p. 174;
Bruner Corporation p. 175

Cover design:
Larrabee Design Associates

CONTENTS

SYMBOLS

New words in each lesson are marked by this symbol

Main ideas in each lesson are marked by this symbol

PREFACE

Clothes, Clues, and Careers is an introductory clothing textbook. Its purpose is twofold: to provide a comprehensive study of the many facets of clothing and to encourage further study of these facets.

The ten units deal with a broad range of topics. Unit One is concerned with why people wear clothes, where clothes came from, what shapes clothes have, and the reasons why people decorate clothes.

Unit Two surveys the history of clothes in the United States from 1600 to the present time, then goes on to speculate about the future. Major events in each century are summarized so that learners may identify these events with the general characteristics of clothes of that century.

The meaning of clothing is explored in Unit Three. The individual's concern for clothing as it affects appearance is described. In addition, examples are presented to show how clothing communicates.

Unit Four views clothing with other factors which affect appearance. The advantages of physical well-being, personal grooming, and social skills as other factors of appearance are analyzed.

Unit Five explains elements and principles of design and suggests ways in which they apply to clothes.

Buying clothes is the topic of Unit Six. Making decisions about clothes and plans for purchases are considered. There is information about fibers, fabrics, and finishes. Consumer information found in advertisements and on labels and hang tags is explained. Guidelines for the selection of some types of garments commonly worn are presented.

Unit Seven deals with the topic of clothes care and the factors which affect that care.

Unit Eight introduces some construction techniques which have useful applications. For example, sewing skills are a human resource that provides an alternative in making decisions about how to secure clothing. In other words, the person who has learned some of these techniques is not entirely dependent on ready-to-wear garments. Further, construction skills may be used to make or alter clothes to emphasize one's individuality. If one has some sewing ability as well as skill in the comparison and selection of ready-to-wear garments, clothes can more readily become a means of self-expression.

Unit Nine centers on some of the techniques one can use in making alterations and repairs of clothing.

Work and careers are the topics of Unit Ten. Types of jobs, working conditions, and special training required are discussed. Special consideration is given to the effects of work on one's lifestyle and some practical steps to take in preparation for a vocation. Learners are encouraged to investigate careers in retailing, production, maintenance, teaching, research, and communications.

Throughout the text illustrations support and emphasize main ideas. There are suggested learning activities to encourage further study and the application of these ideas or concepts. All units are broken into a series of short lessons, eighty-eight in all. Each focuses on a number of major concepts which appear at the beginning of each lesson.

Important new vocabulary words are introduced with each lesson. Review questions appear at the end of each lesson to encourage recall of the major concepts.

The Teacher's Guide summarizes the conceptual structure of the text, outlines instructional objectives and learning outcomes, and provides duplicatable evaluation devices for each unit.

Teachers should enjoy teaching and students should enjoy learning. The text and teacher's guide were designed to contribute to the teaching and the learning about clothing.

Margil Vanderhoff

CLOTHES BEGIN

UNIT ONE

If someone asked you the question "What are clothes?" your answer might be "Clothes are materials used to cover and decorate the body," or something similar. You probably would think that was a pretty easy question to answer.

Now think for a minute about the clothes you have on. Look around you and see what others are wearing. Think about the clothes worn today by people in other parts of the world and about how people dressed and decorated their bodies long ago. These thoughts may raise some questions about clothes that aren't so easy to answer. Why do people wear clothes today? Why did people start to wear clothes? When did people start to wear clothes? How did the different types of clothes develop? Why aren't clothes the same in all parts of the world? These are just some of the many questions you might ask yourself.

In this unit we will explore some of the possible answers.

LESSON ONE
WHY PEOPLE WEAR CLOTHES

 anthropologist   modesty

prehistoric   adornment

theory

 when people began to wear clothes

why people began to wear clothes

why people wear clothes today

The many variations of clothes we know today had their beginnings thousands of years ago. It is not known exactly how long ago the custom of wearing garments and body ornaments began. However, *anthropologists* and historians believe that people decorated their bodies and wore clothes many thousands of years before written records were kept. Anthropologists study early civilizations and the way groups of people live in the present.

It may have been more than 20,000 years ago that humans first decorated and covered their bodies with materials they found around them. Body ornaments of sea shells and bone have been found in areas of Europe and Asia where it is known that *prehistoric* peoples lived. Prehistoric people are those who lived before written records were kept. Ancient drawings, statues, tools, and remains of materials for making clothes are some other evidences that clothes have been worn for many thousands of years. Written records are later sources of information about clothes and body adornment.

ADORNMENT

Although it is generally agreed that clothes are a basic human need, there are many ideas, or theories, about why people began to

wear clothes. The theory most authorities agree on is *adornment,* or decoration. This theory is that human beings first felt the need to make themselves more attractive and developed ways to do so. People learned to paint parts of their bodies and tattoo designs on their skin. They made ornaments of bones, feathers, animal teeth, and fur. They learned how to color materials they wore with dyes made from plants. They spent time on the art of making their bodies beautiful and attractive. The theory of adornment also says that people probably started to paint or decorate their bodies a long time before they began to wear clothes.

Today, people still feel the need to make themselves attractive with clothes and body adornment. Clothes of different colors and fabrics, jewelry and other accessories, and cosmetics are just a few examples of ways people decorate their bodies today.

PROTECTION AND SURVIVAL

Another theory about the beginning of clothes is that they were needed for *protection and survival.* It is believed that the extreme climates in some parts of the world made clothing necessary for survival. However, there is record of some groups of people wear-

Statues, cloth, and other relics from the past tell of the ornamentation and clothing people wore.

ing little body covering yet surviving in extreme climates.

Much clothing today in the United States and other parts of the world protects people from the climate and environmental conditions. Some examples are raincoats, winter coats, and wide-brimmed sun hats. However, even though clothing provides protection, it is usually also designed to be attractive.

The theory of protection also suggests that people began to wear clothes as protection against evil spirits. Clothes worn by witch doctors is one example of clothing which protects against evil spirits. The same idea is present when someone wears a "lucky hat" or

carries a "lucky charm." The page to the left shows illustrations of how people protect themselves with special clothing.

Clothes have also provided protection from visible enemies in battle. This may or may not have been the reason people first wore clothes. Helmets, partial body shields, suits of armor, and bulletproof vests are some examples of clothing that has been developed for protection in battle. Today, protective clothing is not limited to military equipment. Padded suits, helmets, and protective aprons are some types of clothing designed to guard workers in hazardous occupations.

MODESTY

Still another theory about the beginning of clothes is that of *modesty*. Modesty refers to ideas about the proper way to dress to cover the body. The theory of modesty is that people started to wear clothes to cover their bodies. However, throughout the world there are different ideas about the parts of the body that should be covered. Many people now think that ideas of modesty were developed after people started to wear clothes. Some think that modesty is not the reason people began to wear clothes.

OTHER REASONS PEOPLE WEAR CLOTHES

Today, there are many reasons people wear clothes. Usually it is a combination of reasons. In the United States customs and laws dictate that the body be covered. Some religious groups, social groups, and schools have their own customs and rules about the way to dress. Protection from climate and occupational hazards influence the choice of clothes, too. The way people live and the things that are important to them also influence the way people dress. What are some other reasons you can think of for people wearing the clothes they do?

 **PUTTING IT TOGETHER**

1 How long ago did people begin to wear clothes?
2 What are some things which show that humans wore clothes before history was recorded?
3 What are some theories about why people began to decorate their bodies and wear clothes? Give some examples of present clothing practices to support these theories.
4 What are some reasons people most everywhere in the world wear clothes? Why are so many different kinds worn?

LESSON TWO
WHERE CLOTHES CAME FROM

 resources

natural environment

Industrial Revolution

technology

 some materials in the environment used for clothes

some technical skills and tools for making clothes

manufactured materials for clothes

some effects of communication and trade on clothes

Humans have used many different *resources* from the *natural environment,* or things from nature, for making things they needed. The first materials for clothing were likely from plant and animal sources. These sources still provide much of the raw material for fibers used in clothing today.

NATURAL RESOURCES

In parts of the world where it was cold, people tended to move about to hunt and trap animals for food. It is believed that animal skins provided the first clothes for these people. The skins, or *fur pelts,* were logical choices since they were available and provided protection against the cold.

At first the skins may have been worn just as they were removed from the animals. However, without treatment, the skins were stiff and not comfortable to wear. It was discovered that scraping the fat from the inside of the skin then beating the skin made it soft enough to be comfortable. Stone and bone were used to make knives to skin the animals and scrapers to scrape the fat from the skin. Several means were developed to soften

the skin. Some groups of people beat the skin with stone implements. Some chewed the skins. Others repeatedly beat the skin, wet it, and rubbed it with oil. Using *tannic acid,* a substance from the bark of certain trees, to treat animal skins was developed later. This treatment kept the skins soft for long periods of time.

Later people learned to remove the fur or hair from the animal skins. The *hide,* or animal skin without fur, is called *leather.* The hides were used for clothing. This practice was common among groups of people who hunted and trapped and lived in warmer climates. Processes were developed to use the fur or hair for making several other kinds of materials for garments.

Birds and other animals that didn't bear fur or hair were also used for clothing or adorning the body. For example, people found that skins of snakes could be made into belts, pouches, and other decorative articles. Alligator skins were sought as still another source of clothing. Many birds have provided plumage for ceremonial headdresses, hats, fans, and other ornamental clothing. Blue-green peacock feathers and multicolored parrot feathers made colorful body ornaments. They were fashioned into capes and skirts. Shells and seeds were strung to make necklaces.

Eventually people discovered that certain animals and plants could be raised to provide food and clothing. This meant that they really didn't have to spend as much time hunting. It also meant that people could settle in one place rather than move from place to place. More time could be spent developing tools and other implements and in finding other ways to make clothing.

People in warmer climates discovered ways to use parts of plants and trees and grasses for clothing. Inhabitants of the Polynesian and Melanesian islands in the South Pacific and some areas of Central Africa learned to use grasses for body coverings. Other plants and parts of plants required some kind of treatment or processing before they were suitable for making fabrics. One example is *tapa cloth,* or *bark cloth,* made from the paper mulberry tree. Bark was stripped from the tree, then soaked until it was pliable. Next, a special beater was used to beat the bark thin to form a large piece of cloth. The leaf of the pineapple plant was also used to make cloth.

Cotton and *flax* are other plants that grew in warm climates. When people discovered

People used natural resources to make clothes.

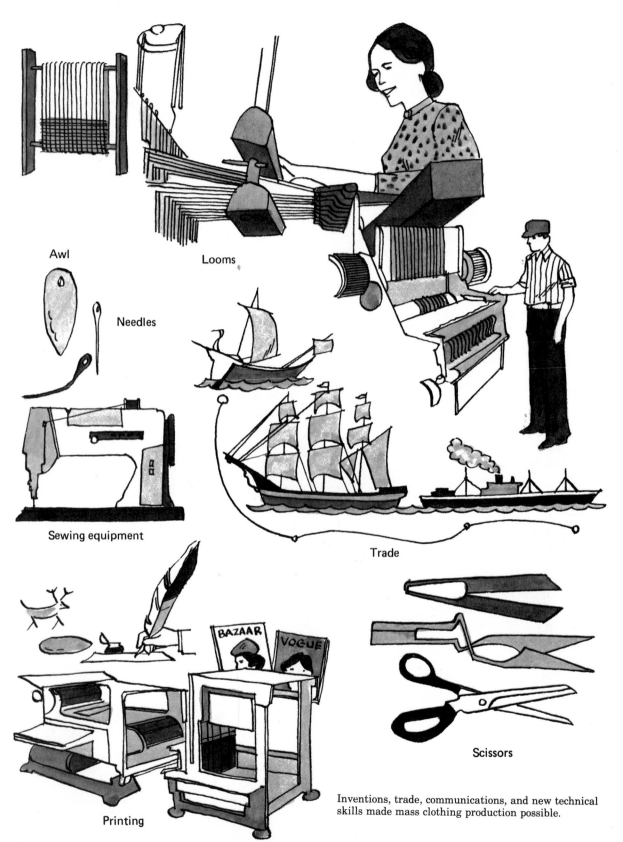

Awl

Looms

Needles

Sewing equipment

Trade

BAZAAR

VOGUE

Printing

Scissors

Inventions, trade, communications, and new technical skills made mass clothing production possible.

that cotton and flax could be processed and made into yarns for making fabric, they started to cultivate these plants. Tools for spinning and weaving these fibers into cloth were invented. Flax may have been grown in Egypt as early as 8000 B.C. Linen is the cloth made from the stalk of the flax plant. Cotton has been a useful crop in widely separated areas of the world since at least 3000 B.C. when it was grown in India. It was also cultivated in Peru and Mexico by early inhabitants there. From these early beginnings, cotton and flax still remain important resources for clothing today.

There is a legend which tells of a Chinese princess discovering how to soften the cocoon of the silkworm to obtain fibers for making fabric in about 2600 B.C. Whether this legend is true, no one really knows. However, silk production is still limited to only a few places because of the special climate needed for mulberry bushes on which the silkworms feed.

DISCOVERIES AND INVENTIONS

Changes in ways to provide materials for garments and ways to make garments have resulted from discoveries, inventions, or improvements in technology. *Technology* involves special ways to make things using science and inventions and discoveries. For example, the invention of the awl made it possible to bind animal hides together for clothing. The needle made it possible to sew pieces of fabric together and to decorate clothes. When people discovered how to work with metals, shears were developed to cut wool from sheep. Later adaptations made it possible to cut fabric.

After the *Industrial Revolution,* scientists became interested in making artificial silk, since raising silkworms was unsuccessful in many places. Several processes were tried, and a fiber now known as *rayon* was finally developed as a result of the experiments. Since that time many manufactured fibers have been developed, using chemicals as the main raw materials. This has made people less dependent on natural sources in the environment for clothes.

COMMUNICATION

As different ways of living developed and people had contact with each other and started to trade, ideas and practices related to clothing were exchanged. One group of people would take information learned from another group and adapt it to their way of life and the materials around them. Or, people might get actual clothing or fabric in trade for something else. This made it possible for people to have fabric and clothes made from materials from faraway places. For example, Europeans got silk from the Orient in exchange for their goods from Europe.

Today, as a result of technology, communication around the world is rapid and travel to many places in a short time is possible. Many countries produce fabric or clothing and then trade with other countries. People are no longer limited to producing cloth and making or wearing garments and body ornaments from materials in their own environment. Ideas about clothing have spread rapidly.

Technology has also helped with the conservation of natural resources and the protection of endangered species of animals and birds. Manufactured materials which resemble animal fur, leather, snakeskin, and feathers replace many natural materials once used for clothing.

 **PUTTING IT TOGETHER**

1 What are some natural resources from the environment that have been used for clothing since clothes were first worn? Describe some ways they have been used.

2 What are some reasons that clothes are not the same as they were when people first started wearing clothes?

LESSON THREE
THE SHAPE OF CLOTHES

 draped garments

fitted garments

wrapped garments

seamed garments

combination garments

 characteristics of draped, fitted, and combination garments

how different types of garments were developed

where today's styles come from

It may seem like clothes have changed a great deal since people began to wear clothes. It is true that styles have changed and that many different garments were developed in different parts of the world. However, with all this variety there are still only three basic ways clothes are made. These classifications of garments are *draped or wrapped garments, fitted or seamed garments,* and those garments which are a combination of draping and fitting.

A fitted or seamed garment is made by cutting material into pieces to fit different parts of the body, then joining these pieces together. Draped or wrapped garments are made from flat pieces of cloth or other material large enough to be wrapped around the body or draped over it. A *combination garment* is made by combining techniques of draping and seaming and fitting.

FITTED GARMENTS

It is believed that the first fitted garments were made in the colder regions of the world. Animal skins were used to cover the body. In the beginning, the skins were probably tied around the body with a *sinew,* or string made

from the hides. However, with the development of the *awl,* a pointed instrument for making holes, it became possible to puncture pieces of hide and bind them together with sinews to fit the body. The closely fitted garments provided more warmth than hides simply tied around the body.

One of the first fitted garments was likely the *parka.* Adaptations of this garment are seen in clothing today in parts of the world other than the Arctic where it was developed thousands of years ago. The first pants were probably skins fitted around the legs to allow for body movement while providing protection. *Churidars* and *kurta* are types of pants developed in India and have been worn for many centuries. Pants of various types are seen today in many countries.

DRAPED GARMENTS

Draped or wrapped garments are believed to have originated in warmer parts of the world, such as in the Mediterranean region. The climate was favorable for growing plants and raising animals for fibers. The techniques for spinning the fibers into yarns and weaving the yarns into cloth were then developed. It

Here are examples of fitted garments
from the past and the present.

Here are examples of draped garments.

is believed that the first woven cloth had *selvages,* or tightly woven edges, on all four sides. To prevent raveling, the cloth was not cut but draped over the body or wrapped around the body in one piece in order to form the garment.

Some examples of early draped garments are the *chiton* and *himation* worn by the Greeks about six thousand years ago. The *tunic, toga,* and *stola* were draped garments worn by the ancient Romans. In northern Africa and other desert regions, garments were developed for protection from the scorching sun and cold winds of the desert climates. The *haik, aba,* and *burnus* are draped garments still worn by people who live in desert areas. The *poncho* was worn in North and South America by natives before Columbus made his first expedition into the western hemisphere. In India the *sari* and *dhoti* have been worn for thousands of years. The sari is also found in Java, Bali, and East Africa. A

wrapped garment called the *sarong* has also been worn for many centuries in Malaya.

Throughout the years, many garments have reflected the characteristics of the first draped garments. Today, it is possible to see the true draping of long ago or designs which appear to be draped, in ponchos, caftans, capes, and other garments.

COMBINATION GARMENTS

Evidence indicates that combination garments first appeared in the Orient about three or four thousand years after the first civilization in the Mediterranean area. The Orient includes China, Japan, and other countries of the Far East. Here, the people learned to cultivate the silkworm and weave silk into fabric. Much of the clothing was cut and sewn yet was not fitted closely to the body so it also had a draped effect. The *Chinese robe* and *Japanese kimono* are examples of early garments using both draping and

Chinese robe

Mumu

Kimona

1800

Middle ages

Bloomer 1800

Modern

Here are examples of combination garments.

seaming. These garments are still worn today in the Orient. Adaptations can be seen in clothing in other parts of the world.

Much of the clothing today combines draping and seaming techniques in its construction. Few garments are draped without some cutting and seaming.

 **PUTTING IT TOGETHER**

1 What are the characteristics of draped or wrapped garments? How were they developed?

2 Give some examples of draped or wrapped garments. Which of these types of garments are still worn today?

3 What are the characteristics of fitted or seamed garments? How were they developed?

4 List some examples of fitted or shaped garments.

5 Describe the characteristics of combination garments. What are some examples?

6 Review this list of garment names. Tell which garments are fitted, which are draped, and which are combinations. Find the country or countries from which each comes.

chiton	haik	tunic	parka	poncho
himation	sari	aba	kimono	sarong
kurta	dhoti	choli	robe	
stola	toga	churidars	burnus	

LESSON FOUR
MORE THAN CLOTHES

 batik
ikat
embroidery
applique

reverse applique
quillwork
beadwork

 some reasons people decorate clothes

some techniques used to decorate clothes

Ever since clothes were developed people have found ways to enhance their own appearances and express beauty by adorning or decorating their garments. Painting, dyeing, stitching, and attaching ornaments are just some of the ways people have decorated clothes. Today many individuals still think of clothes as more than just body coverings. The clothes people wear show that they are concerned with appearance and the expression of beauty.

The techniques, or methods, for decorating clothes developed many centuries ago were hand methods. Some are still done by hand today, although many have been modified or changed to be done by machine. Other techniques once used to ornament clothes are no longer in use today. However, many museums have collections showing examples of these and other ways people have decorated clothes.

PAINTING

Painting with dyes made from natural materials in the environment has been done for thousands of years. The Polynesians painted designs on *tapa cloth,* or *bark cloth,* made from the paper mulberry tree. Indians who lived in the plains regions in North America painted animal skins that they prepared for clothing. Today people still do hand-painting on fabric, but machine methods of printing designs and colors are used for producing large quantities of fabric.

DYEING

Batik is a dyeing process developed many centuries ago in the Indonesian island of Java. Batik dyeing is done by covering parts of cloth with wax before the cloth is dyed. The waxed areas do not absorb dye and leave a pattern of uncolored areas against a dyed background.

Batik is still done in some areas of the world and by people who enjoy producing hand crafted products. The appearance of batik can be imitated by factory processes which produce thousands of yards of fabric rapidly. The batik-like fabric sold in fabric stores and used for ready-to-wear garments has probably been produced by printing the design on the surface of the fabric in a factory process. Hand produced batik may be found in some specialty shops and import stores.

Tapa, or bark cloth, is made from the paper mulberry tree. Here it is being painted.

14

CLOTHES, CLUES, AND CAREERS

Ikat, or tie-dyeing, is another process using dye for decorating cloth. This art was developed in Japan and India more than a thousand years ago. To tie-dye, parts of cloth are folded and knotted or tied in such a way that the tied areas do not absorb dye when the cloth is put into the dye solution. When the tied areas are loosened they leave an uncolored pattern on a dyed background.

Many fabrics today which appear to be tie-dyed are made by machine. However, like the batik process, tie-dyeing by hand is still done today. The Yorubas of Nigeria are skilled in ornamenting cloth with individualized patterns using the tie-dyeing process. You may have tried tie-dyeing or may know someone who decorates fabric in this way.

STITCHING

Embroidery is still another technique for decorating cloth that was developed many centuries ago. This process involves using a needle and thread to apply patterns and colors to fabric or other material. Ancient paintings and carvings found in Egypt show that

This is an example of batik dyeing.

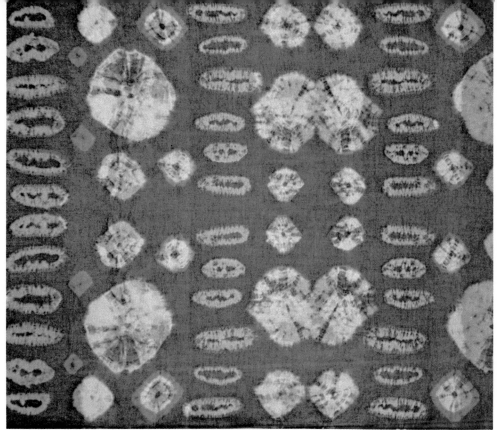

This is an example of ikat, or tie-dyeing.

This is another example of tie-dyeing.

This pouch is decorated with a beautiful design created with silk embroidery.

embroidered garments may have been worn as long ago as 1500 B.C. The Greeks had learned the art of embroidery by the fourth century B.C. On the other side of the world the Chinese were using embroidery to ornament clothes by 200 B.C. The Japanese made elaborately embroidered kimonos in the seventh century A.D. Wealthy families and royalty had garments of expensive fabrics embroidered with gold strands and colored yarns. Those who were not wealthy nor members of royalty embroidered designs on their clothes by making use of any materials that were available to them.

Embroidery remained totally hand done until 1829 when the first embroidery machine was invented. This invention made it possible for machine-produced embroidery to be applied rapidly to ready-to-wear garments. Most embroidery found on ready-to-wear garments today is machine-produced.

The Cuna, or Kuna, Indians of the San Blas Islands in the Caribbean produce a distinctive type of applique called *reverse applique*. This process was developed about 100 years ago so it is relatively new when compared with other techniques described in this lesson. The reverse applique design is made by stitching together several layers of cloth. Then top layers are cut out to expose lower

Appliqued designs decorate these garments made by Cuna (Kuna) Indians.

layers, thus creating a design with the combination of colors. This is the reverse of the regular applique process in which cloth pieces are attached on top of a base layer of fabric to create a design. Whether the regular applique process or the reverse applique process is used, a multi-layered fabric results from the applique process.

When several colors are combined to form the different layers an elaborate and colorful design is created. Fine hand stitching is done to attach the layers of the reverse applique design and to secure the edges of the cutout areas to the lower layer of fabric.

You may be familiar with regular applique which is used to ornament garments such as jackets, children's wear, and loungewear. Stitching for applique work on home-sewn garments can be done by hand or machine. High-speed factory equipment is used when applique ornamentation is put on ready-made garments.

ATTACHING ORNAMENTS

Quillwork was developed by the Plains Indians in the northern half of the United States and Canada. It was unique as an American Indian art and was not practiced or copied anywhere else. In quillwork, porcupine

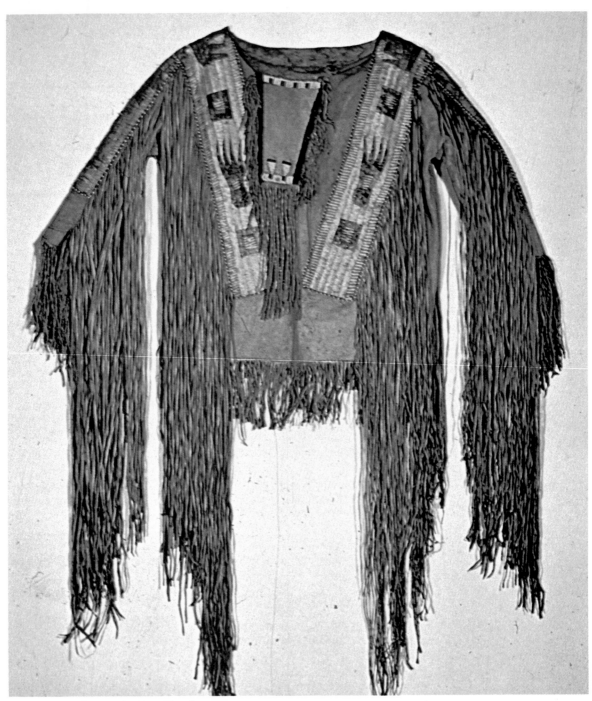

Here is a shirt decorated with quillwork and beadwork.

quills are attached to garments and other objects as a form of ornamentation. Porcupine quills are hollow, round, and about one and one-half inches in length. They are white with a black tip. Although the quills are hard, they can be soaked until they are flexible enough to be bent and twisted to form a pattern. The quills were softened, then dyed with natural plant dyes. Quills were stitched to clothing in shapes of flowers and leaves as well as geometric forms.

Before traders came to the area, quillwork was applied to leather garments the Indians wore. Later, when cloth could be obtained from traders, cloth garments were ornamented with quillwork.

Beadwork was another means the North American Plains Indians used to ornament their clothes. They made the beads from shells, seeds, animal bones, and teeth. About 1800, traders came to the central and the northern regions and brought European-made beads, called trade beads, as well as the cloth they traded. Gradually, these beads from trade were used instead of quills and native beads. The art of quillwork became less known until the process was totally lost. Beadwork using the manufactured beads brought by traders became the predominant technique for ornamenting clothes.

Some modified forms of beadwork are still used to ornament clothes today. This type of applied ornamentation is usually found on more elaborate garments.

PUTTING IT TOGETHER

1 Describe some evidence from the past to illustrate that people wanted clothing to do more than provide protection and physical comfort. What are some examples of this today?
2 What are some ways that clothes have been decorated in the past? In what ways have these techniques changed in recent years?

TAKING ANOTHER STEP

1 Prepare a bulletin board which illustrates how clothes fulfill the need to express beauty.
2 Use maps to point out how trade routes were a means to spread clothing styles and materials.
3 Prepare a display of means of communication that have helped spread clothing styles and technology. Show both past and present means of communication.
4 Find facts and give reports about the history of particular types of garments. Some topics to investigate might be hats, shoes, handbags, gloves, capes, blouses, petticoats, muffs, pants, and shirts.
5 Investigate one of the hand-decorating techniques or machine techniques described in this lesson.
6 Find out about a hand-decorating technique and try using it.
7 Ask your librarian to help you find a book of well-known art pieces or paintings of early times. Check details of clothing and body adornment. Try to find out why the people wore these clothes, what materials were used to make the clothing, and the reasons for using the materials that were used.
8 Find out about early types of clothing. Based on your research, make garments for dolls or hand-made figures. Make up cards to go with each figure telling the approximate dates the garment was worn, the material used for clothing, reasons for the type of clothing, any decoration used, and other related information. Use this material for a display in your classroom, the library, or display case.

HISTORY SPEAKS

UNIT TWO

Look around you. See the different kinds of clothes that people are wearing. Fashions in clothes differ very much from country to country, and within each country. If someone were to ask you "Why do styles vary so much?" you might answer, "People like different things. They come from different cultural backgrounds. They work at different jobs. Each person has his or her own way of living." But then you ask, "How did these differences come about? What events of the past have influenced the clothes that one sees today? How do the outfits worn today look like or look different from ones that were worn in the 1600s?" Can you explain some of the reasons for the answers you might give?

Exploration and settlement of new territories, wars, new inventions, and discoveries in new technology are historical events. In this unit you will have a chance to see how these events come together to tell the story of clothes and fashion from early times in America to the present.

LESSON ONE
SEVENTEENTH CENTURY (1600–1699)

 natural resources

raw materials

durable

linsey-woolsey

 where the American colonists came from

the importance of hand skills and use of resources to the colonists

some types of clothing worn by the colonists

EVENTS

While Europeans were changing their ways of living and thinking, it was a time of accepting challenge and fighting for survival for those just arriving in the New World.

Some of the resources used to make a living in Colonial America.

New opportunities for freedom, adventure, wealth, and a better quality of life encouraged the exploration and settlement of the North American continent. The English colonies along the east coast of America were surrounded during the 1600s by the French on the north and west and by the Spaniards on the south. Before the English arrived in America,

the Spaniards had already claimed Florida, as well as the southwest regions which later became Texas, New Mexico, and Arizona. The French established permanent settlements in Canada and moved west and south through the Great Lakes and the Mississippi River Valley.

The *natural resources* of America were used to produce numerous *raw materials*. The Pilgrims and Puritans of the Northeast found it was difficult to make a living by farming. Some of them turned to shipbuilding, trade, fishing, and raising sheep for wool. The Middle colonies had no single major product to support them, but their rich land yielded a wealth of grains and fruits; agriculture became their way of life. The Dutch, who settled in the Hudson Valley, were skilled in dyeing and weaving woolens, but also helped to make New York a fur trading center. People in the southern colonies cultivated a new plant called tobacco. It, along with rice and indigo, were their main products. They also experimented with *sericulture,* or the production of silk from silkworms, and cotton.

There was an abundance of lumber in the New World to answer every settler's needs and still become a profit-making export. The French, in their domination of the northern regions, introduced to the New and Old World alike, a wide selection of furs and leathers.

Most colonists were farmers, whether it was to feed their families or to make a living. Except for the services of the skilled shoemakers and bootmakers, blacksmiths, and wagonmakers, who traveled between the small villages to practice their trades, the colonists depended on imports from England to provide the goods and other products which they could not make for themselves. The farmers in the Middle and Northeast colonies settled in small villages and had small farms. In the South, many well-to-do farmers lived on plantations, or large farms, and had many people living and working there. Traders, merchants, ships' captains, and skilled workers settled in the seacoast towns, where the trade of the colonies centered.

CLOTHING

The various styles and constructions of clothing in early America were reflective of the wearer's background, occupation, and social position. The Pilgrims and Puritans of New England dressed plainly in keeping with their religious beliefs, although those Puritans who became leaders in business and government used elegant English materials and designs in their clothing. The Quakers, who arrived with William Penn, were often well-to-do and kept up with current fashions, but avoided over-ornamentation. The plantation owners of the South enjoyed the many luxury fabrics, such as brocades, taffeta, satins, and calicos, which were imported from England.

For other than the rich, styles changed slowly in seventeenth century America. Most colonists made their own clothing and wanted it to be *durable,* to last as long as possible. Of necessity, most of the clothing, footwear, and accessories came from materials close at hand.

Men and women of the 1600s led rigorous lives. Much of their work was out-of-doors; indoors there was no central heating. It was essential that their clothing be sturdy, manageable, and in the colder climates, warm. Women achieved this warmth by wearing long, full skirts with many petticoats underneath, some of which were *linsey-woolsey,* a coarse fabric of linen and wool. The general *silhouette,* or overall appearance, of men's clothes included some variation of *knee breeches,* woolen hose, a *doublet* or vest, and an ankle-length coat. In the late 1600s wealth became more widespread and dress more elaborate. The wig was introduced from England and became popular. To complement this vanity, men also began to carry *muffs* of rich materials with fur linings. As the life along the eastern seacoast became easier and daily tasks less difficult, more time could be spent following and copying the latest fashion trends from London and Paris.

Large families were common in the seventeenth century. Every child who survived the rigors of early life was an extra pair of hands to help raise crops and livestock, to mind the shop, and to improve the family's general welfare and productivity. Children were expected to share adult responsibility. Clothing a child often meant cutting down the somewhat worn or outgrown outfit of a parent or older brother or sister; the style remained identical to that of the previous owner. Even when a child received a new suit of clothing, it was a miniature adult suit.

 **PUTTING IT TOGETHER**

1 What story do clothes tell about the early settlers in America?
2 The early colonists exported their raw materials to England in exchange for imported manufactured goods. How would this affect the price of clothing?
3 List some factors that influenced the colonists' clothing choices.
4 Describe the activities of a child in early America.

EIGHTEENTH CENTURY (1700–1799)

flying shuttle   steam power

wool carder   cotton gin

cotton printer   textile

spinning jenny   wearability

spinning mule   lawn

power loom

⊙ some things that happened in the eighteenth century

some clothes people wore

EVENTS

The great distances and slow methods of transportation caused a communications gap between England and her new colonies. Life was different in the New World. The colonists began to develop ideas and ways of living more suited to this new life. As the century progressed, the colonists built new industries and explored and settled new territories. The colonies expanded southward into Georgia and took possession of all of the land between

Some of the major inventions which marked the beginning of the textile industry.

Cotton gin

Cotton printer

Power loom

Shuttle

Spinning jenny

Steam spinner

1725

1760

1776

1790

the coastal colonies and the Mississippi River. A more complete road system was developed. Trade, travel, and a common political experience brought the colonies closer together. By sharing and comparing ideas the colonies became more unified. They declared their independence in 1776. England refused to accept the independence of the colonies and the *Revolutionary War* broke out. When the fighting was over, the colonists formed a new government and elected George Washington as the first president of the United States in 1789.

The separation from England lifted many of the restrictions which had controlled the colonists' contacts with the world. Ships brought materials from all over the world to the seaports of the United States. The *Industrial Revolution* was just beginning in England. This was a time when new methods and machinery for manufacturing were developed. At the same time, the colonists were also experimenting with and improving the quality of their own raw materials. Eli Whitney's invention of the *cotton gin* made the cultivation and large-scale production of cotton practical. Samuel Slater, borrowing from English innovations, built the first cotton mill in Rhode Island. Piece by piece, as first the *flying shuttle,* and then the *wool carder, cotton printer, spinning jenny* and *mule, power loom,* and *steam power* were developed, the colonists began to make their own textiles. New industries, such as textiles, were

beginning. Established ones, such as shipbuilding, were expanding. These factors and many others helped the new nation to play a larger role in world trade.

CLOTHING

Day-to-day life and responsibilities did not change much. Strength and purpose were still important factors in the choice and design of clothing. Trade and communication with other countries increased. Contact with other countries led to more elaborate forms of clothing in the United States. Fashion dolls came to the colonies every four or five months. They showed the styles and materials being worn in London and Paris. Political leaders paid close attention to fashion. When traveling, much of their time was spent having clothes made according to the styles of the places they visited.

Special attention was paid to the detail work of women's clothing. *Flounces, quilted petticoats,* and lace caps were all added to the low-cut bodices and full-skirted gowns of the time. Men, still in *breeches* and *waistcoats,* also showed a greater interest in fussy extras. With low shoes, and the new silks available, great care was given to the selection of hosiery. Shirt collars and sleeve cuffs were made of *lawn,* a thin, cotton material, or lace. In this century, children were still regarded as miniature adults. They were dressed to look like the European fashion dolls.

PUTTING IT TOGETHER

1 How did increased world trade affect life in the United States?
2 Give some examples of technological developments that helped to develop the textile industry.
3 What design trends distinguish eighteenth-century clothing from that of the early colonists?

NINETEENTH CENTURY (1800–1899)

 manpower

immigration

industrialization

Industrial Revolution

manufactured fibers

 some things that happened in the nineteenth century

some clothes people wore

EVENTS

The United States of America extended from coast to coast by the end of the 1800s. The development of the steamboat and the railroad encouraged expansion and settlement. The excitement of the California gold rush drew many people across unexplored territories to the West Coast. Samuel Morse's telegraph and Alexander Bell's telephone pulled the distant corners of the country closer together. Massive *immigration* from European and Asian countries provided the additional *manpower* that helped to make the country an *industrial power*. The first women's rights convention was held in Seneca, New York. Women decided that they too wanted to take part in, and benefit from the development of higher education, industrialization, and a democratic system of government.

The development of transportation and communication encouraged expansion and settlement.

1830

1815

1855

Preceding the Civil War, about 1830, America began to experience its own *Industrial Revolution*. Independence of thought and action played a major part. New inventions and methods of production were accepted as natural by-products of the forward-moving country. Four of these developments had a very specific effect on the clothing industry.

First, were fashion magazines such as *Harper's Bazaar*. In addition to illustrating French fashions, which still had a strong influence, these magazines kept different parts of the country in close touch with the latest styles. Ebenezer Butterick and James McCall created ready-made paper patterns. These helped tailors and seamstresses to follow fashion trends to the last detail. The sewing machine, first introduced by Elias Howe, and then by Isaac Singer, was the most important invention that influenced clothing. This opened the doors to the industrial production of ready-made clothing. In home use, it freed the homemaker from hours of hand sewing. Lastly, experimentation began with *manufactured fibers*. In the nineteenth century, American textile mills used only natural fibers, but rayon was produced in France in the late 1800s.

CLOTHING

Styles passed through many phases in the nineteenth century. The shape and accent of women's dresses changed continually. With

the assistance of *petticoats, hoops,* padding, *bustles,* and *horsehair crinolines,* hips and shoulders were wide or narrow. Bosoms and posteriors were accented or made slight of and material was used abundantly or sparingly. Men donned their first long trousers, *tophats,* and shorter *waistcoats.* As the 1800s drew to a close, men wore the outfit which became the forerunner of the traditional business suit. Children continued to dress like adults but there was a growing concern as to how adult-like they really were.

 **PUTTING IT TOGETHER**

1 How did the increased and better means of transportation and communication influence fashion trends of the nineteenth century?

2 Straight pins, snaps, safety pins, and zippers were also inventions of the nineteenth century. How would these items add to the usefulness of the sewing machine?

3 What effects did the development of manufactured fibers have on the textile industry in the nineteenth century?

LESSON FOUR
TWENTIETH CENTURY (1900–1949)

 technology
assembly lines
mass production

work force
lifestyle
child labor laws

 some things that happened between 1900 and 1949

some clothes people wore

EVENTS

The invention of new machinery and the growth of industry continued in the 1900s. Mass-produced goods and *convenience,* which were to be so important in the twentieth century, resulted directly from this *technology.* The increased use of electrical power and electrical appliances—refrigerators, washing machines, irons—took over many time-consuming household tasks. New factories, the *assembly line,* and *mass production* decreased the need for home production of food, clothing, and other necessities. Industry drew more people out of the home and into the work force. Employees had to adjust to regularly scheduled hours, days off, and planned vacation periods. There was more free time and there were more ways to spend it. The routines and attitudes that influenced lifestyles, or the ways people worked, played, and dressed, were beginning to change.

Trains, and eventually cars and planes, allowed for more travel for business and for pleasure. Improved methods of communication and transportation brought together the ideas and attitudes of people from all over the world. People no longer had to wonder what was happening in Paris, Peking, or other faraway places. They saw the news in motion picture houses, heard it on the radio,

and by the late forties, saw it on television. World events and politics became subjects of daily discussion and debate.

Technology also introduced new materials and methods of production to manufacturers. The increased efficiency of new power sources allowed time for more research. In the textile industry, this research resulted in several new manufactured fibers.

CLOTHING

In the early twentieth century people were beginning to select their clothing to suit their own needs and ways of life instead of choosing clothes that required a great deal of care and preparation. In earlier times, Americans waited months to see the accepted season's styles from Paris and London. Because of faster communications, it became possible to follow each new trend as it developed. There was a new freedom to accept or reject a style as it fit individual tastes. The variety of and opportunity for choice became a major characteristic of American life.

Still, change comes more slowly to people than to things. Many of the ideas and fashions of the late 1800s carried over into the early 1900s. Women's clothes were still binding and cumbersome. They were designed for appearance rather than for practicality. Men's business suits were solid black or dark stripes. World War I brought all the concern with expensive fabrics and "proper" dress to a halt. Creative efforts and the production of materials were directed toward winning the war. Many women joined the work force to replace the men who had joined armed services. Some women also enlisted in the armed services. When the war was over, many women didn't want to give up their newly found sense of independence and achievement. They continued to progress towards equality in the women's rights movement of the 1920s. Women found the ease and practicality of the uniforms which they wore for many jobs and in the armed services qualities they were unwilling to give up. They cut their hair short, put on tailored suits and tubular-shaped dresses, and moved to take a larger part in the business world. After work, they maintained this new sense of daring with shorter skirts, lower necklines, and close fitting, straight designs.

The 1920s were years of *affluence,* or widespread wealth. While women were testing their new freedoms, men were busy finding new ways to spend their time and money. Sports became serious pastimes and professional occupations. *Sportswear* became part of everyday dress. Men added new and brighter colors to their business suits. *Separates,* such as jackets and slacks, blazers, and sport shirts became popular.

The *stock market crash* in October of 1929 resulted in a *depression* with high unemployment. Even the very rich were caught short of money. Life became much more serious. People were striving to regain stability in their lives. The world situation and the *economy* were very uncertain. The conflicts between femininity and boyishness in women's clothing calmed for a time. Hemlines moved downward and the shirtwaist dress became common. In men's clothing, there was much less difference between the clothing of the very wealthy and those with average income. The manufacture of ready-made clothing created new jobs and cut clothing costs. Most types of clothing were available to everyone in a variety of fabrics, designs, and prices.

During the early 1940s, ready-made clothes were again scarce due to World War II. Women took up jobs outside the home in larger numbers than ever before. Slacks became acceptable women's wear. Clothing purchases were based on practicality and easy maintenance or care. Shortages lasted until

1903

1923

1913

1928

the end of World War II in 1945 and for a few years after. When more fabric became available, skirts became fuller and hemlines dropped to just above the ankle. Padded shoulders became fashionable in both men's and women's suits. The *trenchcoat* was popular. This coat first appeared in imitation of the World War I uniform and again in other forms in the first half of the twentieth century.

Child labor laws had been passed in the late 1800s. Children became the subject of more attention and study. The new laws determined that no child was capable of han-

dling the same physical labor and working hours as those of an adult. The laws no longer allowed children to work in factories. It was accepted that the characteristics and needs of children are very different from adults. Children were encouraged to find playtime activities and were relieved of many responsibilities. It was no longer appropriate to dress them as miniature adults. These new activities indicated a need for a whole new industry. This industry specialized in the design and manufacture of children's clothes. These clothes, made especially for growing,

active children, included *rompers, snowsuits,* and one-piece *jumpsuits* or *coveralls.* Busy parents looked for sturdy, comfortable, and easy-to-care-for children's clothing.

As these children grew to their teens, they were fascinated with fads and unusual combinations. This fascination created and supported a booming, independent industry.

PUTTING IT TOGETHER

1 What technological developments changed life in the early 1900s? How did these changes in lifestyle affect clothing trends?

2 How would a shortage of materials affect clothing styles.

3 Describe the early twentieth century attitude toward clothing.

4 What caused manufacturers to gear a part of the clothing industry especially to children?

LESSON FIVE
TWENTIETH CENTURY (1950–TO THE PRESENT)

- **technological expansion**
- **standard of living**
- **environment**
- **individual responsibility**
- **consumer**
- **lifestyle**
- **manufactured fibers**
- **youth-oriented industry**

some things that have happened since 1950

some clothes people wear

EVENTS

By the middle of the twentieth century, the *technological expansion* which continued after the Civil War was moving faster than ever. There were many changes in a short period of time. The exploration of space became possible. In 1969, the first successful moon landing was completed. Today, news travels around the world in a matter of minutes. The *standard of living* continues to rise. The standard of living is the amount of necessities and luxuries people are able to buy. *Modern conveniences* are available to many more people. These changes cause confusion as people try to balance the old with the new. Action is being taken to provide equal opportunities for men and women and for those who are of different races, ethnic backgrounds, and incomes. Young people want to participate more actively in decision making. Women feel ready to take on more responsibilities outside of the home.

A rapid rise in the population after World War II created new problems. The United States, once with land and natural resources to spare, is now faced with overcrowding and shortages. One problem is the drain on the supply of natural resources, such as the raw materials which are needed for production and energy. Another is the misuse of those resources and abuse of the *environment*.

Solutions to problems sometimes indicate the need for a new approach. As people are learning to deal more effectively with their surroundings, new laws and *safety standards* are being created. Agencies to protect the consumer and the environment are being formed. Recent developments indicate the need for people to participate actively to help find solutions and to accept more individual responsibility. The strong emphasis on personal development and responsibility is directly related to the new freedoms also evident in today's society. Individuals are more free to determine their own values and goals. The variety of options is greater. As each person is free to choose and support his or her own beliefs and causes and those of society, he or she is also free to choose a unique *lifestyle*.

CLOTHING

The variety of options is also apparent in the clothing industry. "Proper" dress is much harder to define in these times. For most occasions women were formerly expected to wear a hat, gloves, and a dress, suit, or skirt. Pants are now appropriate for every occasion. Men were limited to business suits, or matching jackets, slacks, vests, and white shirts. Now sport jackets and slacks are not unusual business wear. Shirts are made in a variety of colors, stripes, and prints. Neckties are less conservative.

Changes in fashion are now less a function of the designer's whim and more an expression of the consumers' *budgets* and preferences. An ever-increasing variety of styles, separates, and mix-and-match sets add to more relaxed and individualized appearances.

In the 1960s, clothing styles and fabrics from other parts of the world besides the fashion centers in Europe began to have a very strong influence on styles in the United States. Clothing and fabric from Africa, Russia, China, and India are just a few examples which are commonly seen today.

New developments in *manufactured fibers,* fabric-making techniques, and *fabric finishes* have made possible easy-care, comfortable clothing at prices most people can afford. These developments go along with the greater freedoms and opportunities in all areas of living and allow people to choose clothes which are practical and more suited to climate, occupation, and lifestyle than to specific fashion codes.

The *youth market,* begun in the late 1940s, continues to grow. Beginning in early childhood, most young people have more money and more opportunities to spend it than ever before. They now dominate a large part of the consumers' market. Mass communication and expanded travel have broadened young people's exposure to the trends of their peers and to that of adults. Some manufacturers have sensed their obvious moods. An entire industry, separate from the rest of clothing production and design, is all geared to the

1951

1955

1958

specific wants and needs of the young. Fashion changes with lightning speed in this *youth-oriented* industry. It is a challenge to every manufacturer to keep up with the latest fads while keeping in mind the spending allowances of the buyers in their market. *Options,* or different choices, are now a big part of young people's lives, too. It can no longer be said that the young are an imitation or miniature of anything. They have their own unique ways of looking at life and all of its opportunities.

 **PUTTING IT TOGETHER**

1 Technological growth means change. What are some changes that have occurred within your lifetime?

2 What are some problems that have concerned people since the 1950s? What do you think are some solutions to these problems?

3 The standard of living has risen steadily throughout the twentieth century. How do you think this has affected youth?

4 If the standard of living does not continue to rise, what do you think might happen to the youth-oriented market? To clothing for all age groups?

 **TAKING ANOTHER STEP**

1 Use a map to point out areas of colonization in North America from 1600–1699.

2 Prepare and give a report on craftspeople of the colonies who produced articles of clothing.

3 Prepare a report on Samuel Slater and his cotton mill.

4 Find out more about hoops that were worn with fashionable dresses in the early 1700's.

5 Prepare a report on the invention of the sewing machine.

6 Prepare a bulletin board which shows conditions of home life in 1900 contrasted with those of today.

7 Make a bulletin-board display and pair some currently popular fashions with similar styles from the past.

8 Compile a report of fashions worn by Presidents and Presidents' wives. A booklet on this subject may be obtained from the Smithsonian Institution, Washington, D.C.

9 Do you live near a college or university which has a Home Economics department? Find out whether the department has a historic costume collection. Ask the person in charge of the collection to tell your class about one or two outstanding items in the collection.

10 Contact the director of your state historical museum to determine whether any historic clothing is included in the exhibits. If there is a collection of historic clothing, find out more about it and report to the class.

CLOTHES COMMUNICATE

UNIT THREE

You communicate whenever you send a message to another person. Whenever you receive a message from someone else, that person is communicating with you. When two or more persons are sending and receiving messages they are communicating.

Frequently, communication involves speaking, listening, writing, and reading. This is communicating by use of *verbal symbols*, or words. Besides verbal symbols, there are other means of communication. Pictures, diagrams, colors, and sounds are *nonverbal symbols* that can carry messages. For example, a siren is a sound that sends a warning message. The colors used in traffic signals send messages to drivers and pedestrians.

Posture, facial expression, and gestures are other nonverbal symbols which send messages to others. They express feelings such as surprise, anger, fear, and happiness. Still other nonverbal symbols are the clothes we wear. They tell others something about the wearer.

Of course, communication is successful only if the meanings of the verbal and nonverbal symbols are understood by both the person sending the message and the person who receives the message. If the sender and receiver do not have the same meaning for the symbols, a breakdown in communication might take place and cause a misunderstanding.

In this unit, you will see how the way you look and dress are nonverbal symbols that send messages to others.

LESSON ONE
YOU AND YOUR APPEARANCE

 communication   self-concept

impression   self-image

 the "you" others see

some reasons people are concerned about appearance

You and your clothes go places together. When others see you they actually see you and your clothes. Your face, hair, body shape and dimensions, your posture, and the gestures you use are also parts of the "you" others see.

What did others see when they saw you today? How did other persons react to your appearance? Do any of these reactions sound familiar?

"Hey, you look great!"

"Fantastic!"

"Is that a new sweater?"

"What did you do to your hair?"

"Please take off your hat in the classroom."

"I like you in that jacket."

"Have you lost weight?"

"Where are you going looking like that?"

Reactions such as these tell you that others are aware of your appearance. Nonverbal reactions, such as a frown, a smile, or a stare also tell you that others are aware of your appearance. They have received a message about you. If you are pleased by the reactions of others, you feel comfortable about your appearance. The message received is the one you sent; the communication is successful.

If you are concerned about the way you look, you are like many other young people. Most persons are concerned about their appearance. One reason is that people care about the *impression* they make on others. This means they are concerned about what others think.

A favorable impression, either with people you have just met or with people you already know, makes you feel comfortable. You feel secure in the way you look and are accepted. Wanting to belong and be accepted are feelings almost everyone has.

One way people try to be accepted is by trying to make their appearance similar to others. You and your friends may like to wear similar clothes and hairstyles. These are nonverbal symbols which identify you as being part of a group and accepted by others.

Even though most people like to feel they belong, they also want to be known and seen as individuals. You may wear clothes like those of your friends, but you probably choose different styles and colors to express your individuality.

Another way people try to be accepted is by wearing what is considered acceptable for certain occasions. They try to give the appearance they think others want them to have. You may dress one way for a job interview, another way for chores or for school.

You may tell people about your personality by your appearance. What you wear tells others about you. For example, a shy, quiet person might dress differently from a more outgoing person. Think about some people you know. Do they say things to you about their personalities by their appearances?

Some people like to imitate others in the way they dress. A person may try to look and

act like a favorite teacher, singer, fashion model, movie star, or other person he or she thinks highly of. Young children may imitate older children or adults. Adults may imitate other adults or young people. This is one way people learn about themselves and others. Usually it is part of finding one's identity as an individual.

Because appearance is a type of communication, there is always the chance that the message sent is not the message received. For example, you and your friends may spend time making your appearances similar. You are accepted by each other and you all belong to the same group. The messages among you and your friends are received as they are intended. However, other people may think that your appearance means something else and form a different opinion just because of your appearance.

Another example is an older person wearing clothes intended for a younger person.

Here the older person may want to be seen as a younger person and tries to do this through his or her appearance. Instead of seeing this person as being young, the message received by others might be something else. Can you think of other times the message sent by appearance is not the message received by others? When this happens, communication with clothes is not successful.

Another message sent by the way you appear to others is how you see yourself. In other words, your appearance can tell others about your *self-concept* or *self-image*. Self-concept includes ideas you have about yourself. This image may be positive or negative or somewhere in between. If you see yourself as a person who makes a good impression, you will probably make that kind of impression. If you have this kind of self-concept, you will probably work at trying to present yourself in a positive way and your appearance will show this to other people.

 **PUTTING IT TOGETHER**

1 How does communication take place?
2 What is a first impression?
3 What are some messages people send by their appearances? Explain why the messages may not be the ones received.
4 What does self-concept mean? What can clothes and appearance tell about the wearer's self-concept?

CLOTHES COMMUNICATE

LESSON TWO
CLOTHING SPEAKS

 ceremony

ritual

symbol

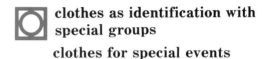 clothes as identification with special groups

clothes for special events

You can often learn something about a person by his or her clothes if you know the meaning of certain garments. For example, some garments identify the wearer as male or female, although the differences in clothing for males and females in the United States are not as distinct as they once were. Dresses and skirts are still considered garments for girls. However, jeans and slacks are worn by both males and females as are high-heeled shoes and boots, earrings, and necklaces.

Clothes may give clues about the age of a person. You can notice differences in dress among age groups. Because an adult's body shape tends to change over the years, clothes for older people may be designed differently from those for younger people.

Deciding whether a person is male or female or old or young by clothing is not always easy because the clues given by the clothes may not be accurate. It is easier to know something about a person when the clothes he or she wears identify a special

Special clothing is worn for special ceremonies.

group such as a band or sports team or community organization. Clothing is used in this way to communicate to others that the group exists. For example, you know your school band because of its *uniform*. Also, an individual band member can be identified when apart from the band if he or she is wearing the uniform. The uniform tells people that he or she is a part of that special group. Cheerleaders can be recognized by their special outfits. Football players and basketball players wear special uniforms. Chorus members may wear similar robes or outfits when they perform. Special garments, pins, and rings are other symbols worn to identify members of a club or student body of a school. *Symbols* sewn onto the back of a jacket or on a sleeve are other examples.

Community organizations may also have special garments to identify them. The scout uniform is one example. Candy Stripers who are volunteers in hospitals have special uniforms to identify them.

Special clothes are also associated with special events. In addition to the special clothes, a *ceremony* or *ritual* may call attention to the individual and the event. Sometimes garments may be purchased or made or rented for a particular ceremony, then never be worn again by the same individual.

Ceremonies help to preserve *traditions* and give continuity to families, communities, and organizations. Families and individuals who value traditions may preserve some garments worn for special ceremonies so they can be handed down for later use by other members of the family when they experience the same special event.

A special event early in the lives of some individuals is the *christening* ceremony or baptism. Sometimes a special garment is worn by the young child for this event. In some families, the christening dress may be one which has been handed down and used through several generations.

Another religious ceremony is the ritual involved with becoming a full member in a church or other religious group. Different faiths have different ceremonies for this event, which may include the wearing of a special garment.

Formal *initiation* into a social, educational, or service organization often includes accepting and wearing the symbols and special garments of the particular organization. For example, the scout uniforms and badges are distinctly special to the scout organizations. Another example is the Future Homemakers of America organization which has its symbol to be worn by members. Also, the Future Farmers of America has a symbol which is frequently worn attached to the back of the FFA jacket. These are only a few examples. Different organizations have their own symbols which show that individuals are members of the organization.

Graduation ceremonies recognize completion of academic requirements for a school diploma, a certificate, or a college degree. The traditional garment worn by graduates at these ceremonies is the academic gown and mortar board, or cap and gown.

The wedding ceremony in its many forms is performed when two people marry. Often there are special clothes worn by the bride and groom for this event. If there are attendants, these people may also wear special clothes. Wedding rings may be exchanged by the couple at the ceremony and worn after-

wards as visible symbols of the ceremony. Like the christening dress, a wedding dress may be preserved as a visible reminder of an important event in the family's history. Or it may be saved to be used later by other women in the family when they get married.

There are also ceremonies and special clothes associated with the end of life. Religious ceremonies may be performed at death, at funeral services, and at burial. The dead may be buried in special clothes or symbols associated with an organization to which he or she belonged before death. The mourners may wear black, the traditional color of mourning clothes in the United States.

PUTTING IT TOGETHER

1 Why is it sometimes difficult to tell whether a person is male or female by the clothes that person is wearing?
2 How are teams, clubs, and other organizations identified through clothing and other symbols?
3 Why are ceremonies carried out to observe special events? Of what value are traditions to families and communities?
4 What are some events for which special clothes may be worn? Describe the clothes for each event.

CLOTHING SPEAKS FOR THE JOB

 occupational clothing

standards of dress

uniform

 clothes can identify what one does

some reasons why some jobs require special clothes

Clothing identifies people in some occupations. It is possible to tell what some people do by looking at the clothes they wear to work. Sometimes this clothing is called *occupational clothing*. This term refers to clothes that are associated with certain jobs or types of work. Occupational clothing may also be clothing a worker obtains and uses only to carry out his or her occupational responsibilities.

There are many reasons people wear what they do on the job. Some employers have rules about clothes that workers may wear. Employers may set some standards for their employees with the expectation that their places of business will appear more attractive to customers. They may do this to make the businesses operate more efficiently. In this case, the workers dress as they do because they are following the employers' standards and rules, trying to work efficiently.

Examples of businesses where employees may be required to meet certain *standards of dress* include large banks, department stores, other retail stores, travel agencies, and insurance agencies. Although a uniform is not required, an employee may be expected to choose clothing which meets certain standards. Men may be required to wear business suits or slacks and sport jackets. Women may be asked to wear dresses, tailored suits, or pant suits in particular styles which are considered suitable to their jobs.

In some occupations special clothing is required to protect the worker from possible injury. Safety for the worker is essential for fire fighters, construction workers, miners, employees in some manufacturing processes, police personnel, and military personnel. Examples of garments which are designed to protect the worker are hard hats, helmets, fireproof suits, and rubber or asbestos fireproof aprons. White gloves and yellow slickers of the traffic police officers make them more easily seen when visibility is poor. Traffic controllers may also wear yellow or orange vests, so they can be clearly seen. In some instances it is essential for the protection of the worker not to be seen. Military personnel in combat assignments depend on clothing that hides them from the enemy.

Another reason for special clothes at work is sanitation or cleanliness. This is especially important in the medical profession, food service occupations, and food processing plants. Special uniforms may be required of cooks and waiters or waitresses in restaurants and cafeterias. Workers in food processing plants may be required to put on special garments when they enter the plant so the food will not be contaminated. A variety of covering garments are used by workers in the medical profession to maintain cleanliness.

Personnel who provide protection to the public are usually identified by *uniforms* so they can be readily identified. These include fire fighters and police and military personnel. These protection specialists have responsibility for public safety. When the services of these people are required it is important that they be easily recognized.

Besides protection specialists, uniforms are standard dress for many types of service personnel. This includes the transportation industries with services provided by bus drivers, airline personnel, and train crews. Also, postal service workers are usually uniformed. The service industries have many types of uniformed personnel including appliance repair personnel, hairstylists, delivery personnel, bell captains, sky caps, security guards, parcel delivery persons, maintenance workers, and household service employees.

 **PUTTING IT TOGETHER**

1 What is occupational clothing?
2 What are reasons why occupational clothing may be required on the job?
3 What are examples of occupational clothing? Give reasons why each of these types of occupational clothing may be required.

TAKING ANOTHER STEP

1 Survey class members to determine the sources (such as friends, parents, movies, magazines, stores) which influence their choices of clothes for different situations. Report your findings. Which influence seems to affect clothing choices of the class members most frequently?

2 Survey parents of class members or other adults to determine sources which influence their choices of clothing. Are these influences the same as those which affect clothing choices of class members?

3 Plan a bulletin board or display of clothing identified with special events.

4 Make a bulletin-board display showing typical dress that is associated with certain occupations.

5 Describe a character in a TV program or a movie you have seen recently. Did the character's clothing tell you something about his or her personality traits? Did clothing help to explain his or her role in the story? Try describing the character without mentioning clothing.

6 Notice descriptions of clothing the next time you read a biography or an autobiography. When you are making a book report for literature class include an accurate description of clothing worn by the characters in the book. Or illustrate your report with sketches of the clothing.

7 Join the dramatics club or the theater arts group in your school and volunteer for the costume committee. You should understand the personality traits of the characters and choose costumes to fit these traits.

APPEARANCE COMMUNICATES

UNIT FOUR

A person's appearance leaves an impression on others. Attractive clothing can help you create a pleasing appearance, but clothing alone cannot make you an attractive person.

Physical attractiveness begins with good health. Health is affected by what one eats, by cleanliness that one practices, by exercise, and by posture. Add a knowledge and skill of selecting and caring for clothes and you have the resources to maintain a pleasing physical appearance. Part of the task of growing up is the development of personal habits that will help in the maintenance of an attractive appearance. This means that to a large extent you control your appearance through the everyday decisions you make about eating, sleeping, keeping clean, exercising, and having good posture.

Actions and behavior, together with one's behavior toward others or with others, can add or take away from one's personal attractiveness. All make up your appearance. You feel good to be you when you know that you look right. You feel good about how you look when you know that others approve of your appearance.

In this unit we are going to look at these things which make up a person's appearance and influence the way one feels about oneself.

LESSON ONE
FOODS YOU NEED

 nutrient

Basic Four
Food Plan

Basic Four

Basic Four
Food Groups

citrus fruit

refined

 some ways food affects the
way you look and feel

types of food your body needs

The foods you eat every day affect how you look and how you feel. The condition of your skin, eyes, teeth, and hair depends on the foods you eat. Body weight can be controlled to a great extent by what you eat. Energy and enthusiasm as well as your resistance to disease and what your health will be as you grow older are related to what you eat.

Your body needs certain *nutrients* for growth and development, for resistance to disease, and for maintenance of all body functions. These nutrients are *vitamins*, *minerals*, *proteins*, *carbohydrates*, and *fats*.

BASIC FOUR FOOD GROUPS

One way to get all the nutrients you need is to follow the *Basic Four Food Plan*. This means choosing certain amounts of foods every day from four different groups. The groups are: milk and milk products, meat and meat substitutes, fruits and vegetables, breads and cereals. You may have heard them called the *Basic Four* or the *Basic Four Food Groups*.

You need three or four servings of *milk* or *milk products* each day. Foods made with large amounts of milk can provide part of the four glasses of milk you need. If you do not care to drink the total amount of milk you need, good substitutes are cheese, ice cream, ice milk, and puddings made with milk.

You need two or more servings daily from the *meat group*. The main dishes of many meals usually consist of foods from this

THE FOUR FOOD GROUPS
Every day you need:

MILK
4 or more glasses
to drink and in foods like these

MEAT and EGGS
2 or more servings

COTTAGE CHEESE

BEANS

or some
of these alternates

Have one dark green
or yellow vegetable

VEGETABLES
and FRUITS
4 or more servings

Have one citrus fruit

BREAD and CEREALS
4 or more servings

OATMEAL

RICE

enriched or whole grain

group. Lean meats, fish, poultry, eggs, and cheese supply a wide range of choices, and each of these foods can be prepared in a variety of ways. Meat substitutes, such as dried beans, peas, nuts, and peanuts are also included in this group. When you eat a meat substitute, add to it a glass of milk or an egg or a piece of cheese or other similar food. This combination can take the place of meat, fish, or poultry.

Include a dark green or a deep yellow vegetable or yellow fruit in your four servings of *vegetables* and *fruits* each day. Apricots, carrots, pumpkin, cantaloupe, mangoes, sweet potatoes, squash, and persimmons are considered deep yellow vegetables and fruits. Kale, chard, spinach and other leafy greens, and broccoli are dark green vegetables.

One of your servings from the vegetable and fruit group each day should be a *citrus fruit,* that is an orange, grapefruit, lemon or lime, or the juice from one of these fruits. A large serving of tomato juice, tomatoes, cantaloupe, broccoli, or strawberries can be substitute choices for citrus fruits.

You need four or more servings daily from the *bread* and *cereal group.* Some examples are cooked or ready-to-eat cereals, sandwich buns, bread, toast, rice, crackers, noodles, macaroni, and spaghetti. Enriched or whole-grain products are recommended. *Enriched* products have vitamins and minerals added; *whole grain* products are made with grains that have not been *refined,* or processed to remove any parts.

EXTRAS

There are many foods you may know that are not included in any of the Basic Four Food Groups. Some of these are soda, jam, jelly, honey, sugar, candy, chocolate, potato chips, pretzels, butter, popcorn, pickles, catsup, salad dressings, and gravy. Foods such as these are not in any of the food groups because they do not provide enough nutrients. It is all right if you eat foods that are not in the Basic Four as long as you eat them in addition to the recommended amounts from each of the Basic Four. When you eat these "extras" instead of foods from the Basic Four, your body will not get the nutrients it needs.

CONTROLLING WHAT YOU EAT

If you are still hungry after you have eaten the recommended foods from the Basic Four, choose additional servings from the four food groups. You may also want to choose some "extras" to add variety.

The amounts of food people need daily vary with each person. An adequate amount of food for a person depends on age, physical activity, body size, and other conditions. Eating more food than your body can use will result in a weight gain. If you find you are gaining weight, but not growing taller, you may be eating too much. Cut back on extras, but do not stop eating the recommended amounts from the Basic Four.

A small snack between meals can help to keep you from becoming so hungry that you overeat at mealtime. You can learn to control the snacks you eat if you plan them as part of the food you need. A few snacks that can be counted as part of your body's total daily food needs are a glass of milk, a serving of ice cream, some raw fruits or vegetables or a meat sandwich.

Eating too little food can have the immediate effect of leaving you without enough energy, too tired to carry on your activities. Long-time results of eating too little food or not enough of the foods your body needs are lowered resistance to disease and infection and poor body development.

Right now, from day to day, you are forming habits of eating particular types of foods in particular quantities. Eating patterns which are based on the foods you need will help you maintain general good health and an attractive appearance. Continued use of these patterns will benefit you in adulthood.

 **PUTTING IT TOGETHER**

1 How does the food you eat every day affect the way you look and feel?
2 List the Basic Four Food Groups and give examples of foods in each group. How many servings do you need from each group every day?
3 Give examples of foods not included in the Basic Four Food Groups. When might you decide to eat these foods? What might make you decide not to eat these foods?

LESSON TWO
POSTURE AND EXERCISES

 muscles
posture
alignment
exercise

 how posture and exercise are important to health and appearance

some ways to improve posture

some exercises for posture and health

Your body is made up of many substances such as water, vitamins, minerals, proteins, fats, and carbohydrates. These substances, or *nutrients,* combine in special ways to make bone, body fat, and muscle. Bones give your body a framework, or structure, and protect the organs of the body. One purpose of fat is to be a cushion around certain organs. Muscles work to hold the body in place when standing, sitting, and lying down. They also work to produce body movements.

When muscles are strong and healthy, you have *good posture.* This means that you stand and sit and walk and move about with your body held as it should be. Your body is in *alignment,* that is all the bones, muscles, and organs are lined up correctly. You also move easily and have energy. Good posture and easy body movements add to your health and appearance.

The picture at the right and the three pictures on page 55 show some ways to stand, sit, walk, and move with good posture.

Standing. Stand with your head centered over the rest of your body. Keep your back straight and shoulders back, but relaxed. Pull your abdomen in and up while tucking your hips under slightly. Bend you knees a little, but keep relaxed.

Standing

Sitting

Walking

Bending

Walking. As you walk, hold the upper part of your body as you should for standing. Swing your legs from the hip as you step. Be sure to keep your toes pointed straight ahead and your feet parallel.

Sitting. Sit with your back straight and your hips touching the back of the chair. Keep your neck in line with your upper back. If you are working at a desk or table, lean forward from the hips.

Bending. Move with your back straight. Bend from the knees to pick up things from the floor. Picking up objects from the floor or low places while bending from the waist can damage your back.

Standing, sitting, and moving in these ways may seem awkward, but it is important for health as well as for appearance. Incorrect posture may cause back injury or other problems because the body is not aligned properly. Poor posture may also cause you to feel tired and give you aching muscles. Practice every day will make correct posture much easier for you to achieve and maintain. Finally then good posture will become a comfortable, regular habit for you.

Muscles need regular *exercise* to work as they are intended to work. Your general health and well-being benefit from exercise. Exercise also improves blood circulation and helps your body digest foods and eliminate wastes. If you don't regularly play sports, walk briskly, swim, play tennis, run, or engage in an exercise program, you probably are not getting enough exercise. Your muscles will become "lazy" and will not work as well as they should.

Here are some exercises to help improve your posture, keep your muscles in good condition, and keep you healthy. If you are not used to doing exercises, do only a few of each and do them slowly. Gradually work up to the number recommended in each exercise. If you have a bad back or other physical problem, check with your doctor before doing any type of exercise.

EXERCISE 1

STEP 1. Do this exercise barefoot. Hold on to a chair or other object to help keep your balance.

STEP 2. Keep your legs straight while doing this exercise.

STEP 3. Place your feet about 8 inches (20 cm) apart. Slowly lift your heels until you are standing on your toes. Then slowly lower your heels.

STEP 4. Repeat step 3 25–50 times.

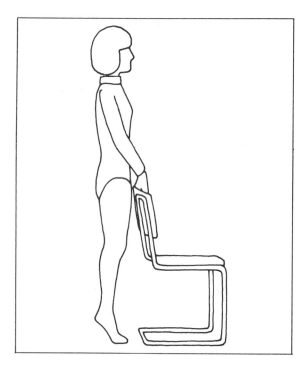

EXERCISE 2

STEP 1. Do this exercise barefoot.

STEP 2. Breathe through your mouth while doing this exercise.

STEP 3. Start by slowly running in place. Lift your feet off the floor. When you put your foot down, put your toes down first, then your heel.

STEP 4. Work up to a more rapid pace and keep running in place until you begin to feel tired.

STEP 5. Return to a slower pace before you stop.

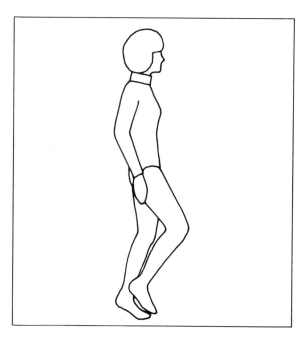

EXERCISE 3

STEP 1. Sit on the floor with your legs out in front of you.

STEP 2. Keep your knees flat while doing this exercise.

STEP 3. Lift your arms up over your head. Slowly bend from the waist and stretch to touch your toes. If you can, bring your hands down so your fingertips go over your feet.

STEP 4. Repeat step 3 10–20 times.

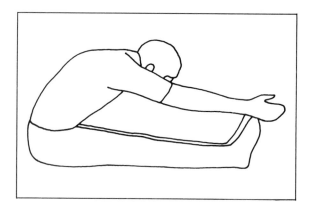

EXERCISE 4

STEP 1. Stand with your back flattened against a wall. Bend your knees if you need to.

STEP 2. Slowly straighten your legs and move your back up the wall. Stop when you can no longer keep your back flat against the wall.

STEP 3. Lift your hands up over your head and touch the wall. Then lower your arms. Keep your back flat against the wall.

STEP 4. Repeat step 3 10–15 times.

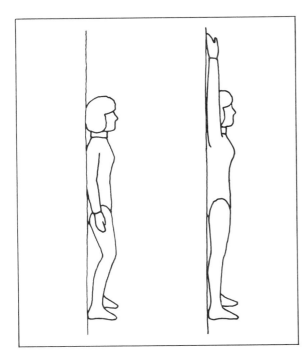

EXERCISE 5

STEP 1. Place your feet about 18–24 inches (45-60 cm) apart. Place your hands on your hips.

STEP 2. Bend over from your hips and slowly make a circle with your upper body. Try not to move the lower part of your body.

STEP 3. Repeat step 2 making a circle in the opposite direction.

STEP 4. Repeat steps 2 and 3 15–25 times.

EXERCISE 6

STEP 1. Lie on your stomach on the floor. Put your arms from elbows to wrists on the floor in front of you.

STEP 2. Lift the middle part of your body off the floor until your whole body is in a straight line. Lower the middle part of your body to the floor.

STEP 3. Repeat step 2 15–20 times.

EXERCISE 7

STEP 1. Lie on your back on the floor. Put a small pillow under your back.

STEP 2. Keep your elbows straight as you do this exercise.

STEP 3. Lift your arms up over your head to touch the floor. Breathe in deeply as you do this.

STEP 4. Bring your arms down to your sides. Breathe out hard as you do this.

STEP 5. Repeat steps 3 and 4 20–30 times.

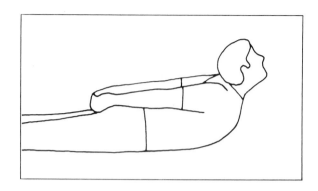

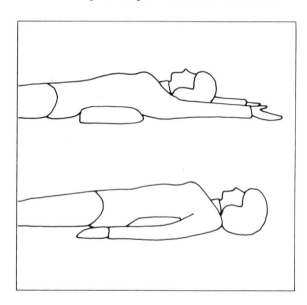

EXERCISE 8

STEP 1. Lie on your stomach on the floor.

STEP 2. Clasp your hands behind your back. Lift up your head and shoulders as far as you can and hold the position as long as possible.

STEP 3. Lower your head and shoulders; return your hands to the floor.

STEP 4. Repeat steps 2 and 3 5–15 times.

EXERCISE 9

STEP 1. Lie on your back on the floor. Have someone hold your feet to the floor. Or put your feet under the edge of a heavy chair or sofa.

STEP 2. Keep your back straight as you do this exercise. Try to keep your legs straight. If you can't, change your position so your knees are slightly bent.

STEP 3. Clasp your hands behind your head and slowly sit up. Then slowly lie down.

STEP 4. Repeat step 3 15–30 times.

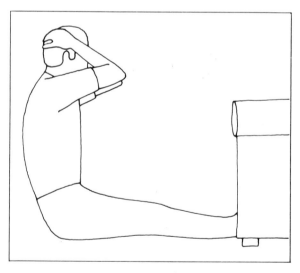

 **PUTTING IT TOGETHER**

1 Explain why posture and exercise are important to health and appearance.
2 How is exercise related to posture?

LESSON THREE
CARING FOR YOUR SKIN, TEETH, AND NAILS

 deodorant cuticles

antiperspirant callus

acne   plaque

antibacterial tartar

manicure cavities

pedicure

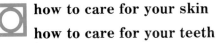 how to care for your skin

how to care for your teeth

how to care for your nails

Your skin, teeth, and nails are important to your appearance. Eating the right foods helps keep you healthy and helps give your skin, teeth, and nails, a healthy, attractive appearance. Keeping clean is also important to health because it helps prevent disease.

SKIN CARE

There are many ways to keep your body clean. You can take a tub bath, a shower, or a sponge bath. A *sponge bath* is taken similar to the way you wash your face. A sponge bath is convenient when you cannot take a *tub bath* or a *shower*. However you choose to keep your body clean, be sure to rinse all the soap from your skin. If soap is not rinsed away it can cause irritation.

Calluses, or areas of hardened skin, are caused by constant rubbing of the skin; they may appear on your hands and feet. Gently scrub calluses with a brush each time you take a bath or shower and apply a lotion or cream to soften them. Also, be sure your shoes fit correctly since shoes that do not fit can cause calluses.

If your skin is dry or itchy, you may want to use body lotion after a bath or shower. Body lotion helps add moisture to your skin and makes dry skin softer and more comfortable. To prevent body odor, use an underarm *deodorant* or *antiperspirant* every day and after a bath or shower. An *antiperspirant* also helps to prevent wetness from perspiration.

Acne, pimples, and oily skin are sometimes problems. *Acne* is a skin disease and may need treatment by a doctor. Pimples and oily skin often can be helped by special care.

Whether you have skin problems or not, it is important to eat the right foods. If you have acne, pimples, or oily skin, avoiding greasy foods and sweets and eating plenty of vegetables and fruits may help. If you are under a doctor's care, follow the instructions given to you about what to eat.

Another thing you can do to help your skin is to wash your face often with a special soap for your particular skin problem. Some soaps are labeled *antibacterial*. This means that there are ingredients in the soap which help destroy bacteria which can cause infections. Antibacterial soaps may help clear up acne and

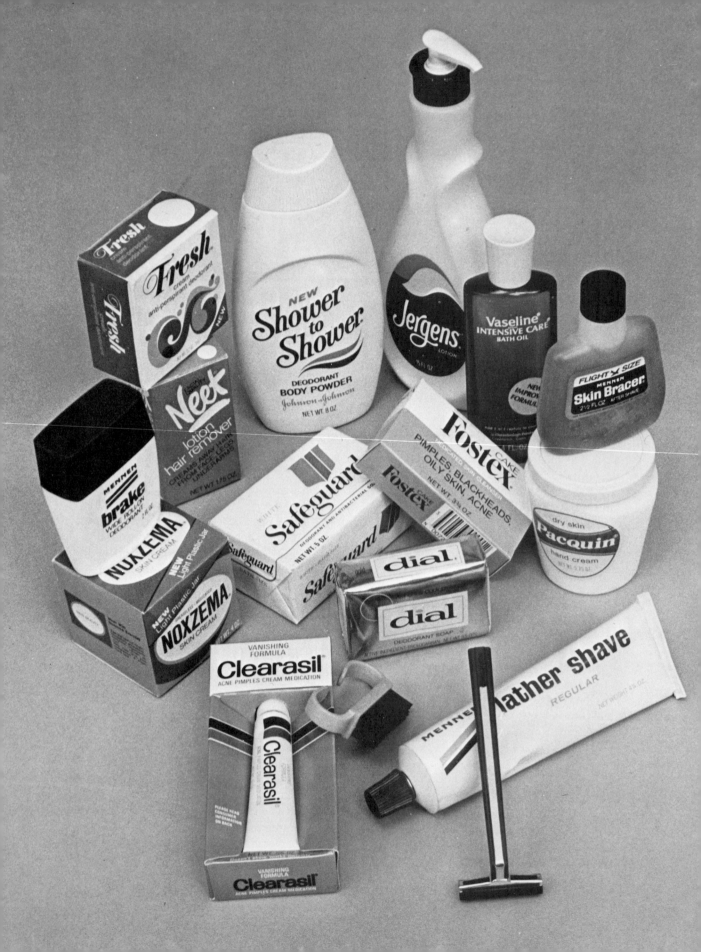

These are some products used for skin care.

pimples. Other soaps are for oily skin, dry skin, or normal skin. Try to find one that works for you. You may want to try a special lotion or ointment for clearing up pimples or acne.

Washing your hands often is important for many reasons. Clean hands and fingernails help prevent spreading germs and dirt from the things you touch and work with every day. Clean hands and nails also add to your appearance. If the skin on your hands is dry or rough, use hand lotion or hand cream often.

NAIL CARE

Grooming your fingernails is called a *manicure*. Grooming your toenails is called a *pedicure*. A basic manicure or pedicure includes shaping the nails by cutting or filing or both. The fingernails can be rounded according to the shape of your fingers. Toenails should be cut straight across to avoid ingrown toenails which can be painful. Push back the *cuticle*, or skin around the nails, with the towel each time you dry your hands and feet. This helps prevent hangnails and gets rid of dead skin cells. You may also want to use an orangewood stick or other special tool to push back the cuticle. If you use nail polish, apply it to clean nails.

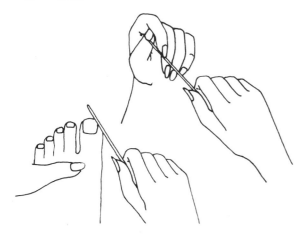

STEP 1.   Clip or file the nails to the length you want them. Shape toenails straight across to prevent ingrown toenails. Fingernails can be shaped into ovals.

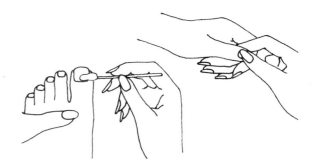

STEP 2.   Soak your nails in soapy water or wash your hands. Use a cotton-wrapped stick or a towel and your fingers to gently push the cuticle back. Or use cuticle remover according to directions on the label.

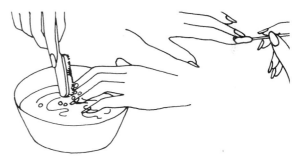

STEP 3.   Scrub the nails with a nail brush and soapy water if necessary. Clean under the nails with a cotton-wrapped stick or metal instrument for this purpose.

CARE OF THE TEETH

Your teeth and gums also need attention for health and appearance. Eating the right foods, brushing, using dental floss, and visiting the dentist regularly are all part of caring for your teeth. Choosing foods from the *Basic Four* will help you be sure you are eating the right foods for healthy teeth and gums. Milk and milk products and citrus fruits are especially important.

Each time you eat, some food particles stick to your teeth or get caught between your teeth. Sometimes these particles are so small you can't see them, but they are still there. If the particles are not removed, bacteria feed on the particles and form *plaque*, a sticky film, on the teeth. Plaque cannot be seen, but this is what is believed to cause tooth decay and gum disease. If plaque is not removed, it hardens into tartar, a substance that is not removed by ordinary brushing.

Brush after you eat to remove food particles. If you can't brush, rinse your mouth with water or try to eat some raw vegetables such as celery or carrots. Rinsing helps remove food particles from the surface of the teeth; raw vegetables help remove food particles from between the teeth. At least once a day, use *dental floss* to remove food particles from between the teeth. If you wear braces to straighten your teeth it is especially important to keep your teeth clean because there are so many places food particles can stick. Follow your dentist's instructions for caring for your teeth.

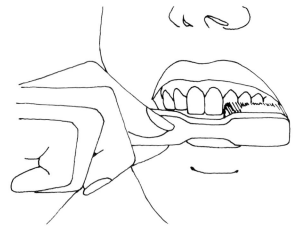

Use a soft brush for brushing teeth.

Brush carefully in an up-down motion.

Use a soft toothbrush for brushing your teeth. A toothbrush with stiff bristles may damage the teeth and gums.

The dentist will check your teeth for decay and the presence of plaque or tartar. If there are *cavities*, or decayed spots, the dentist will fill them so they do not get larger and cause more trouble. Special equipment may be used to remove tartar. Sometimes the dentist will apply a special substance to teeth to help prevent decay.

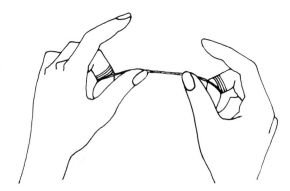

Use dental floss to remove food particles.

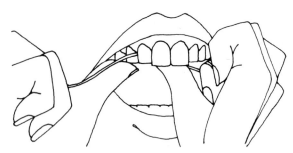

Work dental floss carefully between teeth.

 **PUTTING IT TOGETHER**

1 Explain how the Basic Four Food Groups can affect your skin, nails, and teeth.
2 Why is it important to remove plaque from your teeth through daily care?

LESSON FOUR
HAIR CARE

 shampoo   dandruff

creme rinse   hairstyle

conditioner

 keeping your hair clean

some hairstyles for you

Your hair is one of your most noticeable features. Healthy hair depends on what you eat as well as how you care for it.

Keeping your hair clean is basic to an attractive appearance. Because hair collects

perspiration and dust just as the rest of your body does, it needs to be washed regularly. Hair that needs to be shampooed is apt to appear dull, or it may look streaked and oily. Your scalp may feel irritated. You can soon learn to recognize how often your hair needs to be washed. This may be every three or

These are some of the products which are used in caring for the hair.

four days, once a week, or even less frequently. There is no one rule that everyone can follow about how frequently to wash their hair.

Use a *shampoo* designed for the type of hair you have. There are shampoos for oily hair, dry hair, normal hair, and damaged hair. Try different ones until you find one that is right for you.

Some flaking of skin from the *scalp* is normal. Severe flaking may be a problem. This condition is often called *dandruff*. There are special shampoos and rinses available to control dandruff. If none of these works, you may need to see a doctor for special treatment.

If you have tangles or have trouble controlling your hair, you may need a *creme rinse* or a *conditioner*. These products are applied to the hair after shampooing. Hair-setting products and hair sprays also help control your hair.

Brushing hair between shampoos can help remove dirt and dust. It also stimulates the scalp and distributes oil from the scalp through the hair. Stiff bristles on a brush or brushing too hard may damage the hair and scalp. Wash your brush and comb with soap and water or ammonia and water each time you wash your hair. A dirty comb or brush can put dirt and oil back into your hair.

A *hairstyle* that is in proportion to your size and designed for your facial features helps make an attractive appearance. If you wear glasses, these need to be considered also. Another thing to think about is whether you have curly hair, straight hair, fine hair, or thick hair. Experiment to discover hairstyles that are becoming to you. Look in magazines and newspapers for ideas for arranging hair. Some ideas are shown in the pictures above. A good haircut is usually necessary for a hairstyle to keep its shape.

PUTTING IT TOGETHER

1 Why is regular shampooing necessary for attractive hair?
2 What are advantages of a well-shaped hair cut?
3 How does your hairstyle affect the appearance of your face?
4 Why consider your height, body proportions, and facial features in choosing a hairstyle?

LESSON FIVE
COSMETICS

 cosmetic
Food and Drug Administration
hypo-allergenic

 what cosmetics are
some kinds of cosmetics
what cosmetics can do

According to the *Food and Drug Administration* (FDA), an agency of the federal government, a *cosmetic* is "an article intended to be rubbed, poured, sprinkled, or sprayed onto the body to cleanse, beautify, promote attractiveness or alter appearance."[1] You can probably think of many cosmetics right now.

[1] *We Want You to Know What We Know About Cosmetics,* DHEW Publication No. (FDA) 73–5005, 1973. Food and Drug Administration, Division of Colors and Cosmetics Technology, BF-430.

Makeup; products for hair care, skin care, hair coloring, nail care; antiperspirants; hair removers; and suntan lotions are examples.

The Food and Drug Administration regulates cosmetics in two ways. It prohibits the sale of cosmetics that may be harmful and requires that ingredients be listed on labels.

Until January 1, 1976, the ingredients in most cosmetics sold in the United States did not have to be listed on the labels. Exceptions were antiperspirants, sunscreens or suntan

lotions, and hair removers. Since January 1, 1976, however, the FDA has required that the ingredients in cosmetics be listed on the product package in descending order by weight. This means that the ingredient contained in the cosmetic in the largest amount is listed first. Exceptions are any ingredients that are used as fragrances or as flavors.

Having all of the ingredients listed makes it possible to avoid any cosmetics that contain ingredients to which you may be allergic.

Cosmetics can clean, beautify, promote attractiveness, or alter appearance. Select cosmetics in terms of what you need. Products that make a difference in cleanliness and appearance can contribute to your well-being. Other products may be of no benefit to you.

Read directions on packages and labels before you use any cosmetic. Improper use may cause problems. If you have sensitive skin, look for cosmetics that are labeled *hypoallergenic*. These products have fewer skin irritating ingredients. However, your skin may still be sensitive to this type of product so be careful when making selections.

Many different cosmetic products are available today. If you prefer to be experimental in learning to use cosmetics, inexpensive brands which are packaged in small amounts are available. Find out how the product is meant to be used. The label on the container will tell you what to expect from the product. For best results, follow directions and use a cosmetic product only for its intended use.

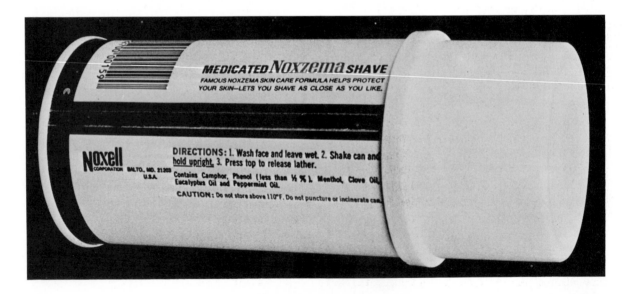

 **PUTTING IT TOGETHER**

1 What is a cosmetic? Give some examples.
2 How does the Food and Drug Administration regulate cosmetics?
3 What information must be given on cosmetic package labels?
4 Why should you read and follow directions for using cosmetics?

LESSON SIX
WHAT TO DO AND SAY

 social skills   **etiquette**

manners   **courtesy**

 your behavior toward others

your behavior when with others

Your behavior toward others and with others can add to your appearance. The world is filled with other people with whom you will come in contact. Some of these may be your family; others may be friends or classmates; still others are those you do not know but meet in stores, at school, or other places. If you do not smile and are not considerate of others, you will probably not be seen as an attractive person by others. Learning and using basic social skills are important in making your associations with other people happy and pleasant experiences. *Social skills* are habits of thoughtfulness which one uses in associating with other persons. *Manners, etiquette,* and *courtesy* are other terms used to describe social skills. Courteous actions make things easier.

Every day you share with others—laboratory equipment, references in the library, a table in the cafeteria. Sharing space and equipment means you often must wait patiently for your turn. When your turn comes for using equipment, work as quickly as possible, then leave the equipment as you would want to find it. Follow the rules in using reference books. Before leaving the cafeteria, pause long enough to tidy the space you used. Leave laboratory equipment clean. Thoughtful actions don't take much time.

When you share work on an assigned project, remember to do just that. You are showing your social skills when you are an asset to a partnership. Deciding how to share the work on a project is part of the fun of working with others. Do your part with the unpleasant tasks as well as with the pleasant tasks. For instance, don't disappear when the time comes to clean up the laboratory after a project has been completed. Think how you would feel if someone left you with all the cleanup. The ability to share responsibility adds to your attractiveness.

Be alert to new ideas and open-minded about the viewpoints presented by other persons. It is not considerate to ask personal questions, nor is it considerate to monopolize a conversation. You are making progress toward being an expert conversationalist when you balance your talking with listening.

Thoughtful acts by others call for a statement of thanks in some form. An immediate thanks, spoken in a direct way, is appropriate for most occasions. "Thank you," or "I appreciate your help," or just "Thanks," are all good ways to say it.

Paid employees in public places of business who give you prompt assistence in the course of doing their work should be thanked for the help they provide. Sales clerks, elevator operators, bus drivers, and school crossing guards are a few of the persons who appreciate an acknowledgement of their services.

Sometimes a short note is an appropriate way to show your appreciation. Some occasions which call for thank-you notes are

when you have received a gift of money, clothing, books, jewelry, or some other item; when you have been an overnight house guest; or when you have received a special favor. Some examples of special favors are when a friend gives a party for you, or an adult friend helps you find a part-time job.

If you are a member of an organization which is served by adult sponsors or advisors you might want to suggest at one of your meetings that your adult helpers should be remembered with a written note at least once a year. If they do something very special, such as furnish some transportation for an out-of-town trip, a note right after the trip would be appropriate.

Being a guest at a meal can be one of the most enjoyable social occasions if you know what to do. You show regard for your hostess or host if you dress appropriately for the occasion. If you are invited to the home of a close friend, you could ask about the usual type of dress worn at meals. If you are invited to a restaurant, you could call the restaurant to ask about appropriate dress.

To arrive on time is an unbreakable rule. Only an emergency should keep you from being prompt. If there is a reason that will cause you to be late, call the hostess and tell her how long you will be delayed. If you have been invited to be a guest at a meal to be served in a restaurant, probably a reservation for a specific time has been made. If the meal is to be at someone's home, plans may have to be changed because of your lateness.

When you arrive, look pleased to be there. A smile is good form in this situation. Accept the greeting of your host or hostess with "It is thoughtful of you to invite me," or "I have been looking forward to coming."

If the table setting differs from that used in your home, watch your hostess and do as she does about the tableware. Not all families follow the same pattern of table service. In a restaurant it is also correct to do as your hostess does about using the tableware.

Accept the food that is served without making negative comments. Families differ in the types of foods they prefer and in the ways they prepare it. The chances are that, because they are serving a meal to company, they are trying to please you. Show that you recognize this by your positive comments.

Be sure to thank your host or hostess when you leave. This part will come naturally if you enjoy being a guest.

Making and receiving introductions are not difficult to do. If you see a new person in class, you may introduce yourself. You might say, "My name is Pat Green and I live at 2521 West Tree Street." The new class member will probably respond in about the same way. Then you could add, "I would be glad to show you around after school." These simple self-introductions would help each of you gain a new acquaintance.

How do you introduce two persons of your own age? To introduce Joe Ricci and Janet Olsen you could say, "Janet, this is Joe Ricci, who transferred to our school last week." To Joe you would explain, "This is Janet Olsen. She put up this bulletin board about the Fall Festival which you noticed."

There are times when you will introduce your friends to your parents or other adults. When presenting friends of your own age, you

might say, "Mom and Dad, I want you to meet Cynthia Bowden and Ron Quintana. Cynthia and Ron are in my 9B English Class."

Depending on the situation, introductions are often followed by casual conversation.

Your social skills are a part of your appearance that shows most clearly. The examples have attempted to show that courteous actions are not attention-getting behaviors. They are just doing things with others in mind. Courteous behavior should not be reserved for special occasions; it can make each day in your life a special day. Good manners grow through everyday use.

PUTTING IT TOGETHER

1 What are social skills? What are some reasons they are important?
2 Give examples of thoughtful gestures toward others.
3 Tell some ways you can thank others for thoughtful behavior toward you.
4 How do you introduce two persons of your own age? How do you introduce your friends to your parents or other adults?

TAKING ANOTHER STEP

1 Prepare a bulletin board or exhibit illustrating easy-to-prepare snacks chosen from foods in the Basic Four Food Groups.
2 Plan meals for two days using the Basic Four Food Groups as a guide. When you include a food on your menu, place the number of the group to which it belongs beside the food you list and circle it.

---

3 Work in pairs or small groups to analyze your posture. Use a three-way mirror to observe standing and sitting postures. Or, if your classroom does not have a three-way mirror, try aligning your body with vertical and horizontal lines marked on bookshelves or on the chalk board. Practice the posture and coordination exercises described in this unit. Keep a record of your improvement in posture and body coordination.

4 Observe the sitting and standing postures of students in several of your classes. As a result of your observations what conclusions did you reach about the posture habits of your classmates? Base your conclusions on specific examples which you observed.

5 Plan a display of skin-care products. Give information about the products (such as what they are supposed to do, comparison of ingredients, and costs, etc.).

6 Invite a dentist to explain the importance of dental hygiene and what a dentist does and to demonstrate some good dental hygiene practices.

7 Plan a display of hair-care products which are suitable for different types of hair.

8 Invite a hair stylist to demonstrate good hair-care practices. Ask the stylist to talk about hair-care products and styles for different types of hair (such as coarse, fine, straight, curly, etc.).

9 Prepare an exhibit of cosmetics which you consider to be essential for everyday use. For each product prepare a small poster or label telling the purpose of the product and how it is meant to be used.

10 Compare the cost per ounce or gram of several different brands of one cosmetic product (such as hand lotion, hair spray, shaving cream, suntan lotion, etc.). If the prices differ greatly, how might you account for these differences? Report your conclusions to the class.

11 Find information about activities of the Division of Colors and Cosmetics Technology, Food and Drug Administration, regarding regulation of cosmetics. See current issues of *FDA Consumer.*

12 Observe people to see how they behave toward others. Think about whether this affects the ways others behave towards them. How might these persons improve their behavior toward others?

13 Observe people when they are with one or more people. What are some ways people act when with others? See if you can tell whether their behavior changes when with different people. Suggest some reasons for this.

14 With friends practice making introductions so you will do this naturally when you have to make introductions.

15 Make a plan for working toward a personal appearance goal.

DESIGN CREATES

UNIT FIVE

Have you ever wondered why you like the way your favorite outfit looks? Or why you may receive compliments when you wear certain clothes you have? It is probably because these clothes were designed well. You might also say the clothes are of good design.

Clothes that are of good design have a pleasing combination of *design elements* or parts. The elements have been combined according to *design principles*. Design elements are color, line, and texture; the principles are rhythm, balance, emphasis, and proportion. You will learn more about design elements and principles in this unit.

Knowing design elements and principles makes it possible for you to choose or make clothes that are of good design. You will be able to recognize these elements and principles of design in other aspects of living, too. Look at some buildings, gardens, parks, or settings in nature to see the elements and principles of design used in different ways. Study them to see how they are pleasing to you. Try using design elements and principles in making a bulletin board, setting a table, preparing and serving food, planting a garden, or arranging books on shelves. Practice in using design elements and principles makes them easier to understand.

LESSON ONE
COLOR CHARACTERISTICS

color wheel

hue

primary color

secondary color

intermediate color

tint

shade

value

intensity

warm color

cool color

some characteristics of colors

the personality of colors

You have characteristics. You have a name and physical features which identify you and distinguish you from others. Colors do too. A *color wheel* is often used to show some of the characteristics of colors. Look at the one in the column at the right.

Hue is one characteristic of color. The word hue refers to a color's name. For example, yellow is a hue, or the name of a color. Notice the names of the twelve colors on the color wheel.

Yellow, red, and blue are known as the *primary colors* because no other colors can be combined to form these three colors. All other colors are made from the primary colors.

Green, orange, and violet are called *secondary colors*. Each of these colors is made by mixing equal parts of two of the primary colors. Green, for example, is made from blue and yellow in equal quantities. Violet is a mixture of red and blue. Orange is a mixture of yellow and red.

The other six colors on the color wheel are known as *intermediate colors*. Each intermediate color is formed by a combination of the hues on either side of it on the color wheel. For example, orange and red form red-

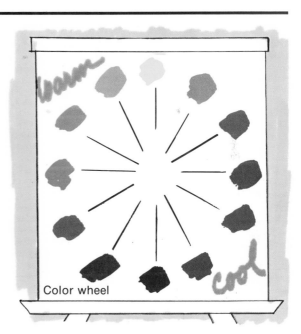

Color wheel

orange. Blue-green results from a mixture of green and blue. What are the combinations which form the other intermediate colors?

Other colors can be made by mixing any of the twelve colors on the color wheel. For example, brown is a combination of red and green. What is another combination?

Value is another characteristic of color. It describes the lightness or darkness of a color. Black or white is added to a color to change its value. A color with white in it is called a *tint*. A color which contains black is called a *shade*. Many different shades and tints of a color can be formed by varying the amount of white or black in the color. Red becomes pink when white is added and becomes dark red when black is added. Study the value scale to see variations of lightness and darkness in color. The scale is in the column at the right.

A third characteristic of color is *intensity*. Intensity describes the amount of color present. A color's intensity can be described as bright or dull. An intense color is a bright color. A less intense color may be described as a dull color. Although a bright hue has more color than a dull hue, the two colors may be equally pleasing to look at.

Colors have personality traits as well as physical characteristics. These personality characteristics of colors might be described as the impressions they make on individuals. For example, orange, red, and yellow are called *warm colors*. Perhaps this is so because at various times during the day the sun may appear to be yellow or red or orange. Also we may associate the warmth of fire with the yellow, red, and orange that we see in the flames. Think of some other examples.

Blue, green, and violet are considered *cool colors*. This is probably because these colors remind us of the coolness of water, forests and trees, and shade. Look at the color wheel on page 73 and see which colors you think are warm and which are cool.

 **PUTTING IT TOGETHER**

1 Define hue.
2 Write the names of the primary colors, secondary colors, and intermediate colors.
3 What characteristic of color is described by its value? What words are used to describe a color's value?
4 What characteristic of a color is described by its intensity?
5 What are warm colors? Cool colors? Give some examples of each.

LESSON TWO
COLOR PLANS

 color harmony
color plan
monochromatic color plan
complementary color plan
split-complementary color plan
triad color plan
adjacent color plan
accented neutral

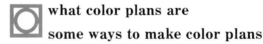 what color plans are
some ways to make color plans

A *color harmony* is a combination of colors that look good with each other. A harmonious color combination is pleasant to see, just as a harmonious combination of musical sounds is pleasant to hear. A group of colors put together at random will be a combination of colors, but they will not necessarily be a color harmony. In order to make harmonious color combinations some knowledge of the ways to successfully combine colors is needed.

One way to combine colors successfully is by using a color plan. A *color plan* is a plan for a special combination of colors based on their location on the color wheel.

Color plans include more than just the combinations of the twelve colors on the color wheel at their fullest intensity and medium value. The many tints and shades of each hue make possible an endless variety of color plans. Different intensities of each hue can be used. Color plans using only bright colors or only dull colors tend to be monotonous. Combinations using both bright and dull intensities are usually more interesting.

When several values and intensities of one color are combined, a *monochromatic*, or *one-color*, *color plan* is formed. Tints may be com-

bined with other tints and shades with other shades. A one-color plan may have much contrast and variation or very little. However, no matter how much or how little the contrast, only one color is varied in the combination.

An *adjacent color plan* is made up of two or more colors that have one hue in common. For example, blue and blue-green make an adjacent color plan; so do yellow, yellow-orange, and orange. As you study the color wheel (page 73) you will see that adjacent color plans are made up of colors next to each other on the color wheel. Such plans are more likely to be harmonious when the colors used are of similar value and intensity.

Colors directly opposite each other on the color wheel are called complements of each other. A *complementary color plan* results when two complements are used together. Each color has only one complement. Values and intensities of complementary colors can be varied in many ways to form imaginative combinations. Usually, dulled complementary colors form more pleasing combinations than complements used together at their fullest intensities. Some examples of complementary color plans are blue-violet and yellow-orange,

Examples of color plans used in clothing.

Monochromatic

Adjacent

Complementary

Split complementary

Triad

Accented neutral

blue and orange, blue-green and red-orange, green and red, yellow-green and red-violet, and yellow and violet.

A *split-complementary color plan* is a variation of a complementary color plan. To get a split-complementary plan, select two complementary colors. Then instead of combining the complementary colors, combine the two colors on each side of one complement with the other complement.

A *triad color plan* is one made up of three colors equidistant on the color wheel. The primary colors form a triad color plan. The secondary colors will also form a triad color plan. If you look at the color wheel (page 73), you will notice that a combination of three equally distant intermediate colors is another example of this color plan.

When a large area of one or more of the neutrals (black, white, or gray) is used with a small area of a bright color, an *accented neutral color plan* results. A gray coat with a bright gold scarf is one example of an accented neutral color plan. Another example is a black and white checked suit with a red scarf. Many combinations are possible with neutrals and vivid colors.

 **PUTTING IT TOGETHER**

1 Explain how each of these color harmonies is produced: (a) monochromatic; (b) adjacent; (c) complementary; (d) split-complementary; (e) triad; and (f) accented neutral. Find examples of each of these color harmonies in your classroom.

2 How do you think you can use your knowledge of color harmonies to advantage in the way you dress?

CLOTHES, CLUES, AND CAREERS

LESSON THREE
CHOOSING COLORS

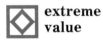 **extreme**   **accent**
value

     contrast

 some ways colors affect your feelings

some ways to use color in the way you dress

Do you feel more cheerful when you wear something red or yellow? Do you feel more relaxed and calm when you wear blue or green? If so, you are not unusual. Colors can cause you to feel warm or cool, gloomy or happy, excited or relaxed.

Because warm colors, such as red, orange, and yellow, remind us of sunlight and warmth, they seem cheerful and exciting. The cool colors, such as blue, green, and violet, suggest quietness, distance, and space.

Some colors may suggest weight or the lack of it. In large amounts, black may seem heavy, somber, and dignified. The same effect may be felt in large areas of deep shades of violet, brown, red, or blue. White and pale tints suggest lightness, softness, and quietness.

Because all of us have different past experiences, a color may also suggest different things to each of us. You may decide to choose colors by how they make you feel or how you want others to feel.

Colors and combinations of colors can be used to make you look larger or smaller. They can be used to emphasize some features and draw attention away from others. Here are some ways to make color work for you.

Warm colors, extreme values, and intense colors seem to advance or cause an object to seem closer and larger than it actually is. An *extreme value* or a strong value is a very dark or very light color. Cool colors, medium values, and dull colors make an object appear farther away or smaller than it actually

is. If you want to appear to be larger, you might choose a warm color or an extreme value or an intense color for your outfit or part of an outfit. If you want to appear smaller, a cool color in a medium value or a less intense color might be a good choice for large areas of your clothing. Experiment to see what is best for you.

Do you like bright, warm colors but do not want to call attention to body size or shape? Use medium values or cool or dull colors for your outfit. Then use bright, warm colors as accents at the neckline or in your accessories. An *accent* may be a scarf or pin or collar which is emphasized because it *contrasts* with, or is a different color, shade, or intensity than your outfit.

Strong value contrasts or contrasts in color intensity in large areas of clothing often call attention to body size. This is because the contrasts, or differences, break up the space into two or more parts. Many contrasts in value or intensities in a garment may result in a cluttered look. Extreme value contrasts in large areas of clothing may call attention to your body size. On the other hand, close values do not break up space and let the eye follow an unbroken line.

Contrasting values can be used to call attention to a particular part of an outfit or to emphasize a feature. A small waist can be accented by a contrasting belt. A light collar on a shirt of medium or dark value will draw attention to the face. Accessories such as

Color can be used to emphasize or to de-emphasize.

scarves, belts, and shoes are more quickly seen when a contrast in value, or intensity, sets them apart from the rest of your clothing. Look at the illustration above.

Bright colors as well as warm colors may lift your spirits on a gloomy day. However, you may find it tiring to wear only intense colors unless you have many changes of clothing in your wardrobe. Because bright colors are readily seen they are more likely to be remembered. Therefore, you may want to buy the garments that you plan to wear longest, such as coats, in less intense colors.

If you never seem to have anything to wear, you may be able to use color to make it appear that you have more clothes than you actually do. When you buy clothes, make your selections so that as many garments as

possible combine well with other garments you have. Decide on one or two main colors as the basis for your wardrobe. Then make your selections in different shades and tints of the color or colors. You can also combine prints, checks, and plaids with plain colors in the same basic color.

More versatile combinations will be possible, too, if you choose mainly medium values rather than extremely light or extremely dark colors. Medium values combine more easily than strong values. White shoes, for example, look better with white or pale colors. However, shoes in gray, beige, caramel, or sand colors blend readily with both darker and lighter values.

There are other ways in which the colors you choose can add to your appearance. For example, your skin, hair, and eyes are

CLOTHES, CLUES, AND CAREERS

complemented by some colors. Other colors may not blend as well with your coloring. Study the illustration above.

One way to tell if a color is attractive on you is by listening to comments of friends or family members. If they compliment you on the color you are wearing, it is probably a good color for you. Another way to tell is by holding different color fabrics close to your face. If you want to emphasize your eyes, choose a color which repeats your eye color. A color which contrasts with your hair will emphasize your hair. Experiment to see what is best for you.

 **PUTTING IT TOGETHER**

1 How can colors affect your feelings? Give some examples.
2 What might be a good choice of color or colors for someone who wants to appear larger? For someone who wants to appear smaller?
3 What can you do with color to emphasize a feature or draw attention away from a feature?
4 How might your coloring (color of hair, eyes, and skin) be important in choosing colors to help you look your best?

DESIGN CREATES

LESSON FOUR
LINE

 line
vertical lines
horizontal lines
diagonal lines

silhouette
structural lines
diagonal lines

some characteristics of line

some effects of lines on clothing design

what decorative and structural lines are

some ways to use lines in the way you dress

In Lessons 1, 2, and 3 you learned about color which is one element of design. Another element of design is *line*. Just as colors have characteristics which identify them and distinguish them from each other, lines also have characteristics. Some of these are direction, straightness, width, and length.

All lines in design are either straight or curved. Usually straight lines and curved lines are combined in any design.

Direction in line can be vertical, horizontal, or diagonal. *Vertical lines* are lines which go up and down. Lines which go from side to side or around an object are *horizontal lines*. *Diagonal lines* are lines which are neither horizontal nor vertical, but slanted. Vertical, horizontal, and diagonal lines are sometimes straight lines. However, curved lines may be used to show direction. For example, a design of wavy lines arranged in a certain way can have the appearance of horizontal direction just as can a design of straight lines arranged in the same way.

The width of lines in a design can vary greatly and give different effects. A narrow line will give a different effect from that of a wide line even though both may have the same direction. The lengths of lines can also vary greatly and give different effects. The appearance of several short lines differs

Horizontal lines

Vertical lines

Diagonal lines

Curved lines

Wide lines

Narrow lines

greatly from the appearance of one long line or several long lines.

Lines in clothing are used in different ways. The shape formed by the outer lines of your clothing is called a *silhouette*. This is probably the most important design line in clothing. The silhouette encloses all other design lines in an outfit. Study your shadow and you will see the general silhouette of the clothes you are wearing.

Lines in garments can be both structural and decorative. *Structural lines* are formed by seams and darts in the making of the garment. Structural lines give a garment shape and help to form the silhouette. *Decorative lines* are present in the fabric design or texture or can be made by applying trim, accessories, or stitching.

The effect of lines in a design depends on their length, direction, straightness, and

Silhouettes

Structural lines

Decorative lines

A variety of silhouettes are formed by the outlines of clothes.

width. For example, long lines may suggest continuity, or unbroken space. Wide lines tend to be more noticeable than narrow lines. Curved lines often add softness to a design, while straight lines may be more dramatic. Some diagonal lines suggest a feeling of action and strength.

If a fabric is plain colored or has a design that is not very noticeable, structural lines will be the most noticeable lines in a garment. Sometimes when a fabric is colorful plaid, or bold stripes, or has rows of trim, decorative lines will be the most noticeable. Decorative lines can also accent structural lines through repetition and contrast. For example, structural lines can be accented by piping or rows of zig-zag stitching. Decorative lines can be created to accent large areas

Lines in clothing can give illusions of height, width, softness, and strength.

LINES AND FACE SHAPES

FACE SHAPES	HOW TO ACCENT THE FACE SHAPE	HOW TO MODIFY THE FACE SHAPE
oval	Repeat the oval shape in the necklines you wear. Wear oval jewelry in bright colors and strong contrasts.	Wear a contrasting-shaped neckline, such as round, square, U- or V-shaped.
round	Repeat the round shape in the necklines you wear, such as Peter Pan collars. Wear collars that emphasize the roundness by contrast, such as a standing collar. Wear round jewelry, short necklaces, or wide neckties.	Wear V-shaped necklines, long, pointed collars, and narrow lapels. Wear long necklaces to make the face seem longer. Wear medium-width neckties.
square	Choose square necklines which outline the squareness of your face. Accent a square face by wearing high, round collars for contrast.	Wear V- or U-shaped necklines to help soften the square lines. Sharp V or U shapes may be softened with either scallops or notches to break the severe lines.
oblong	Wear high, round necklines to emphasize an oblong face by extreme contrast. Accent the face shape with necklines that follow the same vertical line of the face, such as V necklines and pointed collars. Choose strong vertical lines in a dress, suit, or accessories.	Add width to a long, thin face with medium-wide collars, rounded collars and necklines, and rolled collars. Make a long face seem more oval with a horizontal line near the neckline.
heart	Reflect the shape of the face with a V neckline.	Wear a wide, round neckline to make the lower part of the face seem wider. Stand-away collars also add width.
long neck	Choose garments that have V necklines. Wear blouses or shirts with narrow lapels or collars set off from the neck to emphasize a long neck.	Wear stand-up collars, high neckline designs, and turtleneck designs. Choose bulky fabrics. Wear ascots, scarves, neckties, and necklines with horizontal emphasis to conceal a long neck.
short neck	Wear choker-style necklaces, standing collars, turtleneck designs, and wide lapels.	Choose a garment with narrow lapels or a V neckline. Some garments, especially suits in which the jacket closes with a long V line, have a lengthening effect.

through smocking, shirring, applique, and pin tucks. A sewn-in crease in slacks becomes a decorative line.

Decorative lines in clothing can be seen in the fabric as well as in the construction of a garment. The lines in plaids, stripes, corduroys, figured fabrics, and quilted fabrics become a part of a garment's design lines.

The lines in plaid fabrics may be accented by contrast when not all parts of the garment are cut the same way. Also stripes may be accented by contrasting direction of the lines.

What are the best lines for you? How can you choose design lines that will accent your best features and de-emphasize the appearance of others? You can determine becoming clothing lines by analyzing your body shape and facial features.

Try first to select an attractive silhouette. Your body proportions can be emphasized by the outline of your clothing, or they can be de-emphasized. How tall you appear to be is affected by the silhouette you create. If you want to accent height, choose a slim silhouette with predominant vertical lines so that your height is emphasized through repetition of the vertical lines of your figure. A silhouette with horizontal lines will often modify the appearance of a form. The silhouette appears shorter by contrast with the vertical body lines and appears wider.

The shape of your face and the length of your neck can be either accented or de-emphasized by the clothing lines and shapes you wear near your face. Study the chart on page 83 to see some examples.

 **PUTTING IT TOGETHER**

1 How do the characteristics of line affect clothing designs and the way clothing makes you look?
2 Where are structural lines found in a garment? How do structural lines contribute to clothing designs?
3 What are some examples of decorative lines? How do decorative lines contribute to clothing designs?
4 Why might you consider your facial features as well as your body proportions in determining the best design lines for your clothing?

TEXTURE

 texture   soft

bulky   smooth

shiny   rough

dull

 some characteristics of texture

some ways texture affects color

some ways to use texture in the way you dress

Color and line are two design elements described in this unit. Both of these design elements have characteristics which can be described by what you see. *Texture* is another element of design. However, you can feel texture as well as see it.

Texture is found in the thickness of fabric and on the surface of the fabric. Many words are used to describe texture. Some of the words used are loopy, fuzzy, soft, furry, shiny, ribbed, rough, scratchy, crisp, smooth, and sheer. What examples can you think of?

The different textures in fabrics affect one's appearance in clothes.

CLOTHES, CLUES, AND CAREERS

The fiber (or fibers) used to make fabrics is one reason why fabrics have textures, or look and feel the way they do. Silk fibers may give fabric a smooth, shiny texture. How fabrics are made also affects their texture. Variations in weaving or knitting can create ridges in fabric or make fabric smooth, fuzzy, or shiny. Fabric finishes affect the textures of fabrics by making them soft, smooth, shiny, crisp, or by giving them other characteristics.

As with line and color, fabric texture also affects your appearance. Thick, shaggy, fuzzy, and wrinkled textures seem to add to body size because of their own bulkiness. Sleek, glossy, or shiny textures tend to increase apparent body size because a shiny surface reflects more light than a dull surface does. In contrast, smooth, dull textures seem to decrease body size because these textures reflect less light than glossy textures do.

If your hips are large in proportion to the rest of your body, you may want to wear slacks which are made of a fabric which has a smooth, dull texture with a sweater of bulky or shiny texture or to make your hips seem smaller. If you are thin, you may want to choose fabrics which have textures which make you appear heavier. Or you may decide to choose fabrics of textures which emphasize your slimness.

Textures can be combined to create variety in an outfit. A combination of smooth and fuzzy textures can add interest to a monochromatic, or one-color, outfit.

Because different textures reflect light differently the appearance of color often varies with the texture of fabric. For example, colors in shiny textures seem brighter. This means a shiny red satin blouse would seem to be brighter and more intense than a fuzzy sweater in the same color red.

Texture can also affect the way you feel. Fuzzy textures are associated with warmth and may help keep you warm in cool weather. A sheer smooth fabric may make you feel cooler when the weather is warm.

 **PUTTING IT TOGETHER**

1 What is texture? What are some ways it is described?
2 Describe some ways that different textures in fabric are made.
3 Give some examples of ways to use texture in the way you dress.

LESSON SIX
PROPORTION

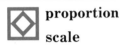 proportion
scale

 what proportion is

what scale is

some ways proportion is used
in design

some ways to use proportion
and scale in the way you dress

In a design, *proportion* refers to the relationship of parts to each other and to the whole, based on the way space has been divided. The principle of proportion has been applied when all parts of a design look good together. Usually proportion is considered good when space is divided slightly unequally.

In clothing, for example, the principle of proportion can be seen in the length of a jacket in relation to the length of pants or skirt and in relation to the whole outfit. You may have had the experience of taking up the hem on a skirt or pants or slacks, but not changing the jacket hem, only to find that the outfit doesn't look quite right. This is because the relationship of the parts to the whole has been changed. Taking the jacket up as well as the pants or slacks or skirt would probably make the proportion pleasing once again.

Using the principle of proportion in the way you dress may be easier to understand by thinking in this way. The human body is divided at the waist. If three-eighths of the total standing height is from the top of the head to the waist and the remaining five-eighths of the total height is from the waist to the floor, it is said that these are *ideal body proportions.* However, few people have ideal body proportions. If the body above the waist is long in relation to the part of the body below the waist, then we say that person is *long-waisted.* If the part of the body above the waist is short in relation to the part of the body below the waist, we say that person is *short-waisted.* When a person is overweight or underweight, the horizontal measurements may not be pleasing in relation to the vertical measurements.

It is possible to have the appearance of ideal body proportions by choosing clothing carefully. For example, a long-waisted person may choose a garment that is not fitted at the waist or one that has a waistline above the natural waistline. To give the appearance of ideal body proportions, a short-waisted person may wear clothes with a dropped waistline or a waistline that does not fit snugly for the same reasons. The use of line and color and texture in clothing can make body proportions seem closer to ideal also.

Scale is the relationship of the size of one thing to that of another. For example, a garment is more pleasing if its parts are scaled to the size of the person wearing it. Small belts, collars, buttons, and other details may look better on a small person. Scale is important in fabric design. A plaid, print, or stripe will be more pleasing when scaled to suit the size of the person wearing it. The garment's design and the effect you want to create are also important. A large person may not choose a large plaid or print because these designs may tend to emphasize his or her body size.

CLOTHES, CLUES, AND CAREERS

Here are examples of how proportion and scale influence people's appearance.

The principles of proportion and scale can be applied in choosing hats, purses, neckties, jewelry, and other accessories. Try on garments with various lines in different styles and fabrics to find out which are best for you.

Only by putting on the garments and the accessories can you tell that the space has been divided in a pleasing way and that the details in the design are scaled in a satisfactory manner.

 **PUTTING IT TOGETHER**

1 What is proportion? How is it used in design?
2 What are some ways the principle of proportion can be used in selecting clothes that look good on you?
3 What is scale? How can you use scale in the way you dress?

LESSON SEVEN
BALANCE

 balance

formal balance

symmetrical balance

informal balance

asymmetrical balance

 what balance is

some ways balance is used in design

some ways to use balance in the way you dress

Another principle of design is *balance*. It exists when the various parts of a design have been arranged so that a feeling of rest or equilibrium results. Balance is closely related to proportion and scale. If a design is not pleasing in proportion or scale, it is not likely to have a feeling of balance.

Balance in a design may be either formal or informal. *Formal balance* is created when the design is the same on each side of the center of the design. Formal balance is sometimes called *symmetrical balance*. *Informal balance*, or *asymmetrical balance,* is created when the design is balanced, but is not the same on each side of the design center.

A jacket with buttons down the center front and pockets of the same size and in the same place on either side is one example of formal balance in clothing design. An example of informal balance is a jacket with an off-center closing and one pocket.

Symmetrical and asymmetrical balance can also be found in fabric design. Some plaids and stripes are designed to have symmetrical balance, others to have asymmetrical balance. Several short lines may balance one longer line. Two or more small shapes may

balance a similar but larger shape. A few thin lines may balance one thick line. Vertical lines may be used to balance horizontal lines. These pictures show examples of symmetrical and asymmetrical balance.

A feeling of balance is produced when large areas of color tints are equalized by small areas of either bright colors or shades. Likewise, large areas of neutrals may be balanced by small areas of bright colors. Warm colors can be used to balance cool colors. Usually smaller amounts of warm colors balance larger amounts of cool colors if they are of the same value and intensity. The principle of balance can be applied by adding a bright yellow necktie to a pale yellow shirt. Or, a bright yellow belt or scarf can be added to a pale yellow dress. A small area of bright color balances a large area of pale color. A gold satin collar on a dark blue velvet dress gives balance through color and also through texture contrast. The lustrous texture of the satin collar balances the larger areas of soft but dull texture. A bright red shirt or accessory with a gray suit shows how a large neutral area is balanced by a small area of intense color.

 **PUTTING IT TOGETHER**

1 What is balance? How is balance created in clothing designs? Point out examples of balance in clothing designs.

2 What are some ways balance can be considered in the way you dress?

CLOTHES, CLUES, AND CAREERS

Here are examples of the effect of balance in clothing design.

LESSON EIGHT
EMPHASIS

 emphasis   contrast

dominate   repetition

 what emphasis is

some ways emphasis is used in design

some ways to use emphasis in the way you dress

Emphasis is present in a design when your attention is attracted to a certain part of the design. It is the center of interest because it *dominates,* or stands out from, the rest of the design.

Emphasis can be created by *contrast* in texture, color, and line, or by the use of unusual shapes, textures, and colors. For example, lace becomes a center of interest on a plain fabric. Fur, metallic fabrics, and vinyl-coated fabrics become accents when used in small amounts with a plain fabric. Scallops, fringes, and ruffles attract attention. Bows, ties, and scarves also are means of emphasis or accent.

Repetition, as well as contrast, can create emphasis. A neckline which repeats the shape of the face will accent the face. One outstanding color in a print, plaid, or striped fabric may be emphasized by repeating the color in a belt or scarf. Lines in a particular garment may become dominant if they are outlined with stitching or trim.

Usually one main emphasis in a design is enough. When too many types of textures, lines, or colors are accented, a design or outfit may have a cluttered look. When several parts of a design or outfit are given equal emphasis, nothing seems to be emphasized and the design lacks interest. Failure to recognize the importance of emphasis can cause disappointment in one's appearance.

Emphasis in clothing can be used to draw attention to a feature or to move the eye away from a feature. For example, if a person wants to appear taller, a point of emphasis high on the body draws the eye upward and creates an illusion of height. If a person wants to appear shorter, an area of emphasis at the waistline or at the neckline and hemline can help to achieve this.

Color can be used to emphasize eye color or hair color. Either a contrasting color or a matching color near the face will do this. Body proportions can be emphasized with bright, warm colors and dramatic prints. Cool colors in medium value and dull textures may be used to de-emphasize body proportions. An accent at the neckline can also call attention away from body proportions.

 **PUTTING IT TOGETHER**

1 What is emphasis in design?
2 Explain how emphasis can be created and used in clothing design.
3 Give examples of how the principle of emphasis can be used to draw attention to features; to move the eye away from features.

Here are examples
of emphasis in a
variety of clothing designs.

LESSON NINE
RHYTHM

 rhythm

repetition

progression

 what rhythm is

some ways rhythm is used in design

some ways to use rhythm in the way you dress

Rhythm in design exists when the parts of the design have been arranged so that your eye moves easily from one part of the design to another. Each part of the design is related to another part. When rhythm is present, there may be an illusion of motion created in the design.

One way rhythm can be created is by *repetition*. This involves repeating lines and shapes in a design. Repetition carries the eye from one part of the design to another. In the structure of clothing, repetition of shapes may be carried out in several ways. The rounded edge of a jacket may be repeated at the neckline in rounded lapels. Or the shape of the lapels may be duplicated in cuffs or pocket tabs. Decorative stitching may repeat some of the structural lines. Stripes of the same width and checks of the same size are examples of repetition in decorative lines. The eye moves from one design part to another with a steady movement.

Progression is another way to create rhythm in a design. Progression involves a series of similar objects ranging from small to large or large to small. A series of wide and narrow stripes is an example of progression. Another example is a series of different sized squares, circles, or other objects.

Rhythm can also be created by the use of continuous line. This can be seen in structural lines of garments when a vertical seam in a jacket lines up with a vertical seam in the slacks or skirt. Examples of decorative continuous line in a garment are stripes or a paisley print.

Rhythm of line can be destroyed when plaids, stripes, or other designs are not matched at seams or in other construction details. Unless breaking the rhythm is a carefully planned part of the design, such as a pocket with horizontal stripes on a jacket with vertical stripes, interrupting the rhythm can be upsetting to the eye.

Some types of rhythm may create emphasis in a design. Two examples are progression and repetition. If you want to avoid emphasizing a feature, make sure that the progression or repetition does not appear in the area you want to de-emphasize. Rhythm created by continuous curved lines may suggest softness and quietness if there are no extreme contrasts in color or line in the design. Choose this design if this is the effect you wish to create.

Progression or repetition of vertical lines may suggest height because these lines tend to carry the eye upward. This gives the illusion of one's being taller than one actually is. If you want to appear taller or to give emphasis to your height, garments with many structural and/or decorative vertical lines may be your choices. Try on several different types of garments and accessories in order to see the effect that the rhythm of the designs has on the way you look.

Progression

Progression and repetition

Continuity

Continuity and gradation

Repetition

Gradation

Here are examples of rhythm created
in a number of clothing designs.

PUTTING IT TOGETHER

1 What is rhythm? How is it used in design?
2 Explain the different ways rhythm can be created.
3 How can the principle of rhythm be used to your advantage in the way you dress? Give examples.

TAKING ANOTHER STEP

1 Read all or part of *Hailstones and Halibut Bones* by Mary O'Neill, Doubleday and Company, Inc., Garden City, New York, 1961. This small book describes colors in terms of feelings, moods, and things we remember. Both the words and the colorful illustrations can expand your sensitivity to colors.
2 Make a color wheel using tempera paints.
3 Experiment by combining colors to see the different values and intensities you can produce.
4 Make a display of clothing and accessories showing different color plans for each outfit.
5 Plan a display showing how colors of clothes can make you look larger or smaller.
6 Analyze the lines in the clothing you have. What different choices might you make in future purchases?
7 Plan a bulletin board which shows the different types of lines. Include examples of structural and decorative lines.
8 Collect fabric scraps and make a notebook of different textures.
9 Give a demonstration with two or more students of different heights. Have each try on sweaters of different lengths to illustrate the effect of proportion. Select the most pleasing sweater length and explain how the principle of proportion is applied.
10 Give a demonstration to illustrate proportion in accessories.
11 Give a demonstration to illustrate the principle of balance.
12 Give a demonstration to illustrate the principle of emphasis.
13 Give a demonstration to illustrate the principle of rhythm.
14 Prepare a bulletin board which shows "What Your Clothes Can Do for You." Illustrate one or more of the suggestions from this unit.
15 Plan a day when each class member will wear an outfit which he or she believes most closely illustrates good design. Each person should be prepared to explain how one or more of the design principles have been applied in creating the design of the outfit.
16 Analyze your own body proportions, facial shape, and personal coloring. Find illustrations of clothing which show good line, texture, and color for yourself. Explain why each of your illustrations is a good choice for you in terms of design principles.
17 Start your own file of clippings or a notebook about clothes selection. Organize the information so that it will be useful to you. Try to improve your decisions about what to wear by applying some of the suggestions.

INFORMATION HELPS

UNIT SIX

Some of your clothes are probably ready-to-wear garments made in places where mass production techniques are used. Think about the last time you bought a garment. Did you consider your needs and the money that you had to spend before you went to shop? Or was your selection made on the spur-of-the-moment? Did you compare a variety of garments before you made the final decision? Now that you have made the purchase and have added the garment to your wardrobe, how does it fit in with the other things you have? Are you satisfied with your choice?

Clothing is made by different manufacturers. Therefore size, construction details, location of labels, and care instructions are handled in a variety of ways. By planning the clothes you need, deciding how you will get them, and using some guidelines, such as style and design, fit, durability, and ease of maintenance, you can learn how to make choices which are satisfactory. This unit explains these guidelines and gives information that makes comparison and selection easier. It also explains the kinds of construction and care needed for fabrics in order to make your choices more satisfactory.

MAKING DECISIONS

decision	**advantages**
resources	**disadvantages**
responsibility	

what decision making is
some ways decisions can be made
some things that affect decisions about clothes

When you need clothing, what do you do? If you are responsible for providing your own clothes, you probably will proceed differently from a person who depends on others to provide clothing. However, no matter who is responsible for providing your clothing, many decisions must be made. If some thought is given to making the decisions, what happens will probably be more satisfactory than if the decisions are not thought out.

DECISION MAKING

Satisfactory *decisions* are usually easier if you work out a *system* for making decisions. A system can be thought of as a plan, or a way to do something that is outlined ahead of time. Even small decisions are easier to make if you have a system you follow. Once you find a system that works for you, you can practice using it so that all types of decisions are easier for you to make. Here are some suggested steps to follow in making decisions.

State the problem. Be specific about what the problem is. Otherwise you may have trouble deciding how to solve the problem. For example, if you say a problem is that you are always broke, you may not be able to solve the problem satisfactorily until you figure out why. Stating the problem as "I am broke because I am not careful of how I spend my money" or "I am broke because I do not

have enough money" will give you a better idea of how to solve the problem.

Think of different ways to solve the problem. For some problems that require big decisions, you may want to make a list of the possible solutions. Think about your *resources,* or things you have, which might help you solve the problem. Some examples of resources are time, money, energy, other people, knowledge, skills, equipment, books, schools, community organizations, and abilities. Usually the more resources you have available to you, the more possible ways there are to solve the problem.

Think about the advantages and the disadvantages of each of the possible solutions. This includes thinking about the effect each solution might have on you and on others. It also includes thinking about other decisions you may have to make as a result of the decisions you are making now. For problems that are complicated or require big decisions, you may want to write some of this information down so you can compare the different solutions.

Choose a way to solve the problem. After carefully thinking about the advantages and disadvantages of each way it is possible for you to solve the problem, decide which solution you think is best.

Opposite. There are several solutions to a problem.

Do what you decide. This means carrying out the decision you have made.

Accept the responsibility for the decision you make. This means that if you don't like the results of your decision, you don't make excuses or blame someone else. It means you can say "I made a decision I didn't like," then try another way to solve the problem. *Accepting responsibility* means you learn from your mistakes as well as from your successes.

The kind of decision you have to make may make a difference in the steps you follow. To make a big decision, such as what you will do when you finish high school, you may follow the steps listed or even add others. You may collect information over a period of time. Other decisions may need little thought, and you may skip some of the steps listed above and on page 98. For example, in a matter of seconds you may decide to ride your bicycle rather than to walk to the store. You probably don't think consciously about each step involved in making that decision. Learning which decisions need a lot of thought and which can be made quickly is part of learning how to make satisfactory decisions.

Often you cannot make one decision without making others. For example, if you decide to buy a garment rather than make one or repair one, you then have to decide where to look for the garment, how much to pay for it, and so on. If you try to think about other decisions involved when you make the first decision, the results of all your decisions may be more satisfactory.

Sometimes decisions are made by more than one person. This is common in families or groups of people when decisions will affect many people. Each person may share in each step of the decision. Or one person may make the decisions after listening to suggestions and information from others.

Sometimes people do not like to make decisions so they just let things happen and hope it works out for the best. The situation may turn out the way they want, but often they are disappointed—things sometimes get worse! To "just let things happen" is a kind of decision—a decision not to decide. This is not usually a good solution to a problem.

SOME THINGS THAT AFFECT DECISIONS

If you are part of a family, you may be allowed to make your own decisions about clothes. Or you may share in the decision making. No matter who makes the decisions, however, many things affect these decisions. Income, other expenses, attitudes about clothing, climate, occupation, size of family, and the ages of family members are just some of these things.

Since clothing is only one of the many needs and wants of individuals and families, it is not usually possible to have all the clothes one wants. Housing, food, medical care, taxes, transportation, and recreation are a few of the other expenses which must be considered. How much can be spent for the various needs and wants depends on the amount of income. How the available money is divided among the various needs and wants depends on how important each need or want is. For example, if clothing is important, more money is likely to be used for that expense than if clothing is not so important.

Sometimes families or individuals may decide not to purchase certain articles of clothing new. They may decide to take care of their clothing needs in other ways. At times, for example, clothing may be exchanged among immediate family members, other relatives, or friends. Sometimes a favorite garment may be altered or repaired so that it may be used another season. This decision will depend on income, on the available time and skill to repair and alter clothing, and on attitude toward clothing.

Families differ, too, in the number of individuals for whom clothing must be provided. The clothing needed by individual family members will differ according to their ages and daily activities. Because school clothing is worn every day, it may need to be replaced more often than clothing that is worn for special occasions. When young children are growing rapidly some articles of their clothing are outgrown in a few months. Working clothes are needed by wage earners in the family. For some types of jobs, special clothing may have to be purchased. Community standards, traditions, and customs also influence clothing needed by each individual. This, in turn, affects the decisions that are made about clothing.

The area of the country in which one lives also affects decisions about clothes. In areas where the winter season is severe, clothing is needed that gives protection from low temperatures. In other parts of the country, lightweight or all-weather garments may provide enough protection.

 **PUTTING IT TOGETHER**

1 What are some steps you can follow in making a decision? When might you skip some of the steps? Add some steps?

2 Give some examples of decisions that might require a lot of thought. What are some examples of decisions that can be made quickly?

3 What are some things which influence how much money can be spent for a particular garment? Some things which influence how much of the total income can be spent on clothes?

4 Describe some things which influence decisions about providing clothes.

LESSON TWO
PLANNING YOUR CLOTHES

◇ plan   decisions   ◎ what a plan is

planning   organize   some ways decisions are related to plans

goal   color-coordinated wardrobe   some guidelines to follow

adequate wardrobe

resources

Do you have clothes you don't know where or when to wear? Do you have clothes that do not go with other clothes you have? Perhaps you don't have a plan for your clothes. Or maybe you don't follow the plan you have made because it is too much trouble.

Resources that are carefully used can help one achieve the goal of providing satisfactory clothing.

MAKING A PLAN

A *plan* is a blueprint or a way to do or make something that is outlined ahead of time. *Planning*, the process of making a plan, requires many *decisions*. In making a plan, you first decide what your goal is. That is, you decide what you want the plan to accomplish.

One goal might be to have an *adequate wardrobe,* or enough clothes to make it possible for you to carry out your daily activities. If this is your goal, then you have to decide what kinds of clothes you need, how many you need, and how they will go together.

Another decision to be made in planning is to decide what *resources* you have that can be used to help achieve your goal. If you have skill in sewing, that is one resource. Money is another resource for providing clothes. If you find you don't have any resources for achieving your goal, you may need to rethink your goal.

Another decision in planning is related to how you *organize* your plan. These decisions are about the order in which you will do things to reach your goal. For example, you may decide to get the red slacks you need before you get the blue jacket. Organization helps you carry out your plan.

CARRYING OUT A PLAN

As you carry out your plan, you need to check often to see that the plan is working to help you achieve your goal. If it is not, don't be afraid to make changes. A plan is only a tool or guide to help you achieve a goal. A plan is not useful if it doesn't work.

There may be a number of reasons for making changes in your plans. Resources that were available when you made the plan may no longer be available; or your goals may change. All of these are common happenings. A plan for reaching goals does not have to be completely finished to be useful. A plan has served its purpose as long as it helps you to reach a goal.

PLANNING A WARDROBE

To make a plan for an adequate wardrobe, you must decide what is an adequate wardrobe for you. This decision should be based on your own needs and wants. For example, if most of your activities are centered around school and school-related events, you will need clothes for these activities. If your

school has a dress code, you will probably have clothing needs that would not exist if there were no dress code. If you are a member of the school band, you may need fewer clothes for school events because you will wear the band uniform. If you work part time you may need special clothes or uniforms for the job; if you don't work, you wear different clothes. Think about what an adequate wardrobe is for you. Check the clothes you have to see how many things you already have to meet your needs. Start your wardrobe plan on the basis of these clothes. Then decide what you need to add to make your wardrobe adequate for you. Remember to consider your resources as you make the plan.

Here are some guidelines to consider in making your plan and carrying it out.

Plan to buy, make, or repair only garments that you will use. Buying, making, or repairing clothes that are not suitable for what you do probably means that these clothes will be worn very little or not at all. You probably will not get very much satisfaction from your effort.

Plan for several garments that can be worn together or that can be combined in various ways. Start with the clothing you already have. Plan at the same time the colors and styles of garments you want to buy even though you may actually buy them at different times. If you plan only in terms of single garments that you think you need or want, you may soon have a collection of unrelated items. Your clothing is more likely to combine well if you plan for it to combine.

Plan to buy colors that will permit as many combinations as possible. You will need to follow a color plan over a period of time to develop a *color-coordinated wardrobe,* that is one in which the colors can be used together. Colors that harmonize will allow you to make better use of all your clothing. If you select more solid colors than stripes, plaids, or figured designs, you can combine more items.

What I have

Slacks	Shirts	Sweaters	Shoes	Jeans
gray	brown	tan	brown	2 navy
red	red/white stripe	black	black	1 brown
navy	yellow	blue		
green/brown plaid	navy print			

What I need

Slacks	Shirts	Sweaters	Shoes	Jeans
black	green	green	tennis shoes	
	light blue	white	hiking boots	

Carry a list of the garments you have and their colors when you shop to remind you of your plan. This guide will help you build combinations and avoid collecting unmatched garments. Fabric samples from clothing you already have will help you match or coordinate new garments with that clothing.

Increase your resources by learning to sew, repair, or remake garments.

Plan accessories you need when you plan other additions to your wardrobe. Purses, jewelry, headwear, belts, and other accessories will be useful if they are planned as part of the total design of an outfit. Follow your color plan when you choose these items.

Plan ways to care for the clothing you already have. This will help maintain its appearance and increase the number of wearings you can get from each garment.

Revise and make changes in your plan as your activities, needs, wants, and goals change. Remember, the purpose of a plan is to help your reach a goal. A plan is not useful unless it does this.

 **PUTTING IT TOGETHER**

1 How is a plan helpful to you even though it will need to be revised as you carry it out?
2 In what ways are decisions important in making and carrying out a plan?
3 What are some guidelines for planning a wardrobe? Why might a plan that has been made for an adequate wardrobe never be completely finished?

LESSON THREE

WHERE TO BUY CLOTHES

 variety store

specialty store

department store

services

self-service

discount house

mail-order house

credit

interest

30-day charge account

revolving credit account

layaway plan

 some types of stores

some ways to pay for clothes

SOME TYPES OF STORES

Deciding where to buy clothing is not always a simple decision. There are many types of stores where clothing may be purchased. Some of these are department stores, specialty clothing stores, drugstores, variety stores, supermarkets, mail-order houses, used clothing stores, and discount houses. Each type of store is different from the others. Some offer special *services,* such as free delivery, guarantees, charge accounts, free parking, many salespersons, and mail or phone order services. Special services usually result in higher prices. Other stores may offer no services and have lower prices.

Drugstores and supermarkets usually sell only a few clothing items, such as stockings and socks, underwear, play shoes, and work gloves. Sizes, colors, and styles may be limited. *Variety stores* may have a bigger selection of clothing than supermarkets and drugstores, but it is limited in comparison with

INFORMATION HELPS

that in specialty clothing stores and department stores. Variety stores, drugstores, and supermarkets are often *self-service,* that is you wait on yourself. Salespersons may not be informed about the clothing they sell.

A *specialty store* sells only a few types of clothing or clothing for a special age group or size range. For example, such a store may sell clothing for women and girls, for men, or for children. Or the store may specialize in one type of clothing, such as shoes or hats. The salespersons are usually well-informed about the products they sell. Personal service to the customer may be emphasized. Prices may be higher than in department or discount stores.

Large *department stores* usually sell all kinds of clothing for all family members. There are often special departments for each type of clothing. For example, men's sportswear may be sold in one department, men's

Purchases can be made using cash, credit, or layaway.

Candida's

READY-TO-WEAR

–	00.59	I
–	00.79	I
–	00.49	I
–	00.49	I
–	00.49	I
–	02.85	SUB TOTL
–	00.20	IV
–	01.25	III
–	04.30	SUB TOTL
–	04.30	B

YOUR RECEIPT

THANK YOU

4 8 2 1   9 DEC

TICKET NO.
385

LAY-AWAY

Date _____

Name _____
Address _____
Article _____ Sold by _____
Retail Price _____ Tax ____ Total _____

TICKET NO.
385

Retail Price _____
Tax _____
Total _____

Name _____
Address _____
Article _____ Clerk No. _____

Date	Sales Slip Number	Amount	Balance	Received By

---

1. I understand that this merchandise will be held for me in the Lay-Away Dept. and I agree to pay the balance due by _____
2. I agree to pay $ _____ Every ☐ WK. ☐ MO.
3. I understand that if the merchandise is not fully paid for and called for on or before _____ it will be returned to stock unless special arrangements are made.

Sig. _____
Mfr. _____
Lot No. _____ Date Rec'd. _____

Remarks: _____

Tennis World

15 EAST 48TH STREET, NEW YORK, N.Y. 10017

Customer's Statement

AMOUNT PAID

DATE	STORE	REFERENCE NUMBER	DEPT. NO.	TRANSACTION DESCRIPTION	PURCHASES & OTHER CHARGES	PAYMENTS, RETURNS & OTHER CREDITS

PREVIOUS BALANCE	TOTAL PURCHASES & OTHER CHARGES	PAYMENTS, RETURNS & OTHER CREDITS	FINANCE CHARGE	THIS IS YOUR NEW BALANCE	PAYMENTS OVER DUE	THIS IS YOUR MINIMUM PAYMENT

ACCOUNT NUMBER   BILLING DATE

suits in another, and men's coats in another. A more extensive choice of styles, colors, sizes, qualities, and price ranges is likely to be found in a department store than in any other type of store. Salespersons are usually available to help and often know a lot about what they are selling. Some department stores guarantee what they sell; most allow you to return or exchange things if you are not satisfied.

Used clothing stores may have clothing for all family members in various qualities. But sizes, colors, and styles may be limited because it is not possible for the store manager to plan the types of garments there will be to sell. This is because the clothing for sale is used clothing which may come from many different sources.

Discount houses claim to sell items at lower prices than might be found in department stores. Sometimes this is the case. Many discount houses are self-service, and you may not be allowed to return or exchange things you buy. Some stores that started as discount houses are now very similar to department stores. Depending on the size of the discount house, choices or styles and sizes of clothing may be limited.

Other factors are also important in choosing a place to shop. If time for shopping is limited, the store must be easy to reach. A parking area near the store is a convenience for drivers. Ordering by telephone is a convenience, too, but it is not possible to see the clothing or try it on before buying. It may have to be returned if it is not satisfactory. This is a chance that one takes.

SOME WAYS TO PAY FOR CLOTHES

Depending on where you shop, there may be several ways to pay for what you buy. You may pay cash, use credit, or use a layaway plan. Each way has advantages and disadvantages.

Paying cash for clothes means that you have no payments to worry about and that there are no extra costs for using credit. You also do not spend more money than you have. Some stores give discounts if you pay cash.

The *30-day charge account* and the *revolving credit account* are different kinds of *credit*. Credit is a promise to pay later. Credit accounts or charge accounts are usually made available to people who can prove they have the ability to pay and can be counted on to pay the bill on time.

If you use a 30-day charge account, you agree to pay the entire bill in thirty days. There may or may not be an extra charge for this service if you pay on time. If your payment is late, there is usually an extra charge.

A revolving credit account can often be used the same as a 30-day charge account, that is you can pay your entire bill. However, over a certain minimum amount, you are not required to pay the entire bill at one time. Rather, you make a payment each month. The amount of the payment is based on the total amount you owe. *Interest,* or a charge for using credit, is charged on the amount of money you still owe and is added to your bill.

On a *layaway plan,* the store puts away an item you want. Usually a down payment is required. When the rest of the money is paid, you receive the item. Often there is interest charged on the amount of money owed.

An advantage of buying on credit is that you don't have to carry large amounts of money with you when you shop. However, when you use credit, it is easy to buy more than you can pay for all at once when the bills come in. Then you end up paying more than the price on the price tag because of the interest charged on the money you owe.

 **PUTTING IT TOGETHER**

1 What are some types of stores in your community? What are some advantages and disadvantages of shopping in each one?
2 Describe some different ways you can pay for clothes. What are some advantages and disadvantages of each way?

LESSON FOUR
FIBERS

 fiber

natural fiber

manufactured
fiber

synthesize

generic name

trademark
name

 what fibers are

some natural fibers and what
they are like

some manufactured fibers and
what they are like

Fibers are threadlike strands which can be spun into yarns to make fabrics by weaving, knitting, or some other fabric-making process. Fibers can be separated into two major groups. One is *natural fibers,* or those fibers which are formed by natural processes. Another is *manufactured fibers,* or those which are made in factories from chemicals and other raw materials.

NATURAL FIBERS

The major *natural* fibers used in clothing are cotton, wool, flax, and silk. These fibers are produced by natural processes carried on in plant and animal life. *Wool* and *silk* are fibers produced by animal life. Wool is the coat of sheep and goats which can be sheared from the animals. Silk fibers are the filaments produced by silkworms as they make cocoons during one stage in their life cycle.

Cotton and *flax* are familiar fibers produced by plants. Cotton fibers are formed in the seed pods of the cotton plant as it ripens. Flax fibers are formed in the stalk of the flax plant. Flax fibers are made into linen fabric.

Each fiber has individual characteristics which make it suitable for certain uses. Wool cloth is warm compared to cotton, silk, and linen. Wool clothes are generally good choices in cool climates. Cotton is absorbent and relatively strong. Cotton can be made into sturdy fabrics that wear well. Cotton is a good choice for garments that are worn often and washed often. Flax is absorbent and strong like cotton, but linen garments are generally more expensive than cotton garments. Silk is a soft, luxurious fiber. Silk garments require special care to maintain their appearance and are relatively expensive compared to garments made of other fibers.

The chart on pages 109 and 110 compares the characteristics of natural fibers without special finishes and summarizes differences in clothing made of these fibers.

MANUFACTURED FIBERS

Manufactured fibers are *synthesized,* that is formed from raw materials through planned manufacturing processes in factories.

Manufactured fibers may be divided into groups according to their composition and general characteristics. Each group of fibers has a *generic name.* The list below contains the generic names of manufactured fibers. You may recognize some of them.

acetate	metallic	rayon
acrylic	nylon	rubber
anidex	modacrylic	saran
aramid	novoloid	spandex
azlon	nytril	triacetate
glass	olefin	vinal
lastrile	polyester	vinyon

As with natural fibers, manufactured fibers have characteristics which affect their use. As a result not all of the manufactured fibers are used for clothing; some are used in industry. Those commonly used in clothing are *acetate, acrylic, modacrylic, nylon, rayon, polyester, spandex,* and *triacetate.* The chart on pages 110–112 compares the characteristics of these manufactured fibers and summarizes differences in clothing made of these fibers.

In addition to generic names, manufactured fibers can also be recognized by *trademark* names. Trademark names are given to a fiber by the company that makes that fiber. For example, many companies make polyester fibers. Each company has a different name for the polyester fiber it makes. Fortrel is the trademark name for a polyester fiber made by Fiber Industries, Inc.; Kodel is the trademark name of a polyester fiber made by Eastman Kodak Company.

The chart on pages 110–112 shows some trademark names of manufactured fibers. It also shows characteristics of fibers and fabrics.

NATURAL FIBERS IN THE CLOTHING YOU WEAR

FIBER NAME AND SOURCE	FIBER CHARACTERISTICS	TYPICAL CLOTHING USES	HOW THE FIBER AFFECTS CLOTHING CHARACTERISTICS
Cotton (cotton plant)	strong, durable supports mildew growth absorbs moisture well does not spring back into shape	blouses dresses skirts underwear socks sportswear housecoats shirts jeans	an all-cotton garment will: be comfortable in warm weather wrinkle easily without special finish wash easily if color-fast need to be ironed at high temperature unless it has wrinkle-resistant finish be durable; withstand wear burn readily mildew if stored damp or in a damp place
Flax (flax plant)	strong, durable supports mildew growth absorbs moisture well	blouses dresses skirts suits	an all-linen garment will: be comfortable in warm weather wrinkle easily without special finish wash easily if color-fast need to be ironed at high temperature unless it has wrinkle-resistant finish be very durable; withstand wear burn readily mildew if stored damp or in a damp place

continued on next page

FIBER NAME AND SOURCE	FIBER CHARACTERISTICS	TYPICAL CLOTHING USES	HOW THE FIBER AFFECTS CLOTHING CHARACTERISTICS
Wool (sheep)	warm durable returns to original shape quickly absorbs moisture	knit garments sweaters gloves skirts coats sportswear socks suits slacks	an all-wool garment will: be warmer than cotton, linen, or silk resist wrinkling absorb odors be durable; withstand wear need protection against insects (moth) need careful handling if washed need to be pressed at low temperature
Silk (cocoon of silkworm)	smooth lustrous strong	skirts blouses dresses neckties scarves	an all-silk garment will: feel luxurious need ironing at low temperature show water spots unless it has special finish need to be dry-cleaned, unless carefully handled in washing

MANUFACTURED FIBERS IN THE CLOTHES YOU WEAR

FIBER	FIBER CHARACTERISTICS	TYPICAL CLOTHING USES	HOW THE FIBER AFFECTS CLOTHING CHARACTERISTICS
acetate (generic name) Avicolor Celacloud Chromspun (examples of trademark names)	lustrous does not shrink lacks strength resists damage from moth larvae and mildew	underwear sportswear dresses blouses shirts neckties scarves	an all-acetate garment will: drape well resist fading from sunlight and perspiration be damaged by acetone and nail polish remover need to be dry-cleaned unless carefully handled when wet

FIBER	FIBER CHARACTERISTICS	TYPICAL CLOTHING USES	HOW THE FIBER AFFECTS CLOTHING CHARACTERISTICS
acrylic (generic name) Orlon Acrilan Creslan (examples of trademark names)	lightweight warm does not absorb moisture springs back into shape quickly	sportswear knitted garments ski wear	an all-acrylic garment will: be soft, warm, and lightweight dry quickly resist wrinkles resist damage from sunlight, chemicals, oil tend to build up static electricity tend to "pill" on the surface
modacrylic (generic name) Dynel Verel (examples of trademark names)	lightweight warm springs back into shape quickly does not absorb moisture resists burning	sportswear sleepwear knitted garments fur-like garments	an all-modacrylic garment will: not burn readily be soft, warm, and lightweight dry quickly resist wrinkles tend to build up static electricity withstand wear
nylon (generic name) Antron Qiana Cantrece (examples of trademark names)	strong, durable does not mildew lustrous does not shrink does not absorb moisture	sportswear swimwear hosiery underwear raincoats ski wear	an all-nylon garment will: not mildew absorb oily stains be damaged by strong sunlight tend to build up static electricity be very durable; withstand wear wash easily
rayon (generic name) Avril Coloray Zantrel (examples of trademark names)	absorbs moisture supports mildew growth does not spring back into shape lacks strength heat sensitive	sportswear blouses shirts neckties underwear	an all-rayon garment will: be comfortable in warm weather wrinkle easily without special finish burn readily mildew if stored damp or in a damp place not be as durable as a garment made from some other fibers be damaged by sunlight and acid solutions need to be ironed at a low temperature

continued on next page

FIBER	FIBER CHARACTERISTICS	TYPICAL CLOTHING USES	HOW THE FIBER AFFECTS CLOTHING CHARACTERISTICS
polyester (generic name) Dacron Kodel Fortrel (examples of trademark names)	strong does not absorb moisture absorbs oil and grease springs back into shape quickly heat sensitive	sportswear suits blouses dresses shirts scarves neckties	an all-polyester garment will: wash easily and dry quickly resist wrinkling retain heat-set creases and pleats absorb oily stains melt if ironed at high temperature
spandex (generic name) Lycra Vyrene (examples of trademark names)	stretches strong, durable lightweight heat sensitive	girdles swimwear ski wear support hose garments with stretch	an all-spandex garment will: be lightweight stretch and return to its original shape when wet or dry not be damaged by perspiration, body oils, and most chemicals be durable; withstand wear be damaged by heat
triacetate (generic name) Arnel (example of trademark name)	does not absorb moisture well lacks strength springs back into shape	sportswear dresses skirts garments with pleats	an all-triacetate garment will: maintain a crisp finish not be damaged by heat build up static electricity retain heat-set pleats resist wrinkling dry quickly not be as durable as a garment made from some other fibers

PUTTING IT TOGETHER

1 What are fibers?
2 What are natural fibers?
3 What are manufactured fibers?
4 What are some things which determine how fibers are used?

LESSON FIVE
YARNS

 fiber

yarn

ply yarn

texturized
yarn

texturized
yarn
with stretch

 what yarns are

some ways yarns are made

Fibers are twisted together to make *yarns* from which fabrics are made. Both natural fibers and manufactured fibers are used to make yarn.

The ways fibers are made into yarns affect the appearance of yarn. Fibers can be twisted together in many ways to make a variety of yarns. Short fibers may be twisted together loosely or tightly; so may long fibers. Thick fibers and thin fibers may be twisted together loosely or tightly. Thick fibers may be twisted together with thin fibers. Yarns made in these ways have different appearances. Yarns affect the appearance of a fabric.

Sometimes yarns are made up of two or more yarns twisted together. These yarns may be referred to as two-ply yarns, three-ply yarns, and so on. *Ply* refers to the number of yarns twisted together. Differences in ply yarns are made by twisting two or more similar yarns together or by twisting two or more different yarns together.

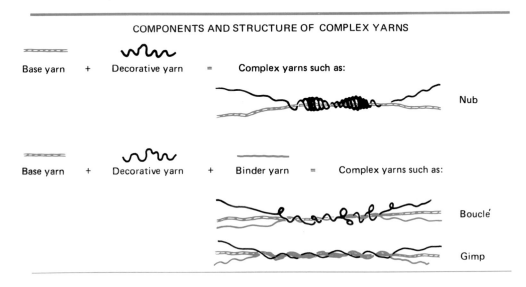

COMPONENTS AND STRUCTURE OF COMPLEX YARNS

Base yarn + Decorative yarn = Complex yarns such as:

Nub

Base yarn + Decorative yarn + Binder yarn = Complex yarns such as:

Bouclé

Gimp

continued on next page

Exceptions to the above are:

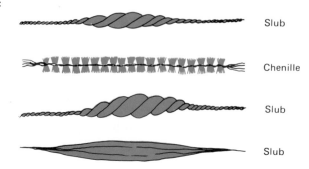

Slub

Chenille

Slub

Slub

TEXTURIZED THERMOPLASTIC FILAMENT YARNS

Textralized yarn
(textured by stuffer box method)

Helanca yarn
(textured by twist-heatset-untwist method)

Taslen yarn
(textured by loop method)

Agilon nylon yarn
(with undeveloped crimp)

The characteristics of fibers also affect the appearance of yarns. For example, silk fibers and some untreated manufactured fibers have the characteristics of luster and smoothness. Yarns made of these fibers also have these characteristics. Some wool fibers are coarse or thick. These characteristics are present in yarns made from these fibers.

The characteristic of manufactured fibers that causes them to be affected by heat can be used to make still other types of yarns. Long, smooth, plain yarns of manufactured fibers are processed in special ways, using heat, to create bulky, airy yarns with a three-dimensional appearance. Yarns made in these ways are called *texturized yarns.* Other processes are used in manufactured fibers to create *texturized yarns with stretch.*

The fiber strength and the way fibers are twisted together both contribute to the strength of yarns. Strong fibers help to make strong yarns. Also, tightly twisted fibers help to make a stronger yarn than loosely twisted fibers.

Yarns may be made of only one fiber type, such as cotton or wool or nylon. Yarns may also be made of two or more fiber types blended together. Common fiber blends are polyester and cotton, wool and nylon, and nylon and spandex.

 **PUTTING IT TOGETHER**

1 What are yarns? Describe some ways yarns are made.
2 Name some things which affect the characteristics of a yarn. Describe how these things affect the characteristics of a yarn.

LESSON SIX
FABRICS

woven fabrics

loom

yarns

grainline

knitted fabrics

knitting machine

layered fabrics

nonwoven fabrics

bonded fabric

what fabrics are

some ways fabrics are made

some ways fabrics behave

Fibers and yarns can be held together in various ways to make *fabric,* or cloth. The two most common methods for manufacturing cloth are weaving and knitting. Some other methods are bonding, felting, braiding, and lace-making. Most clothes are made of either woven fabrics or knitted fabrics, therefore most of this lesson will be concerned with these methods for making fabric.

WEAVING

Woven fabrics are made by interlacing yarns at right angles to each other. The loom is the machine used in the weaving process. First *warp yarns* are threaded on the loom. These yarns produce the lengthwise yarns in the fabric. The warp yarns are crossed over and under at right angles by *filling yarns*, or weft. These yarns produce the crosswise yarns in the fabric.

Every woven fabric has a *lengthwise grainline* and a *crosswise grainline*. Lengthwise grainline refers to the warp yarns; crosswise grainline refers to the filling yarns, or weft.

Different kinds of woven fabrics can be made by varying the interlacing process. Woven fabrics are usually made by one of the three basic weaves. These are the *plain weave,* the *twill weave,* and the *satin weave.*

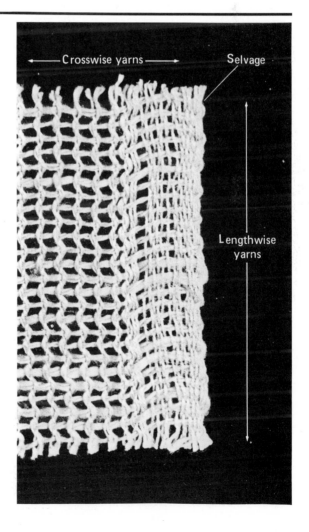

Crosswise yarns — Selvage

Lengthwise yarns

INFORMATION HELPS

Fabrics produced by the three basic weaves differ in appearance and in the way they withstand wear. The chart below compares the three basic weaves.

Pile fabrics, such as corduroy, terry cloth, and velvet, are made by a variation on a plain weave or a twill weave. Extra yarns are woven into the basic weave or anchored into the basic weave to give the pile surface.

Fabrics with designs woven into them are another variation on the three basic weaves.

The yarns used to weave the fabric are controlled in special ways to create the designs.

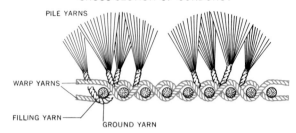

CROSS-SECTION OF CORDUROY

BASIC WEAVES AND THEIR USES

TYPE OF WEAVE	MICROSCOPIC VIEW	FABRIC NAMES	GENERAL CHARACTERISTICS	SOME CLOTHING USES
plain		seersucker broadcloth sailcloth gingham indian head chambray poplin oxford cloth duck organdy shantung percale	varies from sheer and fragile to heavy and sturdy	sportswear blouses shirts sleepwear dresses skirts housecoats jackets coats
twill		denim gabardine ticking serge	diagonal design on the surface very strong and durable	sportswear dresses skirts slacks jeans jackets
satin		satin sateen	smooth, sometimes shiny appearance threads snag easily not durable; will not withstand wear as well as a plain or twill weave	bridal gowns evening wear dresses blouses shirts

KNITTING

If you look closely at a knitted fabric you will see that it is not made in the same way as a woven fabric. *Knitted fabrics* are made by interlooping one or more yarns. *Knitting machines* are used to make knitted fabric for clothes. Circular knitting machines make knitted fabric in tube-like form. Flat knitting machines make knitted fabric in flat form similar to the form of woven fabric.

Wales (lengthwise)

 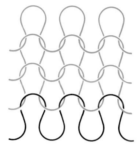

Courses (crosswise)

A *warp knit* is made by interlooping several parallel yarns to form loops in the lengthwise direction of the fabric. A *filling knit,* or *weft knit,* is made by interlooping one yarn to form loops in the crosswise direction of the fabric. Filling knits can be made either on a flat knitting machine or a circular knitting machine. Warp knits are made on flat knitting machines.

Because knitted fabrics are constructed differently from woven fabrics, knitted fabrics have characteristics different from those of woven fabrics. Knitted fabrics generally wrinkle less than woven fabrics without some special treatment; knitted fabrics tend to show wrinkles less than woven fabrics do. Unless woven fabric is made with stretch yarns, woven fabric stretches very little compared to most knitted fabrics. The construction of knitted fabrics gives them the ability to adjust easily to the shape of the body.

The chart below compares some different knits commonly used in clothing.

BASIC KNITS AND THEIR USES

TYPE OF KNIT	MICROSCOPIC VIEW	FABRIC NAMES	GENERAL CHARACTERISTICS	SOME CLOTHING USES
warp		tricot raschel Milanese	generally tighter, flatter, and less elastic than weft knits; stronger and do not ravel	underwear blouses dresses linings for layered fabrics gloves
weft		jersey rib knits purl knits full-fashioned knits pile knits	generally tend to stretch more than warp knits and may run if a stitch is broken	hosiery pile fabrics underwear shirts sweaters dresses sportswear scarves and mittens

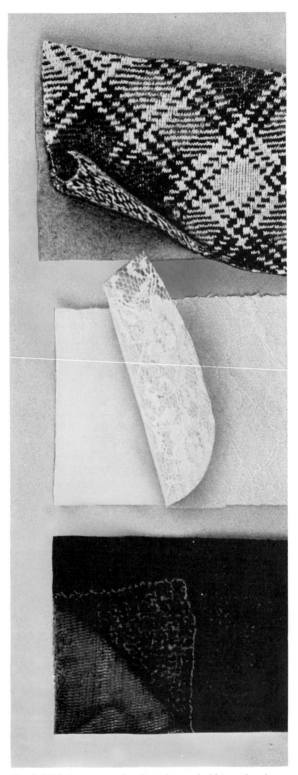

Bonded fabrics are made of two layers held together by chemical, mechanical, or thermal means.

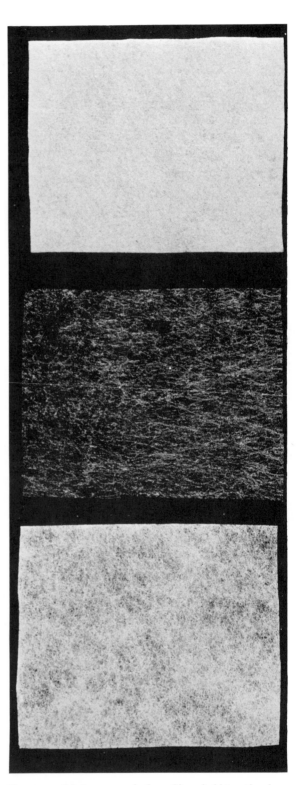

Nonwoven fabrics are made from fibers held together by means other than knitting or weaving.

Double knit fabrics are a variation of weft knitting. Two sets of needles are used in the process, making it possible to knit two layers of fabric at once. The two layers are knit together as they are made. Double-knit fabrics are firm and do not ravel.

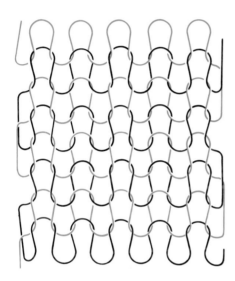

OTHER METHODS OF MAKING FABRICS

Layered fabrics are made from two layers of fabric that are fastened together by some means. A common method uses an *adhesive,* or a sticky, glue-like substance. One layer of fabric may serve as a lining to eliminate the need for a separate lining. The lining may also add support and strength to the outside fabric. Layered fabrics may be made of two similar fabrics, or of two different ones. For example, two knitted fabrics may be fastened together, two woven fabrics may be fastened together, or a knitted fabric may be fastened to a woven fabric or a lace fabric. Sometimes a layer of foam is attached to a layer of fabric. This is common on coats and jackets because it adds warmth.

Bonding and *felting* are two methods used to make *nonwoven fabrics.* Nonwovens are made directly from fibers rather than from yarns. The fibers are held together by means other than knitting or weaving.

Wool fibers are used in the felting process. Heat and moisture are applied to the fibers as they are being pressed together. The scaly quality of the wool fibers causes them to hold together.

Manufactured fibers are usually used in the bonding method of making nonwoven fabrics. The fibers are *bonded,* or held together, by chemical, mechanical, or thermal means. *Chemical bonding* is done with adhesives. *Mechanical bonding* is done with a machine which has many hooked needles. The needles are pushed through the fibers to catch the fibers and interlock them. *Thermal bonding* is done with heat which causes manufactured fibers to melt slightly and stick together.

Nonwoven fabrics are not as strong as most woven or knitted fabrics. Wool felt is used to make some decorative clothing, such as vests, hats, and skirts. Nonwoven fabric made by bonding may be used for disposable clothing and for interfacing fabrics used in clothing construction.

PUTTING IT TOGETHER

1 What are woven fabrics? Describe the three basic weaves and give some advantages and disadvantages of fabrics made by each weave?

2 How are pile fabrics and fabrics with woven-in designs produced?

3 What are knitted fabrics? How are they different from woven fabrics?

4 Describe how layered fabrics are made.

5 What are some ways nonwoven fabrics are made? How do they differ from woven fabrics or knitted fabrics?

LESSON SEVEN
FABRIC FINISHES

fabric finishes

permanent finish

durable finish

temporary finish

renewable finish

what fabric finishes are

some types of fabric finishes

some effects of fabric finishes on fabrics

Fabric finishes are treatments or processes used to improve fabrics in various ways. Some finishes improve the appearance of fabrics while others make the fabric easier to care for. Less desirable characteristics of

fibers can often be controlled by special finishes. For example, untreated cotton fibers tend to wrinkle easily; they also shrink when washed in hot water. Cotton with special treatment, however, can be both wrinkle-resistant and shrink-resistant. Clothing made

Fabrics may have special finishes to improve them.

from specially treated fabrics may serve you better than clothing made of fabrics that have not been treated.

Fabric finishes can be permanent, durable, temporary, or renewable. A *permanent finish* lasts the life of the garment. A *durable finish* lasts through several launderings or dry cleanings, but has a tendency to lose some of its effectiveness over a long period of time. A *temporary finish* lasts until the fabric is washed or dry cleaned. A *renewable finish* is temporary but can be replaced.

Finishes can be grouped according to the ways they affect fabrics. Some common types of finishes are wrinkle-resistant, including permanent press or durable press and wash-and-wear; flame resistant, shrink-resistant, moth resistant, mildew resistant, stain- and spot-resistant, soil release, water-repellent, water-proof, and crisp finish.

Knowing what to expect from a garment which has a specific fabric finish will enable you to choose your clothes carefully for specific purposes. You will also avoid damaging the finish or the garment itself if you follow the directions for cleaning a garment with a particular finish.

The chart on pages 121–122 provides information about types of finishes, common trademark names for these finishes, and ways the finishes affect fabrics and garments to which the finishes are applied.

SOME COMMON FABRIC FINISHES

TYPE OF FABRIC FINISH	WHAT IT MEANS	EXAMPLES OF TRADEMARK NAMES
crisp finish	Fabrics have the appearance of being starched and stay crisp through wear, laundering, and dry cleaning No need to starch garments	Bellmanized Salerized Fresh-tex
flame-resistant	Fabrics will resist burning Special care may be needed to maintain the finish	Fire-Guard Saniflamed
mildew-resistant	Mildew damage is less likely Care in storing clothes is still necessary	Fresh-tex
moth-resistant	Fabrics will resist damage by moth larvae Special care may be needed to maintain the finish	Woolgard Mitin Moth Snub
shrink-resistant (cotton and linen)	Shrinkage controlled to less than 1 percent Garments can be laundered repeatedly without excess shrinkage	Sanforized
shrink-resistant (wool)	Garments can be washed under the conditions described on the label Special care may be needed to prevent excess shrinkage	Lanaset Dylanize Kroy ® Process Bancora Sanforlan

continued on next page

TYPE OF FABRIC FINISH	WHAT IT MEANS	EXAMPLES OF TRADEMARK NAMES
soil release	Aids in removing oil, grease, and dirt during laundering	Come clean Dual Action Scotchgard Fabric Protector Soil-out Zip-Clean
stain- and spot-resistant	Depending on the finish, fabrics resist water-based stains and/or oil-based stains If stain is not removed quickly, the stain will likely be absorbed by the fabric and be difficult to remove	Zepel Unisec Hydro-Pruf Sylmer
waterproof	The fabric sheds water The fabric may be uncomfortable because it will not allow air to pass through	Reevair
water-repellent	Fabrics resist water, but eventually become wet Depending on the finish, it may need to be renewed when the garment is dry cleaned Insufficient rinsing of washable fabrics may make the finish less effective	Cravenette Hydro-Pruf Zelan Zepel
wrinkle-resistant (wash-and-wear)	Garment requires little or no ironing Wrinkles tend to flatten or disappear from garment upon hanging	Sanforized-Plus Bancare Minicare Wrinkle-Shed Tebelized
wrinkle-resistant (permanent press or durable press)	The garment should hold its original shape, pleats, and creases No ironing should be needed if care instructions are followed Unless specially treated, stains may be difficult to remove	Conepress Dan-Press Koratron Super-Crease Penn-Prest Presslokt Never-Press Sharp-Shape

 **PUTTING IT TOGETHER**

1 What are fabric finishes?
2 Give some examples of fabric finishes and describe how garments are affected by each finish.

LESSON EIGHT
UNDERSTANDING ADVERTISEMENTS

 informative   **trademark**
advertisement   **name**

brand name

 what informative advertising is

some ways advertisements encourage consumers to buy

Informative advertisements can be a source of helpful information before shopping. What is an informative advertisement? An *informative advertisement* gives you facts about a product and tells you where it can be purchased. Advertisements let you know what types of clothes are sold by different stores. Also, you can use information from advertisements to make some comparisons among similar garments.

What kinds of information can you expect to find in an informative advertisement? You will find a wide range of useful information presented in words and pictures. An accurate picture of a garment is better than words to tell you about the style. A colored picture is effective in showing you how the garment might combine with the clothes you have. Written descriptions of design and colors are also used in advertisements, but pictures show style and color better than words.

Facts about the fiber content and care of a garment are useful in estimating the time and cost of maintaining it. Look for words such as "Washable" or "Machine Washable" or "Dry Clean Only" to learn how to care for each garment.

Frequently, *brand names* or *trademark names* are included in clothing advertisements. This information is useful if you have been satisfied with a particular brand. The manufacturer of the garment may be identi-

fied in some advertisements along with the trademark name.

In addition to trademark name or brand name, the designer's name may be mentioned. If the designer is well-known, this may attract attention to the advertisement and to the garment being advertised.

The advertisement may include information about sizes that are available in the store. Or, it may tell you the size range in which the garment is manufactured.

The specific price of a garment, or the price range, is useful if you need information about the current price of certain garments you are planning to buy. This information will help you to compare several garments in terms of cost and to make the best buy.

Finally, a clothing advertisement aids consumers when it tells the name and location of the store where the garment is sold. This information saves time for consumers who do not have enough time to search out the products they want to buy. Also, it gives consumers an opportunity to compare similar garments advertised by different stores.

Not all advertisements provide enough facts for consumers who want information about the products they buy and who want to compare products. Some advertisements tell the consumers why they need a particular garment, rather than describe the garment itself. Such advertisements often encourage

the consumer to buy the product, but give few facts about the product. Other advertisements may give information but also encourage the consumer to buy by using information other than the facts. For example, an advertisement may tell you that you will win the approval of others if you buy and wear the advertised garment. Or, an advertisement may suggest that a garment is the "very latest" thing to wear this season. Or, you may be told that the garment is the style "everyone" is wearing. Or, the advertisement may suggest that "people who know" are wearing this style.

Advertisements may appeal to your need for adventure. Clothes may be photographed against backgrounds in faraway places. You are encouraged to believe that when you own the garment it will help to fulfill any wish you have for adventure.

Some advertisements may be designed to appeal to your need for individuality, or your need to be different in some way from others. The advertisements emphasize some unusual or unique features of the garment that will make you and the garment be noticed by other people.

Still other advertisements appeal to you by telling you that wearing a particular garment will give you the personality you want. The advertisement will emphasize that clothes will make you the person you want to be. For example, the advertisement may claim that you will become "the girl he will remember" or "the fellow she will remember" or "hero of the ski slopes."

Advertisements such as these are fun to read. You might even decide to buy some clothes because of one of these advertisements. However, unless what you buy fits into your wardrobe, you may not find it useful.

 **PUTTING IT TOGETHER**

1 What is an informative advertisement?
2 What is some information consumers might find in an informative advertisement?
3 How do some advertisements influence consumers to buy? Give examples.

INFORMATION HELPS

LESSON NINE
UNDERSTANDING LABELS AND HANG TAGS

 label

hang tag

permanent label

detachable label

mandatory information

generic name

voluntary information

brand names

trademark names

 information on labels and hang tags

some ways labels and hang tags help the consumer

Labels and hang tags on garments provide information that may be helpful when you buy clothes. A *label* may be permanently attached to a garment or it may be detachable, that is it can be removed. *Permanent labels* are often stitched to garments. *Detachable labels,* or *hang tags,* are usually attached to garments by a string, a pin, a staple, or a plastic band.

Labels and hang tags are attached to garments in various places. Some may be attached on a seam, neckline, sleeve, button, buttonhole, zipper, belt loop, or shirt tail. When a garment is packaged in a transparent wrapper, label information may be printed on the wrapper.

MANDATORY INFORMATION

Some information on labels is *mandatory,* or required, because of federal legislation governing textile products. The fiber content is one type of information that must appear on an attached tag or label. The *generic name* and percentage of each fiber which make up more than 5 percent of the fabric weight must be listed. Fibers must be listed in order on the label; the fiber making up the largest percentage of the fabric is listed first.

A fiber does not have to be mentioned by name or percentage if it makes up 5 percent or less of the weight of the fabric and if it has no effect on the characteristics of the fabric. The terms "other fiber" or "other fibers" are used on labels to show the presence of fibers making up less than 5 percent of the fabric. If a fiber making up less than 5 percent of a fabric affects the characteristics of the fabric, both the percentage and the fiber name must be listed.

Garment labels must show the name of the manufacturer. Also, labels on all imported products must show the name of the country in which the product has been processed or manufactured.

Care instructions must appear on garment labels. This information must be printed on or woven into material that will withstand washing or dry cleaning for the life of the garment.

- Corduroy jeans that stay the size you buy... designed not to shrink more than 2% to 3%.

- Fine quality midwale textured fabric of 87% cotton and 13% polyester with great feel and look of cotton.

- Lengths proportioned to you... PETITE, AVERAGE, TALL.

- Easy care... machine wash, warm, tumble dry. No bleach.

Sold by THE VILLAGER S

Country Togs

RN 18740
STYLE NO. 6270
SIZE: L

65% Acrylic
30% Linen

SIZE
11–12

100% TEXTURIZED POLYESTER

STYLE 130S   CUT 2887

CASUALS

Linde..

A SPECIAL IMPORT

DOUBLE KNIT

**100% POLYESTER
COMPLETELY WASHABLE
HI-STYLE FASHION**

RN 28403 MADE IN HONG KONG

100% TRIACETATE
Arnel®
CELANESE

TURN OVER FOR
WASHING INSTRUCTIONS

- WASH—**WARM** WATER
- DRY—**LOW** HEAT
- STEAM PRESS AT
  LOW HEAT ALONG
  LENGTH OF SHIRT
  RN 19101

100% TEXTURED CELANESE
FORTREL POLYESTER

DOUBLEKNIT
OF 100% TEXTURED

FORTREL®

This **DOUBLEKNIT** hang-tag is awarded only to knit fabrics of superior performance. Celanese laboratories continuously evaluate fabrics of the same style as in this garment against rigorous performance standards. Fabrics which fail to meet these standards are not awarded this tag.

**Wonderful for travel,
just hang garment up,
wrinkles disappear**

CARE INSTRUCTIONS

- **Machine wash**—wash/wear cycle—low temperatures
- **Drip or tumble dry**
- Can also be hand washed, drip dried
- **NEEDS NO IRONING**

Fortrel is a registered trademark
of Fiber Industries, Inc.   P0035

POLYESTER makes a fabric really carefree. It's machine washable, dry cleanable, crease resistant and resilient.

DOUBLE KNIT means a fabric with just enough "give" to make it comfortable.

CARE INSTRUCTIONS Hand wash or machine wash in sudsy water at medium temperature. Rinse well. Tumble dry. Hang immediately. Garment may be drip dried and steam pressed at low setting. Also may be dry cleaned.

55% FORTREL® POLYESTER • 45% AVRIL® RAYON

Wamsutta® NEVER-PRESS™ FABRIC

featuring **CELANESE® FORTREL®**

FOR PRESS FREE WEARING FOLLOW INSTRUCTIONS BELOW
- WASH—at medium setting use full cycle
- Do not use Bleach
- DRY—Tumble dry using wash & wear setting
- When dry remove promptly
- HANG NEATLY—on wooden or plastic hanger

Fortrel is a registered trademark of Fiber Industries, Inc.   F4869

Of the four kinds of mandatory information, the care instruction label is the only label that must be permanently attached to the garment. Information about fiber content, manufacturer, and country of origin may be printed on hang tags or on detachable labels.

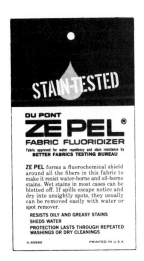

VOLUNTARY INFORMATION

In addition to the mandatory information you will find that certain other information is usually included on labels and hang tags. This information is *voluntary,* that is, it is not required.

Brand names or *trademark names* of manufactured fibers may be included as voluntary information on a label. Besides trademark names for fibers, trademark names or brand names for garments are often included on hang tags. Garment manufacturers may have one or more brand names which identify the garments they produce. The brand name may help you make the best choice if you have found garments with certain brand names

that fit you well. Also, you may have found styles that you like in certain brand names.

Information about the fabric construction may be included. For example, the label may tell you that the fabric is knitted. If the fabric is woven, the common name of the fabric may be given, such as oxford cloth, pique, gingham, or denim. Also, information about size and a special finish may be given on a hang tag.

Sometimes, you will find a guarantee stated for a certain length of wear for a garment. A guarantee may indicate that the garment will be replaced or your money refunded if the garment does not give you the amount of wear stated on the label.

PUTTING IT TOGETHER

1 How do labels and hang tags help the consumer?
2 What are some ways labels and hang tags are attached to garments?
3 What information is mandatory on labels? Give some examples of voluntary information found on labels.

LESSON TEN
CHECKING THE GARMENT

 comparison shopping

comfort

appearance

durability

care

minimum care

 some guidelines for comparison shopping

When you compare garments while shopping, you are *comparison shopping*. Many things about a garment help to determine whether it will serve the purpose you want it to serve. Some characteristics you may want to look at and compare are comfort, appearance, durability, and care.

If a garment is to be worn for a long period of time, *comfort* may be an important characteristic to consider. Clothes that are too warm or too cool, tight, irritating to the skin, or fitted so as to make it difficult to carry out activities are not comfortable. When you are buying think about what the garment will be used for. The fiber content, the fabric construction, the garment design, and the fit of the garment all influence its comfort.

Appearance is another characteristic that may be important. Is current style important to you? Do you want the garment to be for dress-up, casual wear, or for many purposes? Is neatness important to you? The fiber content, fabric construction, garment design, garment construction, and special finishes affect this characteristic of garments.

The *durability* of a garment refers to how long the garment will last and still retain its original appearance. For a garment that will be worn often or one that will be handed down to other members of the family, durability is important. Fiber content, fabric construction, special fabric finishes, garment fit, garment design, and garment construction are to be considered when durability is important.

Care requirements are another garment characteristic that may be important. If a garment needs to be dry cleaned often, the expense of the garment is increased. Also, the garment is not always available to be worn. *Minimum care* garments are ones that require little care to keep them wearable. Minimum care garments usually resist stains and soil, need little or no ironing, and need no special handling for washing and drying. Fiber content, fabric construction, special fabric finishes, and garment construction affect the care of garments.

Some of these characteristics of garments may be more important than others. How important each one is depends on the purpose of the garment and what is important to you or to the person buying the garment. You may want to use the guide lines below for checking and comparing garments when you shop. Compare before you make final choices.

GUIDELINES FOR CHECKING AND COMPARING GARMENTS

ITEM	WHAT TO LOOK FOR
fabric	Is the fabric on grain?
	Do plaids or stripes match?
	Is the fabric tightly woven or knitted?
seams	Does the thread match the fabric?
	Are seam allowances 5/8 inch (1.5 cm) or more?
	Are there seam finishes if necessary?
	Are there 10–12 stitches per inch (6–8 stitches per centimeter)?
	Are seamlines smooth and free of puckers?
	Are seam edges flat, corners flat, and no puckers?

continued on next page

ITEM	WHAT TO LOOK FOR
zippers	Does thread match the fabric?
	Is the stitching even and inconspicuous?
	Is the zipper covered?
	Is the zipper opening smooth and free from puckers?
	Does the zipper open and close easily without catching fabric in the teeth or coils?
buttons snaps hooks eyes	Are the buttons, snaps, hooks and eyes, or other closure securely attached?
	Is there a shank on the button or a thread shank?
	Does the button fit through the buttonhole and lie flat?
buttonholes	Are buttonholes evenly spaced?
	Do buttonholes lie flat?
	Are the buttonholes on grain?
	Are the stitches close together?
hems	Is the hem finish suitable to the fabric?
	Is the hem the proper width for the garment style?
	Does the hem lie flat?
	Is the hem even?
	Is the stitching inconspicuous from the garment outside?
care	Does the fiber content, fabric construction, and/or special finishes resist soil, stains, and wrinkling?
	Is the fabric colorfast to cleaning and sunlight?
	Can all parts of the garment be cleaned in the same way?
	Can the garment be washed?
	Does the garment require little or no ironing?

PUTTING IT TOGETHER

1 Give some examples of times when comfort in a garment would be important; when minimum care would be important; when durability would be important; when appearance would be important.

2 Suppose you are shopping for the following garments. List some characteristics you think would be important and explain why.
   Tennis outfit
   Bathing suit
   Garment for a special occasion
   Clothes for school

LESSON ELEVEN
CHECKING THE FIT

 body measurements

body structure

stage of physical development

size charts

one-piece outfits

proportioned sizes

inseam measurement

some guidelines for checking garment fit

some ways to use size charts

When you are shopping for clothes, it is helpful for you to know your correct size. This is not always easy because clothes are made in so many different sizes.

FINDING THE SIZE

How do you find your correct size? First you need to know certain *body measurements.* Look at the illustration to see where these measurements are taken.

In addition to body measurements, you also should know your height and your *body structure* or your *stage of physical development* to help find your correct size. Your body structure depends on your height in relation to weight, your bone structure, and the location of your waistline in relation to your chest or bust and hips. Your stage of physical development means how much your body has grown and how well developed your muscles and bones are.

Have someone take your measurements for you. This is more accurate than trying to take them yourself.

Height. Stand against a wall and make a mark level with the top of the head. Measure from the mark to the floor.

Chest or bust. Measure around the fullest part of the chest or bust. Keep tape straight across the back.

Waist. Measure around the smallest part at the natural waistline. Hold tape snugly but not tight.

Hips. Measure around the fullest part of the hips. Keep tape straight around body.

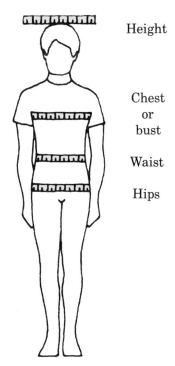
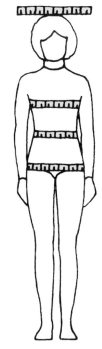

Height

Chest or bust

Waist

Hips

Inseam. Measure the inside leg seam of a pair of slacks, pants, or jeans that are the right length.

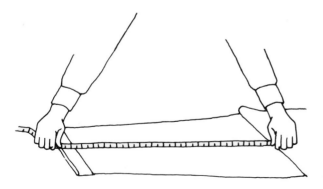

Neck. Measure the collar from the middle of the collar button to the end of the buttonhole on a shirt that is comfortable around the neck.

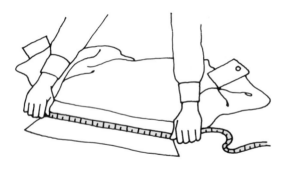

Sleeve. On a shirt that fits, measure from the center back at the collar, along the back of the arm, to the cuff at the wristbone.

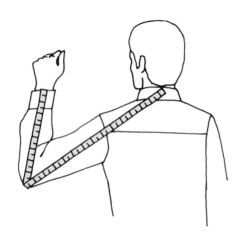

When you have the information about your measurements, body structure, and physical development, you can compare it with different *size charts* to find your size. Several size charts are included in this lesson to help you.

You may find that your measurements do not correspond exactly with those in the measurement charts. If not, choose the size that most closely matches your measurements. If only one of your measurements is different from those in the size you have chosen in the chart, you may have to try different size garments to see which size fits best. For example, if your waist and bust measurements correspond with size 9, but your hip measurement is a size 11, you may have to try both size 9 and size 11 garments to see which fits best. Usually it is better to buy clothes to fit the larger measurement because it is easier to take in clothes than to let them out.

After you find a garment in your size, it is a good idea to try it on and check the fit. Manufacturers do not always base their sizes on the same measurements. You may find that garments in the same size but made by different manufacturers may not fit exactly the same. Some brands may fit better and feel more comfortable than others. You may have to buy several different sizes, all of which may fit. For example, in Brand X you may wear size 14, while in Brand Y you may need size 16.

It is also a good idea to try on a garment to check its fit because the garment style or design and the fabric used to make the garment may affect the fit. For example, you may need a smaller size in a loosely fitted garment than in a garment which is designed to fit closely to the body. Garments made of knitted fabrics sometimes fit more closely than similar garments made of woven fabrics. Therefore you should try different sizes to find which fits you best.

Beginning on the next page is some information to help you find your correct size. There are also some guidelines for checking the fit of various garments. You may want to write down some of this information to take with you when you shop.

ONE-PIECE OUTFITS

One-piece outfits are made in many styles and of many fabrics for different occasions. Some examples of one-piece outfits are dresses, jumpsuits, and skimobile suits. One-piece outfits are often made in several sizes for different figures, or body structures, and for different stages of physical development. In addition, some one-piece outfits are made in *proportioned sizes*, that is for persons of different heights. Some examples of size charts for one-piece outfits for fellows and for girls are on pages 136–141.

Finding a one-piece outfit that fits well can be a problem if your measurements are not in proportion according to the size charts. If your hips are large in proportion to the rest of your body, you may find that a one-piece outfit that fits the upper part of the body will be tight in the hip area; if it fits in the hip area, it may be too large for the upper part of your body. You may find that two-piece outfits are more satisfactory for a comfortable fit.

Here are eleven guidelines that you can use in checking the fit of one-piece outfits.

1. Neckline fits smoothly and comfortably

2. Shoulder length is comfortable

3. Armhole does not bind

4. Bust darts are at fullest part of bust

5. Enough ease across the bust or chest and through the back; no pulling or stretching

6. Sleeves are comfortable and an attractive length

7. Center front and back seams are right length; no pulling or stretching when moving; comfortable when sitting down

8. Waistline is located at waist; belt stays smooth

9. Enough ease through the hips and seat

10. Hem is parallel to the floor

11. Length is attractive for height and is current style

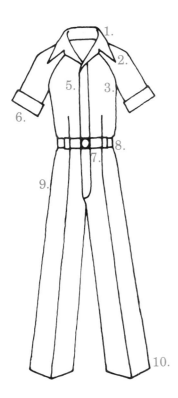

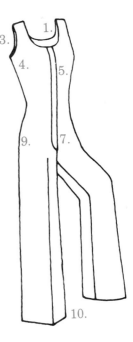

REGULAR GIRLS' SIZES   For girls whose figures are average and undeveloped in bust and hips.

size		7	8	10	12	14	16
height	in	49½–52	52–54	54–56	56–58½	58½–61	61–63
	cm	125.5–132	132–137	137–142	142–148.5	148.5–154.5	154.5–160
chest	in	25½–26½	26½–27½	28–29	29½–30½	31–32	32½–33½
	cm	65–67.5	67.5–70	71–73.5	75–77.5	78.5–81.5	82.5–81
waist	in	22½–23	23–23½	24–24½	25–25½	26–26½	27–27½
	cm	57–58.5	58.5–59.5	61–62	63.5–65	66–67.5	68.5–70
hips	in	27½–28	28–29	29½–30½	31–32½	33–34½	35–36½
	cm	70–71	71–73.5	75–77.5	78.5–82.5	84–87.5	89–92.5

SLIM GIRLS' SIZES   For girls whose figures are slim and undeveloped in bust and hips.

size		7S	8S	10S	12S	14S	16S
height	in	49½–52	52–54	54–56	56–58½	58½–61	61–63
	cm	125.5–132	132–137	137–142	142–148.5	148.5–154.5	154.5–160
chest	in	24–25	25–26	26½–27½	28–29	29½–30½	31–32
	cm	61–63.5	63.5–66	67.5–70	71–73.5	75–77.5	78.5–81.5
waist	in	20½–21	21–21½	22–22½	23–23½	24–24½	25–25½
	cm	52–53.5	53.5–54.5	56–57	58.5–59.5	61–62	63.5–65
hips	in	25½–26	26½–27	27½–28½	29–30½	31–32½	33–34½
	cm	65–66	67.5–68.5	70–72.5	73.5–77.5	78–82.5	84–87.5

CHUBBY GIRLS' SIZES   For girls whose figures are heavier and undeveloped in bust and hips.

size		8½	10½	12½	14½	16½
height	in	52–54	54–56	56–58½	58½–61	61–63
	cm	132–137	137–142	142–148.5	148.5–154.5	154.5–160
chest	in	29–30	30½–31½	32–33	33½–34½	35–36
	cm	73.5–76	77.5–80	81.5–84	85–87.5	89–91.5
waist	in	26½–27	27½–28	28½–29	29½–30	30½–31
	cm	67.5–68.5	70–71	72.5–73.5	75–76	77.5–78.5
hips	in	31–32	32½–33½	34–35½	36–37½	38–39½
	cm	78.5–81.5	82.5–85	86.5–90	91.5–95	96.5–100.5

YOUNG TEEN GIRLS' SIZES For girls whose figures are beginning to develop. Height 4 ft 4½ in to 5 ft 4½ in or 133.5 cm to 164 cm in stocking feet.

size		6	8	10	12	14	16
bust	in	28–29	29–30	30–31	31½–32½	33–34	34½–35½
	cm	71–73.5	73.5–76	76–78.5	80–82.5	84–86.5	87.5–90
waist	in	21½–22½	22½–23½	23½–24½	24½–25½	25½–26½	26½–27½
	cm	54.5–57	57–59.5	59.5–62	62–65	65–67.5	67.5–70
hips	in	30½–31½	31½–32½	32½–33½	34–35	35½–36½	37–38
	cm	77.5–80	80–82.5	82.5–85	86.5–89	90–92.5	94–96.5

JUNIOR SIZES For girls and women who are fully developed and have smaller, more defined waists, higher bustlines, and shorter back waist lengths than Misses. Height 5 ft 2 in to 5 ft 6 in or 152.5 cm to 167.5 cm in stocking feet.

size		5	7	9	11	13	15	17
bust	in	30½–31	31½–32	32½–33½	34–35	35½–36½	37–38	38½–39½
	cm	77.5–78.5	80–81.5	82.5–85	86.5–89	90–92.5	94–96.5	98–100.5
waist	in	21–21½	22–22½	23–24	24½–25½	26–27	27½–28½	29–30
	cm	53.5–54.5	56–57	58.5–61	62–65	66–68.5	70–72.5	73.5–76
hips	in	32½–33	33½–34	34½–35½	36–37	37½–38½	39–40	40½–41½
	cm	82.5–84	85–86.5	87.5–90	91.5–94	95–98	99–105	103–105.5

PETITE JUNIOR SIZES For girls and women whose measurements and body structures are the same as for Juniors, but whose heights are under 5 ft 2 in or 152.5 cm in stocking feet.

TALL JUNIOR SIZES For girls and women whose measurements and body structures are the same as for Juniors, but whose heights are over 5 ft 6 in to 5 ft 11 in or 167.5 cm to 180.5 cm in stocking feet.

MISSES SIZES For girls and women who are fully developed and of average proportions. Height 5 ft 3½ in to 5 ft 7 in or 160 cm to 170 cm in stocking feet.

size		6	8	10	12	14	16	18
bust	in	31–31½	32–32½	33–34	34½–35½	36–37	37½–38½	39–40½
	cm	78.5–80	81.5–82.5	84–86.5	87.5–90	91.5–94	95–98	99–103
waist	in	22–22½	23–23½	24–25	25½–26½	27–28	28½–29½	30–31½
	cm	56–57	58.5–59.5	61–63.5	65–67.5	68.5–71	72.5–75	76–80
hips	in	33–33½	34–34½	35–36	36½–37½	38–39	39½–40½	41–42½
	cm	84–85	86.5–87.5	89–91.5	92.5–95	96.5–99	100.5–103	104–108

continued on next page

continued from page 135

PETITE MISSES SIZES For girls and women whose measurements and body structures are the same as for Misses, but whose heights are under 5 ft 3 in or 160 cm in stocking feet.

TALL MISSES SIZES For girls and women whose measurements and body structures are the same as for Misses, but whose heights are over 5 ft 7 in to 6 ft or 170 cm to 183 cm in stocking feet.

BOYS' SIZES For young boys of average build.

size		6	8	10	12
height	in	44–48	48½–50½	51–54½	55–58½
	cm	112–122	123–128	129.5–138.5	139.5–148.5
weight	lb	up to 53	54–60	61–74	75–88
	kg	up to 24	24.5–27	27.5–33.5	34–40
chest	in	24½–25½	26–27	27½–28½	29–30
	cm	62–65	66–68.5	70–72.5	73.5–76
waist	in	22–22½	23–24	24½–25	25½–26
	cm	56–57	58.5–61	62–63.5	65–66
hips	in	24½–25½	26–27	27½–28½	29–30½
	cm	62–65	66–68.5	70–72.5	73.5–77.5

SLIM BOYS' SIZES For young boys with slender build.

size		6	8	10	12
height	in	44–48	48½–50½	51–54½	55–58½
	cm	112–122	123–128	129.5–138.5	139.5–148.5
weight	lb	up to 47	48–54	55–66	67–78
	kg	up to 21.5	22–24	24.5–31	31.5–35.5
chest	in	23½–24	24½–25½	26–27	27½–29
	cm	59.5–61	62–65	66–68.5	70–73.5
waist	in	20–20½	21–22	22½–23	23½–24
	cm	51–52	53.5–56	57–58.5	59.5–62
hips	in	23½–24	24½–25½	26–27½	28–29½
	cm	59.5–61	62–65	66–70	71–75

HUSKY BOYS' SIZES   For young boys who are heavier than average.

size		8	10	12
height	in	48½–50½	51–54½	55–58½
	cm	123–128	129.5–138.5	139.5–148.5
weight	lb	61–68	69–82	83–96
	kg	27.5–30.5	31–37	37.5–43
chest	in	27–28	28½–29½	30–31½
	cm	67.5–71	72.5–75	76–80
waist	in	25–26	26½–27	27½–28
	cm	63.5–66	67.5–68.5	70–71
hips	in	27½–29	29½–30½	31–32½
	cm	70–73.5	75–77.5	78.5–82.5

TEEN BOYS' SIZES   For boys of average build who are beginning to develop.

size		14	16	18	20	22	24
height	in	59–61½	62–64½	65–66½	67–68½	69–71	69–71
	cm	150–156	157.5–163.5	165–169	170–174	175–180	175–180
weight	lb	89–101	102–116	117–127	128–139	140–153	154–169
	kg	40–45.5	46–52	52.5–57	57.5–62.5	63–69	69.5–86
chest	in	30½–32	32½–33½	34–35	35½–36½	37–38	38½–39½
	cm	77.5–81.5	82.5–85	86.5–89	90–92.5	94–96.5	98–100.5
waist	in	26½–27	27½–28	28½–29	29½–30	30½–31	31½–32
	cm	67.5–68.5	70–71	72.5–73.5	75–76	77.5–78.5	80–81.5
hips	in	31½–32½	33–34½	35–36	36½–37½	38–38½	39–40
	cm	80–82.5	84–87.5	89–91.5	92.5–95	96.5–98	99–101.5

SLIM TEEN BOYS' SIZES   For boys of slender build who are beginning to develop.

size		14	16	18	20
height	in	59–61½	62–64½	65–66½	67–68½
	cm	150–156	157.5–163.5	165–169	170–174
weight	lb	79–91	92–105	106–116	117–127
	kg	35.5–41	41.5–47	47.5–52	52.5–57

chart continued on next page

SLIM TEEN BOYS' SIZES   For boys of slender build who are beginning to develop.

size		14	16	18	20
chest	in	29½–30½	31–32	32½–33½	34–35
	cm	75–77.5	78.5–81.5	82.5–85	86.5–89
waist	in	24½–25	25½–26	26½–27	27½–28
	cm	62–63.5	65–66	67.5–68.5	70–71
hips	in	30–31	31½–33	33½–34½	35–36
	cm	76–77.5	80–84	85–87.5	89–91.5

HUSKY TEEN BOYS' SIZES   For boys of heavier build who are beginning to develop.

size		14	16	18	20
height	in	59–61½	62–64½	65–66½	67–68½
	cm	150–156	157.5–163.5	165–169	170–174
weight	lb	97–113	114–131	132–144	145–157
	kg	43.5–51	51.5–59	59.5–64.5	65–70.5
chest	in	32–33½	34–35½	36–37	37½–38½
	cm	81.5–85	86.5–90	91.5–94	95–98
waist	in	28½–29½	30–30½	31–31½	32–32½
	cm	72.5–75	76–77.5	78.5–80	81.5–82.5
hips	in	33–35	35½–36½	37–38	38½–39½
	cm	84–89	90–92.5	94–96.5	98–100.5

MEN'S SIZES   For boys and men who are fully developed. Height over 5 ft 7 in to 5 ft 11 in or 170 cm to 180.5 cm in stocking feet.

size		34	36	38	40	42	44	46	48
chest	in	34	36	38	40	42	44	46	48
	cm	86.5	91.5	96.5	101.5	106.5	112	117	122
waist	in	30	32	34	36	38	40	42	44
	cm	76	81.5	86.5	91.5	96.5	101.5	106.5	112

SHORT MEN'S SIZES   For men whose body structures and measurements are the same as for Men's Sizes, but whose heights are 5 ft 3 in to 5 ft 7 in or 160 cm to 170 cm in stocking feet.

TALL MEN'S SIZES For men whose body structures and measurements are the same as for Men's Sizes, but whose heights are 5 ft 11 in to 6 ft 3 in or 180.5 cm to 190.5 cm in stocking feet.

EXTRA TALL MEN'S SIZES 40 to 46 For men whose body structures and measurements are the same as for Men's Sizes, but whose heights are over 6 ft 3 in or 190.5 cm in stocking feet.

SKIRTS

Skirts are made in a variety of styles and lengths. You can combine skirts with other garments, such as sweaters, blouses, jackets, and vests, to increase the number of outfits in your wardrobe. Skirts are sized by waist and hip measurements or as for dresses or one-piece outfits. They may also be available in proportioned sizes. If your hips are in proportion to your waist according to the size chart, choose a skirt that fits well in the waistline. If your hips are large in proportion to your waist, you may need to buy a skirt according to your hip size and take it in at the waistline. Some examples of size charts for skirts are on pages 142–143.

1. Waistband fits snugly and lies flat

2. Skirt hangs smoothly at the hip line and is comfortable when sitting down

3. Hem is parallel to the floor

4. Length is attractive for height and is current style

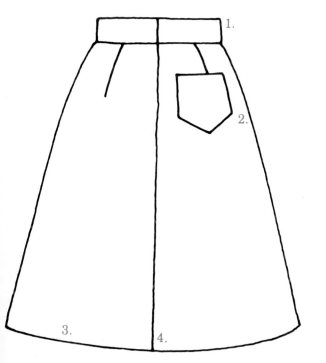

REGULAR GIRLS' SIZES   For girls whose figures are average and undeveloped in the hips.

size		7	8	10	12	14	16
height	in	49½–52	52–54	54–56	56–58½	58½–61	61–63
	cm	125.5–132	132–137	137–142	142–148.5	148.5–154.5	154.5–160
waist	in	22½–23	23–23½	24–24½	25–25½	26–26½	27–27½
	cm	57–58.5	58.5–59.5	61–62	63.5–65	66–67.5	68.5–70
hips	in	27½–28	28–29	29½–30½	31–32½	33–34½	35–36½
	cm	70–71	71–73.5	75–77.5	78.5–82.5	84–87.5	89–92.5

SLIM GIRLS' SIZES   For girls whose figures are slim and undeveloped in the hips.

size		7S	8S	10S	12S	14S	16S
height	in	49½–52	52–54	54–56	56–58½	58½–61	61–63
	cm	125.5–132	132–137	137–142	142–148.5	148.5–154.5	154.5–160
waist	in	20½–21	21–21½	22–22½	23–23½	24–24½	25–25½
	cm	52–53.5	53.5–54.5	56–57	58.5–59.5	61–62	63.5–65
hips	in	25½–26	26½–27	27½–28½	29–30½	31–32½	33–34½
	cm	65–66	67.5–68.5	70–72.5	73.5–77.5	78–82.5	84–87.5

YOUNG TEEN GIRLS' SIZES   For girls whose figures are beginning to develop. Height 4 ft 4½ in to 5 ft 4½ in or 133.5 cm to 164 cm in stocking feet.

size		6	8	10	12	14	16
waist	in	21½–22½	22½–23½	23½–24½	24½–25½	25½–26½	26½–27½
	cm	54.5–57	57–59.5	59.5–62	62–65	65–67.5	67.5–70
hips	in	30½–31½	31½–32½	32½–33½	34–35	35½–36½	37–38
	cm	77.5–80	80–82.5	82.5–85	86.5–89	90–92.5	94–96.5

CHUBBY GIRLS' SIZES   For girls whose figures are heavier and undeveloped in the hips.

size		8½	10½	12½	14½	16½
height	in	52–54	54–56	56–58½	58½–61	61–63
	cm	132–137	137–142	142–148.5	148.5–154.5	154.5–160

CHUBBY GIRLS' SIZES   For girls whose figures are heavier and undeveloped in the hips.

size		8½	10½	12½	14½	16½
waist	in	26½–27	27½–28	28½–29	29½–30	30½–31
	cm	67.5–68.5	70–71	72.5–73.5	75–76	77.5–78.5
hips	in	31–32	32½–33½	34–35½	36–37½	38–39½
	cm	78.5–81.5	82.5–85	86.5–90	91.5–95	96.5–100.5

JUNIOR SIZES   For girls and women who are fully developed and have smaller, more defined waists, higher bustlines, and shorter back waist lengths than Misses. Height 5 ft 2 in to 5 ft 6 in or 152.5 cm to 167.5 cm in stocking feet.

size		5	7	9	11	13	15	17
waist	in	21–21½	22–22½	23–24	24½–25½	26–27	27½–28½	29–30
	cm	53.5–54.5	56–57	58.5–61	62–65	66–68.5	70–72.5	73.5–76
hips	in	32½–33	33½–34	34½–35½	36–37	37½–38½	39–40	40½–41½
	cm	82.5–84	85–86.5	87.5–90	91.5–94	95–98	99–105	103–105.5

PETITE JUNIOR SIZES   For girls and women whose measurements and body structures are the same as for Juniors, but whose heights are under 5 ft 2 in or 152.5 cm in stocking feet.

TALL JUNIOR SIZES   For girls and women whose measurements and body structures are the same as for Juniors, but whose heights are over 5 ft 6 in to 5 ft 11 in or 167.5 cm to 180.5 cm in stocking feet.

MISSES SIZES   For girls and women who are fully developed and of average proportions. Height 5 ft 3½ in to 5 ft 7 in or 161 cm to 170 cm in stocking feet.

size		6	8	10	12	14	16	18
waist	in	22–22½	23–23½	24–25	25½–26½	27–28	28½–29½	30–31½
	cm	56–57	58.5–59.5	61–63.5	65–67.5	68.5–71	72.5–75	76–80
hips	in	33–33½	34–34½	35–36	36½–37½	38–39	39½–40½	41–42½
	cm	84–85	86.5–87.5	89–91.5	92.5–95	96.5–99	100.5–103	104–108

PETITE MISSES SIZES   For girls and women whose measurements and body structures are the same as for Misses, but whose heights are under 5 ft 3 in or 160 cm in stocking feet.

TALL MISSES SIZES   For girls and women whose measurements and body structures are the same as for Misses, but whose heights are over 5 ft 7 in to 6 ft or 170 cm to 183 cm in stocking feet.

BLOUSES, SHIRTS, AND TOPS

Blouses and shirts and tops can also add to the number of outfits in your wardrobe if they are planned to coordinate with other garments. They can be worn with skirts, jumpers, vests, pants, and jeans to name a few examples.

Blouses, tops, and shirts for girls and women are sized in different ways. They may have the size listed as the bust or chest measurement or be listed as small, medium, or large. Blouses, tops, and shirts for girls and women may also be sized the same as one-piece outfits.

Shirts and tops for boys and men are sized in different ways also. Sport shirts and some dress shirts may be sized as small, medium, large or extra large. Many dress shirts are sized according to neck size and sleeve length. Still other shirts may be sized by chest measurements or they may be sized the same as one-piece outfits. Some size charts that are commonly used for shirts, blouses, and tops are on pages 145–148.

1. Neckline fits smoothly and comfortably

2. Shoulder length is comfortable

3. Armhole does not bind

4. Bust darts are at fullest part of bust

5. Enough ease across the bust or chest and through the back; no pulling or stretching

6. Sleeves are comfortable and an attractive length

7. Bottom stays tucked in when moving

EXAMPLES OF SIZE CHARTS FOR BLOUSES, SHIRTS, AND TOPS

GIRLS' SIZES For girls who have not begun to develop.

size		small	medium	large
chest	in	26–27½	28–30½	31–32
	cm	66–70	71–77.5	78.5–81.5
height	in	49½–53½	54–58	58½–60½
	cm	125–136	137–147.5	148.5–153.5

GIRLS' SIZES For girls who have not begun to develop.

size		7	8	10	12	14	16
chest	in	25½–26½	26½–27½	28–29	29½–30½	31–32	32½–33½
	cm	65–67.5	67.5–70	71–73.5	75–77.5	78.5–81.5	82.5–85

TEEN GIRLS' SIZES For girls whose figures are beginning to develop.

size		small	medium	large
bust	in	28½–30	30½–32½	33–34
	cm	72.5–76	77.5–82.5	84–86.5

TEEN GIRLS' SIZES For girls whose figures are beginning to develop.

size		6	8	10	12	14	16
bust	in	28–29	29–30	30–31	31½–32½	33–34	34½–35½
	cm	71–73.5	73.5–76	76–78.5	80–82.5	84–86.5	87.5–90

JUNIOR SIZES For girls and women who are fully developed and have smaller, more defined waists, higher bustlines, and shorter back waist lengths than Misses.

size		5	7	9	11	13	15	17
bust	in	30½–31	31½–32	32½–33½	34–35	35½–36½	37–38	38½–39½
	cm	77.5–78.5	80–81.5	82.5–85	86.5–89	90–92.5	94–96.5	98–100.5

chart continued on next page

JUNIOR SIZES For girls and women who are fully developed and have smaller, more defined waists, higher bustlines, and shorter back waist lengths than Misses.

size		small	medium	large
bust	in	30½–32	32½–35	35½–38
	cm	77.5–81.5	82.5–89	90–96.5

size	small (5–7)	medium (9–11)	large (13–15)

MISSES SIZES For girls and women who are fully developed and of average proportions.

size		6	8	10	12	14	16	18
bust	in	31–31½	32–32½	33–34	34½–35½	36–37	37½–38½	39–40½
	cm	78.5–80	81.5–82.5	84–86.5	87.5–90	91.5–94	95–98	99–103

MISSES SIZES For girls and women who are fully developed and of average proportions.

size		small	medium	large
bust	in	30–32	34–36	38–40
	cm	76–81.5	86.5–91.5	96.5–101.5

size	small (8–10)	medium (12–14)	large (16–18)

MISSES SIZES For girls and women who are fully developed and of average proportions.

size		30	32	34	36	38	40
bust	in	32–32½	33–34	34½–35½	36–37	37½–38½	39–40½
	cm	81.5–82.5	84–86.5	87.5–90	91.5–94	95–98	99–103

BOYS' SIZES For young boys of average build.

size		6	8	10	12
height	in	44–48	48½–50½	51–54½	55–58½
	cm	112–122	123–128	129.5–138.5	139.5–148.5
weight	lb	up to 53	54–60	61–74	75–88
	kg	up to 24	24.5–27	27.5–33.5	34–40
chest	in	24½–25½	26–27	27½–28½	29–30
	cm	62–65	66–68.5	70–72.5	73.5–76

TEEN BOYS' SIZES For boys of average build who are beginning to develop.

size		14	16	18	20	22	24
chest	in	32	33	34	36	38	40
	cm	81.5	84	86.5	91.5	96.5	101.5

TEEN BOYS' SIZES For boys of average build who are beginning to develop.

size		small	medium	large
chest	in	24½–27	27½–30	30½–33
	cm	62–68.5	70–76	77.5–84

MEN'S SIZES For boys and men who are fully developed.

sizes are neck and sleeve measurements, such as 15/32 or 16/34

neck	in	14½	15	15½	16	16½	17
sleeve	in	32	32	32	32		
		33	33	33	33	33	33
			34	34	34	34	34
			35	35	35	35	35

sizes are neck and sleeve measurements, such as 38/84 or 42/89

neck	cm	37	38	39.5	40.5	42	43
sleeve	cm	81.5	81.5	81.5	81.5		
		84	84	84	84	84	84
			86.5	86.5	86.5	86.5	86.5
			89	89	89	89	89

tapered cut: for slender build   regular cut: for average build   full cut: for heavy build

MEN'S SIZES For boys and men who are fully developed.

size		small	medium	large	extra large
neck	in	14–14½	15–15½	16–16½	17–17½
	cm	35.5–37	38–39.5	40.5–42	43–44.5

chart continued on next page

MEN'S SIZES   For boys and men who are fully developed.

size		small	medium	large	extra large
chest	in	34–36	38–40	42–44	46–48
	cm	86.5–91.5	96.5–101.5	106.5–112	117–122

SWEATERS

Sweaters are made in many styles and lengths and of many fibers and fabrics. They can be combined successfully with other garments to add to your wardrobe.

Sweaters for girls and women are usually sized according to bust or chest measurement or are labeled small, medium, or large. Sweaters for boys and men are sized similarly. Labels usually state the chest measurement or show sizes of small, medium, large, or extra large. Sweaters for both men and women may be made in proportioned sizes. Here are guidelines for checking the fit of sweaters.

1. Neckline fits smoothly and comfortably

2. Shoulder length is comfortable

3. Armhole does not bind

4. Fits comfortably across bust or chest; no pulling or stretching

5. Sleeves are comfortable and an attractive length

6. Front opening stays neatly closed; no gapping between buttonholes

7. Rib knit at lower edges fits snugly

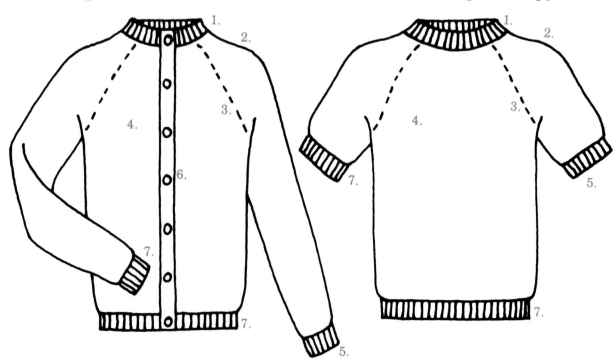

SLACKS, JEANS, AND PANTS

Slacks, jeans, pants, and suit trousers are made in a variety of styles and fabrics. They may be part of an outfit, such as a suit, or they may be separate items. As with blouses and shirts, skirts, and sweaters, they can be combined with other garments in your wardrobe.

Slacks, jeans, and suit trousers for boys and men are sized according to sizes for one-piece outfits or according to waist measurement and inseam measurement. *Inseam measurement* is the length of the inside seam of the pant leg. Labels may show the inseam measurement in inches or as *short, medium,* or *long.*

Pants and jeans for girls and women may be sized according to waist size as for skirts or according to sizes for one-piece outfits. They may also be sized according to waist, hip, and inseam measurements. Often slacks and jeans are available in proportioned sizes. As with skirts, if your hips are in proportion to your

waist according to the size chart, choose pants or jeans that fit well in the waistline. If your hips are large in proportion to your waist, you may need to buy pants or jeans according to your hip size and take them in at the waist.

1. Waist fits snugly at waist (or at hips if hip-huggers)

2. Fits smoothly through hips and seat

3. Center front and back seams are right length; no pulling or stretching when moving; comfortable when seated

4. Leg length is attractive for height and is current style

Some sample size charts for slacks, jeans, pants, and suit trousers are shown on pages 150–154.

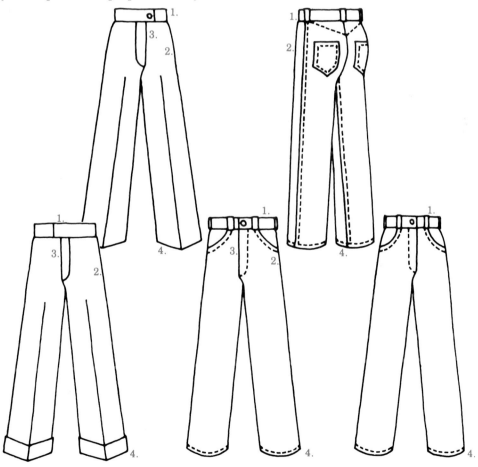

EXAMPLES OF SIZE CHARTS FOR SLACKS, PANTS, AND JEANS

GIRLS' SIZES For girls whose figures are average and undeveloped in the hips.

size		7	8	10	12	14	16
hips	in	27½–28	28–29	29½–30½	31–32½	33–34½	35–36½
	cm	70–71	71–73.5	75–77.5	78.5–82.5	84–87.5	89–92.5

YOUNG TEEN GIRLS' SIZES For girls whose figures are beginning to develop.

size		22	23	24	25	26
waist	in	22	23	24	25	26
hips	in	31–31½	32–32½	33–33½	34–35	35½–36
inseam	in	29 or 31 for all sizes				

size		56	58.5	61	63.5	66
waist	cm	56	58.5	61	63.5	66
hips	cm	78.5–80	81.5–82.5	84–85	86.5–89	90–91.5
inseam	cm	73.5 or 78.5 for all sizes				

JUNIOR SIZES For girls and women who are fully developed and have smaller, more defined waists, higher bustlines, and shorter back waist lengths than Misses.

size		5	7	9	11	13	15	17
waist	in	21–21½	22–22½	23–24	24½–25½	26–27	27½–28½	29–30
	cm	53.5–54.5	56–57	58.5–61	62–65	66–68.5	70–71	73.5–76
hips	in	32½–33	33½–34	34½–35½	36–37	37½–38½	39–40	40½–41½
	cm	82.5–84	85–86.5	87.5–90	91.5–94	95–98	99–101.5	103–105.5
inseam	in	31 or 33 for all sizes						
	cm	78.5 or 84 for all sizes						

MISSES SIZES For girls and women who are fully developed and of average proportions. Height 5 ft 3½ in to 5 ft 7 in or 161 to 170 cm in stocking feet.

size		6	8	10	12	14	16	18
waist	in	22–22½	23–23½	24–25	25½–26½	27–28	28½–29½	30–31½
	cm	56–57	58.5–59.5	61–63.5	65–67.5	68.5–71	72.5–75	76–80

MISSES SIZES For girls and women who are fully developed and of average proportions. Height 5 ft 3½ in to 5 ft 7 in or 161 to 170 cm in stocking feet.

size		6	8	10	12	14	16	18
hips	in	33–33½	34–34½	35–36	36½–37½	38–39	39½–40½	41–42½
	cm	84–85	86.5–87.5	89–91.5	92.5–95	96.5–99	100.5–103	104–108

PETITE MISSES SIZES For girls and women whose measurements and body structures are the same as for Misses, but whose heights are under 5 ft 3 in or 160 cm in stocking feet.

TALL MISSES SIZES For girls and women whose measurements and body structures are the same as for Misses, but whose heights are over 5 ft 7 in to 6 ft or 170 cm to 183 cm in stocking feet.

BOYS' SIZES For young boys of average build.

size		6	8	10	12
height	in	44–48	48½–50½	51–54½	55–58½
	cm	112–122	123–128	129.5–138.5	139.5–148.5
weight	lb	up to 53	54–60	61–74	75–88
	kg	up to 24	24.5–27	27.5–33.5	34–40
waist	in	22–22½	23–24	24½–25	25½–26
	cm	56–57	58.5–61	62–63.5	65–66

SLIM BOYS' SIZES For young boys with slender build.

size		6	8	10	12
height	in	44–48	48½–50½	51–54½	55–58½
	cm	112–122	123–128	129.5–138.5	139.5–148.5
weight	lb	up to 47	48–54	55–56	67–78
	kg	up to 21.5	22–24	24.5–31	31.5–35.5
waist	in	20–20½	21–22	22½–23	23½–24
	cm	51–52	53.5–56	57–58.5	59.5–62

continued on next page

HUSKY BOYS' SIZES   For young boys who are heavier than average.

size		8	10	12
height	in	48½–50½	51–54½	55–58½
	cm	123–128	129.5–138.5	139.5–148.5
weight	lb	61–68	69–82	83–96
	kg	27.5–30.5	31–37	37.5–43
waist	in	25–26	26½–27	27½–28
	cm	63.5–66	67.5–68.5	70–71

TEEN BOYS' SIZES   For boys who are beginning to develop.

size is waist and inseam measurements, such as 27/30 or 30/31

waist	in	26	27	28	29	30	31	32
inseam	in	29	28	29	30	31	30	31
			30	31	32	33	32	33
				33	34		34	

size is waist and inseam measurements, such as 71/84 or 76/78.5

waist	cm	66	68.5	71	73.5	76	78.5	81.5
inseam	cm	73.5	71	73.5	77.5	78.5	77.5	78.5
			76	78.5	81.5	84	81.5	84
				84	86.5		86.5	

TEEN BOYS' SIZES   For boys who are beginning to develop.

size is waist and inseam measurements, such as 31/29 or 40/34

waist	in	30	31	32	33	34	36	38	40	42	44
inseam	in			28	28	28	28	28	28	28	28
		29	29	29	29	29	29	29	29	29	29
		30	30	30	30	30	30	30	30	30	30
		31	31	31	31	31	31	31	31	31	31
		32	32	32	32	32	32	32	32	32	32
		33	33	33	33	33	33	33	33	33	33
				34	34	34	34	34	34	34	34
				35	35	35	35	35	35	35	35
				36	36	36	36	36	36	36	36
				37	37	37	37	37	37	37	37

TEEN BOYS' SIZES For boys who are beginning to develop.

size is waist and inseam measurements, such as 76/84 or 91.5/76

waist	cm	76	78.5	81.5	84	86.5	91.5	96.5	101.5	106.5	112
inseam	cm			71	71	71	71	71	71	71	71
		73.5	73.5	73.5	73.5	73.5	73.5	73.5	73.5	73.5	73.5
		76	76	76	76	76	76	76	76	76	76
		78.5	78.5	78.5	78.5	78.5	78.5	78.5	78.5	78.5	78.5
		81.5	81.5	81.5	81.5	81.5	81.5	81.5	81.5	81.5	81.5
		84	84	84	84	84	84	84	84	84	84
				86.5	86.5	86.5	86.5	86.5	86.5	86.5	86.5
				89	89	89	89	89	89	89	89
				91.5	91.5	91.5	91.5	91.5	91.5	91.5	91.5
				94	94	94	94	94	94	94	94

MEN'S TRIM SIZES For boys and men who are fully developed and of average build.

size is waist and inseam measurements, such as 30/S or 36/M

waist	in	30	32	34	36	38
inseam	in	S (29½)	S (29½)	S (29½)	S (29½)	S (29½)
		M (31)	M (31)	M (31)	M (31)	M (31)
			L (33)	L (33)	L (33)	L (33)

size is waist and inseam measurements, such as 76/S or 86.5/M

waist	cm	76	81.5	86.5	91.5	96.5
inseam	cm	S (75)	S (75)	S (75)	S (75)	S (75)
		M (78.5)	M (78.5)	M (78.5)	M (78.5)	M (78.5)
			L (84)	L (84)	L (84)	L (84)

MEN'S REGULAR SIZES For boys and men who are fully developed and heavier through the seat and legs.

size is waist and inseam measurements, such as 36/M or 42/L

waist	in	36	38	40	42	44
inseam	in	S (29)	S (29)	S (29)	S (29)	S (29)
		M (30)	M (30)	M (30)	M (30)	M (30)
		L (32)	L (32)	L (32)	L (32)	

chart continued on next page

MEN'S REGULAR SIZES   For boys and men who are fully developed and heavier through the seat and legs.

size is waist and inseam measurements, such as 91.5/M or 101.5/L

waist	cm	91.5	96.5	101.5	106.5	112
	cm	S (73.5)	S (73.5)	S (73.5)	S (73.5)	S (73.5)
		M (76)	M (76)	M (76)	M (76)	M (76)
		L (81.5)	L (81.5)	L (81.5)	L (81.5)	

GIRLS' AND WOMEN'S   Conversion charts for those who buy boys' and men's jeans.

teen boy's waist size	in	25	26	27	28	29	30	31	32
girls' hips	in	29–30	30½–31½	32–33½	34–35	35½–36½	37–37½	38–39	39½–41½

men's waist size	in	29	30	31	32	33	34	36
women's hips	in	34–35	35½–36½	37–37½	38–38½	39–39½	40–40½	41–42

teen boy's waist size	cm	63.5	66	68.5	71	73.5	76	78.5	81.5
girls' hips	cm	73.5–76	77.5–80	81.5–85	86.5–89	90–92.5	94–95	96.5–99	100.5–105.5

men's waist size	cm	73.5	76	78.5	81.5	84	86.5	91.5
women's hips	cm	86.5–89	90–92.5	94–95	96.5–98	99–100.5	101.5–103	104–106.5

COATS AND JACKETS

Coats and jackets are sometimes parts of outfits, such as suits, or they may be separate items designed to combine with other garments. Jackets and coats for girls and women may be sized as one-piece outfits are sized (see pages 136–141) or according to chest or bust measurement. Labels may also show sizes as small, medium, or large. Many styles are available in proportioned sizes. Jackets and coats for boys and men are sized in the same way. Some examples of size charts for jackets and coats begin at the bottom of page 155 and continue through page 158.

Here are nine guidelines to use when checking the fit of coats and jackets.

1. Neckline fits smoothly, comfortably

2. Shoulder length is comfortable

3. Armhole does not bind

4. Bust darts are at the fullest part of the bust

5. Enough ease across the bust or chest and through the back; no pulling or stretching

6. Sleeves are an attractive length and are comfortable

7. Waistline is at the waist

8. Hem is parallel to the floor

9. Length is attractive for height and is current style

EXAMPLES OF SIZE CHARTS FOR COATS AND JACKETS

GIRLS' SIZES For girls who have not begun to develop.

size		small	medium	large
chest	in	26–27½	28–30½	31–32
	cm	66–70	71–77.5	78.5–81.5

chart continued on next page

EXAMPLES OF SIZE CHARTS FOR COATS AND JACKETS *chart continued from page 155*

GIRLS' SIZES   For girls who have not begun to develop.

size		small	medium	large
height	in	49½–53½	54–58	58½–60½
	cm	125–136	137–147.5	148.5–153.5

sizes	small (7–8)	medium (10–12)	large (14)

TEEN GIRLS' SIZES   For girls who have begun to develop.

sizes	small (6–8)	medium (10–12)	large (14)

JUNIOR SIZES   For girls and women who are fully developed and have smaller, more defined waists, higher bustlines, and shorter back waist lengths than Misses.

size		5	7	9	11	13	15	17
bust	in	30½–31	31½–32	32½–33½	34–35	35½–36½	37–38	38½–39½
	cm	77.5–78.5	80–81.5	82.5–85	86.5–89	90–92.5	94–96.5	98–100.5

sizes	small (5–7)	medium (9–11)	large (13–15)

MISSES SIZES   For girls and women who are fully developed and of average proportions.

size		6	8	10	12	14	16	18
bust	in	31–31½	32–32½	33–34	34½–35½	36–37	37½–38½	39–40½
	cm	78.5–80	81.5–82.5	84–86.5	87.5–90	91.5–94	95–98	99–103

MISSES SIZES   For girls and women who are fully developed and of average proportions.

size		small	medium	large
bust	in	30–32	34–36	38–40
	cm	76–81.5	86.5–91.5	96.5–101.5

BOYS' SIZES   For boys who have not begun to develop.

size		6	8	10	12
height	in	44–48	48½–50½	51–54½	55–58½
	cm	112–122	123–128	129.5–138.5	139.5–148.5

BOYS' SIZES For boys who have not begun to develop.

size		6	8	10	12
weight	lb	up to 53	54–60	61–74	75–88
	kg	up to 24	24.5–27	27.5–33.5	34–40
chest	in	25	26½	28	30
	cm	63.5	67.5	71	76

SLIM BOYS' SIZES For slim boys who have not begun to develop.

size		6	8	10	12
height	in	44–48	48½–50½	51–54½	55–58½
	cm	112–122	123–128	129.5–138.5	139.5–143.5
weight	lb	up to 47	48–54	55–66	67–78
	kg	up to 21.5	22–24	24.5–31	31.5–35.5
chest	in	23½–24	24½–25½	26–27	27½–29
	cm	59.5–61	62–65	66–68.5	70–73.5

HUSKY BOYS' SIZES For heavier boys who have not begun to develop.

size		8	10	12
height	in	48½–50½	51–54½	55–58½
	cm	123–128	129.5–138.5	139.5–148.5
weight	lb	61–68	69–82	83–96
	kg	27.5–30.5	31–37	37.5–43
chest	in	27–28	28½–29½	30–31½
	cm	68.5–71	72.5–75	76–80

SLIM TEEN BOYS' SIZES For slim boys who have begun to develop.

size		14	16	18	20
height	in	59–62	63–64	65–66	67–68
	cm	150–157.5	160–162.5	165–167.5	170–172.5
weight	lb	80–90	91–105	106–116	117–127
	kg	36–40.5	41–47	47.5–52	52.5–57
chest	in	30	32	33	34
	cm	76	81.5	84	86.5

continued on next page

TEEN BOYS' SIZES   For boys who have begun to develop.

size		14	16	18	20	22	24
height	in	59–62	63–64	65–66	67–68	69–71	69–71
	cm	150–157.5	160–162.5	165–167.5	170–172.5	175–180.5	175–180.5
weight	lb	91–105	106–116	117–127	128–139	140–153	154–169
	kg	41–47	47.5–52	52.5–57	57.5–62.5	63–69	69.5–76
chest	in	32	33	34	36	38	40
	cm	81.5	84	86.5	91.5	96.5	101.5

BOYS' AND TEEN BOYS' SIZES

size	small (6–8)	medium (10–12)	large (14–16)	extra large (18–20)	extra-extra large (22–24)

MEN'S SIZES   For boys and men who are fully developed.

size is chest measurement and length, such as 36 short or 40 long

chest	in	36	37	38	39	40	42	44	46
short		X		X		X	X		
medium		X	X	X	X	X	X	X	X
long				X	X	X	X	X	X

size is chest measurement and length, such as 94 medium or 99 long

chest	cm	91.5	94	96.5	99	101.5	106.5	112	117
short		X		X		X	X		
medium		X	X	X	X	X	X	X	X
long				X	X	X	X	X	X

MEN'S SIZES   For boys and men who are fully developed.

size		small	medium	large	extra large
chest	in	36–38	39–41	42–44	45–47
	cm	91.5–96.5	99–104	106.5–112	114.5–119.5

PUTTING IT TOGETHER

1 Explain why garments labeled the same size may not fit you the same.
2 Give some reasons why it is important to try garments on before you buy.

TAKING ANOTHER STEP

1 Look through your closet and dresser and write down all the clothes you have. Are there some you don't wear? Why? Make a plan of all the clothes you can wear. See how many different outfits you can create by combining different separates and accessories. Make a plan for getting any new items.
2 Think of a garment you plan to buy or would like to buy. Check different stores to find out prices and ways you can pay. Look at prices of the same brand name in different stores to see if there is a difference in price. Find out about services which the stores offer. How do these services affect prices? What are the different ways to pay for the item? Find out if you can get a discount if you pay cash.
3 Prepare a bulletin board which illustrates clothing made of knitted fabrics.
4 Observe a demonstration of the weaving process on a hand loom.
5 Examine samples of the three basic weaves with a magnifying lens. Explain how they differ in appearance. What are some of the other characteristics of fabrics which have been made by each of these basic weaves?
6 Examine samples of knit fabrics with a magnifying lens. After studying close-up views of knits explain how "interlooping" yarns differ from weaving yarns.
7 Report the differences between water-repellent and waterproof finishes. Point out the advantages and disadvantages of each of these two types of fabric finishes. You might show two all-weather coats with different finishes, and demonstrate the effectiveness of each coat in keeping the wearer dry. You might find out the price of renewing a water-repellent finish.
8 Work in groups to collect a variety of clothing labels that state the trade names of fabric finishes. For ideas consult the chart on pages 121–122. The labels might be grouped together according to the type of finish. Have a contest to see which group can collect labels with all the trademarks listed on the chart.
9 Keep a notebook of ads. Show which ones are informative and the kinds of helpful information given. Show which ones are mainly trying to get the consumer to buy.
10 Make a display of labels and hang tags. Show different ways you can save them and organize them so they are useful to you after they have been removed from the garment.

continued on next page

continued from page 159

11 Make a bulletin board to display sample labels and hang tags. Show the information on each that is required by law. Also point out information that is useful but not required by law.

12 Collect information about a type of garment or accessory you expect to purchase soon, such as socks, slips, sweater, shirt, or jeans.

13 During the last twelve months how many of the following items of clothing did you purchase by yourself with no suggestions or advice from anyone?

    coats
    sweaters
    raincoats
    skirts
    slacks, pants, or jeans
    blouses or shirts
    dresses
    shorts, other sportswear
    socks
    hosiery
    underwear
    gloves
    scarves
    other items (list these)

If you paid for any of the items purchased from your earnings, allowance, or gifts of money, how much did you spend?

14 Do you ever buy clothing which you pay for from earnings, allowances, or gifts, taking suggestions or advice from other people? Who helps you with your choices?

CARE
SHOWS

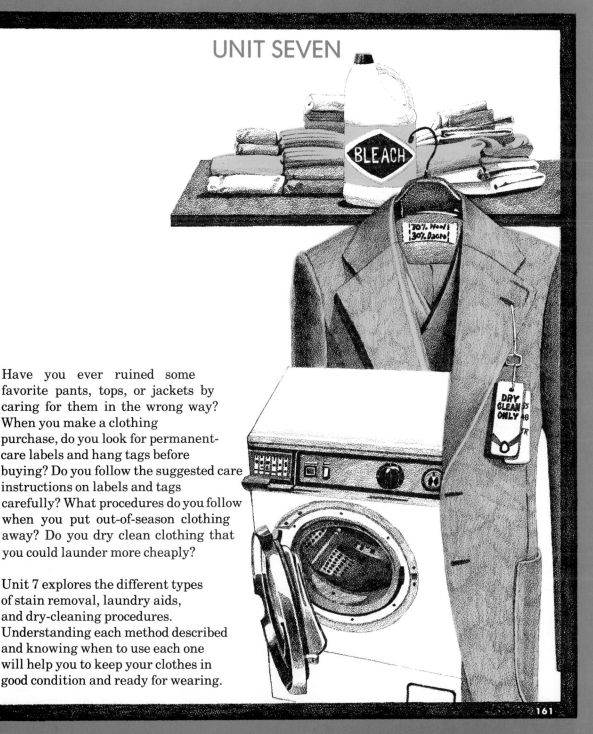

Have you ever ruined some favorite pants, tops, or jackets by caring for them in the wrong way? When you make a clothing purchase, do you look for permanent-care labels and hang tags before buying? Do you follow the suggested care instructions on labels and tags carefully? What procedures do you follow when you put out-of-season clothing away? Do you dry clean clothing that you could launder more cheaply?

Unit 7 explores the different types of stain removal, laundry aids, and dry-cleaning procedures. Understanding each method described and knowing when to use each one will help you to keep your clothes in good condition and ready for wearing.

LESSON ONE
FACTORS THAT AFFECT CLOTHES CARE

◈ absorbency

resiliency

heat sensitivity

strength

 some ways fiber content affects clothes care

some ways fabric construction affects clothes care

some ways fabric finishes affect clothes care

some ways garment construction affects clothes care

The most satisfactory care for a particular garment is not determined by any one thing. Usually a combination of several characteristics of a garment determines the care it should have. The fiber content, the fabric construction, the fabric finish, the design, and the garment's construction are all factors that affect the way in which a garment should be cared for. Information about each one of these factors will help you understand the care directions attached to a specific garment. Also, this information may help you care for garments when exact directions are not available.

FIBER CONTENT

The kind of fiber that is used to make a fabric is one thing that affects the care a garment needs. This is because of the characteristics which different fibers have.

Moisture absorbency, or the ability to absorb water, is one characteristic of fibers. Many manufactured fibers commonly used in clothing do not absorb water. Polyester, nylon, and spandex are examples of these fibers.

When fabrics made of these fibers are washed, water cleans the outside of the fibers but does not penetrate inside. This gives fabrics of these fibers the ability to dry quickly. In contrast, the natural fibers (cotton, wool, silk, and flax) absorb water readily. Fabrics made of these fibers take longer to dry.

Although many manufactured fibers do not absorb water, they may absorb oily stains. Once an oily spot is in the fiber, it is difficult to remove because water and soap will not penetrate the fiber to remove the stain. An oily stain is likely to be permanent unless the fabric has been treated to resist this type of stain.

Another characteristic of fibers is *resiliency.* This is the ability of a fiber to return to its original size and shape after it is twisted or crumpled. Most manufactured fibers have good resiliency, or are wrinkle-resistant. The natural fibers wool and silk are more wrinkle-resistant than cotton and flax, but less resilient than some of the manufactured fibers. Fabrics of 100 percent cotton or of flax fibers are not wrinkle-resistant unless they are specially treated. They require also ironing after washing, and may require touch-up pressing between wearings.

Strength is another fiber characteristic that affects garment care. Cotton and flax and most of the manufactured fibers are strong when either wet or dry. This means they wear well and are not weakened in washing. Wool and silk fibers are much weaker when wet than when dry. Garments of these fibers must be handled carefully in order to prevent damage if they are washed. This is one reason it is often recommended that garments made of wool and silk be dry cleaned rather than washed.

Many fibers are *heat sensitive,* or damaged by high temperatures in washing, drying, or ironing. Most manufactured fibers will melt when ironed at too high a temperature. Using very hot water in washing garments of these fibers or drying them at too high a temperature or leaving them in the dryer too long can set in wrinkles. These wrinkles may not press out and the garment may need to be washed and dried again to remove the wrinkles. Heat is also damaging to wool fibers since it can cause them to shrink. This is especially true when heat is combined with moisture and agitation as in washing. This is another reason it is often recommended that wool garments be dry cleaned.

Often, fibers are combined in making a fabric. This is so the fabric will have some characteristics of each fiber. For example, cotton and polyester fibers are commonly combined in one fabric. The fabric will dry faster and will have more wrinkle-resistance than a fabric of 100 percent cotton. A garment of cotton and polyester will be more comfortable to wear than one of 100 percent polyester because the cotton will absorb moisture from the skin.

The care required for *blends,* that is, fabrics made of more than one fiber, depends on the fibers making up the fabric. If there is no care label, a general suggestion to follow is to care for the garment according to the most sensitive fiber in it. For example, if a fabric is a blend of wool and nylon, it should be handled carefully when wet because of the wool fiber content. Twisting or stretching would not damage the nylon fibers, but it might very well damage the wool fibers.

FABRIC CONSTRUCTION

The *construction of a fabric,* or the way it is made, is a second factor that affects garment care. The two most common types of fabric construction used for clothing are weaving and knitting.

The looseness or firmness of the weave or knit in a fabric affects the care the fabric needs. A closely woven or firmly knitted fabric will withstand more handling without stretching than one that is loosely woven or knit. When there are few yarns per square inch, fabrics tend to pull apart easily. Such fabrics need careful handling in hanging up, washing, drying, and pressing.

Garments of knitted fabrics are often easier to care for than garments of woven fabrics. The knitted construction gives fabric more resiliency, or wrinkle-resistance, than the woven construction. This means that most knitted garments can be stored flat or folded in a drawer or box without becoming wrinkled. Most garments which are made of woven fabrics need to be hung up in order to prevent wrinkles from forming.

Because of their resiliency, garments made of knitted fabric usually do not need to be pressed between wearings as garments of woven fabric often do. Firmly woven fabrics generally do not stretch out of shape when being pressed. However, knitted fabrics may require extra care in pressing in order to prevent stretching the garment out of shape. This is because the knitted fabrics generally have more "give" than do woven fabrics.

Of course, the fiber content, fabric finishes, and garment construction also affect the care garments need. So some woven fabrics may require less care than some knitted fabrics.

A *layered fabric* is made when two layers of fabric are permanently attached together. Sometimes two woven fabrics or two knitted fabrics are fastened together; sometimes a knitted fabric and a woven fabric may be fastened together.

Care of layered fabrics depends on the construction of the two layers of fabric as well as the fiber content, fabric finish, and garment construction. Some dry-cleaning solvents may dissolve the substance used to fasten the two layers of fabric together. For this reason it is important to follow directions for care of the garment. High temperatures or improper pressing may also damage the substance holding the layers together.

FABRIC FINISHES

Some undesirable characteristics of fibers have been overcome by special finishes given to fabrics made from these fibers. For example, there are shrink-resistant finishes for fabrics that shrink and wrinkle-resistant finishes for fabrics that wrinkle easily. These and other finishes usually make it easier to care for a garment. However, like most conveniences, fabric finishes are not always perfect. Clothing may be slightly uncomfortable

because of finishes which have been applied. For example, a water-repellent finish may close the spaces between yarns in a fabric, making it impossible for perspiration to evaporate. As a result you feel warm in a water-repellent garment because of unevaporated perspiration on the skin.

Some fabric finishes are designed to last as long as the garment. Others may need to be reapplied when the garment is cleaned. How long a finish lasts or how effective it is will depend on the care the garment receives. A fabric which has special finishes may need different care from that of the same fabric without finishes. For example, white cotton fabric can be bleached with chlorine bleach. However, if white cotton has been treated with a permanent-press finish, bleaching with chlorine bleach will eventually destroy that finish. Another type of bleach should be chosen for use.

Permanent-press garments are treated to hold their original shapes, pleats, and creases. When cared for properly, no ironing should be needed. Proper care for a permanent-press garment includes rinsing in cold water. This is because warm or hot water sets in wrinkles which are hard to remove. Also, if permanent-press garments are machine-dried, removing them from the dryer as soon as the cycle is finished will prevent setting in wrinkles. Otherwise the garment may need to be pressed.

Flame-resistant finishes are applied to some children's clothing. Many of these finishes are destroyed if the garments are not washed correctly. Read the label to find out how to maintain the finish.

Other types of special finishes include water-repellent finishes, waterproof finishes, stain-resistant finishes, moth-resistant finishes, mildew-resistant finishes, and others. To get the most benefit from special finishes

follow the directions on the label that is attached to the garment.

GARMENT CONSTRUCTION

Specific construction details will affect the care that a garment needs. Such things as applied trim, seam finishes, seam allowances, pockets, lapels, and other details are some things to consider.

Buttons, belts, braid, and ribbon should require the same care as the rest of the garment. If not, such trims may need to be removed for washing or dry cleaning, or the garment may need special care because of the trim. Pockets, lapels, ruffles, and other construction details add to the care of the garment if the fabric of which they are made requires ironing or pressing.

Finished seams are considered to be a good construction feature, especially if the garment is to be machine-washed often. Raveled seam allowances cause a shaggy appearance inside, and the seams become weaker as the seam allowances disappear in ravelings.

None of these factors which affect clothes care can be considered without thinking about the other factors. Fiber content, fabric construction, fabric finishes, and garment construction all influence the care a garment requires. Be sure to read the labels to find out the best way to care for garments.

 **PUTTING IT TOGETHER**

1 How do the characteristics of fibers affect the care required by clothes made of the fibers? Give examples.
2 How does the looseness or firmness of the fabric affect the care a garment requires? What are some differences in care required by knitted fabrics and woven fabrics?
3 What are some things to remember in caring for fabrics with special finishes?
4 How do specific construction details affect the care of garments?
5 Give some examples of how the factors that affect clothes care are related.

LESSON TWO
PERMANENT CARE LABELS

 permanent care labels

negative care instructions

 what permanent care labels are

some things permanent care labels tell you

Since July, 1973, clothing manufacturers have been required to attach permanent care labels to the garments they manufacture. A *permanent care label* is a label which provides instructions for the care of the garment and is attached securely to the garment.

Although most of the clothes you buy are now required to have permanent care labels, there are a few exceptions. These include sheer garments where the label would show and inexpensive items which can be sold for $3.00 or less.

Care labels must be made of durable material and may be attached to the garment by stitching or an adhesive. Regardless of how they are attached they must remain attached and be readable for the life of the garment.

You may find permanent care labels sewed to the back of the neckline in blouses, shirts, jackets, robes, and sweaters. In pants, shorts, and skirts the label will likely be attached to the center back of the waistband. In some garments without a waistband you will find the label sewed into a seam on the inside of the garment. If the garment must be bought in a sealed package the care instructions are to be printed on the package.

The requirement for permanent care labels applies to fabrics for home sewing as well as to ready-to-wear clothes. When you buy fabric by the yard, you should receive a label to sew in the garment. The label you need will be identified by a code at the end of the fabric bolt. Check to see that the code on the label you are given matches the code at the end of the bolt. Sew the label into your garment in the same place where you would expect to find a care label on a ready-to-wear garment.

Care labels provide information about the basic care procedures of washing, drying, ironing and pressing, and dry cleaning. A combination of procedures is often necessary to properly care for a garment. If this is so, directions must state all the procedures that should be followed. Also, labels must list procedures that are not suitable for the garment and which should not be used. Directions which tell you not to do something are *negative care instructions*. Labels may also include special instructions about the use of bleach or how to remove stains.

Washing instructions will tell whether the garment should be machine washed or hand washed. The directions may state that the garment may be either machine washed or hand washed. Water temperatures for machine washing and rinsing are often included in directions for operating the machine.

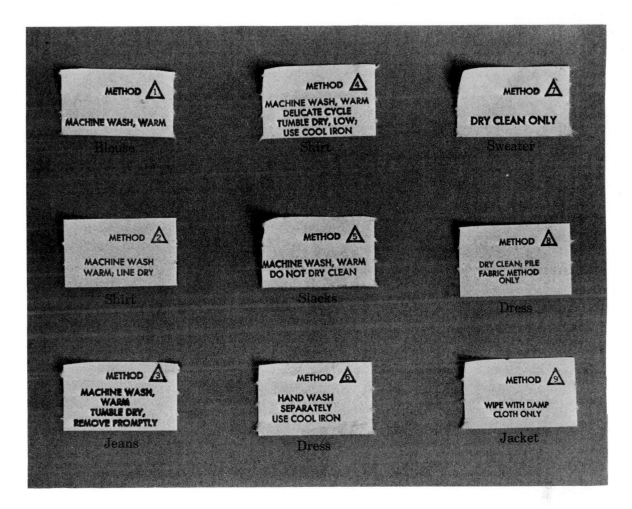

METHOD ⚠1
MACHINE WASH, WARM
Blouse

METHOD ⚠4
MACHINE WASH, WARM
DELICATE CYCLE
TUMBLE DRY, LOW;
USE COOL IRON
Shirt

METHOD ⚠7
DRY CLEAN ONLY
Sweater

METHOD ⚠2
MACHINE WASH
WARM; LINE DRY
Shirt

METHOD ⚠5
MACHINE WASH, WARM
DO NOT DRY CLEAN
Slacks

METHOD ⚠8
DRY CLEAN; PILE
FABRIC METHOD
ONLY
Dress

METHOD ⚠3
MACHINE WASH,
WARM
TUMBLE DRY,
REMOVE PROMPTLY
Jeans

METHOD ⚠6
HAND WASH
SEPARATELY
USE COOL IRON
Dress

METHOD ⚠9
WIPE WITH DAMP
CLOTH ONLY
Jacket

When the terms "Dry Clean" or "Dry Clean Only" are used this means the garment should be sent to a commercial dry cleaner. Or, it may be done in a self-service laundry which has dry-cleaning machines that are coin-operated.

 **PUTTING IT TOGETHER**

1 How do permanent care labels in ready-to-wear clothes help you?
2 Where are usual places that care labels are attached to ready-to-wear garment?
3 How can you obtain a care label to sew in a garment you are making for yourself?
4 What basic care procedures are listed on permanent care labels? What are negative care instructions? How can negative instructions be helpful?
5 Explain what each of these labels tells you. Which label gives the most complete information? If any are confusing, how would you change the directions to make them easier to understand? stand?

LESSON THREE
STAIN REMOVAL

 stain
water-borne stain

oil-borne stain

 some types of stains
some ways to remove stains

Stains or soiled spots caused by food or other substances are special problems in caring for clothes. They require special treatment to remove them without causing damage to the fabric. It may be possible to remove spots or stains from washable clothes by rubbing the spot with detergent or by soaking, followed by the usual washing procedures for the garment. However, many stains require more elaborate treatment. Check the care label before attempting any stain-removal procedure.

Some stains are classified as water-borne stains, while others may be oil-borne stains. *Water-borne stains* are those with a water base and will dissolve in water. *Oil-borne stains* have a greasy or waxy base and usually need treatment with a dry-cleaning product for removal.

Home dry-cleaning products are manufactured in fluid form and powdered form. Using a dry-cleaning product at home requires caution. Some are flammable and should not be used if there is any risk involved.

A variety of substances cause fabric stains.

Causes of water-based stains

Causes of oil-based stains

**IF YOU DO NOT UNDERSTAND THE DIRECTIONS, OR
IF IT IS NOT POSSIBLE FOR YOU TO FOLLOW THE DIRECTIONS,
DO NOT USE THE DRY-CLEANING PRODUCT.**

There are many guides for removing specific stains. One such stain guide appears below. Others can be found in books about taking care of clothes and in booklets published by the government and other organizations. It is difficult to remember exact directions for removing a particular stain from a specific fabric without using such a guide. Even if you use a guide, try out any stain-removal procedure on a fabric sample or inside seam before you use it on the garment itself. This allows you to see how the fabric reacts to the treatment. Some procedures change the color or appearance of fabric.

The sooner a stain is treated, the better the chances are for success in removing it. If a stain remains untreated, it may become permanently set in the fabric. Also, you may forget what the stain is which makes it difficult to treat it properly.

In attempting to remove a stain—especially an unknown stain—there is always some risk of damaging the fabric. If the stain has been in the garment for some time, or if a heavily soiled spot has been pressed over, it may be very difficult or impossible to remove the spot or stain. Dry cleaners often have special equipment and cleaning products which make it possible for them to remove some stains that cannot be removed at home. Many have special training and can determine what unknown stains are and treat them properly.

The chart below summarizes suggestions on how to remove some common stains. Notice that a particular stain is treated differently depending on whether or not the fabric is washable. This shows the need to consider the fabric as well as the type of stain. Some of the procedures involve several steps and require patience in carrying them out. When you stop to consider the problems involved in removing stains from fabrics, you can understand why it is worth the effort to avoid staining your clothes.

TREATMENT OF SOME COMMON STAINS

STAIN	WASHABLE FABRIC	DRY-CLEANABLE FABRIC
blood	Soak in cold or lukewarm water. Rub in detergent.	Send to dry cleaner.
	Wash; use bleach if recommended for fabric.	
catsup	Scrape off with knife.	Send to dry cleaner.
	Soak in cold water about 30 minutes.	
	Rub in detergent and wash using chlorine bleach if recommended.	
carbonated drinks	Sponge or soak in cold water immediately.	Take to dry cleaner while stain is fresh.
	Rub in detergent and wash.	Sponge with water if no risk of leaving ring.
	Stain may be difficult to remove after it dries.	

continued on next page

STAIN	WASHABLE FABRIC	DRY-CLEANABLE FABRIC
cosmetics	Rub in detergent to loosen stain. Wash.	Send to dry cleaner.
deodorants and anti-perspirants	Rub in detergent and wash. Use type of bleach if recommended for fabric.	Send to dry cleaner.
grass (fresh stain)	Rub in detergent to loosen stain. Wash; use bleach if recommended for fabric. May not be possible to remove old stain.	If wool, sponge stain with rubbing alcohol. Or, send to dry cleaner.
mildew	If fresh stain, wash using bleach if recommended for fabric.	Send to dry cleaner. May not be possible to remove old stain.
mud	Brush dried stain to remove dirt particles. Soak in cold water about 30 minutes. Wash in hot water, if safe for fabric.	Brush off dried particles and send to dry cleaner.
perspiration	Rub in detergent, or soak in detergent-water solution. Wash.	Send to dry cleaner. May not be possible to remove stain on some fabrics.
ballpoint pen ink	May be difficult or impossible to remove. Use home dry-cleaning fluid on the spot. Then wash, following usual procedure.	May be difficult or impossible to remove. Try dry-cleaning powder on rough-textured fabric. Or, send to dry cleaner.

 **PUTTING IT TOGETHER**

1 What kinds of stains can be removed by treatment with detergent or by soaking before washing?
2 Why should you read the care label on a garment before you attempt any kind of stain removal?
3 Why is caution necessary when you use a home dry-cleaning product?
4 When is it a good idea to send a garment to a dry cleaner to remove a stain instead of trying to remove the stain at home?

LAUNDRY AIDS

 soap   hard water

detergent   soft water

syndet

 some types of laundry supplies

some things that affect choice of laundry supplies

Have you ever noticed the number of washing products in a store? Have you counted the many boxes, bottles, and plastic containers of various sizes and shapes? How do you decide which ones to use?

DETERGENTS AND SOAPS

Detergents, or washing products, of many kinds are used for keeping clothes clean. Soap is one kind of detergent and is manufac-

tured from fat and lye. *Syndet,* or synthetic detergent, is another type of detergent. It is a nonsoap product so the raw materials used to make a syndet are different from those used to make soap.

Even though soaps and syndets are both detergents, most people refer to soap as "soap" and call syndet "detergent." This is the way in which these terms will be used in this book.

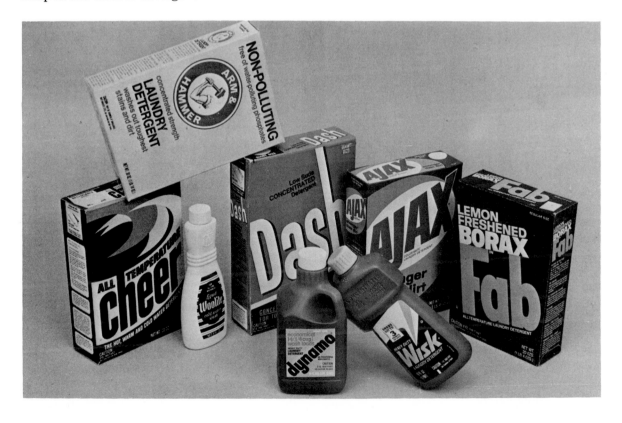

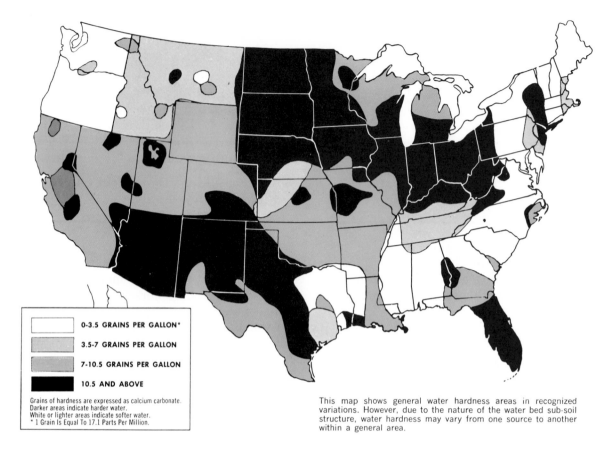

This map shows general water hardness areas in recognized variations. However, due to the nature of the water bed sub-soil structure, water hardness may vary from one source to another within a general area.

0-3.5 GRAINS PER GALLON*

3.5-7 GRAINS PER GALLON

7-10.5 GRAINS PER GALLON

10.5 AND ABOVE

Grains of hardness are expressed as calcium carbonate.
Darker areas indicate harder water.
White or lighter areas indicate softer water.
* 1 Grain Is Equal To 17.1 Parts Per Million.

Many types of detergents and soaps are available. *Light-duty detergents* and *soaps* are suitable for delicate fabric and clothes that are only lightly soiled. *All-purpose* or *heavy-duty detergents* and *soaps* are suitable for sturdy fabrics and heavily soiled clothes. *Cold water detergents* and *soaps* are manufactured especially for use in cold water, but are effective in warm water as well.

Whether water is *hard* or *soft* determines to a great extent whether soap or detergent will clean clothes effectively. Water hardness depends on the amount and type of minerals in the water. All water which comes from the ground contains dissolved minerals. Water hardness is measured and described as grains of minerals per gallon. Water with 0–3 grains per gallon is considered soft; with 3–7 grains, as moderately hard; with 7–10 grains, as hard; and with more than 10.5 to 30 grains, as very hard. The map above shows general water hardness areas.

Soap works best in hot water that is soft, or contains few dissolved minerals. If soap is used in hard water, few suds will form. Instead, the soap will combine with the minerals and form a scum which is deposited on the clothes during washing. Detergents dissolve and make suds more easily than soap in cold water and in hard water.

Some parts of the country have laws which prohibit the use of some detergents. This is because some of the chemicals in detergents are thought to contribute to pollution. If soap is used, clothes washing problems due to hard water can be solved by removing the dissolved minerals which cause water hardness.

WATER SOFTENERS

One way to remove dissolved minerals from water is by using a *mechanical water softener*. This system is installed so that the water supply for the house passes through it before being used. The principle applied in these water-softening devices is to remove by chemical reaction minerals which cause water hardness. The hard water flows into a tank where it filters through materials which reduce the mineral content of the water. The water then flows into the household water system. Eventually the materials which remove the minerals causing water hardness become saturated. These same materials are renewed, and the process is continued.

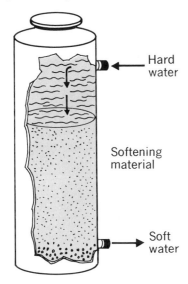

Another method of dealing with water hardness is to add water-softening products directly to the wash water. *Powdered water softeners* can be added to the hard water at the time it is used. The dissolved minerals causing water hardness are not removed, but their effect on soap is lessened. Soap can then dissolve in the water more easily and make suds. The amount of water softener required depends on the hardness of the water.

DISINFECTANTS

Laundry disinfectants may be added to the wash cycle or final rinse to kill bacteria on clothes. This step is important when there is need to control or eliminate infections among family members. When clothes are washed in a coin-operated commercial laundry, disinfectant may be used as a precautionary step to avoid infections. Disinfectants are particularly useful in reducing bacteria on clothes that must be washed in cold or warm water. A hot water temperature of at least 140° F (60° C) will kill bacteria, but hot water temperatures are not recommended for some garments. Chlorine bleaches also reduce bacteria in the wash, but chlorine bleaches are not recommended for some types of fabrics.

BLEACHES

Bleaches are used to maintain the original white appearance of white fabrics. Also, some stains can be removed from clothing with the aid of bleaches.

There are two general groups of bleaches. These are *chlorine bleaches* and *nonchlorine bleaches*. Each type affects fibers and fabric finishes differently. The best way to find out whether a particular brand of bleach belongs to one group or the other is to read the product description on the container. If the word chlorine is in the description it is very likely a chlorine-type bleach. If the description says definitely that the product is not a chlorine bleach, or that it does not contain chlorine, or if the word chlorine is not included in the list of ingredients, you know that the product is a nonchlorine bleach. Chlorine bleaches are recommended for washing white cottons and linens which do not have crease- and wrinkle-resistant finishes. Chlorine bleaches are not recommended for washing fabrics of manufactured fibers, wool, silk, and fabrics with crease- and wrinkle-resistant finishes. When a chlorine bleach is used in very hard water it may cause brown stains on the clothing. Nonchlorine bleaches are milder than chlorine bleaches in their action on fibers and fabric finishes. They can be used when a chlorine bleach is not recommended.

Both chlorine and nonchlorine bleaches can be bought in several forms. Powder, liquid, and tablet are some of these. Instructions on the various products tell correct amounts to use. Bleaches are added to the washing water and removed with the rinse. A liquid bleach should be dispersed in the wash water and removed

with the rinse. A liquid bleach should be dispersed in the wash water before the clothes are added. Powders and tablets should be dissolved in the water before clothes are added. The bleach solution should be thoroughly removed from the clothes by rinsing before the washing process is completed. If any bleach is left in the fabric, the fibers may be weakened.

FABRIC SOFTENERS

The fibers in clothes washed often in hard water with syndets tend to become somewhat stiff and harsh. *Fabric softeners* are available in several forms to help improve this condition. These substances coat the fibers and give the fabric a soft feel and reduce static electricity in garments made of manufactured fibers. Fabric softeners also help prevent wrinkles and make clothes easier to iron.

Many liquid fabric softeners are added to the final rinse. However, some have been developed so they can be added at the beginning of the wash. Read the directions to find out how much fabric softener to use and when to add it.

Liquid fabric softeners build up on fabrics after repeated uses and tend to reduce the absorbency of the fibers in the fabric. To prevent this buildup, add the fabric softener to every other washload or to every third washload.

Other forms of fabric softeners are designed to be used in the dryer. Some manufacturers of dryers do not recommend the use of fabric softeners in the dryer. If you decide to use this type of fabric softener, check to see that it is guaranteed not to damage either the dryer or the fabrics.

STARCH

Starch gives crispness and body to fabrics. Of course, fabrics with a special crisp fabric finish do not require starching to have this appearance. And clothes with wrinkle-resistant finishes have a smooth, somewhat crisp appearance without the help of starch.

Starching also provides fabrics with some resistance to soiling. Dirt particles cannot cling to a smooth, slick surface so easily as to a rough surface.

Starching products are sold in powdered or in concentrated liquid form. Water is added to the powder or the concentrated liquid according to directions. The solution is then added to the final rinse water.

Spray starches are also manufactured. This product is applied to the clothes after they have been washed, and then either dried or partially dried. It is sprayed onto the clothes as they are ironed. This product is convenient for stiffening small areas when other parts of the garment are to be left untreated. For example, by using a spray starch a collar might be given some crispness while the rest of the garment is left untreated.

PUTTING IT TOGETHER

1 Define these terms: detergents, synthetic detergent, syndet.
2 What is hard water? How do soaps react in hard water? What can be done to make hard water soft?
3 What are some reasons for using a laundry disinfectant?
4 What are the two general groups of bleaches? How can you tell whether a particular brand of bleach belongs in one group or the other?
5 What are some reasons for using a fabric softener?
6 Why is starch used in clothes care? What forms of starches are manufactured?

LESSON FIVE
STEPS TO SUCCESSFUL LAUNDRY

pretreating

prewashing

presoaking

color-fast

agitation

automatic dispenser

drip dry

line dry

dry flat

some ways to do laundry

some ways to solve laundry problems

Certain procedures used in washing and drying clothes help them maintain their original size, shape, color, and overall appearance. To do this, it is important to sort clothes, pretreat heavy soil and stains, and choose laundry aids carefully and use them correctly. Also, the water temperature; length of the washing cycle; and the drying method, temperature, and time are important factors.

PRETREATING HEAVY SOIL AND STAINS

Pretreating heavily soiled areas in clothes may require only rubbing detergent into the fabric where the soil is. However, if the entire garment is heavily soiled, it may require *prewashing* or *presoaking* before washing. Many washing machines have prewash or presoak cycles. If so, follow directions for the machine. If not, fill the machine with enough warm water to cover the clothes, add detergent, let it dissolve, then add the clothes. Use the amount of detergent for the size load you are soaking. Allow the clothes to soak for about a half hour, drain the water,

then wash in the usual way. For ways in which you can treat stains, refer to Lesson 3, pages 171–172.

LAUNDRY AIDS

Using the right laundry aids for the type of wash you are doing helps to get clothes clean and to keep their color. Using the correct amount also contributes to good results. For example, too little detergent or soap can lead to such problems as graying, yellowing, or making clothes dingy. Too much detergent or soap may give a stiff, harsh feel to clothes. Chlorine bleach used on polyesters causes these fibers to turn yellow. Nonchlorine bleach used in water at too low a temperature will not be effective. If fabric softener that is designed to be added in the final rinse is added with the detergent or soap, it does not make the fabric soft. Instead, the fabric softener combines with the soap and forms a sticky substance which is left on the clothes. To prevent these and other problems, read and follow the directions for using the various laundry aids.

Detergents and packaged water conditioners
are not compatible with most fabric softeners.

Ammonia should not be used with chlorine bleach
and detergent.

SORTING

Clothes should be sorted according to color, fiber content, fabric finish, garment construction, and amount of soil. These things are important when deciding on water temperature, length of washing cycle, wash and spin speeds, and laundry aids.

Separate white clothes from colored clothes and dark-colored clothes from light-colored ones. Then sort these piles of clothes so that those which are to be washed in hot water are separate from those to be washed in warm water and cold water. Or sort them according to the different cycles on the washing machine, such as delicate or permanent press. Heavily soiled clothes should not be put in to wash with lightly soiled clothes. The heavily soiled clothes may not get clean and may make the lightly soiled ones dingy.

WATER TEMPERATURES

Knowing the appropriate water temperatures for different fabrics and washing problems may help you decide how to sort your clothes. *Very hot water* provides the most soil removal and sanitizing, or disinfecting. It is suitable for white cottons and linens and heavily soiled articles which are *color-fast,* or colors which do not run. Very hot water will cause wrinkles in fabrics made of manufactured fibers and may cause some fabrics to lose their colors.

Lightly soiled cottons and linens in white or in color-fast colors usually wash clean in *medium hot water,* although water at this temperature provides no sanitizing. A disinfectant may be added to the wash if it needs sanitizing.

Warm water is suitable for silks and washable woolens and garments made of manufactured fibers. When possible, garments with permanent-press or wrinkle-resistant finishes should be washed in warm water or medium hot water instead of in cold water. The heat in warm or medium hot water helps release wrinkles in garments caused from wearing the garment. Warm water is also a comfortable temperature for hand washing. Water at this temperature provides no sanitizing so you may want to add a disinfectant.

Cold water may be recommended for clothes in colors that run, lightly soiled clothes, clothes of some manufactured fibers, or thoroughly pretreated garments. Water at this temperature gives the least cleaning and provides no sanitizing. A disinfectant added according to directions will be needed if you want to sanitize clothes in cold water. Since cold water causes minimum wrinkling of

manufactured fibers, it is recommended for rinsing permanent-press garments.

WATER LEVELS

A choice of water levels is a feature many washing machines have. This is good when there are small loads to wash. Be sure to allow enough water for each load. Too many clothes for the amount of water keeps clothes from getting clean and causes wrinkles.

AGITATION AND SPIN SPEEDS

Many washing machines have at least two agitation and spin speeds. *Agitation* is the action of the washing machine during washing and rinsing. The faster speed of spinning and agitation results in better soil removal from heavily soiled clothes, but may cause wrinkles in garments of manufactured fibers or with permanent-press finishes. Slow agitation and spinning speeds are good for delicate fabrics and those with wrinkle-resistant or permanent-press finishes. If the washer has special cycles for delicate clothes, permanent-press garments, and regular loads, the agitation and spinning speeds are automatically controlled when the dials are set.

Heavily soiled clothes need to be agitated longer than lightly soiled clothes. Delicate fabrics may be damaged by too much agitation. Garments of manufactured fibers and with permanent-press, wash-and-wear, or soil-release finishes should be washed for a short length of time. Water does not penetrate manufactured fibers or those with some special finishes. This means that garments made of manufactured fibers or those with special finishes clean faster than untreated natural fibers. Washing for too long a time may put soil from the wash water back on the clothes.

MACHINE WASHING

Choose the correct cycle or agitation and spin speeds, water temperature, and length of wash cycle for the load you are washing. (See

RECOMMENDED WASHING PROCEDURES

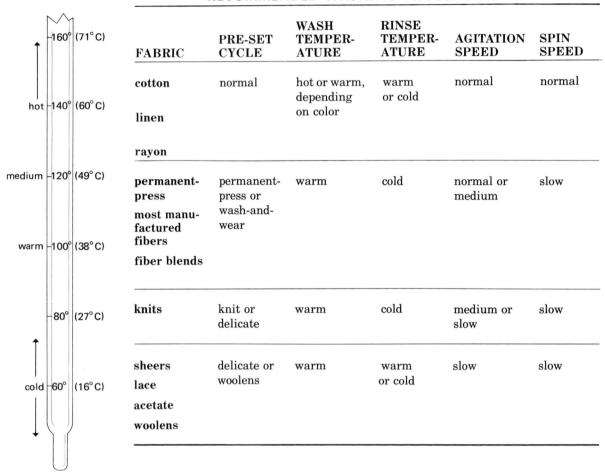

FABRIC	PRE-SET CYCLE	WASH TEMPER-ATURE	RINSE TEMPER-ATURE	AGITATION SPEED	SPIN SPEED
cotton	normal	hot or warm, depending on color	warm or cold	normal	normal
linen					
rayon					
permanent-press **most manu-factured fibers** **fiber blends**	permanent-press or wash-and-wear	warm	cold	normal or medium	slow
knits	knit or delicate	warm	cold	medium or slow	slow
sheers **lace** **acetate** **woolens**	delicate or woolens	warm	warm or cold	slow	slow

Thermometer scale:
160° (71° C)
hot 140° (60° C)
medium 120° (49° C)
warm 100° (38° C)
80° (27° C)
cold 60° (16° C)

the chart above for suggestions.) If the washing machine has automatic dispensers for laundry aids, follow the instructions for using these features. *Automatic dispensers* add laundry aids to the wash and rinse water at the time they should be added. If there are no automatic dispensers, add the detergent or soap, bleach, disinfectant, water softener, and other laundry aids after the water has started to fill the machine. Read the instructions on the package labels for the correct amounts to use. Add the clothes after the machine has filled with water and the agitation has dissolved the soap or detergent. Undissolved detergent or soap may stick to the clothes and not rinse out. Add fabric softener according to the directions.

HAND WASHING

To hand wash, use as hot water as possible for the fabric and finish. Add the detergent or soap and other laundry aids in amounts suggested on the package labels and swish them around in the water until dissolved. Pretreat spots and stains, then add the clothes and swish them around until they are wet. If necessary, let them soak for twenty or thirty minutes. Otherwise wash immediately. Use warm or cool water to rinse. Rinse until the water is clear. If using fabric softener, add to last rinse.

DRYING

Care instruction labels on some garments may recommend drip drying, line drying, or drying

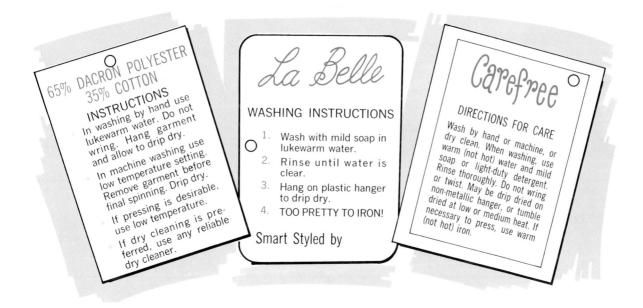

65% DACRON POLYESTER 35% COTTON

INSTRUCTIONS

In washing by hand use lukewarm water. Do not wring. Hang garment and allow to drip dry.

In machine washing use low temperature setting. Remove garment before final spinning. Drip dry.

If pressing is desirable, use low temperature.

If dry cleaning is preferred, use any reliable dry cleaner.

La Belle

WASHING INSTRUCTIONS

1. Wash with mild soap in lukewarm water.
2. Rinse until water is clear.
3. Hang on plastic hanger to drip dry.
4. TOO PRETTY TO IRON!

Smart Styled by

Carefree

DIRECTIONS FOR CARE

Wash by hand or machine, or dry clean. When washing, use warm (not hot) water and mild soap or light-duty detergent. Rinse thoroughly. Do not wring or twist. May be drip dried on non-metallic hanger, or tumble dried at low or medium heat. If necessary to press, use warm (not hot) iron.

flat. *Drip dry* means to hang the garment dripping wet, without squeezing or wringing any water from the garment after it is rinsed. This is often recommended for permanent-press or wash-and-wear garments if they cannot be machine dried. *Line drying* is drying by hanging clothes after they have been spun in the machine or as much water as possible has been squeezed out after rinsing. The instruction to *dry flat* means the garment should be placed on a flat surface, shaped to its original shape, and allowed to dry. Line drying may stretch out of shape a garment that should be dried flat; machine drying may also cause a garment to stretch out of shape or it may cause a garment to shrink.

Permanent-press and wash-and-wear garments dry smoothest in the dryer. The heat smoothes out the wrinkles. These garments often require at least touch-up ironing if line dried or drip dried. Any clothes dried in an automatic dryer should not be dried for too long a time. Overdrying sets in wrinkles and may cause the fabric to feel harsh and stiff. Some garments may also shrink. Drying too many garments at one time and leaving garments in the dryer after it stops causes wrinkles. Garments removed from the dryer just before they are dry often can be smoothed with the hands when being folded or hung so they need no ironing or pressing.

Some dryers have a temperature control. This allows you to choose the correct temperature for the fabric. Check the care labels on your garments to find out which drying temperature to use.

 **PUTTING IT TOGETHER**

1 What are some laundry problems you have had? What are some things you learned in this lesson that will prevent them from happening again?
2 What are some reasons for sorting clothes before washing?
3 In what ways does water temperature affect clothes during washing? How does agitation and spinning speed affect clothes?
4 What difference does it make how long the clothes are agitated during washing?
5 Describe some different drying methods.

LESSON SIX
DRY CLEANING

 dry cleaning

coin-operated dry cleaning
machines

professional dry cleaner

 purpose of dry cleaning

coin-operated dry cleaning

professional dry cleaning

"Dry Clean Only" is the recommended cleaning method for some ready-to-wear garments as well as for some fabrics sold by the yard for home sewing. *Dry cleaning* is the process of cleaning clothes or other textile products with nonwater solvents or absorbent materials. When "Dry Clean Only" is recommended, this means the garment cannot be cleaned satisfactorily by washing.

Dry cleaning can be done in coin-operated dry-cleaning machines, or clothes may be sent to a professional dry cleaner. It usually costs less to clean clothes in a coin-operated machine than to have them done by a professional dry cleaner. However, if you do not have time, or if there are stains in the clothing, you may decide to have them professionally cleaned.

SELF-SERVICE DRY CLEANING

Dry-cleaning machines are often located in coin-operated laundry establishments. Satisfactory results depend on the careful preparation of clothes and on following instructions when using the machine.

Prepare clothes at home before you go to the coin-operated cleaning center. There may be neither the space nor the equipment available to prepare clothes at the center.

Brush dust and dried soil from the outside of the garments.

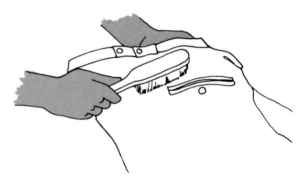

Brush lint from the insides of cuffs and pockets and from the undersides of collars.

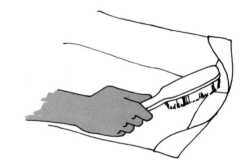

Check the garment care label for instructions about removing trims. Some types of trims are damaged by dry-cleaning solvent, and the label should tell this. Remove trims that will not withstand dry cleaning. Repair rips and broken seams to prevent further damage during cleaning. If there are stains on the garment, consider taking it to a professional dry cleaner rather than trying to clean it yourself.

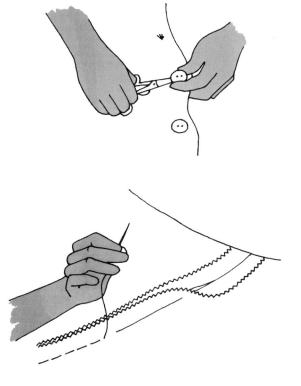

Sorting is an essential step in preparing clothes for dry cleaning, just as it is for washing clothes. Similar kinds of garments may be cleaned in the same machine load. For example, heavy clothes such as coats and suits may be combined. Lightweight, thin garments should be separated from heavy articles to avoid damage to the lightweight garments. Separate white and light-colored clothes from black and dark-colored clothes.

At the dry-cleaning center weigh garments together that you intend to clean together. Load the machine as directed, putting in only the number of pounds the machine will hold. The operating cycle for a coin-operated dry-cleaning machine is set. This means that all clothes will be processed the same length of time. The cleaning-drying cycle is usually a little less than one hour. During this time clothes will be cleaned and dried without requiring further attention.

After the cycle is completed remove garments immediately and hang them up before wrinkles are formed. You may need to shake them lightly and pat out wrinkles that were formed during the drying step. Some garments will be ready to wear without further treatment. Others will require pressing. Allow the garments to air out before storing in a closed space.

Some coin-operated cleaning centers have pressing equipment. However, garments can be pressed at home.

PROFESSIONAL DRY CLEANING

Whenever you take your clothes to a professional dry cleaner you are buying clothes care service. A *professional dry cleaner* has had specialized training in the techniques of dry cleaning.

In a large dry-cleaning shop a garment may be handled by several clothes care specialists before the cleaning service is completed. The first step begins when garments are inspected for special handling they may require. Trims that cannot be dry cleaned are removed before other treatment is done. A spotter examines the garment for spots and stains that cannot be removed in the regular machine process. An expert spotter must understand fabrics, dyes, and garment construction in order to select the best treatment for each garment.

Clothes are cleaned in dry-cleaning machines similar to the coin-operated machines you may use in self-service establishments. However, the professional dry cleaner has much larger machines which process many garments in each load. Garments are sorted and similar garments are cleaned together, in the same way in which this step would be done if a coin-operated machine were being used.

Pressing the cleaned garment is part of professional dry-cleaning service. This step is done in the finishing department where steam and air are used to return the shape to the garment and take out wrinkles. Expert pressers carry out this step.

If a garment needs minor repairs this may be done before it is returned to the customer.

PUTTING IT TOGETHER

1 What is the purpose of dry cleaning?
2 How should clothes be prepared for cleaning in a coin-operated dry-cleaning machine?
3 What final steps are necessary after clothes are removed from a self-service coin-operated dry-cleaning machine?
4 What kind of clothes care service do you buy when you take your clothes to a professional dry cleaner? What steps are included in professional dry-cleaning service?
5 What kinds of clothes care services must you be able and willing to provide for yourself when you use a coin-operated dry-cleaning center?

LESSON SEVEN
PRESSING AND IRONING

 press

iron

press cloth

soleplate

 the difference between ironing and pressing

some equipment for ironing and pressing

general guidelines for ironing and pressing

The terms ironing and pressing are sometimes used as if they mean the same thing. Actually these terms refer to two different processes. *Ironing* is the process of removing wrinkles from damp, washable clothing. Heat and pressure from an iron are combined with moisture in the clothing to smooth wrinkles. The wrinkles are flattened and the original appearance of the clothing is restored. Moisture in the clothing is removed during the ironing process. Ironing usually is done with a gliding motion.

"Touch-up ironing" means that only a few places in the garment are ironed. Wash-and-wear garments generally resist wrinkling during washing but seam, collar, or buttonhole areas may need a small amount of touch-up ironing.

Pressing is also a process for removing wrinkles from clothing. However, instead of sliding the iron on the fabric, the iron is placed on the fabric, then lifted. Moisture may be used in pressing, but it is added in the form of steam from a steam iron or damp pressing cloth. Wool clothing and clothing with wool-like texture are always pressed, not ironed. Also, washable clothing is sometimes pressed between wearings, although it may be ironed after washing.

EQUIPMENT

An iron, an ironing board or other large, flat surface, a press cloth, a sleeve board, and a tailor's ham are some common equipment used in ironing and pressing. Other equipment is available, but is not necessary to basic pressing and ironing.

Irons are available in four basic types. These are dry irons, steam-dry irons, steam-spray-dry irons, and travel irons. A *dry iron* is designed to iron or press without steam. There is no place in a dry iron for water to produce steam and no holes in the soleplate for steam to pass through when the iron is being used. Dry irons are useful if most items to be ironed need to be dampened first. Pressing with a dry iron usually requires the use of a *press cloth*. A press cloth is dampened and placed over the item to be pressed. The heat from the iron combines with the moisture in the press cloth to produce steam.

Steam-dry irons have an opening for pouring in water which produces the steam. There are holes in the soleplate which allow the steam to come through to dampen the fabric when the iron is being used. A *steam-spray-dry iron* is similar to a steam-dry iron with the added feature of being able to spray a

CARE SHOWS

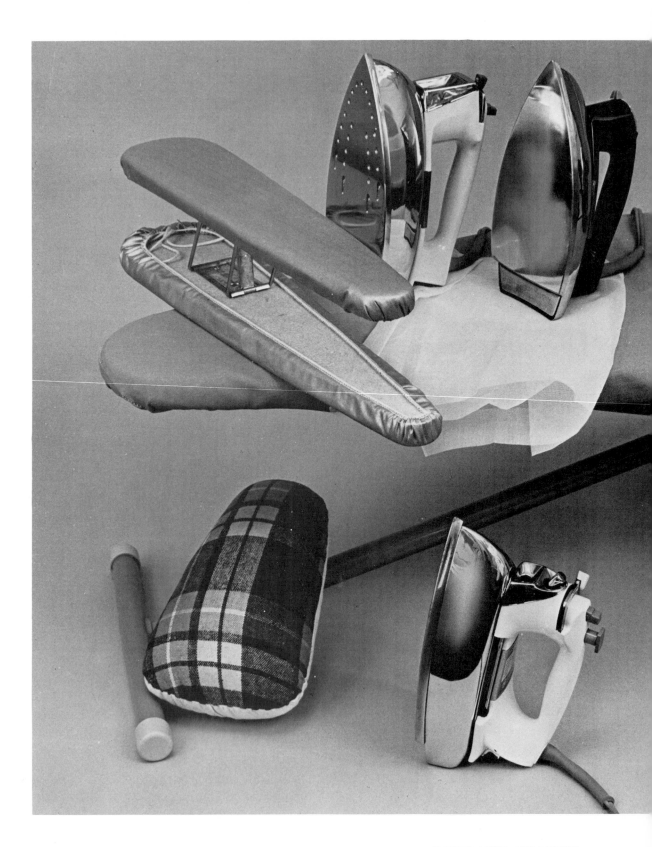

fine mist of steam on a particular area of a garment. Steam-dry irons or steam-spray-dry irons are suitable for pressing garments without predampening them or for pressing wrinkles from lightly wrinkled garments. They can also be used as dry irons.

Travel irons are small and lightweight so they will fit into a suitcase easily without adding too much extra weight. Some travel irons are dry irons and others have a steam attachment.

CARE OF EQUIPMENT

Proper care will keep an iron in the best condition. Distilled water is recommended for steam-dry irons and steam-spray-dry irons to avoid clogging the iron with mineral deposits. Empty the water immediately after you have finished using the iron.

When the iron is not in use, store it on the heel rest to protect the ironing surface.

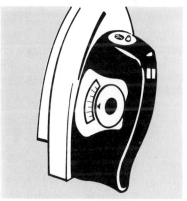

Use the correct temperature for each fiber. This will protect both the clothes and the iron. For example, most manufactured fibers are heat-sensitive; they become soft and melt at high temperatures. The fabric, of course, will then be damaged and particles will stick to the soleplate. Also, if starched cotton is ironed at a high temperature, starch may stick to the soleplate and scorch.

If anything becomes stuck to the soleplate, check instructions for using the iron to find out how to remove sticking substances. On some irons a dampened cloth may be used to wipe off anything stuck to the soleplate. On stainless steel soleplates, a powdered household cleanser may be used. Do not clean an aluminum or nonstick soleplate with anything that might scratch the finish.

Ironing boards, sleeve boards, and tailor's hams should be well padded and have a clean cover. Covers may be purchased or made from old sheets or pillowcases. Some ironing boards are adjustable in height. This makes it more comfortable and easier to iron or press without becoming tired quickly.

GUIDELINES FOR IRONING AND PRESSING

An ironing board or a large flat surface is best to use for ironing or pressing large flat areas. Curved areas of garments, such as darts, retain their shape when pressed over a rounded surface such as a tailor's ham. A sleeve board is convenient to use when pressing sleeves, sleeve caps, and small flat areas of garments.

Here are some guidelines for pressing and ironing to help preserve a garment's original appearance.

1. Press or iron on the wrong side dark fabrics which have a dull surface. Or press them on the right side, using a dampened press cloth. This prevents shiny areas from appearing on the right side of the garment.

2. Press or iron on the right side of fabrics which have a shiny surface. This helps preserve the desired shiny appearance.

3. Use a piece of wool fabric and a press cloth when pressing wool. Place the piece of wool on top of the garment, then cover the wool with a dampened press cloth. Do not press wool without added moisture as it will make the fabric shiny and harsh to the touch.

4. Press napped fabric, such as corduroy or velvet, on the right side by holding the steam iron close to the fabric but not touching it. Or steam it from the wrong side by running the steam iron very lightly over the surface. The use of pressure while pressing napped fabric will flatten the nap. A damp press cloth may be used with a dry iron.

5. Press or iron with the grainline to avoid stretching the fabric. Fabric stretches and causes a garment to lose its shape when yarns are pulled apart or out of line.

6. Press or iron darts and curved garment areas over a tailor's ham to maintain their rounded shape.

7. Press or iron long plain seams open. This gives the garment a smooth outside appearance. When pressing seams open in an unlined garment, slip a strip of paper under each edge of the seam to prevent the outline of the seam from showing on the outside of the garment.

8. Press or iron first collars, cuffs, facings, pockets, and other garment areas where there is more than one layer of fabric. Press

Characteristics of a Well-pressed Garment

* The garment is free of wrinkles
* The original texture has been preserved
* The original shape of the garment has been maintained
* Outline of inside details such as darts, facings, and hems, do not show on the outside
* Inside seams have been pressed as originally pressed

small garment areas, such as yokes and sleeves, and curved areas, such as darts, next. Then press the large flat areas. Pressing garment areas in this order prevents wrinkles from forming in other areas already ironed or pressed.

9. Use the correct temperature for the fiber content. Too high a temperature may damage some fabrics. Too low a temperature may not remove wrinkles from other fabrics. Complete care directions will tell the appropriate temperature or you can follow the fabric and temperature guide on the iron. For fiber blends and layered fabrics, use the lowest temperature required for any of the fibers in the fabric.

PUTTING IT TOGETHER

1 In what ways are ironing and pressing different?
2 What are some things you can do to take care of an iron?
3 Describe some ways to press or iron in order to keep a garment's original appearance.
4 How would you describe a well-pressed or well-ironed garment? What clues would tell you that the garment had been pressed or ironed correctly?

LESSON EIGHT
CLOTHES STORAGE

 storage principles

 some guidelines for clothes storage

some ways to improve clothes storage

A satisfactory clothes storage system saves time and energy; makes maximum use of the storage space; and protects fibers, fabrics, and shapes of garments. The way you arrange clothes and accessories affects the time and effort you spend in dressing every day. Time is often wasted in aimless searching for clothing and accessories that are not stored in a systematic way. Small articles are easily misplaced when there is no storage plan.

PLANNING STORAGE

If you plan exactly how you will use your storage space, you are more likely to use all the space available and use it efficiently. The following *storage principles* may help you to plan an effective storage system.

Store each item as close as possible to the place where it will be used or put on. For example, less time and energy is used if coats, jackets, and other clothing worn outdoors is stored near an outside door. If jewelry or accessories are to be put on in front of a mirror, they should be stored near a mirror.

Store items together that are used together. Underwear can be stored in one place rather than in several places to save steps and avoid opening several drawers when dressing.

Store clothes and other items so that they are easy to locate at a glance. Storing many items on a deep shelf means that you cannot see what is behind the first row of items. You may forget you have some things. Also, if you want something in back, you have to remove whatever is in front to get it. Time and energy are used in doing this. A turntable or step shelves might be used so that things are easier to reach.

Store items that are used frequently where they are easily reached. A sweater that you wear often is more conveniently located in a place other than the top shelf of a closet. Items that are not used often can be stored in places that are more difficult to reach.

Store similar articles together. Storing sweaters, pajamas, and underwear in the same drawer makes it difficult to find what you want. Mixing shirts, jackets, jeans, and pants in the closet means you have to sort through several things to find what you want. Arranging shirts together, jackets together, and so on means that you only need to look through a few things to find what you want. Drawer dividers can be used to separate items in drawers if the space which you have to use is limited.

Use all the space you have. If it is mainly separates that are to be hung in a closet, they might be hung on two rods, one above the other. If there is not room for two rods, but still space at the bottom of the closet, a shelf, shoe rack, foot locker, or box for storage can be put in that space.

PROTECTING FIBERS, FABRICS, AND SHAPES

Clothes remain wearable longer when fibers, fabrics, and shapes are protected. This is another way you benefit from a good storage plan. Seasonal clothing, when it is not being worn, might be stored in specially designed, zippered clothes bags. Also, individual garments can be covered by plastic bags of the type used by dry cleaners. Use transparent tape or masking tape to close the top and bottom. Wool garments can be protected from moth damage this way.

Fabrics that can be damaged by mildew should be stored clean, dry, and in a dry storage area. This is a good practice for clothes in daily use as well as for seasonal clothing. Freely circulating air in a well-ventilated closet will discourage mildew growth.

The odor on clothes caused by mildew can be removed by washing the clothes, if they are washable. Mildew stains may be difficult to remove.

Some types of clothes collect odors easily and need to be aired between washings or dry cleanings. All-wool and wool-blend fabrics tend to retain odors more than others. Wool jackets, coats, skirts, and sweaters are typical garments which may require frequent airing. Cotton garments may acquire a stale odor if they hang for a long period of time in an unventilated room.

Ideally, garments should be aired outside in clean, fresh air, but outdoor airing is not always practical. In some areas where there are concentrations of smoke and car-exhaust fumes, hanging clothes outside may leave new odors in the clothes rather than airing away the old ones. Moreover, when there is dust and soot in the air the clothes may become soiled from being hung outdoors.

One possible substitute for outside airing is to circulate air around clothes indoors with an electric fan. Hang the articles on a clothes rack and direct the fan so that air freely circulates around them. Or you can air out the entire closet, or other storage space, in the same way.

Another way to deal with odors on clothes is to use a vacuum cleaner on them. The upholstery attachment can be used on clothing fabrics the same as on furniture upholstery fabrics. Vacuum cleaning the clothes will pull loose dust from the surface as well as agitate the air in and around the fabric.

Sometimes automatic clothes dryers are used to freshen clothes. If this is done, use the no-heat setting, especially when freshening woolens. The no-heat setting may be the last five to seven minutes of the drying cycle or it may be a separate cycle that is indicated.

Garment shapes, as well as fibers and fabrics, should be considered in storing garments. Knit garments stretch easily when they are not handled carefully. Hanging causes knits to stretch unnecessarily. Therefore, knit clothes, such as sweaters and jerseys, should be folded and stored flat. Woven stretch fabrics can be stored the same way. This is true of sportswear which you might ordinarily store flat anyway. Some garments of stretch fabrics can be hung just as you would hang other clothes. After each wearing, a garment of woven stretch fabric requires some time to return to its original shape.

Sport coats and suit jackets keep their shapes if hung on hangers shaped especially for these garments. Pants and slacks keep their shapes when hung on pants hangers.

Heavy clothes and loosely woven fabrics need some special consideration to preserve their shapes. A heavy garment, such as a winter coat, might best be hung on a wide wooden hanger or a padded hanger. A wire hanger may not support it evenly across the shoulders. If the coat is to be stored several months, a wire hanger is likely to leave a ridge in the fabric across the shoulders and spoil the appearance of the coat.

Loosely woven fabrics need firm support, too. Hang each skirt evenly, attaching both the front and back of the waistband to the hanger. Check hems to see that they hang evenly all around. Button a jacket so that the front does not sag.

 **PUTTING IT TOGETHER**

1 Explain how your clothes storage system can conserve your time and energy.
2 Give examples of how you can make maximum use of your clothes storage space.
3 How does good storage protect the appearance of a garment?
4 Explain how garments can be protected from moth damage and mildew damage.
5 What are some ways odors can be removed from clothes?
6 In what ways can garment shapes be protected by good storage procedures?

 **TAKING ANOTHER STEP**

1 Make a list of the clothes you have. Then write down how you take care of them and keep them clean. List the reasons they require the care you give them.
2 Work in small groups or individually to examine clothing labels and the garments to which they are (or were) attached. New garments might be loaned by class members or stores. Garments that have received some wear might also be examined if their lables can also be supplied. After examining the labels and the garment, try to answer these questions: Does the label provide a clear explanation of the care required by the garment? If not, what information is missing?

continued on next page

---

continued from page 195

3 Prepare a display of products that can be used for stain removal. Provide information about the kinds of stains each product will remove.

4 Demonstrate the correct ways to remove some common stains, such as soda, grease, chocolate, etc.

5 Prepare an exhibit of washing products, including soaps, detergents, bleaches, and fabric softeners. Group similar types of products in your exhibit. Write a definition of each type of product (soap, detergent, bleach, fabric softener). For each group of products in the exhibit prepare labels which define the products and explain the correct use.

6 Find out the degree of water hardness in your community. How does water hardness affect washing clothes?

7 Demonstrate how to sort clothes using a basket of soiled clothes. Or, using several different garments, tell best water temperature, length of washing time, and whether the article requires hand washing or can withstand machine washing.

8 Survey two or more local dry-cleaning stores and ask the cost of dry cleaning several common garments such as a coat, jacket sweater, slacks, and skirt. Survey two or more local coin-operated dry-cleaning machines in self-service laundry centers to determine the cost of having the same articles cleaned in a coin-operated machine. Compare prices from activities 1 and 2. Discuss other advantages and disadvantages of each alternative.

9 Demonstrate the correct way to use a steam iron.

10 Point out the characteristics of a well-pressed garment on an actual garment.

11 Study the ways you store clothes at home. See how you might improve your own clothes storage by applying one or more of the storage principles described in this unit.

12 Get together with some classmates and think of some ideas for making the most of storage space. Make illustrations of these ideas and create a bulletin board.

13 Make a box for questions about clothes care. Plan a time to discuss questions that have been put in the box.

14 Take a field trip to a local coin-operated laundry center for a demonstration of self-service dry cleaning.

TECHNIQUES MATTER

UNIT EIGHT

The knowledge and skill required in sewing serve several purposes. For some people, they are a means to be used to repair or remake a favorite outfit. For others who are responsible for clothing children they are a means to modify hand-me-downs. To others, being able to sew is a means to save money by creating a wardrobe at lower cost. To these persons and to others, sewing is a means to express creativity. It allows for personalized selection of fabrics, color combinations, and designs. These things together enable one to create a special look or style that is distinctly one's own.

The lessons in this unit will help you to make a garment. You will see that learning to sew involves a series of steps. With practice, each step can become a skill to be used in making garments and in doing other sewing. Sewing can be for recreation, pleasure, necessity, or for the development of an important skill in one's vocation.

LESSON ONE
THE SEWING MACHINE

 stitch-length regulator

reverse stitch control

tension

bobbin

bobbin case

presser foot

feed dog

hand wheel

presser bar lever

spool pin

thread guide

thread take-up

tension unit

bobbin winder

 basic parts of sewing machines

how to use sewing machines

how to care for sewing machines

The sewing machine is the most valuable piece of equipment you will use when you sew. The ability to use it and care for it properly is an important step towards developing and improving your skill in sewing.

Even though there are different models and makes of sewing machines, the way in which they work and the care they need are similar. You probably have seen many different types of machines. If there is one in your home, it may be different from the ones at school. The machines at school may not all be alike. Look at the ones in your classroom to see what kinds there are. Do you know of any sewing machines that are not electric? Although some people still use nonelectric sewing machines, most people today have electric ones. For this reason the information in this lesson refers to electric sewing machines. If your machine is not electric, ask your teacher for directions.

SEWING MACHINE PARTS

It is important to learn the names of the sewing machine parts. If you do not know these names and cannot recognize the parts on the machine, it will be hard for you to follow the directions for the operation of the machine. Also, it will be hard to ask or answer questions about the machine without knowing the correct names of its parts.

The location of some parts of the sewing machine may vary with different machines, but each machine has similar parts which serve similar purposes. The illustration on page 199 shows the basic parts of a sewing machine. The chart explains the purpose of each part. If you cannot find these parts on your machine, study the instruction book for your machine.

THREADING THE MACHINE

Before you start to thread the machine, make sure the needle is at its highest point. Find out which direction the *hand wheel* on your machine turns. Turn the hand wheel to raise the needle to its highest point. Also, the *presser foot* should be up unless there is some fabric under it. Use the *presser bar lever* to raise the presser foot.

Now you are ready to thread the upper part of the machine. Put a spool of thread on the *spool pin*. Then run the thread through

SEWING MACHINE

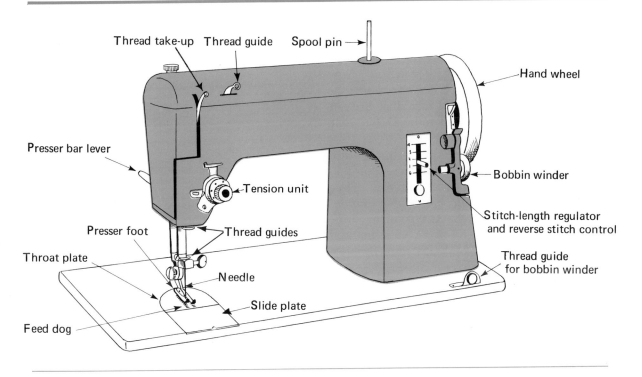

Thread take-up   Thread guide   Spool pin →

Hand wheel

Presser bar lever

Tension unit

Bobbin winder

Stitch-length regulator
and reverse stitch control

Presser foot

Thread guides

Throat plate

Needle

Thread guide
for bobbin winder

Slide plate

Feed dog

hand wheel   turns by hand to raise and lower the needle to make stitches

spool pin   holds the spool of thread for sewing

thread guides   hold thread in place while stitching and while winding the bobbin

tension unit   controls the tightness of the upper thread in sewing

thread take-up   pulls the thread to help make stitches

presser bar lever   raises and lowers the presser foot

presser foot   holds the fabric in place while stitching

throat plate   covers the area around the feed dog

feed dog   moves the fabric under the presser foot while stitching

bobbin winder   holds the bobbin as it is wound

stitch-length regulator   changes the length of stitches

reverse stitch control   allows the machine to backstitch

slide plate   covers the bobbin and bobbin case

the various parts in this order: *thread guide(s), tension unit, thread take-up*, thread guide(s), and needle. Check how to thread the machine you are using by following the directions in the instruction manual for your machine or check with your teacher. After you have studied the directions, practice threading this part of your machine.

Before you thread the lower part of your machine, there are some things you need to do. First, make sure the needle is still at its highest point and that the presser foot is raised. Then find the part of your sewing machine which slides, opens, or lifts to expose the underneath parts of the machine. Now remove the bobbin or the bobbin and *bobbin case* from the machine. Since all machines are not alike, read the instruction manual for your machine or ask your teacher how to do this.

The next step is to wind the bobbin. Follow the instructions in the manual for your machine or ask your teacher to help you. Then remove the bobbin from the *bobbin winder* and thread the bobbin. Each type of machine is threaded differently so check your manual or ask your teacher to help you. Practice threading the bobbin several times.

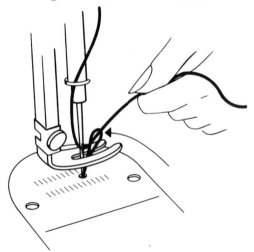

The last step in threading the machine is to bring the bobbin thread up to meet the upper thread. To do this, hold the upper thread loosely in one hand. Then turn the hand wheel one complete turn so that the needle goes all the way down and returns to its highest point. Next, pull on the upper thread until the thread from the bobbin shows. Then pull on the loop with your other hand until the end of the bobbin thread comes out of the needle hole. Always pull both threads away from you and back between the presser foot "toes" as the next step. This helps avoid thread tangles when stitching.

USING THE SEWING MACHINE

Guidelines for stitching are marked on many sewing machines. Some markings are in inches and fractions of inches. Other markings may be in centimeters and parts of centimeters. Unless the directions say otherwise, seams are stitched at ⅝ inch (1.5) cm from the edge.

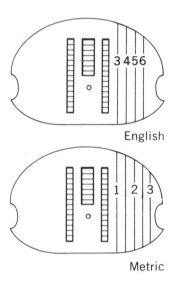

To practice stitching a seam, fold a scrap of fabric in half so that the raw edges match. Place the fabric next to the seam guideline. Lower the needle into the fabric and lower the presser foot. Start to stitch by turning the hand wheel and pressing lightly on the foot or knee control. When the machine starts stitching, use your right hand to guide the fabric, keeping the seam width at ⅝ inch (1.5 cm). The *feed dog* moves the fabric under the presser foot so you don't need to push or pull the fabric through. Stop the machine before you get to the edge of the fabric. Do the last few stitches turning the hand wheel by hand. Stop with the needle at the highest point and raise the presser foot. Pull the piece of fabric toward the back of the machine and cut the threads on the thread cutter or with scissors. Practice stitching until you can control the speed of the machine and stop and start smoothly.

HOW TO AVOID TANGLES WHEN STITCHING

STEP 1. Be sure thread take-up is at its highest point. Pull thread ends back between the toes of the presser foot.

STEP 2. Turn the hand wheel and lower the needle into the fabric. Then lower the presser foot. Check to be sure the threads are still pulled back as in Step 1. Then stitch the seam.

STEP 3. When you finish stitching, be sure the thread take-up is at its highest point.

STEP 4. Wind thread on an empty bobbin. Check that the thread is wound evenly on the bobbin. Use the same thread for both upper threading and bobbin.

Sometimes you have to adjust the length of the stitch. Locate the *stitch-length regulator* on your sewing machine. Read your instruction manual or check with your teacher to find out how to change the stitch length. Make samples of long stitches and short stitches. Then reset the stitch-length regulator to 12 to 15 stitches per inch (5 to 6 stitches per centimeter). This is the setting you will use most of the time.

Most machines have a *reverse stitch control.* This allows you to backstitch at the beginning and end of a seam. Find the reverse stitch control on your machine. If there is one, find out how to use it and make a seam with backstitching at the beginning and end. Follow the directions to the right to do this.

HOW TO BACKSTITCH

STEP 1. With presser foot raised, place fabric under presser foot.

STEP 2. Turn the hand wheel to lower the needle into the fabric on the seam line ¼ inch (6 mm) from the top edge of the fabric.

STEP 3. Lower the presser foot.

STEP 4. Backstitch to the top edge of the fabric.

STEP 5. Stitch to the end of the seam.

STEP 6. Backstitch 4 or 5 stitches at the end of the seam.

STEP 7. Turn the hand wheel until the thread take-up is at its highest point.

STEP 8. Raise the presser foot.

STEP 9. Pull the fabric back and cut the threads.

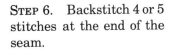

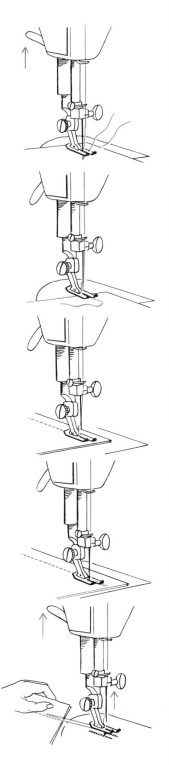

THREAD AND NEEDLE CHOICES FOR MACHINE SEWING

FABRIC	THREAD TYPE AND SIZE	NEEDLE SIZE[1]	MACHINE SETTING FOR STRAIGHT STITCHING
sheer[2] of natural[3] fibers	mercerized cotton A or 50	11 or fine	12–15 stitches per inch or 5–6 stitches per centimeter
of manufactured[3] fibers or blends containing manufactured[3] fibers	regular cotton-covered polyester		
lightweight[4] of natural[3] fibers	mercerized cotton A or 50	11 or 14, or fine or medium	12 stitches per inch or 5 stitches per centimeter
of manufactured[3] fibers or blends containing manufactured[3] fibers	regular cotton-covered polyester		
medium[5] of natural[3] fibers	mercerized cotton A or 50	14 or medium	12 stitches per inch or 5 stitches per centimeter
of manufactured[3] fibers or blends containing manufactured[3] fibers	regular cotton-covered polyester		
medium heavy[6] of natural[3] fibers	heavy duty mercerized cotton	16 or medium coarse	10 stitches per inch or 4 stitches per centimeter
of manufactured[3] fibers or blends containing manufactured[3] fibers	heavy duty cotton-covered polyester		
heavy[7] of natural[3] fibers	heavy duty mercerized cotton	18 or 19, or coarse	8 stitches per inch or 3 stitches per centimeter
of manufactured[3] fibers or blends containing manufactured[3] fibers	heavy duty cotton-covered polyester		

[1]Use ball point needle for knitted fabrics.

[2]*sheer fabric:* chiffon, voile, organdy, organza.

[3]See listing of natural and manufactured fibers in Unit 6, Lesson 4.

[4]*lightweight fabric:* gingham, percale, tricot, some single knits, some broadcloth, some seersucker, flannelette.

[5]*medium fabric:* some broadcloth, poplin, flannel, some corduroy; velveteen, some double knits, some single knits, some seersucker, some terry cloth, taffeta, some bonded fabrics.

[6]*medium heavy fabric:* some coating fabrics, heavy denim, some double knits, some upholstery, some corduroy (wide-wale), some terry cloth, quilted, some bonded fabrics.

[7]*heavy fabric:* some coating fabrics, some upholstery, some double knits, canvas, fake furs.

When stitching with a sewing machine, the thread from the bobbin locks with the upper thread to form a stitch. How well a stitch is formed depends on the adjustments of the upper and lower tensions. For example, if the *tension*, or tightness, of either thread is wrong, the stitches will be too tight or too loose. Both the upper tension and the lower tension need to be correct for the threads to be interlocked with the right tightness. The tensions are set correctly when the stitching is flat and smooth and looks the same on both sides of the fabric.

Both tensions correct.

Loose upper tension.
Tight lower tension.

Tight upper tension.
Loose lower tension.

Check the stitching on the samples you made. Does the stitching look the same on both sides? Is it flat and smooth? If your answer is no to either one or both of these questions, find out from your teacher how you adjust the tension on your machine.

The amount of pressure on the presser foot can be controlled too. Exact directions as to how this can be done are in your machine's instruction manual. This pressure is sometimes adjusted for different weight fabrics or fabrics with special characteristics.

It is important to change the sewing machine needle if it is the wrong size or if it is bent or blunt. This is not hard to do. Follow the directions in your sewing machine manual or ask your teacher. Look at the chart on page 202 for the correct size needle. Throw away a bent or blunt needle. Each time you sew, it is a good idea to check how the needle is put in. If the needle is backwards you will probably have stitching problems.

While using your sewing machine, pay attention to what you are doing. Talking to a friend or daydreaming may cause an accident. Keep scissors away from the machine's electric cord to avoid cutting it and getting an electric shock. Follow instructions in the sewing machine manual for cleaning the lint from the machine and for keeping the machine properly lubricated, or oiled. If you have problems, ask your teacher what to do.

SEWING SUGGESTIONS

broken needle might be caused by:	Improper size of needle for thread and material.
	Needle bent.
	Pulling of material when stitching.
	Needle striking improperly fastened presser foot or attachments.
	Crossing too thick a seam with too small a needle.
broken needle thread might be caused by:	A knot in needle thread.
	Improper threading.
	Upper tension too tight.
	Needle not inserted in needle clamp as far as it will go.
	Needle blunt or bent.

continued on next page

broken needle thread might be caused by:	Needle in backwards.
	Thread too coarse for needle.
	Roughened hole in throat plate.
	Improper arrangement of thread when starting to sew.
broken bobbin thread might be caused by:	Improper threading of bobbin case.
	Bobbin thread tension too tight.
	A knot in bobbin thread.
skipped stitches might be caused by:	Needle not inserted in needle clamp as far as it will go.
	Needle in backwards.
	Needle threaded incorrectly. Thread from long groove side to short groove side.
	Needle blunt or bent.
	Needle too small for thread.
	Needle too short.
puckered seams might be caused by:	Tension too tight.
	Stitch too long for material being sewn.
	Wrong presser foot. Use only the presser foot provided for each particular machine, as they are, in some cases, not interchangeable.
	If machine runs heavily, clean and oil it.

PUTTING IT TOGETHER

1 What are the parts that you will find on all sewing machines? Point out these parts on a sewing machine or on a diagram of a sewing machine.
2 What are some parts of the sewing machine that you can learn to adjust to keep it running smoothly? Describe how these parts can be adjusted.
3 What is the sequence of steps to follow in threading a sewing machine? Demonstrate them on a sewing machine.
4 Explain some ways to avoid tangles when you begin to stitch.
5 What might cause each of these problems in using the sewing machine?
   a broken needle
   b broken needle thread
   c broken bobbin thread
   d skipped stitches
   e puckered seams

LESSON TWO
SMALL SEWING EQUIPMENT AND SUPPLIES

gauge

shears

scissors

tracing wheel

dressmaker's carbon

pinking shears

pressing ham

point presser

sleeve board

pressing cloth

seam ripper

hem marker

some types of equipment and supplies

storage of equipment and supplies

In order for you to sew you need certain tools or equipment to work with. These tools require a place in which they can be stored and ready for use. They may be kept in a box, a basket, or perhaps an especially-made sewing kit.

Some tools are necessary to have. Others are nice to have, but not essential. A tape measure, a yardstick or meterstick, a small ruler or *gauge, shears, scissors,* a *tracing wheel, dressmaker's carbon,* an iron, an ironing board, a pressing ham, pins, hand needles, a thimble, and a pin cushion are usually considered necessary sewing equipment. *Pinking shears,* a *seam ripper,* a *press cloth,* a *point presser,* a *sleeve board,* and a *hem marker* are useful but not always necessary for beginning sewers.

MEASURING EQUIPMENT

A tape measure can be used on either flat or rounded surfaces. A tape measure can be used for taking body measurements. A yard-stick or meterstick or hem marker is good for marking a hem. To measure a small amount, such as a hem turn-up, a small ruler or gauge is useful. So, for measuring you should have a tape measure, a yardstick or a meterstick, a small ruler, or hem gauge. The right measuring tools will make your work easier.

Now turn to page 206 and see if you can identify each of the tools that are to be used for measuring as they are shown in the photograph.

CUTTING EQUIPMENT

Several tools are designed for cutting fabric. Shears and scissors are not the same. Each is designed to do different cutting jobs. Shears are generally larger and have longer blades than scissors. Shears are used for cutting out pattern pieces. Scissors are used for cutting threads, for clipping, and for trimming. Pinking shears cut a zig-zag edge and are used for trimming seams. They should not be used for

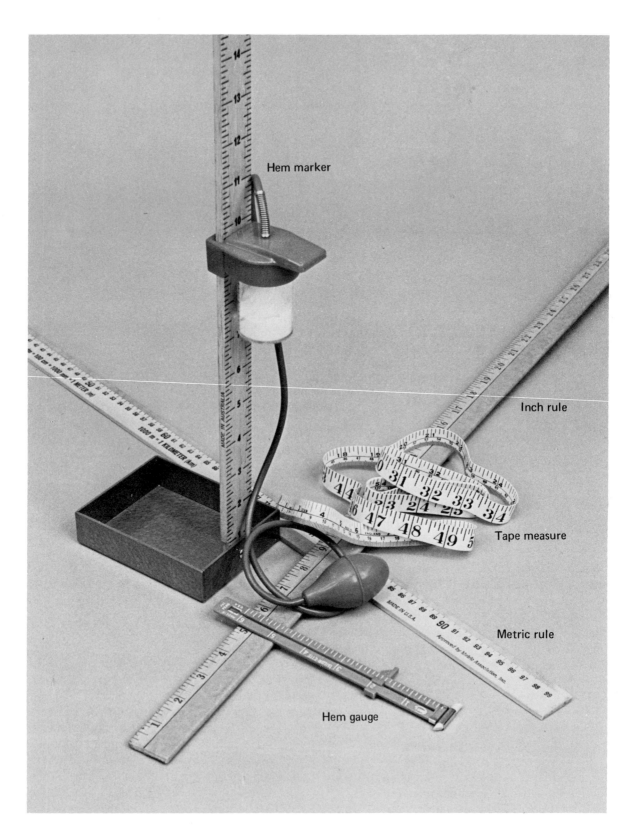

Hem marker

Inch rule

Tape measure

Metric rule

Hem gauge

CLOTHES, CLUES, AND CAREERS

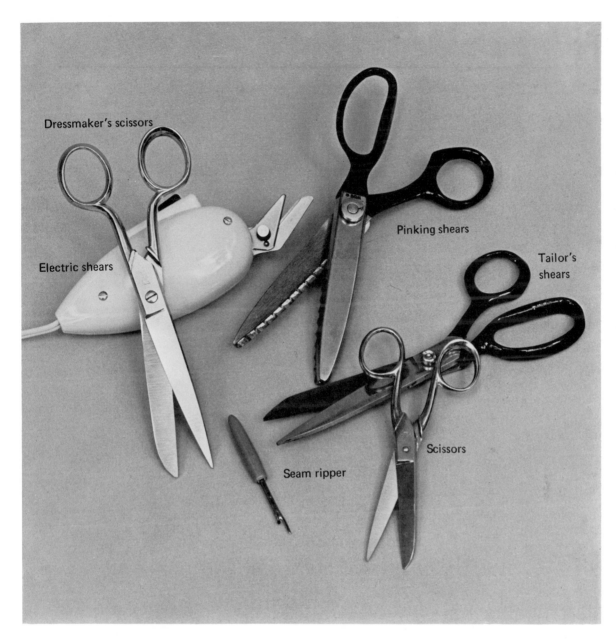

Dressmaker's scissors

Electric shears

Pinking shears

Tailor's shears

Seam ripper

Scissors

cutting out pattern pieces. Both shears and scissors should be sharp and easy to use. Dull cutting tools or ones that stick can ruin fabric.

A seam ripper is handy to have if you need to take out stitching. Notice the seam ripper in the photograph above. It has a pointed end for picking up a stitch to be taken out and a razor-like edge for cutting just the stitch and not the fabric around the stitch.

Look at the photograph above again and see if you can identify the shears and the scissors. Notice how they differ.

MARKING EQUIPMENT

Marking tools include tracing wheel, dressmaker's carbon paper, and chalk. Dressmaker's carbon paper, or tracing paper, and a tracing wheel are often used to transfer pattern markings to fabric. A tracing wheel with

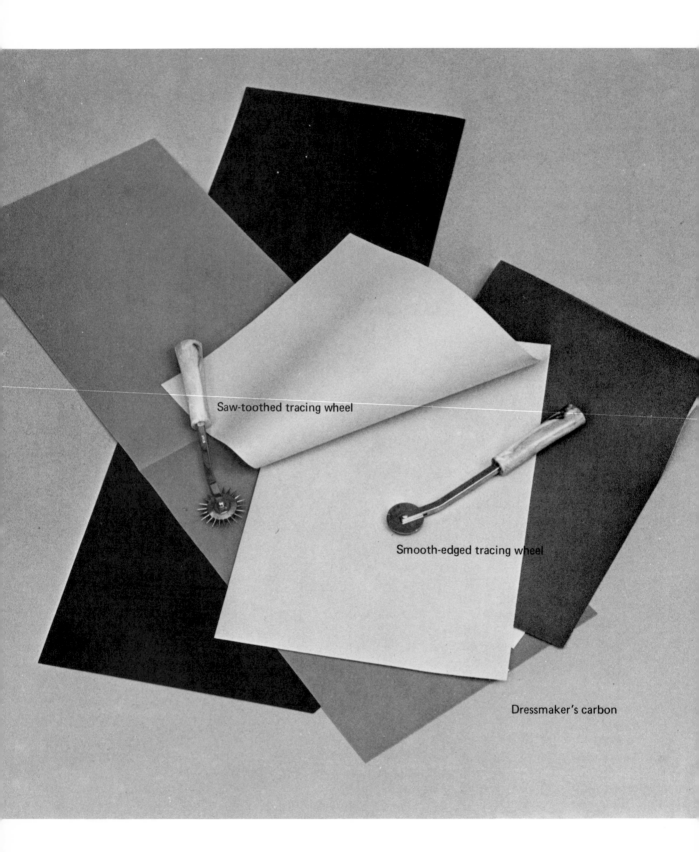

Saw-toothed tracing wheel

Smooth-edged tracing wheel

Dressmaker's carbon

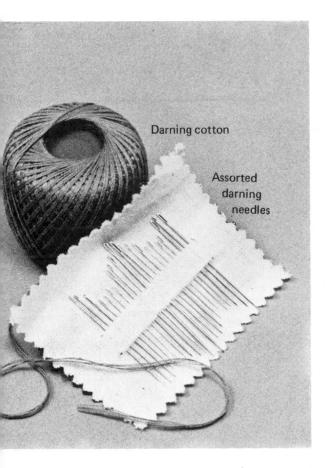

Darning cotton

Assorted darning needles

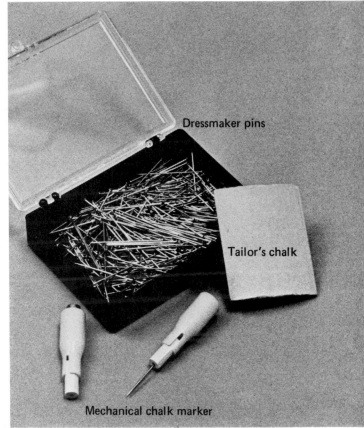

Dressmaker pins

Tailor's chalk

Mechanical chalk marker

a serrated, or saw-toothed, edge is a good tool to use when you are marking fabrics which have smooth surfaces. However, knits, and certain other fabrics which may snag easily, may better be marked by using the tracing wheel which has a smooth, rather than a saw-toothed edge.

There are instances when it is best not to use carbon markings at all. There are other ways to transfer pattern markings. For example, a heavy pile fabric cannot be successfully marked by using carbon paper and a tracing wheel. When carbon paper markings are not suitable to use on some particular fabrics, there are other means. Darning cotton or cotton thread may be used to make tailor's tacks. Chalk and pins may also be used to indicate the markings which are needed.

In the photograph to the left and in the ones above are examples of marking equipment. Identify each one.

PRESSING EQUIPMENT

Good pressing equipment is important to good sewing. The ironing board can be used for pressing straight seams and flat areas of a garment. A tailor's cushion or pressing ham is used when pressing rounded or curved seams and parts of a garment which might be pressed out of shape on a flat surface. A point presser is helpful when pressing points such as those in shirt collars. Sleeve boards are small ironing boards which make it easier to press sleeves and other small rounded areas. In pressing some fabrics, a press cloth must be used. The press cloth is placed on top of the fabric to be pressed to allow heat and steam to pass through but prevent shine on the fabric itself.

In the photograph on page 210 are examples of a tailor's ham, point presser, ironing board, sleeve board, iron, and a press cloth.

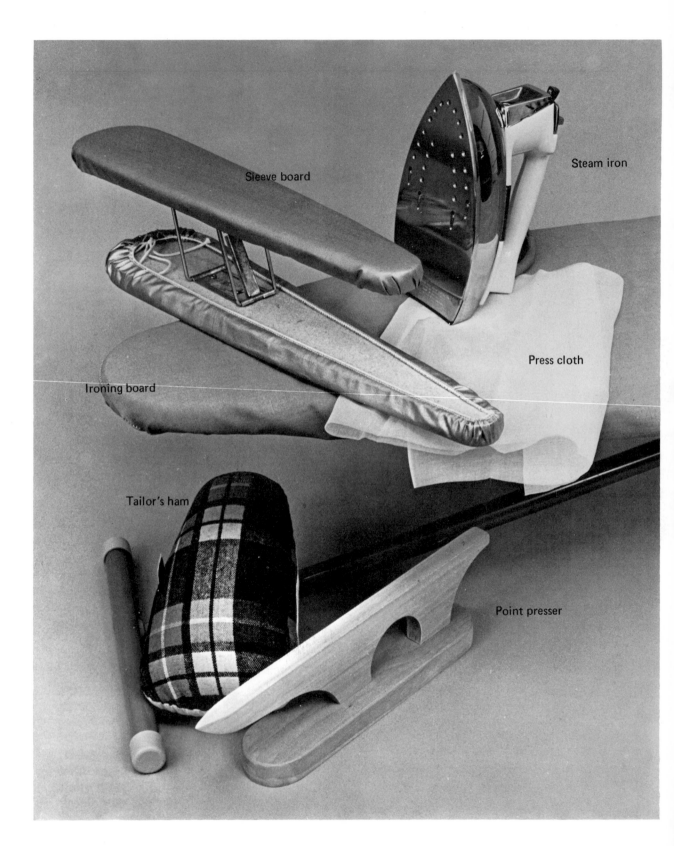

Sleeve board

Steam iron

Press cloth

Ironing board

Tailor's ham

Point presser

OTHER EQUIPMENT AND SUPPLIES

Plenty of pins are necessary for pinning while you sew. If you are using a woven fabric, be sure the pins have sharp points. Dull pins may snag the fabric. For knit fabrics ball point pins are a good choice. A pin cushion, rather than a box, is better to keep the pins handy and to prevent spilling.

You will need a thimble and hand needles for hand sewing. A thimble protects your finger as you push the needle through fabric. Choose one that fits your middle finger comfortably. Learn to use the side of the thimble rather than the end. Be sure hand needles are the correct size for your fabric. Check with your teacher to be sure. Ball point needles are for use with knit fabrics.

Some of the small sewing equipment you need may be in your classroom so you won't need to buy all of the equipment and supplies mentioned. If you buy your own equipment, mark it with your name so you do not lose it. If you are sharing equipment, be considerate of others and take turns.

STORAGE OF EQUIPMENT AND SUPPLIES

You may already have a sewing box in which to store sewing equipment and supplies. If not, you may want to buy one or make one. Your sewing equipment is easier to find and use when you have a special place for it. Whether you make or buy a storage box, it should have a top handle for easy carrying and compartments for separating small articles so that they are easy to find. Shears, scissors, pins, needles, and any sharp objects should be stored safely in a place where they won't be damaged. The latch should be secure in order to keep the box from opening unexpectedly.

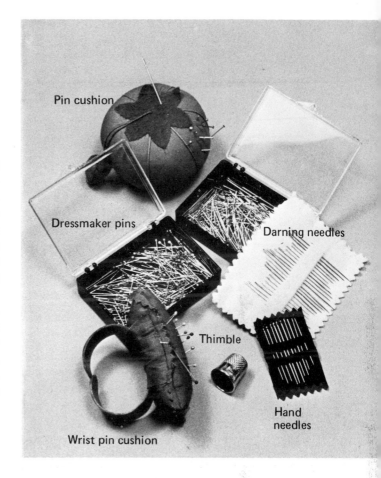

Pin cushion

Dressmaker pins

Darning needles

Thimble

Hand needles

Wrist pin cushion

 **PUTTING IT TOGETHER**

1 What are some kinds of measuring equipment for sewing? Describe some ways each piece can be used.
2 What are some cutting tools for sewing? Describe how they are used. Explain the difference between scissors and shears.
3 Name some kinds of marking equipment and describe how each is used.
4 What are some kinds of pressing equipment used when sewing. Explain how this equipment is used.
5 What are some ways other than those suggested in this lesson for storing sewing equipment?

LESSON THREE
FABRICS

 closely woven fabric

double knit fabric

on grain

care instructions

straightening fabric

 choosing fabric

information to look for when buying fabric

how to prepare fabric for cutting and sewing

Some fabrics are easier to work with than others. Therefore some are better choices than others for first sewing projects. You are likely to have success with your first sewing project if you choose a fabric which is firmly woven or firmly knitted; does not ravel easily; is of medium weight; is on grain; looks the same on both sides; and has a small design or is a solid color.

SELECTING A FABRIC

Closely woven fabrics and double knit fabrics are less likely to ravel and stretch out of shape than loosely woven fabrics and some single knit fabrics. A *closely woven fabric* is one in which many yarns have been woven in both the lengthwise and crosswise directions

of the fabric. The illustrations below show examples of a closely woven fabric and a loosely woven fabric. You may want to look at some samples of cloth under a magnifying lens to see the differences in the number of yarns used to make different fabrics. *Double knit fabrics* are made up of two layers of knitted fabric. These layers are knitted together as the fabric is made. The fabric is firm and does not "run" as some single knits do. Examples of "runs" can be seen in nylon hosiery and dropped stitches in hand knitting.

When choosing a fabric, check to see that it feels firm and is not slippery. Feel the weight of the fabric. Thick, bulky fabrics and sheer, thin fabrics are difficult to pin, cut, sew, and press. A medium weight fabric is easier to work with.

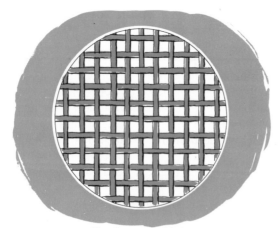

Closely woven fabric

Loosely woven fabric

Woven fabric that is *on grain* has the lengthwise and crosswise yarns at right angles to each other. Look closely to see that the fabric is on grain. Some off-grain fabrics can be straightened. Off-grain fabrics with finishes set by heat cannot be straightened. Garments made from fabrics that are off grain may not fit or hang properly.

Fabrics in solid colors or small patterns are usually good choices for first projects. Small mistakes often do not show on a patterned fabric. Stripes, plaids, and large designs all require careful planning before cutting. They need to be matched when the garment is sewn. This may take more time than you have to complete your project.

As you look at different fabrics, read the information on the ends of the bolts and on the attached labels. This will tell you what the fabric is made of and how to care for the fabric. Fiber content and care instructions are required by law to be stated.

Care instructions should include washing instructions or tell you that dry cleaning is required. A complete label for a washable fabric will give the suggested washing temperature and the pressing instructions. A care label should be attached to the end of a fabric bolt. When you buy a fabric, the salesperson should give you a care label to sew onto your completed garment.

The information on the ends of bolts and on attached labels may also include special finishes on the fabrics. If you are concerned about shrinkage, look for information about shrinkage-control finishes. If easy care is important, look for finishes that are wash-and-wear or permanent-press.

Write down the information you will need to remember, such as the width of the fabric. If you find two or three different fabrics you like, you may want to write down information about each one so that you can compare them before you decide which to buy.

It is a good idea to buy your pattern before you buy fabric. You will then know the right amount of fabric to buy. You will also be able to buy thread, zipper, buttons, and any other things you need to complete your garment.

PREPARING FABRIC

For good results, some preparation of your fabric is necessary before you start to sew. Special treatment is needed to make sure that the fabric is on grain and will not shrink after your garment is completed.

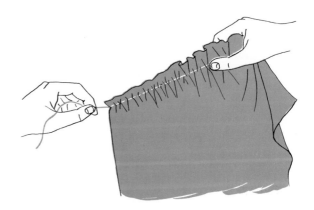

Ends of the fabric should be straight so that when the fabric is folded lengthwise, the crosswise grainline can be matched exactly on both thicknesses of fabric. To find out if a woven fabric is on grain cut each end of the fabric piece on a crosswise thread. Pull a thread as a guide for cutting straight across the fabric. Cut as close as possible to the end of the fabric piece. Now fold the fabric in half lengthwise. Do the ends match and do the corners form right angles? If not, it may be possible to correct this by pulling the fabric straight. Pull evenly, but firmly, from opposite corners until the lengthwise and crosswise yarns form right angles.

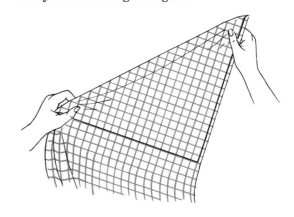

Cotton and other fabrics with heat-set finishes cannot be straightened by pulling the corners. Therefore, look at the grainline of the material carefully before you buy to be sure that it is straight. If you buy a fabric that has this type of finish but is slightly off grain you must accept the idea that your finished garment may be slightly off grain. You may have more satisfactory results in sewing fabrics with wash-and-wear finishes if you choose plain colors rather than prints, checks, or plaids. Slight irregularity in the grainline will not show as readily in a plain fabric.

If you are unsure about shrinkage in your fabric it will be worth the extra time to preshrink it. You can straighten your fabric at the same time. Use the following procedure for woven cotton fabrics. First, straighten the ends by pulling a thread and cutting across the fabric along the crosswise grain. Fold the fabric lengthwise and pin or baste the ends. Soak it in lukewarm water until thoroughly wet. Squeeze out as much water as possible. Roll it in a bath towel to remove more water. Spread the fabric on a water-resistant table top. Use one table corner and side as a guide to straighten the ends and sides of the material. When the fabric is dry, press it.

If a knit fabric has been wound closely on the bolt it may be stretched when you buy it. Before you cut and sew, allow the fabric to relax and recover its unstretched condition. Preshrink knit fabrics if there is no information on the fabric bolt that tells you that it has been preshrunk. Soak polyester knits a few minutes in lukewarm water and dry flat, if possible. Or fold ends evenly and hang over a drying rack. Dry as you might drip dry a ready-to-wear polyester garment.

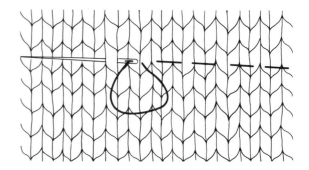

Straighten the ends of the knit fabric by marking along a line of loops across the fabric with a thread. Cut along the thread mark to make straight ends for folding the fabric and laying out the pattern. Straightening the ends of the fabric does not mean you have straightened the fabric. You may need to do that, too. Try pulling the fabric gently while you and a partner hold opposite corners of the fabric. Fold the fabric and line up the fabric edges with one corner and edge of a table. It may not be possible to straighten the fabric if it has been heat set slightly off grain during the manufacturing process.

If your fabric is on grain and does not need to be preshrunk, press it before you lay out the pattern. Pattern layout and cutting will be more accurate if there are no rough folds or wrinkles in the fabric.

PUTTING IT TOGETHER

1 Why are plain colors and small patterned fabrics easier to work with than stripes, plaids, and large designs?
2 Why are closely woven fabrics and double knits generally good choices for your first few sewing projects?
3 What facts should you look for when you buy fabric for sewing? How can information about the fabric help you in making the garment and caring for it? Give examples.
4 How should the fabric be prepared for cutting and sewing?

LESSON FOUR
FINDING YOUR PATTERN SIZE

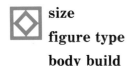 size figure type body build	measurement chart	figure types and body builds why measurements are important how to select a pattern

If you have looked in a pattern book you have probably noticed that patterns are made in many different sizes. You may also have noticed that each section of the pattern book is labeled with a special name, such as Girls, Juniors, Misses, Men, Teen Boys, and so on. Pattern sizes are based on body measurements. Patterns are designed for different figure types and body builds, which are based on physical development and body structure. When you choose a pattern you need to consider both *body measurements* and *figure type* or *body build*. Pattern sizes are not the same as sizes for ready-made clothing.

BODY MEASUREMENTS

To obtain accurate measurements you should work with a partner. Write down each of your measurements on a card or slip of paper. Refer to this card when choosing the correct *size* pattern for you.

Measure over the undergarments you usually wear. Do not measure over heavy outer clothing as this adds width; measurements will be incorrect. A measurement taken over a heavy waistband will not be accurate either. Measure your height with shoes off. Stand up straight. When you measure, read the instructions which follow and use the series of illustrations on page 216 as guides.

One measurement girls will need is the *bust measurement*. Fellows will need the *chest measurement*. To measure the chest or bust place the measuring tape under the arms and around the fullest part of the chest or bust. Be sure the tape is straight around the body and does not slant.

Two measurements both girls and fellows will need are the *waist* and *hip measurements*. The waist measurement is taken at the natural waistline, or the smallest area between the bust or chest and hips. It may be helpful to tie a string around your waist to show clearly where your natural waistline is. The string should be snug but not tight. The hip measurement is taken around the fullest part of the hips. This is usually 7 to 9 inches (17.5–22.5 cm) below the waistline. Be sure the tape is straight around the body.

Another measurement girls will need is the *back waist length measurement*. This measurement is taken from the bone at the base of the neck to the waistline at the center back. Fellows will need to take *neck* and *sleeve measurements* for shirts and *inseam measurement* for slacks. The neck is measured around its fullest part. Sleeve length is measured from the bone at the base of the neck, across the shoulder, and down to the wristbone. Inseam length is the length of slacks or jeans along the inside leg seam.

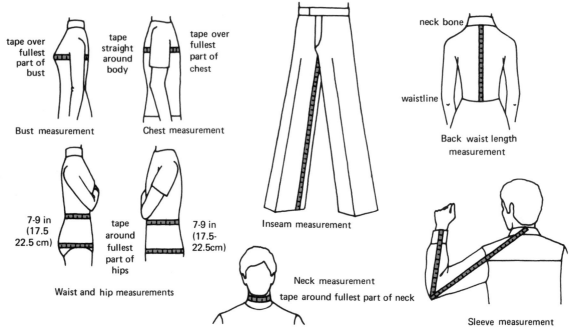

Bust measurement — tape over fullest part of bust

Chest measurement — tape straight around body; tape over fullest part of chest

Waist and hip measurements — 7-9 in (17.5 22.5 cm); tape around fullest part of hips; 7-9 in (17.5-22.5cm)

Inseam measurement

Neck measurement — tape around fullest part of neck

Back waist length measurement — neck bone; waistline

Sleeve measurement

FIGURE TYPE AND BODY BUILD

After you have your measurements, you are ready to determine your figure type or body build. Read the descriptions of figure types and body builds given with the Measurement Charts on pages 216–219. Find your figure type or body build. Compare your measurements with those given in the charts to find your size within the correct figure type or body build.

MEASUREMENT CHARTS FOR GIRLS AND WOMEN[1]

GIRLS young figure, not yet beginning to develop

	English						Metric					
size	7	8	10	12	14		7	8	10	12	14	
bust	26	27	28½	30	32	in	66	68.5	72.5	76	81.5	cm
waist	23	23½	24½	25½	26½	in	58.5	59.5	62	65	67.5	cm
hip	27	28	30	32	34	in	68.5	71	76	81.5	86.5	cm
back waist length	11½	12	12¾	13½	14¼	in	29	30.5	32.5	34.5	36	cm
height	50	52	56	58½	61	in	127	132	142	149	155	cm

[1] from Johnson, Clawson, Shoffner, *Individualized Sewing System*, Copyright 1974, by Ginn and Company.

YOUNG JUNIOR/TEEN (about 5 ft 1 in to 5 ft 3 in or 1.55m to 1.60m) developing pre-teen and teen figure; high youthful bust, short waist

	English							Metric						
size	5/6	7/8	9/10	11/12	13/14	15/16		5/6	7/8	9/10	11/12	13/14	15/16	
bust	28	29	30½	32	33½	35	in	71	73.5	77.5	81.5	85	89	cm
waist	22	23	24	25	26	27	in	56	58.5	61	63.5	66	69	cm
hip	31	32	33½	35	36½	38	in	78.5	81.5	85	89	92.5	97	cm
back waist length	13½	14	14½	15	15⅜	15¾	in	34.5	35.5	37	38	39.5	40	cm

JUNIOR (about 5 ft 4 in to 5 ft 5 in or 1.63m to 1.65m) mature figure, higher bustline and shorter waist than Misses'

	English							Metric						
size	5	7	9	11	13	15		5	7	9	11	13	15	
bust	30	31	32	33½	35	37	in	76	78.5	81.5	85	89	94	cm
waist	22½	23½	24½	25½	27	29	in	57	59.5	62	65	68.5	73.5	cm
hip	32	33	34	35½	37	39	in	81.5	84	86.5	90	94	99	cm
back waist length	15	15¼	15½	15¾	16	16¼	in	38	39	39.5	40	40.5	41.5	cm

JUNIOR-PETITE (about 5 ft to 5 ft 1 in or 1.52m to 1.55m) similar figure to Junior, but shorter, more petite

	English							Metric						
size	3	5	7	9	11	13		3	5	7	9	11	13	
bust	30½	31	32	33	34	35	in	77.5	78.5	81.5	84	86.5	89	cm
waist	22½	23	24	25	26	27	in	57	58.5	61.5	63.5	66	68.5	cm
hip	31½	32	33	34	35	36	in	80	81.5	84	86.5	89	91.5	cm
back waist length	14	14¼	14½	14¾	15	15¼	in	35.5	36	37	37.5	38	39	cm

continued on next page

MEASUREMENT CHARTS FOR GIRLS AND WOMEN *continued from page 217*

MISSES' (about 5 ft 5 in to 5 ft 6 in or 1.65m to 1.68m) mature figure, fully developed; lower bustline and longer waist than other figure types

size	English								Metric							
	6	8	10	12	14	16	18		6	8	10	12	14	16	18	
bust	30½	31½	32½	34	36	38	40	in	77.5	80	82.5	86.5	91.5	96.5	101.5	cm
waist	23	24	25	26½	28	30	32	in	58.5	61	63.5	67.5	71	76	81.5	cm
hip	32½	33½	34½	36	38	40	42	in	82.5	85	87.5	91.5	96.5	101.5	106.5	cm
back waist length	15½	15¾	16	16¼	16½	16¾	17	in	39.5	40	40.5	41.5	42	42.5	43	cm

MISS PETITE (about 5 ft in to 5 ft 4 in or 1.57m to 1.60m) similar figure to Misses' but shorter

size	English							Metric						
	6mp	8mp	10mp	12mp	14mp	16mp		6mp	8mp	10mp	12mp	14mp	16mp	
bust	30½	31½	32½	34	36	38	in	77.5	80	82.5	86.5	91.5	96.5	cm
waist	22½	23½	24½	26	27½	29½	in	57	59.5	62	66	70	75	cm
hip	32½	33½	34½	36	38	40	in	82.5	85	87.5	91.5	96.5	101.5	cm
back waist length	14½	14¾	15	15¼	15½	15¾	in	37	37.5	38	39	39.5	40	cm

MEASUREMENT CHARTS FOR BOYS AND MEN[2]

TEEN BOYS slender build, youthful body not fully matured

size	English					Metric				
	14	16	18	20		14	16	18	20	
neck	13½	14	14½	15	in	34.5	35.5	37	38	cm
chest	32	33½	35	36½	in	81.5	85	89	92.5	cm
waist	27	28	29	30	in	68.5	71	73.5	76	cm
hip	32½	34	35½	37	in	82.5	86.5	90	94	cm
height	61	64	66	68	in	155	163	168	173	cm

[2] from Johnson, Clawson, Shoffner, *Individualized Sewing System*, Copyright 1974, by Ginn and Company.

CLOTHES, CLUES, AND CAREERS

MEN'S (about 5 ft 10 in or 1.78m) mature build; fully developed body

	English									Metric								
size	**34**	**36**	**38**	**40**	**42**	**44**	**46**	**48**		**34**	**36**	**38**	**40**	**42**	**44**	**46**	**48**	
chest	34	36	38	40	42	44	46	48	in	86.5	91.5	96.5	101.5	106.5	112	117	122	cm
waist	28	30	32	34	36	39	42	44	in	71	76	81.5	86.5	91.5	99	106.5	112	cm
hip	35	37	39	41	43	45	47	49	in	89	94	99	104	109	114.5	119.5	124.5	cm
neck	14	14½	15	15½	16	16½	17	17½	in	35.5	37	38	39.5	40.5	42	43	44.5	cm
sleeve	32	32	33	33	34	34	35	35	in	81	81	84	84	86.5	86.5	89	89	cm

OTHER INFORMATION

Sometimes girls' body measurements are not exactly the same as those on the measurement charts. If you want to make a blouse, dress, or jumper, choose a pattern closest to the bust measurement within the correct figure type. If you choose a pattern for slacks, shorts, or a skirt, choose the pattern size which is closest to the hip measurement within the correct figure type.

For fellows whose body measurements are not exactly the same as those on the chart, choose a shirt pattern closest to the correct neck measurement within the correct body build. For slacks, choose a pattern to fit waist or hip measurement, whichever is larger, within the correct body build.

 **PUTTING IT TOGETHER**

1 What are some figure types for girls' and women's patterns? What are some body builds for men's and boys' patterns?
2 What measurements do you need to determine your pattern size and figure type or body build?
3 What is your pattern size and figure type or body build?

LESSON FIVE
UNDERSTANDING PATTERNS

 view

pattern envelope

pattern guide sheet

cutting layout

sewing directions

 what the pattern envelope tells you

what the pattern pieces tell you

how the pattern guide sheet helps you to use the pattern

Patterns for home sewing are packaged in envelopes. If you look at a *pattern envelope,* you can see that the envelope is more than a protective wrapper for the pattern pieces. It has helpful information to be used when you are deciding what pattern and fabric to choose for a garment. See illustrations on pages 221–222.

PATTERN ENVELOPE FRONT

Often a pattern makes two or more different styles. A drawing or photograph on the front of the pattern envelope shows the style or styles the pattern pieces can make. For example, a shirt may be shown with long sleeves and with short sleeves. This means that pattern pieces are included for both styles. If a dress is shown with a V-neck and a round neck, there are pattern pieces for both styles. Sometimes one style of a garment is shown in different fabrics. A blouse may appear in a plain fabric in one style and in a different fabric in another style. Instructions are included for making both styles. The different styles are usually called *views* and may be labeled View 1, View 2, and so on.

The pattern identification number appears on the front of the pattern envelope. This tells you that the envelope contains the design you have selected from the pattern book. Patterns for women and girls show the sizes and figure types. Examples are Junior size 9, Misses size 10, or Young Junior/Teen size 13/14. Patterns for men and boys indicate the body build and size, such as Teen Boys size 16 or Men size 40. When you choose your pattern, check to make sure that it is the style you want and that the size and figure type or body build are correct. Sometimes patterns cannot be exchanged or returned. For this reason be certain that you have made the right choice that will satisfy you.

Other information may also be shown on the front of the pattern envelope. A few words may tell you that the pattern should be used only with knitted fabrics. Or a statement may tell you that the garment is considered to be one that is easy to make. Sometimes the pattern envelope indicates that the pattern is especially good for beginners to use.

PATTERN ENVELOPE BACK

The back of the pattern envelope has important information, too. The back view of each garment the pattern pieces will make is given.

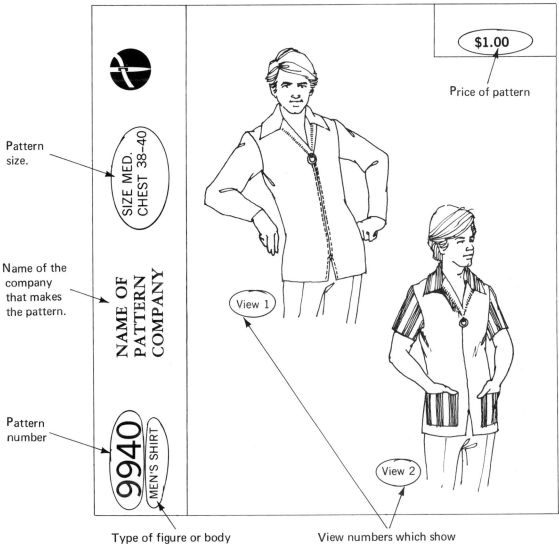

Pattern size. → SIZE MED. CHEST 38-40

Name of the company that makes the pattern. → NAME OF PATTERN COMPANY

Pattern number → 9940

MEN'S SHIRT

Type of figure or body build the pattern is for.

$1.00

Price of pattern

View 1

View 2

View numbers which show the style the pattern makes.

There also the number of pattern pieces in the envelope is listed. Each pattern piece is illustrated to show the shape of each piece. If there are pattern pieces for two or more garments, such as a vest and pants, the pieces for each garment are shown together. Information about the number of pattern pieces and the shape of each is helpful in deciding whether you can work easily with the pattern. A garment with straight lines and few pattern pieces is easier to make than one with curved lines and many pattern pieces.

A chart on the back of the pattern envelope shows the amount of fabric required for each view. Since not all fabrics are made in the same width, the amount needed will depend on how wide the fabric is you are buying. To find out how much fabric you need, look in the left column of the chart and find the view you are to make and the width fabric you plan to buy. Draw an imaginary line across the chart from that point. Then look along the top of the chart to find the pattern size you have. Draw an imaginary line down the chart from this point.

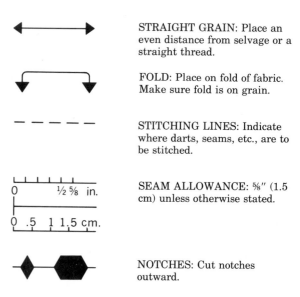

9940

Johnson, Clawson, Shoffner, Individualized Sewing System © Copyright, 1974, by Ginn and Company (Xerox Corporation) All Rights Reserved Home Office, Lexington, Massachusetts 02173

MEN'S SHIRT

Size		Small	Medium	Large	Extra Large
Standard Body Measurements	Neck	14–14½	15–15½	16–16½	17–17½ Ins.
	Chest	34–36	38–40	42–44	46–48 Ins.
	Waist	28–30	32–34	36–39	42–44 Ins.
	Hip	35–37	39–41	43–45	47–49 Ins.
Fabric required					
View 1					
35″–36″ with nap		2⅞	3¼	3⅝	4 Yds.
44″–45″ with nap		2½	2½	2⅞	3 Yds.
58″–60″ with nap		1⅞	1⅞	2⅛	2⅜ Yds.
View 2					
35″–36″ with nap		2⅜	2⅜	3¼	3⅜ Yds.
44″–45″ with nap		1⅞	1⅞	2¼	2⅜ Yds.
58″–60″ with nap		⅞	⅞	1¼	1¼ Yds.
Contrasting sleeves, collar, and pockets					
35″–36″ with nap		1	1	1⅛	1⅛ Yds.
44″–45″ with nap		¾	¾	⅞	1 Yds.
58″–60″ with nap		⅝	⅝	⅝	⅝ Yds.
Interfacing for collar 35″–36″ or 44″–45″ woven		¼	¼	¼	¼ Yd.
Finished back length		30	30½	31	31½ Ins.

MEN'S SHIRT: Collared shirt has set-in sleeves, separating zipper. View 1 has long sleeves; view 2 has short sleeves.

NOTIONS: Thread, seam tape, 22″ separating zipper

FABRIC SUGGESTIONS: cotton broadcloth, denim, double knit, seersucker, corduroy, madras, gingham

English measurements

Pattern Panel 6, Fig. 2

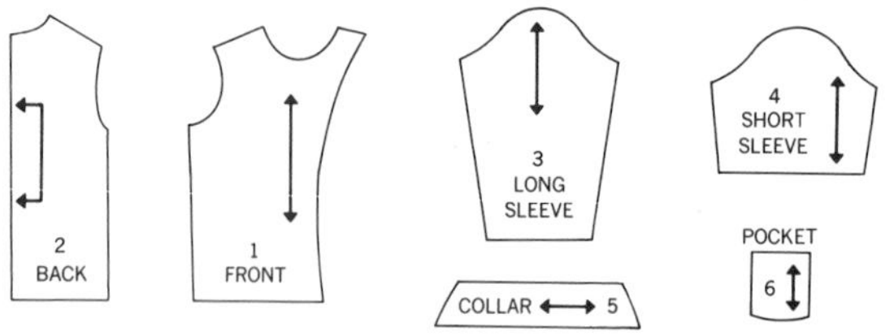

The point where the lines meet tells you the amount of fabric you need. If interfacing fabric is necessary for the garment, the amount you need will also be given in the chart. If a view has trim, the amount needed is given.

A description of each view sometimes appears on the back of the pattern envelope along with suggestions for fabrics to use for each view. Sometimes suggestions about fabrics not to use are also included. Sewing notions such as thread, buttons, and zippers are listed.

PATTERN PIECES

Inside the pattern envelope are the pattern pieces. These are labeled by letter and name. The pattern number and size are also included. Markings on the pattern pieces show the seamline and construction details such as darts or pleats. Usually there are directions for how many pieces of each pattern piece you should cut.

STRAIGHT GRAIN: Place an even distance from selvage or a straight thread.

FOLD: Place on fold of fabric. Make sure fold is on grain.

— — — — —

STITCHING LINES: Indicate where darts, seams, etc., are to be stitched.

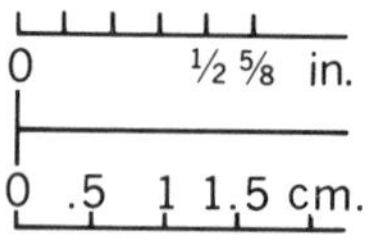

SEAM ALLOWANCE: ⅝″ (1.5 cm) unless otherwise stated.

NOTCHES: Cut notches outward.

Choose the pattern pieces for the view you are to make and put the rest back into the envelope. Write your name on all pattern pieces so they will not be lost.

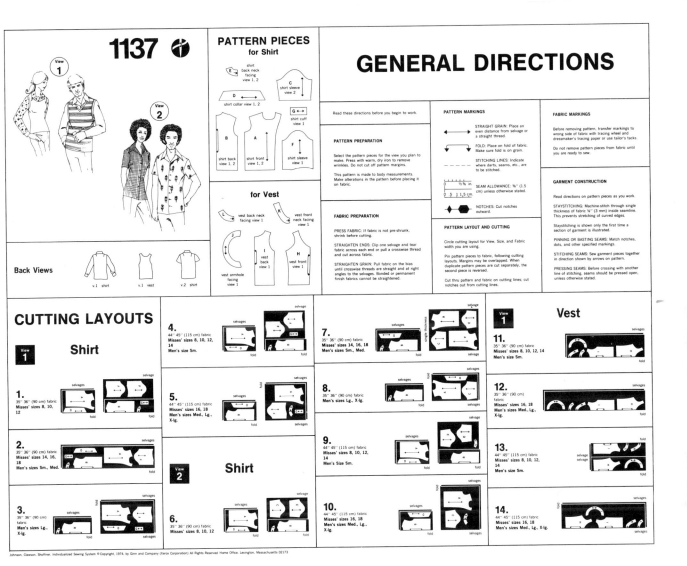

PATTERN GUIDE SHEET

The pattern guide sheet shows the front and back views of each garment and the pattern pieces needed for making each view. There are special directions for preparing your pattern and fabric for layout and an explanation of the various markings on your pattern pieces. There are also suggested ways to transfer markings from the pattern pieces to fabric and definitions of any special terms which are used in the directions. See guide sheet above.

Other information on the pattern guide sheet includes the *cutting layouts* and *sewing*

directions. The cutting layouts are diagrams which show how to position the fabric for laying out the pattern pieces and how to place each pattern piece on the fabric according to view, pattern size, and fabric width. When you are ready to lay out your pattern, draw a circle around the correct layout on the guide sheet for easy reference.

The sewing directions tell how to sew the pieces together. See guide sheet on page 224. Usually each direction includes drawings which make it easier to follow each step. It is a good idea to study the pattern guide sheet before you begin to construct your garment.

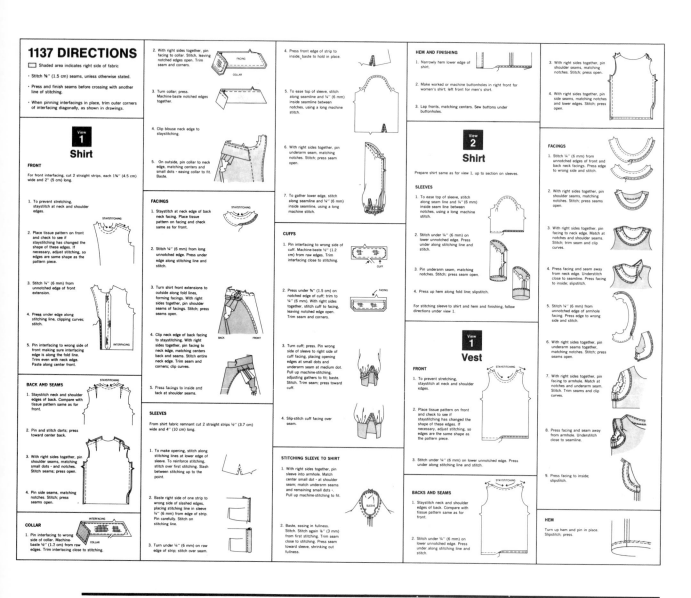

PUTTING IT TOGETHER

1 What information will you find on the front of the pattern envelope?

2 What information can you expect to find on the back of the pattern envelope?

3 How will the pattern guide sheet help you cut and assemble the garment?

LESSON SIX
PLANNING YOUR WORK

 pattern   **plan**
guide sheet

view

 **some reasons for planning
your work**

making a plan

Depending on the garment you are making, the lessons in this unit may or may not be in the order in which you will use them. There may be some you will not use at all. To make it easier for you to use these lessons, this lesson will show you how to plan your work. After you have made your *plan,* you will know the order in which you will use the lessons and those lessons you will not use.

Making such a plan helps you to organize your work and use your time effectively.

To make your plan you will need your *pattern guide sheet* and a form similar to the one below. Find the directions on your pattern guide sheet for the *view* you are making. Read through the directions and make note of each step you must follow. Be sure you write down the steps in order.

Name _____ *Pat* _____

Garment _____ *Jeans* _____

Steps to make garment according
to my pattern guide sheet

Lesson number and pages in
Clothes, Clues, and Careers

*1. Staystitch waistline edges
of front pieces*

Lesson 10, pages 241-242

*2. Pin front sections together
and stitch seams*

Lesson 12, pages 247-248

3. Clip curves, press seam

Lesson 13, pages 250-251

*4. Press front extensions along
fold lines*

Pattern guide sheet

continued on next page

continued from page 225

Steps to make garment according to my pattern guide sheet	Lesson number and pages in <u>Clothes, Clues, and Careers</u>
5. Baste facings to upper garment edge	Lesson 9, pages 237
6. Put in zipper	Lesson 17, pages 261-269
7. Make and attach pockets	Lessons 15 and 16, pages 254-260
8. Staystitch waistline edges of back pieces	Lesson 10, pages 241-242
9. Pin back sections together and stitch seams	Lesson 12, pages 247-248
10. Clip curves; press seam	Lesson 13, pages 250-251
11. Pin front to back at side seams and inner leg seams, stitch seams	Lesson 12, pages 247-248
12. Press seams	Lesson 13, pages 250-251
13. Make and attach waistband	Lesson 22, pages 286-290
14. Sew on hook and eye	Lesson 26, pages 310-311
15. Hem	Lesson 27, pages 312-317
16. Final touches	Pattern guide sheet

When you have completed this part of your plan, refer to the checklist of sewing steps on page 227. Look at the first step you have written down and find it in the checklist. On your plan, fill in the lesson and page numbers in this book you will need to use to carry out this step. Do the same for each step. If directions for some steps are not in the checklist, use the directions on your pattern guide sheet. Ask your teacher for help if necessary.

CHECKLIST OF SEWING STEPS IN THIS UNIT

 **PUTTING IT TOGETHER**

1 How can making a plan for your work help you?
2 What might happen if you do not have a plan?

PATTERN LAYOUT AND CUTTING

 layout

lengthwise grain

lengthwise fold

crosswise grain

crosswise fold

selvage

 how to lay out the pattern pieces

how to cut the pattern pieces

Careful pattern layout, marking, and cutting, are necessary steps in making a garment that fits well and looks good. If you do not follow directions carefully, the garment pieces may not go together easily and the finished garment may not fit comfortably.

Before laying out your pattern make sure your fabric and pattern pieces are smooth and wrinkle-free. Keep your *pattern guide sheet*[1] handy so you can refer to the suggested *cutting layout*[2] for your fabric and pattern size as you place pattern pieces on the fabric.

If the cutting layout you are to use shows the fabric folded for pattern layout, do this before placing any pattern pieces on the fabric. The fold may be lengthwise or crosswise.

To make a *lengthwise fold*, fold the fabric on the *lengthwise grain* so the *selvages*, or tightly woven edges, are opposite the fold.

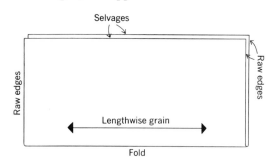

[1] See pages 222–223. [2] See pages 222–223.

A *crosswise fold* is made on the *crosswise grain* and forms right angles with the selvage and lengthwise grain.

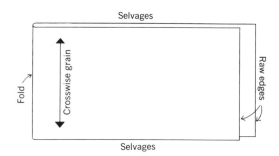

Sometimes the fabric is not supposed to be folded exactly in half. When this occurs, the folded part must be even in width. To do this with a lengthwise fold, measure the distance from the fold to the selvage in several places.

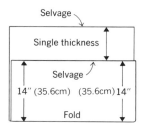

Make sure that the distance between the fold and selvage is the same at all points. On a crosswise fold the selvages should be on top of one another. You may need to use some pattern pieces to test how much the fabric is to be folded. When your fabric is folded correctly you are ready to place the pattern pieces on the fabric.

Place the pattern pieces on the fabric as shown in the cutting layout you are using. Put one pin in the center of each piece to keep it in place until you are sure you have placed all pattern pieces correctly and close enough to each other so they fit on the fabric. This helps to avoid any waste of fabric.

Markings[3] on your pattern pieces tell you how each pattern piece should be pinned in relation to the grainline of the fabric. Follow these pattern markings carefully because this will give you the correct grainline in your completed garment. A lengthwise grainline marking on a pattern piece should be on the lengthwise grainline of the fabric. To pin on grain, remove the pin from the center of the pattern piece and place it at one end of the grainline arrow. Place the end of a tape measure at the end of the arrow where the pin is and measure to the selvage. Move the pattern piece until the other end of the arrow is the same distance from the selvage as the other and place a pin in that end of the arrow. Check again to make sure the measurement from each end of the arrow to the selvage is exactly the same.

To pin the rest of the pattern piece in place, smooth the pattern toward each corner and place a pin in each corner at right angles to the seam line. Make sure the pins do not go beyond the cutting line. Place more pins about 3 to 4 inches (8 to 10 cm) apart around the edge of the pattern piece, smoothing the pattern as you go.

Pattern pieces which are marked with a fold line will be on grain if the fold line of the pattern is on the fold of the fabric. Place the fold line exactly on the fold of the fabric. Place a pin at each end of the pattern piece along the fold line and a pin in between these two pins. Continue pinning as for pattern pieces with a grainline marking.

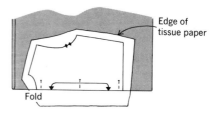

Some pattern pieces are to be placed on fabric that has not been folded. If this is true in the suggested layout you are using, follow the instructions for that layout. Before cutting, check with your teacher to be sure all the pattern pieces are placed correctly. By doing this you will avoid making mistakes.

If the pattern piece to be cut from a single thickness of fabric has a fold line marked on it, place the pattern piece on the fabric as shown in the suggested cutting layout. Use the fold line as the grainline. Put pins along the fold line so the pins can be used as hinges. Fold the pattern piece from one side to the other to be sure there is enough room to cut the whole piece. If there are any other pattern pieces to cut, outline with pins the area of fabric to be used for the pattern piece with a fold line. Put the other pattern pieces to be cut from a single thickness of fabric into place. When you are ready to pin the pattern piece with a fold line in place for cutting, leave in the pins that are along the fold line. Pin the pattern piece to the fabric, placing

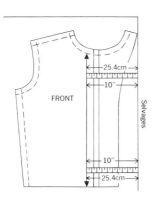

[3] See page 222.

the pins at right angles to the seamline about 3 or 4 inches (8 to 10 cm) apart.

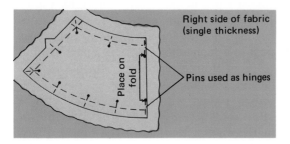

When you are ready to cut, cut on the cutting line, but not along the fold line nor into the area where the pattern piece will be folded.

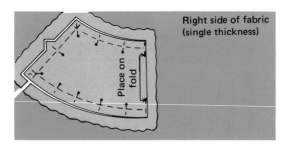

Then remove the pins from the pattern piece except along the fold line. Fold the pattern piece to the other side using the pins as hinges. Pin the pattern piece into place and cut along the cutting line.

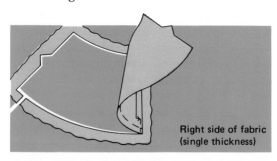

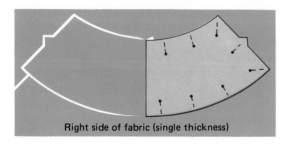

A different procedure is followed if a pattern piece to be cut from a single thickness of fabric has a grainline rather than a fold line. If you are to cut two garment pieces from the same pattern piece, place the pattern piece right side up in the position shown on the suggested cutting layout.

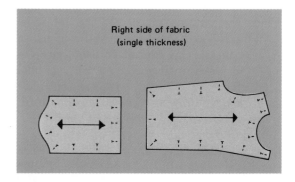

Place the pattern piece as close to the edge of the fabric as possible so there will be enough room for cutting the second piece and any other pieces that are to be cut from the single thickness of fabric. Make a pin line around the pattern piece at the cutting line. Remove the pattern piece, turn it over, and place it wrong side up as shown in the suggested layout. Be sure that the cutting line of the pattern piece does not extend beyond the pin line that marks where the first piece is to be cut.

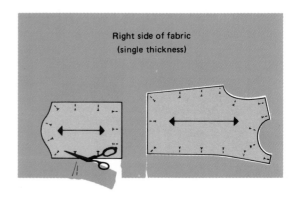

When you are ready to pin the pattern piece in place for cutting, pin it in the correct position for the pattern piece being right side up. Check to be sure it is on grain. Remove the pins which mark the outline. Read the directions in this lesson for cutting, then cut around the pattern piece. To pin the pattern piece a second time, turn your fabric over and place the pattern piece in the correct position. The garment piece just cut out should still be pinned to the pattern piece. Pin the pattern piece into place making sure it is on grain. Cut out the second piece.

It is extremely important that you turn your fabric over before cutting out the same pattern piece a second time. If you do not, you will have two garment pieces for the same part of your body. For example you will have two right sleeves instead of one right sleeve and one left sleeve.

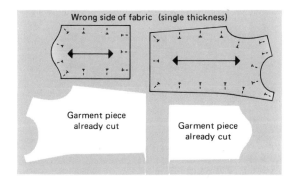

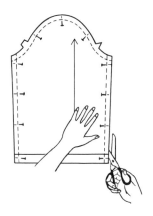

When all your pattern pieces are pinned correctly you are ready to cut them out. If you are right-handed, hold the shears in your right hand with the thumb through the larger hole of the handle. Use your left hand to hold the fabric in place. Try not to lift the fabric with your hand or the shears because this may stretch the fabric out of shape as you cut. If you are left-handed and have left-handed shears, hold them in your left hand with the thumb through the larger hole. Use your right hand for holding the fabric in place. Use long strokes for long spaces, such as straight side seams. Use short cutting strokes for short spaces, such as cutting around notches.

Be sure to cut on the cutting line. Cut out around notches away from the seamline. Cut double or triple notches as one by cutting straight across the point rather than cutting between each notch. Leave the pattern pieces pinned to the fabric.

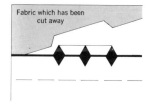

 **PUTTING IT TOGETHER**

1 Explain how to make lengthwise and crosswise folds in fabric.
2 How can you be sure pattern pieces are pinned to fabric on grain?

LESSON EIGHT
TRANSFERRING PATTERN MARKINGS

 pattern markings   **tracing wheel**

dressmaker's carbon   **tailor's tacks**

 some ways to transfer pattern markings

Pattern markings are transferred to your material after you have finished cutting. Darts, small and large dots, center front and center back, fold lines, and buttonholes are usually marked. *Pattern guide sheets*[1] give suggestions about the markings you will need.

A *tracing wheel*[2] and *dressmaker's carbon paper*[3] will transfer markings satisfactorily on most lightweight and washable fabrics. A dull table knife might be used instead of a tracing wheel. Use light-colored carbon paper on white and light-colored fabrics.

Tracing wheels differ so you can select the kind you need. The wheel may have a sharp-toothed edge or a smooth edge. Use a smooth edge for knits to avoid snagging the fabric.

Arrange the carbon paper so that all markings will be on the inside of the garment when it is finished.

Arrange dressmaker's carbon this way when fabric is folded with wrong sides together.

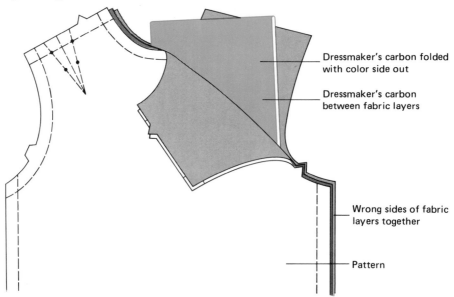

Dressmaker's carbon folded with color side out

Dressmaker's carbon between fabric layers

Wrong sides of fabric layers together

Pattern

[1] See pages 222–223.   [2] See pages 207–209.
[3] See pages 207–209.

Arrange dressmaker's carbon this way when fabric is folded with right sides together.

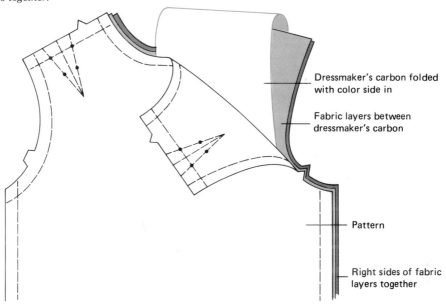

Dressmaker's carbon folded with color side in

Fabric layers between dressmaker's carbon

Pattern

Right sides of fabric layers together

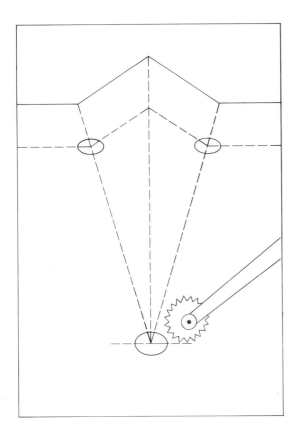

Mark the ends of darts with a straight line.

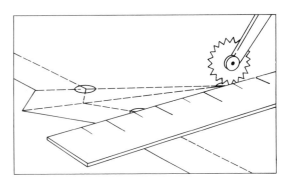

Use a ruler when marking straight lines.

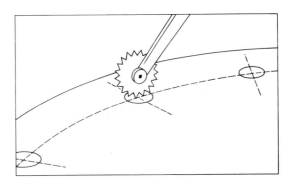

Mark dots by making X's.

Chalk[4] and pins may be used to mark thicker fabrics such as corduroy. Put pins through the pattern and fabric where marks are to be transferred. Look at the illustrations shown here to see how to mark fabric using chalk and pins.

Mark this way when fabric is folded with right sides together.

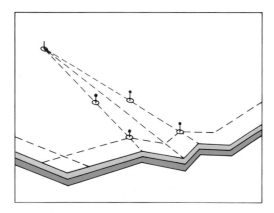

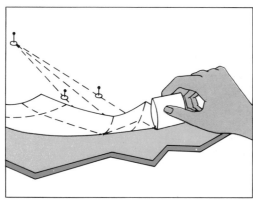

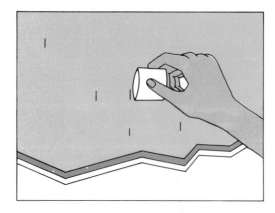

Mark this way when fabric is folded with wrong sides together.

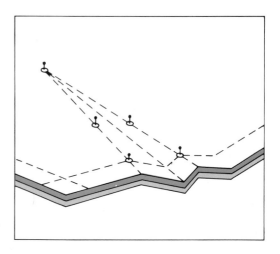

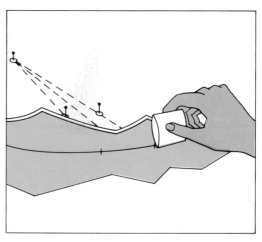

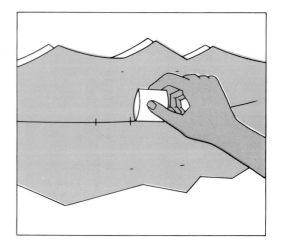

[4]See pages 207–209.

Tailor's tacks can be used on very thick fabrics which may not pick up carbon paper marks or chalk. Use double thread to make a loose stitch through both layers of the fabric where you want markings.

Next, clip the threads on top of the pattern and between the fabric layers. Tufts of thread remain to mark the garment pieces. Remove the threads when the markings are no longer needed.

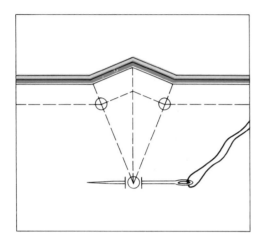

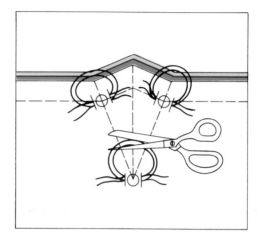

Repeat the loose stitch to form a loop. Make thread loops at all places where you want markings.

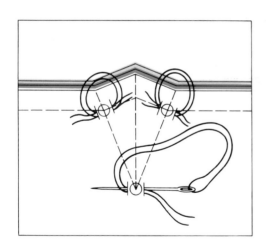

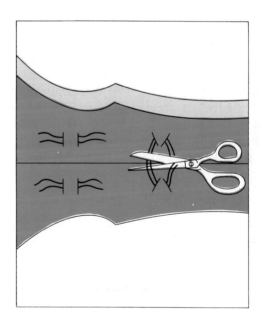

PUTTING
IT
TOGETHER

1 How can you transfer pattern markings using a tracing wheel and dressmaker's carbon paper?
2 When are chalk and pins useful equipment for transferring markings?
3 What are the steps in making tailor's tacks? On what fabrics might they be used.

LESSON NINE
HAND STITCHING

 hand stitches

temporary hand stitches

permanent hand stitches

 some reasons for hand stitching

some kinds of hand stitches

how to hand stitch

When you sew you will often need to use *hand stitches*. These are stitches made by hand using a needle and a single thread.

There are different hand stitches for different purposes. Some are *temporary hand stitches*. These are taken out before the garment is worn. Temporary hand stitches hold fabric in place until permanent stitches are made. For example, you might hand baste a pocket in place before it is machine stitched to the garment. *Permanent hand stitches* are left in the garment and are not visible from the garment outside. Some examples are hand stitching done on hems, sewing on hooks and eyes, and sewing on snaps.

GUIDELINES FOR HAND SEWING

STEP 1.   Use a needle and thread of the right size for your fabric. (Refer to the chart on page 240.) For woven fabrics use a regular needle; for knitted fabrics use a ball point needle. A regular needle may snag the fabric.

STEP 2.   Use a single thread 18 to 24 inches (46-61 cm) long. Too long a thread tangles easily.

STEP 3.   Tie a knot in the thread by following the motions in the next four illustrations. Practice until you can make a knot that is neat and will hold.

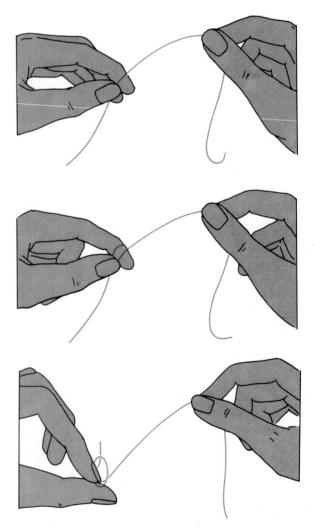

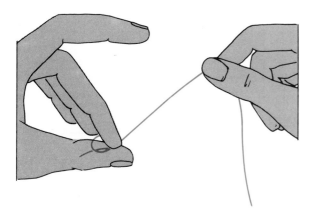

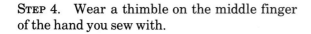

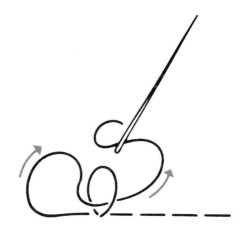

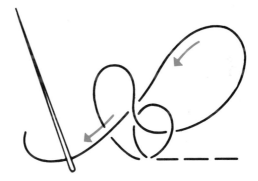

Step 4. Wear a thimble on the middle finger of the hand you sew with.

Step 5. Keep stitches loose to avoid puckering of the fabric.

Step 6. To secure the thread in the fabric when you begin, make a few small stitches in one place or make a knot.

Step 7. To end hand stitching, make several stitches in one place or make a knot. This keeps stitches from pulling out.

Step 8. To make a knot in thread as you end hand stitching, use the three illustrations that follow as guides. Be sure to notice the directions of the arrows. After you look at the illustrations, practice making knots to end a line of hand stitching.

Here are directions for making hand stitches that are commonly used. Some of these will be referred to throughout this unit.

BASTING STITCH

Step 1. Work from right to left.

Step 2. Make stitches ¼ inch (6 mm) long in lightweight fabrics. Make longer stitches in heavier fabrics

Step 3. Make stitches the same length on both sides of the fabric.

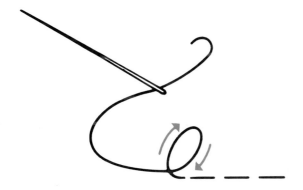

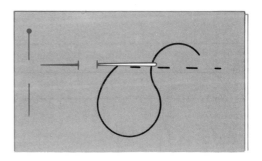

On pages 236 and 237 you have studied the guidelines for hand sewing. You have practiced making a knot in a thread by twisting it with your fingers. You know how to end a line of hand stitching by knotting the thread.

You have studied the illustrations and the steps to be taken when doing the basting stitch. You know that the basting stitch is the first basic stitch for hand sewing.

Now on this page and the following one you will see illustrations of some of the other basic stitches that are used in hand sewing. In order for you to become skilled in sewing by hand, you must practice. Try practicing each of the following stitches. Follow each of the steps that precede the illustrations. Be sure that you start each type of stitch in the direction that is given with each illustration.

As you make various kinds of garments you will find that the skill you have gained in hand sewing will pay off.

OVERCAST STITCH

STEP 1.   Work in either direction.

STEP 2.   Keep stitches evenly spaced and of the same depth.

STEP 3.   Make stitches about ¼ inch (6mm) deep in lightweight fabrics. Take deeper stitches in heavier fabrics or in fabrics which ravel easily.

STEP 4.   Keep stitches loose enough so that the cut edge of the fabric does not curl.

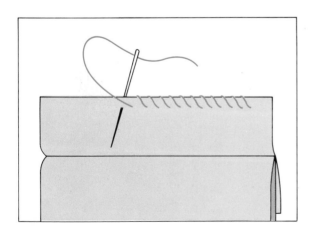

BUTTONHOLE STITCH

STEP 1.   Work from right to left.

STEP 2.   Keep stitches evenly spaced and the same depth.

STEP 3.   Make stitches about ¼ inch (6 mm) deep on lightweight fabrics. Take deeper stitches in heavier fabrics or on fabrics which ravel easily.

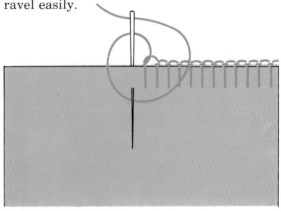

HEMMING STITCH

STEP 1.   Work from right to left.

STEP 2.   Space stitches evenly. Make stitches ¼ inch (6 mm) apart in lightweight fabrics. Make stitches farther apart on heavier fabrics.

STEP 3.   Take small stitches in the garment so that stitches cannot be seen on the right side of the fabric.

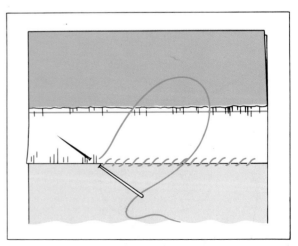

RUNNING STITCH

STEP 1.   Work from right to left.

STEP 2.   Space stitches evenly. Make stitches ⅛ inch (3 mm) or shorter for permanent stitching. For easing or gathering, make stitches ⅛ inch to ¼ inch (3 mm to 6 mm) long.

BACKSTITCH

STEP 1.   Work from right to left.

STEP 2.   Make stitches on top ⅛ inch (3 mm) or shorter. Stitches on the underside will be twice as long as those on the top.

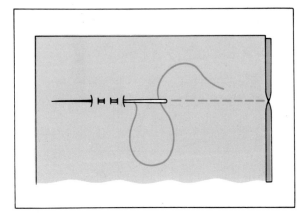

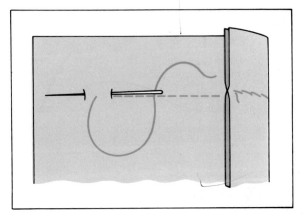

SLIP STITCH

STEP 1.   Work from right to left.

STEP 2.   Make stitches ⅜ inch (9 mm) apart on lightweight fabrics. Make longer stitches in heavier fabrics.

STEP 3.   Take small stitches in the garment so stitches cannot be seen on the right side of the fabric.

CATCH STITCH

STEP 1.   Work from left to right.

STEP 2.   Make stitches ⅜ inch (9 mm) apart on lightweight fabrics. Make stitches farther apart in heavier fabrics.

STEP 3.   Take small stitches in the garment so stitches cannot be seen on the right side of the fabric.

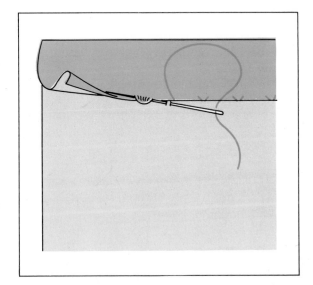

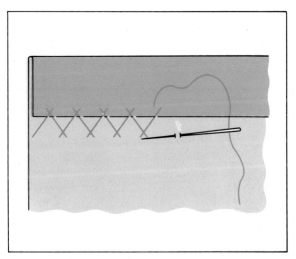

THREAD AND NEEDLE CHOICES FOR HAND SEWING

FABRIC	THREAD TYPE AND SIZE	NEEDLE SIZE[1]
sheer[2]		
of natural[3] fibers	mercerized cotton A or 50	9, 10
of manufactured[3] fibers or blends containing manufactured[3] fibers	regular cotton-covered polyester	
lightweight[4]		
of natural[3] fibers	mercerized cotton	8, 9
of manufactured[3] fibers or blends containing manufactured[3] fibers	regular cotton-covered polyester	
medium[5]		
of natural[3] fibers	mercerized cotton A or 50	7, 8
of manufactured[3] fibers or blends containing manufactured[3] fibers	regular cotton-covered polyester	
medium heavy[6]		
of natural[3] fibers	heavy duty mercerized cotton	6
of manufactured[3] fibers or blends containing manufactured[3] fibers	heavy duty cotton-covered polyester	
heavy[7]		
of natural[3] fibers	heavy duty mercerized cotton	4, 5
of manufactured[3] fibers or blends containing manufactured[3] fibers	heavy duty cotton-covered polyester	

[1]Use ball point needle for knitted fabrics.
[2]*sheer fabric:* chiffon, voile, organdy, organza.
[3]See listing of natural and manufactured fibers in Unit 6, Lesson 4.
[4]*lightweight fabric:* gingham, percale, tricot, some single knits, some broadcloth, some seersucker, flannelette.
[5]*medium fabric:* some broadcloth, poplin, flannel, some corduroy; velveteen, some double knits, some single knits, some seersucker, some terry cloth, taffeta, some bonded fabrics.
[6]*medium heavy fabric:* some coating fabrics, heavy denim, some double knits, some upholstery, some corduroy (wide-wale), some terry cloth, quilted, some bonded fabrics.
[7]*heavy fabric:* some coating fabrics, some upholstery, some double knits, canvas, fake furs.

PUTTING IT TOGETHER

1 What is the difference between temporary hand stitching and permanent hand stitching?
2 What length should a thread be for hand sewing? Why?

STAYSTITCHING

 staystitching
stitching with
the grain

 what staystitching is
some reasons to staystitch
how to staystitch

Staystitching is a line of stitching made through a single thickness of fabric to prevent stretching while a garment is being made. Since *curved areas* or *bias edges* are most likely to stretch, these are the areas that need to be staystitched. Examples of such edges are a curved neckline, a curved facing, an armhole, and a shoulder seamline.

STITCH LENGTH

For staystitching set the *stitch length*[1] at 10 to 12 stitches per inch (4 to 5 stitches per centimeter). This is the same stitch length that you will use for stitching seams. The stitching is done ½ inch (1.2 cm) from the garment edge if the seam allowance is ⅝ inch (1.5 cm). If staystitching is done accurately, it will not extend beyond the seamline. This means it will not show when the garment is finished. If the staystitching does not show on the outside of the garment, there is no need to remove this line of stitching after the garment is assembled.

DIRECTION OF STITCHING

The direction in which staystitching is done is as important as where the staystitching is placed. Stitching in the wrong direction can stretch the fabric out of shape. To find the right direction for staystitching, rub a finger gently along a curved or bias edge on one of

[1] See page 201.

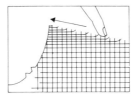 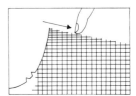

your garment pieces. In one direction the threads will be roughed up; in the other direction the threads will smooth down. The correct direction in which to stitch is the direction which makes the threads lie smooth. Stitching in the direction which smooths the threads is called *stitching with the grain*. Staystitching should be done with the grain.

HOW TO STAYSTITCH

Look at the illustration on page 242 to see examples of garment pieces which need to be staystitched and the direction in which staystitching should be done. Find the garment front piece and notice the direction of the arrows at the neckline. You will notice that there are two arrows and that each arrow points to the center front of the piece. This means that the staystitching is not done in one continuous line on this part of the garment piece; it is done in two steps. To staystitch this piece or a garment piece which has been cut on the fold, follow these directions.

STEP 1. Place the garment piece on the sewing machine with the wrong side up. Start

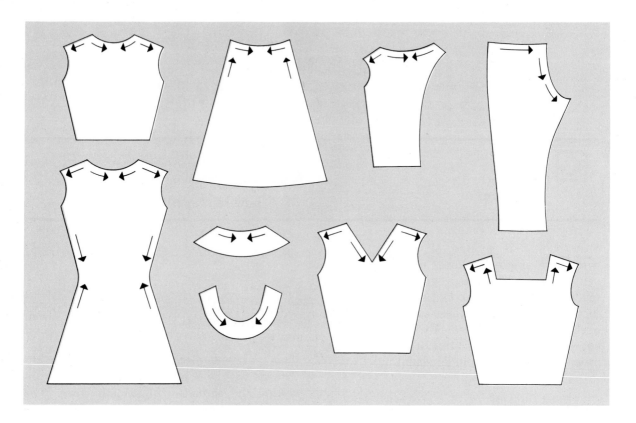

stitching ½ inch (1.2 cm) from the seam edge. Stop when you reach the center front. Clip the threads.

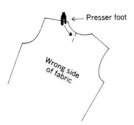

← Presser foot

Wrong side of fabric

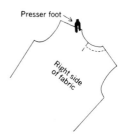

Presser foot

Right side of fabric

STEP 2. Turn the garment piece over so the right side is up. Start stitching ½ inch (1.2 cm) from the seam edge. Stop when you reach the center front. Clip the threads.

When you staystitch on pieces that have not been cut on the fold, some will have the right side up and others will have the wrong side up when stitching with the grain. Whether the wrong side is up or the right side is up does not matter. The important thing is that the staystitching is done in the right direction, that is with the grain.

PUTTING IT TOGETHER

1 What is staystitching?
2 What garment pieces may require staystitching?
3 Where is the staystitching located in relation to the seam allowance on garment pieces?

LESSON ELEVEN
DARTS

Darts are basic construction details in many garments. They have a wide part and taper to a point in order to give shape to clothes so that the clothes will fit the human body.

Some places darts are found are at the waist, shoulders, bustline, elbows, and neckline. Depending on the design of a garment, a dart may be curved or straight, or long or short.

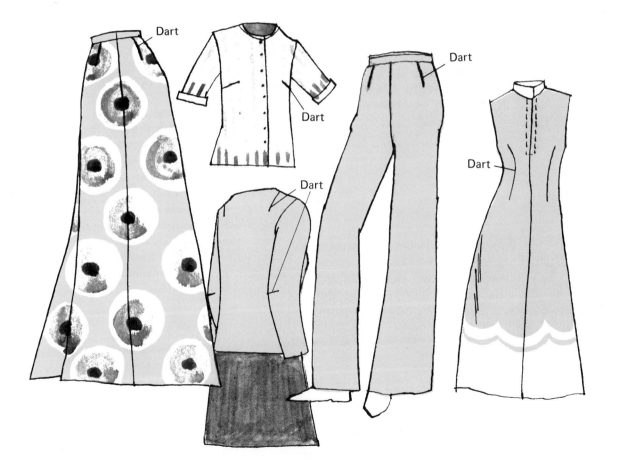

Single-pointed dart   Double-pointed dart

Many darts have one point tapering from the wide part. These are called *single-pointed darts*. Other darts have a point at each end with a wide part in the middle. This type of dart is called a *double-pointed dart* and is made of two single-pointed darts joined at the wide part.

Dart lines are one type of *pattern markings*[1] that should be transferred to your fabric. If you have not done this, transfer the markings now. There should be three lines on your fabric for each dart. These are the fold line and the two stitching lines.

MAKING DARTS

PINNING A SINGLE-POINTED DART

To make a single-pointed straight dart fold the garment piece along the fold line. Make sure that the right sides of the fabric are together. Hold the garment piece so the wide part of the dart is in your left hand.

Put a pin through the folded garment piece on the stitching line at the widest part of the dart. The pin should come through the stitching line on the other side. Finish pinning the dart to the point. The pin points should point toward the wide part of the dart.

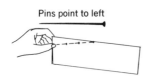

Pins point to left

Some single-pointed curved darts do not have a fold line as the center marking. Instead the directions may tell you to cut along the center line before pinning and stitching the dart. If this is what your pattern guide sheet directs you to do, follow the directions. Then with the right sides of the fabric together, match the stitching lines. Hold the garment piece so the wide part of the dart is in your left hand. Put a pin through the stitching line at the widest part of the dart. The pin should come through the stitching line on the other side. Finish pinning the dart in this way. Be sure the pin points point toward the wide part of the dart. Keep the pins in an even line.

STITCHING A SINGLE-POINTED DART

To stitch a single-pointed dart place the wide end of the dart under the presser foot and lower the needle into the stitching line at the cut edge. Lower the presser foot and remove the first pin.

Needle

Stitch on the marked line up to the next pin. Stop the machine with the needle in the fabric and remove the pin. Continue stitching and removing pins until you have almost reached the point of the dart. Use the *hand wheel*[2] to make the last 3 or 4 stitches so you are sure the dart tapers to a point and ends exactly where it is supposed to. Do not *backstitch*[3] at the end of a dart, but leave about 3 inches (7.5 cm) of thread so you can tie a knot at the end. Tie the knot and trim the threads to ½ inch (1.2 cm). The dart stitching is then secure.

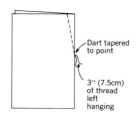

Dart tapered to point

3″ (7.5cm) of thread left hanging

[1] See page 232.

[2] See page 198.   [3] See page 201.

It is very important to stitch a dart to a sharp point exactly on the stitching line. An incorrectly stitched dart will not lie smooth and may cause a wrinkle or bubble at the end of the dart. Look at darts 1 and 2 below.

1 This is good. The dart is stitched to a sharp point.
2 This needs improvement. The blunt end will cause a wrinkle or bubble on the outside.

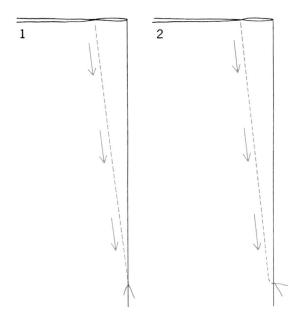

PINNING AND STITCHING A DOUBLE-POINTED DART

Each half of a double-pointed dart is made like a single-pointed dart. Begin the pinline at the center of the dart at the widest part. Pin from the wide part to the point, keeping the wide part to the left and the point to the right.

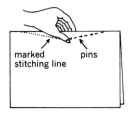

marked stitching line   pins

Stitch this part of the double-pointed dart as for a single-pointed dart. Turn the garment piece over and repeat the process for the other half of the dart.

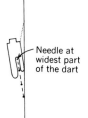

Needle at widest part of the dart

TRIMMING, SLASHING, AND CLIPPING DARTS

Some types of darts need to be trimmed, slashed, or clipped before they are pressed. Refer to your pattern guide sheet to see if you need to clip, slash, or trim any darts in your garment and when this should be done.

Double-pointed darts are clipped at the widest point and sometimes above and below this point. *Clipping* is done with the points of shears from the fold line to about ¼ inch (6 mm) from the stitching line.

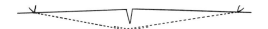

To *slash* a dart make a clip from the fold line toward the stitching about ½ inch to 1 inch (1.2 to 2.5 cm) above the point of the dart. Be careful not to cut through the stitching. Then cut along the fold line from the wide part of the dart to the cut.

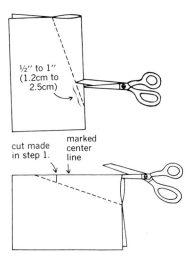

½" to 1" (1.2cm to 2.5cm)

cut made in step 1.   marked center line

To *trim* a dart put a pin in the dart about ½ inch to 1 inch (1.2 to 2.5 cm) from the point. Then cut away all but about ¼ inch (6 mm) of the fabric between the wide end of the dart and the pin.

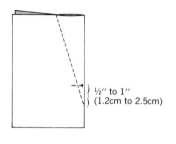

½″ to 1″
(1.2cm to 2.5cm)

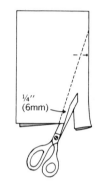

¼″
(6mm)

PRESSING DARTS

After a dart is stitched, the fabric is no longer flat but molded into a curve. Therefore, darts should be pressed on a curved surface, such as a *tailor's ham*,[4] rather than on a flat surface, such as an ironing board.

[4] See page 209.

To press a dart, place the dart over a tailor's ham with the right side of the fabric down. Press vertical darts toward the center front or center back of a garment. Press horizontal darts downward.

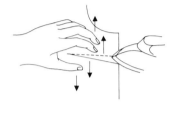

Slashed darts and trimmed darts are pressed open except for the point which is flattened.

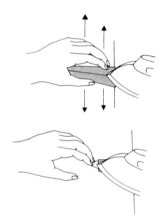

Gently pull the fabric down over the tailor's ham so it fits smoothly with no wrinkles. Press with the point of the iron.

PUTTING IT TOGETHER

1 How do darts give shape to clothes?
2 Where are darts usually located to give shape to clothes?
3 Why press darts over a rounded surface?
4 What are some other guidelines for pressing darts?

LESSON TWELVE
PINBASTING AND STITCHING PLAIN SEAMS

 seam

plain seam

pinbaste

stitch with the grain

 pinbasting

stitching plain seams

A *seam* is one or more lines of stitching which join two pieces of fabric together. A *plain seam* is made with one line of stitching with the right sides of the fabric pieces together. Plain seams are used more often than any other type of seam.

Seam edges should be pinned together before they are stitched. The pins hold the edges together so the layers of fabric do not slip. It is important that seams be stitched in a certain direction and that pins be on top for stitching. For this reason you have to know the direction of stitching before you place any pins in the seam edge.

DIRECTION OF STITCHING

If you have *staystitched*[1] certain edges of any garment pieces, you have done this *stitching with the grain*[2] of the fabric to prevent stretching the edges of garment pieces out of shape. You must also stitch with the grain when stitching seams. To find which direction is with the grain, rub your finger along the edge of the fabric in both directions. In one direction the threads of the fabric will be roughed up; in the other smoothed down. The direction in which the threads are smoothed

down is *with the grain* of the fabric and is the direction in which seams are to be stitched. Be sure to check for the direction of the grain of your fabric before you start to stitch.

PINBASTING

To *pinbaste*, or pin the edges of seams together for stitching, follow these instructions. Check your *pattern guide sheet*[3] to find out which garment pieces are to be sewn together first. With the wrong side down, place one garment piece on a table. Be sure the piece is placed so that the edge to the right is on grain if you rub the threads toward you. With the wrong side up, place the other garment piece on top of the first one matching seam edges and notches. The right sides of

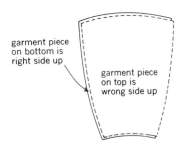

garment piece on bottom is right side up

garment piece on top is wrong side up

[1] See pages 241–242.   [2] See page 241.

[3] See pages 222–223.

the garment pieces should be together. Place a pin at each end of the seam. The pin should go in one side of the seamline and out the other with the point away from the seam edge. Place the next pin at the notch. Then place pins about halfway between pins already in the fabric. Keep dividing the space with pins until there are pins about every 3 or 4 inches (8 to 10 cm) along the seam edge. Be sure the pins go through both thicknesses of fabric.

STITCHING

To stitch the seam, place the garment piece under the *presser foot*[4] with the pins on top. Most of the fabric should be to the left of the presser foot. Put the needle through the fabric on the correct seam width about ¼ inch (6 mm) from the top edge of the fabric. Lower the presser foot and *backstitch*[5] just to the top edge of the fabric. Then stitch the seam on the seamline. You may stitch over the pins if you stitch slowly. Stop at the edge of the fabric and backstitch 4 or 5 stitches. Move the *hand wheel*[6] so that the needle is in its highest position; lift the presser foot; pull the garment pieces out; and clip the threads.

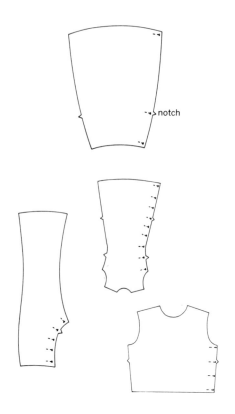

notch

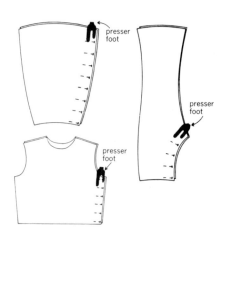

presser foot

presser foot

presser foot

[4] See page 198.   [5] See page 201.   [6] See page 198.

PUTTING
IT
TOGETHER

1 Why is it important to stitch seams with the grain of the fabric?
2 Describe how to pinbaste a seam edge.

LESSON THIRTEEN
TRIMMING, LAYERING, CLIPPING, NOTCHING, AND PRESSING PLAIN SEAMS

 trim
layer
grade

clip
notch

 how to trim and layer plain seams

how to clip and notch plain seams

how to press plain seams

Each seam should be pressed before it is crossed with another line of stitching. This is important to the finished appearance of the garment. Some seams can be pressed without anything else being done to them after they have been stitched. Other seams must be *trimmed, layered, notched,* or *clipped* before they are pressed.

TRIMMING SEAMS

Trimming a seam is cutting away a part of a seam allowance parallel to the seamline. Seams are trimmed to make the stitched edge less bulky.

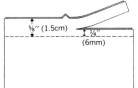

Seams are also trimmed at corners to eliminate bulk when the corner is to be turned right side out. A corner with a right angle is trimmed diagonally about ⅛ inch (3 mm) from the stitching.

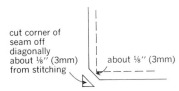

Other types of corners are trimmed as shown below.

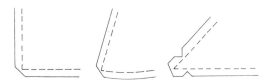

LAYERING OR GRADING SEAMS

Layering, or *grading,* is a method of trimming a seam when there are two or more thicknesses of fabric in a seam allowance. Layering means to trim each seam allowance to a different width. The garment seam allowance is left wide: the facing seam allowance is trimmed to a narrow measure. Any layers of fabric in between are trimmed more than the garment seam allowance but less than the facing seam allowance. When layering, the facing seam allowance is trimmed to ¼ inch (6 mm). The next layer is trimmed to ⅜ inch (9 mm) and the next layer to ½ inch (1.2 cm).

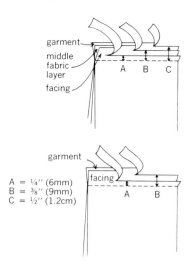

CLIPPING SEAMS

Clipping is done on seams where there is an inward curve so the seam will be smooth when the garment is turned right side out. To clip a seam, use the points of scissors or shears to cut into the seam allowance at right angles to the seamline. The clips should be made almost to the seamline about every ½ inch (1.2 cm) around an inside curve.

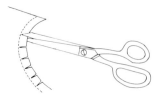

NOTCHING SEAMS

When a seamline forms an outside curve, the seam allowance is *notched.* To notch a seam use the points of scissors or shears to cut out V-shaped pieces from the seam allowance. Notches should be made every 1½ inches (4 to 5 cm) on an outside curved edge.

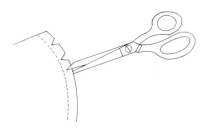

PRESSING SEAMS

Depending upon its shape, a seam is pressed either on a flat surface or on a rounded one. Curved seams are pressed on a rounded surface, such as a *tailor's ham.*[1]

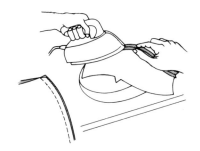

Flat seams are pressed on a flat surface, such as an ironing board. Before pressing a seam, be sure to read your *pattern guide sheet*[2] to see if the seam is to be pressed open, to one side, or up or down.

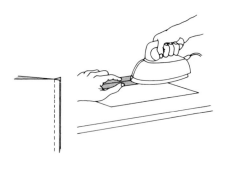

[1] See page 209.   [2] See pages 222–223.

To press a seam open, place the fabric on the correct surface with the wrong side up. Gently pull the fabric over the surface so it is smooth. Use your fingers to open the seam at the beginning. Use the tip of the iron to press the seam open. Keep using your fingers to make sure the seam stays open as you press.

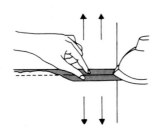

To press a seam to one side or up or down, place the fabric on the correct surface with the wrong side up. Gently pull the fabric over the surface so it is smooth. Use your fingers to keep both seam edges in the right direction. Press along the seamline.

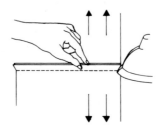

Be sure to carefully press any seam before it is crossed with another line of stitching. If you skip this step, the seams will not lie smooth and you may be disappointed with the finished appearance of your garment.

 **PUTTING IT TOGETHER**

1 Why is it important to press seams before they are crossed with another line of stitching?
2 What is the purpose of trimming? Of layering? Describe how each is done.
3 Describe how to clip a seam and how to notch a seam.

SEAM FINISHES FOR PLAIN SEAMS

 seam finish

pinked finish

pinked and stitched finish

zig-zag finish

◯ why seam finishes are used

some types of seam finishes

how to finish seams

Threads on the edges of a seam allowance which is not enclosed sometimes pull apart as a garment is handled and worn. Washing, drying, and ironing may also cause threads on unprotected seam edges to separate. For these reasons seam finishes are sometimes applied to seam edges. *Seam finishes* are special ways of sewing or trimming seam edges to prevent raveling and stretching. Seam finishes also keep the inside of the garment neat looking.

There are several very satisfactory ways to finish plain seams which are exposed. Which seam finish to use depends on the fabric you are using and the use the garment will get. The three types of seam finishes shown in this lesson are suitable for firmly woven or knit fabrics of medium weight. Some fabrics, such as double knits, may not require a seam finish. Any seams that are enclosed, such as a facing seam, do not require a seam finish.

PINKED

If you have a fabric that does not ravel, but you want a neat appearance along the seam edges that might be seen, such as in a jacket, a *pinked seam finish* may be all that is needed. Pinking shears are used to make the zig-zag cut edge for this finish. Pink the seam edges before pressing the seam. Trim the

seam through both fabric layers close to the seam edge.

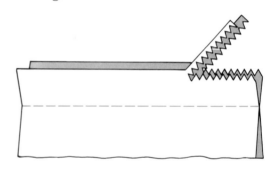

Then press.

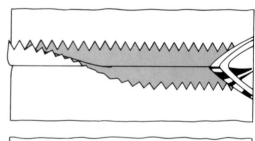

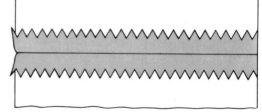

PINKED AND STITCHED

For fabrics that ravel slightly a *pinked and stitched finish* may be appropriate. Use pinking shears to trim the seam close to the seam edges before the seam is pressed.

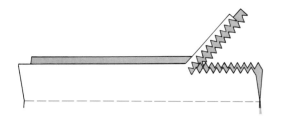

Stitch through each seam allowance separately close to the pinked edge. Then press the seam.

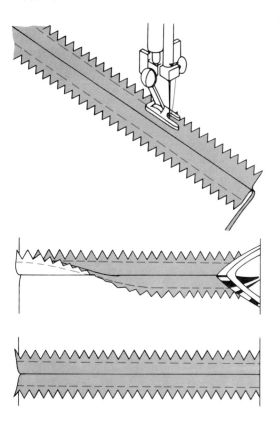

ZIG-ZAG

A *zig-zag seam finish* is good to use on fabrics that ravel. This seam finish is done with a sewing machine that makes zig-zag stitches or a sewing machine with an attachment that makes zig-zag stitches. Zig-zag stitching may be done close to the seam edge or over the edge of a seam. Experiment on a scrap of fabric to find out the best stitch width and length to use and the best placement of the stitching. Press the seam before you apply this seam finish to each seam allowance.

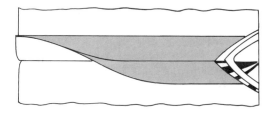

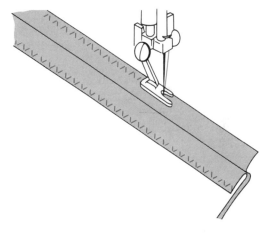

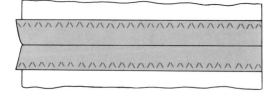

 **PUTTING IT TOGETHER**

1 What are some reasons for applying a seam finish?
2 What are some of the seam finishes for plain seams?
3 When is a seam finish not needed?

LESSON FIFTEEN
PATCH POCKETS

 patch pocket

edge stitch

slip stitch

miter a corner

hand baste

machine baste

 deciding where to place patch pockets

some ways to make patch pockets

some ways to attach patch pockets

A *patch pocket* is sewn to the outside of a garment. It may be square or rectangular, have two rounded corners, or be in the shape of an object, such as an apple or a flower. Your pattern may include a patch pocket or you may decide to add one or more to your garment as an individual touch.

If a patch pocket is part of a pattern design, there are *markings*[1] on the pattern piece to be transferred to the garment to indicate where the pocket is to be placed. You may want to place the pocket according to these markings or you may want to change the placement. After you have made the pocket, experiment to see where you want to attach it.

If you have one or more patch pockets on your garment, you will need to decide on the size, shape, and location of each one. Your knowledge of *design elements and principles*[2] will help you with these decisions. You will also need to make a pattern for each one of the pockets which you decide to add to your garment. Test the size of each pocket to make sure that it is the right size in relation to the space where it is to be and in the right proportion for the garment.

MAKING PATCH POCKETS

SQUARE OR RECTANGULAR PATCH POCKETS; PATCH POCKETS WITH ROUNDED CORNERS

To make square or rectangular patch pockets or patch pockets with rounded corners, follow these directions.

STEP 1. Make a pattern from tissue paper or a lightweight paper bag. Allow 1½ inches (3.8 cm) at the top for a hem and ⅝ inch (1.5 cm) at the sides and bottom for turning under. Mark the *grainline*[3] parallel to the sides of the pocket. Place the pattern piece or pieces on the fabric, pin in place, and cut out.

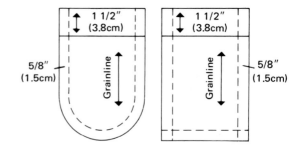

[1] See page 232.
[2] See pages 72–95.

[3] See pages 212–214.

Patch pockets come in many styles and sizes.

STEP 2. Apply *hem tape*[4] to the hem edge. Or turn under the hem edge ¼ inch (6 mm), press, and stitch close to the fold.

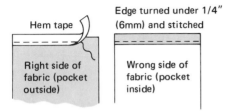

STEP 3. Fold the hem to the right side and stitch on the seamline. *Trim the seam and corners.*[5] Turn the hem right side out and press. *Hand stitch*[6] into place.

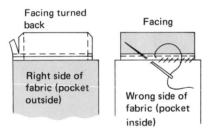

STEP 4. If your pocket is square or rectangular, you will need to *miter the corners* at the bottom. To miter corners, follow these directions. Turn under and press the ⅝ inch (1.5 cm) allowance on the sides and bottom. Gently unfold the seam allowances at the bottom corners and refold each corner diagonally, making a crease with your fingers.

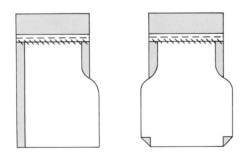

Trim each corner to ⅛ inch (3 mm) from the fold. Refold so the corners are square again; press again if necessary. Pin the edges under and *hand baste*[7] into place. Remove the pins.

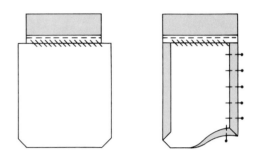

STEP 5. If your pocket has rounded corners, *machine baste* ⅜ inch (9 mm) from the raw edge. Machine basting is a line of stitching with 5 or 6 stitches per inch (2 stitches per centimeter). Gently pull on the lower thread so the ⅝ inch (1.5 cm) allowance folds under and lies flat. Remove the pins. Press the pocket, then *cut notches*[8] from the rounded areas to eliminate extra bulk. Press the pocket again, then pin and *hand baste*[9] the turned under part in place.

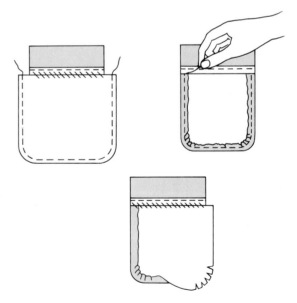

[4]See page 316.
[5]See pages 249–251.
[6]See pages 236–240.

[7]See page 236.
[8]See pages 249–251.
[9]See page 236.

PATCH POCKETS SHAPED LIKE OBJECTS

To make a pocket shaped like an object, follow these directions.

STEP 1. Make the pattern from tissue paper or a lightweight paper bag. Allow ⅝ inch (1.5 cm) on all sides for seam allowance. Mark the *grainline*[10] vertically through the center of the shape. Place the pattern piece on the fabric according to grainline and cut it out. Use the same pattern to cut another piece for lining from a lightweight fabric.

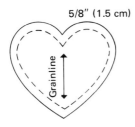

STEP 2. Place the lining on the pocket with right sides of the fabric together. *Pinbaste*[11] and stitch on ⅝ inch. (1.5 cm) seamline, leaving an opening to turn the pocket right side out. *Trim and notch*[12] the seam.

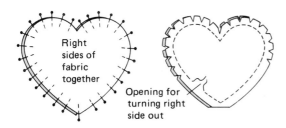

STEP 3. Turn the pocket right side out. Turn under the seam edges at the opening and

[10] See pages 212–214.
[11] See pages 247–248.
[12] See pages 249–250.

press the whole pocket. Make sure the lining doesn't show on the right side of the pocket. *Slip stitch*[13] the opening and press the pocket again.

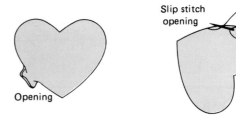

ATTACHING PATCH POCKETS

You can attach patch pockets by machine, using an edge stitch, or you can use a hand *slip stitch.*[14] The machine edge stitch can be seen on the outside and can be considered a decorative trim. The hand slip stitch will not be visible when it is completed. The machine stitch is a faster method than the hand stitch. If the garment is to be machine washed, the machine stitch will likely be more durable. If the garment is to have hard wear, machine stitching is better to use than hand stitching.

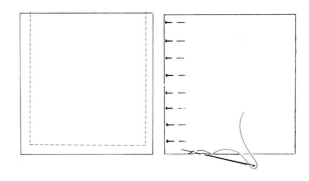

[13] See page 238.   [14] See page 238.

PUTTING IT TOGETHER

1 What is a patch pocket?
2 How can you use your knowledge of design elements and principles whenever you plan the size, shape, and location of a patch pocket?
3 What are two ways to attach patch pockets? What type of stitch is suggested for attaching the patch pocket by hand?

LESSON SIXTEEN
SEAM POCKETS

 seam pocket

 how to make seam pockets

some ways to attach seam pockets

A *seam pocket* is a pocket sewed into the side seam or side front seam of a garment. Often seam pockets are part of the design of a skirt, slacks, shorts, or jumper. If your garment does not have a seam pocket, you may want to include one.

Use tissue paper or a lightweight paper bag to make a pattern. Notice the shape of the pocket in step 1 on page 260. Draw the *grainline*[1] parallel to the side, measuring 6 ½ inches (16.4 cm).

You will need enough fabric to cut pieces for each pocket. If your garment fabric is lightweight, you may use the same fabric for the pocket. If your garment fabric is heavy or thick, a lightweight fabric in a color that matches or blends with your garment fabric should be used. This will keep the pocket from being too bulky.

The piece of fabric you use for cutting seam pockets may be large enough to fold so you can cut both pocket pieces at the same time. If so, make the fold on the *lengthwise grain.*[2] If you are using scraps of fabric, be sure that the fabric is folded or arranged so that both right sides are together or that both wrong sides are together. Also, make sure the lengthwise grain of one piece is placed in the same direction as the lengthwise grain of the other piece. Be sure to *pin your pattern on grain*[3] before cutting.

Here is one way to join a seam pocket to a garment.

STEP 1. Measure the straight side edge of your pocket. Leave an opening the same length in the seam where the pocket is to be attached. For example, if you are putting a seam pocket in slacks and your pocket measures 6 ½ inches (16.4 cm) along the straight side edge, make a mark 6 ½ inches (16.4 cm) from the top edge of your slacks at the side seam. *Pinbaste*[4] and stitch the side seam up to the mark.

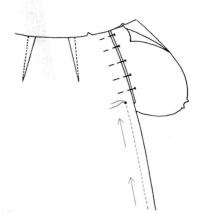

STEP 2. With the right sides of the fabric together, pin the straight side edge of one pocket piece to one seam edge. With the right sides of the fabric together, pin the straight

---

[1] See pages 212–214.   [2] See page 228.   [3] See page 228.   [4] See pages 247–248.

Each of these different garments has some type of seam pocket.

side edge of the other pocket piece to the other seam edge of the opening. The right sides of the fabric of the pocket pieces should be together.

STEP 3. Stitch each pocket piece to the seam allowance from the bottom of the pocket to the top with a ⅜ inch (9 mm) seam.

STEP 4. Stitch the pocket pieces together with a ⅝ inch (1.5 cm) seam. Start where the seam stitched in step 1 ends. The pocket seam and the garment seam should meet exactly.

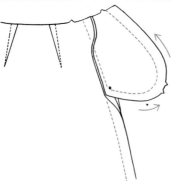

STEP 5. Turn the completed pocket to the front and press. When the waistband is attached, the raw edge at the top of the pocket will be enclosed.

Here is another way to attach a seam pocket.

STEP 1. Assemble the pocket first. With the right sides of the fabric together, *pinbaste*[5] and stitch the curved outside edges of the pocket together. Sew a ⅝ inch (1.5 cm) seam. Start stitching at the bottom of the pocket ⅝ inch (1.5 cm) from the straight side edge.

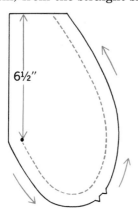

6½"

[5] See pages 247–248.

STEP 2. Pinbaste and stitch the garment seam, leaving an opening the same measurement as the straight side seam of your pocket.

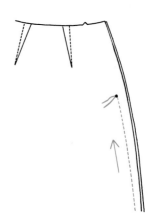

STEP 3. Pin the open pocket edges to the open seam allowances of your garment. *Hand baste*[6] in place if necessary, then machine stitch the pocket into place.

STEP 4. Turn the pocket to the front and press in place.

[6] See page 236.

PUTTING IT TOGETHER

1 What is a seam pocket?
2 Describe two ways to attach a seam pocket.

CLOTHES, CLUES, AND CAREERS

LESSON SEVENTEEN
ZIPPERS

- placket
- lapped zipper application
- slot zipper application
- fly front zipper application
- invisible zipper application

- kinds of zippers
- some types of zipper applications
- deciding which zipper application to use
- some ways to apply zippers

You probably have many garments that have *zipper plackets.* A zipper placket is an opening with a zipper closing. You may have noticed that the type of zipper and the way it is applied in each garment is not always the same. Depending on the garment, the fabric, and the location of the zipper placket, different types of zippers and different ways of sewing them into garments are used.

Some zippers have metal teeth and cotton tape; others may have nylon coil and nylon or polyester tape. Some zippers have large teeth and heavy or thick fabric. Lightweight zippers are used in garments that are made of lightweight fabric.

Three types of zipper applications for a regular zipper are the lapped zipper, the slot zipper, and the fly front zipper. Another type of application is used for the invisible zipper. This is a special type of zipper which, when applied, cannot be seen from the outside of the garment.

In a *lapped zipper application,* the zipper is stitched in place so that the seam allowance on one side of the placket covers the zipper. This application is used in center front and center back openings, side openings, and in fitted sleeves that have zipper plackets. The lapped application is best suited for fabrics of light and medium weight.

In a *slot zipper application,* the zipper is centered in the seam and stitched with equal amounts of fabric on both sides of the opening. This application may be used in center front or center back openings or in fitted sleeves that have zipper plackets. A slot zipper application is usually more satisfactory than a lapped zipper application in a heavy fabric. It is also suitable for use in light and medium weight fabrics.

The *fly front zipper application* is used most commonly in pants, shorts, slacks, and jeans. The seam edge of the placket is wider than ⅝ inch (1.5 cm) because of an extension that is either cut as part of the garment or sewn to the seam edge. This extension adds strength and forms a wide lap over the zipper when it is sewn into the opening.

The *invisible zipper* is best suited for use in garments made of lightweight or medium weight fabrics. The zipper may not work well in thick fabrics or fabrics with a napped, or fuzzy, surface. The invisible zipper is often chosen if the design of the garment or fabric is better emphasized when the stitching for a zipper is not seen. If there is a seam at the zipper opening, such as the waistline seam in a dress, the invisible zipper may be difficult to insert.

On the next page you will see a photograph showing a variety of zippers available in stores. See if you can identify each zipper. Then decide on which particular garment each zipper is used and where.

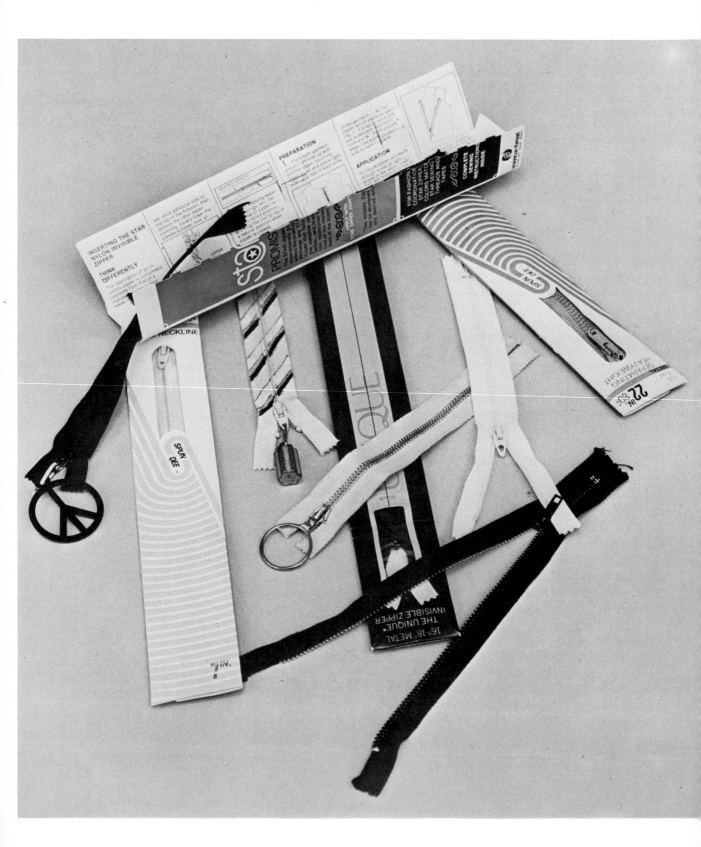

CLOTHES, CLUES, AND CAREERS

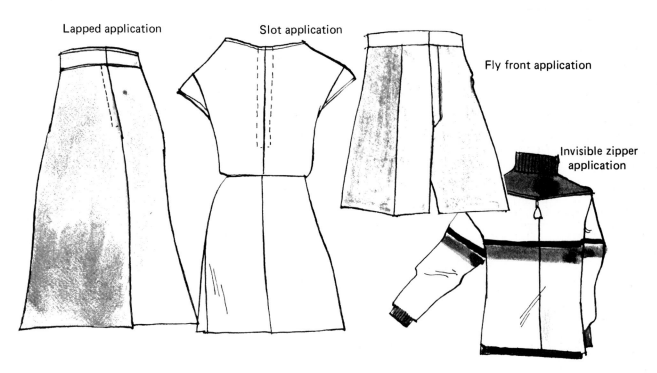

Lapped application

Slot application

Fly front application

Invisible zipper application

Follow these directions to make a slot zipper placket. In a collarless blouse, shirt, or dress the zipper may be sewn in either before or after the neck *facing*[1] is attached. Garments with a *collar*[2] or *waistband*[3] must have the zipper inserted before the collar or waistband is attached.

STEP 1. Mark the seam for the zipper opening if you have not already done so. To do this, place the zipper on the seamline so that the teeth or coil part at the zipper top is ⅝ inch (1.5 cm), or the seam allowance, plus ¼ inch (6 mm) from the top edge of the garment. Be sure the zipper is flat and the fabric is not stretched. Mark your fabric where the teeth or coils end at the bottom of the zipper.

STEP 2. *Pinbaste*[4] and stitch the garment seam at ⅝ inch (1.5 cm), *backstitching*[5] at the mark where the zipper opening begins. Clip the threads. *Machine baste*[6] the zipper opening at ⅝ inch (1.5 cm). If the facing has been

attached, continue the basting right on through the facing.

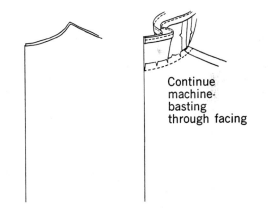

Continue machine-basting through facing

STEP 3. *Press the seam open.*[7]

STEP 4. Attach the zipper foot to the sewing machine and adjust it to the right side of the needle. Open the zipper. Place it face down on one seam allowance with the teeth edge at the seamline and the teeth or coil part at the top of the zipper ⅞ inch (2.2 cm) from the top seam edge. Sew through the tape and seam allowance only.

[1] See pages 277–279. [2] See pages 291–294.
[3] See pages 286–290. [4] See pages 247–248.
[5] See page 201. [6] See page 256.

[7] See pages 250–251.

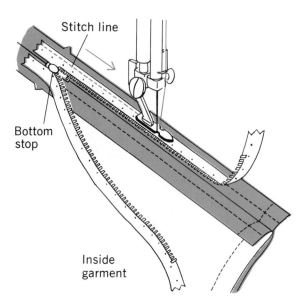

Stitch line

Bottom stop

Inside garment

STEP 5. Adjust the zipper foot to the left side of the needle. Place the other side of the opened zipper on the other seam allowance with the edge of the teeth at the seamline and the pull tab turned up. Begin stitching at the turned up pull tab and sew through the zipper tape and seam allowance.

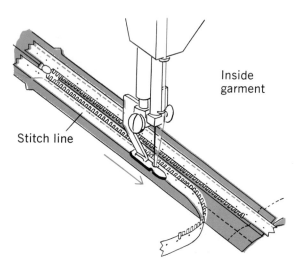

Inside garment

Stitch line

STEP 6. Close the zipper and spread the garment flat. Begin stitching at the top edge on the wrong side. Sew down one side of the zipper, across the bottom, and up the other side through the zipper tape, seam allowance, and garment. To keep your stitching even, follow the guideline on the zipper. Clip the threads.

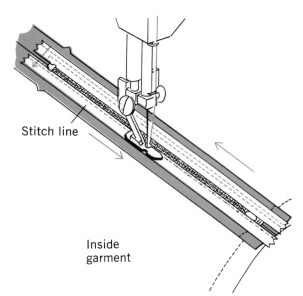

Stitch line

Inside garment

STEP 7. Remove the machine basting from the seamline after carefully clipping the stitching every few stitches. Press the placket from the inside of the garment. Place a towel under the placket and a moistened press cloth over the zipper. Hold the iron lightly over the placket and allow steam to penetrate the cloth. If the placket seam is curved, use a *tailor's ham*[8] to protect the garment shape during pressing.

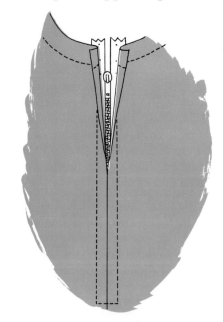

[8]See page 209.

LAPPED ZIPPER APPLICATION

Here are directions to make a lapped zipper placket. If you are making a collarless blouse, shirt, or dress, you may sew the zipper in place either before or after the neck *facing*[9] is attached. If your garment has a *waistband*[10] or *collar*[11] the zipper must be sewn in before the waistband or collar is attached.

STEP 1. Follow steps 1–3 as given for the making of a slot zipper placket.

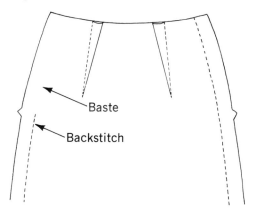

Baste

Backstitch

STEP 2. Attach the zipper foot to the sewing machine and adjust it to the right side of the needle. Open the zipper and place it face down on the back seam allowance with the teeth or coil at the seamline. The top of the coil or teeth should be ⅞ inch (2.2 cm) from the top seam edge of the garment. Sew through the zipper tape and back seam allowance only.

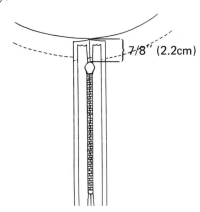

7/8″ (2.2cm)

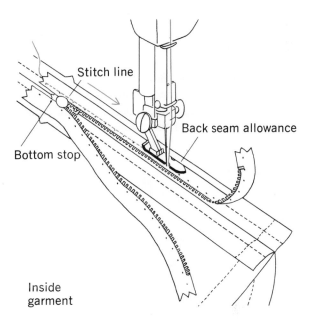

Stitch line

Back seam allowance

Bottom stop

Inside garment

STEP 3. Adjust the zipper foot to the left side of the needle. Close the zipper and turn it face up. Finger press the fabric away from the zipper, making a narrow fold in the back seam allowance along the zipper.

STEP 4. Stitch close to the fold beginning at the bottom of the zipper. Sew through the fold and the tape only.

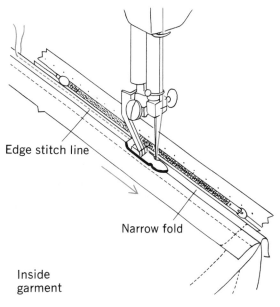

Edge stitch line

Narrow fold

Inside garment

STEP 5. Spread garment flat with the zipper face down on the front seam allowance,

[9]See pages 277–279. [10]See pages 286–290.
[11]See pages 291–294.

thus forming a pleat at the lower end of the placket. Stitch across the bottom of the zipper, make a square corner, and stitch up the side of the zipper. Sew through the zipper tape, seam allowance, and garment front piece. Stitch along the guideline on the zipper tape to keep your stitching even.

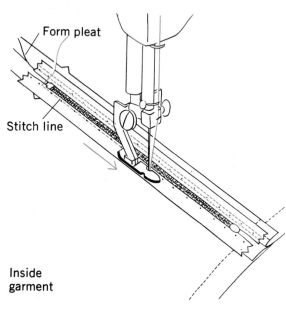

STEP 6. Follow step 7 as given for making a slot zipper placket on page 264.

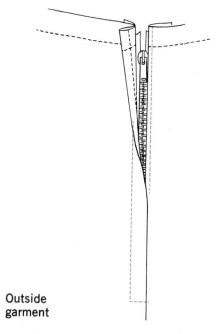

FLY FRONT ZIPPER APPLICATION

There are many ways to make a fly front zipper placket. Here is a simple method. If your *pattern guide sheet*[12] has different directions, follow your pattern guide sheet.

STEP 1. If you have not *transferred* the center front, fold line, and stitching line *markings*,[13] do this now.

STEP 2. *Staystitch*[14] the center front seam as shown here. Turn a square corner at the marking for the bottom of the fly opening. Use the points of shears to *clip*[15] to the stitching in the corner. Be careful not to cut through the stitching.

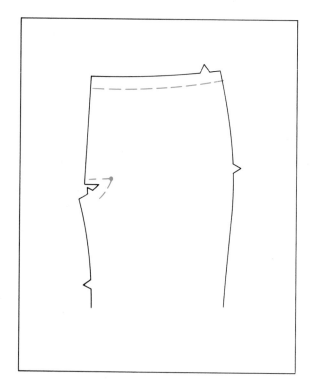

STEP 3. With the right sides of the fabric together, *pinbaste*[16] and stitch the seam to the marking for the bottom of the fly opening. *Clip the curves*[17] and *press the seam open.*[18]

[12] See pages 222–223. [13] See page 232.
[14] See pages 241–242. [15] See page 250.
[16] See pages 247–248. [17] See page 250.
[18] See pages 250–251.

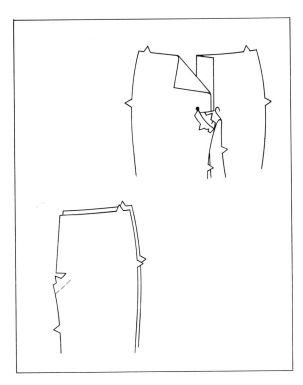

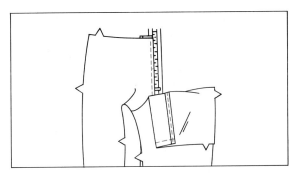

STEP 4. Press the left extension to the inside along the center front line and baste it in place at the top edge. Press the right extension to the inside along the fold line and baste it in place at the top edge.

Step 6. Attach the zipper foot to the sewing machine and adjust it to the left side of the needle. Stitch the zipper in place close to the fold.

STEP 7. Lap the left front over the right front. Match the center front markings and pin the left front to the right front as shown. *Handbaste*[19] along the center front line.

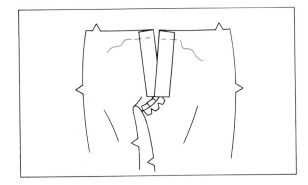

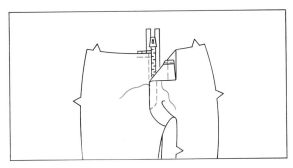

STEP 5. With the zipper closed, place the zipper under the right front edge with the fold close to the zipper teeth or coil. Pinbaste in place. The lower end of the zipper should be at the bottom of the opening. If you are using a zipper with metal teeth, do not worry if the top of the zipper extends above the top seam edge.

STEP 8. Pinbaste the left front of the garment to the zipper. Stitch along the stitching line. Remove the pins and handbasting. If you have used a metal zipper that extends beyond the top seam edge, cut the zipper off even with the top edge and *overcast*[20] between two teeth just below the seamline on each side of the zipper.

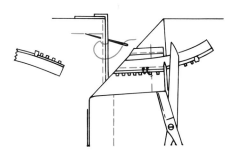

[19] See page 236. [20] See page 239.

Remove the teeth above the overcasting.

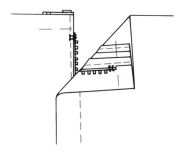

STEP 9. Press as directed in step 7 for the slot zipper placket.

INVISIBLE ZIPPER APPLICATION

If you are using an invisible zipper, you will need a special zipper foot to sew the zipper into the garment. To sew an invisible zipper into a garment, follow these directions. The zipper should be applied before the *facing,*[21] *collar,*[22] or *waistband*[23] is attached.

STEP 1. Open zipper. Press zipper using a synthetic setting on the iron. From the wrong side, press coils flat so that the two rows of stitching show.

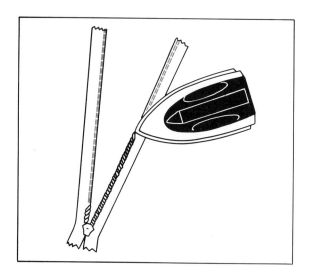

STEP 2. Leave the entire seam open. Open the zipper and place it face down on the right

[21] See pages 277–279. [22] See pages 291–294.
[23] See pages 286–290.

side of the fabric. Place the zipper teeth along the seamline with the tape extending into the seam allowance. The teeth at the top of the zipper should be ⅞ inch (2.2 cm) from the top seam edge. Pin the zipper in place.

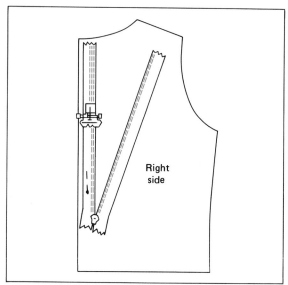

Right side

STEP 3. Attach the special zipper foot to the sewing machine and adjust it so that the needle comes down through the hole in the center of the zipper foot. Lower the needle into the zipper tape; then lower the attachment over the zipper teeth so the teeth fit in the groove on the attachment. Stitch from the top edge to the zipper tab. Take each pin out as you come to it.

STEP 4. Close the zipper and place the side of the zipper that is not stitched on the right side of the second garment piece. Line up the zipper teeth along the seamline with the zipper tape extending into the seam allowance and the teeth at the top of the zipper ⅞ inch (2.2 cm) from the top seam edge. Then pin the zipper in place.

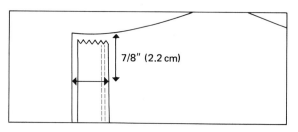

7/8" (2.2 cm)

Step 5. Open the zipper and stitch from the top edge to the zipper tab. Be sure that the zipper teeth are in the groove on the zipper foot and that you take each pin out as you come to it.

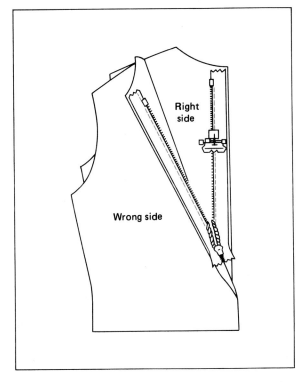

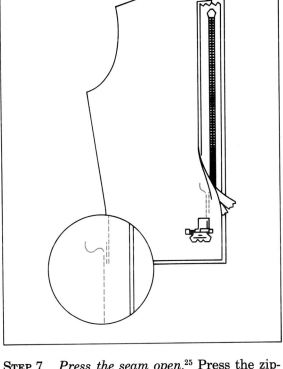

Step 6. Close the zipper. *Pinbaste*[24] the seam from the zipper bottom to the seam end. Slide the special zipper foot to the left so the needle lines up with the edge of the zipper foot. Lower the needle into the fabric at the point where the stitching for the zipper ends. Stitch slowly to the seam end along the seamline. Remove each pin as you come to it.

[24]See pages 247–248.

Step 7. *Press the seam open.*[25] Press the zipper placket as directed in step 7 for the slot zipper (page 264) Hand sew or machine stitch the bottom ends of the zipper tape to the seam allowances.

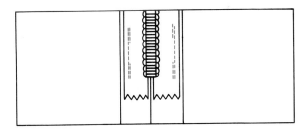

[25]See pages 250–251.

 **PUTTING IT TOGETHER**

1 What are some types of zipper plackets? Where are they used?
2 If you are making a garment from a heavy or thick fabric, which zipper application would probably be most satisfactory?
3 Which zipper application(s) can be used for light or medium weight fabrics?
4 What are some advantages of the invisible zipper? Some disadvantages?

LESSON EIGHTEEN
EASING AND GATHERING

 easing

gathering

 what easing is

what gathering is

reasons for easing and gathering

how to ease a seam

how to gather a seam

Sometimes a pattern calls for two seam edges to be sewn together that are not the same length. If your *pattern guide sheet*[1] tells you to "ease a seam" or to "gather a seam," you will know that one seam edge is longer than the other.

Easing is done when one seam edge is slightly longer than the other. If one seam edge is much longer than the other, the longer seam edge may be *gathered* to make it fit the shorter seam edge. Some seams in a garment that may be eased are the shoulder seam, the armhole seam of a set-in sleeve, and the curved seam at the bustline in a princess style dress or blouse. Gathered seams may be found at the armhole of a set-in sleeve. The waistline seam of a skirt or dress may be gathered to fit the waistband; the bodice front or back may be gathered to fit the yoke in a shirt. Another gathered seam may be found where a full sleeve and cuff are sewn together. Eased seams and gathered seams may be curved or straight.

Often extra stitching is needed to ease extra fabric into a seam. Extra stitching is always used when gathering a seam edge. Look at your pattern guide sheet to see if extra stitching is needed. There are special ways

in which easing and gathering can be handled successfully.

EASING A SEAM WITH PINBASTING

PINBASTING EXTRA FABRIC INTO A STRAIGHT SEAM

When extra stitching is not required in an eased seam, a special way of *pinbasting*[2] is used to fit the extra fabric into the seam.

Follow these directions for pinbasting extra fabric into a straight seam.

STEP 1. With right sides of the fabric together, pin the garment pieces together at each end of the seam and at the notches.

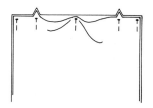

STEP 2. Place additional pins halfway between pins already in the fabric. Spread the extra fabric equally on each side of each pin.

[1] See pages 222–223.

[2] See pages 247–248.

Eased seam

Eased seam

Eased seam

Eased seam

Gathered seam

Gathered seam

Gathered seam

Gathered seam

Keep pinning between pins until there are pins about every ½ inch (1.2 cm) for the part of the seam that is eased. Pins should be 3 or 4 inches (8 or 10 cm) apart in the rest of the seam.

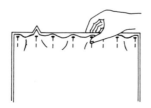

STEP 3. Sew the seam with the easing on top. If necessary, you may break the rule about *stitching with the grain*[3] of the fabric. Stitch slowly and use your fingers to keep the fabric smooth in front of the presser foot. When the seam is completed there should be no tucks along the seamline.

STEP 4. Press the seam.

PINBASTING EXTRA FABRIC INTO A CURVED SEAM

Follow these directions for pinbasting extra fabric into a curved seam.

STEP 1. *Staystitch*[4] the curved edge on the part to be eased. On an inward curve, *clip*[5] to the staystitching.

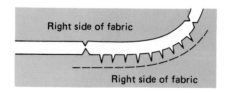

Right side of fabric

Right side of fabric

STEP 2. With right sides of the fabric together, pin the garment pieces together at each end of the seam and at the notches.

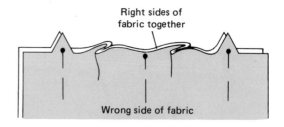

Right sides of fabric together

Wrong side of fabric

STEP 3. Place additional pins halfway between each pin already in the fabric. In the part of the seam being eased, distribute the extra fabric equally on both sides of each pin. Keep pinning between pins until there are pins about every ½ inch (1.2 cm) where the seam is eased and about every 3 or 4 inches (8 or 10 cm) where the seam is not eased.

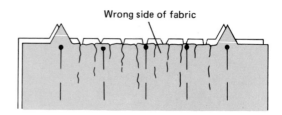

Wrong side of fabric

STEP 4. Sew the seam with the easing on top. If necessary, you may break the rule about *stitching with the grain*[6] of the fabric. Stitch slowly and use your fingers to keep the fabric smooth in front of the presser foot. When the seam is completed, there should be no tucks along the seamline.

STEP 5. Press the seam.

EXTRA STITCHING FOR EASING OR GATHERING

When your *pattern guide sheet*[7] calls for extra stitching to ease or gather a seam, follow these directions.

STEP 1. Set the *stitch-length regulator*[8] so your machine will make 8 to 10 stitches per inch (3 to 4 stitches per centimeter). Place

---

[3]See page 241.   [4]See pages 241–242.   [5]See page 250.

[6]See page 241.   [7]See pages 222–223.   [8]See page 201.

the seam edge to be eased or gathered under the presser foot and insert the needle ⅝ inch (1.5 cm) from the seam edge at the point where you are to begin gathering or easing. This point is usually a notch.

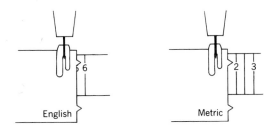

STEP 2. Stitch at ⅝ inch (1.5 cm) to the mark at the end of the part of the seam to be eased. Do not *backstitch*[9] at the beginning or end. Leave about 2 inches (5 cm) of thread at each end.

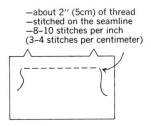

—about 2″ (5cm) of thread
—stitched on the seamline
—8–10 stitches per inch
(3–4 stitches per centimeter)

STEP 3. Make another row of stitching in the seam allowance ¼ inch (6 mm) from the first line of stitching.

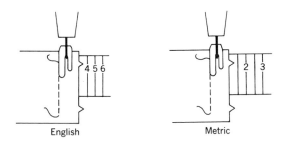

STEP 4. Return the stitch-length regulator to the position for 12 to 15 stitches per inch (5 to 6 stitches per centimeter).

[9] See page 201.

EASING A SEAM WITH EXTRA STITCHING

Here are directions for easing a seam with extra stitching.

STEP 1. With the right sides of the fabric together, pin the garment pieces together at each end of the seam and at the notches. Put a pin at the center of the part of the seam to be eased.

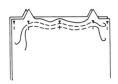

STEP 2. Pick up the ends of the easing threads. Gently pull both threads at the same time and slide the fabric along the thread toward the center of the seam with the other hand. Continue pulling the threads until the larger piece of fabric fits the smaller piece between one end and the center of the part being eased.

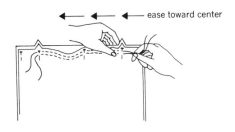

ease toward center

STEP 3. Use your fingers to distribute the extra fabric evenly along this part of the seam. *Pinbaste*[10] the part you have eased.

ease toward center

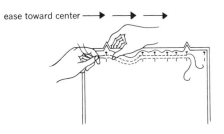

[10] See pages 247–248.

Step 4. Follow steps 2 and 3 for the other half of the seam to be eased.

Step 5. Check to be sure pins are 3 or 4 inches (8 or 10 cm) apart where the seam is not eased; pins should be about ½ inch (1.2 cm) apart in the eased part.

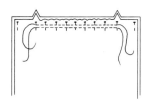

Step 6. Stitch the seam along the seamline. The easing should be on top. If necessary, you may break the rule about *stitching with the grain*[11] of the fabric. Stitch slowly and use your fingers to keep the fabric smooth in front of the presser foot. When the seam is complete, there should be no tucks along the seamline.

Step 7. Remove the ease stitching and press the seam.

GATHERING A SEAM

Gathering is done much the same as easing with extra stitching. The difference is that with gathering there is more extra fabric than with easing. This means the seam is not smooth and flat when the seam is completed. There are small tucks along the seamline.

To gather a seam, follow the directions for easing with extra stitching. Keep pulling the threads until the longer seam edge fits the

[11] See page 241.

shorter edge. Distribute the gathers, or small tucks, evenly along the seamline.

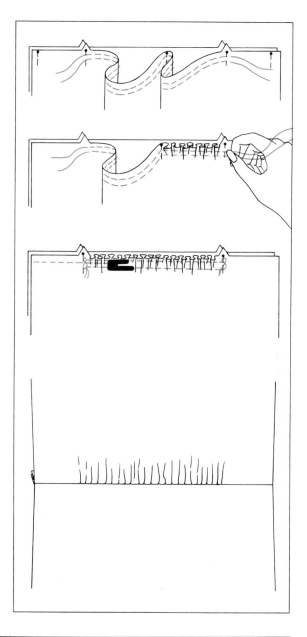

 **PUTTING IT TOGETHER**

1 When does a seam need to be eased or gathered?
2 What is the difference between easing and gathering?

LESSON NINETEEN
INTERFACING

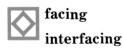

◆ **facing**

interfacing

○ **what interfacing is**

some places interfacing is used

some fabrics for interfacing

some ways to apply interfacing

A *facing* is a piece of fabric which finishes a raw edge of a garment. It may be cut as part of the garment or sewn to the garment edge and turned under. An *interfacing* is a layer of fabric placed between the facing and the garment in certain areas to reinforce, hold shape, or prevent stretching. Interfacing is used as reinforcement under buttons and buttonholes; it helps collars, waistbands, cuffs, and collarless neck edges hold their shapes.

Your pattern may call for interfacing in certain parts of the garment you are making. If so, choose a fabric that is firm and lighter in weight than the garment fabric. Any interfacing to be used in garments of woven fabrics should be woven fabric or a special *nonwoven fabric*.[1] Interfacing for garments of lightweight woven fabrics in plain colors can be cut from the same fabric as the other parts of the garment. Print, plaid, or striped fabric may show through if used for interfacing. For this reason, a solid color fabric is a better choice. Heavy or thick fabrics may require a medium weight fabric for interfacing. A garment of knitted fabric should have interfacing of nylon net or lightweight knitted fabric. A very lightweight, flexible nonwoven fabric is also suitable for interfacing for knitted fabrics.

In the illustration to the right are several examples of where facings are used in garments.

[1] See page 119.

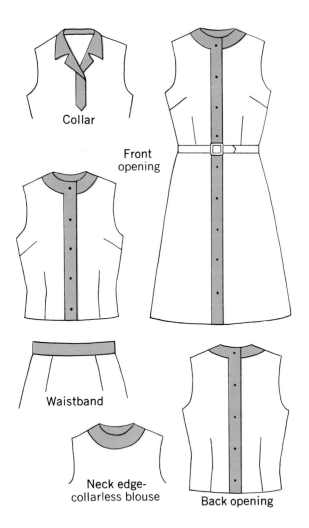

Collar

Front opening

Waistband

Neck edge—collarless blouse

Back opening

If separate pattern pieces for interfacing are not included in the pattern envelope, pattern pieces for *facings*[2] may be used to cut interfacings. Pin and cut each interfacing piece on the same *grainline*[3] as the facing and garment part being interfaced unless the pattern tells you otherwise.

Follow these instructions to attach interfacing to a facing piece or to the garment.

STEP 1. Cut corners off the interfacing pieces. This eliminates bulk in the seam allowance at corners when the garment is turned right side out.

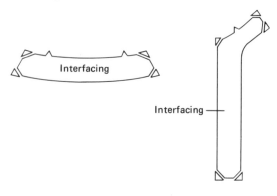

STEP 2. Check your *pattern guide sheet*[4] to see whether you are to attach the interfacing to the facing or to the garment. *Pinbaste*[5] the interfacing in place, matching notches and other markings. Stitch at ½ inch (1.2 cm) on all sides where there will be a seam. Do not machine stitch along a fold line.

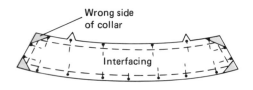

[2] See pages 277–278. [3] See pages 212–214.
[4] See pages 222–223. [5] See pages 247–248.

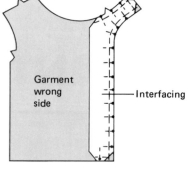

STEP 3. *Trim*[6] the interfacing close to the stitching.

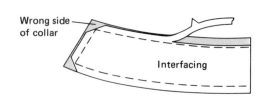

STEP 4. If the interfacing fits along a fold line, *catch stitch*[7] the interfacing to the garment fabric along the fold line. Stitch carefully so the stitches do not show on the outside of the garment.

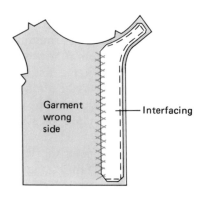

[6] See pages 249–250. [7] See page 238.

 **PUTTING IT TOGETHER**

1 What is interfacing? Why is it used in garments?
2 Where might interfacing be placed in a garment?
3 What are some things to think about when you choose a fabric to use for interfacing?

LESSON TWENTY
MAKING FACINGS, ATTACHING FACINGS, AND UNDERSTITCHING

facing

extended facing

attached facing

understitching

what facings are

where facings are used

how to make and attach facings

purpose of understitching

how to understitch

A *facing* is a piece of fabric used to finish a raw edge of a garment or garment piece. For example, a shirt has facings along the front edges where the buttons and the buttonholes are located; a sleeveless, collarless blouse has facings to finish the neck edge and the armholes.

A facing may be an *extended facing* or a *fitted facing*. An *extended facing* is part of a garment piece which turns back or under to form a finished edge. Front edges of shirts may have this type of facing. A *fitted facing* is a separate piece of fabric that is sewed to a raw edge. Fitted facings are cut the same shape as the parts of the garment to which they are sewn. Fitted facings are found at necklines, waistlines, and armhole edges.

Fitted armhole facing

Extended facing

MAKING FACINGS

Fitted facing pieces sometimes need to be sewn to one or more other facing pieces before the facing is attached to the garment. To prepare fitted facing pieces for attachment to a garment, follow these directions.

STEP 1. *Staystitch*[1] any inside curved edges.

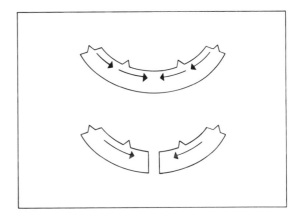

[1]See pages 241–242.

STEP 2. Lay the facing pieces on a table with the wrong sides up and the notched edges together. This means that the right sides of the fabric will be together as you work.

STEP 3. With the right sides together, *pin-baste*[2] the seams. Be sure to match notches. Sometimes corners of edges on neck facings will not match. This is right as long as the facing edges at the seam allowances match.

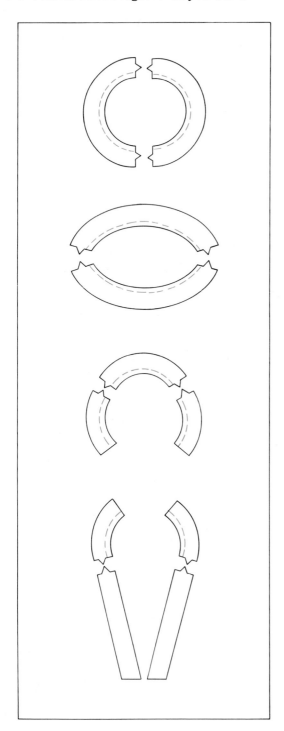

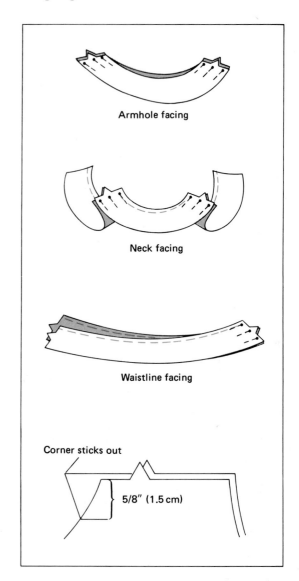

Armhole facing

Neck facing

Waistline facing

Corner sticks out

5/8″ (1.5 cm)

STEP 4. Stitch the seams; *trim*[3] them to ¼ inch (6 mm); then *press them open.*[4]

STEP 5. *Finish*[5] the outside edges of facing pieces as you would a seam.

[2] See pages 247–248. [3] See pages 249–250.
[4] See pages 250–251. [5] See pages 252–253.

Follow these directions to attach a fitted facing piece to an extended facing piece.

STEP 1. *Staystitch*[6] any inside curved edges.

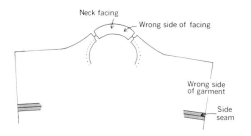

STEP 2. Lay the garment piece with the extended facing and the fitted facing piece on the table with the wrong sides up and the notched edges together.

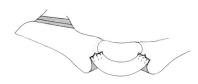

STEP 3. Follow steps 3–5 as given for preparing fitted facing pieces for attachment to a garment (page 278).

ATTACHING FACINGS

Here are directions for attaching facings to a garment.

STEP 1. If you are working with an extended facing or a fitted facing attached to an extended facing, turn the facing to the outside of the garment with the right sides of the fabric together. Match notches if there are any and *pinbaste*[7] the facing in place.

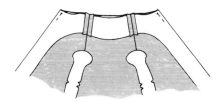

STEP 2. If you are working with a fitted facing, place the right side of the garment against the right side of the facing. Match notches, seamlines, and other markings. Pinbaste the seam edges in place.

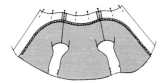

STEP 3. Stitch the seam at ⅝ inch (1.5 cm).

STEP 4. *Trim*[8] or *layer*[9] and *clip*[10] or *notch*[11] the seam edge.

UNDERSTITCHING

When a garment is completed and the facings are turned under, the facings should not show from the garment outside. *Understitching* is a line of stitching through the facing and both seam allowances after the facing is attached to the garment. Its purpose is to help keep the facing turned under.

STEP 1. Place the garment on the sewing machine with the right side of the garment up. The wrong side of the facing will be up. Be sure the garment part is to the left and the facing is to the right.

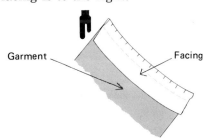

[6] See pages 241–242.   [7] See pages 247–248.

[8] See pages 249–250.   [9] See page 250.
[10] See page 250.   [11] See page 250.

STEP 2. Lift up the facing and pull it to the right so the right side of the fabric is up and the facing covers the seam edges.

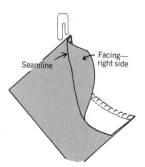

STEP 3. Place the facing under the presser foot. Insert the needle into the fabric just to the right of the seamline so the seamline is along the inside of the left-hand toe of the presser foot. The needle should go through the facing and both seam allowances.

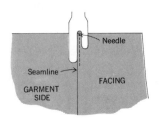

STEP 4. Understitch the facing. Do not *backstitch*.[12] With your hands pull the facing gently to the right to keep the seam flat. Stop and straighten out the fabric when it is necessary. Be sure to keep the seam edges to the right underneath the facing as you stitch. Leave threads about 2 inches (5 cm) long.

[12] See page 201.

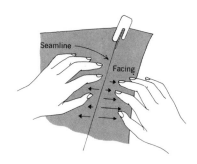

STEP 5. It is not possible to understitch all the way into the corners of facings which have corner seams. When understitching any corner seams, begin and end the stitching about 1 or 2 inches (2.5 cm to 5 cm) from the corners.

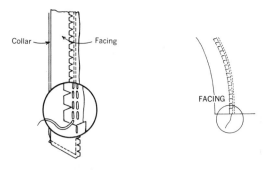

STEP 6. On the wrong side of the facing, pull the understitching thread until a loop of stitching comes through the fabric. Use a pin to pull on the loop until the end of the thread comes through. Tie.

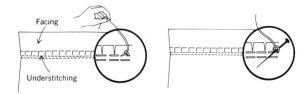

STEP 7. Press the facing in place. Be careful to see that the facing doesn't show on the outside of the garment.

PUTTING IT TOGETHER

1 What is a facing? Describe the difference between a fitted facing and an extended facing.
2 Why should facings be understitched? How is this done?

LESSON TWENTY-ONE
CASINGS

 casing   self-casing

applied casing   bodkin

 what casings are

where casings are used

some ways to make casings

You may have garments which have casings as part of their design. A *casing* is a garment part which encloses a piece of elastic or a drawstring and allows the fabric to be drawn up to fit the part of the body where the casing is located. Casings are used on waistlines of dresses, skirts, slacks, swim trunks, and shorts; on sleeve edges of blouses, shirts, and dresses; and on necklines of blouses, shirts, and dresses.

Some casings are formed by turning back or under an extension of the garment piece. These facings are *self-casings*. Other casings are made by sewing a separate piece of fabric to the garment. These are called *applied casings*.

SELF-CASINGS

SELF-CASING FOR ELASTIC

One way to make a self-casing for elastic is shown here.

STEP 1. On a lightweight fabric turn the raw edge to the inside ½ inch (1.2 cm) and press. On fabrics that are bulky, *finish*[1] the raw edge as you would a seam.

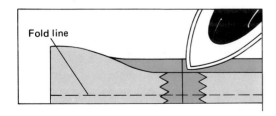

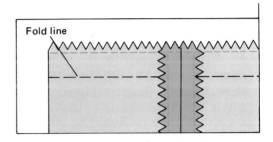

STEP 2. Turn the garment edge to the inside along the fold line. Press along the fold and *pinbaste*[2] the casing in place.

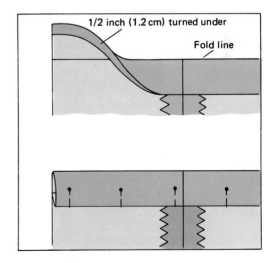

STEP 3. Stitch along the pinned edge about ¼ inch (6 mm) from the edge. For ¾ inch (1.9 cm) or wider elastic, leave about 2 inches (5 cm) unstitched at a seam so you can insert

[1]See pages 252–253.

[2]See pages 247–248.

the elastic. For elastic narrower than ¾ inch (1.9 cm), leave about 1 inch (2.5 cm) not stitched.

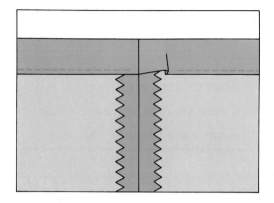

STEP 4. Measure the part of the body where the casing is to fit. Add 2 inches (5 cm) to this measurement and cut a piece of elastic this length. Insert the elastic in the casing at the opening. Pull it through using a safety pin or bodkin. A *bodkin* is a blunt, needle-like instrument designed for pulling elastic or other material through a casing. Overlap the ends of the elastic and pin them together.

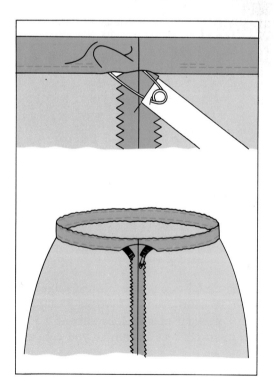

STEP 5. Try on the garment to check the fit at the casing. Unpin and adjust the elastic until you have the fit you want. Cut off more elastic if you need to, but be sure to allow at least ½ inch (1.2 cm) for sewing the two ends together. Pin the elastic together and take the garment off. Stitch the elastic together with the ends overlapped.

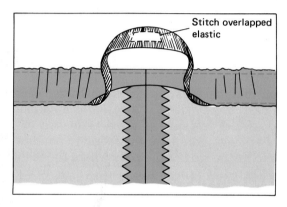

Stitch overlapped elastic

STEP 6. Complete the casing by stitching the opening. To keep the fabric flat, stretch the elastic as you stitch.

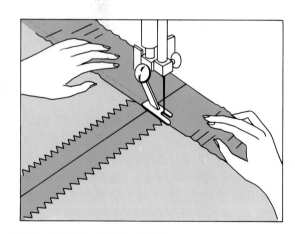

SELF-CASING FOR A DRAWSTRING

Here is one way to make a self-casing for a drawstring.

STEP 1. Find the seam where the drawstring is to be inserted. If you have already stitched the seam, use a *seam ripper*[3] to make an

[3] See page 207.

opening in the outside casing seam (not the part folded under). Start at the fold line and make the opening ¼ inch (6 mm) shorter than the width of the casing. For example, if the casing is 1 inch (2.5 cm) wide, make the seam opening ¾ inch (1.9 cm) long. *Backstitch*[4] over the stitching above and below the opening so the stitching won't pull out. If you haven't stitched the seam where the drawstring is to be inserted, leave an opening in the outside casing seam ¼ inch (6 mm) shorter than the width of the casing. Backstitch above and below the opening.

STEP 4. Insert the drawstring into the opening using a safety pin or *bodkin,* a special instrument for pulling elastic or other material through a casing.

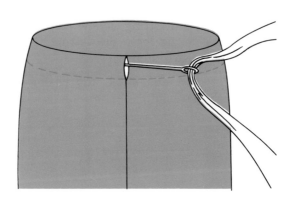

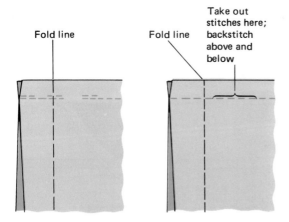

Fold line

Fold line

Take out stitches here; backstitch above and below

STEP 2. Follow steps 1 and 2 as given for making a self-casing for elastic (page 281).

STEP 3. Stitch around the pinned edge about ¼ inch (6 mm) from the edge. Overlap the stitching by about 4 or 5 stitches; do not backstitch.

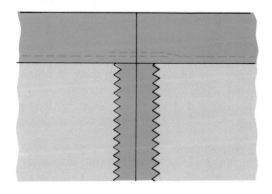

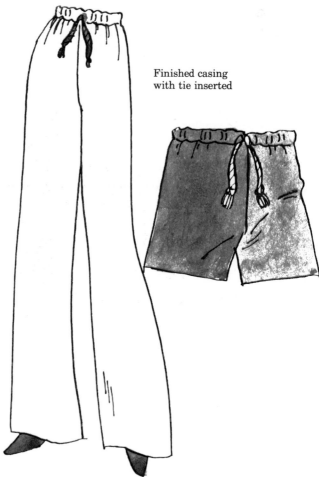

Finished casing with tie inserted

[4]See page 201.

APPLIED CASINGS

APPLIED CASING AT A RAW EDGE

To make an applied casing at a raw edge, follow these directions.

STEP 1. For a drawstring, follow step 1 for making a self-casing for a drawstring (page 282). For elastic, go to step 2.

STEP 2. *Pinbaste*[5] and stitch the casing to the edge of the garment.

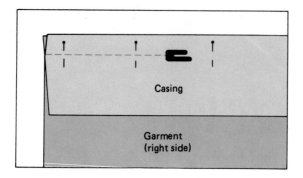

STEP 3. *Press*[6] the seam toward the casing and *understitch*.[7]

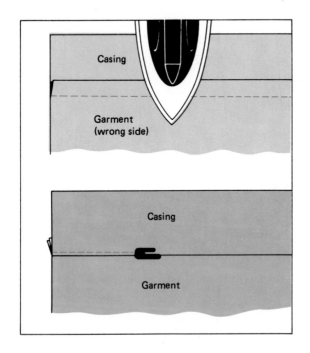

Press the casing to the garment inside. Use the tip of the iron.

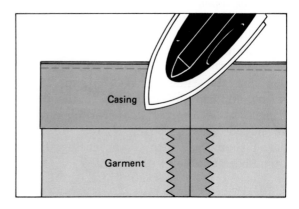

STEP 4. Turn under and press the raw edge of the casing or apply a *seam finish*.[8] (See step 1 on page 281.)

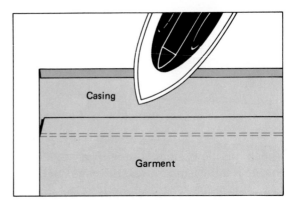

STEP 5. For elastic, follow steps 2–6 under making a self-casing for elastic. For a drawstring, follow steps 3 and 4 under making a self-casing for a drawstring.

APPLIED CASING NOT AT A GARMENT EDGE

To make an applied casing that is not at a garment edge, follow these directions. If you are to insert a drawstring, start with step 1. For elastic, begin with step 2.

STEP 1. Follow the directions for step 1 given for making a self-casing for a drawstring. Instead of a fold line, there will be

---

[5]See pages 247–248. [6]See pages 250–251.
[7]See pages 279–280.

[8]See pages 252–253.

two marked lines for positioning the casing. Make the opening in the seam between these two lines.

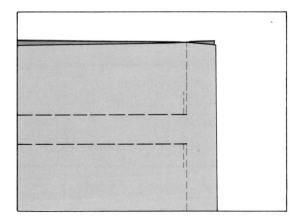

STEP 2. Turn under both long edges of the casing piece and press in place. If you are using packaged bias tape, the edges are probably already turned under.

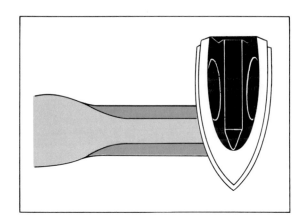

STEP 3. Pin the tape along the marked lines for the casing. Turn under the raw edges where the ends of the casing meet. Stitch along the top and bottom edges about ¼ inch (6 mm) from the fold. Do not stitch the opening where the ends of the casing meet.

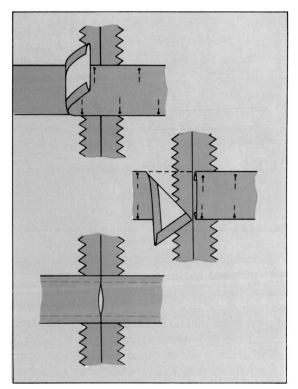

STEP 4. For inserting elastic, follow steps 4 and 5 for making a self-casing for elastic (page 282). For inserting a drawstring, follow step 4 for making a self-casing for a drawstring (page 283).

STEP 5. *Slip stitch*[9] the opening in the casing on the garment inside.

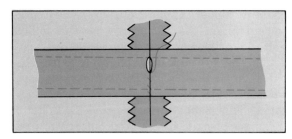

[9] See page 238.

PUTTING IT TOGETHER

1 What is a casing? Where in a garment might a casing be used?
2 What are two types of casings? Describe the differences between these two types.

LESSON TWENTY-TWO
WAISTBANDS

waistband
overlap
underlap

belt loops
topstitching

what a waistband is

some ways to attach waistbands

how to attach belt loops

A *waistband* is a fitted belt-like garment piece stitched to the waistline seam of skirts, shorts, slacks, jeans, or pants to finish the seam edge. Unlike a *facing,*[1] a waistband can be seen from the garment outside after it has been attached to the garment.

Usually one end of the waistband laps over the other so that *hooks and eyes,*[2] a *button* and *buttonhole,*[3] or some other type of fastener can be applied to keep the waistband closed while the garment is being worn.

If the garment has a *slot, lapped,* or *invisible zipper*[4] application in the back seam, the waistband *overlap* is on the left. The waistband *underlap* is on the right. For a slot, lapped, or invisible zipper application in the side seam, the overlap should face toward the back of the garment. For a garment with a fly-front zipper application, the waistband overlap is on the same side as the folded fabric edge covering the zipper. On some waistbands, the overlap may be even with the folded fabric edge along the zipper placket. On other waistbands, the overlap may be *extended.* This means it goes beyond the edge of the zipper placket. Check your pattern to find out if your waistband has an extended overlap.

Some waistbands include belt loops as part of their design. These are attached at the time the waistband is attached.

The method used to attach a waistband to a garment depends on the fabric and design of the garment. On many garments the waistband is attached in one continuous piece after the zipper has been sewn in and all other vertical seams have been sewn. However, on some boys' and men's slacks or jeans, the waistband is attached in two pieces. The center back seam is left open and a waistband piece is attached to each half of the garment. Then the center back seam is sewn.

There are many ways to attach belt loops and waistbands. If your pattern does not call for attaching belt loops and waistband by one of the ways shown here, follow the special directions on your *pattern guide sheet.*[5]

WAISTBANDS WITH TOPSTITCHING

These directions show how to attach a waistband with a final machine stitching on the outside. This method is often used on light or medium weight fabrics for garments that are casual or sporty or have *topstitching,* or stitching on the garment outside, as part of the design. It can be used for garments which call for waistbands to be attached in either one piece or two pieces.

STEP 1. If the garment has belt loops, make them according to the pattern directions. With the right sides of the fabric together,

[1] See page 277.
[2] See pages 310–311.
[3] See pages 307–310.
[4] See pages 261–269.
[5] See pages 222–223.

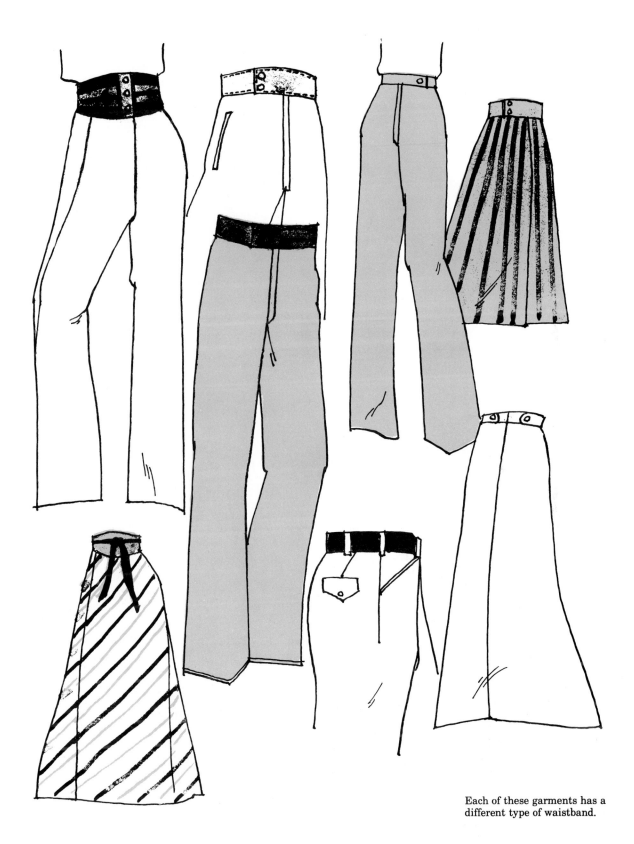

Each of these garments has a
different type of waistband.

pinbaste[6] the belt loops to the garment with the upper edges even. *Machine baste*[7] or *hand baste*[8] in place.

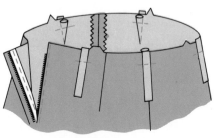

STEP 2. Turn under the seam allowance on the unnotched edge of the waistband and press it into place. *Trim*[9] the seam edge to ¼ inch (6 mm).

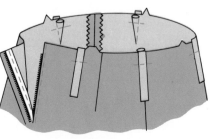

STEP 3. Work from the inside of the garment. With the right side of the waistband against the wrong side of the garment, pinbaste the notched edge of the waistband to the garment. Be sure the overlap and underlap are in the right positions.

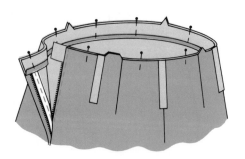

STEP 4. Stitch the waistband to the garment on the seamline. *Layer*[10] the seam allowances, then press the waistband and seam allowances up.

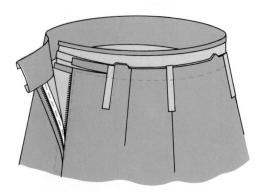

STEP 5. Fold the ends of the waistband at the zipper opening, right sides together. Pinbaste and stitch in place on the seamline. *Trim the seams*[11] and *clip the corners.*[12]

STEP 6. Turn the ends of the waistband right side out. Make sure the corners are sharp. Press.

STEP 7. Pin the folded edge of the waistband in place so it just covers the first machine stitching. The waistband should be the same width all the way around. Measure and make adjustments before you stitch.

---

[6]See pages 247–248.   [7]See page 256.
[8]See pages 247–248.   [9]See page 249.

[10]See page 250.   [11]See page 249.
[12]See page 250.

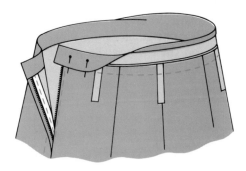

STEP 8. *Hand baste*[13] the waistband in place if you think the fabric may slip. Stitch the waistband to the garment on the outside close to the folded edge. Press.

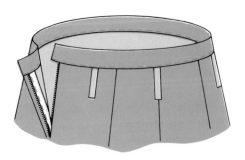

STEP 9. If you are making a garment in which the center back seam has not yet been sewn, pinbaste the seam. Stitch on the stitching line to the top of the waistband and *backstitch*.[14] Press the seam open.

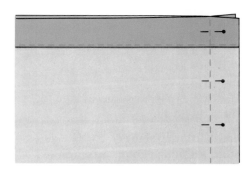

Turn under the corners and *slip stitch*[15] the edges to the inside of the waistband.

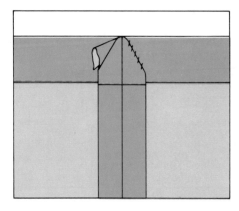

STEP 10. If you attached belt loops to the garment in step 1, turn the belt loops up and turn the raw edges under ⅜ inch (9 mm).

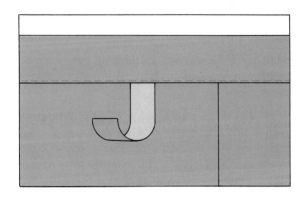

Pinbaste to the outside of the waistband, then stitch in place.

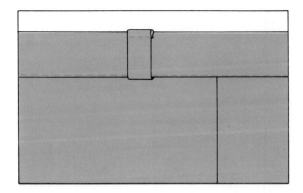

[13] See page 236.   [14] See page 201.

[15] See page 238.

STEP 11. Fasten the waistband with *hooks and eyes*[16] or a *flat hook closure*.[17] If there is a lapped zipper application you may want to use a *button and buttonhole*.[18] Also, design may suggest that a button and buttonhole or *special snap fastener*[19] be used.

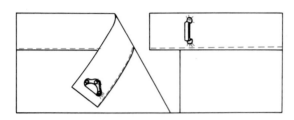

WAISTBANDS WITH HAND STITCHING ON THE INSIDE

Here is how to attach the waistband with a final hand stitch on the inside. This method is often used when it is desired that no stitching show on the garment outside.

STEP 1. Follow steps 1 and 2 as given for attaching a waistband with final stitching on the outside.

STEP 2. With right sides of the fabric together fold the waistband so that the pressed fold is at the seamline on the notched edge. *Pinbaste*[20] and stitch the waistband ends in place. *Trim the seams*[21] and *clip the corners*.[22] Turn the ends right side out and press.

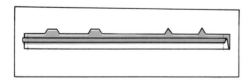

[16]See pages 310–311.   [17]See pages 310–311.
[18]See pages 307–310.   [19]See pages 310–311.
[20]See pages 247–248.   [21]See page 249.
[22]See page 250.

STEP 3. Work from the outside of the garment. With right sides of the fabric together, pinbaste and then stitch the waistband to the garment. Match notches and other markings.

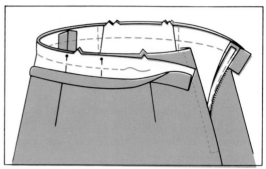

STEP 4. *Layer*[23] the seam allowances, then press the waistband and seam allowances up.

STEP 5. Turn the waistband to the inside and pinbaste the fold along the stitching line. *Slip stitch*[24] in place.

STEP 6. Follow steps 9–11 as given for attaching a waistband with final machine stitching on the outside.

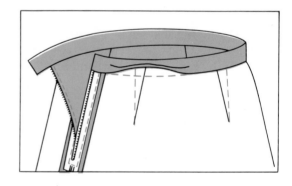

[23]See page 250.   [24]See page 238.

 **PUTTING IT TOGETHER**

1 How is a waistband different from a facing?
2 Why is there an overlap and an underlap on a completed waistband?
3 Describe two ways to attach a waistband. What are their similarities and differences?

LESSON TWENTY-THREE
MAKING COLLARS

 round collar

pointed collar

standing collar

bias turnover collar

layer

clip

understitch

notch

 different collar styles

some ways to make collars

Think about some of the clothes with collars you have seen. A Peter Pan collar, or a round collar that lies flat, is one kind you may know. A pointed collar is another type. There are also standing collars and bias turnover collars. What are some other collar styles you can think of? In the illustration below are examples of collars.

Low round   Mandarin   Low bias roll   High bias roll   Middy

Tailored   Chelsea   Wing   Jabot   Shawl   High round   Ruff

TECHNIQUES MATTER

FLAT COLLAR

Even though there are many collar styles, the ways collars are sewn together before they are attached are similar. Here are the steps for making flat round or flat pointed collars.

STEP 1. If you are *interfacing*[1] the collar, *pinbaste*[2] and *staystitch*[3] the interfacing to the wrong side of the facing. *Trim*[4] the interfacing close to the stitching.

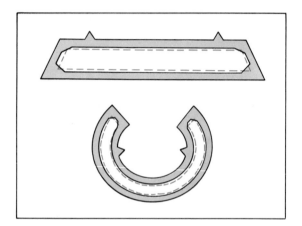

STEP 2. With the right sides of the fabric together, pinbaste and stitch the collar and facing pieces together. Match notches and other markings, making sure that the outside edges are even. Stitch only on the unnotched edge. The notched edge must be left open so the collar can be turned right side out.

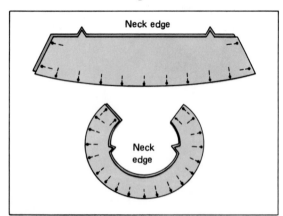

STEP 3. *Layer*[5] the seam allowances.

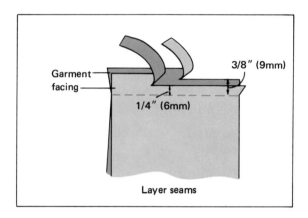

Layer seams

Clip corners[6] if the collar is pointed.

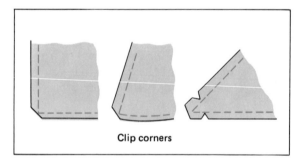

Clip corners

Clip curves[7] if there are inside curved edges where you have sewed the seam; *notch*[8] any outside curves.

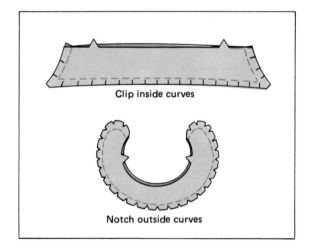

Clip inside curves

Notch outside curves

---

[1] See pages 275–276. [2] See pages 247–248.
[3] See pages 241–242. [4] See page 249.

[5] See page 250. [6] See page 250.
[7] See page 250. [8] See page 250.

STEP 4. *Understitch*[9] the seam allowances to the facing.

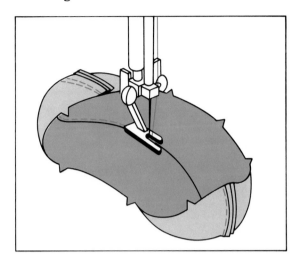

STEP 5. Turn the collar right side out and press it carefully. Be sure that the facing does not show at the seamline on the upper side of the collar. The facing may extend slightly beyond the collar on the unstitched edge.

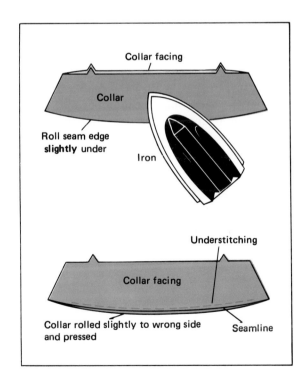

Collar facing

Collar

Roll seam edge **slightly** under

Iron

Understitching

Collar facing

Collar rolled slightly to wrong side and pressed   Seamline

[9] See pages 279–280.

STANDING COLLAR OR BIAS TURNOVER COLLAR

Here is how to make a standing collar or a bias turnover collar.

STEP 1. *Pinbaste*[10] and stitch the *interfacing*[11] to the collar. Trim interfacing close to stitching. If the collar is cut in one piece with a fold line at the top, do not machine stitch the interfacing along this edge. Instead, *catch stitch*[12] the facing to the collar at the fold line. Be careful to see that the stitches do not show on the garment outside.

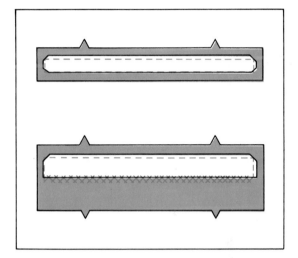

STEP 2. Turn under on the seamline the notched edge of the facing or the notched edge of the collar part away from the interfacing. Press in place, then *trim*[13] the seam allowance to ¼ inch (6 mm).

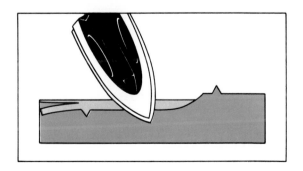

[10] See pages 247–248. [11] See pages 275–276.
[12] See page 238. [13] See page 249.

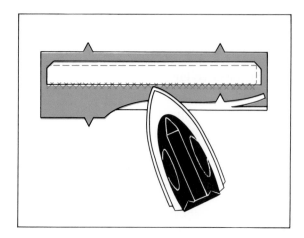

STEP 4. *Layer*[14] the seam edges and clip the corners.

STEP 5. *Understitch*[15] the facing if the collar and facing are stitched together rather than in one piece.

STEP 3. With the right sides of the fabric together, pinbaste and stitch the collar to the facing. If the collar is in two pieces, stitch only along the unnotched edges. The notched edge must be left open so the collar can be turned right side out. For a collar cut in one piece, fold the collar in half the long way so the right sides are together. Pinbaste along each end and stitch. Leave the notched edge open.

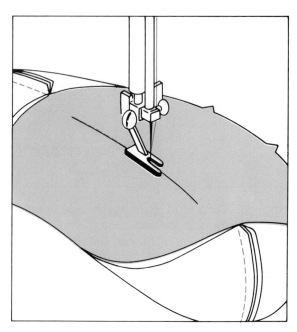

STEP 6. Turn the collar right side out and press it carefully. Be sure the facing does not show at the seamline on the upper side of the collar. The facing may extend slightly beyond the collar on the unstitched edge.

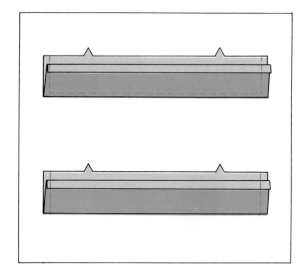

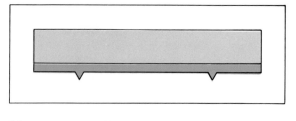

[14]See page 250.   [15]See pages 279–280.

PUTTING IT TOGETHER

1 What is the purpose of understitching?
2 What might happen if you don't clip or notch seams on curved edges?
3 Why is it important to press seams after they are stitched?

LESSON TWENTY-FOUR
ATTACHING COLLARS

 clip **layer** **understitch**   **some ways to attach collars**

There are several different ways to attach a collar to a garment. Three methods commonly used are shown here.

WITH COMPLETE NECK FACING

The first one is for attaching a collar when there is to be a *facing*[1] around the entire neck edge.

STEP 1. *Prepare the facing*[2] for attachment to the neck edge.

STEP 2. *Machine baste*[3] the neck (notched) edges of the collar together.

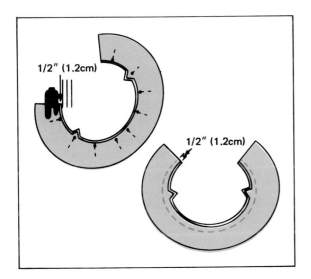

1/2" (1.2cm)

1/2" (1.2cm)

STEP 3. Using points of shears, *clip*[4] the garment neck edge to the *staystitching*.[5]

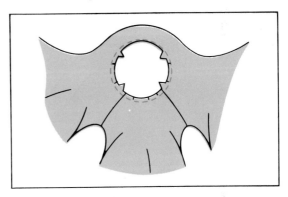

STEP 4. With the collar facing against the right side of the garment, *pinbaste*[6] the collar to the garment at the neck edge. Match the notches and other markings.

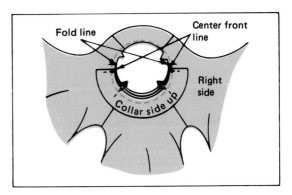

Fold line

Center front line

Right side

Collar side up

---

[1] See page 277.   [2] See pages 277–278.
[3] See page 256.

[4] See page 250.   [5] See pages 241–242.
[6] See pages 247–248.

STEP 5. Machine baste the collar to the neck edge at slightly less than ⅝ inch (1.5 cm). Remove the pins.

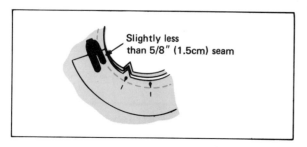

STEP 6. Place the right side of the garment facing against the right side of the collar. Match notches and other markings and pinbaste the facing in place.

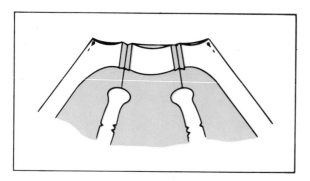

STEP 7. Stitch through all thicknesses with a ⅝ inch (1.5 cm) seamline. Stop the machine with the needle down to straighten the fabric if necessary.

STEP 8. *Layer*[7] the seam allowances and *clip*[8] the curved edges.

STEP 9. *Understitch*[9] through the facing and seam allowances at the neck edge.

STEP 10. Press.

[7]See page 250. [8]See page 250. [9]See pages 279–280.

WITH PARTIAL NECK FACING

This type of collar attachment is often used on shirts or other garments which have extended front facings. To attach a collar when the facing goes only to the shoulder seams, follow these directions.

STEP 1. *Finish*[10] the outside edges of the facings as you would a seam.

STEP 2. Using the points of shears, *clip*[11] the garment neck edge to the *staystitching*.[12]

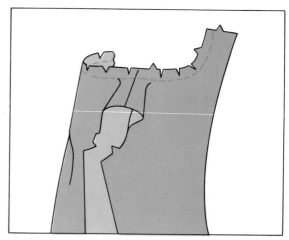

STEP 3. *Pinbaste*[13] the collar and facing to the garment neck edge from the shoulder seams to the collar ends. Match notches and other markings. Pinbaste the collar facing to the garment neck edge between shoulder seams. Match notches and other markings.

STEP 4. *Machine baste*[14] the collar and facing to the garment neck edge from the shoulder seams to the collar ends. Machine baste the collar facing to the garment neck edge between the shoulder seams.

[10]See pages 252–253. [11]See page 250.
[12]See pages 241–242. [13]See pages 247–248.
[14]See page 256.

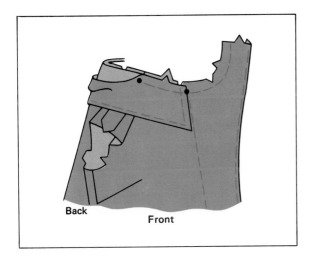

Back   Front

STEP 8. *Layer*[15] the seam allowances and *clip the corners.*[16] Clip any curved seams.

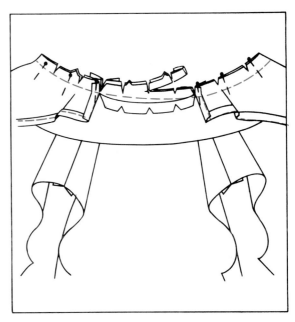

STEP 5. Turn the garment facing back on the fold line so the right side of the facing is against the collar. Match notches and other markings. The shoulder edge of the facing should be at the seamline. Pinbaste in place, then machine baste. Remove the pins.

STEP 6. Clip through all layers of fabric to the seamline at the ends of the garment facings. Turn back the collar away from the seamline at the neck edge.

STEP 9. Turn garment facings right side out and press.

STEP 10. Press seam allowances between shoulder seams toward the collar. Press the upper collar edge under on ⅝ inch (1.5 cm) seamline and trim to ¼ inch (6 mm).

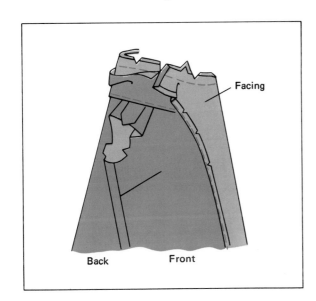

Facing

Back   Front

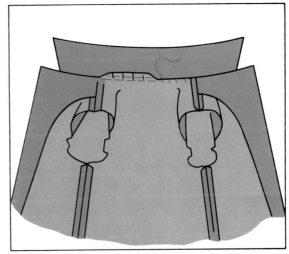

STEP 7. Stitch the neck edge as basted. Be careful not to catch the collar in the stitching between the shoulder seams.

[15] See page 250.   [16] See page 250.

STEP 11. Place the fold on the collar edge against the stitching line and pinbaste in place. Be sure the seam allowances are toward the collar under the folded edge.

STEP 12. *Slip stitch*[17] or *machine stitch*[18] the pinned edge in place.

STEP 13. Press.

STANDING COLLAR OR BIAS ROLL COLLAR

Here is one way to attach a standing collar or a bias roll collar to a garment.

STEP 1. *Clip*[19] the neck edge of the garment to the *staystitching*.[20]

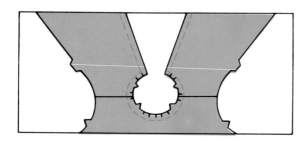

STEP 2. Place the right side of the collar against the right side of the garment neck edge. Match notches and other markings. *Pinbaste*[21] just the collar edge to the garment. Leave the facing free.

STEP 3. Stitch the collar to the neck edge. Be careful not to catch the collar facing in the stitching.

STEP 4. *Layer*[22] the seam allowances and *clip the corners*.[23] Clip curved seam edges.

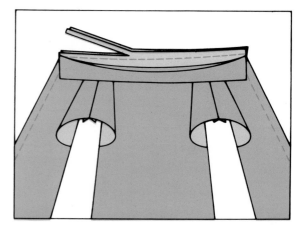

STEP 5. Press the seam allowances toward the collar.

STEP 6. Place the folded edge of the collar facing against the stitching line and pinbaste in place. Be sure the seam allowances are toward the collar under the folded edge.

STEP 7. *Slip stitch*[24] the pinned edge in place.

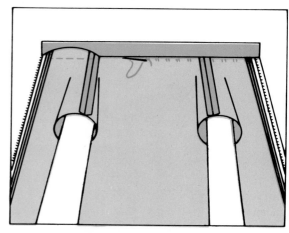

STEP 8. Press.

[17] See page 238.   [18] See page 279.
[19] See page 250.   [20] See pages 241–242.
[21] See pages 247–248.   [22] See page 250.
[23] See page 250.

[24] See page 238.

PUTTING IT TOGETHER

1 Why is it important to clip curves? To layer seam allowances?
2 What might happen if you don't understitch the seam allowances to the facing?

LESSON TWENTY-FIVE
SLEEVES

 set-in sleeve

raglan sleeve

kimono sleeve

reinforce

 some types of sleeves

how to reinforce underarm seams

how to make kimono sleeves

how to make and attach raglan sleeves

how to set in sleeves

There are three basic types of garment sleeves. These are kimono sleeves, raglan sleeves, and set-in sleeves. The *kimono sleeve* is cut in one piece with the garment. The *raglan sleeve* is attached to the garment by a diagonal seam from the underarm into the neckline. A *set-in sleeve* is attached to the garment with a seam around the armhole from the underarm, over the shoulder, to the underarm.

KIMONO SLEEVES

To make kimono sleeves, *pinbaste*[1] and stitch the long seam which is made by the side seam of the garment and the underarm seam of the sleeve. Stitch carefully around the curved area so the fabric is not stretched out of shape. Do not pull or stretch the fabric as you stitch on the machine.

In a garment with kimono sleeves, a sharp curve is formed by the underarm seam. The curved part should be *clipped*[2] so the seam will lie flat when the garment is turned right side out. Because this underarm area is a place where there may be extra strain when

the garment is worn, it is necessary to *reinforce,* or strengthen, the clipped area. Otherwise the seam may not be strong enough and the stitching will pull out. The fabric may also split where it has been clipped.

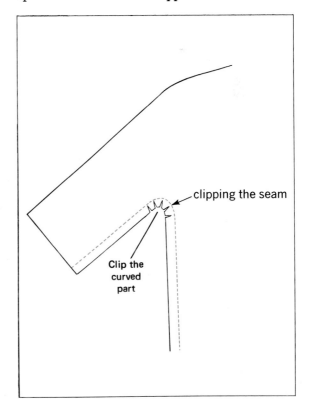

clipping the seam

Clip the curved part

[1] See pages 247–248. [2] See page 250.

Circular flounce

Short

Long

Kimono

Puffed

Angel

Raglan

Bishop

Cuff

Leg-o-mutton

REINFORCING UNDERARM SEAM

There are several ways to reinforce the curved underarm seam. One satisfactory way is to make a zig-zag machine stitch along the seam. Start by clipping the seam carefully in several places. *Press the seam open.*[3] Since this is a very curved edge, try pressing it over a *pressing ham*[4] rather than on the flat surface of the ironing board. Stitch on the inside of the garment. The stitch should follow the seam line exactly. Of course, thread and fabric should match.

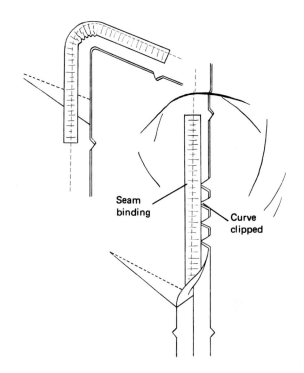

Seam binding

Curve clipped

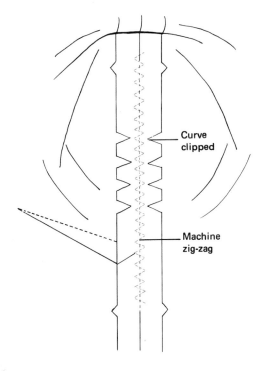

Curve clipped

Machine zig-zag

RAGLAN SLEEVES

Here are the directions to make and attach raglan sleeves.

STEP 1. On each sleeve, *pinbaste*[8] and stitch the dart at the shoulder. *Slash the darts*[9] and *press them open.*[10] If there are elbow darts, pinbaste, stitch, and press them also.

There is another way to reinforce a clipped seam which does not require special equipment, as the zig-zag stitch does. Sew a strip of seam binding on the seam in the curved area. You may want to *baste*[5] it in place first, using the stitches on the underside of the seam as a guide. The stitches which hold the seam binding in place permanently should follow the seam exactly. *Clip*[6] along the curve and *press the seam open.*[7]

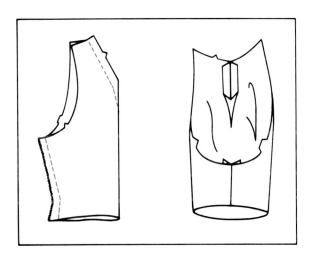

[3] See pages 250–251.   [4] See page 209.
[5] See page 238.   [6] See page 250.
[7] See pages 250–251.

[8] See page 244.   [9] See pages 245–246.
[10] See page 246.

STEP 2. With right sides of the fabric together, pinbaste, stitch, and press the underarm seam on each sleeve. Turn the sleeves right side out.

STEP 3. If the garment side seams have not been stitched, pinbaste, stitch, and press them. Leave the garment wrong side out.

STEP 4. Put the left sleeve inside the garment and into the left armhole so the right sides of the fabric are together. Match notches, underarm seams, and other markings. Pinbaste the sleeve in place.

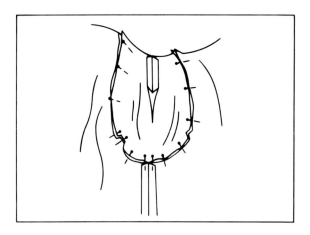

STEP 5. Stitch the seam in one line starting at the neckline edge. Stop with the needle down to straighten fabric if necessary. Stitch again close to the first stitching between the notches. Remove pins.

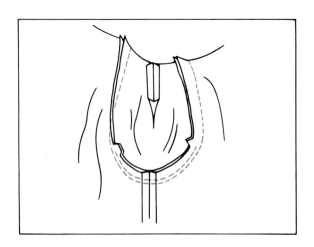

STEP 6. *Clip any inside curves*[11] and *notch any outside curves.*[12] Press the seam open above the notches. Press the seam at the underarm between the notches toward the sleeve.

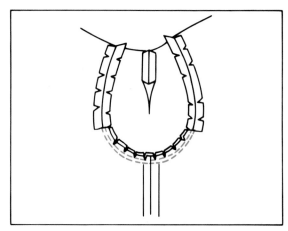

STEP 7. Repeat steps 4–6 for the other sleeve.

SET-IN SLEEVES

Set-in sleeves may be set into, or sewn into, the armhole either before or after the garment side seams and sleeve underarm seams are sewn and pressed. Some set-in sleeves are designed to be smooth and free of puckers at the seamline. Others may have gathers along the seamline. A puff sleeve is an example of a set-in sleeve with gathers at the seamline. The same methods can be used to set in a sleeve that is smooth at the seamline and one that is gathered at the seamline.

SETTING IN SLEEVES BEFORE SIDE SEAMS AND UNDERARM SEAMS ARE SEWN

Here is the way to attach set-in sleeves to a garment before the garment side seams and sleeve underarm seams are sewn.

STEP 1. If there are *darts*[13] at the elbow of the sleeves, *pinbaste,*[14] stitch, and *press.*[15]

[11] See page 250.   [12] See page 250.
[13] See pages 243–246.   [14] See page 244.
[15] See page 246.

STEP 2. *Machine baste*[16] two rows of stitching around the cap of each sleeve between the notches. These stitches are used to make the sleeve into a shape that will fit the armhole. Put one row of stitches on the seamline. Place the second row in the seam allowance about ¼ inch (6 mm) from the first line of stitching. Leave thread ends about 2 inches (5 cm) long. Do not *backstitch*.[17]

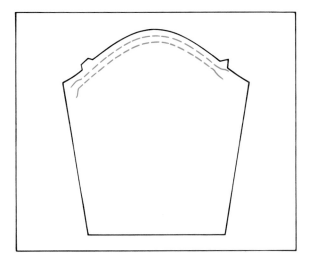

STEP 3. On the left sleeve, begin to form the sleeve cap into a rounded shape by pulling lightly on the two rows of basting stitches.

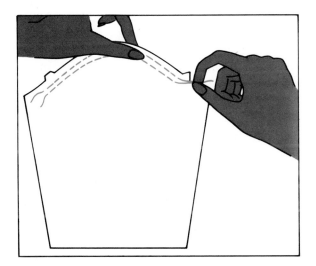

Continue pulling until the sleeve cap is about the same size as the armhole.

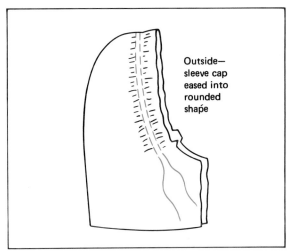

Outside—sleeve cap eased into rounded shape

STEP 4. With the right sides of the fabric together, *pinbaste*[18] the sleeve into the left armhole. Match notches and other markings. Adjust the basting threads so that the sleeve fits the armhole exactly. For a sleeve that is to be smooth at the seamline, be sure there are no little tucks along the line of basting. If the sleeve is to have gathers at the seamline, be careful to distribute the gathers evenly along the basting threads.

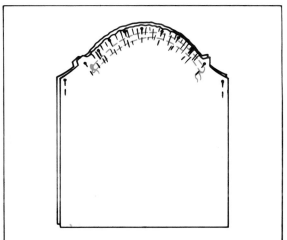

[16] See page 256.   [17] See page 201.   [18] See pages 247–248.

STEP 5. Carefully unpin the sleeve and place the sleeve cap over the end of a *sleeve board.*[19] Using only the point of a steam iron, press the seam allowance lightly to shape the sleeve cap. Press only to the seam line because this is the area which must fit the armhole.

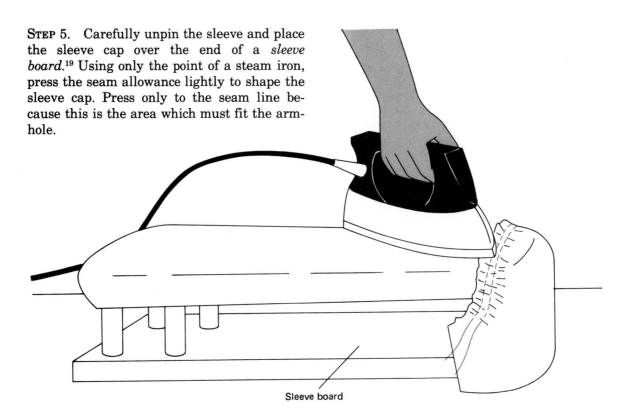

Sleeve board

STEP 6. Repin the sleeve into the armhole, matching notches and other markings. *Hand baste*[20] in place.

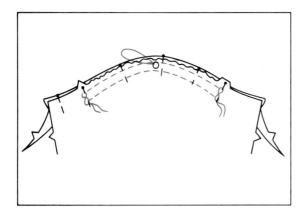

STEP 7. If you want to check the outside appearance before you stitch the sleeve in permanently, try on the garment.

STEP 8. Machine stitch along the seam line. Make a second row of stitching next to the first. Work slowly to avoid puckers. *Trim the seam allowances*[21] to ⅜ inch (9 mm) if your fabric is bulky.

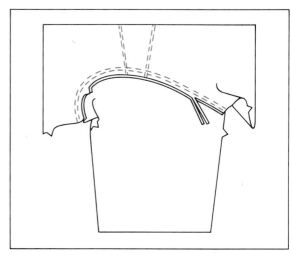

[19] See pages 209–210.   [20] See page 236.

[21] See page 249.

Step 9. *Clip*[22] the seam in the armhole area between the notches.

Step 10. Press the seam toward the inside of the sleeve. Use a *sleeve board*[23] to press the small area around the sleeve. Be careful not to change the shape of the cap you made in step 5.

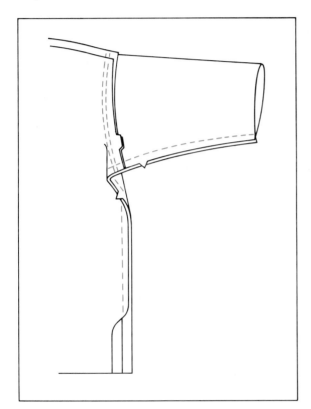

Step 11. Repeat steps 3–10 for the other sleeve.

Step 12. Stitch the underarm seams; press them open.

SETTING IN SLEEVES AFTER SIDE SEAMS AND UNDERARM SEAMS ARE SEWN

To set in a sleeve after the garment side seams and sleeve underarm seams have been stitched, follow these directions.

Step 1. Turn the sleeves right side out. Leave the garment wrong side out.

[22] See page 250.   [23] See pages 209–210.

Step 2. Follow steps 2 and 3 given for setting in a sleeve before the garment side seams and sleeve underarm seams are stitched (page 303).

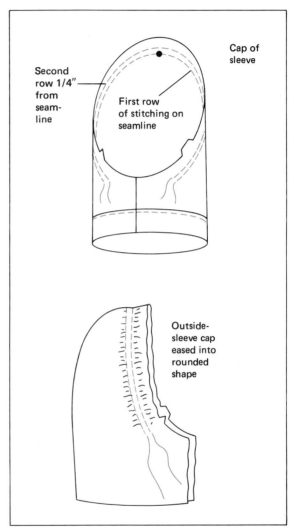

Step 3. Put the sleeve into the armhole so the right sides of the fabric are together. Match notches and other markings. Adjust the basting threads so that the sleeve fits the armhole exactly. For a sleeve that is to be smooth at the seamline, be sure there are no little tucks or gathers along the lines of basting. If the sleeve is to have gathers at the seamline, distribute the gathers evenly along the basting threads (see drawing, page 306).

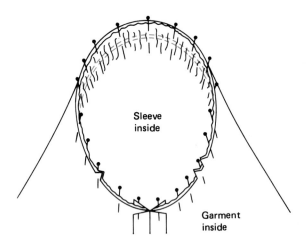

Sleeve
inside

Garment
inside

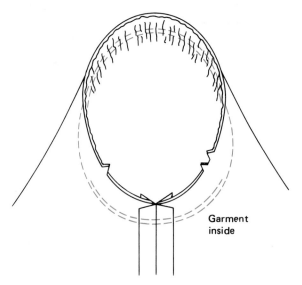

Garment
inside

STEP 4. Follow steps 5–7 as given for setting in a sleeve before the garment side seams and sleeve underarm seams are stitched (page 304).

STEP 5. Machine stitch along the seam line. Start at the notch before the underarm seam and stitch carefully all the way around the seam. Make a second row of stitching next to the first between notches. Work slowly to avoid puckers. *Trim*[24] the seam allowances to ⅜ inch (9 mm) if your fabric is bulky.

STEP 6. Follow steps 9 and 10 as given for setting in a sleeve before the garment side seams and sleeve underarm seams are stitched (page 305).

STEP 7. Repeat steps 2–6 for the other sleeve.

[24] See page 249.

 **PUTTING IT TOGETHER**

1 Why does the underarm seam in a kimono sleeve need to be reinforced?
2 What is the purpose of two rows of basting stitches when you are setting in a sleeve?
3 Why is it important to clip inside curved seam edges? To press seams after they are stitched?

LESSON TWENTY-SIX
BUTTONS AND BUTTONHOLES AND OTHER FASTENERS

 fastener

worked buttonhole

shank button

buttonhole stitch

bar

 some types of garment fasteners

how to make worked buttonholes

how to attach hooks and eyes and snaps

If you have looked closely, you may have noticed the different ways in which garments are fastened or held together. Buttons and buttonholes are one type of *fastener.* Snaps are another type of fastener. What are some other types of fasteners you have seen that are used to keep a garment closed?

BUTTONHOLES

Some garments, such as coats, may have buttonholes made from fabric strips cut and sewed in place. However, most garments have *worked buttonholes,* or buttonholes with hand stitches or machine stitches around the edges. *Hand-worked buttonholes* are usually not as durable as *machine-worked buttonholes.* A garment that will be worn frequently and washed in a machine will probably be much more satisfactory with machine-worked buttonholes.

Both handmade buttonholes and machine-made buttonholes can be made with thread that matches the garment or thread which contrasts with the color of the garment. Hand-worked buttonholes can also be made with yarn or *embroidery floss*[1] to add a decorative touch. If the garment fabric is washable, then the yarn or embroidery floss should also be washable.

Worked buttonholes are always made on a garment after it is otherwise completed. They should be placed far enough from the edge of the garment so that the buttons will not extend beyond the edge when the garment is buttoned. If you use buttons the same size as recommended on your pattern, follow the directions for marking buttonhole placement given in this lesson. If you choose buttons much larger or much smaller than those suggested in your pattern, you may have to adjust the placement of the buttonholes.

The number of buttonholes and buttons to use on a particular garment may be a design problem for you to solve. Usually the pattern

[1]See page 338.

suggests the number of buttonholes to make. However, you may want to consider the type of button you plan to use and the length of the opening to be buttoned before you decide on the number of buttons to use.

Mark the location for buttonholes by *hand basting*[2] or *machine basting*[3] through all layers of fabric—garment, *interfacing,*[4] and *facing.*[5] In girls' and women's garments that are to button in front the buttonholes are made on the right-hand side. If the garment is to button in back, the buttonholes are made on the left-hand side. In both boys' and men's clothing buttonholes are made on the left-hand side of the front or on the right-hand side of the back.

MARKING THE PLACEMENT OF HORIZONTAL BUTTONHOLES

Here are directions for marking the horizontal placement of worked buttonholes at the center front or center back of a garment.

STEP 1. Determine the length the finished buttonhole or buttonholes should be. To do this, measure the diameter of the button and the thickness of the button and add the two measurements. The total of the two measurements is the length the buttonhole or buttonholes should be. For example, if the button is ¾ inch (1.9 cm) in diameter and ⅛ inch (3 mm) thick, the finished buttonhole should be ⅞ inch (22 mm) long.

STEP 2. Make a vertical line to mark the center front or center back.

STEP 3. Make a second vertical line ⅛ inch (3 mm) from the first one on the side closer to the garment edge.

STEP 4. Make a third vertical line where the end of the buttonhole will be. The distance between this line and the second vertical line (step 3 above) should be the finished length of your buttonhole (see step 1 above).

STEP 5. Make a horizontal line where each buttonhole is to be made. If there is to be

more than one buttonhole, be sure there is equal space between each line.

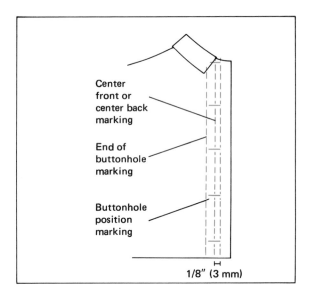

MARKING THE PLACEMENT OF VERTICAL BUTTONHOLES

Follow these directions to mark the vertical placement of worked buttonholes on any garment which has buttonhole closings at center front or center back.

STEP 1. Follow steps 1 and 2 for marking the horizontal placement of worked buttonholes at the center front or center back of a garment, as given in the column at the left.

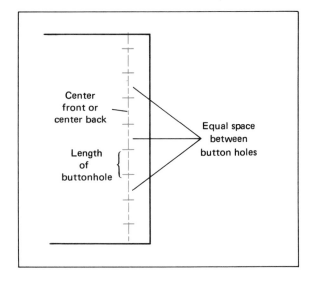

[2]See page 236. [3]See page 256.
[4]See page 275. [5]See page 277.

STEP 2. Make two horizontal lines for each buttonhole across the center front or back marking to mark the buttonhole position. The distance between the two lines should be the length of the finished buttonhole. (See step 1 in the left-hand column on page 308.) If there is more than one buttonhole, the distance between the bottom of one and the top of the next should be the same.

If your garment has buttonhole closings at places other than the center front or center back, or if the buttonholes are diagonally placed, use the pattern markings to mark placement of these buttonholes. Make two lines to both ends of each buttonhole and one line to mark the position of each buttonhole.

MAKING A HAND-WORKED BUTTONHOLE

Follow these steps to make a hand-worked buttonhole.

STEP 1. Stitch around the mark for the buttonhole as shown. For a horizontal buttonhole, round the end nearer the garment edge. For vertical and diagonal buttonholes, make square corners at both ends.

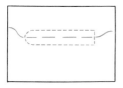

STEP 2. Cut the buttonhole on the center marking and *overcast*[6] the edges.

STEP 3. Work the *buttonhole stitch*[7] over the edges, working from right to left. Start at the straight end on a horizontal buttonhole; at either end on a vertical or diagonal buttonhole. Bring the thread from the needle eye around under the needle point from right to left, forming a ridge of stitches. Place the ridge of stitches exactly on the cut edge. Continue making these stitches close together until you reach the other end of the buttonhole.

[6]See page 239.   [7]See page 239.

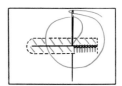

STEP 4. On a horizontal buttonhole, form a fan with the stitches as shown. Keep the center stitch of the fan in line with the cut. On vertically and diagonally placed buttonholes make a *bar* at the end. To do this, take several stitches across the end and work the buttonhole stitch over the threads and through the garment fabric.

STEP 5. Work the buttonhole stitch along the other edge of the buttonhole to the end; then make a bar. (See step 4 above for directions.) The finished horizontal buttonhole will have a fan at one end and a bar at the other end. The finished vertical or diagonal buttonhole will have a bar at each end.

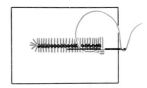

Machine-made buttonholes are made with a special sewing machine attachment or by using a zig-zag stitch in a special way. To make machine-worked buttonholes, follow the directions with your sewing machine or with the buttonhole attachment.

BUTTONS

Buttons that close a garment at the center are sewed on opposite a horizontal buttonhole on the center front or back line. If the buttonhole is a vertical one, mark the upper end on the opposite side and sew on the button ⅛ inch (3 mm) below this mark. If the closing is off-center or slanted, close the garment and then put a pin through the end of the buttonhole nearer the edge if it is horizontal, or through the upper end if vertical. Then position the button ⅛ inch (3 mm) from this mark. The location of buttons which have no matching buttonholes but are used for trimming or for attaching an extra part of a garment is indicated on patterns by small dots. On heavy fabrics, use heavy duty or special button thread for sewing on buttons. Use a double thread.

1.   A button which is to go through a buttonhole should have a *shank,* or stem, to allow room for the extra fabric between button and garment. When a button has no shank, place a heavy pin, toothpick, or kitchen match on top of the button and sew over it. Then remove the pin and wind the thread under the button around the stitches, forming a stem. Fasten securely. If the button has four holes, there are decorative ways of sewing.

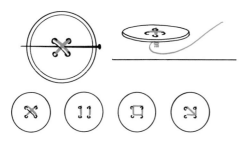

2.   If the shank is metal or plastic, it is not necessary to sew over a pin unless the fabric is very thick. But if the shank is of cloth, then a thread stem should also be made. When sewing shank buttons, keep the stitches small and parallel to the edge of the fabric.

3.   Buttons that will receive extra strain or are sewed on a single thickness of fabric should be *reinforced.* On the inside of the garment, directly under the button location, place a small flat button or a square of fabric. Sew through button or fabric when attaching the outside button.

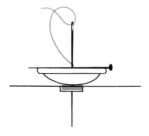

HOOKS AND EYES AND SNAPS

Hooks and eyes and *snaps* are made in many size and weights. Small hooks and eyes or snaps are usually satisfactory on lightweight fabrics. For medium and heavy weight fabrics larger hooks and eyes or snaps may be necessary. There are special large flat hooks and eyes for use on *waistbands*[8] of skirts, slacks, shorts, and pants. Large snaps or special gripper snaps are sometimes used in place of buttons on medium and heavy weight fabrics. The *pattern guide sheet*[9] usually suggests the type of hook and eye or snap fastener to use on a garment.

Gripper snaps must be attached according to the directions on the package in which they are sold. Hooks and eyes and snaps can be sewn to the garment with either the *overcast*[10] stitch or the *buttonhole stitch.*[11]

SEWING ON SNAPS

Here are the directions for sewing on snaps.

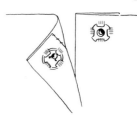

STEP 1.   Place the part of the snap with the rounded extension on the underside of the garment part that overlaps. To prevent the snap from being seen while the garment is being worn, be sure the snap is placed at least ⅛ inch (3 mm) from the garment edge.

STEP 2.   Sew the snap to the *facing*[12] and *interfacing*[13] only. Stitches should not show on the garment outside. Take about six stitches in each hole. Carry the thread under the snap when going from one hole to the next. Finish by *overcasting*[14] two or three times around the threads in the last hole close to the fabric.

[8]See pages 286–290.   [9]See pages 222–223.
[10]See page 239.   [11]See page 239.
[12]See page 277.   [13]See page 275.
[14]See page 239.

STEP 3. To mark the position for the other part of the snap, press the rounded extension of the attached snap part onto the underlap.

STEP 4. Place the center of the unattached snap part over the indentation and sew it in place on the underlap following the directions in step 2 above.

SEWING ON HOOKS AND STRAIGHT EYES

To sew on a hook and straight eye, follow these directions.

STEP 1. Place the hook on the underside of the overlap at least ⅛ inch (3 mm) from the garment edge.

STEP 2. Take about six stitches in each loop at the end opposite the hook, then carry the thread under the hook to the end. Make three or four *overcast*[15] stitches at the hook end to hold the hook flat against the garment. Finish with one or two overcast stitches in the threads close to the fabric.

STEP 3. Lap the garment edge over the underlap so the garment is as it will be when it is worn. Mark with a pin the spot directly under the end of the hook.

STEP 4. Center the straight eye over the pin and sew the eye in place. Make about six stitches in each end. Finish with one or two overcast stitches in the threads close to the fabric.

SEWING ON HOOKS AND ROUND EYES

To attach a hook and round eye, follow these directions.

STEP 1. Sew the round eye to the *facing*[16] and *interfacing*[17] only. Place it so the round edge extends slightly from the garment edge. Make about six stitches in each of the two loops opposite the round edge.

STEP 2. Hook the eye in place and bring the garment edges together. Sew the hook to the facing and interfacing only, making sure the garment edges stay together. Follow the directions given at the left for sewing on a hook. Unhook the hook and eye for making the overcast stitches at the hook end.

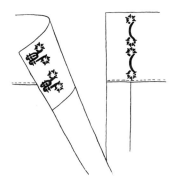

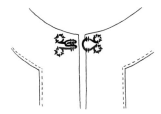

[15] See page 239.

[16] See page 277.   [17] See page 275.

 **PUTTING IT TOGETHER**

1 What are some different types of fasteners for keeping garments closed? Describe how each type works and give some examples of where they are used.

2 Suggest some fasteners that might be used on the following garments. Give reasons for your choices.
   waistband of skirt
   waistband of jeans
   shirt front
   blouse back
   child's play jacket
   coat

LESSON TWENTY-SEVEN
HEMS

 hem   flat hemming   how to make hems

hem finish   inside hemming   some types of hem finishes

gauge   hand stitches in hems

hem with fullness

A *hem* is the finished bottom edge of a garment or garment part. It is made by turning under the fabric and sewing it in place by hand or by machine. Some places where hems are used are at the bottoms of skirts, dresses, pant legs, shirts, blouses, and sleeves.

There are many types of *hem finishes,* or ways hems can be made. The type of hem finish to be used depends on the location of the hem and the fabric type and construction. The width of the hem varies according to the shape of the hem, that is whether it is curved or straight. When completed, a hem should lie flat. The hem width and hand stitching should not show on the outside of the garment if the hemming is correctly done.

When your garment is ready to be hemmed, let it hang for twenty-four hours before you hem it. Sometimes garments stretch slightly after hanging. It is better for this to occur before the hem is made.

MARKING HEMS

MARKING HEMS ON SKIRTS, COATS, AND DRESSES

To mark a skirt, coat, or dress hem, follow these directions. Have a friend help you so that the marking will be accurate.

STEP 1. Try on the garment wearing the undergarments and shoes that you will wear with the garment.

STEP 2. Experiment to find out which length you like and find comfortable. To do this, turn the hem under and pin it in place. Try turning under different amounts until you find the length you want. Sit down and stretch and move about to see if the length is comfortable and attractive.

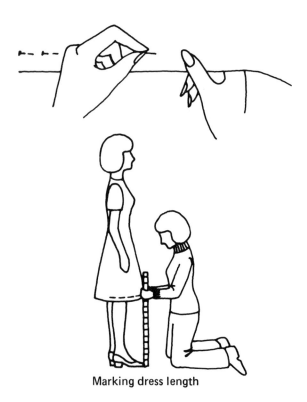

Marking dress length

STEP 3. Measure the distance from the floor to the folded hem edge all the way around the garment. Adjust this fold and repin the hem until the distance between the folded edge and the floor is the same all the way around the garment.

STEP 4. Take the garment off and follow the directions which start on page 314 for preparing a hem for sewing.

MARKING HEMS ON SLACKS OR PANTS

To mark a hem in slacks or pants, follow these steps. Have a friend help with the marking so it will be accurate.

STEP 1. Follow steps 1 and 2 as listed above for marking the hem in a skirt, dress, or coat.

STEP 2. Measure the distance from the floor to the folded hem edge all the way around each pant leg. It should be the same for each leg. Adjust the fold and repin the hem until this distance is the same for each leg. Do not worry if each pant leg is turned under a different amount. This often happens because many people have one leg that is slightly shorter than the other.

STEP 3. Follow step 4 as given for marking the hem in a skirt, dress, or coat.

MARKING HEMS ON SLEEVES AND BOTTOMS OF JACKETS, BLOUSES, AND SHIRTS

To mark a hem on sleeves and the bottoms of jackets and blouses and shirts that are not tucked in, follow these directions.

STEP 1. Try on the garment with the under-garments, outer garments, and shoes you will wear with the garment.

STEP 2. Experiment to find out which length you like and find comfortable. See which one looks good with the garments you will wear with the garment you are checking for length.

STEP 3. Turn under the hem and pin it in place. On jackets and shirts and blouses measure from the floor to the folded edge to check

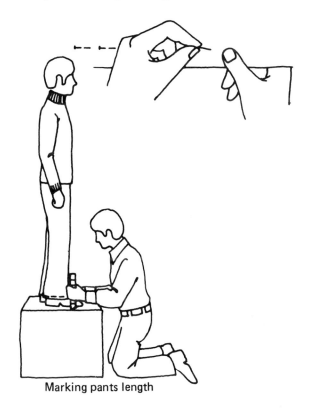

Marking pants length

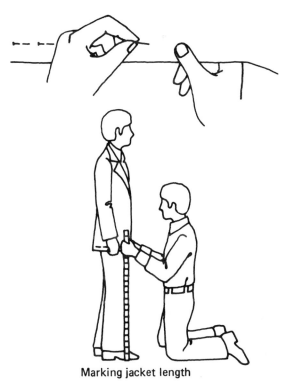

Marking jacket length

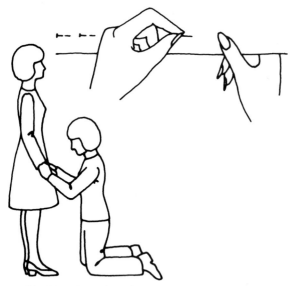

Marking sleeve length

that the folded edge is the same distance from the floor all the way around. On sleeves, be sure the folded edge rests on the same place on both arms. In each case, do not worry if the amount turned up is not the same all around the hem.

STEP 4. Take the garment off and follow the directions which follow for preparing a hem for sewing.

PREPARING HEMS FOR SEWING

After the hem is marked, you need to prepare the hem for sewing. Here are directions for doing this.

STEP 1. Pin the hem in place close to the folded edge.

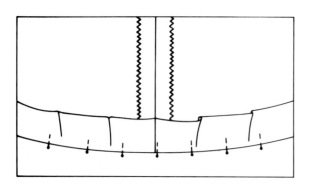

STEP 2. *Hand baste*[1] around the entire hem about ¼ inch (6 mm) from the fold. Remove the pins.

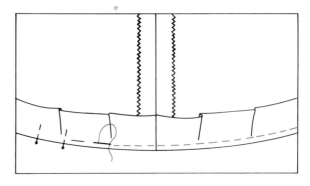

STEP 3. Gently press just the folded edge.

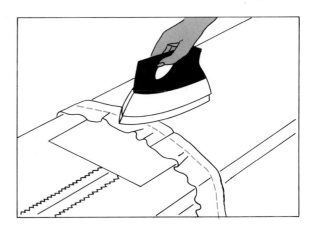

STEP 4. Using a *gauge*[2] or a small ruler, measure the width of the hem you need. Mark the width of the hem with pins or chalk.

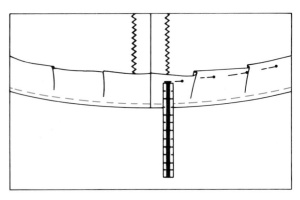

[1] See page 236.　[2] See page 205.

STEP 5. Cut away the extra material along the line you marked in step 4 above.

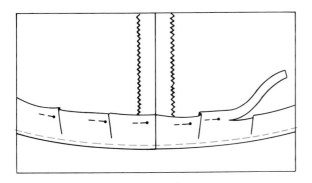

STEP 6. If the hem is flat, or if there is no fullness, go to pages 316–317 to find the hem finish you will use and follow the directions. Straight skirts, pants or slacks with straight legs, and some shirts and blouses have flat hems.

STEP 7. If the hem has fullness, that is if it doesn't lie flat when turned under, make a row of machine stitching ¼ inch (6 mm) from the raw edge. The *stitch length*[3] should be about 8 to 10 stitches per inch (3 to 4 stitches per centimeter). The hems of A-line skirts; flared skirts; and bell-bottom pants, jeans, and slacks are examples of garments which have hems with fullness.

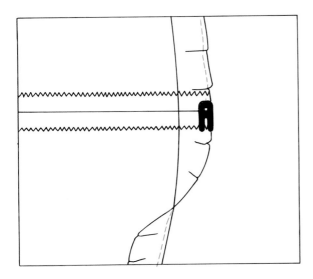

[3] See page 201.

STEP 8. Keeping the garment flat, pull the thread slightly in several places to make the raw edge fit against the area to which the hem will be sewn.

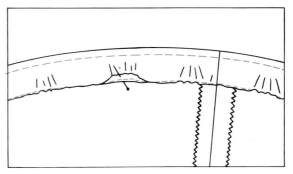

STEP 9. Place a strip of paper cut from a paper bag between the hem and garment. Gently press the entire hem so it lies flat. In some fabrics the fullness will shrink out. In others, there will be several small tucks or gathers along the stitching line. Be sure these are pressed flat.

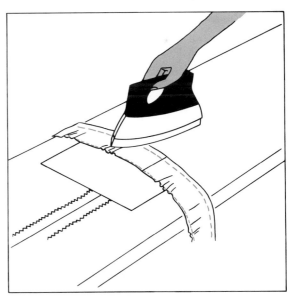

STEP 10. You are now ready to choose the hem finish you will use. Choose the method from among those on pages 316–317 that is best for the fabric and garment and follow the directions.

HEM FINISHES
ZIG-ZAG

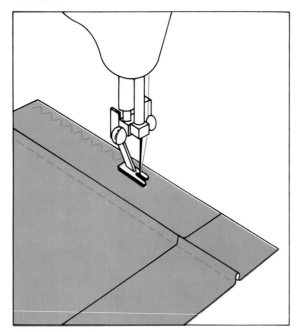

TURNED AND STITCHED

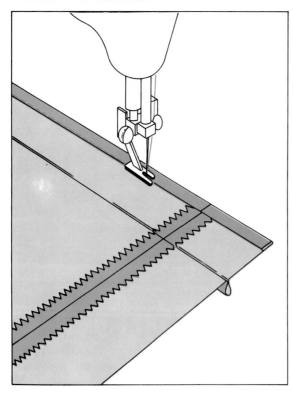

ATTACHING HEM OR SEAM TAPE

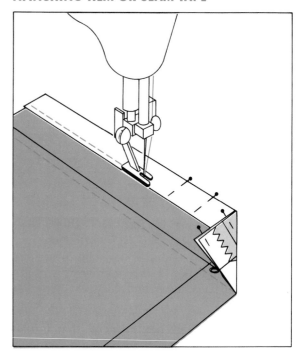

ATTACHING LACE TAPE

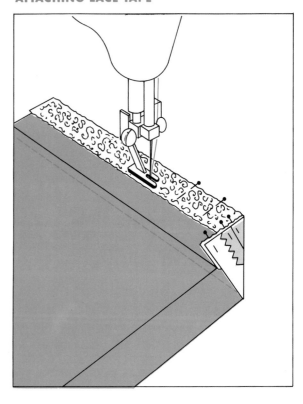

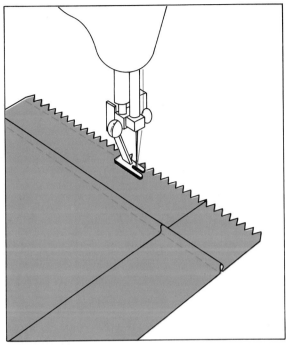

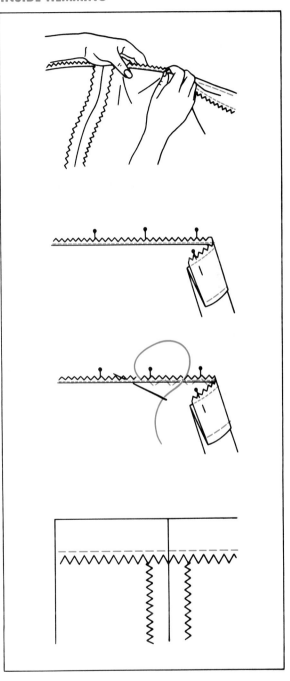

FLAT HEMMING

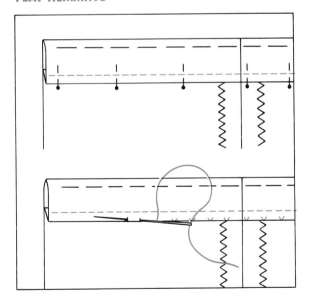

PUTTING IT TOGETHER

1 Why is it helpful to work with a partner when marking a hem?
2 What must you think about when choosing a hem finish?

 **TAKING ANOTHER STEP**

1 Review vocabulary as you learn new terms in each lesson.
2 Make a "question box" or "problem box" for use throughout this unit. Write good questions and deposit them in the box to let your teacher know the special problems you are having with your work. Your teacher could have a short answering session once a week.
3 Throughout this unit share questions and answers through a bulletin board such as this:

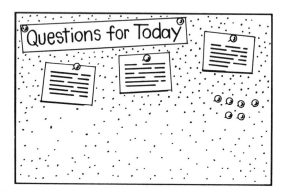

Write questions on a piece of paper. Leave space on the paper for answers. Or write questions and leave space on the bulletin board for answers to be pinned below the questions.
4 Demonstrate the proper way to care for a sewing machine.
5 Plan a display of small equipment and supplies for sewing. Arrange the items in two groups: one for equipment that is necessary, the other for equipment that is useful but not necessary to have for beginning sewers.
6 Plan an exhibit of easy-to-sew fabrics, or "fabrics for beginners" based on ideas from this unit and other sources.
7 Demonstrate the proper way to measure for finding the correct pattern size.
8 Prepare a bulletin board which shows the various symbols on patterns and what they mean. Leave the information up so you and your classmates can refer to it throughout the unit.
9 Prepare a display which shows the different ways to number pattern markings. Show each step in making the markings.
10 Find out ways to transfer pattern markings other than those shown in this unit. Demonstrate one of these methods to the class.
11 Demonstrate the correct way to staystitch.
12 Prepare a display of garments or pictures of garments with different types of darts in different locations. Use the lesson in this unit as reference.
13 Prepare a picture display of garments which have straight seams. Identify the parts of the garments which have straight seams.

14 Prepare samples of (a) a seam that has been layered or graded; (b) a seam that has been notched; (c) a seam that has been clipped.

15 Prepare a display of garments which have curved seams. Use pictures and circle or identify the garment parts where the curved seams are located.

16 Find out ways to finish seams other than those shown in this lesson. Demonstrate these to the class or prepare a display showing each one.

17 Prepare a display of garments or a bulletin board of pictures of garments which have patch pockets. Try to show as many types as possible.

18 Make a bulletin board of pictures showing a variety of seam pockets in various types of garments.

19 Find out when the zipper was invented and trace the changes it has gone through since then. How did people fasten garments before the zipper was invented? How would you fasten your garments if there were no zippers?

20 Prepare a display of fabrics which can be used for interfacing. Show the interfacing fabrics with the fabrics with which they should be used.

21 Demonstrate the correct way to understitch a facing.

22 Prepare a display of garments which have casings as part of their designs.

23 Make a display of drawings, photos, or actual garments showing as many different collar types as you can.

24 Make a bulletin board or display showing as many different styles of sleeves as you can.

25 Show the proper ways to attach different kinds of buttons.

RECYCLING COUNTS

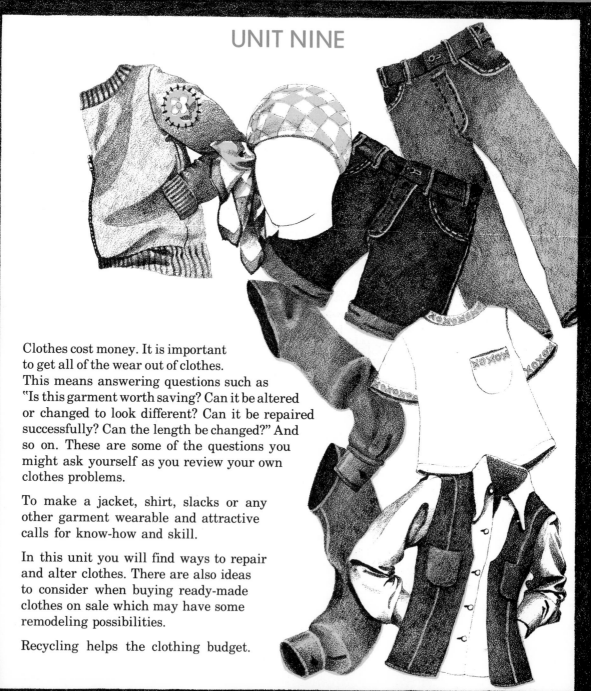

UNIT NINE

Clothes cost money. It is important to get all of the wear out of clothes. This means answering questions such as "Is this garment worth saving? Can it be altered or changed to look different? Can it be repaired successfully? Can the length be changed?" And so on. These are some of the questions you might ask yourself as you review your own clothes problems.

To make a jacket, shirt, slacks or any other garment wearable and attractive calls for know-how and skill.

In this unit you will find ways to repair and alter clothes. There are also ideas to consider when buying ready-made clothes on sale which may have some remodeling possibilities.

Recycling helps the clothing budget.

DECIDING TO ALTER GARMENTS

 alter   alteration

hem   facing

 some ways to tell if a garment can be altered

When deciding whether a garment can be *altered*, or changed, there are certain things you can look at which will tell you if alteration is possible. These are garment fabric, fabric finish, garment design, construction details, seam width, and the age of the garment. Alterations might be needed to make a garment smaller or larger, shorter or longer, or to change the style.

HEM WIDTH

If a garment needs more length, look to see if there is enough *hem*[1] width to be let down and still have a hem. If there isn't enough material to let down, you will need at least enough extra fabric to attach a *facing*[2] which can be turned under for a hem.

SEAM WIDTH

Seams should be wider than ⅝ inch (1.5 cm) if the garment needs to be let out. When seam allowances are left too narrow after alterations, seams are more likely to pull out. Some knit garments have no seam allowances. Therefore, it is not possible to add width by changing these seams. If seams are adequate, a garment with several vertical seams has greater possibility for being let out than does a garment with few vertical seams. This is because each seam can be let out. The more seams, the bigger you can make the garment by letting out the seams.

WEAR MARKS

If a garment has wear marks along seams and hems or has a durable-press or permanent-press finish, it probably will not have a satisfactory appearance even if you have enough fabric to let out the seams or let down the hem. The wear marks and permanent creases will show. However, these could be covered by a trim or braid. Garments with wear marks or permanent-press finishes can be made smaller or can be shortened satisfactorily because the creases or wear marks will not show.

DARTS

Darts[3] are another construction detail you will need to examine. Darts might need to be lengthened, shortened, or moved to improve fit. Two clues will tell you if dart changes are possible. If dart ends have been marked by small punch holes, then alterations are limited. If the darts have been *slashed and pressed open*[4] changes will be limited, or perhaps impossible. If you find that dart alterations are needed, examine the inside of the garment to see whether the alterations you want to make are possible, before you decide to buy it.

[1] See pages 312–317.   [2] See pages 277–280.

[3] See pages 243–246.   [4] See pages 245–246.

Garments can be changed in style to make them as interesting as when new.

Darts can also be added to a garment to improve the fit. In this case the problem is determining where the dart should be located and deciding on the size of the dart.

GRAINLINE

Grainline[5] is also important for good fit and appearance. If a garment has been cut off grain it may not be advisable to spend time on alterations.

FABRIC

What will the fabric tell you about alterations? A loosely woven fabric is likely to stretch as a result of much handling. A firmly woven fabric will be better able to withstand alterations which require ripping and restitching seams.

Examine the fabric carefully in a garment you think might need some alterations. A fabric which ravels easily is difficult to handle. However, if no other improvement is needed, the garment could be made more durable by *finishing the seams.*[6]

Permanent holes are left in some fabric when stitches are removed. It is not always possible to determine whether or not this will happen just by examining the fabric, but it is most likely to occur in fabrics which have been treated with wrinkle-resistant or wash-and-wear finishes. Check the label for information.

[5] See pages 212–214.

[6] See pages 252–253.

 **PUTTING IT TOGETHER**

1 How can you tell by examining a garment whether or not it can be altered successfully? What construction details would you examine?
2 How does the fabric limit alterations that can be made?
3 What are some of the ways in which permanent-press and durable-press finishes limit alterations that can be made?

LESSON TWO
DECIDING TO REPAIR OR MAKE A GARMENT MORE DURABLE

 durable

reinforcement

shank

 some ways to tell if a garment can be repaired or made more durable

some ways to make repairs

some ways to strengthen garments

"Can the garment be repaired?" or "How can I make the garment more durable?" are some questions to think about when buying any clothes on sale, buying any used clothing, or deciding what to do with some clothes you already own. Fabrics that are very worn all over or garments which have many large *holes or tears*[1] may not be worth repairing, but many times garments can be repaired easily or made more durable.

You can expect clothes that you wear frequently to require some occasional repairs. A few stitches at the right time may help you avoid major repairs later. Give immediate attention to minor tears, broken seams, and worn places. Small holes and tears can often be repaired.

Some types of repairs can be done equally well either by hand or at the sewing machine. Many repairs are more durable when they are done with the sewing machine. However, it is possible to make very durable repairs by using hand sewing.

[1] See pages 332–336.

FASTENERS

Snaps,[2] *buttons,*[3] and *hook-and-eye*[4] fasteners are useful only when they are securely attached. A few additional stitches may be all that is necessary to hold them more firmly. If fasteners are missing, it is usually easy to replace them.

Would additional fasteners improve the appearance of the closings? Perhaps a firmer closing depends on more fasteners at the neck or waistband. Is a larger fastener needed where there will be much strain? In this case, small-size snaps and hooks can be replaced by larger ones. Coats, heavy skirts, and sportswear may need sturdy fasteners.

Plastic buttons may be damaged if they are washed in too hot water or ironed with too hot an iron. Therefore, if the garment has plastic buttons and will require this type of care, more durable buttons are necessary. Also, some types of buttons cannot be dry cleaned satisfactorily.

[2] See pages 310–311. [3] See pages 307–310.
[4] See pages 310–311.

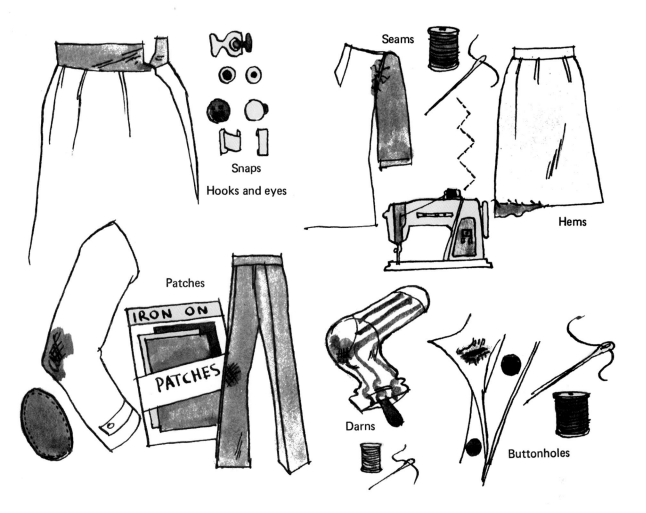

Seams

Snaps

Hooks and eyes

Patches

IRON ON
PATCHES

Hems

Darns

Buttonholes

Your dry cleaner can tell you whether or not a particular button is likely to survive the dry-cleaning process. The size button to use, of course, depends on the buttonhole size. However, you can probably get buttons of the same size as the original ones but made of more durable material.

A *reinforcement*[5] may be sewed under the button location. If fabric is loosely woven or will receive strain in the button area, sew a small flat button underneath each outer button area in order to strengthen coat and jacket closings. Stitch through both buttons at the same time. Make a *shank*[6] under the outer button to provide enough room for the thickness of the buttonhole. This prevents the button from

pressing into the fabric when the garment is buttoned. A small piece of washable fabric is suitable for reinforcing a lightweight, washable article. This type of reinforcement may be specially useful on a washable garment which does not have interfacing under the buttons.

Are the *worked buttonholes*[7] in the garment stitched closely? If there are too few threads, the buttonhole will probably stretch easily from ordinary wear. As a result, the fabric may tear unless it is made more durable. Buttonholes may be reworked by hand. There is no need to remove the original stitches. Use a matching thread. Stitch closely, being sure to cover the fabric around the buttonhole completely.

[5] See page 310. [6] See page 310.

[7] See page 309.

SEAMS

Seams are another construction detail that may need repair. Look at seams for stitches that are too long, for broken stitches, and for loose hanging threads. Tie loose threads securely and cut them off close to the seam. The underarm seams of sleeves and the back, front, and inside leg seams of pants and slacks receive more strain than some other seams. It might be worthwhile for you to restitch these and other seams, particularly if garments are to be worn and washed frequently.

Normal wear will cause plain seams to ravel. If material ravels easily, seam allowances will soon be frayed. Too much raveling will weaken a seam. A garment is useful longer if plain seams are *finished*[8] before the garment is worn. The fabric and the use of any garment determine the best finish. A machine zig-zag stitch is a quick seam finish. Also, machine edge stitching would take very little time. Either of these methods is satisfactory for a washable garment. If you have no machine available, *hand overcasting*[9] is another solution.

If fabric is worn or torn in the seam area, it may be difficult to repair. You may want to try taking out the stitches, reinforcing the fabric with iron-on patches, then restitching the seam. This is satisfactory when the repair is in a place that is not seen or when appearance is not important.

[8] See pages 252–255.   [9] See page 239.

GARMENT SHAPE

A coat or jacket may become misshapen across the shoulders when it must be hung on a hook every day. A pointed hook may damage the lining and perhaps cause stitches which hold the lining to the outer fabric to break at the neckline. One way you can protect a coat or jacket is by sewing a lightweight chain hanger at the neckline. This type of chain may be attached by a hand stitch at the eyelet ends. Some ready-to-wear coats and jackets made for rugged wear have this feature. Or, instead of a specially designed chain, you might use other materials such as braid or twill tape.

PUTTING IT TOGETHER

1 What are some reasons you might decide to repair a garment or make it more durable? When might it not be worth the time to repair a garment?
2 What are some reasons to sew a reinforcement under a button?
3 How can you tell whether a buttonhole needs to be made more durable?
4 What are some ways seams can be made more durable?
5 How can you make a coat or jacket more durable by using the suggestions from this lesson?

LESSON THREE
CHANGING LENGTHS OF GARMENTS

 hem   facing   how to shorten garments

how to lengthen garments

Garment length is one of the marks of good fit and current style most readily noticed. It may be the only difference between an attractive, comfortable garment and one that is not.

SHORTENING A GARMENT

Shortening a garment by taking up the *hem* usually does not present a problem. To do this, take out the present hem, then follow the directions for making a hem in Lesson 27 on pages 312–317.

LENGTHENING A GARMENT

Lengthening a garment by letting the hem down may present special problems. When the hem is let down, a crease may show. If the garment has a permanent-press or wrinkle-resistant finish or is made of manufactured fibers such as polyester, nylon, or acrylic, creases are likely to be permanent. Pressing will not remove them. In older garments the turned edges may show wear. If this is true, you may want to plan a suitable way to cover the evidence of the old hem line. You might use a fabric trim or some decorative stitching that has been planned to go with the design of the rest of the garment.

Another problem with lengthening a garment occurs because there is not always enough fabric to extend the length. When there is not enough fabric at the bottom to make a hem, a garment may be finished with a *facing*.[1] Ready-made hem facings can be purchased in a variety of fabrics and colors. A facing of fabric similar to the garment fabric may be made and attached. To make and attach a hem facing, follow these steps.

ATTACHING A HEM FACING

STEP 1. Take out the present hem stitching and press the garment flat at the hem to remove the crease. Then *mark the hem.*[2]

STEP 2. Mark the hemline with a *basting stitch,*[3] then *trim*[4] the raw edge so the garment edge is ⅜ inch (9 mm) from the marked hemline.

STEP 3. If you are not using ready-made hem facing, cut bias strips 2 inches (5 cm) wide from a fabric similar to that of your garment. Press under ¼ inch (6 mm) along one long edge.

[1] See pages 277–280. [2] See pages 312–317.
[3] See page 238. [4] See page 249.

STEP 4. If the facing is to be applied to a garment which is to have a straight hem, go to the next step. For facing a curved hem or one with a definite bias edge, prepare the facing by steam-pressing it into the curved shape of the hem. With facing you make, be sure the facing is shaped so the folded edge will fit the raw hem edge.

facing

STEP 5. Open the folded edge of the facing and match it to the bottom edge of the skirt. Make sure the right side of the facing is against the right side of the garment. *Pin-baste*[5] the facing to the garment, starting one end of the facing at a seam line in the garment.

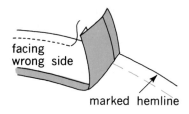

facing
wrong side

marked hemline

Outside
garment

[5] See pages 247–248.

STEP 6. Stitch the facing to the hem using the crease in the facing as a guide. Overlap the ends slightly to close the facing ends.

start

STEP 7. If you made your own facing, *prepare the raw edge as you would for a hem.*[6] If you used ready-made facing go to the next step.

STEP 8. Using the marked hem line as a guide, turn the facing to the inside. Pin, then *hand baste*[7] the fold in place.

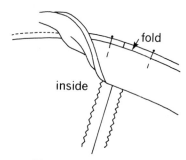

fold

inside

STEP 9. If you used ready-made facing, *slip stitch*[8] the facing in place. Do not pull the stitches too tight or the outline of the facing will show on the outside of the garment. If you made your own facing, follow the directions in Lesson 27 for *hemming.*[9]

[6] See pages 312–317. [7] See page 238.
[8] See page 239. [9] See pages 312–317.

PUTTING IT TOGETHER

1 What are problems that may occur in lengthening a garment? Do these same problems occur in shortening a garment? Why or why not?
2 What are some ways to solve the problems related to lengthening a garment?

CLOTHES, CLUES, AND CAREERS

CHANGING COLLARS, CUFFS, AND TRIM

 **interfacing**

cuffs

collar

 some things to think about before changing collars and cuffs or trim

some ways to change trim

how to change collars and cuffs

DECORATIVE TRIM

Perhaps the simplest type of change to make in garments is either adding, removing, or changing the location of decorative trims. *Decorative trims* include belts, ribbons, bows, ties, pinned-on ornaments, buttons, buckles, and similar attached articles.

In planning this type of alteration, *design principles*[1] can be applied—proportion and scale, emphasis, balance, and rhythm. Remember, the overall appearance of a garment is produced by the combination of all its parts. Therefore, if you study the design of a garment you may be able to see how changing one part may improve the design and make it more pleasing to you.

Consider some specific examples which show how design principles can be applied in improving the general appearance of garments. For instance, belt width may be studied in terms of proportion and scale. If a wide belt is out of proportion for your measurements, you can replace it with a narrower belt or you can remove the belt.

[1] See pages 72–95.

Attached trim, such as buttons or a belt, may provide poorly located accents. These accents can be relocated to provide a more suitable accent for your particular figure. The same type of alteration is possible for fake pocket tabs which have been attached as trim.

Consider balance and rhythm in the design of the garment. Too much trim applied to a particular article of clothing may give a spotty appearance. Too many different shapes used together may result in the same effect.

A garment may be made more useful and more attractive through carefully planned changes in decorative trim. A change of decorative trim may make it possible to combine a garment successfully with clothes you already have. Buttons which are too ornate can be replaced with plainer buttons. The colors of added belts, pins, and buttons on a particular garment may limit the way it can be satisfactorily combined with other clothes. It might be possible and desirable to remove colored trim which limits the use of the garment. Also, when trims are scaled to your proportions your appearance in the garment is improved.

If you plan to remove trim or garment details and not replace them, think about the age of the garment and the type of fabric. Some fabrics show holes from stitching. Also, if a garment is not new, the fabric may be slightly faded in areas not covered by trim or other garment details.

COLLARS AND CUFFS

Sometimes collars and cuffs wear out before the rest of a garment. With time and patience it is often possible to change them and make a garment wearable for a longer time. Collars and cuffs can be changed if you decide the design will be more attractive.

Replacement collars for some jacket styles and for men's and boy's shirts can sometimes be purchased. Jacket cuffs can also be purchased. If the style or size collars or cuffs you want are not available you can make your own from fabric of similar weight, construction, and fiber content. Choose a color that matches or contrasts with the fabric of the garment. Here is how to change collars and cuffs.

STEP 1. Carefully remove the stitching that attaches the collar or cuffs to the garment. Then take the collar or cuffs apart. Since you will use the collar or cuffs as a pattern for cutting new ones, be careful not to stretch the fabric. If it is stretched, the new collar or cuffs will not have the same shape as the ones you have removed.

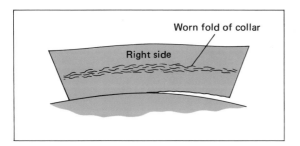

STEP 2. Press the collar or cuff pieces.

STEP 3. Place the collar or cuff pieces on the fabric *according to grainline*[2] and pin in place.

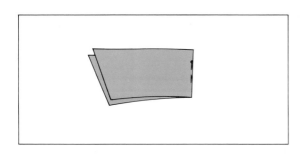

STEP 4. Plan to use *interfacing*[3] in the new collar or cuffs you are making. If the fabric for the collar and cuffs is lightweight and does not have a design that will show through, use the same fabric for the interfacing. Otherwise choose a lightweight fabric

[2] See pages 228–231. [3] See pages 275–276.

in a solid color for the interfacing. If there is no interfacing piece from the old collar or cuffs, use the facing piece as a pattern.

STEP 5. Pin the interfacing piece to the fabric according to grainline. Cut out each piece carefully.

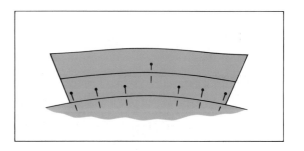

STEP 6. For a collar, follow the directions for *making and attaching a collar*[4] in Lessons 23 and 24 in Unit 8. If the collar is attached differently than shown in the Lesson 24, attach it in the same way as the one you removed.

STEP 7. For cuffs, *pinbaste*[5] the interfacing to the wrong side of the cuff facing and *staystitch*[6] in place. *Trim*[7] the seam to ⅛ inch (3 mm).

STEP 8. With right sides of the fabric together, pinbaste the cuff and facing together. Stitch on three sides, leaving open the edge which will be attached to the garment.

STEP 9. *Layer the seams,*[8] *clip*[9] or *notch*[10] any curved seams, and *trim the corners.*[11] Turn the cuffs right side out and press.

STEP 10. Attach the cuffs to the garment in the same way the old ones were attached.

[4] See pages 291–298. [5] See pages 247–248.
[6] See pages 241–242. [7] See page 249.
[8] See page 250. [9] See page 250.
[10] See page 250. [11] See pages 249–251.

PUTTING IT TOGETHER

1 When might you decide to change trim or collars and cuffs?
2 What are some ways you can change trim on a garment?

DARNING, PATCHING, AND DECORATIVE STITCHING

tear
hole
mend
patch

darn
decorative stitching
applique

how to darn
some types of patches
how to apply some types of patches
ways to make some decorative stitching

Garments sometimes need repair because of a hole or tear. Often the words hole and tear are used as if they are the same thing, but they are not. A *hole* is a cut or damaged spot in fabric which results in the absence of threads or yarns. A *tear* is a cut or slash or damaged spot in fabric which results in some broken threads or yarns; none of the threads or yarns are missing.

A garment with a hole or tear in it can be *mended,* or repaired, by either darning or patching. There are advantages and disadvantages in each method.

DARNING

Darning is a method of repairing a hole or tear by following the grainline and by anchoring new yarns in the fabric on all sides of the hole or tear. Darning a tear involves covering the broken yarns; darning a hole involves replacing the missing yarns.

Darning a hole can be done either by hand or machine. Hand darning can be done so the darned area is invisible. Machine darning is often stronger than hand darning, however, it may not be invisible.

To darn a tear or hole by hand so it cannot be seen, the knit or weave of the fabric must be duplicated exactly. On some fabrics this is not easily done. For example, on double knit fabrics and fabrics knitted or woven from very fine yarns the exact structure is very difficult to see. If you cannot see the knit or weave so that you can copy it exactly, the results will not be invisible. When appearance is important, the end result may be more satisfactory if you take the garment to a department store or tailoring shop that has special services of reweaving or restructuring fabrics. If it is not important that the darning be invisible, or if the fabric structure is easily seen, you may want to darn the tear or hole rather than having it professionally done.

GUIDELINES FOR DARNING

1. Use a *fine needle*[1] and a short length of thread or yarn. A long thread may stretch the tear or hole.

[1] See page 202.

2. Choose yarn or thread that matches the fabric.

3. Work from the outside so you can see how your work looks.

4. Use a single thread and do not tie a knot when beginning or ending stitching. Leave the ends about 1 inch (2.5 cm) long.

5. Try to bring the threads or yarns from the needle through the yarns of the fabric rather than in and out of the material. This is done by holding the needle against the fabric when stitching rather than sticking the needle down through the fabric and back up through the fabric.

6. Keep stitches loose enough to avoid puckering but tight enough to avoid making a bubble.

DARNING A TEAR IN WOVEN FABRIC

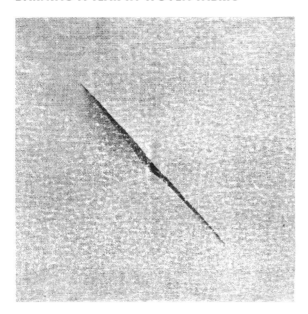

STEP 1. Start darning ¼ inch (6 mm) from one end of the tear. Form a series of rows across the tear using small stitches. Follow the *grainline*[2] and the weave of the fabric. Continue until the stitches extend ¼ inch (6 mm) beyond the other end of the tear.

[2] See pages 212–214.

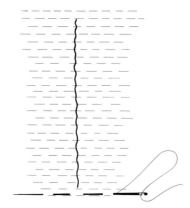

STEP 2. Form a series of rows at right angles to the rows made in step 1 above. Weave the needle thread or yarn in and out of the fabric yarns according to the weave.

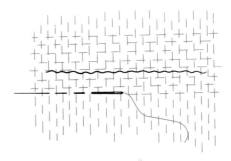

STEP 3. Catch the needle thread or yarn under the last row of stitching before clipping the thread or yarn.

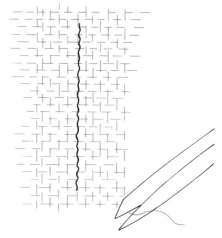

A tear in a woven fabric can be mended quickly by using a zig-zag sewing-machine stitch. Cut a piece of fabric the shape of the tear and stitch it underneath the tear for re-inforcement. Use a lightweight fabric the same color as that of the garment. Close the tear by stitching across all of the torn edges. Follow the machine directions for correct setting of the stitches.

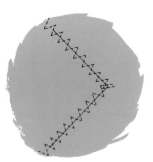

DARNING A HOLE IN WOVEN FABRIC

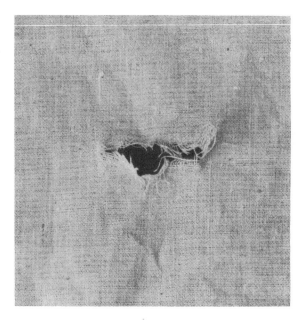

STEP 1.   Trim the frayed edges of the hole if there are any.

STEP 2.   Imagine that there is a circle around the hole and start darning at the bottom of this circle. Take two or three stitches following the *grainline*[3] and weave of the fabric.

[3] See pages 212– 214.

STEP 3.   Continue making rows of stitches the same distance apart as the yarns of the fabric. Slightly increase the length of each row as you work toward the middle of the imaginary circle; then slightly decrease the length of each row as you work from the middle to the top of the imaginary circle.

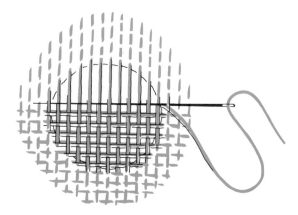

STEP 4.   Form a series of rows at right angles to the rows made in step 3 above. Weave the needle thread or yarn in and out of the fabric yarns according to the weave.

STEP 5.   Catch the needle thread or yarn under the last row of stitching before clipping the thread or yarn.

DARNING A HOLE IN A SOCK OR STOCKING

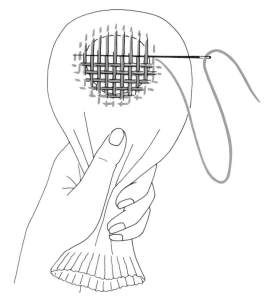

CLOTHES, CLUES, AND CAREERS

To darn a hole in the toe or heel of a sock or stocking, follow steps 1–5 above; make a plain weave in step 4. Slip the sock or stocking over a darning egg or other rounded surface while darning. A *darning egg* is an egg-shaped tool made of a hard material. It usually has a handle to make it easy to hold the item you are darning. Make the darning stitches carefully so there are no rough spots or knots. Otherwise, these might cause blisters or sore spots when the socks or stockings are worn.

MENDING A HOLE IN PLAIN KNIT FABRIC

It is possible to mend a hole in a garment made with a plain knit stitch. An example is a plain hand-knit sweater. Choose matching yarn and a needle with a blunt point especially made for sewing hand-knit garments.

STEP 1.   Carefully make a horizontal cut above the hole and one below the hole.

STEP 2.   Ravel the yarns to the ends of these cuts. Then run a thread through the loops to prevent more raveling.

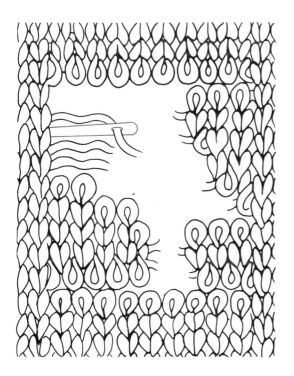

STEP 3.   Thread the loose yarns at the sides of the hole and weave them into the stitches on the wrong side of the fabric. The area to be mended should be a rectangular shape.

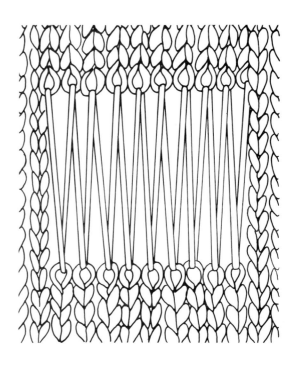

STEP 4.   Thread the blunt needle with yarn for mending. Do not make a knot, but weave the yarn into the stitches on the wrong side of the fabric to anchor the yarn. Start near the upper left corner of the rectangle.

STEP 5.   Bring the yarn up through the loop at the top left corner and down through the loop at the bottom left corner. Continue to make these lengthwise rows of yarn until all the loops have yarn through them. Keep the rows loose or the mended area will pucker. If there is not much yarn left on the needle, weave the yarn into the stitches on the back of the fabric and clip it, leaving about ½ inch (1.2 cm). Otherwise go to step 7.

STEP 6.   If you are starting with a new piece of yarn, follow the directions in step 4 for anchoring the yarn in the fabric.

STEP 7.   Working from the right side of the fabric, bring the needle up through the loop at the lower right hand corner. Put the needle behind the row of yarn in the loop and bring it out on the other side of the row; put the needle down through the same loop and bring it up through the loop next to it on the left.

STEP 8. Continue making these stitches back and forth across each row to fill in the hole. End by weaving the yarn into several stitches on the back of the fabric.

PATCHING

Patching consists of covering a hole or tear with matching or contrasting fabric or fitting a piece of matching fabric into a hole. A patch is more suitable than darning for mending a large hole. Patches that cover a hole take less time than darning and are sometimes stronger and more durable than darning. Patches can also be decorative. Think about the use the garment will get before deciding whether to darn or patch when mending a hole or tear.

Patches are available in several common woven fabrics, including denim, broadcloth, and corduroy. Also, for repairing socks, pajamas, and other knit items, soft knit patches may be purchased. Both types of fabric patches are available in a variety of colors. You can also create your own patches from some garment that you may be discarding. Some patches must be sewn on. Others are iron-on patches, which are bonded to the garment by applying heat and pressure.

When and where ready-cut patches might be best used depends on the type of garments and the expected wear. In choosing the type of patch to use, the fabric construction and texture must be considered. Generally woven fabric patches are more satisfactory on woven fabrics and knitted patches are more satisfactory on knitted garments. If a patch of the same fabric as the garment cannot be obtained, one of similar texture and weight can sometimes be used successfully. Broadcloth patches, for example, might be used with other firmly woven plain weave fabrics as well as on broadcloth. Consider color, too, in selecting a patch. If the patch cannot be matched exactly with the garment to be mended, the mend is likely to be easily noticed. A patch of contrasting color and texture might be used decoratively.

Decorative patches in special shapes and of contrasting colors or textures may be used effectively for some mending. These patches are called *appliques*. You can buy them ready-made or make them yourself. When applied, an applique is both a trim and a patch. Whether or not this is a suitable choice to make depends on the garment and its use. The shape and color of the added trim should be considered in relation to the rest of the garment design.

A precut iron-on patch is laid on the place to be mended. When heat and pressure are applied on the prepared patch it is bonded, or fused, to the garment by an adhesive on the back of the patch. Follow directions with the patches for the correct ironing temperature and for the time that heat and pressure

Patches become interesting parts of clothing design.

should be applied. If properly applied, iron-on patches may be expected to withstand either dry cleaning or washing, as labeled.

If a patch must be sewed to a garment, pin it in place before stitching. Stitching may be done by hand or machine; however, machine stitching will likely be more durable than hand stitching.

DECORATIVE STITCHING

Decorative stitching, such as *embroidery* or *crewel*, can be applied over darning that is not invisible or around the edges of patches. Or decorative stitching can be applied to fabric that has not been damaged and mended. Plan the size and location of any decorative stitching in relation to the garment. Use the principles of design in Unit 5.

The special stitches for crewel and embroidery are the same. The difference is in the material used to make the stitches. Embroidery is done with strands of *embroidery floss*, a special cotton yarn for doing embroidery. Crewel is done with *crewel yarn* of various weights. Usually this yarn is wool or wool-like. Whichever yarn you choose, make sure that it can be cared for in the same way as the garment on which it is used. For example, if the garment is to be washed, the decorative stitches should also be washable. Special needles are available for crewel and embroidery. These are sold either in packages or singly.

Here are the directions for some of the basic stitches you can use for doing designs in crewel and embroidery.

CHAIN STITCH

STEP 1. Work from right to left as shown.

STEP 2. Keep stitches the same length.

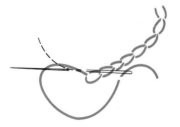

CROSS STITCH

STEP 1. Start at either right or left.

STEP 2. Keep stitches equal in length and evenly spaced.

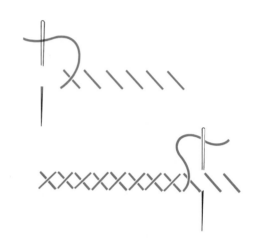

OUTLINE STITCH

STEP 1. Work from left to right.

STEP 2. Keep thread on same side of the needle for each stitch.

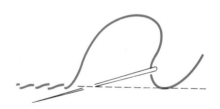

BACK STITCH

STEP 1. Work from right to left.

STEP 2. Keep stitches the same size.

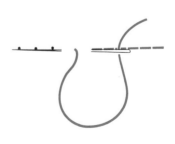

FRENCH KNOT

LAZY DAISY STITCH

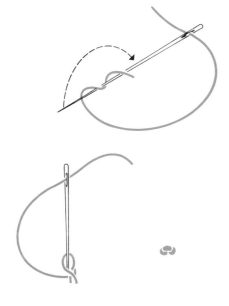

 **PUTTING IT TOGETHER**

1 What is the difference between a tear and a hole?
2 When might it be a good idea to take a garment with a tear or hole to a place that specializes in restructuring fabrics? When might it be a good idea to make the repair yourself?
3 What are some different types of patches? Explain when these patches might be used.
4 When might you decide to apply decorative stitching to a garment?

 **TAKING ANOTHER STEP**

1 Prepare a display or bulletin board which shows different ways to change the lengths of garments.
2 Change the length of one of your own garments or a garment of another family member.
3 Plan a demonstration of different ways to change the trim on garments. Have each person show a different method.
4 Plan laboratory sessions in which you learn how to darn, and how to patch a tear or rip. If some class members do not have garments which need repair, perhaps other class members could bring several articles to repair. Or collect items for repair from a children's home or a home for the aged. Consult your guidance counselor, school nurse, or teacher for information about other sources of clothing to repair.
5 Make a display which shows how patches can be used as decoration as well as for mending.

continued on next page

RECYCLING COUNTS

continued from page 339

6 Make a bulletin-board display or an exhibit which shows ideas for altering ready-to-wear garments. Clipped illustrations might be used with appropriate comments. Use "before" and "after" illustrations if these are available.

7 Make a bulletin-board display or an exhibit which shows ways to reinforce new garments. Use real garments, samples, or illustrations.

8 Make a bulletin-board display or an exhibit which explains the steps in a frequently used repair.

9 Arrange an exhibit of supplies for clothing repairs. Materials might include prepared hem facing, buttonhole twist, iron-on patches, and darning needles.

10 Plan laboratory sessions during which sewing skills are used to alter ready-to-wear garments. Each class member may plan an individual project for improving the appearance or durability of a ready-to-wear garment. Afterwards, have an exhibit or modeling session to explain the "before" and "after" condition of each garment. Determine the dollars-and-cents-values of your work by finding out the probable cost of each type of alteration. Also keep a record of the time required to complete each project.

11 Instead of individual projects and supervised laboratory work, plan one or more demonstrations on ready-to-wear alterations.

12 Find out the cost of several types of alterations by inquiring from retail stores, dressmakers, tailor shops, dry cleaners. Compare the information to see if the cost of a particular alteration is the same regardless of where it is done. Compare the cost of several types of common alterations. Which are most expensive? least expensive?

13 Make a plan for repairing your own clothes. If your mother or another family member has always done this for you, plan to assume some of this responsibility. Find information about the type of repairs you need to make. Plan a specific time to work on this each week. Keep a record of the type of repairs you attempt during half a semester, or an entire semester.

14 Plan laboratory sessions in which clothing is repaired so that it might be donated to a charitable agency for distribution. Ask your teacher to help you plan such a project.

CAREERS CHALLENGE

UNIT TEN

Each person must find a
place in the world of work.
Each must decide what to do.
This decision may affect how you
will live, where you will live,
the amount of income you will have
to spend on the things you want
for yourself and for your family,
and the people with whom you will
associate. So it is a decision not to
be taken lightly.

The choices are many. In this unit
you will explore some of the career
choices that are available in the related
fields of clothing and textiles.

LESSON ONE
THE WORLD OF WORK

 vocation

lifestyle

service industries

 some effects of work on your lifestyle

some things to expect on the job

Sometime in the future you will have a *vocation,* that is you will find a place for yourself in the world of work. During your working years you may even have more than one vocation. For example, you may be a teacher, then decide you would like to be a doctor and go back to school to learn a new vocation. You might have more than one vocation at a time. An example of this is someone who is an engineer during the week and an author on weekends; or someone who is a carpenter and a parent.

The decisions you make about the work you want to do are important decisions. One reason is that the work you do as an adult will affect your lifestyle. A *lifestyle* is the combination of conditions, things, goals, decisions, and experiences that make up the way a person lives. Everyone has a different lifestyle because many combinations of conditions, decisions, and experiences are possible. Your lifestyle includes the choices you make about where you live and the type of living space you have. It is goods and services you choose to buy. And it is also the type of recreation you choose and the persons who share your everyday environment.

How will the work you do affect your lifestyle? The type of work you do will affect where you will be working. It may be outdoors or indoors. It may be in a large city or a small town. In turn, where you are employed will

affect where you live so you can get to your job. Your occupation will affect your daily schedule, particularly the hours you will spend working. Also, your job will affect your *income* and the money you will have to spend on the goods and services you want. Your vocation will also affect the amount of money you will have when you retire and no longer have income from employment. Your occupation will determine somewhat the persons you will know and the social life you will have.

Another reason the decisions you make about work are important is that many adults can expect to spend forty to forty-five years or longer working to earn income. This means a major portion of your life span will be spent in working. The forty years or more that you spend working will probably be more satisfying if you have an occupation which gives you satisfaction as well as makes possible the lifestyle you choose.

What conditions can you expect in the world of work? Jobs and employment conditions are changing constantly. It is not possible to predict what employment will be like throughout your entire lifetime. However, some conditions today are likely to continue. Jobs will increase in *service industries.* This means more employees will be needed in jobs that provide services to others. For example, services related to clothing include cleaning and laundry services, storage, repairs, and

alterations. Also, education services related to clothing will continue to be needed in both schools and businesses. Researchers and specialists who deal with consumer problems will be needed.

Some types of jobs that exist today will no longer be needed and will disappear. New jobs requiring different skills will be created. This trend is expected to continue, so you may need to learn new skills during your working years in order to be prepared for different kinds of work. You should think seriously about these new skills you will need.

Whatever work you choose, you will need to continue learning while working. If you have the same job for many years, you will need to continue learning to keep up with new information related to your job. If you are promoted or transferred or change jobs, you will need new knowledge and skills. Many employers require employees to take certain courses or to learn new skills related to their jobs. Some employers feel that continued learning is so important that they give employees time off to take courses, pay tuition costs for special courses, or arrange for on-the-job training.

 **PUTTING IT TOGETHER**

1 What are some reasons why the decisions you make about work are important?

2 What does lifestyle mean? How will the employment you have affect your lifestyle?

3 Give some reasons why continued learning is important throughout the working years.

LESSON TWO
PREPARING FOR A VOCATION

 personal traits

reliability

responsibility

basic communication skills

basic mathematics skills

 some traits and skills to develop

learning about vocations

The time when you will become an employee may seem far in the future. You cannot predict exactly the type of job you will have, nor the place where you will work. On the other hand, your day-to-day activities now will help to determine your future opportunities. In today's complex world, employment requires preparation.

PERSONAL TRAITS

One thing you can do now is develop positive personal traits. *Personal traits,* or personal characteristics, are those special qualities that identify you. They are qualities others see in you. These qualities are part of your usual behavior.

What are some positive personal traits that will help you succeed in the world of work? *Reliability,* or dependability, is one of these traits. Being reliable or dependable means you can be trusted to do what you say you will do. People have confidence in you because you don't let them down. Another positive trait is *responsibility.* Being responsible means that you do what you are supposed to do without having someone remind you each time. It also means that if you make a mistake,

you accept the blame. *Being able to get along with others* is still another positive trait. No matter what job you have there are other people involved. The ability to be considerate and pleasant, to be concerned, and to get along well with others is important. It is more pleasant and easier to do a job when workers try to get along with each other.

Cheerfulness is another positive trait. Even when everything seems to be going wrong, it helps to look for the good things in a situation. It may not always be easy, but it can make you feel better. You know how unpleasant it is when someone else is always gloomy and looks only for the bad things. Soon everyone starts to avoid that person because he or she spoils the fun.

Interest and *willingness to learn* are other traits that will help you in the world of work. Take an interest now in the events and individuals in your daily environment. Try to have a positive attitude about yourself and your ability to do things. Be willing to learn from new experiences. If you make mistakes, you can learn from these mistakes. You may never develop new skills or discover new ideas if you make a habit of saying, "It's too hard," or "I can't."

There are other positive traits you probably can think of. Developing these traits takes practice. You must work at making them habits and part of your individual behavior. Think about how you like others to be and how you like to be treated by others. If you practice being the way you like others to be and treat others the way you like to be treated, you will be strengthening and developing positive personal traits.

BASIC SKILLS

Besides developing personal traits, there are other things you can do to prepare yourself for employment. One is to become skillful in the use of basic communication skills. *Basic communication skills* include the ability to read, write, and speak. Most occupations require you to read directions, write messages, and exchange information with others. Many occupations also require the ability to use *basic mathematics skills*. These are addition, subtraction, multiplication, and division. You can develop and strengthen your knowledge and ability to use basic communication and mathematics skills while you are in school. Seek help if needed. Practice on your own. Work to improve your skills.

OCCUPATIONS

To prepare yourself further, you can study different vocations. Find out what *occupations,* or jobs, interest you. Compare their advantages and disadvantages. Start by making a list of questions that you might ask. For example, what is the job like? What are the working conditions? What kind of preparation or special training is required?

What is the job like? You will want to know the usual activities you can expect on the job. When you spend many hours each day at work, it is important to know what you must do. Does the work involve selling, sewing, using special mechanical equipment, assisting others with clothes care, answering questions, thinking new ideas, teaching others, or other activities?

What are the working conditions you can expect? An important question to ask is "Where will I work?" Some jobs are available only in large cities. Other jobs are found in both large and small communities. Also, you will probably want to know whether the working hours are regular or irregular. A job may involve extensive travel. Are you willing to spend days or weeks away from home? You might consider this either an advantage or a

Basic Communication Skills
* *write sentences*
* *read messages*
* *answer questions*
* *give directions*
* *understand directions*
* *explain situations*
* *fill in forms*
* *write letters*

disadvantage depending on the kind of working conditions you prefer. If continuous air travel or travel by car and staying in hotels is not an acceptable working condition for you, then you may not find jobs which involve travel to be what you want. Not all conditions in any job are ideal. No matter what you choose there will always be some disadvantages. It is good to know this before you make your choice.

What kind of preparation or special training is required for the job you want to do? A high school education and willingness to keep on learning are sufficient preparation for some types of work. A college degree or more is required preparation for other occupations.

Occupational training, available in vocational and technical schools and on the job, is necessary for still other types of work. Most training and education beyond high school costs money so this is a consideration when thinking about different vocations. Scholarships and loans are available to help pay for college or special training if you or your family do not have the money. You may decide that you should work after high school to save money, then go to school. Or you may decide to work and go to school at the same time. Whatever the preparation, any job requires a willingness to keep on learning after you are on the job.

◭ PUTTING IT TOGETHER

1 Define personal characteristics or personal traits.
2 What are some positive personal traits that will help you in the world of work? Give some examples.
3 What are basic communication and mathematics skills that you can develop and strengthen now while you are a student? Give examples of these skills that might be used every day in many jobs.
4 What are some questions you can ask in studying different vocations?

LESSON THREE
RETAILING

 retailing
salesperson
buyer
fashion
coordinator

stock clerk
entry level
job
salary
commission

 some types of jobs
what working on these jobs is
like
special training needed

Do you like fashion? Are you interested in helping to provide customers with the things they want? If so, you may be interested in working as a salesperson, buyer, fashion coordinator, or stock clerk. These are only some of the many jobs related to *retailing,* or selling goods to customers.

RETAIL SELLING

If you enjoy meeting people and working with clothing and fabrics, you may enjoy being a salesperson. A *salesperson* sells directly to the customer. Knowledge of the products and how to care for them and use them is important. Customers often ask questions and want answers before they decide to buy. A salesperson also may be expected to attend sales meetings to become familiar with new products.

Salespersons must be in good health and have a reasonable amount of physical endurance. Usually many hours are spent standing and walking about. Communications skills are useful in selling. The salesperson must be able to understand the customer's needs and be able to explain the different products to the customer. Basic arithmetic skills are also essential to a salesperson in order to carry out the necessary work to close a sale. A salesperson must also be dependable, courteous, and have a neat appearance.

Usually a high school education is required for an *entry level job,* or a beginning job, in retail selling. However, some specialty stores and large department stores may give preference to applicants with some additional education. Depending on the store, it is often possible to move up from a sales position to a position as an assistant buyer or buyer after additional experience and training.

Salespersons can expect to work regular hours. Sometimes evening hours are part of the work schedule when stores are open to serve customers in the evening. During special sales and holiday seasons sales personnel may be asked to work extra hours in addition to the usual work schedule.

Part-time salespersons, or those working fewer than 35 to 40 hours a week, are usually paid an hourly wage. *Full-time personnel,* or those working a full 35 to 40 hour week, may be paid an hourly wage, a salary rate, or a salary plus a commission on sales. A *salary* is a certain amount of money for a particular job; no extra pay is received for time spent working beyond the usual 35 or 40 hour week. A *commission* is a percentage of the dollar amount of sales.

Depending on the size of the store, paid vacations, holidays, and sick days, plus insurance benefits may be provided for full-time employees. Often salespersons are given a discount on merchandise sold in the store.

CAREERS CHALLENGE

STOCK CLERK

Being a stock clerk involves working with merchandise before it is put on the selling floor. Some duties performed by a stock clerk are these: receiving merchandise; counting merchandise to see that delivery is correct; checking the condition of merchandise; handling damaged merchandise; preparing and attaching price tags; keeping stock records, and distributing merchandise to departments. To be a stock clerk it helps to have good health and eyesight; skills in math, typing, and filing; knowledge of textiles and clothing; the ability to work quickly and accurately; and the ability to work with others.

For an entry level job, a high school diploma is usually required. *On-the-job-training* teaches the various tasks and responsibilities related to a stock clerk job. Advancement from stock clerk to a more responsible position is possible. Supervisory positions, such as stockroom manager, require more training.

Stock clerks are usually paid on an hourly basis. Full-time work, or a 35 or 40 hour week, generally entitles an employee to paid holidays, paid vacation days, insurance benefits, and other benefits.

BUYER

A *buyer* is in charge of buying merchandise for a department. The buyer may be responsible for the department's success as well. Some tasks a buyer must do are these: find out what customers want; find the best place to buy these goods according to the quality and price; stay within a budget; set prices and check to see that items are marked right; introduce new merchandise to salespeople; plan sales promotions and advertising; and train assistant buyers.

Traveling to New York and other clothing and fashion centers is often a part of a buyer's job. Decision-making abilities, a good sense of business, a good sense of fashion, creativity, and knowing what styles and prices will be accepted are important qualities for a buyer to have. Also, a buyer must be enthusiastic, organized, diplomatic, and easy to work with. Energy and good health are essential because long hours of work are often required when deadlines have to be met.

It is sometimes possible to work up to a buyer's position from that of a salesperson, but additional education and training may be required. Opportunities in large stores may be

limited to those persons who have college backgrounds in retailing or merchandising.

Buyers are paid a salary. Paid holidays and vacations, life insurance, and health insurance are some benefits provided by most employers. Specific benefits depend on the size and location of the store.

FASHION COORDINATOR

Fashion coordinators are responsible for promoting new fashions. Depending on the size and location of the store, this may include planning and producing fashion shows, determining publicity for new fashions, planning and putting together store and window displays, and preparing television commercials.

A sense of fashion, imagination, creativity, artistic ability, a sense of humor, energy and good health, and the ability to work under pressure are some qualities needed to be a fashion coordinator. Also, the abilities to make decisions and adapt to many situations are important.

A college or art school background with emphasis on fashion and fashion history, advertising, psychology, and textiles is usually required. It may be possible to advance to a position as fashion coordinator without special training or from the position of a salesperson or buyer. However, this depends on the size and the policies of the store.

A fashion coordinator receives a salary and receives benefits similar to those of a buyer.

There are employment opportunities in retailing in all areas of the country and in cities of all sizes. If you are interested in this type of work you have a wide choice of where you can work.

 **PUTTING IT TOGETHER**

1 What is retailing? Describe some jobs related to retailing.
2 Define the following terms: entry level job; salary; commission; part-time work; full-time work. Give some examples of each term as it applies to retailing.
3 What are some of the characteristics that a buyer, a salesperson, a stock clerk, and a fashion coordinator should have?

LESSON FOUR
PRODUCTION OF CLOTHING

 mass production

patternmakers

cutter

assorter

sewing machine operator

finisher

presser

custom sewing

designer

 some types of jobs

what working on these jobs is like

special training needed

Most of the ready-to-wear clothing that is produced today is made in large quantities by apparel manufacturers. Manufacturing in large quantities is called *mass production*. The manufacture of clothing is a major industry in the United States. Some clothing producers specialize in one type of garment, such as men's shirts, women's blouses, or girls' dresses; other producers manufacture a wide range of garments.

If you enjoy sewing or designing clothes, you may want to think about a job related to the production of clothing. Some of these jobs are directly involved with cutting or sewing clothes or some other specialized task related to making clothes. Other jobs may include many specialized tasks. Designing clothes is another job related to the production of clothing.

QUANTITY CLOTHING PRODUCTION

Large quantity clothing production requires a variety of workers who have specialized skills. Each skilled employee does one step in the manufacturing process. For example,

the *patternmaker* makes the original pattern that is used to cut hundreds of garments of the same style. Garment pieces are cut by a skilled *cutter* who must be an expert in operating a cutting machine. Garment pieces are sorted and tied in bundles by the *assorter*. *Sewing machine operators* sew the pieces into garments. Many sewing machine operators work in assembling a garment. Each operator may complete only one small part of a garment. After the garment is assembled, any hand sewing that is required is done by *finishers*. Finishers may hand sew hems, attach buttons, or add decorative parts to the garment. *Pressers* are skilled in pressing the garments as assembled and completed.

Clothing production workers must be skillful in handling materials and using equipment. Good vision, physical endurance, speed, and accuracy are essential in the mass production of clothing. Workers in the ready-to-wear apparel industry need special training on industrial machines. Industrial sewing machines and cutting equipment differ from those used for home sewing. Some vocational schools provide courses in industrial sewing.

However, some ready-to-wear manufacturers prefer to train their own employees.

In clothing manufacturing plants with many employees, workers can expect to work regular hours. Wages depend on the amount of skill required in the job and years of experience on the job. Sometimes workers are paid according to the work they are able to complete each day.

The wage scale may be determined by the employees' union.

Production employees in large ready-to-wear manufacturing plants may receive paid vacations each year. Also, workers may receive a pension upon retirement if they continue a certain number of years on the job with the same company.

CUSTOM SEWERS

Some clothing is produced by custom clothing shops. *Custom sewing* means making garments for individuals to fit their own particular requirements. Custom clothing producers may specialize in certain types of garments such as tailoring men's suits, or making wedding gowns and attendants' dresses. Other custom clothing shops may design and make any type of garment ordered by the customer.

Skilled employees in custom clothing work usually need to have a wide range of skills. Instead of only one process, an employee may be responsible for sewing and fitting the entire garment for a customer. However, custom sewing may require the skills necessary to produce only one type of garment. For example, the custom sewer may need the tailoring skills essential for making suits.

There are opportunities for employment in custom sewing shops that employ many skilled construction employees. However, custom sewing is also done by persons who work alone in their own homes or in small shops they own themselves. Self-employment in custom sewing is a career opportunity for individuals with expert sewing skills and the ability to manage a business. As in large custom sewing shops, the self-employed custom sewer can limit orders to special garments.

Experts in custom sewing need a wide range of clothing production skills. Advanced courses in dressmaking, tailoring, pattern drafting, and draping can provide basic skills for this type of career. After basic skills are learned, speed must be developed through experience in making garments. Speed is just as essential in custom sewing work as in large quantity manufacturing.

The self-employed custom sewer needs expert skills, too, in order to satisfy customers. A self-employed sewer can control the type of orders and the amount of work that he or she will accept.

In custom sewing shops the work schedule may depend on the number of orders that must be filled each week. A self-employed custom sewer can control the number of orders and his or her own work schedule.

Employees in custom tailoring shops may be paid according to the amount of skill they have or according to the number of garments they are able to complete each day or week. Self-employed custom sewers can determine what they will charge for their services.

DESIGNER

There are career opportunities in designing ready-to-wear clothing and accessories. The *designer* must be able to create fashions that have customer appeal. New fashions must be designed for seasons, therefore the designer must search constantly for new ideas. The designer plans clothing months before the garments are scheduled to reach stores. This means a designer works on the next summer's fashions in September or October. The successful designer must be able to create fashions every season. The success of the manufacturer's business depends much on the designer's ability to produce saleable designs.

A clothing designer must have a broad knowledge of designing techniques, a sense of fashion, artistic ability, and originality. Knowledge of fabrics and construction tech-niques is also essential. Art and design courses as well as textile courses are useful in preparing for a career in designing. A college or art school degree may or may not be necessary. Good health and physical endurance are other essentials since long hours of work are often necessary before a show.

Designers are usually paid a salary. For beginners, the pay is usually low. However, as a designer becomes known, pay usually improves. Benefits of paid vacations, sick days, and insurance are often provided by employers.

Ready-to-wear clothing manufacturers are located in most geographic areas of the United States. Their plants are located in small towns, cities, and suburban as well as metropolitan areas. This is true of custom shops. Self-employed sewers can work wherever they are. Opportunities for designers are usually limited to large cities, especially New York.

 **PUTTING IT TOGETHER**

1 What are some kinds of jobs in the production of ready-to-wear clothing? Describe the kind of preparation needed for each job.
2 What is custom clothing production? How is it different from mass production of ready-to-wear clothing?
3 What skills must a designer have in order to be successful?

ALTERATION, REPAIR, AND MAINTENANCE

- service occupations
- alteration expert
- repair expert
- laundry specialist
- marker
- spotter
- finisher
- self-service

- some types of jobs
- what working on these jobs is like
- special training needed

In this age of ready-to-wear clothing, persons skilled in alterations, repair, and maintenance of clothing are in demand. These occupations are *service occupations,* that is occupations in which a person performs a task for someone else in exchange for pay.

ALTERATION AND REPAIR EXPERTS

An *alteration expert* is usually expected to have skills to carry out a variety of common alterations. Making alterations in ready-made clothing includes improving the fit of garments by adjusting seams and darts, changing hem lengths in coats and dresses, and adjusting trouser length. Also, an alterations expert may be expected to adjust the fit of garments to meet the needs of physically handicapped persons. *Repair experts* need skills in replacing zippers, relining coats and jackets, mending seams, and so on.

Large department stores usually maintain alteration and repair departments for the convenience of their customers. Custom dressmaker shops and tailoring shops make garments for customers according to their individual measurements. These shops may also handle alterations and repairs. There are also opportunities for skilled sewers to work in their own homes. Some dry-cleaning shops employ skilled sewers to make alterations and repair clothing.

The major qualification for employment as an alterations and repair expert is better-than-average sewing skill. A knowledge of the different fabrics and their characteristics is also essential. It is just as necessary to develop skill in fitting as skill in sewing. Alterations and repair experts must be prepared to work on different types of garments, such as coats, suits, dresses, and skirts. Both speed and accuracy in sewing are important. In order to work profitably, a paid sewer must be able to complete projects rapidly.

There are several ways to prepare for paid employment in alteration and repair. Many high school home economics courses may include some work in clothing construction. In these courses it is also possible to obtain a basic knowledge of the natural and manufactured fibers, fabrics, and their characteristics.

Some vocational and technical high schools have intensive courses in dressmaking. Private trade schools also offer advanced courses in clothing construction. Adult evening courses in public schools are still another way to obtain this type of training.

Experts in alteration and repair may spend some time working directly with people when garments are brought in for repair and when garments must be fitted for alterations. However, most of the time is spent working directly with garments and sewing equipment rather than with people. The ability to work quickly and accurately at a steady pace is important. Good eyesight and a knowledge of

construction techniques and fabrics are also essential in this kind of work.

Experts in alteration and repair employed by department stores, specialty stores, dry-cleaning plants, and custom dressmaking shops can usually expect to work regular hours. Pay may be according to the type of alteration or repair, by the garment, or it may be a regular hourly wage. Paid vacations, sick days, and other benefits may be provided by the employer. Alterationists who are self-employed determine what they will charge for their work and set their own schedules.

CLOTHING CARE AND MAINTENANCE SPECIALISTS

Commercial dry-cleaning plants, commercial laundries, and coin-operated laundries and dry cleaners provide services in the area of clothing care and maintenance.

In commercial dry cleaning, *markers* inspect garments for stains, rips, and damaged areas and mark them for special attention. They also sort garments according to color and fiber content. *Spotters* remove various stains and spots before garments are cleaned. After cleaning, pressing is done by *finishers* who use various kinds of equipment to restore the garment to its original condition. These are just some of the jobs related to dry cleaning. Each task requires handling and treating clothing, so a knowledge and understanding of fibers and fabrics is helpful.

Laundry specialists employed by institutions that maintain their own laundries must also understand fibers and fabrics. Institutional laundries usually have the responsibility to maintain staff uniforms, smocks, and aprons as well as sheets and towels.

Employees in dry-cleaning plants and laundries need skill in operating equipment and in using cleaning products. A complete course in laundry and dry cleaning would be useful preparation. Some vocational high schools offer courses of this type.

Some coin-operated laundries and dry cleaners are *self-service,* that is customers do their own laundry or dry cleaning. Others offer the additional service of doing the laundry or dry cleaning for the customers using the coin-operated equipment.

Managers and attendants in coin-operated laundries and dry cleaners need a general knowledge of fibers and fabrics in clothing, fabric finishes, washing products, and washing and dry-cleaning equipment. For example, customers doing their own laundry may ask the correct way to load a washing machine; what the best water temperature is for certain fabrics; what kinds of clothes to wash together; the amount of detergent to use; what kind of bleach to use; and the correct drying method. Customers doing their own dry cleaning may ask how spots can be treated and which fabrics can be successfully dry cleaned. If the coin-operated laundry or dry cleaner does the work for customers, the attendant must know correct cleaning procedures so no garments are damaged.

Tact and courtesy in assisting customers are essential for both managers and attendants. Also, neat appearance and willingness to help others are useful qualities.

Commercial laundry and dry cleaning employees can expect regular working hours and an hourly wage. Working hours in coin-operated laundries and dry cleaners may vary. Sometimes paid vacations are offered as a fringe benefit.

 **PUTTING IT TOGETHER**

1 What are service occupations? Give some examples.
2 Describe some jobs in the care and maintenance of clothing. What kinds of preparation are needed to gain necessary skills for these jobs?
3 Why must attendants in self-service laundries and dry-cleaning establishments be knowledgeable about fabrics?

TEACHING OTHERS

◈ communication skills

   teacher

   extension agent

   state extension specialist

◎ some types of jobs

   what working on these jobs is like

   special training needed

If you are interested in helping others to learn, you may want to consider teaching. There are opportunities for teaching in public schools, private schools, post-high school vocational and technical schools, state and county extension services, and in some business organizations.

Communications skills are especially important for those who teach. A teacher must be able to explain facts, give directions, discuss ideas, and answer questions. Being able to demonstrate is another useful skill. A teacher must also keep up-to-date on new developments in fibers, fabrics, clothing, sewing

INSTRUCTION ON HOW TO USE.

techniques, and equipment. Generally this means spending time reading; attending meetings; examining new equipment, fabrics, and garments; and practicing new techniques. Usually a teacher is expected to appear in a manner that is acceptable in the community. He or she is expected to meet and get along with persons of different ages.

Nearly all jobs which involve teaching about clothing require some preparation beyond a high school education. A college degree and a teaching license are required for teachers in public schools and also in most private schools.

SECONDARY SCHOOLS

Clothing courses are usually included in home economics programs in public and private schools. Classes may be taught in middle school, junior high school, or high school. A home economics teacher may teach several areas of home economics including clothing or specialize in teaching clothing courses. Clothing courses may emphasize consumer problems, the study of fibers, how fabrics are made, history of clothing, or sewing techniques.

Vocational Home Economics Programs in high schools may have two kinds of clothing courses. Courses in general home economics programs, also called consumer and homemaking programs, provide general knowledge of clothing. Other courses are planned to teach specialized skills leading directly to gainful employment.

Four or five years of college preparation are required to become a qualified teacher licensed to teach in secondary schools.

ADULT COURSES

Public schools may offer some evening courses especially planned for adults in the

CAREERS CHALLENGE

CLOTHES, CLUES, AND CAREERS

community. Adults may enroll to seek practical help with clothing problems or to develop skills for leisure-time activities. Adult courses may focus on various kinds of topics such as clothing construction techniques, clothing care, recycling clothing, consumer problems, and others.

There are opportunities to teach adult evening courses in both smaller communities and larger cities. Employment may be full time or part time depending on the demand for such courses. Usually, teachers in adult education are expected to have qualifications similar to those of regular teachers on the school faculty.

POST HIGH SCHOOL VOCATIONAL AND TECHNICAL SCHOOLS

Some post high school vocational and technical schools offer courses in commercial clothing construction, clothing repair, and maintenance services. Courses are planned to prepare students with specialized skills for employment. Usually teachers who teach courses leading to gainful employment are expected to have some work experience that is related to the skills they are teaching. A college degree, a teaching license, and some work experience may be required for teaching positions in vocational and technical schools.

COOPERATIVE EXTENSION SERVICE

The Cooperative Extension Service in Agriculture and Home Economics has offices in each county as well as at the state level. Working as an *extension agent* at the county level involves teaching adults about clothing and textiles and other subjects through classes and workshops. It may also include writing material for use in teaching by radio, television, and newspapers. A *state extension specialist* in clothing trains the extension agents, prepares leaflets and bulletins, gives presentations, and may teach some courses at the college level.

Training and preparation for extension work is similar to that required for teachers in public schools.

BUSINESS-SPONSORED CLASSES

There are some opportunities for teaching business-sponsored sewing classes. These are classes sponsored by stores that sell sewing equipment or fabrics. Sometimes such courses are scheduled during the summer months to attract young people. Other classes may be held just before Christmas or other special days to teach basic skills for sewing gifts. A few large stores may sponsor classes all year to attract customers into the store.

Employment in teaching these courses may be part time or full time. An individual with excellent sewing skills may be able to work regularly, teaching classes for several stores. This may mean teaching at different locations each day. Rather than a regular salary, pay may be on an hourly rate. The store may supply fabrics for use in constructing sample garments.

A college degree and a teaching license are not essentials for teaching business-sponsored classes. However, in some instances, an employer may require the teacher to have a college degree with some special training in clothing and textile studies.

Usually, there are opportunities to teach business-sponsored courses in small cities as well as in large, metropolitan areas. Stores which have a large volume of business are likely to sponsor such classes.

PUTTING IT TOGETHER

1 What communications skills do teachers need? Why are these skills necessary?

2 Describe some types of jobs which involve teaching. What are some similarities and differences among them?

LESSON SEVEN
RESEARCH AND COMMUNICATIONS

 researcher

communications specialist

writer

editor

 some types of jobs

what working in these jobs is like

special training needed

RESEARCH

Research in the area of clothing and textiles may interest you if you enjoy science and experiments. A *researcher* may help to develop new products, such as textile fibers, fiber blends, fabric finishes, fabric constructions, and products used in sewing. A researcher may also test products that have been developed to see if they meet the needs of consumers. The preparation of written reports, recommendations for changes and improvements in products, and studies of consumer complaints may also be tasks performed by researchers.

Patience in carrying out tests, attention to detail, and accuracy in performing tests and recording results are needed characteristics for researchers. The ability to work alone is an important quality for many research jobs, although some research requires that one work as a member of a team.

The training requirements for research jobs may range from a two-year technical school program to several years of college. Courses in science with laboratory experience, and courses in clothing and textiles are emphasized. Individual research may be part of the training. Pay is usually a salary. Benefits may vary with each employer. Work hours are usually regular. However, there may be overtime required.

COMMUNICATIONS

Communications specialists in clothing and textiles pass along information in various forms to consumers. Books, magazines, newspapers, films, television, and radio are some of the means of communication that are used.

Writers must have the ability to write creatively and well and within a short period of time. They must keep up with the latest information and make what they write interesting and useful to the people for whom it is written. *Editors* are in charge of publishing material that has been written. They are responsible for the accuracy of the information, its organization, and how it is presented and illustrated. Editors may work with books, magazines, films, tapes, scripts for radio or television, or newspaper columns.

People in radio and television may write their own programs or scripts or develop them with others. The abilities to meet people, get along well with others, think and act quickly, and speak in a pleasing voice are necessary qualities. Good health is essential because one is required to work with tight schedules, frequent deadlines, long rehearsal hours, and irregular work hours.

A college degree in home economics with writing, speech, drama, fashion, and art may be required for jobs in communications.

ORLON

LABORATORY

FABRIC TEST

DYE III
VAT 2

WASH
CYCLE
TEST

TEST

1

2

CAREERS CHALLENGE

ON THE AIR

MAGAZINE
CLOSING
DATES
1 18
22 29

WARB

FASHION
TRENDS

Some jobs in communications involve travel. An interest in keeping up-to-date, being creative, and being able to organize time and work under pressure are necessary for most jobs in communications. Work hours may be irregular, depending on the schedules and deadlines. Pay is by salary and increases are usually given according to ability and experience. Benefits may be generous, however they vary with the employer.

PUTTING IT TOGETHER

1 Describe some similarities and differences in the kinds of work done by researchers and communications specialists. What are some similarities and differences in personal characteristics and training needed?

2 What are some jobs in research and communications you can think of that are not mentioned in this lesson?

TAKING ANOTHER STEP

1 Invite three or four young people who work full time or part time to speak to the class about what their first job was like. Ask them to describe working conditions; what was expected of them (in terms of jobs, appearance, and working with others); what reaction they had about their first pay.

2 Find out about a vocation in which you are interested. Look up information in the library and, if possible, talk with people who have jobs like the one you are interested in. Find out about the training you need, the characteristics you need to work well in the job, some advantages and disadvantages of the job, etc.

3 How do workers get started in jobs? Ask employees how they developed an interest in their work. Ask them how they decided on the type of work they do. Share information through group discussion.

4 Invite a member of the local Home Economics Association to tell the class about job opportunities in the clothing field. If there is no local Home Economics group, write to the state president for help. Your home economics teacher is a good resource for this type of information, too. However, you may want more than one viewpoint.

5 If possible, take a field trip to a clothing industry in your community. Find information about the specific types of jobs.

6 Do you have a hobby or special interest that could lead to employment in the clothing industry? Share your hobbies and interests in an exhibit.

7 Find out whether there are courses leading to employment in the clothing industry offered in public vocational schools in your area. Also, obtain information about private vocational schools with courses in clothing skills and fashion design. The guidance counselor may be able to help on this.

8 Brainstorm. Plan an exhibit on the future. Think of new jobs or types of work we may have by the year 2000. How will the human needs of clothing, housing, and food be met? What new products and services will we need and want?

INDEX

A

Aba, 12
Acetate fiber, 108, 109
  characteristics of, 110
  clothing uses of, 110
  effect of, on clothing
    characteristics, 110
  trademark names of, 110
Acne, 59, 61
Acrylic fiber, 108, 109
  characteristics of, 111
  clothing uses of, 111
  effect of, on clothing
    characteristics, 111
  trademark names of, 111
Adornment, theory of, 2–5
Advertisements, 123–125
  appeals in, 124–125
  as a help to consumers, 123
  information to look for in, 123
  informative, 123
  purpose of, 123
  types of, 123
Advertising. *See* Advertisements
Agitation and spin speeds of
    washing machines, 181
  effect of, on cleaning soil from
    clothes, 181
  effect of, on clothes, 181
  selecting, 181, 182
Alteration, repair, and
    maintenance of clothing,
    356
  jobs related to, 356–359
  preparation for jobs in,
    356–357, 359
  working conditions for jobs in,
    356–357, 359
Alterations for garments, 320,
    321
  deciding about, 320–323
  for durability, 323
  of length, 327–328
  of seam allowance, 321
  of trim, 329–330
Anidex fiber, 108
Animal skins, 10, 14
Anthropologist, 2
Antiperspirant, 59

Appearance, 50
  others' reactions to, 50, 42–43
  things that make up, 42,
    50–64
Aramid fiber, 108
Asymmetrical balance, 90
Awl, 9, 10
Azlon fiber, 108

B

Backstitch, 239
Backstitching, 201, 248
  directions for, 201
Balance, 90, 91
  applying principle of, in
    choosing clothes, 90
  creating, 90
  as a design principle, 72, 90
  effect of, on appearance,
    90–91
  types of, 90
  See also, Proportion
Basic Four Food Groups, 51–52,
    61
Basic Four Food Plan, 51
Basic knits, 117
  chart of, 117
  variations of, 119
  See also, Warp knit; Weft knit
Basic skills for employment, 346
Basic weaves, 115
  chart of, 116
  variations of, 116
  See also, Plain weave; Satin
    Weave; Twill weave
Basting stitch, 237
Baths and bathing, 59
Batik, 14, 16
Beadwork, 21
Behavior, 50
  and appearance, 50, 67
  toward others, 50, 67–70
  when sewing, 203
  when with others, 50, 67–70
  See also, Social skills
Bell, Alexander, 29
Belt loops, 286
  as part of a waistband, 286

directions for attaching,
  288–289
Bias turnover collar, 291
  directions for attaching, 298
  directions for making,
    293–294
Bleaches, 175–176, 178
Blouses, 144
  guidelines for checking fit of,
    144
  size charts for, 145–148
Bobbin, 200
  threading, 200
  winding, 200
Bobbin case, 200, 203
Bobbin winder, 199, 200
Body build and structure, 133,
    219
  importance of, in finding
    garment size, 133
  importance of, in finding
    pattern size, 215, 216
Body measurements, 215
  for finding garment size,
    133–134
  for finding pattern size,
    215–216
  how to take, 133–134, 215,
    216
Body proportion, 88
Bonded fabrics, 119
Bonding, process of, 119
  types of, 119
Braiding, 119
Brand names. *See* Trademark
  names
Bread and cereal group, 52
Breeches, 25, 28
Burnus, 12
Business suit, 31, 33, 38
Bustle, 31
Butterick, Ebenezer, 30
Buttonhole stitch, 238
Buttonholes, 307
  checking, on ready-made
    garments, 132
  deciding about, 307–308
  determining length of, 308
  directions for making, 309
  marking for, 308–309

reinforcing, 325
types of, 307
Buttons, 307
directions for attaching, 310
location of, 309
reinforcement under, 325
Buying clothes, 100–101, 103, 105–107

C

Caftan, 12
Callus, 59
Cape, 12
Care of clothing
factors affecting, 162–166
in storage, 192–195
types of, 170–172, 179–195
Cash payment, 107
Casings, 281
directions for making, 281–285
location of, 281
types of, 281–285
Catch stitch, 239
Cavities, 62
Ceremonies, 45–46
Chalk and pins, 207, 209, 234
directions for marking with, 234
Charge accounts, 107
types of, 107
interest on, 107
Child labor laws, 34
Children's clothes
in the seventeenth century, 24, 25
in the eighteenth century, 27, 28
in the nineteenth century, 30–31
in the twentieth century, 34–35, 38–40
Chinese robe, 12, 13
Chiton, 12
Churidars, 10, 11
Civil War, 30
Clipping
darts, 245–246
seams, 250

Clothes and clothing, 1
from animals, 6–7, 9
and appearance, 42–43
beginnings of, 2–5
career choices related to, 341, 348–367
as communication, 41–49
development of, in the United States, 23–30
of the eighteenth century, 27, 28
of the nineteenth century, 30–31
from plants, trees, and grasses, 7, 9, 10, 14
ready-made, 97, 356
reasons for differences in, 6–13, 22
reasons people wear, 2–5
of the seventeenth century, 24, 25
techniques of decorating, 14–21
theories about, 2–5
of the twentieth century, 32–35, 38–40
Clothes storage. See Storage of clothes
Coats, 154
guidelines for checking fit of, 155
size charts for, 155–158
Collars, 291
directions for attaching, 295–298
directions for changing, 330–331
directions for making, 291–294
styles of, 291
Colonists, 23–26, 28
Color and colors
and balance, 90
characteristics of, 73–74
choosing, 77–79
effect of, on appearance, 77–79, 90, 92
effect of, on feelings, 74, 77–78
as an element of design, 72

and emphasis, 92
harmony, 75
intermediate, 73–74
primary, 73
and proportion, 88
secondary, 73
tints of, 74
shades of, 74
warm, 73, 77, 90
Color plans, 75
accented neutral, 76
adjacent, 75
complimentary, 75–76
monochromatic, 75
split-complimentary, 76
triad, 76
Color wheel, 73
Combination garment, 10, 12–13
Communication, 9, 26, 32, 38, 41
breakdown in 41, 43
with clothing, 41, 42–49
with nonverbal symbols, 41, 42–49
with verbal symbols, 41, 42
Communication skills, 346, 360
Communications specialists, in clothing and textiles, 364
jobs related to, 364, 367
preparation for jobs in, 364, 367
working conditions for jobs in, 364, 367
Comparison shopping, 131
Conditioner, for hair, 64
Contrast, 77
in color, 77
in design, 92
Cool colors, 74, 77, 90, 92
Cooperative Extension Service, 363
Cosmetics, 65, 66
directions for using, 65
hypoallergenic, 65
ingredients in, 65
labels on, 65
regulation of, by FDA, 65
Cotton fiber, 7, 24, 108
characteristics of, 108, 109

Leather, 6
Lengthening a garment, 321, 327–328
Lengthwise fold, 228
Lengthwise grainline, 115
Lifestyle, 36, 342
Line, 80
  and balance, 90
  choosing, in clothing, 82, 84
  curved, 82
  decorative, 81
  diagonal, 80
  effect of, in a design, 80–83
  effect of, on appearance, 80–84, 88, 90, 92, 94
  and emphasis, 92
  as an element of design, 72, 80
  horizontal, 80
  and proportion, 88
  and rhythm, 94
  and silhouette, 81
  structural, 81
  vertical, 80
Linen, 9, 25, 108, 109
  See also, Flax
Linsey-woolsey, 25
Loom, 115

M

Mandatory information, 167
  on clothes labels, 167–169
  on cosmetics labels, 65
Manicure, 61
Manners. *See* Social skills
Manufactured fibers, 30, 32, 38, 113
  characteristics of, 108–109
  chart of, 110–112
  trademark names of, 109, 110–112
Marking equipment, 205, 207–209
Mass production, 32, 352
McCall, James, 30
Measurement charts for pattern sizes, 216–219
Measurements
  for garment size, 133–134

how to take, 133–134, 215, 216
  for pattern size, 215–216
Measuring equipment, 205, 206
Meat group, 51–52
Mending, 332–338
  garment of plain knit stitch, 235–236
  See also, Darning; Patching
Men's clothing
  in the seventeenth century, 24, 25
  in the eighteenth century, 27, 28
  in the nineteenth century, 30–31
  in the twentieth century, 33–34, 38
Metallic fiber, 108
Meterstick, 205
Mildew-resistant fabric finish, 121, 166
Milk group, 51
Modacrylic fiber, 108, 109
  characteristics of, 111
  clothing uses of, 111
  trademark names, 111
Modesty, theory of, 5
Morse, Samuel, 29
Moisture absorbency of fibers, 162
  effect of, on clothes care, 162
Moth-resistant fabric finish, 121, 166
Muff, 25

N

Nails
  and appearance, 59, 61
  care of, 61
Natural fibers, 108
  characteristics of, 108
  chart of, 109–110
Natural environment, 6
Natural resources, 6, 24, 36
  conservation of, 9
  and raw materials, 24, 36
  shortages of, 36

Needles, 9, 205, 211, 240
  ball point, 202, 211, 240
  choosing, 202, 211, 240
  for hand sewing, 211, 240
  regular, 202, 211, 240
  sewing machine, 202, 203, 204
  sizes of, 202, 240
Negative care instructions, 167
Nineteenth century
  clothes of, 30–31
  events of, 29–30
Nonverbal communication, 41, 42, 43
Nonverbal symbols, 41, 42
Nonwoven fabrics, 119
  characteristics of, 119
  uses of, 119
Notching seams, 250
Novoloid fiber, 108
Nutrients, 51, 54
  in food, 51
  importance of, in diet, 51–53
  kinds of, 51
Nylon fiber, 108, 109
  characteristics of, 111
  clothing uses of, 111
  effect of, on clothing characteristics, 111
  trademark names of, 11
Nytril fiber, 108

O

Occupational clothing, 47–49
Occupations, 346
  learning about, 346–347
  related to clothing and textiles, 348–367
Olefin fiber, 108
One-piece outfits, 135
  examples of, 135
  guidelines for checking fit of, 135
  size charts for, 136–141
Organizing a plan, 103
Overcast stitch, 238

Proportioned sizes, 135
Protection, theory of, 2–5
Puritans, 25

Q

Quakers, 25
Quillwork, 19–21

R

Raglan sleeves, 299
  making and attaching,
    301–302
Raw materials, 24, 36
Rayon fiber, 9, 30, 108, 109
  characteristics of, 111
  clothing uses of, 111
  effect of, on clothing
    characteristics, 111
  trademark names of, 111
Renewable fabric finish, 121
Repairs on garments, 324
  deciding about, 324–326
  types of, 324–326
Repetition, 94
  creating, 94
  in design, 94
  as emphasis, 92
Research in clothing and
    textiles, 30, 32, 38
  jobs related to, 364
  preparation for jobs in, 364
  working conditions for jobs in,
    364
Resiliency of fibers, 162
  effect of, on clothes care,
    162–163
Resources, 6, 36, 98, 103
  See also, Natural resources
Responsibility, 345
  accepting, 100
  individual, 36
  sharing, 67
Retailing, 348
  jobs related to, 348–351
  preparation for jobs in, 348,
    350, 351

working conditions for jobs in,
    348, 350, 351
Reverse applique, 18–19
Reverse stitch control, 199, 201
Revolutionary War, 28
Rhythm, 94
  applying principle of, in
    choosing clothes, 94
  creating, 94
  as a design principle, 72, 94
  effect of, on appearance, 94
Rituals. *See* Ceremonies
Rompers, 35
Rubber fiber, 108
Ruler, 205
Running stitch, 239

S

Safety standards, 36
Salary, 348
Saran fiber, 108
Sari, 12
Sarong, 12
Satin weave, 115
  appearance of, 116
  characteristics of, 116
  clothing uses of fabric of, 116
  fabric names of, 116
  microscopic view of, 116
Scale. *See* Proportion
Scissors, 205, 207
Seam finishes, 252
  directions for making,
    252–253
  effect of, on garment
    durability, 323
  reasons for using, 252
  types of: pinked, 252; pinked
    and stitched, 253; zig-zag,
    253
Seam pockets, 258
  cutting out, 258
  description of, 258
  joining, to garment, 258–260
  making a pattern for, 258
Seam ripper, 205, 207
Seamed garment, 10, 11
Seams, 247–253

backstitching at ends of, 201,
    248
  checking, on ready-made
    garments, 131
  clipping, 250
  easing, 270–274
  gathering, 270, 272–273, 274
  grading, 250
  layering, 250
  notching, 250
  pinbasting, 247–248
  pressing, 250–251
  reinforcing underarm, 301
  stitching, 247–248
  trimming, 249
  width of, 200, 321
Secondary colors, 73
Self-concept, 43
  and appearance, 43
Self-image. *See* Self-concept
Selvage, 12, 228, 229
Separates, 33
Sericulture, 25
Service industries, 342
Services, of stores, 105, 106
Set-in sleeves, 299
  directions for attaching,
    302–306
  with gathers, 302
Seventeenth century
  clothes of, 24, 25
  events of, 23–25
Sewing, 197
  avoiding tangles when, 201
  by hand, 236–240
  by machine, 200
Sewing equipment, 205
  care of, 200–204, 205–211
  storage of, 211
  types of, 205, 207, 209, 211
  use of, 200–204, 205–211
Sewing machine, 30, 198
  adjusting, 201, 204
  causes of problems with,
    203–204
  electric, 198
  invention of, 30
  location of parts of, 199
  nonelectric, 198
  parts of, 199

ABCDEFGH   079876
PRINTED IN THE UNITED STATES OF AMERICA